P9-AGN-516

THE GODS
DELIGHT

THE CLEVELAND MUSEUM OF ART

NOVEMBER 16, 1988 – JANUARY 8, 1989

THE LOS ANGELES COUNTY MUSEUM OF ART

FEBRUARY 9 – APRIL 9, 1989

THE MUSEUM OF FINE ARTS, BOSTON

MAY 9 – JULY 9, 1989

THE EXHIBITION AND CATALOGUE WERE

UNDERWRITTEN BY AMERITRUST

Support was also received from the

National Endowment for the Arts and the Ohio Arts Council

THE GODS
DELIGHT

The Human Figure in Classical Bronze

ORGANIZED BY

ARIELLE P. KOZLOFF AND DAVID GORDON MITTEN

SECTIONS BY SUZANNAH FABING, JOHN J. HERRMANN, JR.,

AND MARION TRUE

with contributions by Cornelius C. Vermeule III

Published by The Cleveland Museum of Art

in cooperation with Indiana University Press

Note: References to catalogue entries are given in square brackets; thus, [14] refers to the Metropolitan Museum of Art's dancing woman (1972.118.95). The spelling of geographical names usually follows that in Nicholas G. L. Hammond, *Atlas of the Greek and Roman World in Antiquity* (Park Ridge, N.J., 1981). Names of individuals have in most cases been Latinized in the manner of John Boardman et al., eds., *The Oxford History of the Classical World* (Oxford, 1986), in order to make them more recognizable to the general reader. Many technical terms and some names, however, are known only in their Greek transliteration, so that version has been used for the sake of clarity. References that are used in three or more entries or essays are shortened to the authors' name and date of publication after the first citation, and complete titles and publication information are given in the Abbreviated Citations and Bibliography. Other citation abbreviations follow those used in the *American Journal of Archaeology* (see *AJA* XC [1986] 381-394).

Copyright 1988 The Cleveland Museum of Art,
11150 East Boulevard, Cleveland, Ohio 44106
Distributed by Indiana University Press,
10th and Morton Streets,
Bloomington, Indiana 47405
Editor: Jo Zuppan
Designer: Laurence M. Channing, Jr.
Assistant: Patsy D. Kline
Production Manager: Emily S. Rosen
Museum Photographer: Nicholas Hlobeczy
Typesetting by LIVE Publishing Co.
Printed in Great Britain
by Balding & Mansell International Ltd.

Library of Congress Cataloging-in-Publication Data
The Gods delight: the human figure in classical bronze/organized by Arielle P. Kozloff and David Gordon Mitten; sections by Suzannah Fabing...[et al.].
    p. cm.
    "The Cleveland Museum of Art, November 16, 1988-January 8, 1989; The Los Angeles County Museum of Art, February 9, 1989-April 9, 1989; The Museum of Fine Arts, Boston, May 9, 1989-July 9, 1989."
    ISBN 910386-93-5. ISBN 910386-94-3 (pbk.)
    1. Bronze figurines, Classical—Exhibitions.
I. Kozloff, Arielle P. II. Mitten, David Gordon.
III. Fabing, Suzannah. IV. Cleveland Museum of Art. V. Los Angeles County Museum of Art.
VI. Museum of Fine Arts, Boston.
NK 7909.3.G64 1988
730'.0938'074013—dc 19   88-14957
                                        CIP

Contents

cal
NK
7909.3
G64
1988

List of Lenders VII
Foreword *Evan H. Turner* VIII
Preface *Arielle P. Kozloff* X
Introduction *David Gordon Mitten* 1
Note on Patina and Surface Decoration *David Gordon Mitten* 26
Maps 28   Timeline 32

Greek Bronzes *Marion True*

INTRODUCTION 42
1. SEATED MAN 48
2. MANTIKLOS APOLLO 52
3. GODDESS OR FEMALE VOTARY 57
4. ARTEMIS 62
5. KOUROS 66
6. MIRROR WITH CARYATID 69
7. APHRODITE AND EROTES 74
8. HERMES KRIOPHOROS 77
9. HERMES KRIOPHOROS 81
10. DEAD OR SLEEPING YOUTH 86
11. EPIMETHEUS OR HEPHAESTUS 90
12. ATHLETE MAKING AN OFFERING 95
13. RIDER 99
14. DANCING WOMAN 102
15. APHRODITE 106
16. YOUTH DANCING (?) 110

17. APHRODITE 113
18. ASCLEPIUS 119
with Cornelius C. Vermeule III
19. BLACK YOUTH 124
20. BLACK BANAUSOS (?) 128
21. HARPOCRATES 132
22. ARTISAN 137
23. PAIR OF PANS 142
24. BOXER 147
25. EMACIATED YOUTH 151
26. PORTRAIT OF A PHILOSOPHER 154
27. HERMES 160
28. GROTESQUE 164
29. ZEUS 168
30. ANTIOCHUS IV EPIPHANES 172
Cornelius C. Vermeule III

Etruscan Bronzes *Suzannah Fabing*

INTRODUCTION 178
31. APOLLO 187
32. KNEELING ARCHER 190
33. KORE 195
34. DANCER OR MAENAD 199
35. DANCER 203
36. THYMIATERION WITH A
DANCER 207
37. KOUROS 212
38. KOUROS 215
39. TINIA 219
40. WARRIOR 223

41. SILENUS 228
42. SATYR 232
43. TURAN 235
44. WOMAN 240
45. SLEEP AND DEATH CARRYING OFF
SARPEDON 244
46. HERCLE 250
47. YOUTH 254
48. LASA 258
49. NUDE GIRL 263
50. LASA 267

Roman Bronzes *John J. Herrmann, Jr.*

INTRODUCTION 274
51. GENIUS 288
52. GENIUS 294
53. DIANA 296
54. COMIC ACTOR ON AN ALTAR 299
55. SINGER ON AN ALTAR 303
56. PHALLIC DWARF 306
57. BOXING DWARF 310
58. WARRIOR IN A HELMET 312
59. ATHLETE WITH HEADBAND 316
60. MERCURY IN A CLOAK 319
61. HERCULES 323

62. LAR 326
63. TWO MAGISTRATES 329
64. ROMA 333
65. A GODDESS, PERHAPS VENUS 336
66. VICTORY WITH CORNUCOPIA 340
67. BARBARIAN 344
68. QUEEN PENTHESILEA 346
69. FEMALE DANCER 349
70. GIRL BEGGING 353
71. CHILD WITH COMIC MASK 357
72. BOY RIDER 359
73. HERCULES RUNNING 361

Citation Abbreviations and Bibliography 366
Glossary 370

The Brooklyn Museum, New York [73]

Christos G. Bastis [16, 36]

Cincinnati Art Museum, Ohio [18]

The Cleveland Museum of Art, Ohio [12, 13, 20, 21, 24, 34, 45, 50, 61, 62, 66, 67]

The Dumbarton Oaks Collection, Washington, D.C. [11, 25]

The Harvard University Art Museums (Arthur M. Sackler Museum), Cambridge, Massachusetts [43]

Indiana University Art Museum, Bloomington [71]

The J. Paul Getty Museum, Malibu, California [10, 37, 39, 53, 54, 55, 63, 64, 65, 70]

Mr. and Mrs. Lawrence A. Fleischman Collection [29, 47, 48]

The Metropolitan Museum of Art, New York [5, 6, 14, 15, 22, 26, 27, 28, 33, 51]

Museum of Fine Arts, Boston, Massachusetts [2, 4, 7, 8, 9, 19, 31, 35, 41, 49, 56, 57]

National Museum of Natural History, Smithsonian Institution, Washington, D.C. [38]

The Nelson-Atkins Museum of Art, Kansas City, Missouri [30, 40]

Museum of Art, Rhode Island School of Design, Providence [17, 32]

Shelby and Leon Levy [23, 59, 68, 69]

The Toledo Museum of Art, Ohio [46]

Wadsworth Atheneum, Hartford, Connecticut [58]

Walters Art Gallery, Baltimore, Maryland [1, 3, 42, 44, 52, 60, 72]

The attitude toward humanity and its relation to the known and unknown forces of the world that evolved in classical times has been of pivotal importance to the subsequent development of Western culture. The physical ideals, as expressed in classical sculpture, even affected the arts of the Far East. Curiously, however, in our own day, while the impact of the classical world is to be seen all around us, probably never—certainly not since the Renaissance—has it been so little understood and appreciated.

That our society no longer draws heavily on classical literature may offer a partial explanation. Even so, in a society that is almost frenetic in its pursuit of ambitious exhibitions, presenting grand overviews of various moments in the history of art, all too little is done to elucidate the grandeur of the classical achievement. Of course, Greek, Etruscan, and Roman art—dating let us say, from about 800 BC to AD 400—can be seen in American and European public collections, but usually it is displayed with little method or breadth, because the material is so rare. Broadly speaking, classical sculpture falls into three groups: monumental freestanding figures, the great decorative schemes for temples and public buildings, and the small works made for private worship and delectation. Transporting works of art in the first two groups would be potentially harmful, not to mention costly. It is, however, possible to realize an exhibition of small classical bronzes. Although the small bronze presents its own particular aesthetic problems and solutions, nonetheless, a carefully chosen group can tell much about the evolving attitudes evident in ancient sculpture as a whole.

The idea for such an exhibition was initially conceived by Arielle P. Kozloff, The Cleveland Museum of Art's Curator of Ancient Art. Having followed closely the great spate of collecting activity in this particular area during the past two decades—having even played a considerable role herself—she was fully aware of the distinction of the holdings in the United States and recognized that much of the material had not yet been properly published. In pursuit of this idea, she joined forces with David Gordon Mitten (James Loeb Professor of Classical Art and Archaeology at Harvard University and Curator of Ancient Art at the Harvard University Art Museums). As they followed the American achievement, launched by that most voracious of all collectors, J. P. Morgan, and by the expatriate Bostonian, Edward P. Warren, searching for the Museum of Fine Arts, and pursued methodically the public and private acquisitions made in the years since, they found that even though some areas were better represented than others, the material was certainly available for a significant overview of the subject. Indeed, such an exhibition could include numbers of the very best small classical bronzes to be found anywhere in the world.

The creation of this exhibition has generated all the intellectual electricity of a thoroughly successful seminar. The organizers brought in three eminent scholars: for the Greek bronzes, Marion True (Curator of Antiquities at The J. Paul Getty Museum); for the Etruscan bronzes, Suzannah Fabing (Managing Curator of Records and Loans at The National Gallery of Art in Washington); and for the Roman bronzes, John J. Herrmann, Jr. (Associate Curator of Classical Art at the Museum of Fine Arts, Boston). As a group, the five examined virtually all the small bronzes in the United States. In the process, they each drew on their own expertise, consulted with other scholars and conservators elsewhere, and took full advantage of the many recently developed scientific aids. They experienced splendid cooperation on every side. Thus, as happens all too rarely, thanks to the owners of these works, private as well as public, the exhibition as it has come about is virtually a reflection of the original plan.

Creating a sense of unity in a catalogue written by five authors, who specialize in three distinct areas, is no mean feat. Thus, approaches vary somewhat from section to section, allowing for differing methods in the pursuit of a single goal—the furthering of our understanding of classical bronzes. One of the catalogue's considerable accomplishments is the identification of many problems and puzzles that may be resolved in time, as new material is discovered.

The questions may be many—but, at least, there can be no doubt whatsoever of the splendor and the originality of these small bronzes, works that were greatly admired by connoisseurs when they were made and that have been treasured over the centuries ever since. Perhaps it is only appropriate, therefore, that Ameritrust of Cleveland, Ohio, should have generously agreed to underwrite the greater part of the shared costs of this exhibition. That commitment was supplemented with a deeply appreciated grant from the National Endowment for the Arts which epitomizes the interaction between the public and private sectors that has been a goal of the Federal government.

The Cleveland Museum of Art is delighted that two such great American art museums as the Museum of Fine Arts, Boston, and the Los Angeles County Museum of Art have joined forces to assure that this exhibition will have a greater visibility, enabling it to be seen literally from coast to coast. Speaking for the creators of the exhibition, we all extend warm thanks to two directors in Boston—to Jan Fontein, who was the director when the idea was first broached, and to Alan Shestack, who has overseen its realization—and to Earl A. Powell III in Los Angeles. Those involved also greatly appreciate contributions to the text, beyond his own entries, made with characteristic generosity by Cornelius C. Vermeule III, Boston's Curator of Classical Art. The outstanding guidance on specific points of the Metropolitan Museum of Art's Chairman of the Greek and Roman Department, Dietrich von Bothmer, is deeply appreciated. Finally, we warmly thank John Walsh because not only has the J. Paul Getty Trust supported this venture in every conceivable way, but its handsome grant has essentially funded the Los Angeles showing.

As will be repeatedly evident in studying this catalogue, many are to be thanked. The organizers, the authors, and the museums are united in their hope that the best reward for the splendid cooperation we have enjoyed on every hand will be a broader public appreciation of those values stemming from the classical traditions that have so influenced each of us.

Evan H. Turner

According to mythology, bronze was invented by the gods on the island of Cyprus. It was a divine gift to man—the first substance that he could replicate himself by combining raw materials and then fashion into useful and decorative objects. This "divine invention" also occurred in such widely separated locales as Egypt, where numberless small figures of gods appeared, and in China, where elaborately shaped and intricately decorated vessels developed. Bronze, "the plastic of antiquity" (Leo Mildenberg), could be used for manifold purposes. In the Mediterranean classical world, it was used for tools, vessels, jewelry, arms and armor, coins, and sculpture.

The gods undoubtedly delighted in man's transformation of the metal, especially in terms of the divine image itself, for classical deities accepted multitudes of man's bronze votive statuettes, such as the proud Mantiklos Apollo [2], in their shrines and temples. They allowed their images to adorn, to glorify precious wine vessels and intimate objects. Thus, Aphrodite, goddess of love, supports a mirror disc for a lady [7] who hopes the divine charms will reflect well on her. At times they allowed man to use their image for his own, sometimes even borrowing it directly, as in the case of Antiochus IV who appears in the guise of Heracles [30].

Seventy-four such statuettes comprise the exhibition represented by this catalogue. All of them belong to public or private collections in the United States. Only complete statuettes—no portrait busts, vase handles, small couch attachments, or appliqués—were chosen, so that we might explore the classical approach to the human figure in its strictest and most fully realized focus. Shaggy-legged Pans and hooved satyrs have danced their way into the line-up by virtue either of their striking humanity or their equally arresting disdain of same. In contrast to monumental bronze statues, these statuettes were chosen for their intimacy and in most cases for their completeness. Despite its hardness, bronze is not impervious to damage, and the delicacy of the finest examples in this medium has often been the cause of their own destruction.

All seventy-four bronze statuettes of human subjects were chosen for their extraordinary aesthetic quality. Each is far more than an illustration of a subject or a figure type or the representative of a particular period. Each work is a supreme example of classical imagination, thought, design, and craftsmanship in bronze.

The most common method of manufacturing bronze objects—lost-wax casting—has a magical contrariness about it that is most appropriate to a divine invention. It is one of very few media in the full range of the visual arts in which the craftsman or artist does not form the object directly (the method itself is explained in David Gordon Mitten's Introduction). Except for the final stages, the work of art is created without ever feeling its master's immediate touch.

Ironically, this sculpture—shaped without direct manipulation by human hands—reproduces the immediacy of the artist's touch on the wax model, and it has a sensually tactile surface. Though formed in darkness, its surface has a remarkable ability to manipulate light. Even the patina—blue, green, gold, brown, or black—which eventually coats the bronze surface actually enhances these properties. It is the feel of the bronze, the way it directs light, and the versatility with which it can render forms—from voluptuously rounded to razor sharp—that bronze collectors most often mention as attributes that arouse their passion for that medium.

The qualities and properties of bronze are most tantalizing when applied to the human figure—and there has been no time in the history of art when bronzeworkers so fully exploited these qualities in the service of the human figure as during classical times. Greeks, Etruscans, and Romans produced sculptures of gods and men, goddesses and women, heroes and wretches, philosophers and barbarians. Within only four figure types—male nude, male draped, female nude, and female draped—an infinite variety of forms were created as artists used the human shape as an instrument of expression and creativity.

The statuettes comprising *The Gods Delight* reveal man's attempts to express and define his own humanity. The Cleveland athlete [12] reflects the self-conscious beginnings of Polyclitus's era of struggle with the ideal. The Metropolitan's dancing woman [14], once owned by Walter C. Baker, and the Cnidian Aphrodite [17] are the Hellenistic formulation of what centuries later would re-surface in the Italian Renaissance as the seemingly antithetical interpretation of Sacred and Profane Love, divine sensuousness being represented by the nude and erotic sensuality by the totally draped figure. The Etruscans, at first ill at ease with three-dimensionality, gradually fleshed out the human form to produce the most voluptuous of winged goddesses [48, 49, 50]. Late Hellenistic artisans satirized man by misshaping his every feature. Roman bronzeworkers cast the hero Hercules [61] in the guise perhaps of their own patrons—middle-aged, no longer narrow-waisted, yet still intensely virile and perhaps even stronger by virtue of his maturity.

Apollo, Nike, Venus, Hercules—these names survive centuries later in the popular consciousness. They evoke images of ideal, beautiful, or powerful beings that each of us might fantasize either inhabiting or loving. They conjure up the sentiments that might have inspired the Western wordsmith: "What a piece of work is a man! how noble in reason! how infinite in faculty! in form and moving how express and admirable! in action how like an angel! in apprehension how like a god!" (Shakespeare, *Hamlet,* II,ii).

Eighteen of the works included here have never before been published in a scholarly context; of them, fifteen have rarely, if ever, been seen in public. Perhaps the Greek dead or sleeping youth [10] and pair of Pans [23] and the Roman group including the magistrates, Roma, Venus, and Victory [63-66] are the most astonishing. Seven more of the bronzes have previously been published only summarily and are therefore little known. The Etruscan Death of Sarpedon group [45], perhaps the most powerful and finely crafted Etruscan bronze in the United States, is still nearly unknown and hence relatively unappreciated.

The remaining works of art in this exhibition are famous to one degree or another; some, like the Baker dancing woman [14], are internationally celebrated. And yet even the best known and loved sculptures gain from fresh study, new surroundings, and imaginative juxtapositions. In some cases, arguments for new datings have become clear; in others, previously unnoticed links have been connected.

In planning this exhibition the most important requisite was that each author examine the bronzes in (gloved) hand. Close, careful scrutiny allowed them to include much detail in the entries which we hope will be of interest and use to other colleagues and students in their own investigations of classical bronzes. Such physical examination has also resulted in essays written with a greater authority, immediacy, and sensitivity than might otherwise have been possible.

Our delight and sense of revelation in handling such prizes must have equalled their first owners' pleasure in fondling these small bronze works of art before handing them over to the appropriate gods, as they used them, or as in passing by their household shrine (lararium), they stopped to pick up and admire a favorite. The patterning on the underside of the stool on which the Dumbarton Oaks emaciated man sits was incised not merely as a matter of artistic conceit but to enchant the patron who picked it up, turned it over, and detected the secret. Handling these objects is part of their context and content. Since it cannot be part of the museum visitor's experience, however, it must be expressed as fully and vicariously as possible here.

Above all, the sensuous rewards of working with bronze statuettes of such extraordinary quality have made this exhibition the fulfillment of a personal dream. I have asked others to write the catalogue because of their superior knowledge of the period. That their scholarship has not made them immune, but has instead enhanced their vulnerability to the thrill of these treasures, has given intense pleasure throughout this venture.

Much of the in-hand scrutiny, and some of the selection, was done with museum conservators close by. So, it is no small thanks that we give to: Frederick Hollendonner and Bruce Christman at the Cleveland Museum; Jerry Podany at the Getty Museum; David Scott in Malibu; Arthur Beale, Richard Newman, and Leslie Ransick at the Boston Museum; Clifford Crane in Cambridge, Mass.; Carlie Cleveland and Richard Stone at the Metropolitan Museum; and Terry Weisser at the Walters Art Gallery. Each of these individuals spent much time studying and testing the objects in their care, as well as ones in other collections. Special thanks are due to the particular collectors who sent objects to Cleveland for examination. Analyses were made by visual examination (gross and microscopic), x-radiography, and x-ray fluorescence.

The processes of selection and study were greatly aided over two years by the unceasingly generous cooperation of our colleagues—both curators and private collectors. The authors join me in extending our sincere thanks to: at the Boston Museum of Fine Arts, Michael Padgett and Florence Wolsky; at the Brooklyn Museum, Richard Fazzini and Robert Bianchi; at the Cincinnati Art Museum, Daniel Walker; at Dumbarton Oaks, Susan Boyd and Stephen Zwirn; at the Getty Museum, Marit Jentoft-Nilsen, Karen Manchester, Kenneth Hamma, Karol White, Dorothy Osaki; at the Art Museum, Indiana University, Adriana Calinescu, and Danae Thimme; at the Nelson-Atkins Museum, Robert Cohon; at the Metropolitan Museum, Dietrich von Bothmer, Joan Mertens, Elizabeth Milleker, and Mary Moore; at the Museum of the Rhode Island School of Design, Florence Friedman; at the Smithsonian, Susan Crawford, Linda Eisenhardt, Jim Rubinstein, Felicia Pickering, and Candace Green; at the Toledo Art Museum, Kurt Luckner; and at the Wadsworth Atheneum, Jean Cadogan; at the Walters Art Gallery, Ellen Reeder and Carol Benson; and the private collectors, Christos G. Bastis, Lawrence and Barbara Fleischman, and Shelby and Leon Levy. Their enthusiastic and steadfast support was essential to our work.

Special guidance and advice was often sought from and given carefully and generously by two colleagues, Mary Comstock and Dietrich von Bothmer. They have tried to keep us from making major mistakes; we hope that we have not failed them. Each of the authors was at one time or another helped, encouraged, or inspired by George M. A. Hanfmann (1911-1986). We remember him with gratitude and affection.

The following individuals provided information and advice on objects of interest: Brian Aitken, Maxwell Anderson, Alexandra Antoniou, Ernst Badian, Larissa Bonfante, Amy Brauer, Carlo de Simone, Torkom Demirjian, Robert Haber, Robert Hecht, Ariel Herrmann, Silvia Hurter, Quentin Maule, Ingrid and Bruce McAlpine, Edward Merrin, Samuel Merrin, Christo Michailides, Leo Mildenberg, Andrew Oliver, George Ortiz, Carlos Picon, Emeline Richardson, Martin Robertson, Brian Shefton, Thomas Solley, Robin Symes, Annewies van den Hoek, Emily Vermeule, Michael Ward, Melba Whatley, Dyfri Williams, and Paul Zanker.

The Cleveland Museum of Art's Ingalls Library, under Librarian Ann Abid, aided greatly in research during the development and production of this catalogue. We are especially grateful to Georgina Gy. Toth, who checked and systematized the complex notes and bibliographies. Sara Jane Pearman assisted in locating illustrations and reading parts of the manuscript, while Eleanor Schiefele organized many of the illustrations of comparative material.

Four women—two on the staff of The Cleveland Museum of Art, and two volunteers in the Department of Ancient Art—Sharon Herene, Daphne Cothren, Carol Lock, and Diane Kelling were the lifeblood of the entire operation. None of our ideas could have come to fruition without their tireless efforts, and most especially their *esprit de corps* and sense of humor. Judith DeVere assisted in many technical aspects of the production.

From the outset of the project, the Publications Department of The Cleveland Museum of Art was involved in the conception of the catalogue. The authors join me in thanking Laurence Channing for his thoughtful, careful guidance in planning the catalogue and his superb talents at designing the whole.

Assistant Directors William S. Talbot and Lawrence J. Wheeler aided greatly in the development and realization of the project, as have Cleveland's Registrar, Delbert R. Gutridge; Designer, William E. Ward; and Plant Operations Manager, Philip H. Dickinson.

"The bronze team" thank Evan H. Turner, Director of The Cleveland Museum of Art, for his spirited encouragement and unflagging support. More than any other individual involved, his belief in this exhibition and his efforts on its behalf have made the dream come true.

The greatest pleasure in writing this Preface is that it affords me the opportunity to express my sincere admiration for the scholarship, energy, integrity, and sensitivity of all five colleagues—David, Marion, Cornelius, Suzannah, and John.

Arielle P. Kozloff

Introduction

During the late fourteenth century the rediscovery of classical bronze statuettes paralleled that of classical stone sculptures, coins, and gems, as part of the intense study and imitation of all aspects of classical antiquity in Italy. By the fifteenth and early sixteenth centuries, Renaissance bronzecasters, like Benvenuto Cellini (1500-1571), Pier Jacopo Bonacolsi (called "Antico," ca. 1460-1528), and other masters in northern Italian cities, including Florence, Padua, Mantua, and Venice, were producing a steady stream of fine statuettes, small functional objects such as lamps and inkwells, and other works, often closely patterned on ancient models, to keep pace with mounting demand. It is still unknown precisely which ancient statuettes numbered among the models for the major Renaissance bronzes and how they were studied and adapted by Renaissance bronzecasters.[1]

From Renaissance times on, ancient Greek bronzes began to reach western Europe in modern times as travelers, merchants, and diplomats visited Greek lands with greater frequency. Some were brought back as souvenirs; a delightful little late Archaic Peloponnesian Heracles, for example, traveled in the kit-bag of a Hessian mercenary in the late seventeenth century. One of the first Greek statuettes to stray north of the Alps, it is now in the Hessisches Landesmuseum, Kassel. During the eighteenth century, classical bronze statuettes were avidly collected by members of the French court; many of those works now form the nucleus of the great collection of bronze statuettes at the Bibliothèque Nationale, Paris. Likewise, royal, noble, and papal collections constitute the core holdings of the Kunsthistorisches Museum, Vienna, and the Vatican Museums.[2]

With the discovery of and first excavations at Pompeii and Herculaneum in the 1760s, the publications of J. J. Winckelmann, the "Grand Tour" for English noblemen to Italy, and the expeditions of the English Society of the Dilettanti to Greece, a new phase in the collecting, study, and appreciation of classical bronze statuettes began. Connoisseurs like Richard Payne-Knight[3] and artists like the neo-classical Danish sculptor Berthold Thorwaldsen (1770-1844) acquired fine statuettes in Greece and Italy. The intense archaeological activity that began in Greece following its liberation from Ottoman rule in 1833 brought to light many Greek bronze statuettes. Especially notable are the systematic excavations of major sanctuaries like those at Olympia, Delphi, and the Athenian Acropolis, as well as private activities at Dodona and the rustic sanctuaries of Arcadia, all of which uncovered magnificent statuettes. Many of those latter objects eventually found their way to museums in Berlin, Munich, and elsewhere in Europe as well as in America.

In the United States, collecting classical bronze statuettes began only during the last quarter of the nineteenth century. Among the first pieces to enter public collections here were statuettes from the vast accumulation of antiquities obtained by Luigi Palma di Cesnola in Cyprus. Among the ones so acquired by the newly founded Metropolitan Museum of Art in New York is an archaic nude girl created as a mirror support (not in this exhibition).[4] During the 1890s, American merchant princes and notable connoisseurs like Henry Walters, J. Pierpont Morgan, and Edward Perry Warren competed in the European market to acquire fine statuettes—including several examples in this exhibition, as the information about previous owners in the various entries makes clear. The comprehensive collections of classical bronze statuettes in the Metropolitan Museum, the Boston Museum of Fine Arts, and the Walters Art Gallery in Baltimore owe much of their strength and distinction to the taste and indefatigable activity of these pioneer collectors, as well as to the first great museum curators of classical art, such as Edward Robinson in Boston and Gisela M. A. Richter in New York. During the first quarter of the twentieth century, American collectors and curators also added fine Greek,

Etruscan, and some Roman statuettes to smaller university museums like those of Princeton University; Bowdoin College in Brunswick, Maine; and the Rhode Island School of Design in Providence. At the same time, scholars wrote the first systematic, scientific catalogues of classical bronzes in the United States, including Richter's 1915 publication for the Metropolitan Museum. Sumptuous privately printed collection and auction catalogues—for instance, the one C. H. Smith prepared for J. P. Morgan[5]—were also conspicuous products of the years about 1890-1930. In 1929 the first comprehensive handbook of classical bronzes, including statuettes, was published in London: Winifred Lamb's *Greek and Roman Bronzes*.

Since then, our knowledge of classical bronze statuettes has accelerated through continuing scientific excavations and ongoing scholarship. New excavations at Perachora and the Isthmian sanctuary of Poseidon (near Corinth), Katapodi in Boeotia, and Kato Symi Viannou in Crete, as well as renewed excavations at Dodona, the Heraion of Samos, and above all, Olympia have continually revealed still more ancient Greek bronze statuettes from securely excavated, datable contexts. Controlled excavations at the cemeteries of Spina, the houses and villas of Pergamum, Ephesus, Delos, Volubilis in Morocco, Augst in Switzerland, and many other sites throughout the Mediterranean area have greatly enriched our store of Roman and Etruscan bronzes from known contexts. Their discovery in such circumstances shows how in specific cases bronzes were used, seen, stored, and valued by their owners, and also may give valuable information about where they may have been manufactured.

By their acquisitions, major American and European museums have brought many superb classical statuettes to public attention. Major exhibitions since World War II, such as *Ancient Art in American Private Collections* in 1955, *Masterpieces of Greek Art* in 1960, *Master Bronzes from the Classical World* in 1967-1968, have assembled comprehensive selections of classical bronze statuettes or have reexamined great collections in the light of new scholarship (for example, *Guss und Form*, 1986).[6] Accompanying most of them have been detailed scholarly catalogues and symposia discussing bronze statuettes from art historical, cultural, and technical points of view.

Perhaps the most important single factor contributing to the rapid growth of the study and appreciation of classical bronze statuettes, however, has been an international effort by European scholars to publish the major collections of Roman bronzes in the countries north and west of the Alps. Initiated and guided by Heinz Menzel of Mainz, this undertaking has produced excellent scholarly catalogues of collections in France, the Low Countries, West Germany, Switzerland, and Austria. It has also stimulated biennial international working congresses of bronze scholars from Europe and North America, with accompanying detailed scholarly proceedings, many of which appear in the notes throughout this catalogue. Surely this enterprise will intensify during the years to come. The inauguration and growth of exceptional private collections in Europe and the United States focus further attention on bronzes. Discriminating connoisseurs continually demonstrate how many bronzes of outstanding quality can still be brought together. Such efforts, especially when the generous collectors are willing to loan their objects to exhibitions, further enhance our understanding and appreciation of these outstanding works of art.

Possessing an aesthetic and presence distinctively their own, small human figures wrought in bronze rank among the most beautiful and original creations of classical art. By assembling a selection of the finest statuettes to be found in collections in the United States and by concentrating on their special imagery, functions, and aesthetic qualities, we intend to present the human classical bronze statuette for the first time as an art form of major importance. These small figures are uniquely effective in conveying a fresh, immediate understanding of the highest classical aesthetic standards and the most original achievements of Greek, Etruscan, and Roman artists.

Classical bronze statuettes, in themselves, immediately capture our attention with their vitality and beauty. Although evoking the forms and subjects of large-scale statues, they compel us to consider them on their own terms. Their material—cast, then polished, and adorned by incision—is beautiful, durable, and costly. These qualities, as well as their portability, made bronze statuettes especially attractive and convenient as votive offerings to the gods during the more than one thousand years of Greek, Etruscan, and Roman civilization. From the fourth century BC on, bronze statuettes also became increasingly favored ornaments for homes and villas.

Designing, casting, and finishing bronze statuettes required proportionately just as much labor and painstaking care as did the manufacture of monumental bronze statues. Intended by their makers to be seen and perhaps handled at close quarters, they invite appreciation of their technical perfection and artistic beauty through intimate contact and scrutiny—through touch as well as sight. When so viewed, they soon reveal an aesthetic and technical logic all their own, one not derived from monumental sculpture. Because so many have survived, the bronze statuettes also help us to gain a more comprehensive picture of the development and complex entirety of classical sculpture—Etruscan and Roman as well as Greek—filling many of the gaps in our knowledge left by the nearly total disappearance of large-scale works. The finest statuettes frequently attain extraordinary levels of originality and quality. Some, including works in this exhibition, must rank among the great masterpieces of their time on any scale. They speak eloquently for themselves as they celebrate in ways uniquely their own the central subject and focus of classical art—the human form.

Sometime late in the ninth century BC, if not earlier, Greeks began to cast small-scale figures of animals and human beings in bronze. Although we do not yet know the precise chronology of the development of these bronzes, we must posit two or three "generations" for the full maturation of the technically and aesthetically complex statuette groups that populated the sanctuaries of the Greek world by 700 BC. The distinctive regional styles and their interrelations that helped to shape the development of these late Iron Age statuettes are only partially understood. The local workshops active at the Panhellenic sanctuary of Olympia are now well known, thanks to recent detailed studies of the votive animal statuettes in both bronze and terracotta. In concentrating on animal statuettes, however, scholars have neglected their human counterparts; for example, we still have no single comprehensive treatment of small bronze human figures of the eighth century BC.

Human statuettes of the Greek Geometric period are the ancestors of all the gods, athletes, warriors, and grotesques that the Greeks produced. Beginning around 800 BC, these human bronze statuettes appear in rich variety. They can be freestanding figures, parts of groups, or subsidiary components for larger assembled objects, such as tripod cauldrons. Most are male; female subjects remain rare among Geometric bronzes. Their sizes range from minute to more than a foot in height. Some stand, brandishing spears, while others sit on their own bases, as does the earliest statuette in this exhibition, one from the Walters Art Gallery [1]. Others are active: runners, jumpers, or fighters. Some may have represented gods, like Zeus or Ares, as well as human beings.

Virtually all these statuettes were cast for use as votive gifts, to be placed in sanctuaries, places consecrated to particular gods, as enduring reminders to those gods of someone's piety. At Olympia, enough miscast statuettes and fragments of bronzecasters' waste have been found to demonstrate that the bronzeworkers, probably itinerant craftsmen who followed a regular cycle of festivals and games from sanctuary to sanctuary, set up shop on the spot, both to sell finished statuettes from their stock and to execute special commissions. Although the "price" of such statuettes in the pre-monetary economy of late Iron Age Greece is unfathomable, presumably only wealthy aristocrats and merchants had the means to acquire such finished products.

By this time, the bronzecasters' techniques had reached a high degree of versatility and refinement. They could produce blade-thin castings for horses' manes and legs and for the large rectangular catchplates of safety-pin-shaped brooches (fibulae), which provided convenient fields for incised scenes of horses, birds, fish, and ships. The principal casting process was the lost-wax method (cire-perdu). Simply stated, a wax model of the intended statuette was invested with a clay mold and then melted out; the cavity thus left was immediately filled with molten bronze. This produced a solid-cast statuette. For a larger work, the wax model—and therefore the final product—was made around a ceramic core. Iron pins, or chaplets, were inserted to hold the core in place when the wax was melted and poured out and during the casting process.

Where did these techniques originate? Already highly developed for producing jewelry, statuettes, and fittings for metal vessels during the Aegean Bronze Age (ca. 1800-1200 BC), the lost-wax process seems not to have been used for statuette manufacture in mainland Greece during the centuries ca. 1200 to 850 BC, although it was applied during the tenth century BC in making components for large, complex, and expensive tripod cauldrons.[7] Discoveries of imported statuettes at major Greek sanctuaries show that both Near Eastern bronzecasting techniques and Near Eastern and Egyptian bronze statuettes entered the Greek world at an accelerating rate during the eighth and early seventh centuries BC.[8] At this time momentous cultural change revolutionized Greek society from its political structure to its religious organization and affected all aspects of artistic and literary activities. The polis and sanctuary; epic poetry, and mythology; increasingly complex painted, drawn, and sculptured figures and scenes; and the use of writing, all appeared between 770-700 BC. Economic hardship and the search for metals, agricultural land, and adventure sent traders and colonizers to Italy, the Anatolian coasts, and the Black Sea area. Differing styles developed in the new colonial settlements, as well as in established cities like Miletus and Corinth; these eventually transformed the Greek arts—ceramics, metalwork, and sculpture—with their orientalizing motifs and compositions.

The Greek human statuettes of the seventh century exhibit a variety of styles as well as reflect to varying degrees Egyptianizing characteristics of stance, costume, and hairstyle. These features may well be traceable to the presence of imported Egyptian bronze statuettes—some of considerable size—that were dedicated at this time at sanctuaries like the Heraion of Samos.[9] Recognition of these affinities with Egyptian stylistic features led some time ago to the definition of the so-called "Dedalic style" visible in all artistic media during the second half of the seventh century BC. Named after the legendary sculptor, metalworker, and builder, Dedalus, the "Dedalic style" is now understood to be an artificial construct of modern scholarship that codifies and simplifies features visible in a variety of regional styles stretching from the new colonial cities of the Greek West to the mainland, Crete, the Cyclades, and the islands and communities along the coastline of Asia Minor.

At the same time, we have far fewer seventh-century Greek bronze statuettes than eighth-century ones. Two of the most famous, also among the most idiosyncratic, are included in this exhibition. The male figure, now in the Boston Museum of Fine Arts [2], is an impressive creation of geometric volumes assembled with a rigid insistence on bilateral symmetry. The dedicatory inscription, incised on his legs, is written in dactylic hexameter (the verse form in which the *Iliad* and the *Odyssey* were written), and states that Mantiklos dedicated the statuette to Apollo, expecting a benefit in return. It has made this statuette famous as a landmark of Greek art and epigraphy of ca. 700-675 BC. If the figure's hand held a bow, we could identify the bronze as representing Apollo himself. Supposedly found with the Mantiklos "Apollo" is a female figure from the Walters Art Gallery [3]. With an upright, pillarlike body, arms bent at the elbows, and hands extended, her scalloped, wiglike headdress and staring eyes mark her as an early Greek masterpiece of the clothed female form, produced in a provincial workshop, ca. 675-650 BC, already deriving and reinterpreting its stylistic vocabulary from models farther east in the Mediterranean. As in so many statuettes, however, the precise identity of this lady—as goddess or mortal woman—cannot be determined. If the Mantiklos dedication and his consort in the Walters Art Gallery are at least roughly contemporary, they demonstrate just how markedly divergent were the regional Greek styles by the middle of the seventh century BC. Marion True has forcefully argued that the divergent styles of [2] and [3] could have occurred within Boeotia itself.

Figure 1. *Kouros.* Bronze, H. 19 cm. Greek, from a Cretan workshop, ca. 620 BC. Found in Delphi in 1895. Delphi, Archaeological Museum, 2527.

During the later half of the seventh century, the rapid initial development of Greek monumental sculpture in marble and limestone began, producing both draped female figures (korai) and nude young men (kouroi). These large-scale models profoundly affected contemporary bronze statuettes, such as the tense, lean youth of Cretan manufacture found at Delphi,[10] whose energy bespeaks both comprehension and reinterpretation of his larger counterparts (Figure 1).

Only in the early sixth century BC, however, did the first great spurt of creativity in casting Greek human bronze statuettes take place. Large numbers have been found at sites such as Olympia, Delphi, the Athenian Acropolis, the sanctuary of Zeus at Dodona, the Heraion of Samos, and at various smaller sanctuaries in the Peloponnese, central Greece, and in the islands. In most cases, we do not know how they were intended to be mounted and displayed, although there is evidence that some were attached to stepped bases or inserted on top of pedestal- or columnar-shaped monuments. These statuettes from the sixth century range from miniatures less than five centimeters tall to ones half a meter or more high. They occur both as freestanding figures (as well as in groups, although no intact Archaic examples are preserved) and in ensembles for placement on the rims, shoulders, or elsewhere on large bronze kraters, mixing bowls, rod tripods, and other similar vessels. Finally, human figures, usually female, support the discs of hand mirrors, as in the Metropolitan's caryatid mirror [6], probably made in Laconia, the province surrounding Sparta, and the magnificent late Archaic Aphrodite with winged Erotes in the Boston Museum of Fine Arts [7].[11]

Because of their scale, these figures reveal a significantly different aesthetic from that of their monumental counterparts. Small in size, they must be closely examined to be understood completely. Such ease of manipulation also facilitates experimentation with innovative poses and attitudes that would be more difficult to achieve in larger, heavier, and more expensive sculptures—whether carved in limestone or marble, or cast in bronze. Consequently, the aesthetics of bronze statuettes are quite different from those observed in large-scale stone or bronze sculpture, whether freestanding or subordinated to settings on or in great sacred buildings.

The function of freestanding bronze statuettes, however, had not yet developed much beyond that of tiny but sumptuous offerings to the gods, presented either in anticipation of divine favor or in fulfillment of a previous promise or a vow. Although not prohibitively costly, these figures were nonetheless of a beautiful material, plastically shaped and durable; the contemplation of their lustrous surfaces and exquisite details would surely please the gods while continually reminding them of the donors' piety and worthiness. The statuettes thus partake in what seems to be a general principle of how the Greeks visualized their gods: as human-like beings, who loved costly, beautiful gifts. At the same time, such statuettes also informed other mortal viewers of the religious scruples, social status, economic power, and good taste of their dedicants. In the competitive Greek society, to increase one's *arete* (excellence)—i.e., to excel—was supremely important. The competitive striving for arete and the prestige it bestowed provided a dominant motive for the commissioning, manufacture, and dedication of bronze statuettes—indeed, for all votive offerings—as enduring presents to the gods in their most favored earthly haunts.

Because we have only a small sample of original large-scale sculptural works from the Archaic period, the surviving bronze statuettes—both freestanding and designed as vessel attachments—provide invaluable help in our efforts to understand more completely what Greek sculptors achieved during these formative decades. We also gain some idea of particularly favored types of statuettes and where they were especially popular. For instance, fully panoplied warriors, probably made in Laconian workshops (Figure II), were preferred by patrons in the southern

Figure II. *Laconian Warrior.* Bronze, H. 12 cm. Laconian, ca. 520-510 BC. Karlsruhe, Badisches Landesmuseum, 73.1.

Figure III. *Kouros.* Bronze, H. 28 cm. Ca. 540-530 BC. From the Heraion at Samos. Berlin, Staatliche Museen, Stiftung Preussischer Kulturbesitz, Antikenabteilung, 31098.

Figure IV. *"Peplos Kore."* Marble, H. 120 cm. Athenian, ca. 530 BC. Athens, Acropolis Museum, 679. Photo: Deutsches Archäologisches Institut, Rome.

and eastern Peloponnese and also at Dodona in northwestern Greece. Lively little figures of stocky shepherds wearing conical felt caps and thick cloaks, sometimes with animal offerings in their hands, were natural choices in the small mountain sanctuaries of remote Arcadia. The Heraion of Samos abounds in nude male statuettes of the kouros type (Figure III).

Although not from this location, the Metropolitan's youth, formerly owned by Walter C. Baker [5], provides a splendid example. These bronze youths may hold their arms bent at their sides or extend them forward. Their outstretched hands may originally have held saucers for pouring liquid offerings, while their pierced fists may have held weapons or athletic equipment. It is their very ambiguity that makes them so fascinating, because a given nude youth could serve equally effectively as an athlete, warrior, or worshipper, or even as a hero or a god.

Some of the finest Greek Archaic bronze statuettes are unmistakably deities. Hermes—the messenger god, patron of travelers and herders, and conductor of the dead to Hades—wears a short belted tunic, flat conical hat, and high laced boots sprouting wings in two Boston statuettes [8, 9]. In both, he is depicted as holding a small sheep under his left arm, transforming the animal brought as an offering by a mortal worshipper to one under divine protection. The god's distinctive costume makes his identification certain. Presumably the products of Peloponnesian workshops, both statuettes were made about 520-490 BC, although some have suggested that [9] is a superb archaizing work of the first century BC.

An impressive female statuette also in the Boston Museum of Fine Arts [4], found at Mazi, near Olympia, probably represents a goddess. Her long tresses, taut upright pose, and the strong suggestion of torso, buttocks, and legs beneath the skirt of her dress (peplos) make her a miniature counterpart to or descendant of such large-scale marble maidens as the "Peplos Kore" (Figure IV), dedicated on the Athenian Acropolis around 540-530 BC. The stance of the Boston statuette on top of a three-stepped plinth heightens her similarity to monumental Archaic statues of women, which often stood on such bases. The bow that she grasps in her hand, however—the attribute of Apollo's sister, Artemis, huntress and protector of wild animals—suggests that she represents Artemis, an identification fortunately confirmed by the dedicatory inscription incised on the front of her skirt. Besides serving as costly miniature dedications, among the finest known from their time, these three statuettes [4, 8, 9] may also show us how some early large-scale cult images of these gods, placed in Peloponnesian temples during the years 550-520 BC, may have appeared.

As in the example from Mazi, Archaic bronze statuettes are often inscribed, most frequently on a leg, thigh, or skirt. Usually very brief texts, the inscriptions seldom comprise more than the donor's and divine recipient's names (the latter in the dative case), then sometimes the verb for "dedicated." One can imagine a Spartan or Argive aristocratic landowner proudly taking his grandson to Olympia to attend the great four-year festival. There, he would point out the statuette or statuettes inscribed with his name that he had dedicated to Zeus in earlier years, perhaps in thanks for abundant harvests or a safe return from battle, or even in commemoration of an athletic victory. Such offerings would have been an enduring source of pride and prestige for the dedicant, his family, friends, and his city-community.

What we do not know is how the taste, means, and intentions of the dedicant interacted with the creativity, ideas, and technical expertise of the bronzecaster in determining the final form. We suspect that innovations within a developing series—a fiercer warrior, a more individualized kouros, a more realistic Hermes carrying a ram—would often have been desired. In many instances, the dedicants may have visited a bronzecaster's workshop or sales booth near the sanctuary, where a stock of "ready-mades" would have been available for immediate purchase. In others, they would have commissioned a gift according to the opportunity and funds available. In still other cases, however, the pilgrims would have brought statuettes with them from home.

Late in the sixth century BC, Greek statuettes became increasingly active in pose and innovative in their representation of the human figure both in motion and during rest. In these and other ways, they appear to have played a primary—perhaps truly "avant-garde" role—as realistic depictions of the human figure moving freely in space. Mastery of this ability formed the essential transition from Archaic conventions for rendering movement into the early manifestations of the Classical style. These innovative bronzes began to extend into and involve themselves with space, breaking out of their former confines within single planes or blocklike volumes. They also started shifting their weight onto one foot, setting up corresponding tensions and relaxations of muscle groups in ways closely resembling the appearance of the human body in motion or at rest. The statuettes may well have anticipated, perhaps even stimulated, the structural, technical, and aesthetic innovations that large-scale hollow-cast bronze sculpture achieved during the decades 510-480 BC, perhaps the single most important factor in developing the early Classical style in Greek sculpture. Much still remains unknown about this process, how these small figures were influenced by monumental sculpture and vase painting, and vice versa, and how the broader political and military events in Greek society during those years—such as the beginnings of Athenian democracy, the traumatic Persian invasions of Greece, and the sudden, exhilarating Greek victories over the Persians against overwhelming odds—affected and influenced the origins of Classical Greek art.

A shift in Greek votive practices toward commemorating victories at local or Panhellenic athletic festivals may have stimulated this momentous change. During the late sixth and first half of the fifth centuries BC, victorious athletes increasingly wanted to dedicate statues and statuettes in civic market places as well as in sanctuaries, acknowledging—often depicting—the event they had won. In some instances, such a dedication may also have been aimed at winning divine favor prior to the competition. These small bronze athletes—jumpers, wrestlers, discus throwers, and others engaged in activities not yet identified—give us specific glimpses of stages in the progressive innovative mastery of virtually every active pose assumed by the human figure. A series of runners and discus throwers from the Athenian Acropolis—made and dedicated before the catastrophic Persian sack of 480 BC—Delphi, and Olympia is a case in point.

For a few decades after the Persian Wars, to around 440 BC, Greek bronzecasters made many freestanding bronze statuettes of outstanding quality and compelling originality. The newly acquired freedom inherent in the early Classical sculptural style enabled them to create miniature human figures who twist and turn, shift their weight, or pause momentarily. Thus they devised, through a seemingly infinite gradation of gestural and attitudinal nuances, a new language of meaning, of expressing inner psychological states (the quality that the Greeks called "ethos"), revealing and exploring the depicted individual's character, thoughts, and feelings. They created visual counterparts for the representation and shrewd exploration of individual moral dilemmas and emotional states of mind that appear so forcefully in Athenian tragic dramas during the mid-fifth century BC.

Examples of such innovative statuettes appear in this exhibition. A tiny, exquisitely rendered youth, from the J. Paul Getty Museum, bends backward, dying as he falls [10]. He may represent one of the children of Niobe, shot down by the arrows of the angry Artemis and Apollo after Niobe boasted that her children were finer and more numerous than those two gods, the children of Leto. Whatever its identification, this statuette gives us one of the most poignant and vivid images of death created by the Classical Greeks. Arresting, too, in pose and mood is a powerful standing youth in Cleveland [12], perhaps created in a South Italian Greek workshop, possibly Locri or Tarentum, around 450-425 BC. Although his identification is complicated by a missing arm, he may represent an athlete beginning to relax, his weight balanced on one foot, in an alert yet introspective post-victory mood. He is an invaluable example of Classical sculptors' intense preoccupation with the human figure's shift of weight onto one leg, leaving the other relaxed, and the resulting rhythms and tensions caused by this shift. This interest in the ideal human figure standing in repose led to the formulation and creation of ideal athletic figures by Polyclitus of Argos (ca. 450-420 BC), who codified and explained his system of proportions embodied in these figures in a book on his canon (Figure V). Although we do not understand how the canon worked, it seems to have involved a complex system of proportions, related to each other as well as to the entire figure. In very few instances, however, do we find Greek bronze statuettes that merely replicate large-scale models. The Classical Greek art of shaping small-scale human figures in bronze had become far too inventive and innovative for that.

The complex poses newly attained by great masters of miniature bronzecasting, who in some instances may also have been producing large-scale bronze statues, is nowhere seen more clearly than in the striding, twisting male figure in Dumbarton Oaks [11]. This leanly muscled, bearded figure steps forward as he

Figure V. *Youth Holding a Ball.* Bronze, H. 14.7 cm. Probably Argive. Berlin, Staatliche Museen, Stiftung Preussischer Kulturbesitz, Antikenabteilung, 8089.

twists his body, his arms bent backward over his head as if about to deliver a mighty blow. Dating to ca. 460-450 BC, his identity—as the divine smith Hephaistos, another god or hero, or even a mortal man—remains a fascinating enigma.

Around 450-430 BC, Athens reached the height of its political power and cultural influence. The Parthenon with its sculptures— especially the colossal gold and ivory cult statue of Athena Parthenos, richly adorned with subsidiary relief sculptural compositions (like the battle of Greeks and Amazons on Athena's shield) and many other buildings, monuments, and statues taking shape under the partnership of the statesman Pericles (d. 429 BC) and the sculptor Phidias (ca. 450-430 BC)—the general overseer of the Parthenon project and creator of the Athena Parthenos and the slightly later, gold and ivory seated Zeus for his temple at Olympia—generated a supremely influential high Classical style, which is characterized by a new idealization of the human figure and realization of the full expressive potential of drapery. Yet, in comparison with the abundant productivity in bronze statuettes of the immediately preceding decades, surprisingly few have been found that reflect and partake of this new style.

Around 430 BC, there is a noticeable, sudden falling off in the numbers of bronze statuettes of high quality being dedicated in sanctuaries throughout the Greek world. At this time also, the magnificent series of bronze mirrors supported by standing female, and occasionally male, statuettes comes to an end. Although the reasons for this decline have not yet been fully investigated, they appear to be complex. Could the Greeks have substituted other types of gifts at this time? Is this abatement a sign of the general economic and political disruption accompanying the Peloponnesian War? Is it a sign, too, of declining or changing religious piety, a questioning of traditional rites—including the kinds of gifts long customary for the gods—as moral and spiritual malaise gradually pervaded the Greek world? Nothing is certain, but clearly larger trends and forces within Greek society were steadily and decisively altering the patterns of political, intellectual, and religious activities and beliefs that had engendered the "Golden Age" of the Greek bronze statuette.

During the last quarter of the fifth century BC and increasingly into the fourth, however, we find a marked increase in private and secular uses of images—especially small sculptures in terracotta, marble, and perhaps in bronze, too, for the adornment of private residences, first those of the very rich in Athens and the Peloponnese, then of what we might call "middle-class" homes, such as those at Olynthus in southern Macedonia. The expanding popularity of small-scale sculpture for private use during these decades has been carefully documented.[12] This development reveals a rising interest in and effort to obtain personal luxuries of all kinds, perhaps stimulated by a growing consciousness of, and access to, luxury goods from the Persian-controlled lands east of Greece. Few superb Greek statuettes securely datable to the early and middle fourth century BC, however, exist in American collections, which accounts for their virtual absence in this exhibition. An exception, however, is Cleveland's tautly dynamic rider [13], probably made in Tarentum between 400 and 375 BC.

It is significant, too, that practically no bronze statuettes appear among the recent astonishing discoveries of funerary metalwork in rich tombs from Macedonia and Thrace dating to the decades of Macedon's rise to supremacy in the Greek world (ca. 360-300 BC). That such works continued to be made in numbers during the fourth century BC is suggested by anecdotal accounts, such as that of the prolific sculptor Lysippus' creation of a little seated Hercules Epitrapezius—which, as the name implies, was suitable for display on a table or other flat surface in a Macedonian general's villa or military headquarters—as well as colossal works like the exhausted, muscle-bound Heracles Farnese (Figure VI). Although probably a late Hellenistic or early Roman work, the powerful standing god, apparently Zeus, in the collection of Mr. and Mrs. Lawrence A. Fleischman [29], shows the influence of the proportions and style of Lysippus' work as we know it.

Two statuettes in this exhibition also reflect and rework what may have been the most daring innovation in Greek sculpture during the fourth century BC: the goddess Aphrodite depicted in the nude. The famous Aphrodite of Cnidus (Figure VII), by the Athenian master sculptor Praxiteles (act. ca. 370-330 BC), became the prototype for dozens of versions—reinterpretations and replicas, large and small—during ensuing centuries. Praxiteles is known to have created numerous slender, graceful statues of both young male and female personages, often characterized by sensuous S-curves and softly modeled anatomy. The first shown here, from the Metropolitan Museum [15], is a fairly straightforward rendition of the Cnidian Aphrodite, who appears as if just emerging from her bath. It was probably made two centuries after its prototype, conceivably to adorn a mansion or villa. Its proportions and stance adhere closely to what we know of the original. In marked contrast, the tall, elegant hollow-cast Aphrodite in the Museum of Art, Rhode Island School of Design [22], presents a radically different interpretation of the goddess, modeled according to the refined, erotic taste for mortal feminine beauty that late Hellenistic and Roman Republican collectors and connoisseurs would have appreciated. The sophisticated, almost manneristic, version that the Rhode Island Aphrodite portrays must have been popular; less complete bronze counterparts exist in the Metropolitan and Toledo, Ohio, museums. One can imagine such an

Figure VI. *Heracles of Farnese Type.* Marble, H. 42.25 cm. Roman 2nd century copy of original of 330-320 BC by Lysippus. The Detroit Institute of Arts, 68.65.

Figure VII. *Cnidian Aphrodite.* Roman copy of an original by Praxiteles, ca. 350-330 BC. Marble, 205 cm. Rome, Vatican Museum, 812. Photo: Art Resource, New York.

Aphrodite shown near a small fountain among the shrubs and trees of a peristyle courtyard of a villa on the Bay of Naples.

In the late fourth to early third centuries BC in Greek and Greek-influenced lands, the mold-made and painted terracotta statuette became the leading genre of miniature sculpture. Easily manufactured and fired in large quantities, these statuettes were equally suitable as dedications, household decorations, children's toys, and burial offerings (Figure VIII). It may be that the growth of this mass industry and its markets, along with changing religious beliefs and tastes, generally replaced bronze statuettes as votive dedications, which had been their predominant function until late in the fifth century BC. The virtual absence of bronze statuettes that are similar to the terracotta figurines in subject and treatment is nevertheless surprising. One exception is the so-called "Baker Dancing Woman" [14], named for its former owner, Walter C. Baker, who bequeathed it to the Metropolitan Museum. A woman, veiled and swathed from head to feet in complex overlapping layers of heavy costume, twists in the movements of a lively dance. The axes, volumes, and planes set up by her moving figure create a composition that is understandable and interesting when viewed from any angle. The bronzecaster has managed to suggest the differing weights and textures in the layers of her costume—revealing heavier folds beneath a diaphanous outer garment—even retaining the lines left when it had been pressed.[13] Who is represented, where the statuette was made, and why, are not known with certainty, although there are strong reasons for attributing it to an Alexandrian workshop active around 250-150 BC. The superb quality of this dancer and her structure, movement, and presence surely point to the taste of a most discriminating and demanding patron,

Figure VIII. *Dancer.* Terracotta. South Italy, Hellenistic, end 3rd century BC. Museo Nazionale di Taranto. After *Il Tesoro di Taras.*

Figure IX. *Demosthenes.* Marble, H. 202 cm. Roman copy of bronze original erected in Athens ca. 280 BC by Polyeuctus. Copenhagen, Ny Carlsberg Glyptotek, 2782.

conceivably even one of the generals who inherited the conquered lands of Alexander the Great.

Portraiture, in the sense of replicating faithfully an individual's likeness, became fully developed during the first half of the fourth century BC, although the trends leading toward it became increasingly visible from the late sixth century BC onward. In Persian satrapal and Anatolian dynastic courts, for example, portraits were carved into the dies from which silver coins were struck. In the Greek cities (poleis), portraits were most often life-sized standing or seated statues, usually in bronze, of important generals, statesman, poets, or philosophers. The portraits of the philosopher Socrates (ca. 469-399 BC)—of which at least three types are known—bronze portraits of the great fifth-century Athenian tragic poets commissioned by the Athenian state and set up in the Theater of Dionysus, and a generation or more later, the haunting portrait of the Athenian orator Demosthenes (384-322 BC) by Polyeuctus (Figure IX) come to mind as especially important examples of such civic portraiture that could be dedicated both by the state and by private individuals.

These statues seem to have been the visual counterparts of the contemporary rise to prominence of a new literary genre—biography. The likeness of a famous individual carries the visual portrayal of ethos, which we have seen as characteristic of early Classical sculpture, one step further, to the revelation of a specific individual's personality and character that generated deeds and creations worth remembering and emulating. It was in this spirit that successive leaders of the Academy and the other philosophical schools that were being established and developed at Athens and elsewhere during these decades were commemorated through their portraits, a tradition that continued well into Roman times. In this exhibition such portraiture finds vivid illustration through a compelling miniature portrait of an aging philosopher from the Metropolitan Museum of Art [26]. Standing on an Ionic capital, perhaps reproducing in miniature a larger statue mounted on a column, the little figure portrays a stocky elderly man, who, despite his prominent paunch, is still capable of vigorous thought and debate. The direction of his glance and the subtle yet commanding gesture of his right hand reinforce the impression of a thoughtful yet commanding personality. Influencing the vocabulary of his stance and gesture are two leading intellectual forces of his time—oratory and rhetoric—as well as the conventions of acting. Some scholars see him as representing Hermarchus of Mytilene, the philosopher Epicurus' star pupil. Hermarchus succeeded his master as head of the Epicurean school of philosophy, which taught that the absence of pain was the highest good and a good life a predominant goal. Although the Metropolitan statuette appears to be early Roman in date, its prototype was probably produced around the time of Epicurus' death, 270 BC, or slightly later. Without doubt this miniature bronze portrait ranks among the finest achievements in portraiture of its time and is certainly the outstanding example of such statuettes in North America.

The Macedonian domination of the Greek world, followed by Alexander's conquests, which spread Hellenic culture, language, and art throughout and beyond the vast lands of the conquered Achaemenian Persian Empire, created new sources of patronage for bronze statuettes. We know that Alexander himself employed favored court artists whose exclusive task it was to fashion his likeness in sculpture, in painting, on engraved gems, and in other media. Statuettes of Alexander—probably of around 300 BC or slightly later, showing him in nude heroic poses with wiry physique, long limbs, and small head, similar to the proportions that are generally associated with statues by Lysippus—may be small-scale reflections of major commissions commemorating the heroic exploits of Alexander and his companions in hunting and battle, and celebrating his divine nature. Such statuettes might well have served as treasured mementos for his associates and successors, and must have helped to foster his cult and his fascination for later generations. They set precedents, too, for heroizing portraits of his successors, which incorporated the attributes and aspects of gods or heroes. An impressive statuette of the early second century BC, considered on good grounds to represent the Seleucid king, Antiochus IV Epiphanes (175-165/4 BC), a Greek ruler of the Syrian area, as Heracles [30], testifies to the constant need for such statuettes as propaganda, promoting and reinforcing the sovereignty of these rulers and their legitimacy as heirs of Alexander.

The achievement of Greek bronze statuette makers through these centuries can only be appreciated fully, however, if considered alongside that of their Etruscan and Italic counterparts. The immediate Iron Age ancestors of the Etruscans—called "Villanovans" after the site near Bologna where their culture was first defined—were superb bronzecasters. Their convoluted fibulae and complex bridle bits with cheek pieces cast in the forms of stylized horses rank among the masterpieces of Mediterranean bronzeworking of any period. Some of these bronze objects are closely related to ones current throughout the Hallstatt culture of central and northern Europe that possibly represents an early phase of Celtic culture.

With few exceptions, Italic freestanding human bronze statuettes, however, first appeared only during the seventh century BC, apparently in response to the arrival of Near Eastern as well as Greek types and models. As with contemporary Greek statuettes, those manufactured at many Etruscan and Italic centers during the sixth through second centuries BC were largely intended as gifts to the Etruscan gods. They range from individual masterpieces to series of mass-produced statuettes of warriors, women, athletes, and figures of the hero Heracles (Hercules) or the Etruscan Hercle. Some of them are extremely stylized and elongated; many, truly crude. As in other media of Etruscan art, they reveal an original taste for contour, an exuberant love of decorative ornament, and a potential for expressiveness quite distinct from the Greek examples. The Etruscans also went far beyond the Greeks in placing human figures and groups on important parts of larger bronze objects—for example, rod-tripods, braziers, incense burners (thymiateria) [34, 36], candelabras, and as supports for the skillet-shaped paterae [48, 49, 50], as well as handles on the lids of cosmetic boxes (cistae) [45]—forms which are scarce or absent from the known repertoire of Greek bronze vessels and furniture. Many such attachments have been recovered from tombs, both in the major centers of Etruria proper and at outlying commercial settlements like Spina on the Adriatic.[14]

Careful scholarly study and classification have now provided a preliminary organization of these statuettes. The astonishing variety of concurrent Etruscan styles and treatments for the human figure embraces structurally coherent and clearly Hellenizing creations, such as the Fogg Museum's Turan [43], the electrically alive, swinging contours of the Cleveland dancer [34], and the extreme elongation and abstraction of the many warriors and women manufactured in Umbria, as well as in Etruria. The variety goes far beyond anything observable in sixth-through third-century BC Greek bronze statuettes. Archaic features of stance, costume, and physiognomy also often persist alongside more developed Classical features well into the later fifth century BC.

The means by which Greek and eastern Mediterranean prototypes reached major Etruscan bronzecasting centers and the ways in which they were altered and revised are only beginning to be understood. Visible in late sixth-century statuettes, particularly those from sophisticated southern Etruscan centers such as

Vulci, is the unmistakably strong influence of figural styles from the eastern Greek world. The flowing surfaces, broad oval eyes, generously smiling lips, and disproportionately large heads, hands, and feet of many bronze statuettes made at Vulci, ca. 530-500 BC, all betray connections with the sculptural arts of eastern Greek and western Anatolian centers like Ephesus, Miletus, and the Heraion of Samos. These features are immediately apparent in the Morgan Girl from the Metropolitan Museum [33] and in the tiny archer in Scythian costume from the Rhode Island School of Design [32]. At least in some instances, the bronzecasters who executed those statuettes and taught Etruscan metalworkers, too, may have been refugees from the eastern Aegean region, who fled Persian domination.

Patterns of collecting in the United States have brought more Greek bronzes than Etruscan to America, a fact reflected in *The Gods Delight*. However, it is true that more Etruscan than Greek statuettes are actually known in the world today. To what extent this mirrors differences in the votive practices common to Etruscan cults is difficult to determine. Partly responsible, at any rate, for such a rich selection is the discovery of large caches of statuettes in and around Etruscan sanctuaries,[15] something that is not true in Greece, where surviving bronzes have largely turned up only piece by piece. As a whole, the corpus of surviving Etruscan bronze statuettes provides themes, types, and techniques that played crucial roles in shaping the later Roman bronze statuettes in the service of sacred, official, and private constituencies from the decades of the late Republic onward through the Imperial centuries.

The subjects of Etruscan bronze statuettes of the sixth through second centuries BC are extremely varied. As with their Greek counterparts, many ambiguous works could equally well represent deities or mortals. For instance, the fine fragmentary statuette of a draped, bearded man from the J. Paul Getty Museum [39] of around 480-470 BC could as easily represent a priest or worshipper, a hero or a god. Specific identifications for others are equally vague. Thus, the Kansas City striding, bearded male figure of the early fifth century [40] might be a mortal warrior, hero, or a god like Tinia or Maris, the Etruscan Mars. With Uni and Menrva, Tinia formed the Etruscan predecessors of the Roman "Capitoline Triad" of supreme gods: Jupiter, Juno, and Minerva. Most likely representing Turan—the Etruscan counterpart of Aphrodite—is a stately statuette in the Sackler Museum, Harvard University [43], datable to ca. 450-430 BC. Although also conceivably representing a divinity, the late Archaic kouros in the Getty Museum more likely depicts a mortal athlete or worshipper [37]. Even more puzzling is the so-called "Apollo" from the Boston Museum of Fine Arts [31], the earliest Etruscan bronze in this exhibition; it gives no clue whatsoever as to its identity. The Greeks' favorite hero, Heracles, also appears in a myriad of Etruscan and other Italic representations in bronze from the sixth through first centuries BC. They range from crude statuettes, mass-produced as cheap popular dedications, to images of exceptional quality and forceful presence, such as the magnificent late Classical Hercle from Toledo [46].

Figures from the Etruscans' world of subordinate supernatural beings are also prominent, such as the nude, or semi-nude, winged female spirits of love and death, the Lasae, personages that seldom occur in the Greek world. The Cleveland Lasa [50] pirouettes spiritedly as she admires herself in a mirror. She formed the handle of a saucer for pouring liquid offerings (patera) and probably dates to the third or early second century BC. Less clearly supernatural are the nude, sensually plump girls, who also once supported the saucers of paterae, now in the Fleischman and Boston collections [48, 49].

The jolly, ribald crew of Dionysus' companions—the satyrs and silens—are as at home in Etruria as in Greece; two spritely examples close to early Classical Greek models enliven this catalogue. One, from the Walters Art Gallery [42], carries a wine jar (amphora) on his shoulder; the other skips exuberantly ahead, blowing a long curving horn [41]. Both would have formed appropriate decorations, perhaps with others, for a large mixing bowl (dinos), the centerpiece of an Etruscan drinking party.

Human figures are legion, representing the whole range of Etruscan society. Richly clad women may be devotees—like the large, now headless, hollow-cast woman from the Walters Art Gallery [44]—or dancers—like the petite, gesturing girl with lively profile from the Boston Museum of Fine Arts [35]. A partially draped youth of sober mood and impressive stance, an outstanding work of about 480 BC, now in the National Museum of Natural History, Smithsonian Institution [38], may also be a worshipper. The impressionistic modeling and hipshot stance of the Fleischmans' late Classical or early Hellenistic youth with incised inscription [47] may be those of an athlete proudly contemplating a victory.

Dancing girls often cavort atop or support candelabra and incense burners (thymiateria), such as an early fifth-century BC example in the Christos G. Bastis collection [36]. Etruscan and Latin metalworking, especially a school at Praeneste, east of Rome, produced a series of cylindrical, lidded bronze boxes (cistae), with engraved scenes on the bodies and cast handles and feet (see Figure XVI in the introduction to the Etruscan section). Cleveland's handle group [45], in which two winged bearded figures in armor stoop to carry off the body of a dead youth, must have crowned one of the finest such cistae known. The death of Sarpedon, the Lycian king who was a major ally of Troy, received monumental treatment on Athenian red-figure vases at the end of the sixth century BC. Although probably produced at least a century later, the three-dimensional version of the myth shown in the Cleveland cista handle is no less poignant, retaining much of the restraint of its Greek counterparts. Etruscan-style bronze statuettes continued to be made throughout northern and central Italy well into the decades of the late Republic, after 100 BC. Along with Hellenistic Greek statuettes, they provided the precedents and prototypes for many types of Roman bronze statuettes.

It is not always easy to distinguish Greek bronze statuettes made during the Hellenistic centuries from their Roman counterparts. Much more work is needed to identify and define distinctively Hellenistic methods of surface working and treatment, and approaches to rendering the human figure on a small scale. The lack of such research has created a large category of statuettes with no attribution or date beyond the general term, "Greco-Roman." The assignment of more precise dates and attributions should be made an urgent priority in research on bronze statuettes, as indeed for Hellenistic and Roman sculpture in general.

The finest Hellenistic statuettes rival their sixth- and fifth-century forebears. Some are original, if eclectic, creations that freely borrow and combine traits from fifth- and fourth-century predecessors. Others are fairly faithful miniature replicas of famous large-scale statues, a practice that accelerated during Roman times. The series of statuettes replicating or adapting famous large originals—like the Hephaestus of Alkamenes at Athens or the Tyche of Antioch—should be reexamined in order to distinguish, if possible, Hellenistic from Roman versions. Such statuettes undoubtedly formed popular souvenirs for wealthy travelers visiting cultural centers such as Athens or Alexandria. Individual, seemingly original, interpretations of divinities—such as the calm vertical classicizing statuette of the Greek healing god Asclepius now in the Cincinnati Art Museum [18], which reworks fourth-century BC Greek models—illustrate the contrasting styles and moods that such large statuettes of high quality can convey.

Some of the most striking creations of Hellenistic art in general, including bronze statuettes made during the third and second centuries BC, apparently originated in Alexandria, the great cosmopolitan seaport and political and cultural capital of Hellenistic Egypt. Founded in 331 by Alexander the Great (355/6-323 BC) on the Mediterranean coast near the mouth of a western branch of the Nile, Alexandria became under Ptolemy I Soter (d. 283/2 BC) and his successors a world center of culture, learning, and scientific research with the establishment of the renowned Library and its affiliated scholars and scientists, supported by royal patronage. For instance, the scholar and scientist Eratosthenes (b. ca. 275 BC) under Library auspices launched the experiments and measurements that not only enabled him to show that the earth was actually round but also to calculate its circumference with remarkable accuracy.

To serve the Hellenic ruling class and unite it with the vast majority of Egyptians who were little touched, if at all, by Hellenic culture, Ptolemy I commissioned the Athenian sculptor Bryaxis (ca. 350-312 BC) to create the image of a new god Serapis (Figure X). He combined the mature bearded male appearance of Classical Greek gods, like Zeus and Asclepius, with aspects of Egyptian gods, like Zeus Ammon and Osiris. The images of Serapis, whether seated or standing, wearing a bucket-shaped grain measure on his head, were replicated in innumerable versions, large and small, throughout the succeeding centuries. Also created in Alexandria during the Hellenistic Period was the image of the boyish Harpocrates (Horus) in which Hellenic and Egyptian traits were fused; Cleveland's superb, large standing Harpocrates may have been made in Alexandria itself [21].

The strong interest of Hellenistic artists in ethnic types, the grotesque and deformed, and the very young and old seems also to have originated during the

Figure X. *Serapis.* Bronze, H. 26.7 cm. Roman, 1st-2nd century AD. Baltimore Museum of Art, 51.256.

third century BC in Alexandria. Its colorful, cosmopolitan, and ethnically diverse population comprised Greeks, blacks, Egyptians, Jews, and many others. This exhibition is especially rich in magnificent bronzes that illustrate different kinds and treatments of such subjects. For example, the Metropolitan statuette of an old man, perhaps an artisan [22], effectively captures the personality and experience of its subject; both legendary and historical personages have been suggested as identifications for him. A grotesque [28], also in the Metropolitan, is among the finest known representations of hunchbacks, cripples, and dwarves, which are depicted with an almost clinical realism and often with what seems like a perverted sense of humor. These types remained popular subjects for bronze statuettes well into Roman times, as the Boston dwarves [56, 57] show us. The populations of large Hellenistic cities like Alexandria were avid fans of professional athletes. Therefore, it is not surprising to find a statuette such as Cleveland's boxer, the so-called "Dattari Athlete" (named after its former owner) [24].

Representations of blacks are also prominent among such Hellenistic statuettes that are probably of Alexandrian inspiration if not origin. Two of the finest anywhere illustrate the Hellenistic sculptors' fascination with such subjects. Boston's small, exquisitely modeled black youth [19] of ca. 150-50 BC stands in a dignified rhetorical pose; his gesture and costume, similar to those of the portrait of a philosopher in New York [26], may indicate that he was a student philosopher or orator. Radically different in attitude and expression is Cleveland's striking black banausos [20]. With a blackened patina highlighted by copper and silver inlays, he vividly portrays a character from the streets of Alexandria, although a more precise identification eludes us.

Among the most unusual Hellenistic bronzes known is the Dumbarton Oaks celebrated seated statuette of an emaciated sick youth, formerly in the E. P. Warren collection [25]. The forward inclination of the figure and the eloquent downward gesture of the slightly raised hand give the impression of a seriously ill patient awaiting treatment at one of the major sanctuaries of Asclepius, such as those at Epidaurus, Cos, or Pergamum, the sanitaria of antiquity. Since the statuette is unique, the motivation of its maker escapes us. Conceivably, it could have been a votive offering from a physician or a recovered patient to Asclepius.

During the second century BC, the Romans increasingly dominated the Greek East militarily and politically. War with the Achaean League culminated in the sack of Corinth by the Roman Consul and General Mummius in 146 BC. Thirteen years later, Attalus III (138-133 BC), the last king of Rome's ally Pergamum, bequeathed his realm in western Asia Minor to the Roman Senate and people. During these decades, the great Roman patrician families became intensely Hellenized. They read Greek literature, sent their sons to Rhodes and Athens to study, and collected Greek art, particularly statuary. In so doing, Rome fully participated in, and increasingly dominated, the later development of Hellenistic art.

To meet the increasing Roman demand for sculpture, workshops were founded in Greece and Asia Minor, particularly at such established centers of sculptural production as Athens and Aphrodisias, as well as in Italy itself. We know about these workshops from discoveries at Pompeii and Herculaneum, and finds at sites like Delos, Stobi (in Yugoslavian Macedonia), and Pergamum, where large statuettes were found in the ruins of wealthy houses. Their locations suggest that they formed important parts of the interior decoration of these buildings. The large late Hellenistic Pans from Stobi and Pergamum have spectacular colleagues in the Shelby and Leon Levy collection [23]. With their vivacious poses, caught as if in the midst of a swirling dance, and their exceptionally fine casting and detailing, these Pans rank among the masterpieces of late Hellenistic art. Possibly once attached to an elaborate piece of furniture, they must have delighted their proud owner.

By far the largest concentration of bronze sculpture, small as well as large, recovered from any dwelling is the collection discovered in the so-called "Villa of the Papyri" at Herculaneum late in the eighteenth century. This villa was the sumptuous country home of a wealthy Roman of around 100 BC, one of the increasing number of patricians who were then building villas around the Bay of Naples. To judge from the charred examples from his library of papyrus scrolls that have been read so far, the owner was an adherent of Epicurean philosophy, the popular system of belief, originated by Epicurus and his pupil Hermarchus of Mytilene. The bronzes were found by tunneling through the villa, covered by solidified volcanic deposits from the eruption of Mount Vesuvius in AD 79, in most cases where they had been placed originally. They include portrait heads and busts of life-sized actual and imaginary philosophers and poets, half life-sized statues of dancing women, and statuettes of animals, satyrs, and other subjects. All vividly demonstrate the artistic tastes and philosophical beliefs of their wealthy connoisseur owner. Their contexts also show us how bronze statuary, including statuettes, may have been displayed in settings ranging from open fountains, peristyle gardens, and colonnaded walkways to interior dining rooms, libraries, and bedrooms. Although definitive technical and art historical studies of these bronzes have not yet been published, it is already apparent that some are especially manufactured eclectic versions, or even reductions, of larger-scale works, made specifically for the owner of this villa.

The late Hellenistic or early Roman bronze workshops were capable of creating large and small statuettes to order in a variety of figural styles, from archaizing to "rococo," or works combining traits of several styles, to accommodate individual tastes. The finest of these works, such as the Metropolitan's standing Hermes [27], are among the most beautiful and elegant small sculptures created at any time from the fifth century BC through the Renaissance. The artist's interpretation of Hermes is far different from the sturdy bearded rural god that we encountered in the late Archaic Greek statuettes [8, 9]. Polyclitan in his relaxed stance but Praxitelean in his slender physique and elegant proportions, this Hermes appears as a graceful youth clad in a traveling costume. The exceptionally sensitive surface treatment of the Metropolitan Hermes proclaim it as probably produced with philhellene Roman Republican tastes in mind; Marion True feels that it could have been created as late as AD 50. Perhaps also as late as these decades is the exquisite nude boy in the Bastis collection [16], whose fluid backward-bending pose intrigues and puzzles us.

That bronze statuettes were considered valuable works of art by connoisseurs during these decades is shown by their presence aboard shipwrecks loaded with art bound for various Mediterranean markets. Statuettes were found alongside large-scale marble and bronze sculpture on a shipwreck near Anticythera Island, off the southern Peloponnese, part of the cargo of a vessel which can be dated as having sunk sometime between 75 and 50 BC. Large statuettes of dancing dwarves and young gods similar to the Metropolitan Hermes that also look like portraits of Hellenistic princes turned up in a wreck of about 100 BC off Mahdia, near Tunis (see Figure XIX in the introduction to the Roman section). Such recoveries must represent only a tiny proportion of the art, both looted and newly created, that was being transported to various urban centers, especially Rome, to meet increasing demand.

The full extent to which serious Roman collectors actively acquired original Greek and Etruscan statuettes is unknown. One suspects that these intimate, highly appealing miniatures were much prized and commanded high prices in the art market of Rome and the cities of Campania during the first century BC, the final tumultuous decades of the Roman Republic, and into the beginning and middle years of the Roman Empire, under the Julio-Claudian, Flavian, and Antonine emperors. The learned tastes of Roman officials, generals, scholars, and merchants, even wealthy freedmen, would have readily accepted and appreciated the varieties of style available in bronze statuettes, whether originals, adaptations, or copies. The possession of fine statuettes—like owning exquisite silver plate vessels, intaglio gems signed by master carvers, or other works of art—would have enhanced their owner's prestige and have strengthened his or her credentials as a discriminating and learned connoisseur.

The introduction of more bronzes onto the art market in Rome may have occurred following specific historical events, as in 44 BC, with Julius Caesar's resettlement of Corinth, which had been largely abandoned during the century following its sack by Mummius. Roman political control of Egypt, after Octavian's decisive victory at Actium in 31 BC over Antony and Cleopatra VII, probably also made new sources of bronze statuettes available. The geographer Strabo (b. ca. 64 BC) reported that the new settlers of Corinth, largely introduced from Italy, ransacked the cemeteries of that Classical city, seeking the highly prized bronzes, which were called *necrocorinthia*, "from the graves of Corinth."[16] Otherwise, the Romans apparently did not plunder Classical Greek cemeteries systematically. Periodic removal of large numbers of bronze statues from Greek sanctuaries, however, occurred well into the second century AD, and bronze statuettes were probably included among the loot. One suspects that a plentiful supply of Greek bronze statuettes remained available both in sanctuaries and in private hands throughout the Greek East well into the third century AD.

Decades of bitter fighting against Mithridates VI Eupator (King of Pontus, 120-63 BC) and other foes in the eastern Mediterranean and bloody civil wars at home finally culminated in the victory of one man, Octavian. Under his better-known name, Augustus—awarded to him in gratitude by the Roman Senate in 27 BC—he reorganized the Roman state and consolidated the Roman Empire. To promote his wide-ranging program of reform and reconstruction, which included a return to traditional Roman values and religious practices, Augustus sponsored an ambitious cultural program, involving both literature and art. Above all, Augustan art drew on Greek models for its inspiration, as the relief panels and friezes of the Altar of Peace (Ara Pacis) and the contrapposto Polyclitan pose and proportions of Augustus' own standing portrait in military costume from Prima Porta, near Rome, clearly demonstrate. The likenesses of Augustus, his family, and associates, as well as the symbols and mottoes of events and goals in his program, were also universally circulated on coins.

The Augustan artistic program most likely furnished the context within which at least two types of specifically Roman bronze statuettes were created. The most important of them are the Lares—youthful tunic-clad male spirits, who either dance vigorously, holding drinking horns or saucers, or step forward in a more restrained, dignified fashion. The Cleveland Lar is one of the finest [62]. Bronze Lares appear in numbers, through a broad range of size and quality, throughout Italy and the western provinces, although less frequently in the Greek East. For generations, they were probably essential members of collections of statuettes in private household shrines (lararia) in homes and, perhaps, cult and business associations and military establishments throughout the Empire. Associated with the Lares are statuettes of male figures clad in togas, which are also draped over their heads.

Comparison with similarly costumed large-scale portrait statues and figures in state reliefs identifies them as making sacrifices. They are thought to have represented the "genius," or protective spirit, both of Augustus and of the paterfamilias, the head of the Roman household.[17]

Also probably to be dated during the reign of Augustus (27 BC-14 AD) or his immediate successors Tiberius, Caligula, Claudius, and Nero are many standing and seated statuettes of gods, often of very high quality, usually displayed on bases. Some, such as representations of Jupiter, Apollo, Bacchus, and Venus, remain Greek in character, imitating or adapting Classical or Hellenistic Greek sculptural models. Such a statuette is the Getty Museum's elegant Diana [53]. Others, like Mars and Mercury, take on a more distinctively Roman quality. The Cleveland Hercules [61], for example, combines classicizing Greek and more specifically descriptive Roman anatomical features into a highly individualized interpretation especially congenial to early Roman tastes. These works, too, could have served as fixtures in lararia or private chapels, gifts at sanctuaries, portable aids for individual worship, or decorative enhancements for the homes of those able to afford them.

Small-scale copies or adaptations of famous Classical and Hellenistic groups of mythological sculpture were also popular both as public dedications and private furnishings. Thus the meticulously finished Amazon in the Levy collection [68] may originally have belonged to such a composition. If so, she may have represented Penthesilea, the Amazon queen with whom Achilles fell in love just as he slew her.

Although many fine bronze statuettes of Roman deities were produced in long-established centers of manufacture in Italy and Greece, it has become evident that equally fine statuettes, some of exceptional quality and originality, were also produced at various workshops in Gaul and Germany, and in the cities and provinces of central Europe, the Balkans, Asia Minor, and the Levant.[18] More precise localization of these centers depends on the full publication of bronze statuettes in museums and private collections, and further discoveries of statuettes in controlled archaeological excavations, such as those in the Roman city of Augst, just east of Basel.

Until recently, few fine Roman bronze statuettes could be found in the United States, relative to the numbers of Greek and Etruscan statuettes acquired by museums and private collectors. Recently, however, several Roman bronze statuettes of superlative quality and preservation have entered American museums. Outstanding in this respect are several impressive figures that seem to form a group, to judge from their lustrous patinas, ranging from a mustard to a darker green hue, and reports that they were found together. A large Victory in Cleveland [66], with widespread wings and cornucopia held aloft, seems literally to hover in mid-air. Her momentary pose and windswept garments place her in a clear line of descent from such Classical Greek masterpieces as the marble Nike by Paeonius (act. ca. 430-410 BC), erected around 420-410 BC at Olympia. Such standing statuettes of Venus and the city goddess Roma as those in the J. Paul Getty Museum [64, 65] adapt and refer to numerous larger-scale sculptures of these goddesses, sharing basically a classicizing style. These figures are associated with a remarkable pair of male figures wearing togas, also in the Getty [63], cast in relief so high that they are almost completely rendered in the round. Of differing ages, these two men look as if they had just arrived from a state or religious procession, or a meeting of the Senate. Their individualized features show them to be specific men, although precise identification with portraits of known members of the Julio-Claudian Imperial family has not yet been possible. The original setting for these statuettes—a monument of some kind, perhaps an altar or trophy, or an elaborate dedication of statuary in a sanctuary—remains unclear. If it is trustworthy, the association of these bronzes, having commensurately distinguished quality but widely divergent sizes and subject matters, demonstrates how ready the Romans were to combine disparate works to create a powerful whole in the service of state goals, cult functions, or the privileges and aspirations of the wealthiest families.

Because so many of the finest Roman statuettes adhere closely to Greek subjects and styles, it is often difficult to decide whether a given statuette is late Hellenistic or early Roman Imperial in date. A vivid case in point is the nude bearded warrior with Corinthian helmet in Hartford [58]. Its soft generalized anatomy and lively expression could argue equally well for a late Hellenistic eclectic creation in Greece or Asia Minor, or for a learned, generic portrayal of a general or hero appropriate for a late Republican or early Imperial official's cabinet or bedside table. Nevertheless, the technical and stylistic criteria for identifying bronze statuettes as products of Roman workshops are steadily being refined and tested. One trait is the precise, even fussy, attention to meticulous replication of style that characterizes many fine academic copies of Greek originals as well as eclectic adaptations from more than one Greek source. Such a work must be the large dancer on tiptoe in the Levy collection [69], which combines classicizing and baroque stylistic features into an original, eclectic new creation.

These bronze statuettes were sometimes produced in parts, which were then joined in solder. Extensive silver and copper inlays are also often typical of such works, the finest of which may rival their cast Classical Greek prototypes in quality. A superb standing bronze statuette of Hermes in the Louvre (Figure XI), clearly of Polyclitan character, for example, was recently shown by Boucher to be a mag-

Figure XI. *Statuette of a Youth, perhaps Hermes.* Bronze, H. 21 cm. Early Roman, ca. 50 BC– AD 50. Paris, Musée du Louvre, BR183.

nificent version of early Roman origin, not a fifth-century Greek original.[19] It is, in fact, just exactly too perfect but not lively and spontaneous enough to be a Classical Greek original. It reminds us of the athlete, perhaps once carrying a discus, in the Levy collection [59], which descends from several Classical and Hellenistic athletic prototypes. More specifically derived from early Classical models, refined for Roman consumption by alterations in costume, is the standing Mercury in the Walters Art Gallery [60]. Many more examples of such original, although eclectic, statuettes could be mentioned.

Another important criterion for recognizing a statuette as Roman is the nature and extent of surface cold working after casting. Sometimes the facial features, drapery folds, and other surfaces of Roman statuettes are drastically carved, abraded, and faceted, a treatment that seldom occurs as conspicuously in the Greek and Etruscan statuettes of the fifth through second centuries BC, the centuries during which the sculptural models most frequently followed by Roman statuette casters were produced. Similar conventions of deep, extensive drilling were used in Roman marble copies of Greek originals to produce dramatic contrasting effects of light and shadow. Close study of these techniques may eventually provide important information that will enable us to assign more precise dates and regional workshops to many Roman bronze statuettes, as well as to distinguish original creations in the various styles from the whole range of replicas, copies, and adaptations that make up a large percentage of the entire body of Roman bronzes so far known.

Not all Roman bronze statuettes, however, are of purely Classical Greek origin. Many from the Roman provinces in central and western Europe represent native Celtic, Iberian, or Germanic deities, portrayed in mixed native and classical styles. They reflect cultural and religious accommodations between indigenous peoples and the Mediterranean newcomers who were as willing to recognize and worship each other's gods as they were to intermarry and breed generations of descendants who inherited varied combinations of ethnic and religious traditions.

In Asia Minor, the Levant, and Egypt large numbers of bronze statuettes served many exotic local cults, such as those of the Phrygian moon god, Mên; numerous ancient Anatolian mother goddesses, such as Cybele and the Artemis of Ephesus; and the fertility goddesses of the Syro-Phoenician area, often portrayed as plump, pulchritudinous Aphrodites. Among the finest surviving representatives of this world are the youthful figures in elaborate oriental costumes in the Metropolitan Museum and the Walters Art Gallery [51, 52], which may depict the personifications of client or conquered eastern provinces like Armenia or the kingdom of Commagene. The range of statuette types produced in Romanized Egypt, both in the countryside still oriented toward the age-old pharaonic gods and in cosmopolitan centers like Alexandria, where Hellenic and native styles intermingled freely, deserves separate discussion. The Hellenized syncretistic gods, Serapis, Isis, and Harpocrates—the latter based on models like the magnificent late Hellenistic statuette in Cleveland [21]—are represented in innumerable statuettes, large and small, found all over the Roman Empire, not merely in Egypt itself. The winsome dolphin-riding boy in the Walters Art Gallery [72] is also at home in this climate and may originally have adorned a larger piece of furniture. Such works reflect the widespread, almost universal appeal of the cults of Isis and Serapis throughout the population of the Roman world during the first through the third centuries AD.

Many Hellenistic genre and theatrical subjects—actors, dancers, dwarves, blacks, and barbarians—remained popular in the Roman world from the English Channel to the Euphrates. They were sensitively treated in statuettes like

Cleveland's small standing barbarian [67], who may have formed part of a larger group of Dacians or Germans meeting, or submitting to, Roman rulers. The imploring little girl in the Getty Museum [70] was adapted from a well-known early Hellenistic characterization of childhood into a Roman novelty "piggy bank" by a clever bronzeworker. Theatrical types receive new, splendid interpretations for the wealthiest and most demanding clientele, as in the Getty's superb seated comic actor and singing mime, both of whom perch atop incense burners disguised as altars [54, 55]. The pudgy nude little boy in Bloomington [71], who takes a break from his acting chores, comic mask pushed back on top of his head, may also be related to the infant genii of Roman gods like Mars or heroes like Hercules. Intense fascination with the grotesque and bizarre—seeming to verge on the perverted—continued to appear through freakish characters like Boston's multi-phallused dwarf [56], intended to ward off misfortune, and his more energetic "brother," also in Boston, vigorously boxing with an unseen opponent [57].

The later history of the manufacture, distribution, and use of bronze statuettes in the Roman world remains to be written. Fine examples probably continued to be made in Italy, Gaul, the Rhine and Danube watersheds, Greece, Asia Minor, and Egypt, even during the increasingly chaotic decades of the third century AD, when barbarian incursions and social, political, and economic disintegration combined to threaten the Empire's very existence. The lumbering, running Hercules from the Brooklyn Museum [73], with its stylized musculature and summarily rendered, brutal facial features, probably dates from this period. Such bronze statuettes attest to the persistent vitality and importance of long-standing classical types, styles, and images in the late antique art of the third and fourth centuries AD.

To what extent, however, such statuettes were made and disseminated during the later fourth and fifth centuries AD under a Christian regime increasingly restrictive of traditional cult practices and images, is not yet known. Standing, draped gods, philosophers, and orators could become apostles and saints; winged Victories could become angels, while seated figures of Apollo and Orpheus could become the shepherd David or even Christ. The transformation of Classical and Hellenistic mythological subjects into images acceptable to Christian practice and taste has been widely discussed elsewhere.[20] How this process of selection and transformation operated with bronze statuettes specifically needs to be examined carefully. Although a great many types were extinguished or passed out of use, others persisted or were transformed into versions that could serve the aims of the new faith.

The history of the classical bronze statuette essentially ends at this point, only to be revived many centuries later, as cardinals, nobles, and scholars began to appreciate, collect, and imitate them as part of the rediscovery and rebirth of classical art and culture that we call the Renaissance. Both in themselves and as models for human sculptures, large and small, from the fourteenth century to the present, classical bronze statuettes have been powerful agents in the continued revitalization of the classical world's predominant visual creation, the portrayal of the human figure.

David Gordon Mitten

1. E. K. Gazda and G. M. A. Hanfmann, "Ancient Bronzes: Decline, Survival, Revival," in *Art and Technology: A Symposium on Classical Bronzes*, ed. by S. Doeringer and D. G. Mitten (Cambridge, Mass., 1970) 245-270; K. Gschwantler et al., *Guss und Form: Bronzen aus der Antikensammlung* (Vienna, 1986) 11-16.

2. M. Bieber, *Die antiken Skulpturen und Bronzen des Königliche Museum Fridericanum in Cassel* (Marburg, 1915) 51-52, no. 114, pl. XXXVIII, p. 11; E. Babelon and J. A. Blanchet, *Catalogue des bronzes antiques de la Bibliothèque Nationale* (Paris, 1895) I-XLV; K. Gschwandtler et al. 1986, 11-16.

3. N. Penny in M. Clark and N. Penny, eds., *The Arrogant Connoisseur: Richard Payne Knight, 1751-1824* (Manchester, 1982) 68-73, 131-135, nos. 29-41.

4. G. M. A. Richter, *Greek, Etruscan, and Roman Bronzes* (New York, 1915) 13-15, no. 28; J. R. Mertens, "Greek Bronzes in the Metropolitan Museum of Art," *The Metropolitan Museum of Art Bulletin* XLIII (Fall 1985) 22-24, no. 11.

5. G. M. A. Richter 1915; C. H. Smith, *Collection of J. Pierpont Morgan: Bronzes, Antique Greek, Roman, etc.* (Paris, 1913).

6. G. M. A. Hanfmann, *Ancient Art in American Private Collections*, exh. cat. (Cambridge, Mass., 1954); K. Schefold, *Meisterwerke griechischer Kunst* (Basel, 1960); S. F. Doeringer and D. G. Mitten, *Master Bronzes from the Classical World* (Cambridge, Mass., 1967); and Gschwantler et al. 1986.

7. This theory is supported by the excavation of fragments of clay investments (molds) for casting the legs of such tripod-cauldrons excavated at Lefkandi not far from Chalcis on Euboea in contexts of ca. 900 BC. This discovery—near Euboean cities traditionally famous for their metalwork (Chalcis is close to *chalkos*, bronze)—also points to at least one Greek region that took an early lead in the development of bronze-casting metallurgy and later pioneered the search for metals further west, at the Euboean workshop and trading settlement of Pithecusae on the island of Ischia off the Bay of Naples, around 750 BC.

For the molds, see H. W. Catling, *Excavations at Lefkandi*, ed. M. Popham and H. Sackett (London, 1964), 28-29; A. Snodgrass, *The Dark Age of Greece: An Archaeological Survey of the Eleventh to the Eighth Centuries B.C.* (Edinburgh, 1971), 218-285, fig. 101. For Pithecusae, cf. J. Boardman, *The Greeks Overseas: Their Early Colonies and Trade*, new and enl. ed. (New York, 1980), 165-168, nn. 13-23, pp. 276-277.

8. For such statuettes, cf. D. Collon, "The Smiting God," *Levant* VI (1972) 111-134; O. Negbi, *Canaanite Gods in Metal: An Archaeological Study of Ancient Syro-Palestinian Figurines*, Tel Aviv Institute of Archaeology, Publ. V (Tel Aviv, 1976); H. Seeden, *The Standing Armed Figurines in the Levant* (Munich, 1980).

9. U. Jantzen, *Samos VIII, Die Ägyptische und orientalische Bronzen aus dem Heraion von Samos* (Bonn, 1972) 5-37.

10. Delphi Museum, inv. 2527; C. Rolley, *Greek Bronzes*, tr. R. Howell (London, 1986) 84, illus. 56.

11. Cf. U. Gehrig, "Zum samischen Opfertrager in der Antikenabteilung," *Jahrbuch der Berliner Museen* XVII (1975) 45-50; N. DeGrassi, *Lo Zeus stilita di Ugento* (Rome, 1981); S. Karusu, "Fragmente bronzener Volutenkratere," *Athenische Mitteilungen* XCIV (1979) 77-91; D. K. Hill, "Class of Bronze Handles of the Archaic and Classical Periods," *American Journal of Archaeology* LXII (1958) 193-201; L. O. K. Congdon, *Caryatid Mirrors of Ancient Greece: Technical, Stylistic and Historical Considerations of an Archaic and Early Classical Bronze Series* (Mainz, 1981).

12. See V. J. Harward, *Greek Domestic Sculpture and the Origins of Private Art Patronage* (Ph.D. diss., Harvard; Ann Arbor, Mich., 1982).

13. See H. G. Taylor, "The Emperor's Clothes: The Fold Lines," *The Bulletin of The Cleveland Museum of Art* LXXIV (1987) 117-121.

14. E. Hostetter, *Bronzes from Spina*, I: *The Figural Classes* (Mainz, 1986) passim.

15. For these deposits see now M. Cristofani, *I bronzi degli etruschi* (Novara, 1985) 246-260.

16. Strabo VIII.6.381; H. Payne, *Necrocorinthia: A Study of Corinthian Art in the Archaic Period* (Oxford, 1931) xii. One suspects that these bronzes were vessels and mirrors, not statuettes, because not a single scientifically excavated grave in Corinth has so far yielded a statuette.

17. Cf. remarks of J. A. Scott in *Master Bronzes* (1967) 253, no. 243; H. Kunckel, *Der römische Genius* (Heidelberg, 1974) 9-147.

18. See discussions by H. Menzel in *Master Bronzes* (1967) 227-233; idem, *Art and Archaeology* (1970) 221-234; and idem, "Römische Bronzestatuetten und verwandte Geräte: Ein Beitrag zum Stand der Forschung," *Aufstieg und Niedergang des römischen Welt: Geschichte und Kultur Roms im Spiegel der neureren Forschungen*, II.12.3 (Berlin, 1985) 127-169.

19. D. K. Hill, "Note on the Piecing of Bronze Statuettes," *Hesperia* LI (1982) 277-283; S. Boucher, "A Propos de l'Hermès de Polyclète," *Bulletin de correspondance Hellénique* C (1976) 95-102.

20. For example, E. Kitzinger, "The Hellenistic Heritage in Byzantine Art," *Dumbarton Oaks Papers* XVII (1963) 95-115.

Note on Surface Decoration and Patinas

From the eighth century BC on, Greek and Etruscan bronzecasters painstakingly finished and decorated the surfaces of their products. After cleaning and burnishing the surface of the castings and filling the cavities left by gas bubbles with patches, they sharpened details rendered in the wax model and added new ones by incision, either through tracing or engraving. They did this cold working with a variety of fine, pointed metal tools, perhaps miniature needle-, burin-, and chisel-like instruments.[1] Sometimes stamped, punched, and compass-scored motifs were also added, especially on statuettes of the eighth and seventh century BC. Often such work, of extraordinary delicacy and accuracy, still greatly enhances the appearance and overall quality of individual ancient bronze statuettes.

From the early fifth century BC on, Greek bronzecasters also increasingly enriched the surfaces of their statuettes and figural attachments for vases with metal inlays and overlays that contrast colorfully with bronze. The bronze surface itself, when newly cast, finished, and polished, would normally be a gleaming light reddish-orange color. The metals most commonly used for inlays were silver and copper—silver contrasting sharply when polished and copper glowing with its deeper reddish hue.

In Hellenistic and Roman times, the use of metal inlays became more prominent and widespread on statuettes. Copper was commonly used for the lips and nipples on nude male statuettes, while the eyes of both male and female figures were frequently inlaid in silver. Note the prominent presence and effects of such inlays in the black banausos' saucer [20] and the grotesque [28] in this exhibition. Inlaid silver spots also mark the feline pelt worn by the Lasa in Cleveland [50]. Copper ribbons were inlaid in the costumes of dancing Lars from the first century AD onward. We know that metals of contrasting colors—copper, silver, and niello (a black alloy of silver, lead, and sulphur)—were combined to produce brilliant polychrome scenes and effects on the elaborate garments of monumental bronze statues, as on the fragment of a hanging folded garment from the robe (paludamentum) of a statue of Emperor Caracalla (AD 211-217), part of an elaborate chariot group on top of his arch in the Forum at Volubilis, Morocco, and now in the Rabat Museum.[2]

Much silver and perhaps even gold overlay or gilding has been irretrievably lost. Roman bronzes were often gilded, as were the four horses from the chariot team placed in late medieval times over the entrance to San Marco Cathedral in Venice, and the horse ridden by Emperor Marcus Aurelius on the Capitoline Hill in Rome. Our understanding and appreciation of this polychromy in metals on bronze statues and statuettes and in classical metalwork generally is sure to increase as scholars become more aware of it and actively seek further examples.

The beautiful green, blue, gray, and reddish patinas on ancient bronze statuettes today result from the natural chemical transformation of the metals comprising the bronze alloy by combination with oxygen and other elements into a variety of minerals—carbonates, chlorides, oxides, and sulfides—as the bronzes respond over the centuries to conditions of burial or submersion. The cleaning, coating, and handling that objects have undergone since their recovery from the earth or sea also alters or affects their patinas. The predominately green tone of most bronze surfaces results from the oxidation of the copper in the alloy, which produces the durable copper carbonate mineral malachite [$Cu_2(OH)_2CO_3$]. The mottled red cuprite (copper oxide: Cu_2O) and blue azurite (copper carbonate: [$Cu_3(OH)_2(CO_3)_2$]) are two other colorful corrosion minerals frequently found on long-buried bronzes.[3]

Some patinas are unstable, chronically breaking out in powdery light green spots or areas that must be treated to preserve the bronze so affected from progressive destruction. Known metaphorically as "bronze disease," this rapid corrosion is caused by high humidities activating the unstable chloride corrosion products taken up during burial. Treatment of the "bronze disease" is a complex process. There are several ways to deal with the problem; each varies in effectiveness and aesthetic intrusion.[4]

Evidence increasingly suggests that in antiquity at least a few bronze statuettes were subjected to special treatments or were deliberately coated with substances to produce desirable patinas. This is especially true in some bronzes reputedly of Egyptian origin, such as the striking black street character (banausos) from Alexandria in Cleveland [20], whose lustrous dark surface has been recognized as resulting from attempts at deliberate patination.[5] Evidence also exists that in at least a few cases, bronzes were painted, as in a gorgoneion of the fifth century BC and a helmet of the first.[6] Other examples doubtless exist. Such rare, deliberately produced ancient patinas should be distinguished from the shiny black to dark brown varnished or heavily handled and worn surfaces characterizing many bronzes from eighteenth- and nineteenth-century collections. Whether produced through conditions of prolonged burial, deliberate manipulation, or alteration in more recent times, their patinas have always been among the most attractive and distinctive features of classical bronze statuettes.

D. G. M.

1. See A. Steinberg, in *Master Bronzes* (1967), 12-14; and W. J. Young, in *Art and Technology* (1970) 87-89.

2. C. Boube-Piccot, *Les bronzes antiques du Maroc* I: *La Statuaire,* Etudes et travaux d'archéologie marocaine IV (Rabat, 1969) 87-103, pls. 16-37.

3. See R. J. Gettens, "Patinas Noble and Vile," in *Art and Technology* (1970) 57-72.

4. See discussion of destructive corrosion of bronze objects and treatments by C. M. Organ, "The Conservation of Bronze Objects," in *Art and Technology* (1970) esp. 76-84.

5. J. D. Cooney, "On the Meaning of [biȝ-km]," in *Zeitschrift für Ägyptische Sprache und Altertumskunde; Festschrift Rudolf Anthes zum 70. Geburtstag* XCIII, nos. 1-2 (1966) 43-47. Bruce Christman notes that this statuette also has a later black lacquer-like patina.

6. H. Born, ed., *Archäologische bronzen: Antikekunst moderne Technik* (Berlin, 1985) 78-83; I thank J. Hermann for this reference.

The Classical World

BRITAIN

GERMANS

Rhine

GERMANIA

Mosel

SCYTHIANS

SEA OF AZOV

Chalon-sur-Saône

Augst

Weissenburg

Danube

Ottenhusen

Lausanne

GAUL

DACIANS

Lugdunum

DACIA

Kerch (Panticapaeum)

ALPS

YUGOSLAVIA

BALKANS

Varna

BLACK SEA

ITALY

Stobi

PONTUS

CAUCASUS

GREECE

ASIA MINOR

Carthage

PHRYGIA

Nimrud Dagh

HITTITES

Mahdia

ASSYRIA

Constantine

CRETE

Antioch

PARTHIA

CYPRUS

Damascus

Volubilis

PERSIA

MEDITERRANEAN SEA

PHOENICIA

LEVANT

SYRIA

Euphrates

Tigris

Cyrene

Babylon

Alexandria

Naucratis

Memphis

EGYPT

Coptus

Thebes

RED SEA

Nile

ETHIOPIANS

Meroë

Charles Szabla

PADUA

Piacenza

Spina

Po

Bologna

VILLANOVANS

Arno

Pizzirimonte

UMBRIA

Rimini
(Ariminum)

Florentia

Ancona

ETRURIA

Volterra

Arezzo
(Arretium)

Sentinum

Esino

Potenza

Piombino
(Populonia)

Siena

Perugia
(Perusia)

Todi

Macerata
(Apiro)

ELBA

Ombrone

Orcia

Chiusi
(Clusium)

Orvieto
Volsinii

PICENUM

ADRIATIC SEA

Vetulonia

LAKE
BOLSENA

APENNINES

Vulci

Falerii

Tarquinii

Tiber

LATIUM

CORSICA

Veii

Cerveteri
(Caere)

Rome

Gabii

Ostia

Palestrina
(Praeneste)

LAKE
NEMI

Capua

APULIA

Herculaneum

Naples

Beneventum

SARDINIA

Cumae

Mt. Vesuvius

Salerno

Potenza
(Potentia)

Taranto
(Tarentum)

ISCHIA

Picentia

Pithecusae

Pompeii

Paestum

Metapontum

BAY
OF NAPLES

LUCANIA

TYRRHENIAN SEA

Thurii

Riace

Locri

Rhegium

MAGNA GRAECIA

Himera

SICILY

Tunis
(Carthage)

Syracuse

Ron Garrett

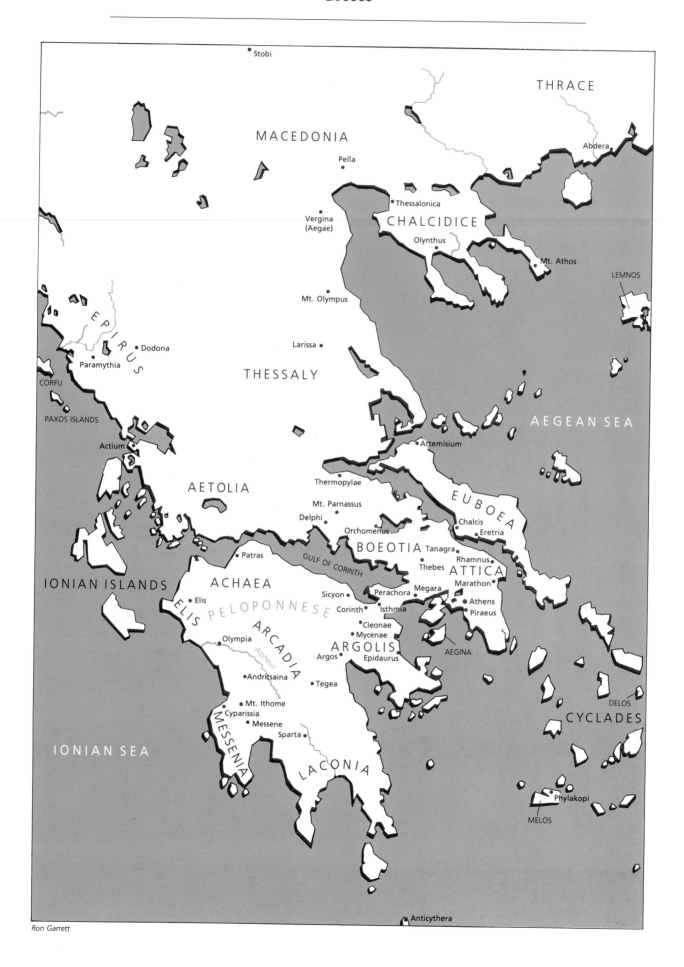

• Stobi

THRACE

MACEDONIA

• Pella

• Abdera

• Thessalonica

CHALCIDICE

Vergina
(Aegae)

• Olynthus

• Mt. Athos

LEMNOS

E P I R U S

• Dodona

• Mt. Olympus

• Paramythia

CORFU

• Larissa

THESSALY

AEGEAN SEA

PAXOS ISLANDS

• Actium

• Artemisium

AETOLIA

Thermopylae

E U B O E A

• Mt. Parnassus

• Delphi

• Orchomenus

• Chalcis
• Eretria

BOEOTIA

Tanagra

IONIAN ISLANDS

• Patras

GULF OF CORINTH

• Thebes

Rhamnus

ACHAEA

ATTICA

• Sicyon

Perachora

Megara

Marathon

ELIS

• Elis

PELOPONNESE

Corinth

• Isthmia

• Athens
• Piraeus

ARCADIA

• Olympia

Alpheus

• Cleonae
• Mycenae

ARGOLIS

• Argos

Epidaurus

AEGINA

• Andritsaina

• Tegea

• Mt. Ithome

DELOS

• Cyparissia

MESSENIA

• Messene

Sparta

CYCLADES

IONIAN SEA

LACONIA

• Phylakopi

MELOS

• Anticythera

Ron Garrett

30

BLACK SEA

BOSPORUS

Izmit

BITHYNIA

Troy
(Ilium)

LESBOS

Mytilene

Pergamum

PHRYGIA

LYDIA

Myrina

Cyme

CHIOS

Sardis

Izmir
(Smyrna)

Apamea

AEGEAN SEA

Ephesus

SAMOS

Magnesia

Priene

Laodicea

Miletus

Aphrodisias

Halicarnassus

COS

Cnidus

LYCIA

RHODES

MEDITERRANEAN SEA

Ron Garrett

Timeline

(Most dates are approximate.)

6000-3000 BC: Neolithic Age

3000-2000: Early Bronze Age

2000-1100: Middle and Late Bronze Age

1100-900: Iron Age

900-700: Geometric period in Greece; Villanovan culture in Italy

825: Greeks begin casting bronze statuettes

800-750: Villanovans begin trade with Greece and Phoenicia

776: Traditional date for founding of Olympic Games

775: Euboean Greeks found Pithecusae (earliest Greek colony in West)

770-700: Greek alphabet is developed; Homer writes *Iliad* and *Odyssey*

753: Traditional date for founding of Rome

733: Corinth founds colony of Syracuse

730-600: Orientalizing period in Greek art, which begins when Eastern influence enters Greece through Corinth and other cities

700: Rise of Etruscan navy; Etruscans adopt Greek alphabet

700-650: Etruscan cities develop on southern and northern coasts of Tuscany; Greek cities develop on southern coasts of Italy and in Sicily; Lycurgus, according to tradition, founds Spartan social and political system

700-600: Etruscans produce bucchero pottery

700-500: Hallstatt period in western and central Europe

664-660: Twenty-ninth Olympiad

650: Nikandre of Naxos dedicates marble kore on Delos (earliest known large-scale Greek stone statue)

650-600: So-called "Dedalic" style

625: Archaic period begins in Greece with rise of Sparta, then Athens

620-610: Marks earliest production of marble kouros statues; Athenian black-figure vase painting begins

594: Solon, poet and chief archon of Athens, promulgates new law code, social and political reforms

590: Bronze statuettes of human beings deposited in large numbers at such Greek sanctuaries as Olympia, Athens, Dodona, Samos

564: Aesop, the fable teller, dies

561-556, 546-527: Pisistratus is tyrant of Athens, succeeded by his sons

550-500: Rise of inland cities of Etruria; Vulci, Tarquinia, Chiusi, and other Etruscan centers produce bronzes, jewelry, painted tombs, and pottery imitating Greek wares

547/6: Cyrus the Great captures Sardis; beginning of Achaemenian Persian empire

540-530: "Peplos Kore" (Figure IV) dedicated on the Athenian Acropolis

530: Athenian red-figure vase painting begins

530: Philosopher/mathematician Pythagoras of Samos is active in South Italy

522-486: Darius rules Achaemenian empire

520-470: Etruscan later Archaic period

514: Harmodius and Aristogeiton murder Athenian tyrant Hipparchus (younger son of Pisistratus); democratic reorganization of Athens follows in 510

509-390: Early Republican period in Rome

500-490: Temple of Aphaea built on Aegina

500-470: Athenian red-figure vase-painters, the Kleophrades Painter, "Berlin Painter," Brygos Painter, and Douris, are active

499-494: Ionian Greek cities revolt against Persian rule

494: Persians destroy Miletus

490: Battle of Marathon, Athens defeats first Persian invasion, led by Darius (d. 486)

490-479: Persian Wars

490-450: Early Classical style, so-called "Severe Style"

490-388: Classical poet-dramatists Aeschylus (active 484-456), Pindar (498-446), Sophocles (468-406), Euripides (455-406), and Aristophanes (425-388) are active, as is Sophist philosopher Protagoras (490-420)

480: Xerxes sacks Athens; bronze "Tyrannicides" (Harmodius and Aristogeiton slaying the tyrant Hipparchus) by Antenor stolen by Persian invaders (replacement made in 470s by Kritios and Nesiotes)

480: Greeks defeat Persian navy at Salamis

480-470: Sculptor Onatas is active at Aegina, pupil Calliteles; Pythagoras of Rhegium erects statue of Olympic victor Euthymos at Locri

478: Delian League founded, led by Athens

477-460: Alkamenes is active as sculptor; Polygnotus of Thasos is active as wall-painter at Athens and Delphi

474: Syracusans defeat Etruscan navy off coast at Cumae; economic decline in Etruria begins

468-406: Athenian tragedian Sophocles is active

465-460: Temple of Zeus built at Olympia

461-451: First Peloponnesian War (Athens vs. Peloponnesian League)

461-429: Pericles rules Athens

460-450: Bronze statue of Zeus made (later lost in shipwreck near Cape Artemisium, recovered 1929)

460-420: High Classical period

460-400: Greek sculptors Polyclitus, Phidias, Myron, Naukydes (brother of Polyclitus), Paionios, and Cresilas of Cydonia in Crete are active

450: Polyclitus completes the Doryphorus (his "canon")

450: Myron creates bronze Discobolus

455-406: Athenian tragedian Euripides is active

455-400: Greek historian Thucydides, author of *Peloponnesian Wars,* is active

447: Construction of Parthenon begins

445-426: Greek "Father of History" Herodotus is active

440-406: Historian Hellanicus of Lesbos is active

431-404: Second (Great) Peloponnesian War; Sparta defeats Athens

430s and 420s: Phidias' major gold and ivory sculptures dedicated at Athens (Athena Parthenos) and Olympia (Seated Zeus)

430: Production of bronze statuettes in Greece suddenly declines

427-354: Greek historian Xenophon is active

424: Paionios' Nike at Olympia dedicated to Messenians and Naupactians, honoring a victory probably over the Spartans at Sphacteria

420-380: Period of the "Rich Style"

413: Athenian expedition to Syracuse defeated

405-401: Monument to victorious Spartan commander Lysander built at Delphi

400-336: Late Classical period in Etruria; artistic and economic renaissance there

399: Greek philosopher Socrates (b. 469) forced to commit suicide

396: Rome conquers Veii in southern Etruria

396-347: Greek philosopher Plato

390-350: Greek sculptor Scopas is active

390-320: Late Classical style in Greek sculpture

390-264: Roman expansion in Italy

385: Plato founds his Academy outside Athens

384-322: Greek orator Demosthenes; philosopher Aristotle (Plato's pupil, Alexander's tutor, and founder of Athenian Lyceum)

364-330: Greek sculptor Praxiteles is active

360-315: Macedonia rises to supreme power in Greek world under rule of Philip II (356-336); sculptor Lysippus of Sicyon is active

358-351: Tarquinia leads Etruscan wars against Rome

350: Sculptors Scopas, Bryaxis, Leochares, and Timotheos decorate tomb of Mausolus at Halicarnassus

350-330: Praxiteles carves Aphrodite of Cnidus and Lycian Apollo

338: Philip II and Alexander (356-323) of Macedonia defeat Athens and Thebes at Battle of Chaeronia; end of independence of Greek city-states

338-324: Orator and statesman Lycurgus champions Athens against Macedonia

336: Alexander (the Great) acceeds to Macedonian throne and dedicates chryselephantine statues of his family in the Philippeum at Olympia

331: Alexander founds the city of Alexandria, Egypt

330: Alexander conquers Achaemenian empire

325: Greek cynic philosopher Diogenes dies

322-286: Theophrastus is head of Lyceum in Athens

321-289: Greek poet of New Comedy, Menander, is active

320-160: Early Hellenistic period

312: Capture of Babylon by Seleucus marks founding of Seleucid dynasty

311: Etruscan League attacks Roman Sutri, ending 40-year truce

307: Epicurus founds school of philosophy at Athens, pupils include Metrodorus and Hermarchus

300-290: Ptolemy I, King of Egypt, founds Museum and Library at Alexandria, commissions Bryaxis to create Serapis statue

300-260: Greek pastoral poet Theocritus and Herodas, Greek writer of mimes, are active

295: Romans defeat coalition of Italic peoples at Battle of Sentinum, winning control of Italy

285-240: Greek poet and scholar Callimachus

280: Polyeuctus completes statue of Athenian orator Demosthenes

279-255: Nicomedes I is King of Bithynia

275: Greek scholar/scientist Eratosthenes is born

270: Hermarchus becomes head of Epicurian school in Athens

264-241: First Punic War; Rome forces Carthage out of Sicily

232-207: Greek Stoic philosopher Chrysippus is active

223-187: Antiochus III (the Great) rules Syria, defeated 190 at Magnesia ad Sipylum by Rome and Pergamum

218-201: Second Punic War; Hannibal invades Italy

211: Romans capture Syracuse

187-175: Seleucus IV Philopater is King of Syria

180: Great Altar of Zeus and Athena built at Pergamum

175-163: Antiochus IV Epiphanes rules Syria and Judaea

160-159: Roman playwright Terence writes six comedies in Latin

150-120: Apollo with cithara carved by Timarchides

150-31: Late Hellenistic (Greco-Roman) period

150-31: Neo-Attic style

149-146: Third Punic War; Carthage destroyed, made Roman province

146: Mummius sacks Corinth; Achaean League defeated by Rome

146-31: Late Republican period

133: Attalus III of Pergamum bequeaths kingdom to Rome

120-63: Mithridates VI Eupator (King of Pontus), arch-enemy of Roman rule in the Greek East

100: Julius Caesar is born

100: Mahdia shipwreck (recovered 1907)

100: Agasias of Ephesus sculpts Borghese Warrior

90 and later: South Italian Greek sculptor Pasiteles is active

88-63: Roman wars against Mithradates VI Eupator

75-50: Anticythera shipwreck (recovered 1900)

70: Crassus and Pompey become Roman consuls

55: Coponius makes sculptures for Theater of Pompey at Rome

53: Crassus defeated and killed by Parthians

44: Julius Caesar is assassinated

44 BC-AD 21: Greek geographer and historian Strabo is active

38-8 BC: Horace leading poet at Rome

30s BC: Zoilos, freedman of Julius Caesar, is a leading citizen of Aphrodisias

31 BC: Octavian conquers Marc Antony and Cleopatra VII of Egypt in naval battle at Actium, becoming sole master of Roman world

31 BC–AD 476: Roman Imperial period

27 BC: Octavian is acclaimed *Augustus* and first Roman Emperor by the Roman Senate; historian Dionysius of Halicarnassus writes *Roman Antiquities*

26-19 BC: Virgil composes the *Aeneid*

13-9 BC: Augustus commissions Ara Pacis Augustae in Rome

AD 14: Augustus dies

AD 14-68: Julio Claudian dynasty rules Rome (Tiberius, 14-37; Caligula, 37-41; Claudius, 41-54; Nero, 54-68)

23-79: Roman scholar, writer, and naturalist Pliny the Elder

41-54: Ara Pietatis is commissioned (see Figure XXVIII)

46-120: Greek philosopher-biographer Plutarch

62: Earthquake shakes Pompeii and nearby Vesuvian towns

69-192: Middle Imperial period

69: Four emperors (Galba, Otho, Vitellius, Vespasian)

69-96: Flavian dynasty rules Rome (Vespasian, 69-79; Titus, 79-81; Domitian, 81-96)

79: Eruption of Mt. Vesuvius on August 21 buries Pompeii, Herculaneum, and Stabiae

90-130: Roman biographer and historian Suetonius

96-98: Nerva is Emperor of Rome

98-117: Trajan is Emperor of Rome

101-106: Dacian Wars; Rome incorporates Dacia into the Empire

101-177: Philosopher, sophist, and philanthropist Herodes Atticus

114: Rome incorporates Armenia into the Empire

117-138: Hadrian is Emperor of Rome

133-188: Greek rhetorician Julius Pollux

138-192: The Antonines rule Rome (Antoninus Pius, 138-161; Marcus Aurelius, 161-180)

140-170: Greek traveler and geographer Pausanias

190-244: Literary biographer Philostratus

192-235: The Severan dynasty rules Rome (Septimius Severus, 193-211; Caracalla, 211-217; interim rulers, 217-218; Elagalabus restores Severan rule, 218-222; Severus Alexander, 222-235)

235-476: Later Roman Empire

235-285: Soldier-Emperors rule Rome

253-268: Gallienus is Emperor of Rome

476: Visigoths sack Rome

Greek Bronzes

Few artifacts preserved from antiquity provide both the visual and intellectual satisfaction of a finely cast Greek bronze. Conceived with a freedom impossible in stone and with a respect for the inherent value of the material that was alien to terracotta, three-dimensional bronze sculpture was the preferred medium of such artists as Myron and Polyclitus in the fifth century BC, and Lysippus in the fourth century. Ancient authors have left tantalizing descriptions of the achievements of the masters in this technique, but few of their monumental bronzes survive. The very qualities of beauty and preciousness for which they were so esteemed by the ancients assisted in their destruction. Many of the most highly prized statues of the Greek cities and sanctuaries were stolen by the Romans, and some were lost in transport. Later, because of the intrinsic value of bronze, especially in times of war, most of the survivors were melted down to be refashioned into weapons and currency.

What has been lost with the groves of statues of gods and heroes that once populated the Greek temples and shrines is irretrievable, but fortunately much of the originality of composition and technical proficiency with which they were created is preserved in miniature form in contemporary bronze statuettes. Still precious because of their medium and unique because they were individually cast in the lost-wax method, these small images are more than a mere supplement to the larger figures. Preserved in far greater quantity and variety, they provide a richer and more complex historical record of the artistic interests and innovations of Greek sculptors, a record that enhances our understanding and appreciation of the rarer monumental images.

The lost-wax method of bronzecasting was nothing new by the time the Greeks encountered it. It had, in fact, been in use in Egypt and the Near East for well over a millennium before the Minoan and Mycenaean artists adopted it with enthusiasm. With characteristic inventiveness and determination, however, the later Greeks mastered the medium and developed its expressive possibilities beyond anything achieved by the earlier craftsmen.

The notion of creative experimentation among Greek artists must always be understood in the context of their status in society, which was inferior. Artists of all calibers, from apprentices to the greatest masters, were considered artisans who produced goods for a competitive market. The expensive, large-scale sculptures were of necessity specifically commissioned by cities or wealthy patrons. Because statuettes were smaller, cheaper, and more easily produced, they allowed for greater freedom of expression but only within the limits of what could be sold.

For *The Gods Delight*, the wealth of inventive imagery demonstrated by the Greek bronzeworkers has been limited to representations of the human or semi-human figures. Still, within these confines, there is nothing repetitious. Man was, after all, for the Greeks "the measure of all things" and a subject of endless fascination. Even the Olympian gods were anthropomorphic—or literally conceived to be of human form—with all the strengths and objectionable foibles of the human character. To focus on the human figure offers perhaps a clearer demonstration of artists' originality than would a broader range of subjects, for it illustrates the diversity of creative reactions when artists of different schools and periods are confronted with similar subjects.

Since they survive in comparatively large numbers, bronze statuettes are important evidence for the definition of chronological developments and the identification of regional distinctions in style. Although the small images were indeed portable, and were surely not infrequently exported in trade, the preserved excavation contexts of many have helped to identify both their time and place of manufacture. And for comparison with images in other media—such as vase painting, stone sculpture, terracotta figurines, and jewelry—they have often proved to be accurate points of reference.

The findspots for many of the pieces discussed here are actually known, and the details of the sculptures often fit quite comfortably with the style generally accepted as characteristic of that region. The features of the Walters' Geometric seated man from Elis [1], near Olympia, for example, are consistent with other Peloponnesian bronzes of this period from Olympia. Both Boston's Mantiklos Apollo [2] and the Walters' standing votary [3] are said to have been found at Thebes in Boeotia, and both can be convincingly allied with representations of human figures on Boeotian relief storage vessels (pithoi) and among the terracotta figurines. Finally, Cleveland's Dattari boxer [24] is said to be from Alexandria, and both its surface finish and comparisons for its hairstyle support this provenance.

Serious efforts to define regional styles accurately have greatly assisted scholars in the interpretation of objects lacking provenances. Thus, the Metropolitan's magnificent nude female mirror caryatid [6] was acquired without any definite information as to its findspot beyond the report that it may have come from Tarentum in South Italy; but Praschniker's earlier work on Laconian mirror caryatids[1] allowed her to be ascribed without question to Spartan manufacture. In the same way, the Getty's dead or sleeping youth [10], which also has no provenance, could be assigned to Athens by comparing it with the well-documented products of Attica, while Cleveland's athlete making an offering [12], once taken for Argive, has recently been convincingly re-assigned to a workshop in Magna Graecia on the basis of comparisons with the products of ancient Locri and Tarentum.

Because of the portability of small bronzes, however, the problem of provenance is not always resolved and is sometimes also complicated by where they were found. Though the Artemis of Chimaridas [4] was actually uncovered at the Greek site of Mazi, she can be connected with Laconia not only by style and dress but by the distinctive letter forms of her inscription as well. Boston's large Hermes Kriophoros [9] is said to have been found at Sparta. Yet, its unusual style does not correspond to the generally recognized products of the Laconian school. In his fundamental study of the early Greek regional styles, Langlotz assigned the image instead to a somewhat nebulous Sicyonian workshop.[2] Since that time, other scholars have tried to explain its peculiarities by identifying it as a Corinthian import or an archaistic product of the late Hellenistic period. Langlotz' original proposal continues to be the most persuasive, however, gaining strength from the later appearance of a related kriophoros in the Stathatos collection and more recent, expanded studies of Laconian and Corinthian sculpture.

Similarly, Boston's statuette of a black youth [19] has frequently been associated with the city of Alexandria, in spite of its having been found in France, together with a large collection of ancient bronzes. As the proposed Egyptian provenance is based exclusively on the Negroid features of the subject rather than any documented relationship with Alexandrian products in style or quality, the Alexandrian connection is weak at best. And as blacks are known from ancient sources to have been common in countries all around the Mediterranean by the Hellenistic period, the place of manufacture must be reconsidered.

Of all the problematic provenances, Alexandria is perhaps the most difficult. Because of its authors and literature, Alexandria came to be associated with an unusual interest in "realism" and caricature, with special attention paid to the outcast and the unfortunate as subjects—the deformed and diseased, slaves, beggars, all the lowlife (banausoi) of this international capital. At least seven of the Greek bronzes in this exhibition have been ascribed at one time or another to the great Hellenistic city, but this assignment has been based for the most part on the subject represented rather than on information about where they were excavated. As each of these bronzes is considered in turn, it becomes clear that the Alexandrian source is actually fairly well-substantiated in five cases. The provenances of the others must remain in question until further information appears to justify their assignment either to Alexandria or elsewhere.

Hellenistic bronzes lacking provenances in general present the greatest difficulties in terms of their regional associations; they also offer the greatest problems in the establishment of an accurate chronology for Greek bronzes. Among the earlier images, there is little difficulty in reconstructing the sequence from the stylized glyph of the Walters' Geometric seated man [1]—whose body is reduced to a wiry scaffolding composed of simple curves and straight lines—to the fully developed dynamism of Cleveland's fourth-century rider [13]—whose finely articulated figure has been distorted only for dramatic effect.

With the turn to the third century, appropriately represented by the Metropolitan's Baker dancing woman [14], the chronological foundations become less firm. The convincing representation of the ideal human form is no longer a primary artistic objective, as the challenge of this subject has been completely mastered. Instead, there is a new interest in the depiction of particular physical and psychological states. The detached ecstasy of dance, the suffering and emaciation of illness, the humiliation of poverty, and the self-absorption of intellectual concentration are all portrayed here in a variety of unusual physical types—young and old, fat and starved, deformed and beautiful. Interest in motion goes beyond the human figure to experimentation with the expressive possibilities of fabric and suggestions of atmosphere. As these images are mostly without parallel, however, they can only be dated generally on the basis of minor details, such as the treatment of drapery folds, the rendering of the curls of hair, the use of ornamental patterns, or the proportions of the body, for which there are comparisons among excavated stone sculptures and the more numerous terracotta figurines. Like reliable provenances, firm dates are rare among the Hellenistic bronzes and they have been expressed here in broader terms than those of the Archaic and Classical periods.

One particularly problematic group of Hellenistic images remains those that apparently reproduce the features of much earlier, perhaps larger sculptures. The late Hellenistic statuettes of the Olympians Hermes, Zeus, Asclepius, and Aphrodite are all variations of figure types known in more than one replica, and they appear to reflect a renewed interest in the Classical, fifth- and fourth-century BC taste for idealized, serene beauty. All have lost the conviction of the original creations, however, and appear to the modern eye as academic reminiscences, finished with great technical facility, but largely lacking in the spiritual or emotional impact exhibited by much earlier, less polished representations like the small Hermes Kriophoros from Boston [8] or the gaunt image of the Mantiklos Apollo [2].

Though a small number of bronze statuettes—such as the Mantiklos Apollo and the Artemis from Mazi [4]—state their votive intentions directly with inscriptions and others—like the mirror caryatids [6, 7]—serve a functional role as figural supports, the original purposes of many small Greek bronzes are not clear. Those that have been discovered in sanctuaries may be considered as offerings, and the freestanding Archaic and Classical figures in particular are generally accepted as dedications. Still, the explanation of the poses of some figures, such as the dead or sleeping youth [10] or the spirited rider [13], is unclear in the votive context, and the distinctions between gods and mortals confusing, as the enigmatic Epimetheus or Hephaestus from Dumbarton Oaks [11] demonstrates so appropriately.

With the later statuettes, the possibilities for interpretation are much more vast. Miniature images furnished personal shrines and households as well as major sanctuaries, where they served votive purposes, and ancient sources describe what pleasure private collectors took in representations of well-known characters from the theater or portraits of writers and philosophers. Even when the original base is preserved, as is the case of the philosopher from the Metropolitan Museum [26], it is difficult to determine whether the figure was intended for public or individual enjoyment. The expanded range of secular imagery, however, illustrates very well the importance of the private market for fine bronzes during this period.

Beyond the purpose for which these bronzes were made, we must ask why are they exhibited together here. It is folly to say that any one object discovered today will rewrite the history of the art of Greece or any other civilization. Too much is known and well documented by controlled excavations and scientific analysis. Still, there is much to be learned from objects that are already recognized as established monuments. The opportunity to reexamine the best-known ancient bronzes in America and to place them side by side, many for the first time, in the company of bronzes that have only recently appeared, must stimulate reassessments, revisions, and hopefully, a few discoveries. Some objects, such as the Asclepius from Cincinnati [18], the philosopher from the Metropolitan Museum [26], and the Zeus from the collection of Lawrence and Barbara Fleischman [29] have been re-dated since their original publications. Once taken to be originals of the fourth or third centuries BC, they are all considered here as late Hellenistic or early Imperial creations, most probably inspired by earlier images of the same subjects. The Aphrodite from the Rhode Island School of Design [17] has also been re-dated, though less drastically, its period extended from the second century BC to include the first half of the first.

Other bronzes have been reconsidered in terms of their origins. Frequently associated with Alexandrian caricature, the small figure of a grotesque from the Metropolitan [28] actually has a venerable Roman provenance, while the emaciated youth of Dumbarton Oaks [25] comes from France. And though trade and travel can be used to explain their findspots, they are unparalleled among known Alexandrian finds.

The review of these master bronzes included in all cases careful physical examination and in some cases extensive technical analyses which have added substantially to the available information on their manufacturing processes. Though the technique of assembling statuettes from separately cast parts has been discussed at some length for Hellenistic and Roman bronzes, it has not been widely mentioned in terms of early Greek images other than mirrors. It is clear, however, that piece-casting was common in the production of bronzes throughout antiquity. X-radiographs show that the left arms of both kriophoroi in Boston [8, 9] were cast separately and attached, explaining the perfection of finish on all sides of the animals they hold. The extended arms of the dead or sleeping youth from the Getty [10] were also joined secondarily to the solid-cast body, allowing for the complexity of the pose, while the right arm of the Cleveland athlete [12] may well have been attached after casting. Besides the evidence they provide for an assembly process with separately made parts, the Cleveland athlete and the Getty dead youth both illustrate that substantial repairs of casting flaws were as common among the best of the early bronzes as they are in the later pieces such as the Metropolitan's artisan [22] and Aphrodite from the Rhode Island School of Design [17] has also been re-dated, though less drastically, its period extended from the second century BC to include the first half of the first.

But ultimately, what is gained from the temporary juxtaposition of the finest examples of any given medium is the provocative experience of seeing familiar objects in unfamiliar contexts. One is forced to look at them anew.

It is difficult to imagine how to improve on the simplicity of the Geometric seated man [1] or the direct emotional sincerity of the Mantiklos Apollo [2] and the standing votary from Thebes [3]. Yet, the much later representation of a seated, emaciated youth [25], though visually and iconographically more complex, conveys something of the same haunting intensity and immediacy of effect. The very different aspects of Aphrodite portrayed in the two nearly contemporary mirror caryatids from Sparta and Aegina [6, 7] point up both the multiplicity of sources for Greek religious imagery and the regional distinctions in style. When these two are placed in proximity with later renditions of the goddess of love, such as the Metropolitan Museum's version of the Cnidian Aphrodite [15] and the Rhode Island School of Design's Aphrodite Stephanusam [17], however, their distinctions are suddenly less pronounced, for they are closer to one another than either is to the sensuous, overtly sexual Hellenistic nudes.

Though he looks very odd standing beside the smaller, blunter image of the same god from the same collection [8], the large Hermes Kriophoros from Boston [9] looks less puzzling when placed beside Boston's Aeginetan Aphrodite [7]—the over-refined late Archaic style of both is immediately apparent. If the date of the mirror can be supported by other related caryatid figures—as it can—there is no need to explain the Hermes as a later, archaistic creation.

The Epimetheus or Hephaestus from Dumbarton Oaks [11] is no less daring and innovative in his extended pose when placed beside the dead or sleeping youth from the Getty [10]. The appearance of the Hephaestus in the first half of the fifth century is somehow less surprising, however, in comparison with the twisted torso of the earlier Getty youth. The fact that the unusual depiction of mood captured in the Metropolitan's artisan [22] finds its closest parallel in the philosopher [26] from the same collection adds a suggestion of nobility to an otherwise pedestrian subject. And though one might not immediately think of Boston's tiny figure of a black [19] when looking at the portrait of the philosopher, their proximity in an exhibition suddenly underlines the similarity in stance and drapery.

The Baker dancing woman [14] does not necessarily remind one of Hermes. When she stands next to the elegant youthful representation of the god from the Metropolitan Museum [27], however, the treatment of the tautly stretched drapery takes on a new significance. And if the association of a black banausos [20] and the infant god Harpocrates [21] is unprecedented, a comparison of these two sinuous dark-surfaced figures from Cleveland shows how the same compositional device and surface treatment could be applied without discrimination, to the advantage of both subjects.

Perhaps the greatest irony revealed by this exhibition of classical master bronzes is the anonymity of the masters represented here. Though the statuettes themselves may carry the inscriptions of donors and votive dedications, the names of the artisans who cast them are lost forever. The bronzes provide a repository of information about the times and places in which they were made: the gods that were worshipped, the styles of clothes and coiffure that were popular, the social roles that were esteemed, and the subjects that were of topical interest. What they do not reveal is the consequence of the nameless personalities who distilled this information into molten metal to cast some of the most memorable and eloquent images of man ever conceived.

Marion True

1. C. Praschniker, "Bronzene Spiegelstütze im Wiener Hofmuseum," *Jahreshefte des Oster-reichischen Archäologischen Instituts in Wien* XV (1912) 219-252.

2. E. Langlotz, *Fruehgriechische Bildhauerschulen* (Nuremberg, 1927) 31, no. 27, pl. 12.

1. Seated Man

At first glance, the spare form of this tiny figure seems little more than a hieroglyph, rather like an artist's flexible wire model whose long tubes of arms and legs are joined to the broader column of the torso and bent into a seated posture on top of a horseshoe-shaped bench. Yet, a momentary reflection on the achievement of convincing three-dimensionality and clarity of image in a work of this scale dispels any doubts about its importance as a work of art. Perfectly composed from every point of view, this is an object of refined sophistication, for all its apparent geometric simplicity.

GREEK, GEOMETRIC, PELOPONNESIAN, CA. 750-700 BC. H. 7.1 CM. WALTERS ART GALLERY, 54.789

Of all the parts of the body, only the head has any substantial volume, which is emphasized by the plastic treatment of its surface. A distinct ridge runs across the forehead between the raised, rounded helices of the ears, intentionally dividing the face from the low rounded cranium. The eyes are defined as simple hollows, unevenly placed on either side of the nose, while the mouth is obscured by the large ovoid object that the figure holds touching the end of its nose. All the features are placed high within the contours of the face, and the smooth cheeks descend to a strong rounded chin that is thrust forward, imparting a sense of alertness consistent with the taut conformation of the limbs.

The neck, relatively thick in relation to the other body elements, joins the broad shoulders without articulation. Under the arms, the columnar torso tapers markedly toward the waist before expanding again at the hips. Though the buttocks are undefined at the back where the figure rests on the bench, the genitals are clearly marked on the front of the pelvis. In profile, the arms appear to run straight from the shoulders to the elbows, but in the frontal or three-quarter view, they form great arcs by the sides of the body before landing firmly on the supporting knees. The thumbless hands that support a bulbous object are indicated as flat extensions of the wrists, with only shallow incisions defining the fingers. The attenuated legs, spread to stabilize the entire composition, end abruptly on the crossbar of the T-shaped base without any suggestion of feet.

This figure is among the few surviving bronzes that document Greek artists' early efforts to incorporate space in the representation of single figures. Unlike the complex figural groups—such as the centaur and hero in the Metropolitan Museum of Art or the hunter with his dogs attacking a predator in the Ortiz collection in Geneva—in which space is an essential component of the composition, the single figure could easily be and often was defined in a more conservative, less ambitious standing pose that required little attention to space beyond the possible extension of a limb. Here, however, with its spidery legs stretched before it and its elongated arms curving out to the sides, the figure occupies a much greater volume of space than its small frame would require if standing.

Changing from every point of view, the shapes of the spaces defined by the limbs are as important to the appreciation of this figure as the body itself, and clearly there is still much here that is expressive of the Geometric stylistic vocabulary. Seen from the side, the triangular voids left between the arms and legs echo the acute angles of the up-thrust knees and the firmly planted elbows; while from the front alone, the arc of the horseshoe-shaped seat and the larger lateral curves of the upper arms can be fully understood. Not the result of an initial experiment, this polished image is the mature product of a well-developed concept, executed with assurance. On the basis of its complex pose and details of surface articulation, it may be dated to the last phase of the Geometric style in the latter half of the eighth century BC, and is most closely related to the bronzes of the Peloponnese.

A number of parallels exist for the pose. Among the preserved statuettes, the most comparable are a bronze figure from the sanctuary of Artemis Orthia, now in the museum of Sparta; a second, formerly in the collection of Leon Pomerance; a third, in the collection of George Ortiz in Geneva; and a fourth, formerly in the Bomford collection and now in the Sackler Museum, Harvard University. Of these examples, however, only the bronzes in the Walters Art Gallery, the Pomerance collection, and the Sackler Museum are seated on stools; while the Ortiz bronze is distinguished by its simian features.

A much larger group of seated figures with elbows resting on their knees and hands holding objects raised to their mouths is found on openwork bronze implements from northern Greece. Formerly referred to as bottle-stoppers, these objects have now been conclusively identified by excavation as ornaments originally sus-

pended from belts or girdles. They are generally more reduced in their definition of surface details and specifically Geometric in their composition; many appear to represent simian subjects.

Though instruments or vessels are sometimes identifiable in the hands of the tiny seated figures, the object held by the Walters bronze is as yet unexplained. As Jantzen has shown, it can hardly be a flute, for it is too broad and has the wrong shape. At the same time, Jantzen's and Lullies' identification (in K. Schefold 1967) of the object as a vessel is not convincing, since the figure appears to hold it to his nose instead of his mouth. Given the oval shape and distinctly tapering ends, Hill's suggestion that this is a bud is far from confirmed. Still, it remains the least objectionable proposal until better evidence appears.

Unfortunately, the original purpose of this statuette is unknown. As it is said to have been found near the Alpheus River that runs through the sanctuary of Olympia, however, it may well have been a votive offering. And, indeed, it is not difficult to imagine the pride with which a Greek would have made this dedication. Immediately comprehensible as a man, the tiny image conveys in its maker's masterful handling of material and space a burgeoning sense of confidence. Here, we find the Greek artist has already focused on the subject that for the next seven centuries presented his primary challenge. Within the available possibilities, he has found a small but supremely satisfying solution.

CONDITION: The figure is solid cast in one piece with the stool and base. The only visible damage is the front leg of the stool, which has been broken away from the base and reattached. The surface is generally covered with a consistent black patina, with areas of lighter green in the crevices around the features of the face, on the front of the torso, and on the insides of the arms; it is also greenish on the underside of the horseshoe-shaped stool and on the top of the base. A small area of the original bronze surface is visible in the center of the small of the back. The surface is rather regularly pitted all over, and there is no remaining evidence of polish or original finish.

PROVENANCE: Said to have been found in the Alpheus Valley in Elis.

EXHIBITED: Baltimore, Md., Walters Art Gallery, 1953, *4000 Years of Modern Art*, no. 15 (brochure).
Cambridge, Mass., Fogg Art Museum, December 4, 1967-January 23, 1968; St. Louis, Mo., City Art Museum, March 1-April 13, 1968; Los Angeles County Museum of Art, May 8-June 30, 1968, *Master Bronzes from the Classical World*, 32, no. 9, entry by D. G. Mitten.

PUBLISHED: E. Buschor, *Die Plastik der Griechen* (Berlin, 1936) 8, illus.
D. K. Hill, *Catalogue of the Classical Bronze Sculpture in the Walters Art Gallery* (Portland, Me., 1949) 77, no. 167, pl. 36.
U. Jantzen, "Geometrische Kannenverchlüsse," *Archäologischer Anzeiger* (1953) col. 63, n. 4.
L. Alscher, *Griechische Plastik* (Berlin, 1954-) 1:21-22, fig. 16.
N. Himmelmann-Wildschütz, *Bemerkungen zur geometrischen Plastik* (Berlin, 1964) 11, figs. 51-53.
R. Lullies in K. Schefold, *Die Griechen und ihre Nachbarn* (Berlin, 1967) 160, pl. 8a-c; also mentioned in passing by Schefold on p. 58.
M. Vickers, "Some Early Iron Age Bronzes from Macedonia," APXAIA MAKE[D]ONIA II, Papers Read at the Second International Symposium Held in Thessaloniki, August 19-24, 1973 (Thessaloniki, 1977) 25, n. 41.
I. Kilian-Dirlmeier, *Anhänger in Griechenland von mykenischen bis zur spätgeometrischen Zeit* (Munich, 1979) 206, n. 18.

G. Ortiz in *Hommes et dieux de la Grèce antique*, ed. K. van Gelder, exh. cat. (Brussels, Palais des Beaux-Arts, 1982) 203-205, under no. 124.

NOTES: On the Geometric group of a hero and centaur in the Metropolitan Museum of Art (17.190.2072), see J. Mertens (*BMMA*) 1985, 18, no. 7.
For the Ortiz Geometric group of a hunter and dogs attacking a predator, see C. Rolley 1986, 66, fig. 35.
For the seated figure from the sanctuary of Artemis Orthia (now Sparta, 2155), see R. M. Dawkins, *The Sanctuary of Artemis Orthia at Sparta* (London, 1929) pl. LXXVII, a; also, N. Himmelmann-Wildschütz 1964, figs. 54-56, and D. Picopoulou-Tsolaki in *The Human Figure in Early Greek Art*, exh. cat. (Washington, D.C., 1987) 70, no. 7. For the seated figure from the Pomerance collection, see *Small Sculptures in Bronze from the Classical World*, ed. G. K. Sams, exh. cat. (Chapel Hill, N.C., William Hayes Ackland Memorial Art Center, 1976) no. 7; also, *The Pomerance Collection of Ancient Art*, exh. cat. (Brooklyn, The Brooklyn Museum, 1966) 79, no. 89. For the Ortiz seated figure, see G. Ortiz in *Hommes et dieux* (1982). He compares also to a similar image with simian features (Ashmolean, 1936.608) and a figure from the sanctuary of Athena Alea at Tegea, no. 329. For the bronze formerly in the Bomford collection and now in the Sackler Museum (1981.41), see P. R. S. Moorey and H. W. Catling, *Antiquities from the Bomford Collection*, exh. cat. (Oxford, 1966) no. 310.
On Geometric flute players, see E. Homann-Wedeking, *Die Anfänge der griechischen Grossplastik* (Berlin, 1950) 15 ff., n. 21; 24.
On the Geometric bronze figures of the Peloponnesian workshop, see L. Alscher 1954, 21-22; also, C. Rolley 1986, 66-70.
For examples of bronze Geometric "bottle-stoppers" crowned by seated figures in similar positions, see I. Kilian-Dirlmeier 1979, 194-208, pls. 61-73; on the archaeological evidence for their correct identification as girdle ornaments, see M. Vickers 1977, 18-19. For ivory and bone figures in similar poses, see R. M. Dawkins 1929, pl. 123, 3 and 169, 3.

2. Mantiklos Apollo

GREEK, PROBABLY
BOEOTIAN,
CA. 700-675 BC.
H. 20.3 CM.
MUSEUM OF FINE ARTS,
BOSTON, FRANCIS
BARTLETT
COLLECTION, 03.997

Few bronzes of any period rival the so-called "Mantiklos Apollo" for either fine execution or visual impact. One of the most imaginative interpretations of the masculine figure ever created, it has been recognized as a major achievement in the development of Western art since it first came to the attention of archaeologists and art historians in the later nineteenth century, and its status has remained unchallenged. The frontally conceived figure stands upright with its left leg slightly advanced; its left arm, bent at the elbow, is raised to hold an attribute that is now missing. Unfortunately, the right arm and both legs below the knees are lost as well. Yet what remains is an image of such direct, expressive power that, once seen, it is never easily put out of mind.

The head appears at first too small in proportion to the elongated body, but the disturbing effects of its inadequate proportions are counteracted by the exaggerated features and the surrounding mass of hair arranged in long, thick coils. Once inlaid with glass or stone, the circular voids of the eyes dominate the face. They are set within the inconspicuously incised lids high in the triangular contours of the face on either side of an enormous, aquiline nose. The carefully described mouth, with lips tightly pursed, is placed well above the cleft, pointed chin.

Pairs of locks frame the face on either side, and five broad tresses are arranged across the back, ending at the shoulders. The hair on the top of the head is divided by a central part running from front to back, and though the individual strands are not indicated on the crown, the long, plump locks that hang below the fillet are scored with roughly horizontal incisions to show the spiraling curls. All are held neatly in place by a fillet, whose convex surface is decorated with an incised zigzag pattern. The hole just above the center of the forehead must originally have held an attached flower; a second hole in the top of the crown may have held another attribute or attachment.

Connecting the head and the wide, rounded shoulders is an exaggeratedly long, flat neck, bisected by a wide vertical groove. This incised central axis continues straight down the front of the triangular torso to end just at the waist above the abbreviated point of the groin. A chain of decorative curvilinear elements, rather like curved teeth pierced for suspension, marks the clavicles and separates the neck from the trunk of the body. Descending incised lines converge at the center of the chest above the shallow curves that underline the pectoral muscles, and an upright chevron is formed by the ascending lines that indicate the bottom of the rib cage. Two horizontal grooves form the belt around the slightly inset, convex waist. A vertical incision corresponding to the front axis marks the spinal column on the back, continuing below the waist to divide the buttocks.

Beneath the belt, the body displays a fullness that is only suggested above in the round curve of the shoulders and the thick locks of hair. The tops of the thighs expand unnaturally into broad hips at the sides and rounded, high buttocks at the back. In front, the thighs are separated at the upper limits only by the carefully modeled genitals and finely incised pubic hair; they then separate below, approximately two-thirds of the way to the knees. Now obscured by the lengthy incised inscription, a low ridge runs down the center front of each thigh, ending just over the small, raised patella. Simple horizontal depressions mark the backs of the knees.

Both the inscription on the front of the thighs and the attribute originally held in the left hand are fundamental to the figure's identification. The two lines of dactylic hexameter in Archaic Boeotian characters run boustrophedon, starting from the right knee up over the thigh and across the groin, then down the left thigh and knee, where they turn to run retrograde, ending beside the spot where they began.

Μάντικλος μ'ἀνέθεικε ϝεκαβόλοι ἀργυροτόχϲοι τᾶς δεκάτας·τὺ δὲ, Φοῖβε, δίδοι χαρίϝετταν ἀμοι [ϝάν]. This inscription may be translated: "Mantiklos dedicated [me] from his tithe to the Far Darter of the Silver Bow [Apollo]; do you, Phoebus, grant gracious recompense." Here, the figure's original votive purpose is articulated; the bronze was surely dedicated in a sanctuary of Apollo, perhaps the Ismenion of Thebes. If the figure's left hand held a bow, then the statuette should be understood to represent Apollo himself, as the archer god whose arrows could visit destruction on mankind. If, on the other hand, the left hand held a spear, then the figure could be the votary Mantiklos represented as a warrior.

The Greek traveler and geographer Pausanias (fl. AD 143-176) records the existence of a famous Mantiklos (IV.xxi.2, 12; xxii.10; xxvi.3). The son of Theokles, he led the Messenian people in the twenty-ninth Olympiad (ca. 664-660 BC), following the second Messenian War in which Sparta invaded and occupied Messenia. The documented period of Mantiklos' prominence approximates the early seventh-century dates generally assigned to the Boston bronze. Since the inscription on the thighs does not have any features connecting it with either the Messenian or the Lacedaemonian dialects, however—but rather fits comfortably within the corpus of known Boeotian Archaic inscriptions—the attractive connection with this historical personage is only a slight possibility at best.

Nor is the evidence provided by a possible attribute any more persuasive for the identification of the figure as the mortal votary. Besides suggesting that the left hand could have held a spear, both Alscher and Vermeule have interpreted the presence of the holes in the forehead and crown as evidence for the attachment of a helmet, and Vermeule has seen the incisions on the chest as the markings of a

corselet. The presence of the decorated fillet and the carefully incised part in the hair would seem to contradict the restoration of a helmet, however; and though a helmet of caplike shape that would fit the top of the head is not without parallels, neither is a flower in the center of the fillet. The unusual incised decoration across the clavicles adds some credence to the possibility of a cuirass; yet, there are neither incisions marking the edges of the armholes nor a noticeable offset to represent the flange at the bottom. As the appearance of a corselet would be unique among the earliest statuettes of warriors, the incisions on the clavicles may be better understood as a necklace of comma-shaped pendants, and a wide belt, which is well documented, is a more likely interpretation for the horizontal parallel lines at the waist.

In the question of identification, the Boston bronze participates in the much larger issue of the original purpose of Archaic kouroi that has never been satisfactorily resolved in most cases, in spite of the firmly stated opinions of various respected scholars. Though the majority of the nude or semi-nude figures are now taken to be generic representations of idealized youths, some must have originally been intended as images of the youthful god Apollo. Found both over graves and in large numbers in certain sanctuaries, especially at Thebes, few preserve their bases, inscriptions, or other external evidence that is helpful for identification. Here, however, the pose corresponds so well to the dedication's description of Apollo as archer that the identification of the statuette as a representation of the god is clearly warranted.

Beyond the question of its identity, the quality of the execution of this figure naturally raises questions about its actual place of manufacture. The reported Theban provenance and strongly Boeotian character of the inscription on the thighs do not, in themselves, prove that the figure is the work of a Theban master. Small and portable, the figure could just as easily have been made elsewhere and transported to a Theban sanctuary for dedication. As has long been recognized, however, details of his anatomy, such as the exaggeratedly long, flat neck, the sausage-like curls, and the staring eyes, find their closest parallels among the early Boeotian terracotta bell idols, statuettes, figures represented on the large relief storage jars (pithoi), and even in the somewhat later monumental Boeotian stone sculpture of the twins Dermys and Kittylos, so the Boeotian provenance, though uncertain, is strongly supported by well-documented evidence.

Although the figure's magnificently stylized anatomy stands at the threshold of the Orientalizing period, it still betrays too many of the characteristics of the earlier Geometric style to be properly considered early Archaic. In its combination of attenuated proportions, simplification of the formal aspects of the body, articulation of the torso with incisions that either exaggerate or invent anatomical features, and the imposition of a kind of linear scaffolding around which the figure is constructed like a piece of architecture, it stands closer to the Geometric tradition.

At the same time, the artist has not conceived of his subject in the purely abstract terms of the Geometric style. Seen from the front, the figure appears like an assemblage of planar forms piled end to end. Yet, when turned in profile, the mass of the thick locks straining under the fillet, the slightly inflated chest, the hemispherical buttocks, and tapering thighs show the extent to which the Greek artist has begun to fill out the wiry form of the hieroglyph with volumes of hair and muscular flesh. And though he still relies heavily on the use of linear incision to clarify the structure of the human form, he has introduced a respect for the individual components comprising the body.

Accuracy of detail is still sacrificed for the expressive power of the whole, however, and rarely has a purpose been achieved more consummately. Thoroughly familiar with the technical possibilities of bronzecasting, the Greek craftsman who created this statuette was not content to accept the established conventions of abstraction. Instead, he chose to reconsider his subject carefully. And from the resources of his imagination and experience, he has distilled no true reflection of natural appearances, but something more profound—a representation of what he understood an Olympian god to be.

CONDITION: The figure is solid cast, with some casting flaws visible in the legs and on the underside of the preserved left arm. The right arm is missing from just below the deltoid. Both legs are missing from just below the knee, the left preserving more of the kneecap than the right. The end of the nose was damaged when the figure was dropped in modern times. The attribute from the left hand and the elements set into the holes at the center of the forehead and the crown of the skull are gone. The irises of the eyes were originally inlaid with glass or stone, and the belt at the waist may have been overlaid with a sheet of precious metal.

The surface is covered with a fairly uniform dark green patina with some heavier blackish-brown encrustation, especially evident between the locks of hair on the back of the head.

PROVENANCE: Said to have been found in Thebes with [3], perhaps from the Ismenion.

EXHIBITED: Buffalo, N.Y., Albright Art Gallery, February 1937, *Master Bronzes: Selected from Museums and Collections in America*, no. 65, illus.

PUBLISHED: W. Froehner, "Apollon bronze archaïque de la collection du Comte Michel Tyszkiewicz," *Monuments et mémoires. Fondation E. Piot* II (1895) 137-143, pl. xv.
W. Deonna, *Les Apollons archaïques; étude sur le type masculin de la statuaire grecque du VIᵉ siècle avant notre ère* (Geneva, 1909) 254, n. 5.
L. Curtius, *Die antike Kunst*, II, I (Berlin, Potsdam, 1938) 80, 84, 91, 97, 100, 102, 139, 171-175, 179-181, 190, 290, 292, fig. 108.
G. H. Karo, *Greek Personality in Archaic Sculpture* (Cambridge, Mass., 1948) 70-71.
G. M. A. Richter, *Archaic Greek Art Against Its Historical Background* (New York, 1949) 22.
L. Alscher 1954, 1:46-49, fig. 41.
A. de Franciscis, "Apollo," in *Enciclopedia dell'arte antica, classica e orientale* I (Rome, 1958-1966) 464, fig. 629.
G. Kaschnitz von Weinberg, *Mittelmeerische Kunst: Eine Darstellung ihrer Strukturen* (Berlin, 1965) 270, 272-274, 277-278, 281, 290, pl. 61.
G. Kaulen, *Daidalika; Werkstätten griechische Kleinplastik des 7. Jahrhunderts v. Ch.* (Munich, 1967) 2-5, 10, 13-15, 20, 126-127, 143; see also review by D. G. Mitten, *AJA* LXXIV (1970) 109-110.
E. Kjellberg and G. Säflund, *Greek and Roman Art: 3000 B.C. to A.D. 500* (London, 1968) 57, pl. 22.
W. Fuchs, *Die Skulptur der Griechen* (Munich, 1969) 21-23, fig. 3-4.
M. Comstock and C. Vermeule, *Greek, Etruscan and Roman Bronzes in the Museum of Fine Arts,* *Boston* (Greenwich, Conn., 1971) 16-17, no. 15 (with extensive earlier references).
R. Brilliant, *The Arts of the Ancient Greeks* (New York, 1973) 44, fig. 2-40.
L. H. Jeffery, *Archaic Greece: The City-States, c. 700-500 B.C.* (New York, 1976) 78, pl. 7.
J. G. Pedley, *Greek Sculpture of the Archaic Period: The Island Workshops* (Mainz, 1976) 20.
J. N. Coldstream, *Geometric Greece* (New York, 1977) 302.
B. S. Ridgway, *The Archaic Style in Greek Sculpture* (Princeton, 1977) 27, n. 16; 55, n. 12.
J. Boardman, *Greek Sculpture: The Archaic Period; A Handbook* (New York, 1978) 10, 30, fig. 10.
P. Devambez, *Great Sculpture of Ancient Greece*, tr. H. Tunikowska (New York, 1978) 90-91.
R. Lullies, *Griechische Plastik: Von den Anfängen bis zum Beginn der römischen Kaiserzeit*, 4th ed. (Munich, 1979) 16, 42, no. 10, pl. 10.
R. Hampe and E. Simon, *The Birth of Greek Art: From the Mycenaean to the Archaic Period* (New York, 1981) 256, 277, 307, pls. 427-428.
A. Schachter, *Cults of Boeotia*, I: *Acheloos to Hera, Bulletin of the Institute of Classical Studies of the University of London*, Suppl. XXXVIII, I (1981) Acheloos to Hera, under Apollo (Ptoion) 73, n. 6; reference to J. Wackernagel, *Zeitschrift für vergleichende Sprachsforschung* XXXIII (NF XIII) (1895) 25-35.
C. C. Vermeule, *The Art of the Greek World: Prehistoric through Perikles (From the Late Stone Age and the Early Age of Bronze to the Peloponnesian Wars)* (Boston, 1982) 80, 83-85, 217, 377-379, fig. 138.
E. Richardson, *Etruscan Votive Bronzes: Geometric, Orientalizing, Archaic* (Mainz, 1983) I:37, n. 86.
J. Barron, *An Introduction to Greek Sculpture*, 1st American ed. (New York, 1981-) 10-11, illus.
O. Palagia and W. Lambrinudakis, "Apollon," *Lexicon Iconographicum Mythologiae Classicae* (Zurich, 1981-) II, 1, pp. 194, 314, no. 14; II, 2, p. 185.
F. Brommer, "Gott oder Mensch," *JdI* CI (1986) 41.

NOTES: The condition statement for this bronze was made with the assistance of Arthur Beale and Richard Newman.

For a discussion of the general characteristics of Boeotian Archaic sculpture, including illustrations of Boeotian terracotta bell idols and other statuettes as well as the figural decoration on Boeotian relief pithoi, see F. Grace, *Archaic Sculpture in Boeotia* (Cambridge, Mass., 1939); more recently J. Ducat, "Les kouroi du Ptoion," *Bibliothèque des Ecoles Françaises*

d'Athénes et de Rome CCXIX, esp. 49-125. Both
Grace and Ducat accept the Mantiklos Apollo
as Boeotian in origin. For the specific associations between Boeotian terracottas and
bronzes, see also H. Goldman, "Some Votive
Offerings from the Acropolis of Halae," Festschrift für James Loeb zum 60. Geburtstag
(Munich, 1930) 67-72, pls. VI-VIII.

For the discussion of the interpretation of
kouroi, see most recently F. Brommer (JdI)
1986; V. Zinserling, "Zum Bedeutungsgehalt
des archaischen Kuros," Eirene XIII (1975) 19-35;
J. Ducat, "Fonction de la statue dans la Grèce
archaïque–kouros et kolossos," BCH C (1976)
239-251; B. S. Ridgway 1977, 49-59; and A.
Stewart, "When Is a Kouros not an Apollo?
The Tenea Kouros Revisited," Corinthiaca;
Studies in Honor of Darrell A. Amyx (Columbia,
Mo., 1986) 54-70.

For a small helmet on the top of the skull, see
C. Rolley, Greek Minor Arts, I: The Bronzes
(Leiden, 1967) pl. 2, fig. 6; pl. 4, fig. 10.

For the rosette at the front of the fillet, see the
kouros in Florence, G. M. A. Richter, Kouroi,
3rd ed. (New York, 1970) no. 70, fig. 239; and
the head in New York, no. 64, fig. 217.

For the belt, compare G. M. A. Richter
(Kouroi) 1970, forerunner fig. 6; forerunner fig.
14; no. 15, fig. 89; no. 17, fig. 94; on the importance of the belt, see also A. Stewart 1986, 57, 59,
n. 18.

For the long sausagelike locks with spiraling
strands incised, see the rear side locks of the
Boeotian twins Dermys and Kittylos, G. M. A.
Richter (Kouroi) 1970, no. II, fig. 77. The caul-
dron attachment in the shape of a siren from
Olympia, now in the Museum of Fine Arts in
Boston (99.458; M. Comstock and C. C. Vermeule 1971, 279, no. 402) shows a similar arrangement of tresses.

D. K. Hill's suggestion, in "One of the Earliest Greek Bronze Statuettes," The Journal of the
Walters Art Gallery II (1939) 30, that the hole in
the top of the head may be taken as an indication that the figure was originally an attachment
on a larger structure is difficult to accept given
the shallowness of the hole and the lack of any
other indications of attachment.

For two-dimensional parallels, compare the
large eyes, aquiline noses, wasp waists, rounded
buttocks, and bulging thighs of Odysseus and
his comrades on the neck of the Proto-Attic vase
by the Polyphemos Painter (fl. 670-640) in the
Eleusis Museum (S. Morris, The Black and White
Style: Athens and Aigina in the Orientalizing
Period [New Haven, Conn., 1984] 36, 52, pl. 6).

3. Standing Goddess or Female Votary

Though seemingly rather distant in style, this standing female figure presents something of the same immediacy and expressive distortion that characterize the Mantiklos Apollo [2], with which she was reportedly found. And like the Mantiklos
dedication, this bronze enjoys a much-deserved reputation as an object of primary
significance in the history of Greek sculpture.

The maiden stands frontally with her face slightly upturned and her hands extended before her to offer attributes or gifts, now lost. Her rather squat proportions are new and unexpected. In contrast to the Apollo and earlier Geometric
seated man [1], her head dominates the figure, comprising approximately one-
quarter of the total height. It is separated from her shoulders by a short, columnar
neck; and the body below is rendered with a minimum of surface articulation—
everything but her arms and feet being hidden beneath the concealing fabric of the
short-sleeved peplos (a long dress, usually made of heavy material, that is fastened
at the shoulders and open on one side). Only the breadth of her unevenly sloping
shoulders and the fullness of her breasts are indicated above her narrow waist,
which is belted. The columnar skirt of her garment falls without a crease, flaring
gradually toward the bottom. The pointed toes of her enormous shoes protrude
beneath its hem. No unnecessary detail detracts from either her lively facial features
or the meaningful gestures of her hands.

The artist has focused most of his creative energies on the statuette's head.
Within the large, rather flat upturned oval of the face, the arching eyebrows are
incised above enormous, staring eyes, whose wide-open lids and circular convex
irises give the visage a rather intense, vivid expression. The brows flow without interruption into the bridge of the sharp, slightly askew nose and the labio-nasal

GREEK, PROBABLY
BOEOTIAN,
ORIENTALIZING,
CA. 675-650 BC.
H. 17.2 CM. H. OF
FIGURE 16.6 CM.
WALTERS ART
GALLERY, 54.773

grooves that run straight down the sides of the nose form the corners of the small, tight-lipped mouth.

The concentrated interest of the sculptor did not stop with the facial features, however, but extended as well to the carefully defined arrangement of the hair, known by the German term *Etagenperücke*, or stepped wig. The head is covered with seven wedge-shaped layers of short, stiff locks. The individual strands of hair, inscribed vertically on the upper surface of each tier, were probably incised in the original wax model from which this figure was cast, not worked in the surface of the bronze, but the crisscrossed incisions on the front of the locks framing the face appear to be part of the cold working.

This particular coiffure is often considered to be a principal characteristic of the so-called "Dedalic style," a special aspect of Greek sculpture usually dated to the seventh century BC and named for its association with Dedalus, the mythical sculptor to whom ancient sources attribute the introduction of lifelike human representations. The Etagenperücke may actually have represented a wig and was most likely inspired by either Egyptian prototypes or Phoenician adaptations. Its appearance on this figure introduces the important issue of foreign influences, particularly from the more developed civilizations of the ancient Near East. As there is a noticeable influx of decorative motifs and figural types borrowed from Assyria, Persia, Egypt, and Phoenicia in Greek seventh-century art, art historians generally refer to this period as the "Orientalizing phase." Besides the Baltimore bronze's hair, the shape of the face and its exaggerated features, especially the eyes, have frequently been connected with Phoenician sources and help to place it firmly within this period.

One other feature of the statuette confirms the presence of oriental influences. Both arms are bent at the elbows and extended forward in the expressive gesture identified as the "Hittite pose" that seems to have originated in the central Euphrates Valley between present-day Turkey and Syria some time in the fifteenth century BC. The attribute in the left hand stood upright in the hole drilled down through the center of the firmly clenched fingers. The right hand's upturned, open palm most likely held a flat-bottomed vessel, probably a phiale. And though the figure has sometimes been identified as the goddess Artemis, the gesture of the right hand is equally appropriate to a votary making an offering to a deity as it is to the deity herself.

In her very thorough publication of this statuette, Hill suggested that the female may have been one of the caryatids or supporting figures from a vessel support (perirrhanterion). This proposal was inspired by the large, deep gouge cut into the back of the figure's skirt close to the base, and the wear on the top of the head. Carefully square-cut with straight edges at the top and bottom, the principal groove in the skirt does indeed seem intentional, and the presence of several smaller incised grooves running parallel above and below suggests that whoever made the cut tried several times before succeeding.

Against Hill's suggestion, however, are a number of factors. The rectangular base on which the figure stands and which is cast together with it shows no signs of attachment to any larger complex and is otherwise without parallel among perirrhanterion caryatids, as are the distinctive gestures of the hands. In addition, except for the gouge in the skirt, there is no sign of attachment elsewhere on the figure—including the top of the head—and the details of the wig, though admittedly cast, are as carefully finished across the back as on the front. The wear on the top of the head might result from other causes, including physical handling and burial conditions, while the convincing explanation of the gouge in the skirt must await the discovery of some parallel or further evidence.

Few introductory surveys of Greek art neglect to mention this standing female figure, but her importance is more difficult to define. The fresh, spirited rendering of the subject, in addition to the hairstyle and the details of the asymmetrical facial features, suggests that the statuette should be dated among the early examples of post-Geometric sculpture. Her origins remain somewhat uncertain, as the traditional provenance of Thebes is undocumented; and even if Thebes could be proven to have been the findspot, this information alone would not prove Boeotian manufacture, as she, like the Mantiklos Apollo, could readily have been imported for dedication at a sanctuary. Still as Goldman observed half a century ago and as the reported Theban provenance of the statuette might have suggested, the closest parallels for the individual features of this image are to be found among seventh-century Boeotian terracotta bell goddesses and the female figures

represented on the large Boeotian relief pithoi; thus, the probability that she is the work of a Theban craftsman is very high.

But whether native or imported, this bronze maiden stands between the abstract reduction of the pure Geometric style, well illustrated here by the Walters seated man [1], and the completely convincing portrayal of the human figure that was achieved in the following decades of the seventh and sixth centuries by the series of Archaic youths and maidens in stone, bronze, and terracotta. The artist has not yet freed himself entirely from the tendency to reduce the human body to an architectonic construction, but he has given the figure greater volume. Reshaping the natural proportions for expressive purposes, he has employed abstraction effectively to draw attention to the most important elements of the image.

An extraordinary vitality is captured in the backward tilt of the face and its jutting jaw, as well as the ingenuously outthrust hands. And though the original attachments will probably never be identified, no offering was ever made with more sincerity or directness. It is unnecessary to imagine this statuette as part of a larger complex. Maiden or goddess, she requires no additional structure to support or explain her existence. Her appearance sometime before the middle of the seventh century BC proved conclusively that the native Geometric style had run its course. Reflecting both the inspiration provided by sophisticated oriental imports and the indigenous fascination with the artistic possibilities of the human form, she heralds the beginning of an epoch of experimentation and innovation that proved one of the most fruitful in the history of Western artistic development.

CONDITION: The well-preserved solid bronze is cast as one piece with the base. The underside of the base is irregular, with a deep hollow penetrating the skirt of the figure. A few casting flaws are visible: one fairly deep hole on the figure's forehead above the proper left eye and two small holes in the thumb of the right hand. A small hole that may have been intentional appears in the top of the right wrist. Besides the deep horizontal groove, most likely intentional, visible near the bottom of the back of the skirt, surface damage is restricted to a squarish gouge on the right cheek close to the hair; a shallow cut approximately at the level of the navel; and a gouge on the front of the skirt.

The surface of the bronze is a wonderful lustrous greenish-black, with some heavier encrustation over the upper torso, down the left side, across the front of the skirt, down the center of the face, on the left cheek, and in small patches in the hair. The proper right side of the back is distinctly greener, while the front of the statuette is mostly blackish in tone.

PROVENANCE: Said to have been found in Thebes with [2], perhaps from the Ismenion.

EX COLLECTION: Count M. Tyszkiewicz.

EXHIBITED: Detroit Institute of Arts, March 23-April 20, 1947, *Small Bronzes of the Ancient World*, no. 55.
Baltimore, Md., Walters Art Gallery, 1953, *4000 Years of Modern Art*, no. 17.
Brussels, Palais des Beaux-Arts, October 1-December 2, 1982, *Hommes et dieux de la Grèce antique*, cat. by K. van Gelder, 188, no. 112.

PUBLISHED: Sale: *Collection d'antiquités du Comte Michel Tyszkiewicz*, by W. Froehner, Paris, Hôtel des Commissaires-Priseurs, 8-10 June, 1898, 48, no. 134, pl. 13.
F. Poulsen, *Die Orient und die frühgriechische Kunst* (Leipzig, 1912) 147-148, fig. 171.
S. Reinach, *Répertoire de la statuaire grecque et romaine* III (Paris, 1920) 93, no. 1.
E. Langlotz 1927, 30, no. 2 (as Sicyon).
W. Lamb, *Greek and Roman Bronzes* (London, 1929) 76, pl. XXII, b.
H. Goldman 1930, 71-72, fig. 5 (mistakenly given as in the collection of the Museum of Fine Arts, Boston).

F. Grace 1939, 49, fig. 64.
D. K. Hill, "One of the Earliest Greek Bronze Statuettes," *JWalt* II (1939) 24-35.
D. K. Hill, Review of F. Grace 1939, *AJA* XLIV (1940) 371.
D. K. Hill 1949, 105, no. 237, pl. 47.
G. M. A. Richter 1949, 22, figs. 36-37.
M. Gjødesen, "Deus ex Machina," *Meddelelser Fra Ny Carlsberg Glyptotek* VIII (1951) 27, fig. 15.
G. Kaulen 1967, 187, n. 85, figs. 4-5 (dated to ca. 690 BC).
G. M. A. Richter, *Korai: Archaic Greek Maidens* (London, 1968) 31, no. 14, figs. 60-62 (dated to ca. 650-625 BC).
L. Kahil and N. Icard, "Artemis," *LIMC* II, 1:630, no. 79; II, 2:448.

NOTES: For the Dedalic style in general, see R. J. H. Jenkins, *Dedalica; A Study of Dorian Plastic Art in the Seventh Century B.C.* (Cambridge, 1936; reprint Chicago, 1978); also B. Ridgway 1977, 17-42.

For the Etagenperücke, see F. Poulsen 1912, 137-160; R. Jenkins 1978, 19-20; and C. Davaras, *Die Statue aus Astritsi. Ein Beitrag zur dädalischen Kunst auf Kreta und zu dem Anfängen der griechischen Plastik* (Bern, 1972) 24-25.

For the "Hittite pose," see E. Richardson 1983, 36-37, with specific reference to the Walters bronze.

For the identification as Artemis, see L. Kahil and N. Icard 1984; as a votary, see K. van Gelder in *Hommes et dieux*, 1982.

For perirrhanteria, see G. M. A. Richter 1968, 27-30.

For the Boeotian bell goddesses and relief pithoi, see H. Goldman 1930; see also F. Grace 1939, pl. 1, fig. 6; pl. 2, figs. 8-9.

4. Artemis

Like a miniature cult figure, the goddess stands on top of a three-stepped base. She is dressed in a sleeveless peplos of Laconian fashion that is belted at the waist, with its skirt arranged to appear straight in the front with the fullness gathered into seven pleats across the back. Its bodice is distinguished by a short overfall (apoptygma). Appropriately for her appearance in the aspect of a young maiden, Artemis' hair is dressed in twelve long, crimped locks, three on either side of her face curving forward from behind her ears and draping over her bodice, while six more spread over her back. Across her forehead, a short fringe ends in curls. A double twisted fillet encircles her head, holding the coiffure in place. Around her neck, she wears a thick choker with a central pendant of a type often found among Laconian bronzes. Her feet, placed side-by-side on the plinth, are shod in plain yoke-type sandals with layered soles.

GREEK, LACONIAN, ARCHAIC, CA. 530–520 BC. H. 19.2 CM. H. OF FIGURE 17.6 CM. MUSEUM OF FINE ARTS, BOSTON, H.L. PIERCE FUND, 98.658

The left hand, raised before the figure, holds the remains of a bow (cast together with the hand)—an attribute that most specifically identifies the goddess of the hunt. A second hole just behind the bow, now empty, probably held an arrow. The right hand, more tentatively extended, is lower and closer to the body; although only part of it is preserved, enough remains to show that this hand was drilled to hold some attribute, which in this case may have been the legs of a small animal, the huntress' unfortunate quarry. In rare confirmation of the identification based on the attributes, the right side of the skirt front carries an inscription in carefully incised Laconian letters: Χιμαρίδας ται Δαιδαλείαι. "Chimaridas [dedicated this] to [Artemis] Daidaleia." On the basis of these letter forms, the figure can be placed in the last quarter of the sixth century BC, which is confirmed by stylistic details, as shown below.

The figure's proportions and especially the features of the head show the sensitivity to human anatomy and precision of execution that distinguishes the best Laconian Archaic bronzes. In spite of the slight anatomical distortions exaggerating the size of head, shoulders, and feet, while minimizing the hips, the contours of the figure are visually satisfying from every point of view—frontal, profile, and three-quarter. Here, the artist acknowledges the volume of the human form, taking obvious delight in the contours of the female figure. The backward thrust of the shoulders emphasizes the fine natural curve of the back and high placement of the small, firm breasts, while the narrow waist sets off the hips and, in profile, the buttocks that swell beneath it. The imposing base underlines the extension of the arms, allowing for the space they invade beyond the outlines of the torso to be included with the contours of the figure.

In the ripe Archaic period to which this bronze rightly belongs, artists were concerned with the accurate observation of anatomical details and, at the same time, with their ability to subordinate these observations to the compositional needs of a work of art. Every contour of the face, for example, is reduced to a curve of refined simplicity. Within its heart-shaped outline, the eyes are set beneath the impossibly symmetrical arches of the brows, with the eyelids curved to reflect both the brows above and the globular forms of the eyes beneath. But with great accuracy, the irises are indicated with fine incision, and the tear ducts are clearly defined. The straight, finely pointed nose ends just above the perfectly matched lips that, while smiling ever so slightly, are naturalistically separated all the way to the corners.

The detailed articulation of the head, on which the artist has lavished his greatest attention, is balanced by the carefully conceived costume and stepped base beneath the figure. The choice of the peplos as costume at a time when the sheerer Ionic chiton and himation were more fashionable in centers of urban power such as Athens and Corinth has been explained as an indication of the figure's provincial origin. The sophisticated use of this garment, however, belies this possibility. Accurately reflecting a fashion popular in the Peloponnese and especially Laconia, the pleats across the back of the peplos skirt also serve an artistic purpose. They contribute a note of visual interest to the otherwise undistinguished length of the skirt, similar in many respects to the effect of fluting on an Ionic column. Serving as a kind of counterpoint to the long tapering strands of hair above, they prevent monotony in the least important aspect of the statuette.

Besides the columnar appearance of the peplos skirt, the recessed steps of the plinth are clearly architectural, adding a dimension of grandeur to the diminutive figure of the goddess that is unusual for a bronze votive statuette of this period and which raises the question of its source of inspiration. Comparisons among the known bronzes of the same period are few, while the closest associations seem to be with monumental stone images such as the figure of Nikandre, the columnar female figures from Samos dedicated by Cheramyes, and the numerous korai found on the Athenian Acropolis. As Neugebauer suggested more than half a century ago, the commanding frontality of the figure on its raised dais and the apparent combination of advanced and traditional features may indicate that the statuette is a slightly later reflection of an earlier monumental cult image, though the epithet *Daidaleia* (Greek for "cunning") is otherwise unrecorded for the goddess.

Only a century removed from the Baltimore votary [3], the Boston Artemis is a world apart from the immediacy and sincerity of the earlier statuette. Yet, although liveliness and energy have been replaced by sophistication, refinement, and increased anatomical accuracy, expressive power has not been lost. Her artist has achieved a harmonious balance between structural simplicity and decorative

surface articulation, hieratic presentation of a sacred subject, and convincing youthful beauty. This is indeed the fair Artemis worthy of Hippolytus' garland, woven from flowers gathered in a meadow where "never shepherd dares to feed his flock nor steel of sickle came," and in which only the pure could set foot (Euripides, *Hippolytos*, tr. A. S. Way, lines 73-81).

CONDITION: The figure is intact except for the upper half of the bow in the left hand and the fingers, part of the palm, and the attribute originally held in the right hand. The surface is covered with a thin black patina, with some areas of the golden bronze fabric visible, especially at the tops of the crimps in the locks of hair and all along the proper left side, where there is evidence of extensive pitting due to corrosion.

Although the figure was solid cast in one piece together with its base, x-radiographs show a small hollow within the head and upper body. This was probably a flaw in the casting process, a result of the molten bronze failing to fill the mold completely.

EX COLLECTIONS: Count M. Tyszkiewicz; Edward Perry Warren.

PROVENANCE: Found at Mazi, in Elis, near Olympia.

EXHIBITED: Buffalo, N.Y., Albright Art Gallery, February 1937, *Master Bronzes: Selected from Museums and Collections in America*, no. 66, illus.
Detroit Institute of Arts, March 23-April 20, 1947, *Small Bronzes of the Ancient World*, intro. by F. W. Robinson, 9, 30, illus. no. 57.

PUBLISHED: M. W. Stoop, "A Laconian Lady?" *Bulletin Antieke Beschaving* XXXIX (1964) 86, no. 6, fig. 3.
C. Leon, "Statuette eines Kuros aus Messenien," *AM* LXXXIII (1968) 179, n. 33.
M. Comstock and C. Vermeule 1971, 20-21, no. 19 with extensive earlier bibliography.
M. Jost, "Statuettes de bronze archaïques provenant de Lykosoura," *BCH* XCIX (1975) 349.
M. Robertson, *A History of Greek Art*, 2 vols. (London, 1975) I:101, 142; II: pl. 44d.
B. S. Ridgway, "The Peplos Kore, Akropolis 679," *JWalt* XXXVI (1977) 54, fig. 5.
L. Kahil and N. Icard, "Artemis," *LIMC* II, 1:630, no. 81; II, 2:741.
B. S. Ridgway, "The Fashion of the Elgin Kore," *The J. Paul Getty Museum Journal* XII (1984) 40.
K. D. Morrow, *Greek Footwear and the Dating of Sculpture* (Madison, Wisc., 1985) 26, 189-190, n. 18.

F. Brommer, "Gott oder Mensch," *JdI* CI (1986) 39-40.
M. Herfort-Koch, "Archaische Bronzeplastik Lakoniens," *Boreas*, Suppl. IV (Munster, 1986) 25, 27, 35, 42, 92, no. K 45, pl. 5, 1-3.
M. Pipili, *Laconian Iconography of the Sixth Century B.C.*, Oxford University Committee for Archaeology, Monograph XII (Oxford, 1987) 44, fig. 57.
E. Walter-Karydi, *Die äginetische Bildhauerschule: Werke und schriftliche Quellen* (Mainz, 1987) 62, no. 9; 64-65, figs. 81-83.

NOTES: The condition statement was made with the assistance of Arthur Beale and Richard Newman.
On the inscription, see L. H. Jeffery, *The Local Scripts of Archaic Greece; A Study of the Origin of the Greek Alphabet and Its Development from the 8th to the 5th Centuries B.C.* (Oxford, 1961) 191, n. 1.
For the peplos with pleats at the back, see M. Stoop (*BABesch*), 85-89 esp., with an extensive list of comparable representations of the fashion in bronzes and other materials; also M. Herfort-Koch 1986, p. 22; compare the Athena (NM 14828) from Tegea illustrated in Jost, *BCH* XCIX (1975) 348, fig. 19; see also, L. H. Jeffery 1961; C. Rolley 1986, 239, no. 243; K. A. Neugebauer in *Antike Bronzestatuetten* (Berlin, 1921) 43-44.
For a parallel for the pendant around the neck, see the bronze kouros found at Delphi but assigned to Laconia (Delphi Museum, 1663), in M. Herfort-Koch 1986, 106, K86, pl. 12, 3; also C. Rolley 1986, 110-111, fig. 84; though significantly larger, this piece shows comparable refinement of facial features (see also [6]).
For the yoke-type sandals, see K. D. Morrow 1985, 26, 189-190, n. 18.
For the monumental stone image of Nikandre, see G. M. A. Richter (*Kouroi*) 1970, 26, no. 1, figs. 25-28; for the figures dedicated by Cheramyes, see ibid., 46, nos. 55-56, figs. 183-189, and the recently discovered statue on Samos, H. Kyrieleis, "Neue archaische Skulpturen aus dem Heraion von Samos," *Archaische und klassische griechische Plastik, Akten des internationalen Kolloquiums vom 22-25 April 1985 im Athen* (Mainz, 1986) 41-43, pls. 20-22.

5. Kouros

At once the most familiar and representative of all the Greek Archaic male figures is the nude youth or kouros. More than two hundred examples of kouroi are preserved in collections around the world. Varying in height from ten centimeters to over five meters, they are made in a wide range of materials besides bronze. In their general aspects, they are much alike. The stance, with the left foot advanced and both feet flat on the plinth, is canonical. Most have their hands at their sides, and few possess any attribute other than a simple fillet in the hair. Yet, remarkably enough, within these very fixed parameters, each kouros is unique, expressive of the Greek artists' intense concern with the representation of both the appearance and potential of the human form.

As already mentioned when describing the Mantiklos Apollo [2], scholars have frequently debated the identity of the kouros figure, raising the possibility that

GREEK, PERHAPS PELOPONNESIAN, CA. 530–520 BC. H. 15.2 CM. METROPOLITAN MUSEUM OF ART, BEQUEST OF WALTER C. BAKER, 1971, 1972.118.101

some, at least, may have been intended to represent the god Apollo himself rather than a generic youth. Since they have been found above graves and as dedications in sanctuaries, it is fairly certain that there are representations of both mortals and the youthful god of the sun among this large series.

Among the preserved examples, the Baker kouros is not only one of the most vital and engaging but also one of the most unusual. Standing frontally on his rectangular base, he is actually a variation on the canonical type, for he extends his left hand before him, and holds an enigmatic object in his right. And though his feet are in the standard positions, his left foot is only slightly forward.

The impression that the head is overlarge for the slender torso is partly due to its thick mass of long crimped hair, but the placement of the facial features contributes to this effect as well, for the features occupy only the lower half of the face, set well beneath the high forehead and dense hair. The unusual treatment of the hair is of special interest: the shorter locks at the front of the crown are parted down the center and combed back to end just before the ears. In back, what appears to be an incised fillet binds the longer strands together just at the level of the top of the helix of the ear; below the horizontal incision, the crimped locks fall in a heavy curtain across the shoulders, tapering toward the bottom and ending well below the shoulder blades. This incision can be interpreted as marking the ends of the shorter forelocks combed back over the top of the head, and indeed, the strands of hair above the fillet do not correspond to those below, appearing to be narrower and more finely crimped. When seen from the front, however, the expansive contours of the tresses below the horizontal division suggest rather that this discontinuity is the result of their having been held together under pressure just above, and the restraining fillet seems a more natural explanation for this feature.

Within the oval contour of the face, the long arcs of the brows are neatly incised over the widely spaced, finely described eyes; the lids as well as the eyes themselves are rendered in high relief and the inscribed circular irises provide a calm direct expression. Set between the flattened cheeks, the small straight nose and the sensitively modeled mouth complete an image of refined beauty that is harmonious with the anatomical treatment evident in the body.

In the torso, the musculature is defined in detail. Although the artist has described the physical structure of his figure with some concern for anatomy, he is more interested in the overall effect of proportions and surface modeling than with accuracy. Only the smallest amount of incision has been used to define the pubic hair and navel. Both shoulders and calves are exaggerated to emphasize the strength and fine conditioning of a practiced athlete, while the waist appears excessively narrow. In a distinct advancement over earlier kouroi, the firm abdomen accurately shows the rectus abdominis above the navel with two rather than three divisions, and the forearms are correctly represented in a semi-pronated position. On the basis of its anatomical sophistication, Richter placed the Baker statuette as a transitional figure between her Ptoon 12 and Ptoon 20 groups, and a date of 530-520—still well within the late phase of the Archaic period—is most acceptable.

Since it lacks a known provenance, only the details of the figure can be used as evidence for its place of manufacture. The tense, carefully detailed anatomy has been employed by Congdon to connect it with the nudes of the Laconian mirrors, while Buschor has taken the unusual treatment of the hair and rather soft, fleshy features to link it with the products of the eastern workshops of Ionia, especially Samos. Its robust vitality is more characteristic of the workshops of the Peloponnese, however, and on the basis of a comparison with a small, slender kouros in the Museum of Fine Arts, Boston, it has been most persuasively linked to Corinth

by Eckstein. Langlotz earlier had taken the Boston bronze to be a product of Cleonae, but as trade and travel had begun to blur the distinctions among the various regional styles by the time this bronze was cast, any definite assignment beyond Peloponnesian is impossible without further evidence.

The gesture of the left hand is unexplained. Its closest parallel is a Laconian votive bronze of a youth, but there the wrist retains part of a pin that held a missing attribute, perhaps a lyre, onto its flat surface. For the identification of the object in the right hand, Eckstein suggested a long jumping weight (halter) of a type described by the Roman author Philostratus, a Sophist of the third century AD (*On Gymnastics*, 55). These weights were always used in pairs. Though an intelligent and learned suggestion, the idea of a three-dimensional representation of an athlete holding only one jumping weight is not at all convincing. And as a weight of this particular shape is otherwise apparently undocumented in sculpture or vase painting, Mertens' cautious identification of the object as the stalk of a flower bud seems more appropriate.

CONDITION: The figure is preserved together with its base, but the lower part of the object held in the right hand has been broken away and lost. Dark, blackish-green patina covers the entire surface, with some irregular areas of red cuprite visible, especially on the proper right thigh.

EX COLLECTION: Walter C. Baker.

EXHIBITED: New York, Century Association, May 17-September 25, 1950, *Greek, Etruscan and Roman Antiquities from the Collection of Walter Cummings Baker, Esq.*, cat. by D. von Bothmer, no. 99A, illus.
Cambridge, Mass., Fogg Art Museum, December 28, 1954-February 15, 1955, *Ancient Art in American Private Collections*, cat. by G. M. A. Hanfmann, no. 206, pl. 61.
New York, Metropolitan Museum of Art, December 17, 1959-February 28, 1960, *Ancient Art*

from New York Private Collections, cat. by D. von Bothmer, no. 133, pls. 44, 48.

PUBLISHED: F. Eckstein, "Zwei amerikanische Kataloge," *Gnomon* XXXI (1959) 643, no. 49 a.
E. Buschor, *Altsamische Standbilder*, IV (Berlin, 1960) 71, figs. 301-303.
H. Cahn, "Antike Kunstwerke aus New-Yorker Privatsammlungen," *Antike Kunst* III (1960) 90, pl. 17, 3.
C. Leon, "Statuette eines Kuros aus Messenien," *AM* LXXXIII (1968) 178, n. 19.
G. M. A. Richter (*Kouroi*) 1970, 135-136, no. 158, figs. 470-473.
E. Langlotz, *Studien zur nordostgriechischen Kunst* (Mainz, 1975) 175, n. 23.
H. C. Ebertshäuser and M. Waltz, *Antiken: Vasen-Bronzen-Terrakotten des Klassischen Altertums* (Munich, 1981) 109, fig. 126.
L. O. K. Congdon 1981, 99, n. 364.
J. R. Mertens (*BMMA*) 1985, 25, no. 13.

NOTES: For the Laconian statuette from Amyclae (now Athens, NM 7570) with his left hand similarly raised, see M. Herfort-Koch 1986, 108, no. K 95, pl. 13, 6; through the back of the left wrist of this figure, however, there is a pin, which

C. Rolley (1986, 108, fig. 80) has suggested may have held a lyre in place on the open palm.
On the hairstyle, see C. Leon, *AM* LXXXIII (1968) 178, and E. Buschor 1960, 71, and compare Buschor's figs. 295-300, 304-306.
For the slender torso and the stance with shoulders pulled back, see Eckstein 1959, who rightly compared it with the Boston statuette (03.996) from Olympia, a piece which he also assigned to Corinth. For the Boston bronze, see also M. Comstock and C. C. Vermeule 1971, 29-30, no. 27; the statuette was assigned by E. Langlotz to Cleonae (1975, 69, no. 19, pl. 35 a).
For the pattern of the incised pubic hair, compare the statuette of Zeus in Munich, Antikensammlungen und Glyptothek (4339), which is assigned by C. Rolley to Corinth (1986, 101, fig. 70).
As a comparison for the object in the right hand, see the bud in the left hand of a female mirror caryatid, also assigned to the northeastern Peloponnese, now in a Swiss private collection (C. Rolley 1986, 105, fig. 75).

6. Mirror with Nude Female Caryatid

In the Archaic period, three-dimensional figures often decorated serviceable objects like vessels and implements, both to enhance them and to suggest some connection with the user. Since the mirror was a feminine toilette object, it comes as no surprise that the overwhelming majority of attachments forming handles or stands for the polished reflective discs are female figures.

In this example, the mirror support (caryatid) is the figure of a girl. Her large head and feet emphasize her youthfulness. She is nude except for the thick choker with a pendant at her throat, the crenelated stephane across her forehead held by a rosette over each ear, and the strap slung diagonally across her chest in bandolier-fashion. On this cord are a knot, a suspended crescent or dolphin, and a ring. And though the small breasts and narrow hips are more appropriate to the figure of an adolescent boy, the incised pubis allows no question of the identification of the figure's sex. Besides these ornaments, the maiden carries a pomegranate, still on its stem, in her left hand; the right hand, raised before her, once held another attribute, perhaps a lotus bud.

The hair is crimped and arranged in short straight locks that follow the curve of the skull at the back—where the surface of the bronze is now worn smooth—and end in little curls. On the sides, a single long curl hangs before each ear; and across the forehead, four shorter locks turn inward on either side of a central part to frame the asymmetrical features of her face neatly. Both her prominent nose and high forehead emphasize the delicate beauty of her slightly slanted and almond-shaped eyes, demure mouth, and pointed chin.

The figure is placed somewhat awkwardly on the body of a lion. Though curled up as if asleep, the carefully modeled features of the beast's face, now obscured by encrustation, show that he is instead awake with his mouth open. Two more crea-

GREEK, LACONIAN, ARCHAIC, CA. 520 BC.
H. 33.8 CM. H. OF FIGURE 16.8 CM.
METROPOLITAN MUSEUM OF ART, FLETCHER FUND, 1938, 38.11.3

tures are attached by their hind feet to the outside corners of the caryatid's shoulders to help distribute the weight of the large engraved disc on her head, but these are griffins, marked as mythical by their fanciful bird-like heads and graceful sickle-shaped wings.

Seen from the front, the mirror flange appears to rest directly on the caryatid's head, held in place from the sides by the front paws of the rampant griffins. In reality, however, the disc is set into a slot in her head and supported at the back by a brace formed of an upright seven-frond palmette that springs from the volutes of two S-shaped tendrils. Fastened by four rivets—one through the caryatid's head just off center beneath the diverging volutes, another through the heart of the palmette, and two near the oculi of the tendrils' outer volutes—the disc is firmly secured to its figural support.

The disc itself is elaborately decorated with a combination of incision and relief ornament. The front, originally the highly polished reflecting surface, is framed by a series of three concentric designs: the edge beaded in relief, a tongue pattern (cymatium) between triple and double lines, and an incised double guilloche with dotted oculi. On the back, a large pinwheel pattern is incised around two concentric circles and a central compass point, and enclosed by a single line near the raised edge. The flange of the mirror disc, separated from the beading at the front edge by a raised line, is decorated with a tongue pattern in relief.

As the individual figural elements are piled one on top of the other in this description, the conglomeration begins to sound more like a surrealist's bizarre fantasy than a utilitarian product of a Greek master craftsman. Yet, strange though the combinations may be, they are artfully joined in a construction that is at once structurally comprehensible and aesthetically pleasing. The disc set on top of the slight figure's head would appear unstable without the supportive griffins, and the body of the lion provides a broad base for the top-heavy object, although the uneven contour of his lower body prevents the piece from standing without external support. Overall, however, the proportions of the complex figural composition and ornamented disc are well matched.

What is perhaps more difficult to comprehend is the logic behind this particular combination of elements, which depends on the identification of the youthful female. Standing as she does on top of one wild beast and assisted in her supportive role by two hybrid monsters, she must be related to the "Mistress of the Animals" (Potnia Theron). An ancient goddess, popular throughout the Near East and the eastern Mediterranean regions, she later became an aspect of both the Olympian Artemis, goddess of the hunt, and Aphrodite, goddess of love and fruitful reproduction.

Since the nude maiden represented here is attached to the reflective disc of the mirror, an object generally associated with feminine beauty, she has often been taken to be a type of Aphrodite, the goddess most concerned with female comeliness. This identification is supported, according to Muthmann, by the presence of the pomegranate in her left hand—a fruit with connotations sacred to Aphrodite—and the flowers on her diadem.

Pipili has recently demonstrated, however, that the pomegranate may also be associated with Artemis Orthia—a goddess who enjoyed great popularity in Sparta—as may the crescent pendant on the baldric. And while the identification of the caryatid figure as the image of the goddess herself seems unlikely, given both her youthfulness and nudity, the possibility that she represents one of the young female acolytes who are known to have performed in the rituals of this goddess is strongly supported by her stylistic connections with the bronzes of Sparta.

Reported to have been found in South Italy, possibly Tarentum, this boyish nude is one of a number of similar caryatids that have been convincingly associated with the bronze workshops of Laconia, or Sparta, an association supported by one example's actually being found on Sparta's acropolis; this association is explained by the fact that Tarentum was, actually, a Laconian colony. The finely described facial features and their placement within the simplified oval contours of the head find parallels among the recognized works of the Laconian craftsmen (for example, compare the features of Artemis [4]), as does the refined, abstracted anatomy of the taut figure.

The superlative craftsmanship of this mirror is evident in nearly every detail. Most likely cast on to her obliging leonine pedestal, the solid figure of the maiden shows no signs of repaired flaws or casting bubbles. There is, however, abundant

evidence for cold working in the details of her hair, the features of her face, and the head, mane, and body of the lion. The griffins, shown in x-radiograph to have been cast onto the figure's shoulders after her initial production, are finished in exquisite detail, down to the incised pattern of feathers on their wing coverts, the hairy tufts on their pointed ears, and the serrated edges of their beaks. And though much obscured by surface encrustation and deterioration, the incised and relief patterns on the mirror disc are executed with masterful precision. Only the careless placement of the rivets on the brace at the back, made more disturbing by the contrast with the general quality of artistry, shows less masterful workmanship.

The artisan who created this mirror achieved a remarkable balance among opposing forces: natural forms and abstract geometry, surface decoration and sculptural attachment, logic and illogic, beauty and practicality. Contrived by an imagination with sources of inspiration on which the modern mind can only speculate, this fantasy reflected more than the face of its ancient owner.

CONDITION: The mirror and stand are preserved intact except for the missing back of the thumb, tips of all fingers but the smallest on the maiden's right hand, and the attribute, probably a bud or flower, that she held. The body of the lion may have rested on a larger, more level base that has been lost. Surface encrustation and blistering have obscured much of the incision on the disc; the designs have been strengthened or, in places where totally lost, reconstructed with white pigment to give the total pattern.

Beneath a wax coating that covers the entire surface, the irregular patina is a rather scaly dark green with areas of red cuprite exposed. Especially on the once-polished disc, the alteration surface has blistered and flaked off in many places.

PUBLISHED: G. M. A. Richter, "An Archaic Greek Mirror," *AJA* XLII (1938) 337-344, figs. 1-7 (as Corinthian).
J. D. Beazley, "A Greek Mirror in Dublin," *Proceedings of the Royal Irish Academy* XLV, C5 (1939) 39, n. 29.
G. M. A. Richter, "Another Archaic Greek Mirror," *AJA* XLVI (1942) 323, n. 11.
M. Gjødesen, "Bronze Paterae with Anthropomorphous Handles," *Acta Archaeologica* XV (1944) 154-155.
G. M. A. Richter, "The Metropolitan's Classics," *Art News* XLIV (June 1-5, 1945) 13.
P. Jacobsthal, *Greek Pins* (Oxford, 1956) 59-61.
E. Homann-Wedeking, "Von spartanischer Art und Kunst," *Antike und Abendland* VII (1958) 68 ff., n. 21, pls. e-f.
J. Boardman, *Greek Art* (London, 1964) 116, fig. 103.
M. Stoop, "A Laconian Lady?" *BABesch* XXXIX (1964) 85, fig. 4; p. 88.
U. Hafner 1965, 12 ff., 21, 25, 33, 149, n. 7.
T. Karagiorga, "Lakoniko Kataptro sto Mouseio tes Spartes," *ArchDeltion* XXA (1965) 96-104, pls. 50-56.
L. Congdon, "Two Greek Mirror Caryatids in the National Museum of Warsaw," *AJA* LXX (1966) 161-165, pl. 43; 164, n. 40.
A. Greifenhagen "Griechische Kleinkunst," in

K. Schefold 1967, 204, no. 147.
C. Christou, *Potnia Theron: Eine Untersuchung über Ursprung, Erscheinungsformen und Wandlungen der Gestalt einer Gottheit* (Thessaloniki, 1968) 113, no. 4, 117.
F. Schaller, *Stützfiguren in der griechischen Kunst* (diss., Wien, 1973) 31-32, 118-119, no. 67.
M. Robertson 1975, 640, no. 147.
H. Jucker, "Der archaische griechische Standspiegel in Cincinnati," *In Memoriam Otto J. Brendel: Essays in Archaeology and the Humanities*, ed. L. Bonfante and H. von Heintze (Mainz, 1976) 28, n. 16; 31.
L. O. K. Congdon 1981, 7, 33, 36, 46, 56, 83, 91-93, 99, and 137, no. 15, illus. 15 a-c, pls. 12-13.
F. Muthmann, *Der Granatapfel, Symbol des Lebens im Alten Welt* (Bern, 1982) 39-40, n. 103, fig. 25.
A. Delivorrias, "Aphrodite," *LIMC* II,48, no. 375, pl. 35.
L. Congdon, "Greek Mirrors," *Source Notes in the History of Art* IV (Winter-Spring 1985) 20, fig. 2.
J. R. Mertens (*BMMA*) 1985, 23-24, no. 12.
M. Herfort-Koch 1986, 34-35, 41, 43, 98-99, no. K 60, pl. 8, 3.

NOTES: For the group of Laconian mirrors with nude female caryatids, see C. Praschniker (*OJh*) 1912, 219-252, and more recently, T. Karagiorga 1965, 96-104, pls. 50-56.

For the use of a lion as a footstool for the nude female caryatid, compare especially the mirror in Munich (Museum Antiker Kleinkunst 3482; M. Herfort-Koch 1986, no. K 58). For an earlier representation of the Near Eastern goddess Ishtar standing on a lion, see the stele from Tell Ahmar, now in the Louvre, illustrated in *EAA* IV:233, fig. 281.

For feline paws, perhaps of griffins, similarly attached to the shoulders, cf. Vienna, Kunsthistorisches Museum (VI 2925; M. Herfort-Koch 1986; 101, no. K66, pl. 9, 5); Berlin, Museen Preussischer Kulturbesitz (Antikensammlung 31084; M. Herfort-Koch 1986; no. K 59); Metropolitan Museum of Art (74.51.5680; M. Herfort-Koch 1986; no. K 61; J. R. Mertens

[*BMMA*] 1985, no. 11); and once Dresden (H4 44/16; C. Praschniker [*OJh*] 1912; 227, figs. 150 a and b).

For the flower bud in the right hand and the pomegranate on a stem in the left hand, compare the lost caryatid once in Dresden (H4 44/16, see C. Praschniker [*OJh*] 1912; figs. 150 a and b).

For the association between Aphrodite and the pomegranate, see F. Muthmann 1982, 39-40. On the interpretation of the subject, see M. Pipili 1987, 77.

On the crescent amulet on the baldric, see J. D. Beazley, *Etruscan Vase Painting* (Oxford, 1947) 30, n. 1; and C. Rolley, "Le problème de l'art laconien." *Ktema* 11 (1977) 130.

7. Aphrodite and Erotes (Mirror Stand)

Magnificently elegant and mannered in style, this statuette of Aphrodite marks the end of the Archaic period's development. A more striking contrast to the earlier boyish nude representation of the goddess on the Laconian mirror than this voluptuous draped figure is hard to imagine. Like the Spartan girl [6], she was intended to support the polished disc of a mirror, but only the large curved cradle and its vertical palmette brace remain mounted on her head. More immediately identifiable as the goddess of love and beauty because of the presence of the two Erotes—her characteristic attendants—this appearance of Aphrodite as a mirror caryatid is far easier to appreciate than the complex iconography of the Spartan example.

The goddess wears a long-sleeved chiton of thin linen. Very fashionable at the time, the style had been borrowed from Ionia. The embroidered neckline is indicated with a fine, incised zizag pattern, and the fabric's fine crinkly folds, which fall in vertical pleats on the front of the bodice and radiate outward around the buttons fastening the garment across her shoulder and down the outside of the proper left sleeve, are carefully described by incised lines. Over the chiton, the goddess has draped a heavier himation, held in place by a large quatrefoil pin at her right shoulder and arranged so that its flattering folds emphasize the fullness of her breasts while disguising the curves of her slender hips. Although apparently not barefoot, no details of her shoes or soft boots are defined.

Standing on a flat disc atop a convex circular base, Aphrodite has caught up a bit of the fabric of her himation with her left hand in a graceful gesture that pulls the material into a series of horizontal folds across her lower body. Between the thumb and first two fingers of her extended right hand, she holds a flower bud, perhaps a lotus, as if offering it to the observer.

Her elaborately dressed hair, divided into long, crimped strands that overlap one another, is parted at the center of her forehead and pulled to the sides beneath two long swags that fall over her temples and are then drawn back over the tops of her ears. A thick, rounded fillet encircles the crown of her head, and at the back, the thick tresses are pulled together by a flat band as they fall over her shoulders. Large pendant earrings, inverted pyramids terminating in single large spheres, are suspended from the lobes of her beautifully detailed ears which are set slightly too low on her head.

With purposeful disregard for anatomical correctness, the artist has made the goddess' head too large, her neck too long, and her shoulders too broad for the rest of her body. Yet, these distortions actually help to create a more comprehensible and harmonious transition between the large polished disc and its intricately worked support, and thus were surely less noticeable when the mirror disc was in place. Just as her figure has been artfully reproportioned for the sake of artistic ef-

GREEK, AEGINETAN, LATE ARCHAIC, CA. 500 BC. H. 25.6 CM. H. OF FIGURE 19 CM. MUSEUM OF FINE ARTS, BOSTON, H.L. PIERCE FUND, 04.7

fect, so too have the contours and finely articulated features of her face. Sharp lids frame her large, narrow eyes, and the pronounced central furrow (philtrum) stresses the fullness of her sensuous lips.

Nor did the creator of this mirror stand spare himself any effort on the minor elements of its composition. The tiny heraldically displayed Erotes, held suspended from the back of the mirror cradle on rivets piercing the coverts of their wings, are executed with the same degree of exquisite detail as the figure of Aphrodite. Wearing only the beaded fillets that surround their carefully dressed heads and low laced boots (kothornoi), they hover around the head of their mother with arms and wings outspread, every feature of their handsome heads and youthful bodies rendered with delight. Only the central palmette and terminal volutes on the mirror cradle itself are incised with a minimum of technical proficiency and ar-

tistic interest. As the mirror brace was the weakest element in the Laconian example as well, this evidence may indicate that an apprentice or assistant assembled the disc and caryatid figure, for it is hard to imagine that the hand of the craftsman who created the figural elements would slip so badly in executing a standard palmette-and-volute pattern.

The marked similarity between this mirror stand and another in the Hermitage has long been recognized, and both have been convincingly identified as the products of the Aeginetan school of bronzeworkers on the basis of their similarities with the pedimental sculptures from the Temple of Athena Aphaea, especially in small details of the locks of hair falling before the ears and the series of small folds at the folded upper edge of the himation. But also like the earliest of the Aegina pedimental sculptures, this statuette represents the end of a tradition. Already apparent in the figures of the Erotes is an interest in the naturalistic representation of the human figure in motion. Stylized drapery, affected posture, and an artificially elaborate coiffure—developed to the furthest possible extent—came to be seen as hindrances to the anatomical accuracy and movement that distinguished the more innovative creations of this great period of experimentation.

CONDITION: Except for the lost mirror disc, all details of the figural elements of the stand are preserved intact. The figure was solid cast in one piece separately from the base to which it was attached mechanically by means of two square tangs on the bottoms of the feet. The mirror cradle was also separately cast and set into a hole in the top of the figure's head with a pin.

The surface is covered with a dark greenish-brown patina. There are some areas of reddish-brown below the right breast, on the left hand, and on the drapery fold below the hand; and a thicker light green encrustation covers the lower parts of the sleeves, front and back, as well as some of the folds of the lower himation and chiton skirt, much of the Erotes' backs, the back of the proper left terminal volute of the mirror cradle, and areas of the base. Rather granular in appearance, the patina does not detract from the minutely defined surface detail.

X-ray fluorescence analysis shows that the metal is a low-lead bronze with moderate tin content; the exact ratios of the bronze alloys vary among the cradle, figure, and Erotes, but the variations are minor.

EX COLLECTIONS: Forman (no. 66); Edward Perry Warren.

EXHIBITED: Detroit Institute of Arts, March 23–April 20, 1947, *Small Bronzes of the Ancient World*, 10, no. 63, illus. p. 35.

PUBLISHED: Sale: *The Forman Collection* by C. H. Smith, London, Sotheby's, Williams and Hodge Sale, June 18, 1899, 10, no. 66, pl. 3. S. Reinach, *Rép.stat.* III:101, no. 2.; idem, IV, 196, no. 1.
B. H. Hill, Boston Museum of Fine Arts, *Annual Report* (Boston, 1904) 57 f.
E. Franck, "Griechische Standspiegel mit menschlicher Stützfigur" (diss., Munich, Ludwig Maximilians Universität, 1923) 12-13, 30 ff., 36, 38, 40, 111, 116 f., 124-125, no. 21.
E. Franck, *AA* XXXVIII (1923-24) col. 374.
G. H. Chase, *Greek and Roman Sculpture in American Collections* (Cambridge, Mass., 1924) 21 f., fig. 24.
E. Langlotz 1927, 99 (Aegina) no. 5, pl. 54b.
J. D. Beazley, "A Greek Mirror in Dublin," *ProcRIA* XLV, C5 (1939) 39.
J. Charbonneaux, *Les bronzes grecs* (Paris, 1958) 77.
L. Congdon, "Greek Caryatid Mirrors: Technical, Stylistic, and Historical Considerations of an Archaic-Early Classical Bronze Series" (Ph.D. diss., Cambridge, Mass., Harvard University, 1963) 16, 38 ff., 76 ff., 97, 105, 147, 220-223, 237, no. 17.
L. Congdon, "Metallic Analyses of Three Greek Caryatid Mirrors," *AJA* LXXI (1967) 150 ff.
M. Comstock and C. Vermeule 1971, 242-243, no. 352.
K. Wallenstein, *Korinthische Plastik des 7. und 6. Jahrhunderts v. Chr.* (Bonn, 1971) 191, n. 410, no. 3.
F. Schaller, *Stützfiguren in der griechischen Kunst* (diss., Wien, 1973) 41, no. 101.
L. O. K. Congdon 1981, 20-21, 36, 50-52, 83-84, 90-92, 94-95, 100, 105, 140-141, no. 19, pls. 16-17; 146, under no. 27, 272, 282.
A. Delivorrias, *LIMC* II, 1, 18, no. 92; 2, pl. 12.
C. Rolley 1986, 104, fig. 74.
E. Walter-Karydi 1987, 69, 105, no. 6; 106-108, figs. 165-167.

NOTES: The condition statement was made with the assistance of Arthur Beale and Richard Newman.

For the closely comparable mirror in Leningrad (Hermitage inv. B815), see E. Langlotz 1927, 99, pl. 54a (side by side with the Boston example); also L. O. K. Congdon 1981, 146-147, no. 27, pl. 24.

For the most recent discussion of Aeginetan sculpture, see E. Walter-Karydi 1987. E. Langlotz' earlier discussion (1927, 99-102), however, remains fundamental.

8. Hermes Kriophoros

Hermes had many widely varied aspects in antiquity. One of the most popular of the Greek gods, he was usually worshipped as the patron of travelers and thieves, and as messenger of the Olympians. He is represented in this small statuette in another guise, one particularly sacred to the Greeks of the Arcadian countryside— the mature protector of the shepherd and guardian of the flocks. Dressed like a herdsman in a short belted tunic (chitoniskos), brimmed hat (petasus), and low laced boots (endromides), he holds a small ram safe beneath his left arm, its front legs firmly grasped in his raised hand. His right arm is bent at the elbow and the hole drilled down through the loosely clenched fingers suggests that he probably had the herald's staff (kerykeion, or in Latin, caduceus) with a snake-entwined finial extended before him to confirm his identification as the Olympian messenger.

Every muscle of this diminutive figure is taut, its energy contained only by its firm body contours. The thick neck, wide shoulders, full rounded buttocks, and massive calves and thighs suggest the god's physical strength, while the features of his head, which is much too large for his body, are extraordinarily alert and confident. His eyes appear to bulge out beneath the relief lids and incised brows, their carved irises staring straight ahead. His large straight nose ends in a sharp point; completely surrounded by his beard and mustache, the carefully modeled, horizontal lips betray no hint of a smile. Six large curls frame his forehead, turning inward from each side toward a central part, while the rest of his wavy hair falls down his back in long strands angled slightly to the left.

The artist has made a great effort to enliven the statuette's surface with a variety of textures, some cast and some incised after casting. The hair of the beard and mustache was neatly cast in waves, with the fine undulations of the strands, as well as the lines separating them, executed in the original wax model. In contrast, the

GREEK,
PERHAPS SICYONIAN,
ARCHAIC,
CA. 520-500 BC.
H. 17.1 CM.
MUSEUM OF FINE ARTS,
BOSTON, H. L. PIERCE
FUND, 04.6

fine hatching that marks the eyebrows, the lines circumscribing the irises in the eyes, and the pattern of zigzags and stitching across the neckline and shoulders were incised in the bronze.

The ram is no less carefully executed than the god himself. The fleece across its back, crimped like the god's hair, forms a herringbone pattern of incised strands, while its belly and inside thighs are smoothly polished on either side of the central pizzle. Its wide-open eyes and finely articulated mouth and nostrils express a lively attentiveness reflected in the tension of its entire body as well, for this creature does not just hang limply in the arms of its protector.

This particular image of the god as shepherd-protector is known in several versions, including the Hermes Kriophoros in the Stathatos collection; the Hermes from Ithome (now Athens, National Museum, 7539); the Hermes from Andrit-

saina (now Athens, National Museum, 12347); the two Arcadian figures in the Staatliche Museen, Berlin (Antikenabteilung 30552 and 10781); and the Hermes from the collection of Walter Baker (now Metropolitan Museum of Art, 1972.118.67). The standard features among these representations are the costume—which consists of the petasus, low boots, and tunic with elaborate incised zigzag patterns around the neck and down the shoulder seams—and the presence of the ram under the left arm. The larger related figure of Hermes Kriophoros in the Boston collection [9] lacks the ornament on the neck of the chitoniskos and is noticeably different in scale and style. Only the Hermes from Ithome (NM 7539), the Hermes from Andritsaina (NM 12347), Berlin 30552, and the Boston Hermes [9] have wings added to the backs of the boots to confirm their identification as the messenger god, but the similarity of pose and specific shared details make it difficult to avoid the conclusion that all represent the same subject and reflect some common source of inspiration, perhaps a cult statue.

Pausanias (V.27.viii) describes one such cult statue of Hermes dressed in a petasus, tunic, and cloak, and carrying a ram under his arm. The creation of the sculptor Onatas of Aegina and his pupil Calliteles, the figure was dedicated at Olympia by the Arcadians of Pheneus. As Onatas is generally considered to have been active in the early decades of the fifth century BC, however, it is not likely that these Archaic bronze kriophoroi reflect his votive statue. Rather, the evidence suggests the existence of an early concept of Hermes well known in the Archaic sculptural vocabulary and perhaps still popular enough to influence the creation of an early Classical master.

The origins of the Boston statuette are much disputed. Langlotz, Kunze, and most recently Rolley have placed it in the Sicyonian workshop, while Neugebauer called it Arcadian and Comstock and Vermeule have stated that, like the Berlin statuettes and the Ithome and Andritsaina Hermes mentioned above, it comes from Arcadia. Indeed, the fact that some relationship exists among all the kriophoroi listed is clear. Yet, it is not at all certain whether this relationship results from the place of manufacture or simply the repetition of an established image of the deity.

Stylistically, the small Boston kriophoros and the Stathatos figure are fairly close, both showing a degree of sophistication in execution that is completely lacking in the bronzes of Arcadian provenance. They are finer than all the others, except for the larger Boston figure [9], which has seemingly little to do with any of the rest. At the same time, the number of other recognized Sicyonian bronzes is small and such strict geographical distinctions are problematic, as Kunze has suggested. Surely the Stathatos and both of the Boston bronzes are from a Peloponnesian workshop, and it is likely that Sicyon may have been the source; but further information will have to be available before this assignment can be confirmed.

Kunze, Comstock, and Vermeule have dated the figure to the decade 520-510 BC, and a late Archaic date is supported by the crimped hair, stylized facial features, and expressively distorted anatomy. Though Kunze placed the Stathatos bronze earlier than the small Boston kriophoros, certain mannered details of the Athens piece such as the winglike treatment of the sides of the beard and the limp, "ragdoll" figure of the ram suggest that it may instead be later. The Boston bronze can rather be dated to the period 530-520, and the Stathatos bronze to 520-510. The larger Boston kriophoros [9] should be dated at the turn of the century.

CONDITION: The figure is solid cast. A noticeable fracture on the left shoulder suggests that the left arm and ram were cast separately and attached, though the method of attachment is still unclear. The god's left ankle and foot, the sheep's left hind leg below the ankle joint, and the attribute held in the right hand are missing. There is an obvious gouge on the right cheek running toward the right nostril and another above the left kneecap. Otherwise the statuette is well preserved with the details still crisp and clear. The entire surface is covered with an even gray-green patina; some additional encrustation is present on the forelocks, the brim of the petasus, and on the hair and chitoniskos at the back.

PROVENANCE: From Arcadia(?).

EXHIBITED: Detroit Institute of Arts, March 23-April 20, 1947, *Small Bronzes of the Ancient World*, 33, no. 60, illus.
Cambridge, Mass., Fogg Art Museum, March 7-April 15, 1950, *Greek Art and Life*, no. 8.

PUBLISHED: B. H. Hill, Boston Museum of Fine Arts, *Annual Report* (1904) 57.
S. Reinach, *Rép.stat.* IV:96, 4.
K. Neugebauer, "Erwerbungen der Antiken-Sammlungen in Deutschland, Berlin," *AA* (1922) col. 72.
W. Lamb, "Arcadian Bronze Statuettes," *BSA* XXVII (1925-26) 137, no. 4.
E. Langlotz 1927, 31, pl. 20a (as Sicyonian).
K. A. Neugebauer, *Katalog der statuarischen*

Bronzen im Antiquarium. Staatliche Museen, Berlin (Berlin, 1931-1951) I:68, n. 1.
J. D. Beazley in O. Burdett and E. H. Goddard, *Edward Perry Warren: The Biography of a Connoisseur* (London, 1941) 358, illus.
E. Kunze, *Drei Bronzen der Sammlung Helene Stathatos,* Winckelmannsprogramm der Archäologischen Gesellschaft zu Berlin CIX (1953) 9-13, figs. 1-2.
D. K. Hill, Review of Kunze 1953, *Gnomon* XXVII (1955) 34.
G. M. A. Richter, Review of Kunze 1953, *AJA* LXII (1958) 236.
H. Sichtermann, "Hermes," in *EAA* IV (Rome, 1961) 2, 4, 7, fig. 3.
K. D. Morrow 1985, 39, 192, n. 50 (who notes that the figure wears endromides, similar to those worn by the Hermes on the Siphnian treasury).

NOTES: The condition statement was made with the assistance of Arthur Beale and Richard Newman.

For the subject of Hermes Kriophoros, see P. Perdrizet, "Hermes criophore," *BCH* XXVII (1903) 300-313, pl. VII, on the Hermes from Andritsaina.

A calf-bearer (moschophoros) in Athens (NM 13053) wears a costume similar to that described above as common among the kriophori, but he carries the calf stretched across his shoulders, holding its forelegs in his raised left hand.

For the sharply outlined and crosshatched eyebrows, D. K. Hill (Review of E. Kunze 1953, *Gnomon* XXVII 1955) shrewdly observed the similarity with the Gorgons' brows on twin hydria handles in Boston, Museum of Fine Arts (01.7474 and 99.462; M. Comstock and C. Vermeule 1971, 288-289, nos. 413-414); strikingly similar also are the six spiraling locks that surround the Gorgons' brows, especially those on 99.462. Both handles have reclining rams flanking the Gorgon attachment and the fleece of the better preserved (99.462) offers a telling comparison with that of the ram held by the Hermes.

For a kriophoros that may be Attic in origin, see D. K. Hill, "A Greek Shepherd," *JWalt* XI (1948) 19-23, 85.

For the kriophoros as subject in marble, see G. M. A. Richter, *Kouroi*, 1970, *AJA* XLVI (1942) 51, no. 14, figs. 84-86, 106 (probably not Hermes, but a nude male figure).

For Hermes carrying a ram in contemporary vase painting, cf. the black-figured oinochoe, Louvre F 159 (ABV 450, 3), by the Painter of Louvre F 161.

9. Hermes Kriophoros

Though iconographically a close counterpart to the other Boston bronze [8], this tall, elegant image of the guardian of the flocks is stylistically much more problematic. Dressed in a short, belted chitoniskos, small-brimmed petasus, and endromides with single wings at the back, the god stands frontally on an oblong plinth with his left foot advanced. Like the other little image [8], he holds a little ram in the crook of his left arm, grasping its front legs firmly together in his left hand. His right hand, placed to the front and slightly to the side, originally extended the kerykeion of the Olympian messenger.

In comparison to his Boston brother, his proportions are much more convincingly natural and the articulation of his features is more anatomically correct. His thick-lidded eyes, though still large, are less prominent within his square, bearded face. His shoulders are exaggerated in breadth, but their size is offset by the extended length of his torso, while his well-developed thighs and massive calves are now harmonious elements in a mature, muscular body.

Yet, for all its sophisticated refinements, this statuette has lost the intensity and liveliness of the other version. The eyes, set evenly beneath pencil-thin raised brows, are not distinguished by incision, and the absence of any indication of pupil or iris gives the face a vacant, abstract lifelessness. The other features are equally well described. The straight nose is beautifully modeled, especially around the nostrils. The contours of the nicely proportioned mouth show the details of the philtrum's arc on the upper lip, and the distinct separation of the lower lip from the beard by five short incised strands of hair. But there is clearly more emphasis on precision than expression.

Nor is this precise description of details limited to the facial features. Beneath the petasus, the god's hair is carefully arranged in a series of ten short, tight curls

GREEK, PERHAPS SICYONIAN, LATE ARCHAIC, CA. 500-490 BC. H. 26.4 CM. H. OF FIGURE 24.9 CM. MUSEUM OF FINE ARTS, BOSTON, H. L. PIERCE FUND, 99.489

rimming his forehead; while longer, finely crimped strands curve from behind his ears to form two pairs of twin locks on his chest, and a solid mass of wavy crimped locks falls down across his upper back. The curtain of hair at the back is divided rather oddly down the center as if the right and left sides were mirror images; the sinuous undulations of both variously meet and part, and the locks on each side overlap one another. This arrangement was defined in the wax original prior to casting instead of being done with more time-consuming incision after the figure was cast. The crimped strands of the short beard, in contrast, are divided by inscribed lines, and the mustache is entirely composed of short, vertical incisions.

Every aspect of the costume shows the same interest in decorative refinement. The short chitoniskos is fastened with buttons across the shoulders, and the belt is knotted in a stylized bow. Perfectly centered, the pleats at the front of the skirt are bunched at the top with a knot of material tied above the bow. Oddly contradictory, these crisp folds suggest that the tunic is made from a heavier fabric than is indicated by the fine crinkly stress lines incised around each button on the shoulder seams. Also carefully described are the low endromides with their high, rounded tongues, raised lacing eyes, and the large bows of their laces corresponding to the bow at the waist.

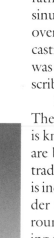

Figure 9a. *Hermes Kriophoros.* Bronze, H. 9.5 cm. Greek, perhaps Arcadian, ca. 550 BC. New York, The Metropolitan Museum of Art, Bequest of Walter C. Baker, 1972.118.67

Even the figure of the animal held on the left arm like a theatrical prop is appropriately enervated. More resigned to its role than its counterpart [8], the little ram holds its feet together and turns its head to the side with an appealing expression. The curls on its forehead are incised with a crosshatched pattern, while the fleece on its body is crimped like the god's hair and beard. A central incised line divides the pelt down the spine, and three overlapping layers of short strands fall down either side, with a small additional partial layer added to cover the fullness of its thighs. Its belly and inside legs are completely smooth, with the navel and testicles standing out in relief; the pizzle is omitted.

Certain details of this figure are singular. Significantly shorter than the tunic of the previous kriophoros [8] and its counterpart in the Stathatos collection, the pleated chitoniskos of this figure is without parallel. The sickle-shaped wing preserved on the back of the left boot has counterparts among known Archaic bronze figures: for example, the Hermes from the Baker collection now in the Metropolitan Museum, the Hermes from Andritsaina (NM 12347), the Hermes from Arcadia now in Berlin (30552), and the androgynous mirror caryatid in Cincinnati (1955.791). None, however, has the bulbous point found on the preserved wing of the Boston kriophoros' boot. The out-turned head of the ram is unique as well among Archaic kriophoroi, although it does have parallels among the recumbent rams on handle attachments.

Because of its uniqueness, the Boston kriophoros has long been the subject of scholarly dispute. According to some, the many unusual features may be explained by its place of manufacture. Although it is reported to have come from Sparta and has many associations with the products of that city, it does not fit comfortably into the series of Laconian bronzes; and Herfort-Koch's recent publication of the Laconian statuettes suggests instead that the Boston kriophoros was a Corinthian import. In his publication on Corinthian Archaic sculpture, however, though Wallenstein recognized the Hermes' relationship to Corinthian products, he set it apart on the basis of its lifelessness. In this, he followed other scholars, most notably Langlotz, Kunze, Schefold, and Fuchs, who have chosen to explain the unusual features by tentatively assigning the bronze to the workshop of Sicyon, known from ancient sources as a center of masterful bronze production. The superb craftsmanship evident in this figure would fit very well with the ancient

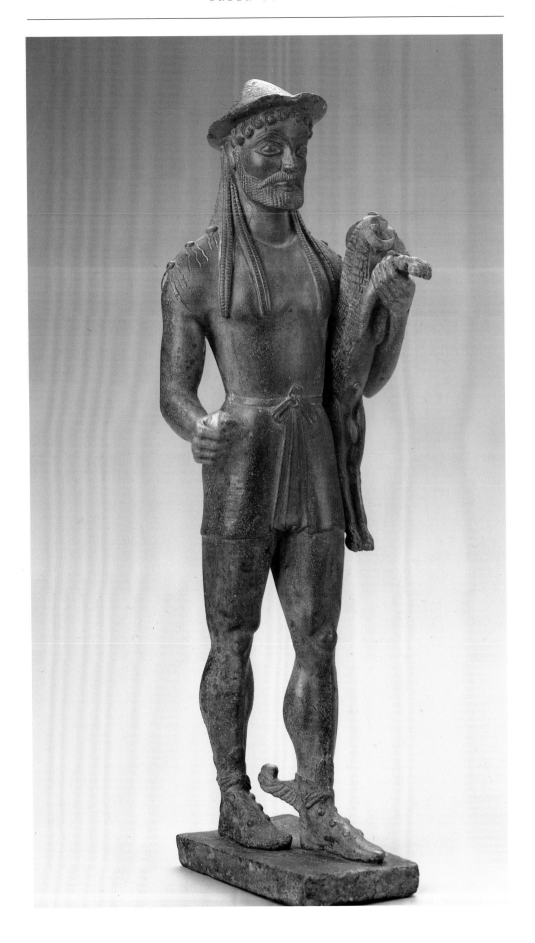

descriptions of Sicyonian products. Unfortunately, the few pieces of preserved evidence for the style of this geographical school offer no strong support for the specific attribution of such a distinctive object.

For other scholars, the statuette's advanced anatomy— especially obvious in the naturalistic treatment of the musculature of the left upper arm that holds the ram—the noticeable lack of vitality, and its academic frigidity have long provoked questions about the accuracy of dating it to the Archaic period. They believe the image's oddness stems from its being not an Archaic Greek original but rather an archaistic imitation—a work of the first century BC imitating an Archaic prototype—as it was identified by Lamb in 1929 and has been interpreted again by such scholars as Eckstein, Young, and Morrow in successive generations.

Though this argument is attractive for some unparalleled elements, one need not look beyond the end of the sixth century for a comparable emphasis on surface ornament and decorative effect at the expense of expressive intensity. The evidence there is still strongly supportive of the opinion that the figure is Archaic. The treatment of specific details of the hair and face find many parallels among the bronzes of the Aeginetan school, which are similarly mannered in their archaism. Comparison with the Boston mirror caryatid [7] shows a similar precision of decorative articulation: the heavy eyelids over rounded orbs, the careful contours of the mouth, the wavy stress-lines around the buttons down the outside of the left chiton sleeve, and the ornamental pattern formed by the wavy strands of hair on the back of the head. Even the large, decorative bows of Hermes' boots and belt can be compared with the large incised bows on the bootlaces of the Erotes. The bronze figure of a warrior in the collection of George Ortiz also offers support for an Archaic date, showing similar thick eyelids, extended eyebrow arcs, carefully modeled nostrils,

twin locks of hair hanging down the chest, and laced boots with incised eyehooks. Assigned with admirable caution to a northeastern Peloponnesian workshop, the Ortiz statuette provides further support for the association of the Boston bronze with this area.

In his publication of the Stathatos kriophoros, Kunze dated the larger Boston kriophoros to the last decade of the sixth century BC; Comstock and Vermeule dated him more cautiously to the previous decade. His serious expression and mannered refinement recall something of the flavor of the late Archaic vase painters, especially the early Berlin Painter, and he may be better placed closer to 500 BC, even in the first decade of the fifth century BC. Cast and finished with unprecedented perfection, this product of a master craftsman marks the end of a long period of artistic development with appropriate acknowledgement of all that had been accomplished.

CONDITION: The statuette is well preserved, still attached to its original base, with the wing of the right boot missing. The solid casting is extraordinarily fine for a figure of this scale, with only a slight flaw on the inside of the right boot just at the ball of the foot. The entire figure appears at first glance to be made in one piece; close examination and x-radiographs have proven, however, that the proper left arm and the ram were cast separately and attached so carefully that the seam is almost impossible to detect without magnification. This piecing of the figure allowed the complex group to be cast nearly flawlessly and to have the figure of the ram finely finished on all sides as well. The base preserves valuable evidence for the original mechanical method of joining the figure; beneath each foot a tang was clearly inserted through the top of the base and hammered out within a square iron washer (now completely mineralized) to hold the figure firmly in place. The base also shows that there may originally have been feet beneath the corners, which have since been filed down.

The surface is covered with a thin, extremely uniform greenish-gray patina overlaid in some small areas with a thicker encrustation of brown, especially on the back. Beneath the patina, the dendritic structure of the bronze is clearly visible, particularly on the chest. This evidence, plus the cast-in details of the hair and the costume, show how little actual cold working of the surface was done after casting.

PROVENANCE: Said to have been found at Sparta.

EXHIBITED: Buffalo, N.Y., Albright Art Gallery, February 1937, *Master Bronzes: Selected from Museums and Collections in America*, no. 69, illus. Basel, Kunsthalle, June 18-September 13, 1960, *Meisterwerke griechischer Kunst*, 38, 61, 178, illus. 181, no. 180, entry by K. Schefold.

PUBLISHED: W. W. Hyde, *Olympic Victor Monuments and Greek Athletic Art* (Washington, D.C., 1921) 108.

F. Poulsen, in P. Arndt and W. Amelung, *Photographische Einzelaufnahmen antiker Skulpturen nach Auswahl und mit Text*, ser. XIII (Munich, 1932) col. 29, under nos. 3760 and 3761.
H. G. Beyen and W. Vollgraff, *Argos et Sicyone; Etudes relatives à la sculpture grecque de style sévère* (The Hague, 1947) 57.
N. Gialouris, "Pteroent Pedila," *BCH* LXXVII (1953) 299, under III, c (winged boots of the type A, "Ionian").
J. H. Young, "Review of G. M. A. Richter, *A Handbook of Greek Art*," *AJA* LXIV (1960) 293.
F. Eckstein, "Review of K. Schefold, *Meisterwerke griechischer Kunst*," *Gnomon* XXXIII (1961) 404.
M. Comstock and C. Vermeule 1971, 25-26, no. 23, with extensive earlier bibliography.
C. C. Vermeule in *Museum of Fine Arts, Boston, Western Art* (Boston, 1971) 161-162, color pl. 12.
K. Wallenstein, *Korinthische Plastik des 7. und 6. Jahrhunderts v. Chr.* (Bonn, 1971) 191, n. 410.
W. Fuchs, *Die Skulptur der Griechen*, 2nd ed. (Munich, 1979) 42-43, figs. 27-28 (as Archaic from the northeast Peloponnese, perhaps of the Sicyon school).
C. C. Vermeule 1982, 136-137, 224, 443-444, fig. 1.
K. D. Morrow 1985, 41, n. 59, 192, pl. 34.
M. Herfort-Koch 1986, 53, n. 193 (as a Corinthian Archaic import found in Sparta).
E. Walter-Karydi 1987, 23, fig. 17; 95.

NOTES: This condition statement was made with the assistance of Arthur Beale and Richard Newman.

For the discussion of the iconography, references to the other Hermes kriophoroi, and an illustration of the Baker Hermes, see [8], especially the reference to P. Perdrizet.

On the Archaic Sicyonian workshop, the fundamental work is still E. Langlotz 1927, 30-53; more recently, C. Rolley 1986, 103-107; for the later sculpture of Sicyon, see H. G. Beyen and W. Vollgraff 1947.

For the discussion of the androgynous mirror caryatid in Cincinnati and arguments for its identification as Laconian, see H. Jucker, "Der archaische griechische Standspiegel in Cincinnati," in *In Memoriam Otto J. Brendel: Essays in Archaeology and the Humanities*, ed. L. Bonfante and H. von Heintze (Mainz, 1976) 25-35, pl. 7.

For the Ortiz warrior, see G. Ortiz and K. van Gelder in *Hommes et dieux* (1982) 215-217, no. 134, with col. illus.

For raised eye-hooks for laces on Archaic boots, see the high flapped boots of the Persian rider in the Acropolis Museum; three eyes are added to the top of the instep in metal; see also the laces on the boots of the Erotes on the Boston mirror [7], which wrap around three eyes and end in large incised bows.

For the knot of fabric above the belted pleats, see the Roman Lar from Paramythia now in the British Museum, in H. B. Walters, *Catalogue of the Bronzes, Greek, Roman, and Etruscan, in the Department of Greek and Roman Antiquities, British Museum* (London, 1899) 37, no. 278, pl. VII; more recently, J. Swaddling, "The British Museum Bronze Hoard from Paramythia, North Western Greece: Classical Trends Revived in the 2nd and 18th Centuries A. D.," *Bronzes hellénistiques et romains, tradition et renouveau, Colloque international sur les bronzes antiques, 5th, Lausanne, 1978* (Lausanne, 1979) 103-106, pl. 53, fig. 10.

For the bulbous end on the sickle wing, compare the wing of the sphinx (Sparta Museum, 2150) from the sanctuary of Artemis Orthia, in M. Herfort-Koch 1986, no. K62, pl. 21,11, ca. 550.

For the pairs of twin locks hanging on the chest, compare Laconian caryatid female figure (Berlin 7933) in M. Herfort-Koch 1986, 95, no. K52, pl. 7, 1-2.

For the recumbent rams with out-turned heads on attachments, see the two hydria handles in the Boston Museum of Fine Arts (01.7474 and 99.462), M. Comstock and C. Vermeule 1971, 288-289, nos. 413-414.

For the Berlin Painter, see J. D. Beazley, *The Berlin Painter* (Mainz, 1974); and D. Kurtz and J. D. Beazley, *The Berlin Painter* (Oxford, 1983) 11-17.

10. Dead or Sleeping Youth

Stretched out on his back, oblivious to his vulnerability, this delicate figure of a youth presents the image of unconscious abandon. Though his physical state is difficult to determine, his exposed body suggests death rather than sleep. His head, with eyes and mouth closed, has fallen sharply backward with the chin turned toward his left shoulder. Both arms are extended in different directions—the left outstretched to the side, the right reaching up before falling back toward the forehead. Both hands, now empty, were closed around attributes. The object in the left hand could only have been a handle, perhaps of a weapon, as the curled little finger would have prevented the insertion of anything longer that might have obscured the incised lines of the palm as well; the right hand may have held a longer shaft of a spear or arrow. The body's original position cannot be reconstructed with certainty, but the curved arc of the spine, the leftward twist of the torso, and the dangling legs suggest that the youth either lay on his upper back across a rock or some other element of landscape, or was supported by at least one other figure. The intentionally drilled hole on the back of his right shoulder was most likely used for one point of attachment.

Unique among surviving bronzes of the Classical period, this extraordinary pose presented the artist with an opportunity to demonstrate his knowledge of human anatomy and his ability to make a figure move in space. For lifeless though it may be, this figure projects in every direction, incorporating in the composition much of the area that surrounds the actual bronze. Although he was surely intended to have one primary point of view from which he could be completely understood, the youth displays such a wealth of detail that every aspect reveals something new.

GREEK
PROBABLY ATTIC,
SEVERE STYLE,
CA. 480-460 BC.
GREATEST EXTENT:
13.45 CM.
J. PAUL GETTY
MUSEUM, 86.AB.530

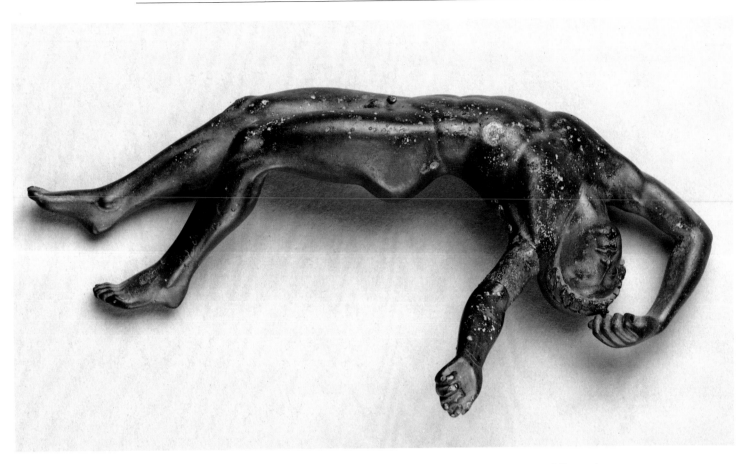

The hair is unusually parted between the front and back by curved lines that run outward from the center of the crown to end just above the ear on each side of the head. On either side of these parts, the individual wavy strands of hair are incised with great delicacy. The short incised locks are bluntly cropped in between spiraling snail-shell curls, inlaid in contrasting reddish copper, that once encircled the head. Of the original twenty-five or twenty-six inlays, only the one before the right ear survives. As an additional note of color, a fillet of inlaid copper runs across the front of the head, ending with the part lines over the ears.

The eyes are plastically rendered as raised orbs beneath the slits that mark the edges of the closed lids. Incised across the centers of the orbs, the lids actually meet too high for the natural depiction of sleep and may be another subtle indication of death. The arched brows—slightly raised but not distinguished by incision—meet at the narrow bridge of the small nose. The philtrum above the upper lip is pronounced, and the full mouth is finely contoured.

Both the features of the face and the hairstyle find their closest comparisons among the sculptures of the Severe Style. The pronounced arch of the brow, the carefully defined lips, the snail-shell curls and the ear-to-ear parting of the hair recall the period of 480-460 BC. His anatomy confirms this date, as the details of the rendering of the abdomen, with the clear divisions of the rectus abdominis within the contour of the lower thorax and the depressed creases in the flesh that form a cross around the navel find their closest parallels in a bronze statuette from the Acropolis (now Athens, National Museum, 6614), that has been dated to the period 470-460 BC.

Though well-toned and slim, the still-undeveloped musculature of the lax body betrays the figure's young age. Ultimately, it is the recognition of his age that

contributes most to both the poignancy and the plausibility of the composition. For, although only the supple figure of a boy could assume this exaggerated pose gracefully, the pose itself suggests a finality whose horror is only increased by the victim's youth and beauty.

Both age and posture suggest a possible identification for the figure. The most closely comparable images associated with fifth-century art are to be found in representations of the unfortunate children of Niobe, who were struck down by the arrows of Apollo and Artemis because Niobe had the hubris to boast that she was a more fecund mother than Leto, mother of the Olympian twins.

The death of the Niobids was evidently very popular in Greece of the fifth century BC. Pausanias describes it among the subjects represented on the throne of Phidias' chryselephantine statue of Zeus at Olympia (V.I.XI,2), and the theme was treated in tragedies by Aeschylus, Sophocles, and Euripides. It has been conjectured that the Niobids were the subject of a monumental wall painting by Polygnotus as well, whose composition may be reflected in one of the best known red-figured vases of the mid-fifth century, the name piece of the Niobid Painter from Orvieto, now in the Louvre. Although none of the ancient works of art that depict the death of the Niobids reproduces the pose of this figure specifically, individual details such as the twist of the torso to expose the chest to greater advantage, the lifeless cast of the head—fallen back and turned outward toward the left shoulder—and the positions of the outflung arms are found among various figures, both freestanding and relief, associated with the original composition. Also, the rocky landscape in which all versions of the Niobids' slaughter takes place provides irregular stone outcroppings that could have supported the sprawling pose. A good parallel for the image and the posture of the bronze is a fallen figure at the bottom of the replicas of the shield of Phidias' Athena Parthenos, especially the nude at the bottom of the Patras replica.

The masterful style and provenance for the closest parallel suggest that this bronze is a product of an Attic workshop. The modeling of the anatomy is sophisticated and confident—exquisite in the details of the face, hands, and feet but without emphasis on the refined musculature at the expense of the overall impression of lifelessness. The torso and limbs are slender and elegant, and the head well proportioned for the body. The structure of the head and the detailed modeling of the features are closest to the discus thrower in Athens (NM 6614), and the style of the hair also finds its closest parallels among the Attic sculptures of youths, although the particular technique for the inlaid curls is unique among known bronzes from Athens and elsewhere.

CONDITION: The bronze is remarkably well preserved, with only the tip of the penis, the tops of the third and fourth toes on the right foot, and the ends of all the inlaid copper curls but one missing. The nipples of the breasts were inlaid in copper as well, the proper left one of which is still preserved. Solid cast, the bronze shows evidence of extensive and extremely careful repairs of flaws. An irregular square patch is visible in the right eye, and a large rectangular patch can be seen in the crown of the head over the left ear. Other repairs can be seen on the upper right of the back, in the right elbow, beneath the left armpit, in the right side of the groin, on the inside of the left knee, and on the lower back of the left calf.

Both arms are made separately and cast on. The large band of corrosion that encircles the upper left biceps beneath the deltoid is not, however, the result of an unsuccessful attempt to cast on the separately made arm and hand, as it does not correspond to the join line visible in the x-radiographs. Rather, it is likely evidence of accelerated corrosion caused by an attachment, perhaps a band of a different, more noble metal such as silver (unpublished report by David Scott, Getty Museum scientist). Casting cracks are still visible in the left foot and ankle, and around the wrist of the right hand. All repairs, including the very large irregular area clearly visible on the right side of the torso, were cast on. A large area of corrosion covers the entire right side of the neck, with a smaller patch on the left side of the abdomen and another beneath the left armpit.

The surface is covered with a fairly uniform greenish-black patina; the corroded section around the upper left arm has differentially altered to a gray-green, as have some areas of the face. A large area on the left breast is only thinly patinated, and the original golden color of the bronze is clearly visible.

PUBLISHED: Recent Acquisition Supplement, "Antiquities," *GettyMusJ* XV (1986) 159, no. 4.

NOTES: The condition report was made with the assistance of Jerry Podany and David Scott.

For the backward falling head and twist of the torso, see the fallen Lapith youth, Parthenon metope 28 South (G. Becatti, *Problemi fidiaci* [Milan, 1951] pl. 32); the Niobid falling backward with arms stretched out above his head, third from the left on the Campana relief in Leningrad (ibid., pl. 75) and third from the left in the second register from the top of the round shield in the British Museum (ibid., pl. 75).

For the fallen Amazon, see the figure beneath the foot of a hoplite at the bottom right of the Strangford shield in the British Museum and of the Patras Shield (perhaps an Amazon; G. Becatti 1951, pl. 64, fig. 191 and pl. 112, fig. 335, respectively).

For the twist of the torso and the pose of the feet and legs, compare the leaping Amazon on the Neo-Attic reliefs from the Piraeus (G. Becatti 1951, pl. 103).

For the twist of the torso and the right arm raised and bent over the head, see the reclining Niobid in the Ny Carlsberg Glyptotek, Copenhagen, which also has an "unusually large hole" in its back between the drapery and the body, perhaps for the attachment of a bronze arrow (B. S. Ridgway, *Fifth Century Styles in Greek Sculpture* [Princeton, 1981] 55-57, figs. 26-30).

For the closest parallels for facial features and anatomy of the torso, see the bronze discus thrower (discobolus) in the National Museum, Athens (6614, in H. G. Niemeyer, "Attische Bronzestatuetten der spätarchaischen und frühklassischen Zeit" *Antike Plastik* III [1964], 26-27, pls. 21, 35b).

For a frolicking satyr taking a very similar pose as he tries to stand on his head, see the Apulian wine jug (oinochoe) in Sale: *Italische Keramik, Münzen und Medaillen AG, November 1984*, 50, no. 75.

The hairstyle with snailshell curls across the forehead, its Persian origins, and its usefulness in dating Greek sculpture have recently been considered by Glenn Markoe, who delivered a paper at the December 1987 meetings of the American Institute of Archaeology entitled, "The Forehead Snail Curl in Greek Sculpture: A Chronological Study" (abstract in *AJA* XCII [1988] 273). Markoe proposed that the terminus post quem for the appearance of this style may be taken from the Bisutun monument (which he dates to 520-519 BC; illus. in K. Schefold 1967, fig. 353a) on which an attendant standing behind Darius has his hair dressed in the incipient form of this fashion. The style gained widespread popularity over the next three decades, appearing on the reliefs from the Persian palace at Persepolis as well as numerous Greek sculptural monuments. It then passed out of fashion in Greece around the end of the first quarter of the fifth century BC. I am grateful to Markoe for providing me with this information which will appear in his forthcoming article (pers. com.). See also G. Markoe, "A Bearded Head with Canonical Cap from Lefkonico: An Examination of a Cypro-Archaic Votary," *Report of the Department of Antiquities Cyprus, 1987* (Nicosia, 1987) 120-121, esp. n. 14.

For the ear-to-ear parting of the hair, see the Severe style head from Volo, B. S. Ridgway, *The Severe Style in Greek Sculpture* (Princeton, 1970) figs. 76-77; the Omphalos Apollo, ibid., figs. 94-95; and the Zeus from Cape Artemesium, ibid., fig. 98; in all cases, the style includes braided strands wrapped around the head, which are not present in the Getty youth. Less similar is the treatment shown by Companion I from the east pediment of the temple of Aegina, ibid., fig. 12, where the hair on the front half of the head is defined with wavy incisions, while the back half is left smooth except for the braids around the bottom.

On the Niobids in general and the various reconstructions of the original compositions, see K. B. Stark, *Niobe und die Niobiden in ihrer literarischen, künstlerischen und mythologischen Bedeutung* (Leipzig, 1863); E. Loewy, "Niobe," *JdI* XLII (1927) 80-136, Suppl. 9-10; idem, "Zu dem Niobiddenkmalern," *JdI* XLVII (1932) 47-68; H. Schrader, "Komposition und Herkunft des Niobidenfrieses," *JdI* XLVII (1932) 151-190; W. H. Schuchhardt, "Die Niobidenreliefs von Zeusthron im Olympia," *AM* (1948) 95-137; R. M. Cook, *Niobe and Her Children, an Inaugural Lecture* (Cambridge, 1964). P. Mingazzini, "Un tentativo di ricostruzione del gruppo dei Niobidi di Firenze," *Bollettino d'arte*, 5th ser., LII (January 1967) 10-16; G. V. Gentili, "Il fregio fidiaco dei Niobidi alla luce del nuovo frammento da Modena," idem, LIX (1974) 101-105.

11. Epimetheus or Hephaestus

The artist has captured his mature subject in a momentary pose that for its period is both an extraordinary depiction of energetic action and a brilliant excuse to demonstrate an impressive mastery of the human figure in motion. Just beginning the forward swing of a heavy implement, he shifts his weight from his right foot, now drawn back with the heel lifted, to the advanced left foot which is firmly planted before him. The weight of the missing object is clear from the tension in his muscles across his chest and back, and the swollen biceps of his upper arms. His massive shoulders are rotated in response to the movement of the head, which is turned to look down to the right. Only the heavy mallet or ax that was once held in his clenched hands is needed to complete the composition.

The head retains more evidence of its original surface than any other portion of the badly corroded statuette. Short locks of hair defined with fine incisions, best

GREEK, PERHAPS
ATTIC, EARLY
CLASSICAL,
CA. 460-450 BC.
H. 21.5 CM.
THE DUMBARTON
OAKS COLLECTION,
36.61
CLEVELAND ONLY

preserved around the right temple, cover the front of the rounded, well-formed skull; either long braids or, less likely, a fillet appears to be wrapped across the back of the head running over the short strands that end bluntly just beneath it. A slight relief contour over the left temple hints that the braids or fillet continued over the forehead, but the surface is now too corroded to be certain. Protected by the raised arm, fine straight incisions still mark the strands of the beard on the right cheek, and the contours of the drooping ends of the mustache are visible in relief around the corners of the mouth. The beard juts out stiffly from the chin in typical late Archaic fashion, while its underside is smooth. The facial features show serious concentration—the mouth determinedly set and the eyes fixed. Unfortunately, much of the impact of the expression has been lost with the missing inlaid pupils, but the direction of the gaze can be fairly accurately reconstructed.

The effects of corrosion have been most damaging to the torso and legs, where the original surface remains only on a small area of the midriff and in the center of the lower back. Though no pose could allow for a finer display of the adult male body, just the general outlines of the musculature can still be read. The raised, flexed arms show the developed deltoids and biceps, while the arched chest and taut back confirm the magnificent conditioning of the torso. Given the carefully modeled nails preserved on the third and fourth fingers of the left hand and the remaining indications of the incised pubic hair, it is easy to imagine the accurate detail with which the anatomy of the abdomen was described. The concentration of energy in the upper torso may have been an intentional artistic device used to emphasize the dramatic posture, as the hips, buttocks, thighs, and calves are also well toned but slender and less muscular. Overall, the general impression is that of a tall, elegantly proportioned man.

Though all the remaining evidence is important in establishing a secure date for this superb bronze, the preserved details of the face and hairstyle are particularly significant. Accepting the likelihood that the hair is dressed with braids wrapped around the back of the head, the figure may be dated on the basis of this coiffure, which was especially fashionable in the early decades of the fifth century BC and was revived only centuries later when a taste for archaizing details again made it popular. It is found combined with the short straight locks on the forehead, stiffly jutting beard, and long drooping mustache in a surviving monumental bronze—the Zeus from Cape Artemisium—which is generally dated to the period of ca. 460-450 BC. It is also found in the Omphalos Apollo that, although known only in Roman copies, has been dated to the early Classical period as well. Both these sculptures offer suitable parallels for the slender proportions of the Dumbarton Oaks statuette; mature masculine figures, their well-formed bodies differ distinctly from the more exaggerated anatomies of the earlier Archaic representations.

In a period of great innovation and experimentation, the artists and patrons of the decades just before mid-century delighted in depictions of the human body in complicated poses. But unlike the spontaneous postures that became popular in the Hellenistic period, the poses of the figures of the Severe and early Classical styles always appear very deliberate and balanced, as if assumed for an effect rather than occurring in the natural course of activity. The emphatic but considered stance of this mature figure thus fits comfortably within this vocabulary as well.

The identification of the subject has indeed provoked some discussion. The great aesthete and collector E. P. Warren, who once owned the piece, first identified it as the god Hephaestus in the act of wielding his ax or mallet. As representations of the Olympian smithy were common enough in the sixth and fifth centuries, especially in scenes of Athena's birth where he assisted in the delivery by splitting open the head of Zeus, this suggestion seems reasonable; at the same time, no known representation of the god shows him with his ax or mallet lifted in a comparable posture. Also, the gaze of the Dumbarton Oaks statuette is directed earthward, not at a figure seated or standing before him.

Langlotz' arguments in favor of Epimetheus—who is represented on a red-figured volute krater in Oxford, standing with a mallet in his hand before the figure of Pandora rising from the earth in the aspect of a fertility goddess reborn—or Picard's suggestion of Lycurgus—who attacked Dionysus' nurses— are based on obscure mythological references and far rarer iconographic sources, but they are not impossible. Both subjects are represented as bearded nude men wielding axes in similar poses, and Picard's observation that the Dumbarton Oaks figure does not have the bearing of an Olympian is not unfounded.

Of the two, Epimetheus is the more persuasive choice, because the figure's concentration on the ground is more appropriate to an earth-breaker than to an ax-murderer. A variation of the Epimetheus figure could be a satyr, as they appear on vases opening the earth for the rising up or rebirth of Kore, or Persephone, the daughter of Demeter. The Dumbarton Oaks figure shows no evidence, however, of the crude facial features, pointed ears, horns, or horse's tail standard among satyr representations of the late Archaic and Severe styles, so this possibility may be excluded. Its handsome head and inherent arrogance are rather more appropriate to a mythical hero or god.

The bronze is said to have been found in Attica, but all efforts either to establish connections between the statuette and major works attributed to the known artists of the period or to connect it with a geographical workshop are undermined

by its poor surface condition and the resulting illegibility of anatomical definition. The attenuated proportions of the figure and the originality of the posture, however, surely recall the Discobolus of the sculptor Myron, who was active at this time.

CONDITION: Though complete except for the ax or mallet once held in the raised hands, the entire bronze figure is very badly corroded with almost nothing left of the original polished surface and the cold working. A large modern repair is visible just above the left elbow, and the toes of the right foot have been broken off and rejoined in recent times. A treatment record from the Fogg Art Museum suggests that the bronze is completely mineralized, and surface cracks on the left elbow and rear of the right thigh indicate its fragile condition.

The rough surface, hardly deserving to be called a patina, is predominantly exposed cuprite, reddish-brown in color; the obvious patches of malachite on the abdomen, the right hip, the rear of the right thigh, the front of the left thigh, the buttocks, and the middle of the back vary from bright to dark green in intensity.

EX COLLECTIONS: Private collection, Athens; Edward Perry Warren, acquired 1897; Mr. and Mrs. Robert Woods Bliss, acquired 1936.

PROVENANCE: Said to be from Attica.

EXHIBITED: Buffalo, N.Y., Albright Art Gallery, February 1937, *Master Bronzes: Selected from Museums and Collections in America* (arrived too late to be included in the catalogue).
Cambridge, Mass., Fogg Art Museum, November 15-December 31, 1945, *A Selection of Ivories, Bronzes, Metalwork, and Other Objects from the Dumbarton Oaks Collection*.

PUBLISHED: E. Langlotz, "Epimetheus," *Die Antike* VI (1930) 1-14, pls. I-III.
C. Picard, "Lycurgue l'édone meneçant une 'nourrice' de Dionysos," *MonPiot* XLV (1951) 22-23, 25, fig. 6.
G. M. A. Richter, *Three Critical Periods in Greek Sculpture* (London, 1951) 11.
G. M. A. Richter, *Catalogue of the Greek and Roman Antiquities in the Dumbarton Oaks Collection* (Cambridge, Mass., 1956) 25-26, pl. IX, no. 14.
G. M. A. Hanfmann, *Classical Sculpture* (Greenwich, Conn., 1967) 315, illus., no. 117.

NOTES: In preparing the condition statement, I drew on a Fogg Museum conservation report from the 1940s.
For a brief discussion of the subject, see G. M. A. Richter 1956, 252-256; E. Langlotz (*Die Antike*, 1930) argues for the identification of Epimetheus; C. Picard (*MonPiot*, 1951) suggests Lycurgus.
For the Oxford red-figured volute krater (Ashmolean Museum 525), see J. D. Beazley, *Attic Red-figure Vase-painters* (Oxford, 1963) 1562,4 (under Alkimachos); also P. Gardner, "A New Pandora Vase," *Journal of Hellenic Studies* XXI (1901) pl. 1.
For the braid of hair wrapped around the back of the head and its appearance on the bronze Zeus from near Cape Artemisium and the Omphalos Apollo, see B. S. Ridgway 1970, 61-64, figs. 94-95, 98-99; for other appearances of this fashion in the Severe and early Classical styles, see S. Stucchi, "Statua di Apollo saettante dalle rovine del Tempio Sosiano," *Bollettino della Commissione Archeologica Comunale di Roma* LXXV (1953-1955) 17-18, n. 36 (the hairstyle of the Dumbarton Oaks bronze appears to be dressed in his third style); B. S. Ridgway 1970, 63, n. 7; E. Harrison, *Archaic and Archaistic Sculpture. The Athenian Agora, XI* (Princeton, N.J., 1965) 143, under no. 156; for a more general discussion of the elaborate treatment of hair in Severe Style sculptures, see W. H. Schuchhardt, "Köpfe des strengen Stils," in *Festschrift für Carl Weickert* (Berlin, 1955) 59-73.
For satyrs wielding axes to break the ground for the rebirth of Kore, see J. D. Beazley, "A Stamnos in the Louvre," *Scritti in onore di Giudo Libertini* (Florence, 1958) 91-95, pls. I-II.
On the rising up, or anodos, of maiden earth-goddesses (both Pandora and Kore), see J. E. Harrison, *Prolegomena to the Study of Greek Religion*, 3rd ed. (Cambridge, 1922) 276-285.

12. Athlete Making an Offering

Serene and confident of his beauty, this adolescent athlete stands in a relaxed pose. The significance of his turned head and the original position of his missing right arm can be reconstructed on the basis of numerous parallels for the stance: he is pouring a libation or making an offering to the gods. His weight, concentrated on the engaged right leg and extended right hip, is artfully counterbalanced by the response of the freed left leg, which is bent at the knee with the foot set back and raised on the ball as if he had just taken a step. His left arm hangs by his side, with his shoulder pulled back slightly and his elbow bent. Although his fingers are curled loosely, they do not appear to have actually held any attribute. His head is not only turned but is also markedly inclined in the direction of the weight-bearing leg, closing the stance effectively. The youth's face is turned down toward the right, presumably so that his glance would focus attention on his right arm and hand.

In rendering this well-conditioned, muscular body, the artist took more pleasure in creating a grand, unified form than in defining minute details. Although the pectorals stand out over the flat abdominal muscles—correctly but cursorily defined, with the nipples inlaid in copper and surrounded by aureoli of incised dots—the ripples of the serratus magnus have been ignored. The contours of the breasts are echoed in the pronounced curves that descend from the iliac crests to the groin, and the pubic hair is done as a series of tiny relief curls. At the back, the specifics of musculature are equally reduced. Only the spinal furrow and the high-set firm buttocks, distinctly separated from the thighs by incised creases, are emphasized. The gentle swinging curve of the stance dominates the visual impression.

Such a long description may seem excessive for so simple a posture, but the achievement that this apparent simplicity represents is indeed monumental and deserves attention. A review of the statuettes preceding it in this catalogue reveals that this is the first image that appears to stand in a convincingly relaxed, natural way. For the history of Western art, this stance itself is a great advancement, for this contrapposto is rightly considered one of the great innovations of fifth-century sculpture.

The facial features, serious and concentrated in expression, are defined with particular care: the eyes, the irises marked by deep voids that originally probably held inlays, are closely set under nearly horizontal brows; the full, rather sullen lips do not meet at the corners, and a pronounced central groove distinguishes the lower lip. The broad flat planes of the cheeks flowing naturally into the curve of the heavy jaw provide the face with a simple, refined contour. Only the slight damage at the end of the straight nose flaws the youth's idealized beauty.

The hair, dressed in a fashion popular around the third quarter of the fifth century BC, is rolled up over a cordlike fillet that rings the head. The finely incised strands of the crown, radiating outward from a central point on the top of the head, are grouped into broader locks; these locks are separated from one another and distinguished from the finer strands by deep, wavy furrows that form a sort of pinwheel pattern over the surface of the cranium. Both furrows and incisions continue over the convex profile of the roll to create an interesting variation in textures. Surely more noticeable when the figure was polished and new, these linear patterns still make an effective contrast with the more subtle articulation of the musculature of the nude figure.

It is the hairstyle in particular that has given the strongest evidence for localizing the place of manufacture of the Cleveland statuette, since the closest comparisons for such details as the curving furrows and the part between the rolled curls over the forehead are to be found among bronzes and terracottas discovered at Locri in Magna Graecia (South Italy). A comparison between the torso and

GREEK, PROBABLY FROM WORKSHOP OF LOCRI OR TARENTUM, CLASSICAL, CA. 450-425 BC. H. 21.2 CM. H. OF FIGURE 19.8 CM. THE CLEVELAND MUSEUM OF ART, GIFT OF THE HANNA FUND, 55.684

representative examples of the various Greek workshops shows that the anatomy is closest to the products of the Argive school (Polyclitan) but is rather more generalized in the execution of details. Its soft, imprecise treatment reflects the inspiration of the Argive style but does not actually reproduce it, which suggests that the statuette is the product of a sophisticated workshop beyond the boundaries but not the sphere of influence of mainland Greece itself. As the wealthy city of Locri is known to have produced some of the finest fifth- and fourth-century Greek bronzes, the Cleveland youth may well be the work of a Locrian master.

The possibility of this South Italian origin, taken together with the large number of athletic offering figures that seem to reflect a similar prototype, has led P. Kranz to identify this statuette as a version of the statue of Euthymos of Locri that was erected to honor his three victories in the Olympic games. The work of Pythagoras of Rhegium, the original sculpture should have been created around 480-470 BC and may have stood in either Locri or the sanctuary of Olympia. If the suggestion that this statuette itself comes from Olympia has any validity, it could be a Locrian athlete's votive offering that reproduced a figure type made popular by a famous earlier victor from the same hometown.

Although the hairstyle is most closely associated with works of the Severe Style, the hipshot stance of this bronze with the unengaged left foot stepping so naturally back and to the side is inconceivable without the intervening influence of the Argive sculptor Polyclitus, who was active around the middle of the fifth century. Thus, whether or not it reflects the original statue of Euthymos, the statuette must be dated slightly later than its coiffure would seem at first glance to indicate, that is, to the third quarter of the fifth century BC.

 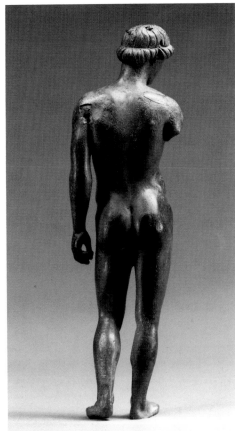

CONDITION: Except for the right arm, which has been lost from just below the deltoid, the hollow-cast figure is very well preserved with surface details still fairly crisp and clearly visible. The right arm was apparently made separately and attached, as a small, roundish hole for a patch on the upper arm just at the break line may have held a pin, and the exposed interior of the arm looks as though it had been prepared for the insertion of a tenon.

The artisan clearly had problems with casting this figure, as its surface is covered with ancient repairs, most noticeably on the cheek at the corner of the mouth, on both the front and back of the right shoulder, on the front and right side of the neck, and in the center of the back. One large rectangular patch is missing from the back of the left shoulder, revealing a deep casting flaw beneath, and there is a small casting flaw on the outside of the upper right thigh. The top of the head shows the greatest amount of repair work, and the incongruous flattening of this area suggests that the piece may actually have been dropped in antiquity. A large, irregular patch covering the crown is marked with obvious cracks, and there is a deep fissure toward the back of the right side.

The fingers of the right hand may have held some attribute, although there is no clear evidence within the loosely closed fingers that the opening was intentionally smoothed or that anything was inserted. The preserved tang on the bottom of the right foot forms a complete U-shaped loop, one end of which is attached to the ball of the foot, and the other to the heel. The two stubs of a similar tang are preserved on the left foot, but in this case the loop ran across the width of the foot with both ends attached to the ball, as the heel was raised.

The figure is completely covered with an alteration surface that is smooth and regular on the back, varying from greenish-gray to greenish-brown; the surface of the front of the figure is less regular, with many patches of heavier encrustation, and the patina varies from bluish-green on the face to green and greenish-black on the torso, and greenish-brown on the right thigh.

PUBLISHED: *Art Quarterly* XXI (1958) illus. 99.
S. E. Lee, "A Bronze from the Age of Pericles," *BClevMus* XLVI (1959) 19-24, illus.
S. E. Lee, "The Art Museum and Antiquity," *Apollo* LXXVIII, no. 22 (1963) 441, fig. 7.
J. Charbonneaux, R. Martin, and F. Villard, *Grèce classique* (Paris, 1969) 137, illus. 148.
B. S. Ridgway, "A Greek Head of the Severe Period," *BClevMus* LVI (1969) 122, fig. 8.
P. Kranz, "Ein Zeugnis lokrischer Toreutik im Cleveland Museum of Art," *Mitteilungen des Deutschen Archäologischen Instituts, Römische Abteilung* LXXXV (1978) 209-255, pl. 101-104, 106.
J. Neils, "A Horseman from Tarentum," *BClevMus* LXVII (1981) 331-332.

NOTES: The condition statement was prepared with the assistance of Frederick L. Hollendonner and Bruce Christman.

For the hairstyle, see P. Kranz (*RM*) 1978, 211, n. 10, with relevant bibliography, and 231, 239.

For the persuasive arguments in favor of its Locrian origins, see P. Kranz (*RM*) 1978, complete; compare especially the following Locrian bronzes: Leningrad, Hermitage (GKH 91), the closest parallel for subject and stance; the mirror caryatid from Locri, now in the museum in Reggio Calabria, ibid., pl. 105, 1, an earlier representation of the stance; mirror caryatid in the form of a draped male figure, museum of Reggio Calabria, ibid., pl. 106, 3-4, for the treatment of the hair.

For the subject of the athlete making an offering, see R. Thomas, *Athletenstatuetten der Spätarchaik und des strengen Stils* (Rome, 1981) 99-126.

For the style of figures of athletes from Magna Graecia, see E. Langlotz 1927, 147-152 (on Pythagoras of Rhegium); U. Jantzen, "Bronzewerkstätten in Grossgriechenland und Sicilien," *JdI* Suppl. XXX (1937) passim, but in particular 7-12 (Locri); E. Langlotz, *Ancient Greek Sculpture of South Italy and Sicily*, tr. A. Hicks (New York, 1965) 246, pl. X; R. Thomas 1981, 162-163.

13. Rider

This young horseman originally sat astride his mount with his knees spread apart to accommodate the breadth of the horse's girth and his unsupported feet turned out and down to the sides, as stirrups were unknown. He has turned his head to look down to the right at something by the horse's side. His arm, bent at the elbow, is pulled back at the shoulder and extended out to his side. The fingers of his right hand still hold the end of a crop or goad. Missing from just beneath his shoulder, the left arm appears from the remaining traces at the back to have been raised outward to the side and somewhat forward, apparently covered by a traveler's cloak (chlamys), of which only a fold across the shoulder remains.

The anatomy of the torso is compartmentalized by an abstract grid of deep furrows that mark, on the front, the groin line, the crease of the waist, and the lower contours of the pectorals; and on the back, the iliac crests. These furrows are bi-

GREEK,
PERHAPS FROM
WORKSHOP
OF TARENTUM,
CA. 400-375 BC.
H. 13.3 CM.
THE CLEVELAND
MUSEUM OF ART,
PURCHASE FROM
THE J. H. WADE FUND,
77.41

sected by continuous vertical grooves defining the spinal column and the crease between the buttocks at the back and the sternum and linea alba, less pronounced, in the front. The head at the top of the central axis, turned to the right, and the genitals at the bottom, pushed toward the left inside thigh, serve to underline the torsion inherent in the pose.

The features of the narrow face are large for its U-shaped contours. The eyes, set within sharp lids, are especially emphasized with drilled pupils, probably once inlaid, though corrosion in the hollows now obscures their original effect. The fine nose is continuous with the brow, and the lips beneath, separated with a deep incision, are defined with precise contours that stress the delicate dip of the philtrum.

Despite the loss of an arm and horse, the rider evokes all the energy and excitement of a race. The linear treatment of his long hair accentuates his motion, apparently swept back by the wind as he speeds forward; his muscles are expressively tense, knotted with the strain of controlling his powerful mount; and his furrowed brow indicates the depth of concentration.

The provenance of the statuette is unknown. The expressive rendering of the anatomy and details of the execution of face and hair have provided important stylistic evidence for the place of manufacture, however. The Cleveland rider has been most persuasively compared with the dancing youth or wrestler from Copenhagen, which Langlotz identified with the workshop of Tarentum, a wealthy Greek colony in South Italy. The Copenhagen figure with its rather squat proportions, exaggerated musculature, and oversized extremities shows much of the same intensity of gaze and tautness of form that distinguish the Cleveland rider. More generally, the deep grooves that appear to segment the body, defining the groin line, the iliac crests, the spinal furrow, and the contours of the pectorals, are not

uncommon among nude male figures in Tarentine sculpture, and they support the rider's relationship with the products of this workshop. Although the interest in exaggerated musculature may at first glance suggest an early date for this figure, the purposeful pose and convincing suggestion of strong movement are rather more characteristic of the early fourth century. Tarentine coins of this period actually bear the image of a youthful rider on one side, and a date in the first quarter of the century seems most appropriate.

The casting of the statuette presents interesting features. Within the torso, a large deep hole runs up from the seat to the shoulder blades, presumably to accept a pin that would attach the figure to a horse. The insides of both thighs are also hollowed out and each preserves part of a pin that originally secured the figure on his mount. Oblivious to the care with which the figure is modeled, these pins were driven through the bronze with remarkably little sensitivity; their broad heads are still clearly visible, the right on the upper surface of the thigh and the left high on the outside of the thigh just before the buttock. Smaller pins were apparently driven through holes in the feet. The left arm appears to have been made separately and attached, the seam disguised in the folds of the chlamys.

CONDITION: The figure has lost its left arm from just below the shoulder and the drapery that covered it. The large toe of each foot and the tops of the next two toes of the right foot are also broken away, as is everything but the handle of the goad in the right hand. Running horizontally across both buttocks is a surface scar; there is also a gouge on the back of the left shoulder and in back of the right armpit. The right arm has been broken and reattached at the shoulder. A break just beneath the knee of the right leg has been repaired recently.

In modern times, the bronze has been cleaned of a heavy encrustation, leaving an irregularly mottled surface. Much of the face and chest are red cuprite, while the back is primarily green malachite with irregular red patches of cuprite on the buttocks. A large area of corrosion on the top of the head has not been removed and may account for the apparently weak incision in the hair around that spot; further cleaning might reveal more detail.

EXHIBITED: The Cleveland Museum of Art, December 28, 1977-January 22, 1978, *Year in Review for 1977*, 38, no. 6, illus.

PUBLISHED: J. Neils, "A Horseman from Tarentum," *BClevMus* LXVII (1981) 331-338, figs. 3-4, 14.

NOTES: The condition statement was prepared with the assistance of Frederick Hollendonner and Bruce Christman.

For horses and horsemanship in antiquity, see J. K. Anderson, *Ancient Greek Horsemanship* (Berkeley, Calif., 1961); on earlier riders, see R. Thomas 1981, 63-71, pls. XXV, 2-XXVIII.

For the Thorvaldsen dancer-athlete, see E. Bielefeld, *AA* (1962) cols. 90-91, figs. 10-11; E. Langlotz 1965, 288, fig. 128; C. Rolley, *Les arts mineurs grecs* I: *Les bronzes* V (Leiden, 1967) 8, no. 25, pl. 25; M. Robertson 1975, 212, pl. 68b; and R. Thomas 1981, 54-56, pl. XXII; the back view is reproduced in J. Neils 1981.

For the incised lines on the throat and the straight incised lines of the pubic hair, see the youth on the 4th-century bronze mirror support from Medma, E. Langlotz 1965, pl. 127.

14. Dancing Woman

Few bronzes in the world enjoy the reputation of this veiled dancer. Mysteriously wrapped in layers of fabric, she dips and twirls with deliberate grace as she executes a complicated step. Only her eyes and left hand are exposed, both defined with extraordinary attention to detail. Every other feature of her body is covered by greater or lesser amounts of material that serve at once to explain and obscure their fascinating subject. As no single view allows the complete appreciation of the pose, the statuette invites the observer to turn it around and thus participate in the vortex of the dance.

While her head turns sharply back to the right in apparent contradiction to the step, her shoulders twist to the left. Covering her head and shoulders is a sheer mantle, through which the knot of hair on the back of her head is visible. Her face is covered by a thin veil stretched across the forehead just below the centrally parted strands of hair and cut out only around her eyes. Her right elbow, bent and raised across her chest, has pulled taut the thin shawl that she has drawn across her mouth and holds close to the opposite shoulder with her muffled right hand. Her left arm draws back, pulling the covering drapery into sharp creases across her left breast; while her left hand, held out to the side, grasps the lower ends of the mantle from which a long fringe flutters out behind in sinuous strands, emphasizing the vigor of her dance movements. Her extended right foot provides the tension that pulls the mantle tightly across her right hip and over the front of her leg, and creates the catenary folds of the chiton skirt over the protruding toe.

Despite the complicated overlays of material, her costume is clearly described. Beneath the mantle covering her head and draping her body to about mid-calf, the vertical folds of a heavier chiton are visible. Belted at her waist with a single overfold (kolpos), this garment provides the voluminous skirt that trails so elegantly behind. The fanned pleats at the bottom edge of the back reflect the forward motion of her twirling step while providing a broad, stable base for the pose.

Artists of the Hellenistic period were frequently inspired by the challenge of convincingly depicting the natural appearance of all things. This tendency accounts for a growing interest in individual portraiture, the accurate representation of bodies in complex active poses or varied physical states—such as sleep or drunkenness—the definition of material surfaces and textures, and the effects of motion or atmosphere.

Many of the most successful representations are achieved with an added element of irony, however, as illustrated here. For while the ability to represent a figure in motion has never been more effectively demonstrated than in this statuette, the body itself is barely visible. Everything is expressed by the drapery. Held tightly then falling freely in voluminous folds, it responds to the dancer's movements while showing completely her momentary posture. This is less the image of a dancer than the portrait of a dance.

So complete is the dancer's absorption in her performance that nothing of her personality or physical appearance is revealed. Her position, however, is unambiguous. As Greek women of the upper classes were traditionally sheltered and were unlikely to have participated in a public display of such frivolity, she must be a professional entertainer. The widespread popular appeal of such performers is attested by the many representations that survive in other media, especially terracotta, from the fifth century on throughout the Greek world.

As Thompson discussed in her thorough and masterful publication of this bronze, the dance that such figures perform may be the baukismos, which was believed to have originated in Ionia. The Greek rhetoretician Julius Pollux (fl. AD 150-200, Naucratis, Egypt) recounts that it was named for a dancer, but the name

GREEK, PROBABLY ALEXANDRIAN, EARLY HELLENISTIC, CA. 250-175 BC. H. 20.5 CM. METROPOLITAN MUSEUM OF ART, BEQUEST OF WALTER C. BAKER, 1971, 1972.118.95

may equally well have been derived from the yellow slippers (baukides) that the dancers and hetairai wore (Pollux VII.94). Indeed, the tip of the soft-tied shoe showing here beneath the folds of the skirt takes on a new significance when one imagines the effect of its brightness set in contrast to some darker color in the swirling drapery. Replete with rapid spins that exploited the fullness of the flowing skirt, the baukismos was a "dance which makes the body fluid and like a whirl-wind" (Pollux IV.100). Like the coy use of the ample drapery and mask, the dancer's enticing movements were surely both modest and flirtatious, suggesting more than they revealed, since the Greek verb *baukidzo* means to "play the prude," and the performance must have relied as greatly on a dancer's skill as an actress as on her ability to execute the complicated choreography.

Thompson has defended the Alexandrian provenance provided by the dealer with the citation of telling details; for example, the transparent mantle with its long soft fringes, which is similar to the fringed shawls found in Egyptian tombs; the use of the veil-like mask and the association of the origins of the combination of dance and masked performances with Egypt; and the unusual extension of the outside ends of the upper eyelids, a characteristic of Egyptian or Egyptianizing sculpture that imitates the applied cosmetic line. Although diaphanous fabrics, especially the sheer silks of the island of Cos, had become popular throughout the Hellenistic world by this time, and their appearance among the charming representations of genre subjects had many applications, the treatment of the eyelid and the presence of the face kerchief that exposes the eyes while covering the rest of the face are surely unusual. The similarly masked faience head found by Petrie in his excavations at Memphis and recently published by Himmelmann offers convincing support for the bronze's Alexandrian origins.

In its virtuoso display of torsion and countertorsion, the pose portends something of later Hellenistic compositions such as the Satyr Turning to Look at His Tail and the Callipygian Aphrodite. At the same time, the proportions of the body show no suggestion of the small heads and elongated legs that distinguish the numerous terracottas from the later part of the second century BC. The sophisticated handling of the overlapping layers of drapery still shows the vigor and interest in interpretation of folds and textures that mark the finest examples of this third-century innovation, and a date in the later third or early second century seems most acceptable. Not content simply to wrap transparent drapery around a static figure to display his ability, the artist has actually created a composition that justifies the brilliant conceit.

CONDITION: The hollow cast statuette is thick-walled (.6-.95 cm. at the lower border), with a noticeable ridge in the metal (approximately 2 cm. up) inside the lower border. A single large hole has been drilled in the back of the proper left shoulder, and the edge of the chiton skirt is broken around the area of the left foot, making the large resting surface unsteady. The bronze is otherwise in superb condition, with the subtle surface details still sharp and quite visible. The surface is covered with a thin dark blackish-brown patina; contrary to Himmelmann-Wildschütz's opinion (1983, 67), careful technical examination suggests that this is the original ancient surface. The gold of the unpatinated bronze is visible along the edges of the drapery folds, and some small spots of cuprite and malachite are scattered over the surface.

PROVENANCE: Perhaps from Alexandria.

EX COLLECTION: Walter C. Baker.

EXHIBITED: New York, Century Association, May 17-September 25, 1950, *Greek, Etruscan, and Roman Antiquities from the Collection of Walter Cummings Baker*, cat. by D. von Bothmer, no. 46, illus.
Cambridge, Mass., Fogg Museum of Art, December 28, 1954-February 15, 1955, *Ancient Art in American Private Collections*, cat. by G. M. A. Hanfmann, no. 221.
New York, Metropolitan Museum of Art, December 17, 1959-February 28, 1960, *Ancient Art from New York Private Collections*, cat. by D. von Bothmer, no. 144.
New York, Metropolitan Museum of Art, October 19, 1974-January 5, 1975, C.I.N.O.A. (La Confédération Internationale des Négotiants en Oeuvres d'Art) exhibition: *The Grand Gallery*.
New York, Metropolitan Museum of Art, December 3, 1975-March 23, 1976, *Patterns in Collecting*.

PUBLISHED: D. B. Thompson, "A Bronze Dancer from Alexandria," *AJA* LIV (1950) 371-385, figs. 1-3, 11, 14.
M. Bieber, *The Sculpture of the Hellenistic Age* (New York, 1955) 96, figs. 378-379.
E. Buschor, *Die Plastik der Griechen*, 2nd ed. (Munich, 1958) 104.
G. M. A. Richter, *A Handbook of Greek Art* (New York, 1959) 189, fig. 288.
D. B. Thompson, *Troy: The Terracotta Figurines of the Hellenistic Period*, Troy Supplementary Monograph III (Princeton, 1963) 104, no. 205.
T. B. L. Webster, *Hellenistic Poetry and Art* (New York, 1964) 171, pl. X.
G. M. A. Hanfmann 1967, 329, no. 229.
H. Kyrieleis, "KATHAPER HERMES KAI HOROS," *AntP* XII (1973) 138-139, n. 44 (the author cites the Baker dancer as evidence for surface polish among the finer Alexandrian bronzes).
M. Robertson 1975, 564, pl. 179 c.
C. Rolley, "Les bronzes antiques: objets d'art ou documents historiques?" *Bronzes hellénistiques* (1979) 17.

Figure 14a. *Stele with a Relief of a Muffled Dancer.* Marble, H. 33 cm. Greek, ca. 3rd century BC. Stockholm, collection of Jack Koert.

N. Himmelmann, "Realistic Art in Alexandria," *Proceedings of the British Academy* LXVII (1981) 196-197.
N. Himmelmann-Wildschütz, *Alexandria und der Realismus in der griechischen Kunst* (Tübingen, 1983) 67-68, pl. 36-39.
J. R. Mertens (*BMMA*) 1985, 48-49, no. 32.
K. D. Morrow 1985, 122, 215, n. 73.

NOTES: For veiled dancers generally, see H. Heydemann, *Verhüllte Tänzerin*, Hallisches Winckelmannsprogramm IV (1870); and C. M. Galt, "Veiled ladies," *AJA* XXXV (1931) 373 ff.

For muffled dancers in terracotta, see C. M. Galt 1931, fig. 3 (MFA 01.7923 and 01.7924); G. Kleiner, "Tanagrafiguren," *JdI*, Suppl. XV (1942) pls. 34, 43; S. Mollard-Besques, *Catalogue raisonné des figurines et reliefs en terre-cuite grecs et romains* II: *Myrina* (Paris, 1963) pls. 129-131; R. Lullies, "Statuette einer Tänzerin," *Studies Presented to David M. Robinson on His 70th Birthday*, I (St. Louis, Mo., 1951-1953) 668-673, pl. 70; K. Schefold 1967, 196-197, pl. VI.

For muffled dancers in stone sculpture (Figure 14a), an unpublished Hellenistic marble stele, said to be from the Chalcidice in Greece, now in the collection of Jack Koert of Stockholm, shows a dancer in mid-performance, moving to the left with her hand drawn up to her face.

For muffled dancers on Greek vases, see C. M. Galt 1931, 374, fig. I, and 389, n. I; M. Robertson, "A Muffled Dancer and Others," *Studies in Honour of Arthur Dale Trendall* (Sydney, 1979) 129-134, especially nn. II, 13.

For the baukismos and baukides, besides Thompson 1950, see A. F. von Pauly and G. Wissowa, *Real-Encyclopädie der klassischen Altertumswissenschaft*, III, I (Stuttgart, 1970) cols. 153-154.

On Alexandrian metalwork and trade, see P.M. Fraser, *Ptolemaic Alexandria*, I (Oxford, 1972) 135 ff.

On Coan silk, see *RE* III, I: col. 678.55, s.v. Bombyx.

For the satyr turning to look at his tail, see W. Fuchs 1979, 136, figs. 124-125; for the Aphrodite Callipygus, see ibid., 243, figs. 265-266.

15. Aphrodite

No sculpture in antiquity enjoyed the renown of Praxiteles' Aphrodite of Cnidus (see introduction, Figure VII). For the Roman author Pliny the Elder (AD 23-79), it was not only the finest work by Praxiteles, but quite simply the finest statue in the world (*NH* XXXVI.20). Carved in marble, the image represented the goddess of love as a voluptuous nude modestly seeking to cover herself, as if surprised at her bath. Though explicit images of nude fertility goddesses were nothing new to the Mediterranean world, which had fashioned and worshipped them since Neolithic times, this naked figure of an Olympian goddess in a remarkably natural human pose was an innovation that inspired the imagination of late Classical artists and changed the iconography of Aphrodite forever. The viewer became, in essence, a voyeur, allowed to behold something that was at once enticing and forbidden. Praxiteles took special care to justify the goddess' nakedness, adding to the sculptural composition on her left a vase with water for her bath, draped with her discarded garments.

Conceived to be appreciated from every point of view, his statue of Aphrodite stood within a round temple on a point of land high on the promontory of Cnidus on the southwestern coast of Turkey, visible from far out at sea. It served as an object of admiration and pilgrimage for several centuries, and though the original sculpture was lost and presumably destroyed in later times, its general appearance is preserved on the coins of Cnidus. This numismatic evidence allowed later art historians and archaeologists to identify the so-called "Cnidian type," which is preserved more or less accurately in numerous copies.

It surely comes as no surprise that this sculpture was widely imitated and adapted by artists of the Greek and Roman world in every medium, on any scale, and this magnificent large bronze statuette, though much ravaged by surface corro-

GREEK,
LATE HELLENISTIC,
150-100 BC.
H. 51.7 CM.
METROPOLITAN
MUSEUM OF ART,
ROGERS FUND,
1912, 12.173

sion, represents only one variation on the Praxitelean original. Standing with her weight resting on her right leg, the goddess has pulled in her abdomen, as she bends her shoulders forward. In an effort to conceal her sex, she holds her outspread right hand across the front of her groin and pulls her left leg, with the knee flexed, closer to the right. Her left arm is raised slightly before her to the left side, where in the marble original the vase of water for her bath and her garments would have been standing, and she has turned her head to glance in that direction.

Her body expresses the Classical feminine ideal: mature and full, with well-rounded hips and buttocks, small waist, and ample breasts. From each point of view, a special aspect of her beauty is stressed: the face in the left view, the buttocks from the back, the breasts in the right, and the pelvis from the front. Though not the firm, slender form of an adolescent, the soft torso gives no suggestion of obesity. Her gestures are decorous, her pose convincingly self-protective, and her head, though sadly damaged, still reflects some shadow of the soft elegance that must have distinguished the original Praxitelean image. Her facial expression is unfortunately much diminished by the loss of the eyes, which were probably inset in glass paste or stone, perhaps with bronze lashes for a surprisingly lifelike effect. The serene beauty of her refined features is still visible, however, despite the loss of most original surface detail.

Three significant aspects of this statuette separate it from the extensive series of Cnidian copies. The left arm, reaching out for clothing from the vase beside it, is extended less to the side here than in other versions, while the head is actually turned more vigorously in that direction. And instead of being bound up in the usual Cnidian fashion of a knot at the base of the neck, the long hair is parted in the center of the forehead and pulled back on either side to form two twisted plaits.

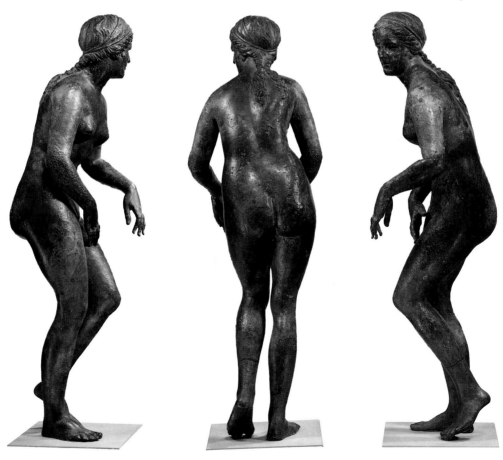

These tresses fall together down over the neck and the back of the right shoulder, and end in a series of loosely curling strands. A broad diadem wrapped across the front of the head tapers in the back, although it shows no evidence of any tie or fastening.

The possible reasons for such variations are many, but most likely is the artist's desire to add some element of originality to a much-loved and often-repeated image. At the same time, a comparison between the bronze and other replicas shows that this statuette has a unique sense of vitality and immediacy missing in most of the known replicas, which are certainly more correct in details but coldly academic. Though this freshness may detract from the goddess' Olympian aloofness, it makes her all the more appealing and desirable.

The surface condition and extensive restoration work make it difficult to appreciate the artistry of the craftsman responsible for this bronze. All but the smallest areas of the original polished surface have been lost, while both legs, both arms, and the upper back have been repaired within the last century, somewhat distorting our understanding of their original shapes and positions. Still, in the fine strands of hair pulled back around the face and the locks that curl sinuously down the back, his attention to detail is evident, as it is in the nervous fingers. The interest in anatomical definition is minimal, with an emphasis placed instead on the exquisite beauty of the smooth, rounded limbs and grand curves of the idealized female body.

In her original publication of the piece, Richter called it a late Greek work, and indeed, the hairstyle in particular has much in common with the post-Praxitelean images of Aphrodite bathing and dressing her hair that became common in the later third and second centuries BC. The harmonious proportions of the figure and its lively pose belong very much within the Hellenistic repertory, however, and a date later than the end of the second century BC seems unlikely.

The suggestion that the bronze may be from Asia Minor is contradicted by another report preserved in museum correspondence that the bronze, came from the Greek village of Hagios Sostis, near Andritsaina in Elis. Richter was told by A. S. Drey, the owner who sold the piece to the Metropolitan, that the statuette was purchased from a Count Palfi at Pressbourg (Bratislava since 1918). The actual provenance may never be established with certainty, but the large statuette remains one of the most sensitive reflections of the Praxitelean masterwork that established forever the place of the female nude in the popular repertoire of Greek sculpture.

CONDITION: The inlaid eyes and attached attributes are missing. The entire left foot and shin are restored. The left arm, broken off at the shoulder and reattached, may also have been broken around the upper arm in antiquity, given the ancient repair on the top of the left shoulder. The right arm was broken around the upper arm and reattached, and there is evidence of restoration above the elbow. The right leg has been damaged around the knee and the thigh just above it; much surface cracking is visible in what appear to be modern fills. There is a crack, which may be the remains of a break, at the base of the neck, and a gouge in the bronze mars the front of the neck. Numerous ancient repairs of casting flaws, both round plugs and square patches, are visible on many parts of the body. The bronze has also suffered extensive surface corrosion with a consequent loss of detail.

The surface is covered with an irregular patina that varies from dark green on the proper right leg and foot to paler green on the shoulders. Some areas of inpainting are difficult to separate from the actual patination, and reddish-brown cuprite is visible beneath the alteration surface.

PROVENANCE: See discussion above.

EX COLLECTIONS: Count Palfi(?); A. S. Drey.

EXHIBITED: Moscow and Leningrad, November 1978-June 1979, *Antichnoe isskustvo iz muzeia*

Metropoliten, Soedinennye Shtaty Ameriki, cat. by D. von Bothmer, no. 64, unpaginated.

PUBLISHED: *BMMA* VIII (1913) 29; idem, 268-269, fig. 6.
G. M. A. Richter 1915, 74-77, no. 121, illus.
G. Elderkin, "The Cnidian Aphrodite and Some of Her Descendants," *Archaeological Papers* II (1941) 8 ff., fig. 2.
M. Bieber, *The Sculpture of the Hellenistic Age*, rev. ed. (New York, 1961) 20, figs. 26-7.
D. M. Brinkerhoff, *Hellenistic Statues of Aphrodite: Studies in the History of Their Stylistic Development* (New York, 1978) 28, pl. II.
A. Delivorrias, "Aphrodite," *LIMC* II:51, no. 401, pl. 38.

NOTES: For the Cnidian Aphrodite in general, see C. S. Blinkenberg, *Knidia; Beiträge zur Kenntnis der praxitelischen Aphrodite* (Copenhagen, 1933); T. Kraus, "Die Aphrodite von Knidos," *Opus Nobile* X (1957); L. Closuit, *L'Aphrodite de Cnide* (Martigny, 1978). Also A. Delivorrias, "Aphrodite," *LIMC* II:50, with extensive bibliography.

On the Cnidian coins that reproduce images of the original statue and the recognition of the Cnidian type by Visconti in the eighteenth century, see C. S. Blinkenberg 1933, 14, 193-199, figs. 70-78.

On the excavations at Cnidus and the discovery of the round temple in which the original Praxitelean statue stood, see I. Love, "Excavations at Knidos, 1970," and "Excavations at Knidos, 1971," *AJA* LXXVI (1972) 70-75, illus. 8-9, fig. 24; and idem, II: 402-403, illus. 6, fig. 18.

16. Youth Dancing(?)

GREEK, LATE HELLENISTIC, CA. 150-50 BC. H. 20.5 CM. CHRISTOS G. BASTIS

With his weight apparently resting on the ball of his left foot, the adolescent steps forward, twisting in an upward-moving spiral that begins at the toes of his retracted right foot and continues through his torso to his raised and outstretched left hand. His knees are bent naturally in response to the step, his torso turns toward the left while leaning to the right, and his head is tossed back, inclined sharply toward his right shoulder. In his upturned face, the drilled pupils of his eyes show that his gaze is directed toward some far distant point high above to his right. To counterbalance the thrust of his head, his left arm, bent at the elbow, is extended out from the side of his body before him, and his fingers are loosely closed. His right arm, now lost from below the deltoid muscle at the shoulder, appears to have been extended across in front of his torso and was perhaps raised as well.

The boy's body is youthfully slim and fit; his legs, especially graceful and lean. But the areas of this solid-cast form that have not suffered extensive surface corrosion suggest that the anatomy was generally treated in a rather summary fashion. Both the abdomen and back are simplified in a manner that emphasizes the pose without concentrating on the distracting details of individual muscles. The pubic hair was defined with small relief curls, now much obscured by corrosion, while the navel is a well-defined oval, sunken at the edges and convex at the center. The missing nipples were inlaid, probably in copper.

The head is large in proportion to the body, related more to fifth-century canons than the fourth, and the features of the oval face are equally substantial and refined. The eyes may have originally been inlaid, presumably with silver, between the thick lids, but this is uncertain. The contours of the parted lips, not inset in another metal, are distinct. The hairstyle is particularly interesting as the short, flame-like locks on the back of the crown radiate in a sort of pinwheel pattern that

III

is Polyclitan in inspiration. The locks around the nape of the neck are longer, curling against it. Coarse incisions individualize strands of hair within the locks.

Although there is no exact parallel for this expressive posture, the most relevant comparisons suggest that the figure was intended to be understood as dancing, captured in mid-step. The twisted torso, the backward thrust of the head, the up-turned face, and unfocused gaze imply the ecstasy of a Dionysiac reveler or maenad, recalling the maenad of Scopas or the dancing faun from Pompeii in the spiraling torsion and the dancing satyr from Izmit in the unfocused expression. Yet, the limbs do not seem to have the purposeful energy and the gestures lack the intensity of those of dancing revelers. Nor does the youth have the ears, horns, or tail of a satyr or any other attribute associating him with the Dionysiac thiasos. Closer is the dancing figure of a boy in Munich, whose head is tossed back with comparable

freedom and whose hands are similarly poised holding castanets (krotala). Another possibility, that he may be a boy at play, tossing or catching a ball, seems less likely, given the lack of persuasive parallels.

Perhaps because of its momentary nature, this figure's pose conveys an uncertainty that does not disappear with readjustment of the stance. Though the weight is on the left foot, it seems insecurely placed, and the torsion of the upper body is somehow incomplete. Distinctly lower than the left, the right shoulder moves in the direction of a spiral but does not carry the momentum suggested by the lower torso and legs. The loss of energy apparent in this part of the figure is intensified by the position of the head that not only does not respond to the spin of the limbs but also appears to contradict it, falling back to the right. Though complex in the number of points of view from which it must be seen to be fully appreciated, the impression of the figure is curiously listless and lacking in vitality in spite of the spontaneous nature of its pose. It is not inconceivable that the figure was actually falling back, perhaps to be supported by another, though no evidence remains on the surface for any points of attachment.

The comparatives for the spiraling pose counteracted by the backward turn of the head, the competent but summary treatment of the anatomy, the slender proportions, and the unfocused gaze, all tend to suggest a date in the later part of the Hellenistic period, that is, around 150-50 BC. More than any other figure in the exhibition, this bronze illustrates the importance of the information that has been lost with the right arm and the base on which he stood. His right hand may have held an identifying attribute, and if his base were preserved, there would be no question about his original position or the explanation for his complicated pose.

CONDITION: Besides its base, the solid-cast figure is missing the entire right arm below the deltoid, the thumb of the left hand between the lower joint and the tip, the big toe and the ends of the small toes of the left foot, the inlaid nipples, and possibly the inlaid eyes. The irregular surface is nearly completely covered with a dark greenish-brown patina, at least part of which may be modern; large areas of the lower abdomen, left thigh, the neck, and the right shoulder show the effects of extensive corrosion.

EXHIBITED: Metropolitan Museum of Art, November 20, 1987-January 10, 1988, *Antiquities from the Collection of Christos G. Bastis*, 202, illus., no. 112, entry by A. Oliver, Jr.

NOTES: For the maenad of Scopas, see A. Stewart, *Skopas of Paros* (Park Ridge, N.J., 1977) 91-93, pl. 32.

For the dancing satyr from Izmit, see H. Philipp, "Eine hellenistische Satyrstatuette aus Izmit (Nikodemia)," *AA* (1987) pt. 1, 131-143, figs. 1-12.

For the dancing faun from Pompeii, see W. Fuchs 1979, 137, figs. 127-128.

On the Polyclitan inspiration for the pinwheel of locks radiating from the crown, see H. von Steuben, *Der Kanon des Polyklet; Doryphoros und Amazone* (Tübingen, 1973) 23-25, fig. 7; this feature is present as well in the locks on the back of the head of the Izmit satyr mentioned above.

For the bronze dancing boy in Munich, similarly posed with head thrown back and arms turned to the left, holding castanets, see W. Lamb 1929, 196, pl. 74 c.

17. Aphrodite

Though close in date and possibly even in source of inspiration for the Metropolitan Museum's large bronze Aphrodite (Figure 17a) adapted from the Cnidia type [15], this statuette conveys a completely different impression of the goddess of love. Unconcerned about her nudity—and apparently assured of her privacy—she stands in a expansive pose that displays the beauty of her body without a trace of modesty. Her torso is more or less frontal, though her head is turned slightly to the left, and she holds her right hand up before her just above the right shoulder. Her weight rests solidly on her right leg, and her right hip is raised correspondingly and thrust to the side in a graceful curve. The right foot and leg below the calf are unfortunately lost, but have been reconstructed. The left leg, bent slightly at the knee, is relaxed and rests close to the right, with the foot placed slightly back and turned out to the side, its heel raised.

GREEK, LATE HELLENISTIC, 150-50 BC. H. 47.1 CM. RHODE ISLAND SCHOOL OF DESIGN MUSEUM OF ART, MUSEUM APPROPRIATION AND SPECIAL GIFT, 26.117

With no sense of shy embarrassment or even awareness of an observer, the goddess looks away. Her small, oval face expresses serene detachment. To heighten the sense of naturalism, the artist inlaid her eyes with silver—still visible beneath the patina—and her lips most probably with copper, which is missing. Both were intended when polished to provide a subtle coloristic contrast with the original golden bronze of her flesh. The pupils of her eyes are drilled to direct her gaze, and the contours of each exquisite feature are sharply defined. The lobes of her ears are drilled for the attachment of earrings, probably silver or gold, and she wears a single silver bracelet around her right wrist.

The most sensuously rendered of all her features, however, is her luxuriant hair, pulled into a knot at the nape of her neck and bound with a fillet that is wrapped twice around the crown of her head. The silver inlay remains in the upper of the two bands, while the traces in the edges of the lower one and the intentionally roughened concave surface of the bronze show that silver was inlaid there as well. In something like a free variation of the melon coiffure, the thick wavy locks are pulled back from the goddess' face in parallel twisted strands. Not content with defining the curling tresses by simple incision, the sculptor has captured their richness, barely restrained by the slender bands of the fillet, with modeling of extraordinary freedom and sensitivity.

The torso and the limbs, in contrast, are smoothed and rounded into sinuous curves of unnatural perfection, and the elongated proportions of the body are mannered and elegant. The head gracing the long neck is small in relation to the figure's height. The firm breasts and the crease that marks the waist are set high on the torso. The hips and buttocks are broad; the legs exceptionally long. Clearly not interested in demonstrating his ability to convey accurately the mundane de-

tails of human anatomy, the artist has concentrated instead on creating an image of lyrical beauty worthy of an immortal.

The original left arm, missing completely from just below the shoulder, was restored in its present position sometime in the late eighteenth or early nineteenth century. Comparison with similarly posed figures of Aphrodite shows that this reconstruction is misleading, if not incorrect. Instead of extending downward and out, with a meaningless attribute in the hand, the left arm was intended either to be raised—in a pose not unlike that of the right, though slightly closer to the body—or extended down but more to the front to hold a mirror. The reconstruction of the arm stretched out before the body is inappropriate to the otherwise harmonious composition of the limbs; the right arm should be extended above the engaged hip if such a gesture was intended.

If the gesture is restored with the left hand raised and the fingers positioned like those of the preserved hand to hold something, the composition becomes infinitely more pleasing. The figure should then belong to a group of images that have often been interpreted as holding out a necklace, and on that basis, identified with a statue attributed to Praxiteles by the ancient authors Pliny (*NH* XXIV.69-70) and Tatianus (*Oratio ad Graecos,* 34; *Contra Graecos* LVI.122)—the so-called Aphrodite Pselioumene. Though the Greek word *pselion* generally refers to a bracelet, the verb *pselioo* may mean to twine or wrap around and, thus, be understood as describing Aphrodite fastening a necklace.

The preserved right hand of the Providence bronze has a deep cavity in the space between its forefinger and the thumb at the upper edge of the palm. Given the position of the hand, it would be likely that if a necklace were to be added, it would have been fastened between the thumb and forefingers from underneath the hand, not behind it, as it could hang more naturally from below. At the same time, two similar cavities are visible deep within the locks on either side of the bun (krobylos) at the back of the head. It is possible that these cavities may have held the attached ends of the silver fillet intended to flutter down the back. Yet, in his original publication of the statuette, which was at that time known to him only from a plaster cast, Reinach—following the earlier observations of Murray on the Pselioumene pose—astutely noted the similarity of the pose with that of the Polyclitan Fillet Binder (Diadoumenos). The obvious accuracy of this iconographic association and the presence and placement of the points of attachment suggest that the ends of the silver fillet did not fall freely, but were attached to the raised hands, and the gesture of the goddess may be restored as pulling tight the ribbon that holds her hair. In an article on a closely related bronze figure, Richter recalls that Praxiteles was also credited by Pliny with an Aphrodite Stephanusam, which may be understood to mean "crowning herself," and as here she is tying on a silver fillet, this designation may be more accurate. But whether she held the ends of her double-wrapped fillet or a necklace, the gesture provided an anecdotal excuse for her arm to be raised and extended to the side, thus completely exposing her splendid torso.

Figure 17a. *Aphrodite*. Formerly in the Haviland collection. Bronze, H. 45.7 cm. New York, Metropolitan Museum of Art, Gift of Mr. and Mrs. Francis Neilson, 1935, 35.122.

The history of this statuette is almost as romantic as its subject. It was first brought to the attention of the scholarly world in the *Revue archéologique* in 1899 by Reinach, who had discovered a slightly embellished cast of the figure in the office of the curator of the Wallraf-Richartz Museum in Cologne. Though unable to discover its provenance or whereabouts beyond the suggestion that it was somewhere in Russia, he recognized its extraordinary similarity to a bronze in the collection of the sculptor Paul Dubois (which came later, after some years in the Haviland collection, into the possession of the Metropolitan Museum of Art, 35.122; see Figure 17a). Having satisfied himself that the cast was not a modern creation based on imitations of the Dubois bronze, Reinach published the photographs of the Cologne plaster, hoping to discover the original. He heard a report of its having been in Finland in 1920, and his efforts were finally rewarded when a Paris dealer named Brummer visited him in 1925, bringing the statuette itself. The bronze was at that time owned by an Austrian collector, Dr. von Frey, who had bought it after it passed through the markets in Paris and Berlin. Reinach subsequently learned that it once had, in fact, been owned by a Russian prince, Bieloselski-Bielozerski, who owned an island villa near Leningrad.

The questions about where the bronze was found and how and when it traveled remain unanswered. As Deonna observed, the statuette appears in its present restored condition in the background of a portrait of Madame Duval-Töpffer painted by Firmin Massot, with the assistance of F. Ferrière, in 1822 (now in the collection of the Musée d'Art et d'Histoire, Geneva). Thus, it must have been discovered sometime in the late eighteenth or early nineteenth century, though this evidence does not support Reinach's theory that it was bought by a Russian nobleman traveling in Campania. Ultimately, on the recommendation of E. P. Warren and through the agency of John Marshall, the bronze came to the Rhode Island School of Design Museum of Art in 1926.

Wherever it was made, the Providence Aphrodite surely reflects the same famous monumental statue of Aphrodite that inspired the Dubois-Haviland bronze in the Metropolitan Museum, as Reinach originally observed, and possibly other images as well. On the basis of the relationship of the pose to that of the Cnidian Aphrodite; the appearance of the double fillet around the hair, which also appears on copies of the head of the Cnidian Aphrodite and on the so-called "Bartlett

Head'' in the Boston Museum of Fine Arts, which is a fourth-century original, contemporary in date with the Cnidia; the similarity of the raised arm to the gesture of the Diana of Gabii; and the possible identification with the Aphrodite Pselioumene, the image that served as the model for these bronzes has been associated with the sculptor Praxiteles.

Richter brought the two bronzes together in New York for detailed comparison and concluded that, though the two were extremely close in every way, the New York version was an earlier and more faithful reflection of the original. She took the Metropolitan bronze to be a nearly contemporary, fourth-century copy, and the Providence bronze to be Roman. Mitten, on the other hand, in his exemplary publication of the Providence piece opted for a date in the last quarter of the second century BC. Other scholarly opinions are divided between the second century BC and the first century AD. Though such a precise date as Mitten's may be difficult to accept, his interpretation of the bronze as late Hellenistic, rather than Roman, would seem to be correct. The comparisons of the torso with those of the Aphrodites of Melos and Cyrene are most instructive. The essentially frontal, serene pose of the Providence goddess would have appealed to the classicizing taste of the later second and early first century BC, and the elongated proportions and reduced interest in anatomical detail are appropriate for a date of 150-50 BC.

CONDITION: The right leg from below the calf and the left arm from just beneath the shoulder are lost, as is the attachment held by the right hand, the ends of the fillet—which were set into the sides of the krobylos—and the earrings. The tip of the small finger on the right hand is also missing. The inlays of silver for the lower band of the fillet and, most likely, copper for the lips are gone, exposing the roughened surfaces of the bronze beneath. A crack around the upper part of the right arm just beneath the shoulder suggests that the raised arm was cast separately and joined on, not broken and repaired. Ancient patches on the right side and front of the neck and in the cleft of the clavicles mask casting flaws. The hollow cast bronze is otherwise well preserved with much of the original surface detail and polish still apparent.

The surface is covered by a dark, reddish-brown patina with areas of bright green malachite irregularly dispersed over the left back, the buttocks, the rear of the right thigh, the lower abdomen, and on the inner thighs.

EX COLLECTIONS: Prince Bieloselski-Bielozerski, Leningrad; Dr. von Frey, Vienna; correspondence in the museum archives from E. P. Warren states that von Frey purchased the statuette: "in 1918 from a Russian banker who had owned it for many years. The banker had it from the Stroganoff family; there was a tale that some Czar had given it to an ancestress of theirs" (D. G. Mitten 1975, 74, n. 1).

EXHIBITED: Detroit Institute of Arts, March 23-April 20, 1947, *Small Bronzes of the Ancient World*, cat. by F. A. Robinson, 11, illus. 42, no. 82.
Northampton, Mass., Smith College Museum of Art, November 18-December 15, 1948, *Pompeiana*.

PUBLISHED: S. Reinach, "Deux statuettes d'Aphrodite," *RA*, 3rd ser., XXXV (1899) 369-375, pl. 21 (cast).
E. Espérandieu, *Réceuil général des bas-reliefs, statues et bustes de la Gaule romaine*, VIII (Paris, 1922) 392, no. 6518.
W. Deonna, "Quelques statuettes d'Aphrodite," *Aréthuse* I (1924) 108-112, fig. 25, pl. XX.
S. Reinach, "Deux nouvelles statuettes d'Aphrodite," *MonPiot* XXVII (1924) 132-139, pls. XIII-XIV (tr. in L. E. Rowe, infra.).
S. Reinach, *Rép.stat.* V,1: 151, 2.
L. E. Rowe, "A Bronze Statuette of Aphrodite," *BullRhISD* XIV (October 1926) 38-42, cover illus.
G. M. A. Richter, "Two Bronze Statuettes," *AJA* XXXVII (1933) 48-51, pls. VII b, VIII b.
K. A. Neugebauer, "Die Venus von Grenoble," *Pantheon* XVII (February 1936) 54, fig. 5.
C. Picard, *Manuel d'archéologie grecque. La sculpture*, III: *Période classique-IVᵉ siècle* (Paris, 1948) 614, n. 2; 615, n. 1; 616-617, figs. 266-267.
R. Lullies, *Die kauernde Aphrodite* (Munich-Pasing, 1954) 65 (as probably modern).
D. G. Mitten, *Classical Bronzes* (Providence, R.I., 1975) 66-76, no. 20, figs. a-m.

D. M. Brinkerhoff, *Hellenistic Statues of Aphro-dite: Studies in the History of Their Stylistic Develop-ment* (New York, 1978) 29, pls. VI-VII.
A. Delivorrias, "Aphrodite," *LIMC* II, 1, 60, no. 492.

NOTES: For the original identification of the Aphrodite Pselioumene type, see W. Klein, *Praxiteles* (Leipzig, 1898) 282-290, figs. 45-50; more recently, A. Delivorrias, "Aphrodite," *LIMC* II:59-60, figs. 482-493.

A close comparison for both the Providence and the New York statuettes is provided by the large bronze Aphrodite once in the de Clercq collection and now in the Toledo Museum of Art (68.72), illustrated in D. G. Mitten 1975, 74, fig. n; also in *Small Sculptures in Bronze* (1976) no. 28.

For the so-called "Bartlett Head" in the Boston Museum of Fine Arts, see M. B. Com-stock and C. C. Vermeule, *Sculpture in Stone: The Greek, Roman and Etruscan Collections of the Museum of Fine Arts, Boston* (Boston, 1976) 39, no. 55.

For a comparable bronze Aphrodite preserv-ing both hands raised, see the Pourtales Aphro-dite in the British Museum, H. B. Walters 1899, 193, no. 1084, pl. V.

For a bronze Aphrodite with the right arm raised and the left arm extended, holding a mir-ror, see K. A. Neugebauer, *Die griechischen Bron-zen der klassischen Zeit und des Hellenismus* (Berlin, 1951) 47, no. 35, pl. 19.

For the Aphrodites of Melos and Cyrene respectively, see W. Fuchs 1979, 230-233, fig. 251; and 244-245, fig. 267.

18. Asclepius

The god of healing and medicine, Asclepius did not come into prominence as a deity until the end of the fifth century BC, though he was surely known much earlier as he is mentioned in Homer's *Iliad* (II.731-732; IV.193-219). Following the introduction of his cult in Athens around 420 BC, however, his popularity grew with extraordinary rapidity, and by the end of the fourth century he was wor-shipped widely in Greece and along the coast of Asia Minor (Turkey), especially at the lavish sanctuaries of Epidaurus, Cos, and Pergamum. His curative powers offered the individual some hope for recovery from illness as well as for personal salvation, prospects that must have appealed greatly to the populations of the Greek city-states that had grown tired of endless wars and plagues, and had become irreverently critical of the more established Olympian gods who seemed to offer neither solace nor assistance.

As an interest in the mythology surrounding his birth and childhood did not arise until his cult was well established, these aspects of the god were not com-monly represented. Rather, the iconographic repertory was primarily limited to the images of his mature appearance as established by the best-known of his cult statues.

Like most surviving figures of Asclepius, this imposing bronze probably re-flects a famous monumental original, although it is impossible to identify at which of the sanctuaries it was housed, as similar images appear from all around Greece and Asia Minor. The noble bearded figure stands calmly with his weight dis-tributed more or less evenly on both feet. His right shoulder is lowered and his legs slightly bent. He is dressed in a himation that passes over his left arm and shoulder from front to back, then wraps around his torso to end in a stack of folds over his left side. Falling in heavy diagonals, the fabric on the back is folded over at the top

GREEK, LATE
HELLENISTIC,
150-50 BC.
H. 23.9 CM.
CINCINNATI ART
MUSEUM, GIFT OF
MICHAEL SCHAIBLE
IN HONOR OF HIS
FATHER, 1957.504

to expose his right shoulder and arm. Across the front of his torso, this folded material is pulled up over his midriff into a thick roll that forms the upper border of a large triangular overfall. The lower corners of the himation are weighted with small spheres, probably made of metal in a real cloth costume. A laurel wreath formed of triple leaf clusters with berries crowns his head, and his feet are shod with sturdy sandals (trochades) with closed heels and open toes, tied at the front of the ankle.

The proportions of the statuette are unnaturally attenuated, and the head and especially the face are small in relation to the figure's total height. Yet, more than any other feature, the head expresses the god's popular appeal. Abundant hair in a series of long, snaky curls frames his serious face. He gazes to his right. The checks furrowed with age and experience, his slightly parted lips, and the deep-set, sensitively modeled eyes effectively convey the sympathetic attitude for which he was revered.

The god's left arm, completely enveloped by his himation, is bent at the elbow and raised, with his muffled hand resting on the back of his left hip. His right arm hangs down by his side in a manner that is not totally relaxed, and the fingers of his right hand appear to have been loosely closed around a missing attribute, which is usually restored as the snake-entwined staff of the god of medicine.

The position of this arm, broken above the elbow with some apparent loss, now filled, and the restoration of this attribute are of some importance for the identification of the god. Bieber clearly established in her original publication of the statuette that its magisterial pose, the pattern of its drapery, and the laurel wreath are completely appropriate for Asclepius, the popular son of Apollo, and she restored the staff in his right hand on the basis of comparisons with close but not identical figures. No trace of the attribute remains in this hand, however, contrary to her information, and the fingers are curled in such a position that neither the shaft nor the top of a staff propped up on the ground beside the body can be easily placed within them. The grip is better suited to a cylindrical object held much less vertically on the right side. Any possible change in the position of the arm only makes it more difficult to restore the staff, as the object held would become almost parallel to the ground.

Ridgway has made the provocative suggestion that the bronze might be identified instead as a Hellenistic poet with Asclepian features, recalling the appearance of the statue of a poet on the relief of the "Apotheosis of Homer" now in the British Museum, and she proposes that the attribute in the right hand, given the position of the fingers, should be restored as a scroll. This interesting possibility is supported by the appearance of a similar triangular overfall of drapery on the himation of the Apotheosis relief figure. The serene dignity of the pose, the idealized and sensitive features, and the thick, peculiarly snaky curls of hair, however, speak against identifying this figure as a mortal. He need only be compared with the Metropolitan Museum's statuette of a philosopher [26], who is similarly dressed and posed, to see that the distinction between god and man is obvious and intentional. The evidence provided by the Cincinnati bronze's relationship to the numerous existing representations of Asclepius, especially those of the Giustiniani and Eleusis types, is ultimately more persuasive, and Bieber's identification of it as a variant of an established image remains unchanged.

Bieber dated the statuette to the second quarter of the third century BC on the basis of its relationship to the Metropolitan's statuette of a philosopher [26], which she dated to the decade 270-260 BC, and to the portrait of Demosthenes by Polyeuctus, which she placed about 280-279 BC. Most scholars have subsequently lowered the date to the late Hellenistic period, to somewhere between the late second century BC (Heiderich) and the first century BC (Vermeule). Vermeule feels that the careful detailing of the shoes, with their open toes, and the weights on the himation indicate that the Asclepius Jameson was fashioned in the late Hellenistic period, about 80 to 50 BC. This was the time when Greek artists were beginning to work for Roman generals and merchants but before the late Republican (Imperatorial) and early Imperial ages which produced the excellent but mechanical copies associated with the bronzes of Pompeii and Herculaneum. The manneristic proportions and the classicizing elegance of the pose surely support a lower date, but it would be difficult to be more precise than 150-50 BC.

The statuette is said to have come from Athens; Heiderich and Ridgway after him have connected it with a workshop of Asia Minor, however, possibly that of Pergamum, on the basis of its similarity in style to a statuette of Asclepius in Berlin that is said to be from Asia Minor. Although most of the small figures of this god were votive offerings and could have easily been transported to any of the various sanctuaries, the Giustiniani type of which this figure is a variant is most closely associated with the fourth-century Athenian sanctuary of Asclepius on the south slope of the Acropolis. Since every urban shrine (hospital or clinic) in the Greek world featured images of the healing god, the possibilities for inspiration were limitless. It is really not until the Greek Imperial period, most notably the second and third centuries of the Roman Empire, that city coins from Thrace to Syria and Egypt show us how popular statues of Asclepius must have been from 350 to 50 BC. There seems no persuasive reason to reject the recorded information and an Attic provenance may be considered reliable until more conclusive evidence is presented.

M. T. and C. C. V. III

CONDITION: The right arm has been broken above the elbow, with some loss of metal, and restored in modern times. Both ankles have been broken and repaired with some filling, and the large toe on the right foot has been broken off and reattached. There is evidence of cooling cracks on the chest beneath the right breast; a casting flaw in the fold of drapery that runs down at the back from the muffled left hand was repaired in antiquity with a circular patch. The body of the statue is hollow cast, and the legs were cast on separately, ending inside just above the skirt of the himation. The right arm does not appear from x-radiographs to have been made separately.

As the entire surface has been coated in modern times with a varnish or wax to give it a polished appearance, the actual condition of the ancient surface is difficult to ascertain. An irregular green patina appears to cover every part of the figure except the feet, which may have been stripped or cleaned in the course of restoration. Their surfaces are more brownish-green, with what remains of the patina preserved in the areas around the sandal straps. A granular surface encrustation is present on the right shoulder and back.

PROVENANCE: Said to be from Athens.

EX COLLECTIONS: Jameson, Paris; Michael Schaible, Cincinnati.

PUBLISHED: Sale: *Collection Arthur Sambon*, by J. Hirsch, Paris, Galerie Georges Petit, May 25-28, 1914, pl. XIV, 60.
S. Reinach, *Rép.stat.* VI:II, no. I.

M. Bieber, "A Bronze Statuette in Cincinnati and Its Place in the History of the Asklepios Types," *Proceedings of the American Philosophical Society* CI (February 1957) 70-92, figs. 1-4.
M. Bieber 1961, 180-181, n. 77, figs. 779-781.
G. Heiderich, *Asklepios* (diss., Freiburg im Breisgau, Albert-Ludwigs Universität, 1966) 107-108 nn., pp. 140, 154.
M. Bieber, "Bronzestatuette des Asklepios in Cincinnati," *AntP* X (1970) 55-56, pls. 46-50.
Sculpture Collection of the Cincinnati Museum of Art (Cincinnati, 1970) 44, illus.
M. Comstock and C. Vermeule 1971, 91, no. 96A.
B. S. Ridgway, "Review of *AntP* X," *Gnomon* XLV (June 1973) 402.
E. G. Raftopoulou, "Remarques sur des bronzes provenant du sol grec," *Bronzes hellénistiques* (1979) 43-47, figs. 1, 3, 5-6.
B. Holtzmann, "Asklepios," *LIMC* II, 1, 880, no. 193; 2, pl. 649, fig. 193.

NOTES: For the god Asclepius, see B. Holtzmann, *LIMC* II, 1, 863-867, 890-897; also K. Neugebauer, *Asklepios: Eine Beitrag zur Kritik römischer Statuenkopien*, Winckelmannsprogramm der Archäologischen Gesellschaft zu Berlin LXXVII (1921); E. J. Edelstein et al., *Asclepius: A Collection and Interpretation of the Testimonies* (Baltimore, 1945); K. Kerényi, *Der gottliche Artz: Studien über Asklepios und seine* Kultstätten (Darmstadt, 1956).

For the Asclepius figures of the Giustiniani type and the association of the original of this type with Athens, see B. Holtzmann, *LIMC* II, 1, 879-882, 894; 2, pls. 647-651; for the Eleusis type, idem, 1, 882-883, 894; 2, pls. 652-654.

19. Black Youth

The boy stands in a rather unsteady pose with his feet side by side, as if he had just paused in the midst of a quiet walk. His head is bent slightly to his right, and his lips are parted, perhaps in mid-speech. A thick himation is draped across his chest, passing over his left shoulder and beneath his right arm. This arm hangs naturally by his side in a relaxed fashion with a missing attribute, perhaps a bookroll, enclosed in the fingers of the right hand. His left arm—completely muffled in the folds of the heavy fabric and bent at the elbow with his hand apparently clenched—is raised to the level of his hip.

GREEK,
LATE HELLENISTIC,
CA. 150-50 BC.
H. 8.1 CM.
MUSEUM OF FINE ARTS,
BOSTON, J. H. AND
E. A. PAYNE FUND, 59.11

The figure's lower legs, bowed and unnaturally short, appear thin in relationship to the fleshy knees and are imprecisely modeled. This summary treatment is equally characteristic of the feet, which appear quite crude by comparison with the other features. It is the legs and feet, however, that account for the convincing sense of uncertainty and spontaneity in the stance. Their bowed outlines may actually be an intentional reference to a physical trait that was considered characteristic of blacks in antiquity ([Aristotle], *Problemata*, XIV.4. 909a; Petronius, *Satyricon*, 102).

The thick disheveled curly hair that stands out from the crown is also treated rather impressionistically, with little specific detail for individual locks. Yet, the suggestion of texture is extremely effective. Similarly generalized are the facial features, set low beneath a large forehead, but they are equally expressive. The tendency to imply details rather than define them precisely is a not uncommon characteristic of works of the late Hellenistic period, and thus a date in the later second or early first century BC would seem most appropriate for the statuette. The momentary nature of the pose of the head and the parted lips suggest the image's spontaneous character, while its flattened nose and broad lips, taken together with the thick woolly hair, identify the subject's Ethiopian origins.

Images of blacks occur early in Greek art and literature. They appeared in Minoan wall paintings of the mid-second millennium BC, and it was among the "blameless Ethiopians" that Zeus was to be found at the opening of Homer's *Iliad* (1.423-425). Their exotic appearance clearly appealed to the Athenian potters and painters of the sixth and fifth centuries BC, as they are popular subjects both among the painted representations and molded vessels made in the shapes of human heads. But it is in the period of the expanded empires of the Hellenistic world that images of blacks become most plentiful. Alexander's conquest of Egypt, the reconquest of the regions of the Upper Nile by the Ptolemies, and the growing importance of Alexandria as a center of trade and intellectual ferment clearly brought the native populations of Africa to greater prominence. At the same time, the artists of the period from the end of the fourth to the first centuries AD showed a remarkable interest in depicting the life and activities of the lower classes. Many of the images are far from flattering. Often captives taken in battle, the Ethiopians who reached the Greek cities were then sold as slaves and, as such, were the object of ridicule and brutal humor.

This image, however, betrays none of these coarser strains of Hellenistic art, since it presents its subject with sympathetic interest and dignity. In their catalogue of the Boston bronzes, Comstock and Vermeule have observed quite correctly that the youth, wrapped in the traditional garb of the privileged classes and especially the intellectuals, is similar in pose to the portraits of philosophers. Indeed, his ungainly stance and apparent preoccupation are closest to one of the best known Hellenistic philosopher portraits, the statuette [26] from the Metropolitan Museum. That the youth may be identified on the basis of this connection as the pupil of one of the great Alexandrian schools of philosophy or rhetoric cannot be

proven, but the sincerity and spontaneity of the image make it equally impossible to accept that this could be intended as a caricature of a philosopher type. This tiny statuette would seem instead to be a genre image of extraordinary sensitivity that has ennobled its subject with intellectual associations.

Although this bronze figure was found in Chalon-sur-Saône in France in the later part of the eighteenth century, it has generally been considered to be Alexandrian in origin on the basis of style and subject, a suggestion that raises the question most recently addressed by Rolley. Must the fine bronzes found in the provincial areas of the Hellenistic and Roman empires, such as Gaul, of necessity be considered to be imports? Many of his objections about the attribution to Alexandria of the splendid bronze black musician in the collection of the Cabinet des Médailles hold equally well for this statuette, with which it was actually found, and also for the emaciated youth from Dumbarton Oaks [25], which was found near Soissons. He maintains that carefully finished surfaces in particular are generally uncharacteristic of the bronzes actually found in Alexandria. And while the foundries of Alexandria continued to produce bronzes for export in the Roman Imperial period, there is also evidence that plaster casts of late Hellenistic Alexandrian models were beginning to be exported when foundries were already established in Gaul. Thus, Alexandria may have provided only the source of inspiration for the motif.

Since the lustrous greenish-black patina of this bronze has been applied, most likely in modern times, it cannot be considered as evidence for finely polished surfaces among either Alexandrian or provincial bronzes. Other figures in this exhibition, however, most particularly the Cleveland Harpocrates [21], persuasively demonstrate that finely polished surfaces do, in fact, exist on bronzes that, though unprovenanced, almost surely come from Alexandria. Still, the definite attribu-

tion to the Hellenistic capital of bronzes found in France on the basis of style and subject alone is problematic. (An Alexandrian provenance is especially difficult to support for this figure, as two similar images of black youths in himatia, Roman in date, have been found at the provincial sites of Avignon in France and Augst in Switzerland.) As little systematic excavation has been done on the great city of Alexandria, generalizations about the characteristics of its products are perhaps still premature. For the fine bronzes found in provincial sites, careful comparative analyses of the alloys, especially of the lead isotopes, may help to determine their places of manufacture.

CONDITION The solid-cast figure has a crack on the inside of the right knee and another in the left ankle, where it may have been broken and repaired. A rivet, apparently ancient, soldered in place in the center of the back may indicate that the bronze was attached to a vessel or support, or was part of a larger composition. It is now surrounded by coarse material that appears to be modern. The surface is rubbed and worn, and file marks are visible on the outside of the top fold and some flat areas of the drapery. The attribute in the right hand is lost, but the figure is otherwise complete. The entire surface is covered with a regular modern greenish-black patina, with some areas of golden bronze showing through on the worn edges of the himation, especially at the back.

PROVENANCE: Found at Chalon-sur-Saône, France, in 1763-1764, in an oak chest containing eighteen superb bronze statuettes.

EX COLLECTIONS: Comte de Caylus; Duc de Caylus.

PUBLISHED: C. C. Vermeule, *Annual Report of the Museum of Fine Arts* (Boston, 1959) 27.
C. C. Vermeule, *Classical Journal* LV (1960) 198 ff., fig. 7.
Fasti archaeologici XV (1960) nos. 208, 671; idem, XVII (1962) no. 243.
F. M. Snowden, *Blacks in Antiquity; Ethiopians in the Graeco-Roman Experience* (Cambridge, Mass., 1970) 28, 89, fig. 64; 186, 194-195.
M. Comstock and C. Vermeule 1971, 78-79, no. 82.
F. M. Snowden, in J. Vercoutter et al., eds., *The Image of the Black in Western Art*, I: *From the Pharaohs to the Fall of Egypt* (New York, 1976) 204, fig. 259.
A. Kaufmann-Heinemann, *Die römischen Bronzen der Schweiz*, I: *Augst* (Mainz, 1976-) 81, under no. 83.
C. C. Vermeule, *Greek Art, Socrates to Sulla* (Cambridge, Mass., 1980) 92, 134, 278-279, fig. 122.
F. M. Snowden, *Before Color Prejudice: The Ancient View of Blacks* (Cambridge, Mass., 1983) 93, 143, n. 157.

NOTES: I thank Arthur Beale and Richard Newman for their assistance in examining this bronze.

On representations of blacks in ancient art, see F. M. Snowden, especially *Blacks in Antiquity* (1970) and *The Image of the Black in Western Art* (1976) with extensive bibliographies; earlier but still useful, G. H. Beardsley, *The Negro in Greek and Roman Civilization: A Study of the Ethiopian Type* (Baltimore, Md., 1929); for a history of the representations of blacks on vases in particular, see E. Buschor, "Das Krokodil des Sotades," *MJb* XI (1919) 33-43; on Hellenistic representations of blacks, see U. Hausmann, "Hellenische Neger," *AM* LXXVII (1962) 255-281, figs. 74-80; for the Alexandrian connections, see N. Himmelmann-Wildschütz 1983, 64-66, also 88-89, pls. 42-43, 49, 62-63.

For representations of children in poses associated with well-known adults, especially the Greek philosophers and rhetoricians, and the significance of the muffled hand in this connection, see G. M. A. Hanfmann, "An Etruscan Bronze," *The Princeton Record* II (1943) 7-9, fig. 5.

For the Chalon-sur-Saône bronzes and the problems of supporting an Alexandrian provenance for the image of the black musician in the Cabinet des Médailles, see C. Rolley 1986, 226-230. Rolley's account of the dispersal of this hoard of figures differs from that of M. Comstock and C. Vermeule 1971; C. Rolley claims only twelve bronzes went to the Comte de Caylus, which all later entered the Bibliothèque Nationale, Cabinet des Médailles, while Comstock and Vermeule state that all eighteen were purchased by the Comte. See also C. Rolley 1986, 16-17.

For the two bronzes representing mantled figures of blacks from the Roman period, see R. Steiger, "Drei römische Bronzen aus Augst," *Gestalt und Geschichte: Festschrift Karl Schefold zu seinem 60. Geburtstag am 26 Januar 1965* (Bern, 1967) 192-195, pls. 62-63; also S. Boucher, *Recherches sur les bronzes figurés de Gaule pré-romaine et romaine* (Rome, 1976) 182-184, 281, figs. 476-478. One of the figures was found in Augst, Switzerland, and the other in Avignon, France, adding further support to the probability that the figural type came to be produced in provincial workshops.

On the evidence for Alexandrian plaster casts and their exportation, see C. Rolley 1986, 216, 230; see also C. Reinsberg, *Studien zur hellenistischen Toreutik; Die antike Gipsabgüsse aus Memphis* (Hildesheim, 1980).

20. Black Banausos(?)

A world apart from the dignified portrayal of a black in the last entry, this image is more in the nature of a caricature than the sympathetic portrayal of a member of the lower strata of society (the banausoi) that struggled to survive by providing physical labor or entertainment, or by begging. He stands with his weight on his right leg, his right hip swung noticeably to the side, and his right arm extended before it. His right hand has been reconstructed in modern times to hold a begging bowl, probably in interpretation of the expression on his face, which is turned to the right with the gaze directed upward. As a profile view shows, the exaggerated hipshot pose is made more emphatic by the marked protrusion of his belly and the corresponding concavity of his back.

The black wears a short tunic (exomis) made of stiff material, perhaps leather. Front and back are tied in a knot over his left shoulder, and the garment is belted in the center front below the distended abdomen. He wears a Phrygian cap that is well known from the Archaic period onward and generally associated with oriental costume. Here, the material must be leather or felt since the cap is stiff enough to hold its rounded peak. It hangs in a long point that covers the nape of his neck and has flaps that stand out beside his ears.

That he is an Ethiopian is clear from the broad, flat nose, the thick lips, the heavy rolls of flesh converging over the bridge of his nose, and the tight corkscrew curls arranged across his forehead. His age, however, is deceptive. Though he appears at first glance to be a young boy, the little goatee and precisely modeled curls of his sideburns are the characteristics of a mature man rather than a child. Besides his swollen belly, his skinny legs and thin arms betray the seriousness of his physical condition, for these are the symptoms of malnutrition, and the unnatural curvature of his spine is due to scoliosis. His large eyes, inlaid with silver into which the upturned pupils have been deeply drilled, and unconsciously parted lips, inset with copper, complete the pathetic image. Yet, in spite of its accurate description of the results of deprivation and the dramatic, almost threatening facial expression, the bronze has none of the emotional impact of the Dumbarton Oaks emaciated boy [25]. For this is not a rendering of human suffering intended to arouse pity in the viewer, but an image skillfully conceived to diffuse the pathos of its subject for the pleasure and even amusement of the observer.

The brilliant artistry of the craftsman is most evident in the skillful interplay of the sinuous contours of the body. The swing of the torso from front to back and side to side can be fully appreciated only after the piece has been studied from all angles, though the primary view is clearly the one in which the figure looks directly at his observer. Nor was the creator of this image insensitive to decorative effects, contriving intentional contrasts in surface textures and colors that distract from the emotional impact of the subject. The fabric of the exomis that stands out over the right hip in broad, stiff points becomes almost transparent at the back, where it clings to the emphatically rounded buttocks. The smooth folds of the cap set off the tight, wiry curls hanging down the forehead and temples around the highly stylized and symmetrical furrows of the brow.

The removal of much of the glossy black lacquer with which the bronze had been coated, perhaps in the last century, revealed that the figure had been covered in antiquity with a fine black patina, most likely artificially induced with sulphide fumes. The flesh was therefore always intended to be the glossy black appropriate for the subject. When polished, the contrast provided by the inlaid silver used for the eyes and the exposed nipple of the proper right breast, and the red copper of the swollen lips could only have heightened their ornamental value, and in the case of eyes and mouth, diminished their expressive importance.

GREEK, PROBABLY
ALEXANDRIAN,
LATE HELLENISTIC,
CA. 100-50 BC.
H. 18.5 CM.
THE CLEVELAND
MUSEUM OF ART,
LEONARD C.
HANNA, JR., FUND
63.507

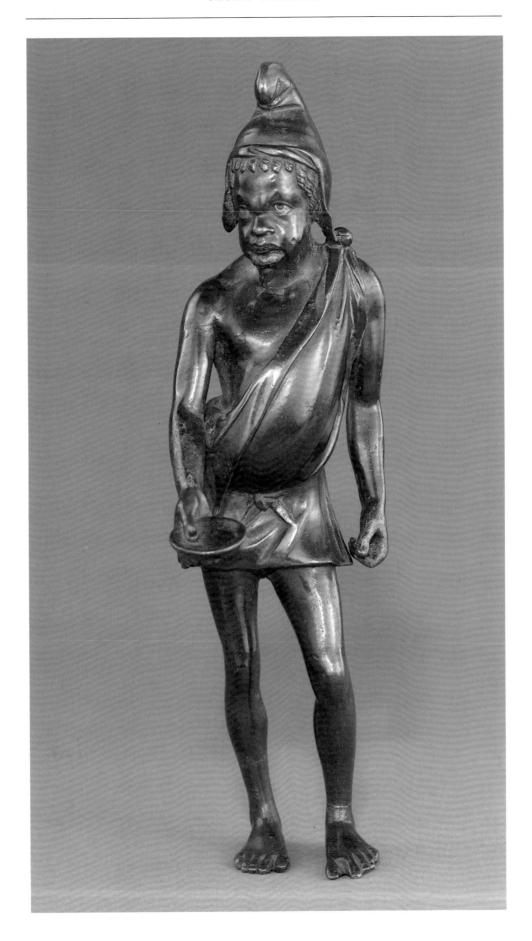

Observant of the characteristic mannerisms of the humble and impoverished, the sculptor has effectively captured the tentative extension of the right arm, the forward thrust of the head that is subtly echoed in the curl of the cap's peak, the rather malevolent stare, and the slack mouth in which the lips are parted not in speech but dull resignation. Whether a beggar, as he has been restored, or perhaps a slave carrying a basket or a lamp, his low station is clear. The artist has allowed no sense of dignity or significance to intrude. Rather, he has taken a banal image that was probably all too familiar in the streets of every Hellenistic city and transformed it into a sophisticated caricature, cynically devoid of emotional content but conceived and executed with a sensuous refinement rarely surpassed among ancient bronzes of any period.

Like most caricatures of blacks, this bronze has been considered a late Hellenistic product of the city of Alexandria since its initial publication by Cooney. The African subject, the intentionally induced black patina, and the interest in a detailed, though decorative, depiction of a lowlife character have been cited persuasively as evidence for this provenance, and the hair treatment in particular provides evidence for a date in the early part of the first century BC. Compositionally and qualitatively, its closest relative is the magnificent bronze musician found at Chalon-sur-Saône, now in the Cabinet des Médailles, which traditionally has been attributed to an Alexandrian workshop as well.

Indeed, the city of Alexandria is known to have produced large numbers of bronzes for the export market, especially in the late Hellenistic and Roman Imperial periods. As mentioned in the previous entry [19], however, scholars such as Rolley have correctly questioned the logic of assigning Hellenistic bronze representations to this Egyptian metropolis on the basis of subject or style, regardless of ac-

tual findspot, pointing out that the popular motifs associated with Alexandrian craftsmen would quickly have become part of an international vocabulary available for repetition in any Hellenistic workshop with greater or lesser degrees of skill. At the same time, ancient literary sources and representations in all media demonstrate that Ethiopians were no strangers in the Hellenistic cities around the Mediterranean, especially in Greece and Italy.

Unfortunately, systematic excavations in Alexandria have not been extensive. To date, no bronze comparable to this figure in quality of surface finish has been recovered from controlled excavations in Alexandria. However, a statuette such as the Cleveland Harpocrates [21] which is difficult to explain as anything other than Alexandrian in origin, offers strong evidence that bronzes with superbly polished surfaces were produced there, together with the more characteristic, rougher casts that show little surface finish. Therefore, though no provenance is known for this statuette prior to its appearance in England in the second half of the nineteenth century, Cooney's original well-argued attribution to Alexandria is most likely correct.

CONDITION: Analysis of the figure by x-ray fluorescence spectrometry has proven that both the proper right hand with attached bowl and the proper right foot are modern restorations; the composition of the metal of these two parts is identical but differs from the composition of the body. The composition of the left foot, which has been broken at the ankle and reattached, is not comparable to either those restorations or the original fabric, and may therefore be an earlier, perhaps ancient, repair. Ancient patches show where the casting flaws were repaired: on the sternum, the left front side of the neck, the upper right arm just beneath the shoulder, the left arm on the outside below the shoulder, and on the back above the elbow. A small casting bubble in the left cheek has left a visible depression. Both arms may have been made separately and attached just below the shoulders. Surface abrasions are visible on the outside and front of the right thigh and the front of the left. The figure is otherwise very well preserved, with all inlays intact. The drilled pupils may have been filled with some secondary material, now lost, but they need not have been for expressive purposes.

The surface is covered with a fairly uniform, black patina, worn thin over the left front of the exomis and the buttocks. Some patches of red cuprite on the surface of the right forearm are evidence of corrosion.

EX COLLECTION: Lord Lonsdale, Lowther Castle, Cumberland, England.

EXHIBITED: The Cleveland Museum of Art, December 1963, *The Year in Review for 1963*, 292, illus. 265, no. 82.

PUBLISHED: "Acquisitions Supplement," *The Burlington Magazine* CVIII (March 1965) 159, fig. 73, 161.
J. Cooney, "Siren and Ba, Birds of a Feather," *BClevMus* LV (1968) 270-271, n. 18.
F. M. Snowden 1970, 73, fig. 43.
J. Cooney, "A Miscellany of Ancient Bronzes," *BClevMus* LVIII (1971) 210-213, figs. 1-4.
A. Adriani, "A proposito di un bronzetto del Museo di Cleveland," *Studi Miscellanei* XXII (1974-1975) 17-20, pls. 1-3.

NOTES: The condition statement was written with the assistance of Frederick L. Hollendonner and Bruce Christman.

See references given with [19] for the role of blacks in antiquity, and images of the Cabinet des Médailles musician and the discussion of its possible Alexandrian provenance.

For the description of the physical features considered by the ancients to be characteristic of the Ethiopian race, see F. M. Snowden 1970, 5-11.

For the intentional black patination of the surfaces of Egyptian bronzes, see J. Cooney, *Zeitschrift für Ägyptische Sprache und Altertumskund* XCIII (1966) 43-47, and *BClevMus* LV (1968) 268-271; idem, LVIII (1971) 212.

For the dating of the image on the basis of hairstyle, see J. D. Cooney (*BClevMus*) 1971, 212; also, compare the dressed hair of the limestone portrait of Arsinoë II, Deified (Metropolitan Museum of Art 20.2.21), no. 123 in B. Von Bothmer, *Egyptian Sculpture of the Late Period, 700 BC to 100 AD*, exh. cat. (Brooklyn, The Brooklyn Museum, 1960) 159-160, pls. 114-115, figs. 307-310.

On the exomis as appropriate garb for the banausoi, see N. Himmelmann-Wildschütz 1983, 77.

21. Harpocrates

The infant son of the Egyptian deities Osiris and Isis, Harpocrates (from *Hor-pa-khred*, meaning Horus the child) was one of the most popular of the oriental gods adopted by the classical world as Alexander expanded the borders of the Macedonian empire. The sun god, the mature Horus, was the conqueror of darkness and evil, and was associated by the fifth-century Greeks with the Olympian Apollo (Herodotus II.144). Although the infant Harpocrates is mentioned in texts as early as the late third millennium BC, the myth of his childhood—in which he was magically conceived by his mother after the death of his father and grew up to avenge his father's murder—seems to have become widespread only in later times, as the vast majority of the preserved images of the god come from the late Hellenistic and Roman Imperial periods. Combining elements of a mystery religion with some hope of a life after death, the story appealed to the troubled populations of the turbulent Hellenistic world. With the foundation of Alexandria, the worship of the Hellenized Harpocrates quickly spread throughout the Mediterranean and beyond, reaching even as far abroad as Britain.

The images of Harpocrates offer some of the best illustrations for the syncretic nature of Hellenistic iconography, as the initially Egyptian deity took on the attributes of several Greek gods. Represented here in his standard Hellenistic guise as a plump child of six or seven, he stands in a languid pose that originally required a support beneath his left arm. Covered with a layer of baby fat, the contours of his torso and limbs are generally reduced to rounded curves that show little interest in the careful description of the underlying musculature, but extraordinary attention to surface finish. As he rests his weight on his elbow, which once leaned on a now-missing support, he thrusts his right hip out to the side above his engaged leg; his left leg bends slightly at the knee and his foot is set forward, the sole flat on the ground. Over his left shoulder, he wears the skin of a feline that was also once draped across the top of the lost support, and the position of his left fingers shows that he originally held something large in the crook of his arm.

The long, thick locks of hair curling softly around his face are held in place by the fillet that encircles his head. Attached to it is a strap that runs directly over the top of his head, tapering from front to back. The strap originates just behind a large cavity in the top of his head, which is partially hidden by the small knot of forelocks pulled up over the center of his forehead (cf. [72]).

The facial features appear surprisingly mature for the childish figure. His large eyes, inlaid with silver sclera, are set far apart on either side of his tiny nose, and the deeply drilled pupils and irises, perhaps originally inlaid with stone or glass, give the bronze an expression that is more wise than naive. This impression is carried further in his mouth whose full lips appear unsmiling and almost sullen.

Were it not for his expressive gesture, the pudgy figure might be mistaken for Eros, the god of love, who also enjoyed enormous popularity during the Hellenistic period and who was similarly represented as a precocious child. His right index finger raised to his mouth is fundamental to his identification as Harpocrates, however. Variously understood by both Roman and later scholars as a reference to an oath of silence—intended for the initiates of his cult—or the finger sucking typical of infancy, this sign may be better interpreted as a reference to the infant god's divine self-sufficiency, that is, Harpocrates as the "self-nourishing Nourisher."

Besides this gesture, other attributes confirm the bronze's identification as the young Horus. Though the most important of them are actually missing from this statuette, they may be reconstructed on the basis of the numerous surviving parallels that attest to the god's popularity. The hole in the front of the head was intended to hold a separately cast miniature double crown of Upper and Lower

GREEK, PROBABLY ALEXANDRIAN, LATE HELLENISTIC, CA. 50 BC. H. 27 CM. THE CLEVELAND MUSEUM OF ART, PURCHASE FROM THE J. H. WADE FUND, 72.6

Egypt (pshent) that was traditionally worn by the pharaohs to signify their unifying control of the country. Assisted by the now-missing column or prop beneath the elbow, the left arm once held a large cornucopia appropriate to the god's role, like that of the Greek infant Plutus, as a provider of fruitfulness and bounty from the earth. The feline skin over the shoulder was borrowed from either the iconography of Heracles, another avenger of evil, or the retinue of Dionysus, with whose mysteries Harpocrates also came to be associated.

Although the preserved images of Harpocrates are plentiful, few are as charming or as well crafted as the Cleveland bronze. The proportions of the large head and fleshy body emphasize the youthfulness of the deity, as do the loosely flowing curls that are in especially high relief around the face. Though borrowed directly from the earlier, more hieratic Egyptian images of the god, the forefinger raised to the lips has been transformed from the significant gesture of a powerful god to the disarming gesture of an innocent child. The effective use of silver inlays for the eyes heightens the intensity of the unusual expression created by their widespread placement in the face. Even the twisted paws of the pelt dangling from the left arm show the artist's extraordinary sensitivity to his medium.

Because so many similar images of Harpocrates exist, Cooney hypothesized in his publication of this bronze that all may reflect a single well-known Hellenistic monument, perhaps the cult figure of an Alexandrian temple. The tremendous variations in scale, quality, and attributes of the surviving images do not contradict this, and their general similarity to the unique marble statue of Harpocrates found in 1936 at Ras-el-Soda, near Alexandria, offers convincing support for Cooney's argument, although the marble is itself a Roman copy of an earlier Hellenistic original.

The hipshot stance common to all the images suggests a Praxitelean inspira-

134

tion, recalling as it does the poses of his Hermes with the Infant Dionysus or the Apollo Sauroctonus. But the sensitive combination in the Cleveland bronze of the naturalistic proportions of the childish body, the minimal interest in anatomical definition, and the sensual and refined treatment of the fleshy polished surfaces can only be the product of a late Hellenistic artist. Comparisons with other representations of Harpocrates and Erotes of similar physical types suggests that a date in the first century BC is most likely.

The Egyptian origins of Harpocrates, together with the Hellenized treatment of the subject, surely support the statuette's reported Alexandrian provenance, but since Harpocrates enjoyed enormous prestige all around the Hellenistic world, this is not proof enough. A smaller but more important piece of evidence may be found in the treatment of the upper eyelids, which are quite comparable in the extended length of their outer ends to those of the Baker dancing woman [14]. As Thompson pointed out in her discussion of its origins, this distinctive feature, unusual in the Greco-Roman world, is characteristic of Egyptian or Egyptianizing sculpture, in which it serves as an indication in relief of the extended cosmetic line. Its presence in the Harpocrates lends further credence to the possibility of an Egyptian, and most likely Alexandrian, workshop.

Among the Greek statuettes included in this exhibition that have been associated with the city of Alexandria, the well-preserved ancient surface of this piece offers the most compelling evidence for the use of fine surface polish on an Alexandrian bronze. Unlike the Boston and Cleveland images of blacks [19, 20]—for which the closest parallels have been found in France and Switzerland—or the Baker dancing woman, which can be compared in style and subject with the terracottas of Asia Minor and Greece as well as those of Egypt, or the emaciated youth from Dum-

barton Oaks [25], which was found in France and is without a convincing parallel, the statuette of Harpocrates has its closest iconographic associations with the terracottas, bronzes, and marble sculpture found in the vicinity of the Egyptian city. And although there may be no evidence for a bronze of similar quality and comparable surface finish excavated in the great Hellenistic capital, neither has an equivalent been excavated elsewhere. In this case, the balance falls in favor of Alexandria, and the Cleveland Harpocrates provides at last some positive justification for the attribution of other unprovenanced bronzes with polished surfaces to the ancient foundries of this enigmatic city.

CONDITION: Besides the base and support on which he leaned his left elbow, the god has lost the miniature pshent, once inset in the cavity on the top of his head; the cornucopia that he held with the tip in his left hand and the horn resting along his arm; and one rear paw and possibly the tail of the feline skin draped over his left arm. The figure is otherwise complete and beautifully preserved.

In order to achieve a uniform perfection of surface in this complex pose, the artist made the hollow-cast statuette in four pieces, which were then assembled. The left arm and its covering skin, the right arm, and the left leg were all cast separately and attached to the torso with added molten metal. Evidence for this process can be seen in the tiny lines of casting bubbles visible around the joints. The clay core remains inside the body and the head and neck appear in x-radiographs to be filled with lead, which prevents learning if it was cast separately. Cracks are visible around both feet, but these appear to be from cooling, not cast-on additions. A casting flaw appears on the left side of the top of the head. The statuette is covered with a smooth marbled greenish-black patina with evidence of corrosion only in the cracks around the ankles.

PROVENANCE: Said to have come from Alexandria.

EXHIBITED: Chapel Hill, N.C., William Hayes Ackland Memorial Art Center, March 7-April 18, 1976, *Small Sculptures in Bronze from the Classical World*, ed. G. K. Sams, no. 33, entry by Edwin L. Brown.

PUBLISHED: J. D. Cooney, "Harpocrates, the Dutiful Son," *BClevMus* LIX (1972) 284-290, figs. 1-3.
A. P. Kozloff, "Harpocrates and the Sacred Goose," *The Ancient World* III (September 1980) figs. 4-5.
American Research Center in Egypt, Newsletter no. 125 (Spring 1984) 11.

NOTES: The condition statement was prepared with the assistance of Frederick L. Hollendonner and Bruce Christman.

On Harpocrates generally, see Plutarch, *Moralia* V, *De Iside et Osiride*, CCCLVIII.18-22, CCCLXVII.38; 367.40; *DarSag* III, 1:12-13; *RE* VIII, 2, col. 2435, s.v. Horus.

For the interpretation of Harpocrates' gesture of the finger to the mouth as an abjuration for silence in Roman times, see Catullus' poem CII, where the name Harpocrates is employed to describe the poet's ability to keep a secret; also poem LXXIV, where a person reduced to silence is referred to as Harpocrates. Both appear in *The Poems of Gaius Valerius Catullus*, tr. F. W. Cornish (Cambridge, Mass., 1976).

For the gesture as an indication of childishness, see Cooney 1972, 286; also, D. K. Hill 1949, 36, no. 68.

For the gesture as a sign of self-sufficiency, see E. L. Brown 1976, with reference to A. M. El-Khachab, "Some Gem Amulets Depicting Harpocrates Seated on a Lotus Flower," *The Journal of Egyptian Archaeology* LVII (1971) 143, especially n. 10.

For the Roman marble statue of Harpocrates found at Ras-el-Soda and discussion of its possible reflection of a famous Hellenistic original, see A. Adriani, "Fouilles et découvertes-Alexandrie," *Annuaire du Musée Greco-Romain* (1935-1939) 140-142, pls. I, LVI.

22. Artisan

In this large statuette of a craftsman or artisan, a Hellenistic artist created an arresting study of introspection and age. The stocky bearded man stands with his head lowered, his chin pressed to his chest, and his brow creased with concentration. His finely articulated features are set quite low in his face, within the tapering contours of the lower half and well beneath his broad forehead. The inlaid silver eyes, closely set on either side of his nose, have incised irises that strengthen the impression of intense absorption. The incisions around the irises are not single continuous lines, however, as one would expect, but short, unconnected strokes in the left and doubled contours in the right, and though straight and small, his nose is displaced noticeably to the proper right side of his face. His mouth is framed by the short strands of his mustache, while his lips are separated by a distinctive deep groove.

His left arm, bent at the elbow, rests on his pronounced paunch, while he holds the flat palm of his hand below his right armpit. The position of his now-missing right arm may be at least partially understood, since what is left of his shoulder indicates that it was extended forward and down. On the basis of parallels in terracotta and bronze, his arm has been tentatively reconstructed as bent at the elbow with the hand raised to support his bowed head. As no evidence remains on the surface of his head to show where his hand may have touched it, this must be accepted as speculative. His preserved left leg is rigid, the foot pressed flat on the ground. The elevation of both the right hip and shoulder that is obvious from the back should indicate that his missing right leg stood out a bit to the front and side, sharing equally in the distributed weight of his solid torso.

The subject's inferior social position is suggested by his costume: he wears a short tunic (exomis) tied over one shoulder, the traditional garb of laborers, fishermen, beggars, and slaves (cf. [20]). The wax tablet (diptych), slipped beneath the knot at the front of his fringed belt, is either the sketchpad of a craftsman or a book intended to suggest the man's literacy. His age is clearly rendered. As if his balding head and furrowed cheeks are not evidence enough, the flaccid flesh of his upper chest and arms, especially clear around his left armpit, and his pendulous belly betray the weakened muscle tone of a tiring body. At the same time, his preserved left leg shows a still-powerful calf while the massive thigh confirms a life of strenuous, heavy labor.

Whatever the man's status, his image has been endowed with a grave dignity uncharacteristic of a genre subject. The stance, as reconstructed, has been conceived as a sensitive balance between physical stability and psychological acuity. Certainly no caricature, the overly large head and self-absorbed facial expression are treated with the seriousness due an important subject. Such textures as the well-defined fleecy curls of his hair, contrasting so effectively with the polished height of his forehead, and the broad folds of the exomis, expressing the coarseness of its heavy fabric, demonstrate the care with which the artist made the statuette.

This noble treatment of an ostensibly prosaic subject has led some scholars to see the figure as a portrait of a well-known Greek of low station. This argument may be supported by the fact that the pose is reflected in varying degrees of accuracy in terracotta figurines and small bronzes, attesting to a fairly widespread knowledge of the original. Dedalus, the mythological inventor and architect; Aesop, the fable-teller and slave; Diogenes, the Cynic philosopher; and Chrysippus, the Stoic philosopher, are among the proposed identifications. To date, however, the most convincing argument has been made for his identification as Phidias. That the most famous of the Classical architects and sculptors should be commemorated in an imaginary portrait during the Hellenistic period is not inconceivable. The exomis

GREEK, PROBABLY ALEXANDRIAN, LATE HELLENISTIC, CA. 50 BC. H. 40.3 CM. METROPOLITAN MUSEUM OF ART, ROGERS FUND, 1972, 1972.11.1

would surely be appropriate to his position as an artisan, and as Bothmer has observed, the bare left shoulder would have permitted the sculptor's mallet-wielding left arm to move more vigorously than the right; the diptych would be the sketchpad of his craft; the once-robust physique is suggestive of his physically demanding profession. But no preserved ancient source records evidence for his deformity and such a dwarfish physique in an imaginary portrait would seem incongruous given his stature as an artist.

Whether the imaginary likeness of a known individual or not, the statue is an extraordinary portrayal of an inwardly focused psychological state. Wrapped up in his thoughts as well as his own arms, he stands pondering, oblivious to everything around him. Such a profound interest in the accurate depiction of a state of mind is characteristic of Hellenistic artists, who explored the expressive possibilities of all media. At the same time, there is an honesty and unflinching directness in the description of the coarsely proportioned, aging body that is far removed from the idealizing tendencies of the earlier Classical style.

The fascination with déclassé subjects and an almost clinical interest in the depiction of psychological character and physical disfigurement has long been associated with Alexandrian artists. Thus, it comes as no surprise that several scholars have assigned this statuette to a workshop in that Hellenistic city and presented some persuasive evidence for this connection. For the subject, Alexandrian bronzes offer no comparisons. Yet, as Himmelmann has pointed out, some Alexandrian terracottas do provide close parallels, especially for such individual details as the diptych in the belt and the hand across the chest. Small, fairly crude, and poorly finished, however, the Alexandrian terracotta genre figures lack the intelli-

gent refinement of the Metropolitan bronze and appear to have been made more for amusement than emotional impact.

Among the other known bronzes from North Africa, one large figure (H. 65 cm.) from Morocco offers a particularly telling comparison for the New York statuette. This is the so-called "Old Fisherman," found in 1943 at Volubilis (Figure 22a). Dated, like the artisan, to the first century BC and attributed to Alexandrian manufacture, this short peasant figure is also old and balding, and dressed only in an exomis. His face has rather more the appearance of a rough caricature than that of a sensitive character study, however. His deeply creased forehead, heavy brows, and clenched teeth—fully described with incision—are exaggerated for an almost melodramatic surface effect. But though the Moroccan piece has little in common stylistically with the Metropolitan bronze, the subject and scale are similar.

The New York artisan is finished as carefully as it has been composed. As the Cleveland Harpocrates [21] has demonstrated that such perfection of finish was well within the capabilities of Alexandrian bronzeworkers, and as the subject of this bronze, if not its style, finds its closest parallels among Alexandrian terracottas, Boucher's original suggestion of an Alexandrian provenance is most probable.

The relatively large scale of this figure is most common among the products of the later Hellenistic period, and the distinctive treatment of the curls with their hollow centers in particular may be compared to the hair of the Stephanos athlete, which has been convincingly dated to the middle of the first century BC. As John Herrmann discusses further regarding the Roman bronzes, this feature is a good criterion for a date around the middle of the first century BC.

Great effort has been expended in repairing the numerous large flaws that disfigured the original cast, and the subtly modeled surface retains evidence of its polish. Without a hint of detachment or superiority, the artist has created a sophisticated image of a laborer, less than perfect in physical form but intelligent and shrewd.

CONDITION: The right arm is missing from just beneath the shoulder; that it was cast separately and attached is clear from the slight flange still preserved above the armpit near the fold of the exomis. The right leg is lost, and lower selvage of the exomis which would have covered the front of it is broken off irregularly; it too was probably cast on separately, attached just within the lower edge of the exomis. The left leg, in contrast, is complete under the drapery and there is insufficient room for the similar restoration of the right. The tips of the index and middle fingers of the left hand are damaged. Sections of the hair on the back and upper sides of the head appear worn, as does the flat forehead.

The hollow cast is generally thick-walled, except for the left upper arm. The casting flaws marring the original surface have mostly been repaired; patches are visible on the left leg's calf, inner thigh, and foot. There also appears to have been an effort to cast on a repair in the weak section of the left upper arm, as fine air bubbles outline the contours of the added metal. The underside of the foot is hollow and appears to retain some traces of lead.

The surface is primarily a warm golden-brown color, close to the original metal, as if little patina survives. Large irregular patches of blackish encrustation are found on the cheeks near the eyes, on the exomis and the bare flesh of the left back and shoulder, and on the back of the left calf, while traces appear between the locks of the hair and beard.

PROVENANCE: Said to have been found in North Africa, probably at Cherchel, Algeria.

EX COLLECTIONS: M. J. Bousquet; M. L. Balsan.

PUBLISHED: S. Boucher-Colozier, "Un bronze d'époque Alexandrine: Réalisme et caricature," *MonPiot* LIV (1965) 25-38, figs. 1, 7, pl. V. New York, Metropolitan Museum of Art, *Notable Acquisitions, 1965-1975* (New York, 1975) 117, illus. J. Frel, *Greek Portraits in the J. Paul Getty Museum* (Malibu, Calif., 1981) 17, fig. 44. N. Himmelmann, "Realistic Art in Alexandria," *ProcBritAc* LXVII (1981) 205-207. N. Himmelmann-Wildschütz 1983, 76-85, pls. 56-58. J. R. Mertens (*BMMA*) 1985, 60-61, no. 41. S. Nodelman, "The Portraits of Brutus the Tyrranicide," in *Ancient Portraits in the J. Paul Getty Museum*, J. Frel et al., 1 (Malibu, Calif., 1987) 78-79, figs. 27a-c.

NOTES: For the suggestion that the figure may be Chrysippus, or another less prominent Stoic, as well as consideration of Aesop and Diogenes, see S. Boucher-Colozier 1965, pp. 35-38.

For the possibility of identification as Dedalus, which he then rejects, see N. Himmelmann-Wildschütz 1983, 78, nos. 283, 284; and *ProcBritAc* LXVII (1981) 205.

For the identification as Phidias, see J. Frel 1981, and most recently, S. Nodelman 1987.

On Alexandrianism, see N. Himmelmann-Wildschütz 1983, with extensive earlier bibliography.

For the Volubilis bronze, see C. Boube-Piccot 1969, 1:169-172, pls. 103-107. I thank Ariel Herrmann for bringing this reference to my attention.

For the flat, fleecy curls of the hair with hollow centers, compare the hair of the copies of the Stephanos athlete, P. Zanker, *Klassizistische Statuen* (Mainz, 1974) pls. 44-45, dated by Zanker to the first century BC (p. 53); also, the bronze head of Heracles in the Istanbul Museum: I. Aksit, *The Istanbul Archaeological Museum* (Istanbul, 1981) unpaginated, col. pl. on [41].

Figure 22a. *Old Fisherman*. Bronze, H. 65 cm. From Volubilis. Morocco, Rabat Museum, inv. V. 193. After Christiane Boube-Piccot, *Les Bronzes Antiques du Maroc* (Rabat, 1969) 1: pl. 103.

23. Pair of Pans

Originally the deity of shepherds in pastoral Arcadia, Pan appealed strongly to the imagination of the Greeks from the fifth century BC on and was perhaps even more popular, though less respected, among the Romans. As a hybrid creature—half goat, half man—he represented an aspect of untamed nature that could delight in the freedom of the woods and fields, and enjoy the bucolic pleasures that had become more and more remote to civilized man in the developing urban centers. A god who appealed to the nostalgia for simpler times, he also came to epitomize the pleasure-seeking self-indulgence associated with paganism. His caprine features were absorbed into early Christian iconography to represent no less than the Devil himself, and Plutarch's description (*De defectu oraculorum*, ch. 17) of the experience of the Egyptian Thamous, who was sailing by the Paxos Islands when he heard a voice three times announce that the great Pan was dead, has been interpreted since the fourteenth century as the divine message signaling the end of pagan religion.

Actually one of the oldest of the native Greek gods, Pan was hardly known outside of Arcadia before his appearance in 490 BC to the Athenian herald Phidippides on Mount Parthenion above Tegea, while on his way to the Spartans to request aid before the battle of Marathon. According to Herodotus (VI.105), Phidippides was accosted by Pan, who asked why it was that, though he had always been a friend to the Athenians, he had never received proper homage. At the conclusion of the war, the victorious Athenians remembered the god's appearance and dedicated a sanctuary to him in a cave on the north side of the Acropolis. His popularity then spread quickly and widely.

Pan's closest associations in myth and iconography are with the nymphs, as he passed his days and nights with them making love, dancing, and playing music on the seven-reeded pipes (syrinx). His identifying features are, in fact, his goat horns, shaggy legs and tail, and the Pan pipes. His upper torso and arms alone are human, while his face may be a variable combination of goat and human characteristics.

Because of his lusty nature and semi-bestial image, Pan's identity was easily confused and intertwined with that of the satyrs and silens. In the fifth century, his images had already become difficult to separate from those of members of the Dionysiac thiasos. One unfortunate aspect of this confusion is that it diminished the god's own stature; he began to appear in multiples instead of remaining a unique deity. He also assumed the servile attendant qualities of the Dionysiac acolytes, and in this capacity, like the satyrs, the figure of Pan comes to be a symbolic reference to the god of wine and fertility, rather than to his own bucolic cult. Especially among the Romans, his image became a popular attachment for banquet furniture, and it is most likely this incarnation of Pan that is represented by this pair of large bronze statuettes.

Stepping forward in a dancelike pose with their right hooves lifted on their cloven tips and both arms raised, these splendid creatures immediately display the rude bestiality of their kind. Their heads are lowered slightly to the left, and the coarse features—huge shaggy brows, broad flat nose, gaping mouth with teeth exposed, and the intent but dumbly threatening expression of the eyes—indicate beings totally lacking in refined sensitivity or intellect. No horns appear on their heads, though two cuts in the head of one (designated here as Pan A) may have once held a pair; but besides their hirsute thighs and hooves, the large scent glands on the sides of their necks, hairlines that extend far down on their foreheads, beards oddly formed of two long locks growing from the sides of their mouths rather than chins, and the spiraling tufts of fur on their bodies proclaim their animal nature. On each, the penis is obvious but not aroused, curving upward on the furry belly

GREEK, LATE
HELLENISTIC,
1ST C. BC.
H. 40 CM.
SHELBY AND LEON LEVY

142

A

to a distinct point; behind, a small curled tail grows out of the base of the spine.

The proper left arm of each is stretched forward to the side, with the hands, palm down, loosely closed. The thumb is flat and straight against the edge of the palm, while the index and small fingers are lifted slightly. The right arms are raised as well, but pulled sharply back to the sides with elbows bent; the semi-closed hands are lifted to the level of the shoulders. Though identical in postures, the Pans seem to have been distinguished by the attributes they held, Pan A in the right hand and Pan B in the left. No trace lingers to suggest what they were, but the size and shape of the hollows between the fingers do not suggest either the syrinx or castanets (krotala).

The artist who modeled the original after which these twins were cast clearly devoted great attention to describing the torso's anatomy. The creatures' muscular power is especially evident at the back, where their shoulders ripple from the tension of the outstretched limbs. An artful play of torsion and countertorsion is created by this extension and retraction of their arms that alternates with that of their legs, giving the pose an extraordinary vitality appropriate to the animalistic subjects.

Certain minor details beyond the attributes in the hands separate the two statuettes. Pan B has no hair actually growing onto his forehead, the whorl of fur on his chest is in lower relief, and his pubic hair is incised with short strokes rather than modeled. Also, the shaggy locks of his legs are less carefully defined. At the same time, his penis is more rounded, the irises of his eyes are effectively raised around the drilled pupils, and his tail curls in a more pronounced spiral. These distinctions suggest that the pair were cast separately in molds made from a single model (or patrix) in which the pose and all the features of the surface were worked out in a general way, but that many of the finer details were added individually in the finishing process. These particulars are minor, however, and in no way detract from the remarkable similarity of the pair.

The unusual occurrence of such twins identical in scale, style, fabric, and patination can be explained most readily by their having been parts of a single original group. The possibility that they were co-attachments to a piece of furniture may be suggested by the presence of a deep hole in the head of Pan B. Images of Pan often served as caryatid figures in the late Hellenistic and Roman periods, together with satyrs and silens, so their appearance supporting a table or tripod would not be unexpected. Satyr A, however, preserves only shallow cuttings on the top of his head, two of which most likely held his horns. It is not impossible, however, that whatever they supported actually rested on the curved surfaces of their horns, which might account for the loss of these features in figures otherwise so well preserved.

The Levy statuettes have much in common with many late Hellenistic representations of hybrid beings in their active stances, superbly modeled torsos, and such details as the stylized spiral tufts of hair on the chests and the glands on the sides of the necks. In all probability, however, these Pans are copies or imitations of an earlier Hellenistic original. Particularly the slack treatment of the fur on the thighs and almost mechanical incision for the strands of the beards are suggestive of repeated formulas, consistent with their basically decorative purpose and justified by their duplication for use as attachments on furniture. Also, the dull expression and the mannered posture that seems more theatrical than momentary may be understood as resulting from their being fine multiple reproductions of a late Hellenistic creation.

Though the Levy Pans are far more vigorous and retain their integrity as individual figures in spite of their roles as caryatids or other attachments, they may

B

A

B

be compared in purpose with the magnificent bronze satyrs that form a tripod from Herculaneum. Dated by Pernice to the Hellenistic period as well, these figures have been reduced more to components of the tripod structure, with their legs joined solidly from hips to hooves which rest on bases at the bottoms. Still, their extended arms and well-developed torsos show a comparable sophistication in modeling and their gestures, a similar theatricality.

Unique documents of a representation of the god that is otherwise unknown, the Levy statuettes must assume a special place in the iconography of Pan. They restore some of the dignity that he had lost in the long course of his assimilation with the Dionysiac thiasos, and together present one of the noblest images of the Arcadian goat-god that has survived from ancient times. No fawning acolyte or sedentary flutist, this Pan recalls again the free spirit of the meadows and woodlands who danced with nymphs and slept in grottos. Strong from his rugged existence and primitive in his instincts, he is the ideal embodiment of uncivilized nature and Arcadian bliss. Though such a time and place never existed, enlightened society has never ceased to mourn its loss.

CONDITION: Both of the figures are hollow cast and show evidence that the arms were made separately for attachment. Their condition is generally excellent. Pan A is missing only the index finger of his left hand, which may have been lost together with the attribute he held; the little finger of the same hand is cracked around its base. There is a small hole in the surface of the throat under the chin and a casting crack in the back of the neck. On the back of the right arm, two large gouges mar the surface.

Pan B holds a kind of tube in the center of his right hand, through which the missing attribute must have passed; he has lost the last knuckle of his left index finger and the last two knuckles of his left small finger. He has a small hole in the top of his head, presumably for attachment. There are ancient patches visible on his right buttock and his left lower back at the side. Pan A is covered with a greenish-gray patina that shows some irregular reddish patches of cuprite on the torso and legs. Pan B shows the same greenish-gray patina on the head and right side of the body; the surface turns a darker green on the back, and much of the left side of the figure is covered with a reddish-brown patina.

UNPUBLISHED.

NOTES: For the subject of Pan see W. H. Roscher, "Pan" in *Lexikon der griechischen und römischen Mythologie*, III (Leipzig, 1881-1904) 1347-1482; *DarSag* IV, 1: 296-302; *RE*, suppl. VII, col. 590-1008; also R. Herbig, *Pan, der griechische Bocksgott; Versuch einer Monographie* (Frankfurt, 1949); P. Borgeaud, *Recherches sur le dieu Pan* (Rome, 1979) with extensive bibliography and discussion of mythical Arcadia; and H. Walter, *Pans Wiederkehr; Der Gott der griechischen Wildnis* (Munich, 1980).

On the lasting influence of mythical Arcadia in later European art and thought, see E. Panofsky, "Et in Arcadia Ego: Poussin and the Elegiac Tradition," in *Meaning in the Visual Arts* (Garden City, NY, 1955) 295-320.

For the spiral tufts of hair on the torsos, compare those on the aged marble centaur in the Louvre (in M. Bieber 1961, fig. 583) and the rosso antico centaur in the Getty Museum (*The J. Paul Getty Museum Handbook* [Malibu, Calif., 1986] 37); this feature also appears on the chest of the Old Fisherman found in Volubilis, now in the Rabat (Museum Figure 21a).

The bulbous glands also appear on the necks of the youthful centaurs as well as on satyrs. See M. Bieber 1961, figs. 570, 576, 582, and 584.

For the beard growing in two long strands from the sides of the mouth, compare the Roman copy of the late Hellenistic group of Pan and Daphnis, in R. Herbig 1949, pl. XVI, 2, and the Pan on a Roman Dionysiac sarcophagus in Dresden, ibid., pl. XXX.

For the tripod of satyrs from Herculaneum, see E. Pernice, *Gefässe und Geräte aus Bronze. Die Hellenistische Kunst in Pompeji* IV (Berlin, 1925) 37, pl. X.

For use of Pans as caryatid figures, see R. Herbig 1949, pls. XXII and XXV; *DarSag*, 300.

For a Roman bronze figure of Pan in a similar pose, see D. K. Hill 1949, 39, pl. 19, no. 78.

24. Boxer

With the confident arrogance of a victor, the athlete stands frontally, his weight resting firmly on his right foot and his unengaged left foot placed back, turned out naturally to the side. His right arm, flexed at the elbow, is extended to the front and side, and he has lifted his gaze to follow the loosely closed right hand raised above his head. His left arm, also extended somewhat to the side, is bent more sharply at the elbow, and the hand, with fingers curled, is raised in front just above the level of his shoulder.

The choice of this self-conscious posture was intentional, for it allowed the artist to focus the observer's attention fully on the beauty of the nude male form. With arms extended to the sides, the thick neck, broad shoulders, and massive chest are shown to maximum advantage, while the copper nipples of the chest, inlaid in squares instead of circles, serve to focus attention on the dominant pectorals.

Though the overall impression is one of refined grandeur, the specifics of the figure's anatomy are treated quite summarily, with little or no reference to the complex underlying musculature. The contours distinguishing one part of the body from another, such as the iliac crests and the inguinal ligament, are softly rounded, as if the skin were inflated instead of stretched taut over rippling muscles. This simplification of detail applies as well to the articulation of the back, arms, and legs; and though the fingers and toes were separated by deep incisions in the wax model, little effort was made to define them more precisely after casting.

This generalization is particularly evident in the face. The athlete raises his head; but his features are modeled softly, more suggestive than descriptive of his actual appearance. This impression may be intensified somewhat by the loss of inlays for his eyes, as the roughened surfaces of the sclera and shallowly drilled pupils

GREEK,
ALEXANDRIAN,
LATE HELLENISTIC,
CA. 50 BC-AD 50.
H. 21 CM.
THE CLEVELAND
MUSEUM OF ART,
LEONARD C.
HANNA, JR., FUND,
85.137

may originally have been covered with silver. But his nose and mouth show little evidence of refinement, and his overall expression indicates that he has more physical than intellectual power.

That he is an athlete is beyond question, as the thick neck and broad chest of his superbly conditioned body show the positive results of years of training. More significant evidence, however, is his hairstyle, cropped short all over the skull except for one lock left long at the crown, the cirrus that hangs down, like a tail, in back. Known from many other representations of athletes, this style is associated with professional fighters. But as these fighters could be wrestlers, boxers, or contestants in combination boxing-kicking-wrestling matches (pancratiasts), other evidence may help to distinguish his special event. From the position of his arms and hands, his complete concentration on his right fist, the hole drilled deeply into his proper right hand between the thumb and index finger, and a corresponding though shallower hole in his left hand between thumb and forefinger, the gesture may be restored as the stretching of the thongs with which he will bind his hands before fighting (see also [57]). As neither wrestlers nor pancratiasts fought with bound hands, he must be a boxer, and his swollen ears are surely the trademarks of a seasoned pugilist.

The reduced interest in surface detail, combined with a contrived but sophisticated posture, may justify a date for the figure in the late Hellenistic period of approximately the first century BC to the first century AD. The works of the Pasiteleans and other classicizing sculptors began to counter the taste for exaggerated poses and explicitly defined surfaces—whether flesh or fabric—by trying to evoke some reflections of the serene dignity of fifth-century art within the expanded vocabulary of Hellenistic imagery. Until now, the cirrus has been found

only on images of later Hellenistic and Roman professional athletes, and the choice of a professional boxer as subject could never have been made in the fifth century, as the Classical athletes were amateurs who played for the love of sport, not money. Yet the image's nobility has far more in common with Myron's Discobolus than with the tangled groups of wrestlers and pancratiasts that better represent the mainstream of Hellenistic realism.

The surface of this bronze has not been finished to a fine, smooth polish, but appears instead to have had little work done after casting. This feature—common among bronzes known to have been found in Alexandria and elsewhere in Egypt—accords well with an Egyptian origin. Since it is well documented as having been in the collection of Giovanni Dattari of Cairo in the early years of this century, an Alexandrian provenance would seem therefore to be reliable.

CONDITION: A superb example of solid casting, this bronze is complete except for the thong that must have been stretched between the hands and, probably, silver inlays in the eyes. The nipples are inlaid in copper. The two legs have been broken around the shins and repaired; the left arm has been broken off and rejoined. Both arms were apparently cast separately and attached. There is a small gash in the proper right side of the head just below the right ear, which is missing the upper corner of the helix. The warm, reddish-brown color appears to be a lacquer patina applied recently, perhaps in the nineteenth century. Some small spots of black and green are scattered over the surface. An encrustation covers the left side of the torso and the entire back.

PROVENANCE: See remarks above.

EX COLLECTIONS: Giovanni Dattari; Arthur Sambon; private collection, Paris.

EXHIBITED: The Cleveland Museum of Art, February 12-April 6, 1986, *Year in Review for 1985*, 62, illus. 38, no. 3.

PUBLISHED: Sale: *Antiquités égyptiennes, grecques et romaines: collections de Feu M. Jean P. Lambros d'Athènes et de M. Giovanni Dattari du Caire*, by J. Hirsch and A. Sambon, Paris, Hôtel Drouot, June 17-19, 1912, 50, no. 433, pls. LII-LIII. Sale: *Collection Arthur Sambon*, by J. Hirsch, Paris, Galerie Georges Petit, May 25-28, 1914, 19, no. 61, illus. D. K. Hill 1949, 67, under no. 142.

NOTES: On boxers and boxing in antiquity, the most useful text is still E. N. Gardiner, *Athletics of the Ancient World* (Oxford, 1930; reprint Chicago, 1980) 197-211, figs. 173-187. The illustrations include ancient representations of boxers stretching the thongs; for poses similar to that of the Dattari athlete, see especially figs. 52 and 174.

For the short-cropped hairstyle with cirrus, see E. N. Gardiner 1980, fig. 74; *RE* III:2, col. 2586; *DarSag*, 1:520, figs. 602-603, s.v. *Athleta*, also D. K. Hill 1949, 67; H. C. Van Gulik, *Catalogue of the Bronzes in the Allard Pierson Museum at Amsterdam* (Amsterdam, 1940) no. 12; S. Boucher, *Bronzes grecs, hellénistiques et étrusques (sardes, ibériques et celtiques) des musées de Lyon* (Lyon, 1970) 61, no. 40; and C. Rolley 1986, 221, fig. 299.

On the characteristic lack of surface finish after casting of Egyptian bronzes, see G. Roeder, "Komposition und Technik der ägyptischen Metallplastik," *JdI* XLVII (1933) 227; idem, "Ägyptische Bronzefiguren," *Mitteilungen aus der Ägyptischen Sammlung* VI (1956) 527 ; H. Kyrieleis, "KATHAPER HERMES KAI HOROS," *AntP* XII (1973) 138 (he notes also in n. 44 that certain finer Alexandrian bronzes were polished, citing as an example the Baker dancing woman [14]), and C. Rolley 1986, 217.

As a parallel for the square-cut inset nipples, see the next entry.

The wasted figure, seated on a backless four-legged bench (diphros), bends forward feebly lifting his left arm before him. With his right, he supports himself on the edge of the stool. Little more than a skeleton, his upper torso is covered by a thin membrane of skin through which every rib is visible. The himation, gathered in thick folds that stand out around the buttocks and over the lap, covers his legs completely, leaving the feet exposed. His left foot is pushed forward from the stool, shod in an open-work sandal (trochas) that is closed at the heel, while his right, shoeless and deformed, is set farther back on a thick pad of cushioning.

By far the most vital part of his body, his head is a portrait of painful endurance and resignation. Short curls cover the well-formed skull and are parted over the center of the forehead. The eyes are set in hollows between the horizontal brows and protruding cheekbones. Inlaid in silver with the pupils drilled, they contrast mark-

LATE HELLENISTIC
OR EARLY ROMAN
AFTER LATE
HELLENISTIC
ORIGINAL,
PERHAPS FROM
ALEXANDRIA,
CA. 50 BC–AD 50.
H. 11.5 CM.
THE DUMBARTON
OAKS COLLECTION,
47.22
CLEVELAND ONLY

edly with the now-dark patina, heightening the intensity of the gaze. His nose is a straight ridge, whose prominence is emphasized by the sunken cheeks on either side. Though his jawline is clear in profile, the chin recedes beneath the slack mouth, contributing further to the overall impression of weakness and suffering.

A small, apparently ancient, intentional drillhole in the underside of his limp left hand may suggest that it rested on a cane or support of some kind. The irregular lumps of encrusted material on the folds of the himation resting across his lap may be the remains of something small that he held in his lap, possibly a pet or some other important personal possession. Three of the legs of the stool are lost and the fourth is actually beneath the piece of drapery, totally separate from the himation, that appears to fall from the back of the chair frame. The woven seat is indicated on the underside by a lattice-work design. Not visible unless the object is turned over, this minor refinement is indicative of the superb degree of finish in the statuette, which must have been intended for a demanding collector.

The straightforward representation of a serious physical condition is startling. Famine and disease were surely never far from mind in antiquity, and the symptoms of terminal illness would have been all too familiar. Yet, on closer observation, it is clear that some anatomical details of the body are far from accurate, most noticeably the two continuous arcs across the chest just beneath the clavicles that are intended to suggest ribs. Yet, they are extraordinarily expressive. Purposeful distortions, these details contribute significantly to the pathos that the figure intentionally arouses. At the same time, they are essential to the symmetrical surface patterns that recall anatomical features but do not reproduce a medical textbook illustration, for this is not a clinical description of a disease, but an artist's interpretation

of the effects of disease. Neither a caricature nor a grotesque in the sense of the Metropolitan's grotesque [28], the subject here has been treated with compassion.

Two dotted inscriptions in Greek letters run across the front of the bronze, one over the knees and the other across the lower selvage of the himation. They offer some evidence for a possible identification. The upper reads: [EUDAMIDAS]; the lower: [PERDIK]. The name Eudamidas is not uncommon in Greek history, as at least one Corinthian, two Spartan kings, and one Laconian commander of this name are documented. Perdik[kas] has been identified as exclusively Macedonian.

In her brilliant discussion of the bronze, Richter offered two possible explanations. The first is that this is a representation of the youth Perdikkas, who is known from the poem, *Aegritudo Perdicae*, to have wasted away for "love of his mother." Eudamidas would thus be the name of the dedicator, and the Perdik the identification of the subject. There is, however, no suggestion that this Perdikkas was crippled. A second possibility derives from the existence of a well-known "lame Athenian huckster," Perdix, whose name came to be associated with delicate or misshapen feet. If this is the inspiration for the inscription, then the dedicator Eudamidas would have been known by the epithet, "Perdik" (for *Perdix*), because he was club-footed. As the right foot is clearly distinguished from the left by both its misshapen contours and the lack of any shoe or sandal, the latter explanation seems more likely.

The letter forms of the dotted inscriptions have been identified as early Roman Imperial. There is no reason to believe that they must be contemporary with the manufacture of the bronze. The "Eudamidas" is, in fact, obscured by the folds of the himation, and the "Perdik" artlessly punched into the fabric between the legs above the hem. But as both the subject and the style of execution are closely related to late Hellenistic bronzes, whose loose chronology surely overlaps the early Imperial period, neither is there any conflict in placing the statuette at the end of the first century BC or the beginning of the first century AD.

The interest in a detailed depiction of a pathological condition has brought this figure into association with the city of Alexandria, a connection that is reasonable as many terracottas, bronzes, and even ivories depicting abnormally shaped or diseased figures survive from that Egyptian metropolis. Perhaps intended as a dedication to Asclepius, the god of healing, this bronze may well be a superlative example of Alexandrian realism that ultimately found its way to Roman Gaul.

CONDITION: The solid figure and stool were cast together as one piece. The three legs of the stool that stood free of drapery are lost, as are the nipples on the chest, which were inlaid as small squares, presumably of copper. Hair curls and edges of the feet show signs of wear, as if the figure had been much handled.

The surface of the metal is covered with a warm greenish-brown alteration surface, with unpatinated bronze visible in the tops of the relief curls, the edge of the right hand, the shod left foot, the toes of the right foot, and the tip of the nose. There are lumps of corrosion on the surface of the lap and on the left knee which may be the remains of an attachment held there.

PROVENANCE: Found near Soissons in France.

EX COLLECTIONS: Vicomte de Jessaint; Wyndham Francis Cook.

EXHIBITED: London, Burlington Fine Arts Club, 1903, *Exhibition of Ancient Greek Art*, 50, no. 50, p. xxvii, B50, pl. LII.

PUBLISHED: A. de Longpérier, "Figurine de bronze du cabinet de M. le Vicomte de Jessaint," *RA* I, 2 (1844-1845) 438-461, pl. 13 (the discussion of this figure is reproduced in A. de Longpérier, *Oeuvres*, II, I [Paris, 1883-1886] 105-109, pl. II).
A. Michaelis, *Ancient Marbles in Great Britain* (London, 1882) 629, no. 29.
S. Reinach, *Rép.stat.* II, 2:691.
C. H. Smith, *Burlington Magazine* II (1903) 255, pl. IV.
C. H. Smith and C. A. Hutton, *Catalogue of the Antiquities (Greek, Etruscan and Roman) in the Collection of the Late Wyndham Francis Cook, Esq.*, 2 vols. (London, 1904-1908) II:109-III, no. 32, pl. XXX.

W. Lamb 1929, 202, pl. 77a.
L. Goldschneider, *Art without Epoch* (New York, 1937) figs. 24-5.
Bulletin of the Fogg Art Museum x (December 1947) illus.
G. M. A. Richter 1951, 32, fig. 57.
G. M. A. Richter 1956, 32-35, pl. XIV, no. 17.
G. M. A. Hanfmann 1967, 331, no. 250.
C. M. Robertson 1975, 558; 726, n. 143; pl. 179 b.

NOTES: For the inscription, see *Corpus Inscriptionum Graecarum auctoritate et impensis academiae litterarum Regiae Borussicae* (Berolini, 1828-1877) IV, 6855b.

For the *Aegritudo Perdicae*, attributed to the Christian poet Dracontius, see A. Baehrens, *Poeti latini minores* v (Leipzig, 1882); also, *RE* v, col. 1644.

On Alexandrian realism and illustrations of pathological conditions, see N. Himmelmann-Wildschütz 1983, esp. 59-64, pls. 44-46, 51-54.

For the identification of the sandal, see K. D. Morrow 1985, on trochades, 84-86, 114-117, 146-147, and esp. fig. 60 (foot of Maussolus).

26. Portrait of a Philosopher

Among the preserved monuments of ancient art, there exists no more sensitive and sympathetic portrait of the Greek intellectual than this bronze statuette of a philosopher. The portly man stands with both feet flat on the base beneath him, looking down to the right as if he had paused abruptly in mid-thought. The deep vertical folds that crease his brow above the bridge of his large nose and the focused gaze of his eyes have captured the intensity of his absorption, while his slightly parted lips suggest the momentary nature of his preoccupation. In unconscious response to the fact that the heavy himation wrapped around his torso has slipped down from his left shoulder, he holds his left arm close to his side and clutches the end of the drapery slung over his raised forearm in his left hand. Nor is his right arm, hanging down by his side, relaxed. His forearm is extended slightly out before him to the right, and his loosely curled long, nervous fingers reflect his tension.

Though the sagging flesh on his cheeks betrays the subject's maturity, every feature of his head expresses a vitality that does not quite accord with the aging body. The unsettling effects of his girth are especially obvious from the back, where the out-turned feet, shod in practical thick-soled sandals, are widely spaced to steady his weight. From the front, large, flaccid breasts hang heavily over his expansive paunch, and the loose flesh at the inside of his armpits shows the extent of physical deterioration due to both age and indulgence.

The individualized appearance of the entire figure, and the successful portrayal of cerebral activity in the bearded head in particular, link this image with the philosopher portraits that became popular during the fourth century BC. Although commemorative images of military heroes and representations of great writers and intellectuals had been erected in the fifth century, they were generally idealized and often imaginary creations. It was only natural, however, that as authors like Aris-

ROMAN WORK OF END OF IST C. BC, INSPIRED BY HELLENISTIC ORIGINAL OF 3RD C. BC. H. OF FIGURE 25.6 CM. METROPOLITAN MUSEUM OF ART, ROGERS FUND, 1910, 10.231.1

totle and Theophrastus analyzed physiognomy as a significant indicator of personality and character, artists and their patrons too would become increasingly concerned with the accurate representation of human appearances. The statue of Socrates, for example, erected by the Athenian government as an act of contrition for his barbarous condemnation and execution in 399 BC had of necessity to reflect the thinker's Silenus-like features, for they had been described by Plato and Xenophon.

The subject of this portrait has long been identified with the members of the Epicurean school of philosophy, most often Epicurus himself or his close follower Hermarchus. Not the self-indulgent hedonist that contemporary and later critics claimed, Epicurus felt that in the uncertain circumstances of the world, each man should seek to attain pleasure and peace in his life, but that effort must be guided by the principles of moderation and harmony with nature. His writings enjoyed great popularity both during his life and after, and he was especially beloved in Rome, where Pomponius stated that he "could not forget Epicurus even if he wanted; the members of our body not only have pictures of him, but even have his likeness on their drinking cups and rings" (Cicero, *De Fin.* V.i.iii).

These images most likely reflected the original portrait of the philosopher erected in the third century within the gardens of his school, the features of which are well-documented today in many surviving Roman copies. Characteristic of the portraits identified by inscriptions are the long narrow head, short hair arranged in a fringe that curls to the proper left over the forehead, a brow furrowed with two or three horizontal creases as well as the vertical folds over a large nose, heavy superorbital folds of flesh that give a gravity to the expression, and a long beard that separates in the center into two distinct curling sides that are balanced but slightly

asymmetrical. And though distinguished by some individual and generally less expressive traits, the portraits of his best-known pupils Metrodorus and Hermarchus are so closely based on the Epicurean model that they are often difficult to separate from those of the master.

Comparisons with the arrangements of locks of hair and beard, the forehead furrows, and other facial features of the inscribed portraits have helped scholars to identify many uninscribed portraits as well, and in this way, the New York statuette has been connected with the Epicureans, as it shows many similar details. Yet, among all the preserved copies recognized thus far, none shows the particular arrangement of hair that appears in this bronze. Here, the short locks over the forehead have been pushed carelessly back to the left side, as if the subject has just run his fingers impatiently through his hair. Nor do the patterns of locks that frame the temples or the outer contours of the beard agree with those on any other copy.

As this statuette is a more original and spontaneous creation than any of the copies of the archetypical portrait types, it is possible that liberties were taken with the standard Epicurean iconography. Against this explanation is the fact that there is also no parallel for the standing pose of the philosopher among the images of Epicurus, who was seriously ill for the last fourteen years of his life and is known only to have been represented as seated. Nor are there comparable images of his disciples. A rather closer comparison for the stance is to be found in a marble figure in the Capitoline Museum in Rome, the so-called "Capitoline Cynic." Though the unkempt, brutish head of the Roman statue has nothing in common with the Metropolitan's philosopher, the aging body is dressed in a very similar fashion, with the left hand grasping the folds of a himation that has slipped off the left shoulder. As the New York bronze's protruding belly and well-made sandals with decorative three-pointed tongues (lingulae) make it unlikely that he should be associated with a philosophy of endurance and self-deprivation, the link here is only to the standing pose and disposition of the drapery.

On the basis of its profound psychological insight and individualized representation, the statuette has been generally dated to the first half or middle of the third century BC, the period which also produced the images of the Epicureans, the Greek dramatist Menander (342-292 BC), the great portrait of the Athenian orator Demosthenes (384-322 BC), and many other well-known intellectuals. The New York philosopher was clearly not intended as an independent statuette, however, for he stands on a elaborately profiled abacus atop an Ionic capital, and these elements must also be considered in the establishment of his date.

The edge of the abacus is beaded above the convex band of ovolo and the reverse curve of the Lesbian cymatium, which are separated from one another by a narrower band of beading. Beneath, the volutes of the capital frame a central two-story flower rising from the addorsed curves that form the lower contours of the canalis. The convex swellings on the balusters of the capital are decorated with vertical lines of large beads, and tendril-like hooks pierce the concave hollows on either end. Formed from the ends of two slender rods that run through from one side of the capital to the other (only the front one of which is completely preserved), these long loops with budlike finials are substantial enough to have held small lamps, garlands, or implements. As the whole complex crowned a column whose height can be restored to about 31.7 cm. (on the basis of the preserved core), nothing very large would have been suspended.

Though figures atop capitals are not uncommon in the Archaic and Classical periods, this particular combination of figure, capital, and attached supports is unparalleled among both Hellenistic and Roman ones; indeed, its only genuine parallels are to be found in the fragmentary Archaic bronze of Orchomenus and the fourth-century candelabrum from Mezek, now in Sofia. The broad expanse of the canalis in proportion to the volutes of the capital recalls Archaic and Classical models, but this is a detail that was revived in Augustan times. Though the beaded treatment of the balusters can support an early or late Hellenistic date, details of the often-repeated Lesbian cymatium on the abacus, such as the short central rib and brief points of the flat leaves, seem to be late. The terminals on the tendril hooks have parallels on handles of the late fourth century as well as Roman implements. But it is the fleshy form of the flower on the face of the canalis that most seriously contradicts the third-century dating, suggesting in its symmetrical disposition of familiar floral motifs a later, even early Imperial date.

Finally, only the positive identification of the subject remains a puzzle. Yet, if his name is in question, his importance among the preserved ancient bronzes is not. One of the most extraordinary portraits ever cast, the Metropolitan Museum's philosopher offers an unsentimental image of contemplation, evocative of an age when the dedication to self-examination and intellectual discipline were considered essential characteristics of a learned man and the philosopher-teacher was among the most respected and influential members of society.

CONDITION: The hollow-cast statuette is completely preserved. The legs were made separately and cast on just within the border of the himation. When purchased in 1910, the figure had lost its left leg. John Marshall found the missing limb in 1911 in the possession of P. Hartwig, and it was restored to the figure. The right ankle has been broken and repaired. The mouth, which has two distinctive cuts in the upper lip and a wide groove between the lips, may have originally been inlaid with copper. Of the original two rods that ran through the front and back of the capital to form the hooks on either side, only the front one is completely preserved; the back preserves the section that runs between the volutes of the capital and the protruding ends. The supporting column is lost, but the core is preserved.

The statuette was cleaned and the patina was removed by Dietrich von Bothmer in the 1960s. Previously, the right leg had not been joined correctly to the figure; the statuette required a wedge under the right foot to stand.

EX COLLECTION: Ludwig Pollak.

PROVENANCE: Said to be from Ostia.

EXHIBITED: Northampton, Mass., Smith College Museum of Art, November 18-December 15, 1948, *Pompeiana.*
Moscow and Leningrad, November 1978-June 1979, *Antichnoe isskustvo iz muzeia Metropoliten, Soedinennye Shtaty Ameriki,* cat. by D. von Bothmer, no. 71, col. pl., unpaginated.

PUBLISHED: E. Robinson, "A Statuette of Hermarchos," *BMMA* (June 1911) 130-134, illus.
R. Delbrueck, *Antike Porträts* (Bonn, 1912) 38-39, illus.
G. Lippold, *Griechische Porträtstatuen* (Munich, 1912) 82.
G. M. A. Richter 1915, 70-74, no. 120.
G. H. Chase 1924, 130-131, fig. 162.
F. Poulsen, "Tête en marbre du philosophe épicurien Hermarchos," *BCH* XLVII (1924) 378.
S. Reinach, *Rép.stat.* V:314, 3.
H. B. Walters, "A Portrait Statuette of Socrates," *JHS* XLV (1925) 258-259, fig. 1.
W. Lamb 1929, 205, pl. 78b.
G. M. A. Richter, *Sculpture and Sculptors of the Greeks* (London, 1929) 37, 65, figs. 230-231, 241.
P. Arndt et al., *Griechische und römische Porträts* (Munich, 1891-1942) no. 1123.
J. D. Beazley and B. Ashmole, *Greek Sculpture and Painting to the End of the Hellenistic Period* (Cambridge, 1932) 95, fig. 204.
J. Pijoan, *El arte griego hasta la toma de Corinto por los Romanos (146 A.J.C.)* (Madrid, 1932) 437, fig. 596.
E. Buschor 1936, 93, illus.
K. Schefold 1943, 124, 211, illus. 125, fig. 4.
L. Curtius, "Griechische Porträts," *RM* LIX (1944) 22.
E. Buschor, *Bildnisstuffen* (Munich, 1947) 179, 183, fig. 78.
E. Buschor, *Das hellenistische Bildnis* (Munich, 1949) 24-5, 28, 32.
G. M. A. Richter, *Sculpture and Sculptors of the*

Greeks, rev. ed. (New Haven, Conn., 1950) 424, figs. 230, 241.

M. Bieber 1955, 68, fig. 230-1.

L. Alscher 1954-, 192, fig. 77c.

G. M. A. Richter, *Greek Portraits* (Berchem-Brussels, 1955-) II:25-26, n. 4, pl. XI, no. 37.

G. M. A. Richter 1955-, III:11, n. 1.

G. M. A. Richter 1955-, IV:40-41, figs. 53, 55.

G. M. A. Richter, *The Portraits of the Greeks*, 3 vols. (London, 1965) II:199, fig. 1220.

S. Boucher-Colozier, "Un bronze d'époque Alexandrine réalisme et caricature," *MonPiot* LIV (1965) 30, fig. 4; 31, n. 1.

E. H. and L. Richardson, Jr., "Ad cohibendum bracchium toga," *Yale Classical Studies* XIX (1966) 257, fig. 5.

C. Rolley 1967, 10, no. 101, pl. 35.

M. Bieber, "Bronzestatuette des Asklepios in Cincinnati," *AntP* X (1970) 55, n. 2.

C. M. Havelock, *Hellenistic Art: The Art of the Classical World from the Death of Alexander the Great to the Battle of Actium* (Greenwich, Conn., 1970), 42-43, pl. 28.

E. Buschor 1971, no. 58, fig. 26, no. 99.

J. Charbonneaux et al., *Hellenistic Art, 330-50 B.C.*, tr. P. Green (New York, 1973) 249, fig. 265.

M. Robertson 1975, 524-525, pl. 158 b.

M. Bieber, *Ancient Copies: Contributions to the History of Greek and Roman Art* (New York, 1977) 120, figs. 535-536.

S. Karusu, "Eines Kandelaber-Kapitell aus Orchomenos," *Boreas* I (1978) 16, n. 38.

E. G. Raftopoulou, "Remarques sur des bronzes provenant du sol grec," *Bronzes hellénistiques* (1979) 43-45, pl. 15, fig. 4.

J. J. Pollitt, *Art in the Hellenistic Age* (Cambridge, 1986) 69, fig. 67, n. 19 (as Roman work after a 3rd-century BC original).

C. Rolley 1986, pl. 173.

NOTES: For identification and discussion of the portraits of Epicurus, Metrodorus, and Hermarchus, see G. M. A. Richter 1955-, II:194-206, figs. 1149-1324; R. R. R. Smith, ed., *The Portraits of the Greeks*, abbr. and rev. (Ithaca, N.Y., 1984) Epicurus, 116-119; Hermarchus, 129-131; Metrodorus, 164-166. See also 172, under Parmenides, a head that is a replica of the Metrodoros type; and B. Frischer, *The Sculpted Word: Epicureanism and Philosophical Recruitment in Ancient Greece* (Berkeley, Calif., 1982) 129-198.

For the Capitoline Cynic, see E. G. Raftopoulou 1979, pl. 17, 11; G. M. A. Richter 1965, II: fig. 1074; R. R. R. Smith 1984, fig. 1.

For the closest parallels for the support with attached tendril hooks, see the Archaic capital with attached feet only, S. Karusu, *Boreas*, 1978, pl. 1, figs. 1-4; also the 4th-century satyr atop an Ionic capital from Mezek, now in Sofia, in B. Rutkowski, "Griechische Kandelaber," *JdI* XCIV (1979) 206, fig. 37a-d; for a Augustan candelabrum with a sphinx seated on an Ionic capital of similar proportions with a relief flower on the canalis, see E. Pernice 1925, 51, fig. 63.

For earlier figures on Ionic column capitals, see G. M. A. Richter 1965, I:67, fig. 233, under Archilochos; R. Thomas 1981, pl. LXXVII (Hermitage GKH 91); G. Ortiz in *Hommes et dieux* (1982) 191, no. 115.

For the Lesbian cymatium in the Hellenistic period, and the development of the floral motifs, see M. Pfrommer, "Eine Bronzebecken in Malibu," *GettyMusJ* XIII (1985) 12-14, fig. 4, and "Kopie oder Nachschöpfüng. Eine Bronzekanne im J. Paul Getty Museum," *GettyMusJ* XV (1987) 15-26.

For the budlike terminals of the attached hooks, see the handles of the bronze situla in the Museum of Fine Arts, Boston (03.1001), which is dated to the second half of the 4th century BC, M. Comstock and C. C. Vermeule 1971, 302-303, no. 428. They also appear on the handles of several Roman bronze implements said to have been found in the Tiber (Getty Museum, no. 82.AC.22)

For a 4th-century representation of a statuette on top of a small column, see the phlyax vase in Leontini, Palazzo Communale, reproduced in M. Bieber, *The History of the Greek and Roman Theater* (London, 1939) fig. 488 a and b.

For the appearance of the lingula on sandals in the late Classical period and after, and the appropriateness of this footwear for a philosopher portrait, see M. Pfrommer, "The Emperor's Shoes: Hellenistic Footwear in Roman Times," *BClevMus* LXXIV (1987) 124-129, esp. n. 15.

27. Hermes

Hermes, the herald and messanger of the Olympians and patron god of travelers and herdsmen, always enjoyed great popularity among the Greeks who admired his craftiness and were amused by his often duplicitous behavior. In Archaic and early Classical art he appears more frequently than any deity except Athena, occasionally as the infant who stole the cattle of Apollo but more commonly as the bearded marshal who conducts a group of gods—such as the trio of Aphrodite, Athena, and Hera, who are to have their beauty judged by Paris—or the souls of the dead on their way to Hades. Hermes is also often depicted as the mature guardian of the flocks, an image well represented in this exhibition by Boston's two superb kriophoroi [8, 9].

GREEK, LATE HELLENISTIC, 50 BC-AD 50. H. 29.1 CM. METROPOLITAN MUSEUM OF ART, ROGERS FUND, 1971, 1971.11.11

During the middle of the fifth century BC, the god's image underwent a notable though somewhat gradual transformation, and he was shown more and more frequently as a beardless youth. This handsome young deity with varied responsibilities was apparently of no less interest to the Greeks. In fact, he seems to have inspired an even wider range of representations than his mature incarnation, and throughout the late Classical and Hellenistic periods, the youthful Hermes often appears—carrying the infant Dionysus to the nymphs, leading the deceased to Hades, fastening his sandals, or resting from his journeys.

In spite of this transformation, the identifying attributes of the god remain remarkably unchanged. He is generally dressed in the large-brimmed hat (petasus) and short cloak (chlamys), the standard apparel for all Greek male travelers. But unlike the mortal wayfarers, he wears boots or sandals on his feet with wings attached to indicate his swiftness. He may also have wings attached to his hat or head, and usually carries a kerykeion to signify his role as messenger.

In this large bronze statuette, the god appears as a radiantly beautiful youth wearing only the chlamys, fastened with braided cords and a round pin over his right shoulder, and small wings at his heels and on his head (now lost). He stands with his weight resting on his right leg, but there is no calm serenity in his posture, for he seems at this moment to have turned his head and torso to the right as well, perhaps to follow the gesture of his arm, now missing, that must have been extended in this direction. His relaxed left leg is drawn up behind, with toes turned out to the side, and his left arm, bent at the elbow, is drawn back sharply within the chlamys, pulling the material tight across his left breast and shoulder as if it were a sling. Only the V-shaped fold of loose fabric at the front of his neck serves to counteract the tension.

The effects on the drapery are further amplified in the back, where the fabric clings to the contours of his protruding elbow, and the right edge of the cloak is pulled from the right shoulder to the left hip in a taut diagonal that is echoed by the series of parallel creases. The explanation for this diagonal strain on the back of the cloak has unfortunately been lost together with the left forearm, but the remaining traces of the directional folds show that the lower lengths of the chlamys were gathered up over his left hip, draped across the top of his left forearm, and allowed to fall in a series of heavy vertical folds intended to offset the stress created between arm and torso.

In contrast to the furrowed surface of the cloak, the sleek body betrays no sign of stress. The anatomy of the torso and limbs is reduced to a series of undulating surfaces that plainly define but do not emphasize any unnecessary details of either skeletal structure or musculature. Only the sinuous line of the pelvis, important for the languid pose, is allowed to interrupt the continuity. Plastically rendered details and incision are sacrificed to the finely polished finish of the bronze, and even

the nipples and pubic hair have been omitted. A simple vertical cut marks the top of the penis, which is set off from the groin by a fold of flesh.

Pairs of small wings are strapped to the god's feet by a series of thin bands; wrapping and crossing over the instep, and tying around the ankles without attachment to any soles, they do not actually qualify as sandals. There is no evidence of a petasus; the god wears a wreath of laurel around his head, and two small rectangular cuttings in the top of the head show that another pair of wings was attached here.

The short curls composing a tight cap over his well-formed cranium are suggested with a minimum of detail, their convex outlines easily confused with the laurel leaves. Beneath this roughly textured surface, the facial features seem exquisitely refined. The large eyes, once inlaid with glass paste or stone, are widely spaced beneath his smooth forehead, while his nose runs straight from the slight indentation at its broad bridge to its rounded tip. Only his finely modeled mouth is too small in relation to the other features. Set deeply within the contours of his cheeks and rounded chin, it adds to the otherwise serious expression a youthful sweetness that complements the graceful posture and elegant proportions of the figure.

As Buitron noted in her fine publication, and as Bothmer had observed in his original study of the statuette prior to acquisition, the Metropolitan Hermes finds its closest parallel in a bronze statuette, now in the Bardo Museum, that was found in the shipwreck discovered off the coast of Mahdia, Tunisia, in 1907. And though the Mahdia bronze lacks the wreath and wings on the head, it preserves both arms and hands as well as the drapery of the chlamys. According to the description in Fuchs' text on the works of art from that wreck, the extended right hand held no attribute, but the left may have held the kerykeion. The New York statuette may be similarly restored on the basis of this evidence.

Though close indeed to the New York statuette, the Mahdia bronze does show some distinctive differences: the muscles of the torso appear firmer and more specifically defined; the head, larger in proportion to the total height of the figure, is turned less to the right; the fabric of the chlamys falls more naturally, especially in the fold before the neck; and the pubic hair is clearly defined with plastic curls. Overall, the pose is less languorous, and the entire image exudes a vitality that is lacking in the Metropolitan piece.

Fuchs has dated the Mahdia Hermes fairly securely on the basis of other contextual material in the shipwreck to ca. 120 BC. This late Hellenistic date is borne out by the decorative use of the drapery. A Hellenistic conceit originating in an interest in conveying natural appearances (seen already in the Baker dancing woman [14]), the device has here become a mere convention employed without compositional purpose.

In the refinement of its curving surfaces, the lack of interest in the specific delineation of the anatomy, the listless elegance of its pose, and the Lysippan proportions, the Metropolitan version must be somewhat later. Close both in spirit and physical details to the classicistic products of the first century BC or the early Imperial echoes of the late Hellenistic period, it recalls the flawless, enervated beauty of the Pasitelean youths, the Roman seated Hermes from Herculaneum, or the bronze youth in Toledo. The New York statuette can thus be dated between the last half of the first century BC and the first half of the first century AD.

CONDITION: The right arm, which was cast separately and attached just below the shoulder, is missing, as are the left forearm, the large toe of the left foot, the inlaid eyes, the wings from the crown of the head, and the inner wing from the right ankle. The rectangular attachment of one of the wings on the head still remains in its cutting; lead is visible within the hollow of the right arm. The beautifully polished surface preserves many ancient patches that repaired the flaws in the original cast: on the chin, on the back of the chlamys at the neck, near the proper left breast, beside the drapery on the left side of the torso and below the left iliac crest, on both legs and on the feet. Patches are missing on the outside near the shoulder of the left arm, on the right side of the neck at the back, and on the back of the proper left calf. The well-preserved surface is covered with a regular greenish-black patina.

EXHIBITED: New York, Metropolitan Museum of Art, December 3, 1975-March 23, 1976, *Patterns of Collecting.*

PUBLISHED: New York, *Metropolitan Museum of Art Annual Report,* 1970-1971 (New York, 1975) 19. New York, *Metropolitan Museum of Art Notable Acquisitions, 1965-1975* (New York, 1975) 117, illus.
D. Buitron, "A Bronze Statuette of Hermes in the Metropolitan Museum," *JWalt* XXVI (1977) 85-90, figs. 1-5.
J. R. Mertens (*BMMA*) 1985, no. 43.

NOTES: For the Mahdia Hermes, see W. Fuchs, *Der Schiffsfund von Mahdia* (Tübingen, 1963) 20, no. II, pl. 20.

For the Pasitelean youths and Toledo bronze boy, see P. Zanker 1974, pls. 42-43, 46; and 33, 5, respectively.

For the seated Hermes from Herculaneum, see W. Fuchs 1979, 276, fig. 301. This figure also provides a good parallel for the wings strapped on at the ankles without attachment to proper sandals.

For similar treatment of the drapery, hair, and inlaid eyes, see also the seated Hermes in the Walters Art Gallery: D. K. Hill 1949, 20, no. 35, pl. II.

On late Hellenistic classicism, see most recently J. J. Pollitt 1986, 164-175; for a more complete discussion, P. Zanker 1974; also, A. Stewart, *Attika*, The Society for the Promotion of Hellenic Studies Supplementary Paper XIV (1979) 34-64.

On the representations of various aspects of Hermes and changes in his appearance, see *DarSag* III, 2, s.v. Mercurius, 1802-1816; *RE* VIII, I, s.v. Hermes, cols. 764-792.

With his enormous head, twisted nose, silver fangs, and the menacing expression of his huge eyes, this little creature appears like the demonic realization of a nightmare. His body is equally deformed. Even through the fabric of his tunic, the hump on his back, his swollen chest, and his enormous phallus are clearly indicated. He stands on spindly legs with his weight spread between two large sandaled feet. The right foot is advanced as if stepping forward, but he has turned his shoulders and head to cast his threatening glance to the left. The parts of both arms not covered by the folds of the unbelted tunic are missing, but their positions can be tentatively reconstructed. The right was bent at the elbow, which is slightly pulled back, and the forearm must have projected straight out from the sleeve; the left appears to have been extended out to the side, perhaps to hold a staff or to gesture.

ROMAN,
CA. 50 BC–AD 50.
H. 10 CM.
METROPOLITAN
MUSEUM OF ART,
ROGERS FUND,
1912, 12.229.6

Yet, if this monstrous apparition arouses primitive fears, he has been created with artistry of extraordinary sophistication. The dominant aspect of the figure, the oversized head, is an intricate combination of exaggerated forms and varied textures and colors that account for its expressive power. Set within hollows under the converging arches of the angry brows, the eyes are inlaid with silver to heighten the contrast with the drilled pupils; the irises incised around the deep holes serve only to focus the gaze further. The thick lips are parted by the silver canines that project like fangs from the corners of the mouth. Across the top of the head, the hair is formed by sheets of foil made of an alloy of copper with an admixture of silver, surely used for coloristic contrast and laid down in sections over the surface; the fine seams between the joints are quite visible at the back of the head and over the proper left ear. The hairline, in relief, recedes on each side of the forehead from

a low central peak and forms the sideburns. In the crown of the head is a curious depression, rather like a tonsure in shape, where one of the inlays of alloy has been lost. Incised strokes are used to indicate the short strands of hair all around this inlay, while the stubble on the unshaven cheeks is suggested with fine stippling. Intruding into the hairline, the fleshy helices of the ears are so massive that they have begun to curl over. The nose changes direction at least twice, forming a great crooked hook that is prominent from any point of view.

Though the body and costume are of less interest than the face, they have been described with no less care. The humps on the back and chest and the large phallus are covered by a short tunic of thick fabric. It is stitched outside on the right sleeve, buttoned down the left sleeve, and open at the left side. The crinkly edges of the woven selvage are clearly rendered with short vertical incisions; the buttons are apparently made of the same copper-silver alloy as the hair. The sandals are thongs with one strap running between the first two of the well-modeled toes, another strap around the ankle, and a third running between the sole and ankle strap on the outside of the ankle. The ankle strap is tied at the front in a knot.

Unlike the statuette of the artisan [22], this bronze offers no suggestion of a sympathetic treatment of its subject by the artist. Neither does it betray the detached clinical accuracy of scientific observation. Intended to fascinate and amuse, it is rather in the genre of the grotesque. Bizarre creations of the imagination that often only exaggerate familiar characteristics, grotesques and caricatures of a wide variety of human types enjoyed tremendous popularity in the ancient world, especially during the Hellenistic period. Surviving literary texts—such as Theophrastus' *Characters*, Menander's comedies, Herodas' fragmentary mimes, and Aristotle's treatise on physiognomy as an indicator of personality—are the most persuasive evidence for this great interest in the identification and classification of human character. They were obvious sources of inspiration for artists as well. Again, because of its association with interest in the realistic observation of lowlife types and disfigurement, Alexandria has often been credited with the creation of many of these figure types. Large numbers of grotesques, including this bronze, have been found elsewhere, especially in Asia Minor and Italy, and the fascination with such images was clearly international.

Various efforts have been made to explain the significance of ancient grotesques. They have been viewed as amulets for warding off the evil eye (see [56]), as representations of mimes—actors who performed character roles without masks in the popular Hellenistic comedy skits that focused especially on the daily life of the lower classes—and as caricatures from the native Italic Atellan farces in which the actors wore masks (see also [54, 71]). The subject here seems more a personification of evil than a charm against it, and though the performers in farce were often dwarfs or otherwise physically deformed figures, it is difficult to imagine any actor achieving this disfigured appearance without the benefit of some props and make-up. Thus, if an actor, he most likely played in a crude Atellan farce.

The unusual combination of the hooked nose, huge ears, and knitted brows, together with the prominent fangs, in particular, recall Etruscan images of Charun, god of the underworld. This demon in later Roman times became "the model for the servant who burnt the defeated gladiators" and, in medieval Christian iconography, the source of inspiration for the image of the Devil. Given the reported Italian provenance for this bronze, it is probable that the image is a late Republican or early Imperial version of the same character who parodies the familiar features of the lord of the dead, likely dating to the later first century BC. Until new evidence provides more persuasive proof, however, it may best be understood as a fine miniature, made both to horrify and amuse.

CONDITION: The right forearm and the left arm from just above the elbow, both made separately for attachment at the edge of the tunic, are missing. The inlay from the top of the crown is also lost. Otherwise the solid-cast figure is complete with its surface details well preserved. It has been cleaned by Dietrich von Bothmer, which brought out the contrast of the inlays. In her original publication, Richter suggested that the pupils of the eyes should have been inlaid; though this is certainly possible given the variety of materials used in the head, such a reconstruction is not necessary for a dramatic expression.

The golden-brown surface of the bronze is covered with irregular patches of dark red and reddish-brown cuprite as well as green malachite.

PROVENANCE: Said to have been found in the excavations on the Esquiline in 1727.

EX COLLECTION: F. de Ficoroni.

EXHIBITED: Buffalo, N.Y., Albright Art Gallery, February 1937, *Master Bronzes: Selected from Museums and Collections in America*, no. 94, illus.

PUBLISHED: F. de Ficoroni, *Dissertatio de larvis scaenicis et figuris comicis antiquorum Romanorum ex Italica in Latinam linguam versa*, 2nd ed. (Rome, 1754) pl. 9, no. 2.
F. Wieseler, *Theatergebäude und Denkmäler des Bühnenwesens bei den Griechen und Römern* (Göttingen, 1851) 92, pl. XII, no. II.
DarSag I:514-515, fig. 597, n. 30 (with information on Roman provenance and discovery date).
A. Dieterich, *Pulcinella: Pompejanische Wandbilder und römische Satyrspiele* (Leipzig, 1897) 151-152, n. 2, illus.
S. Reinach, *Rép.stat.* II:815, 3.
G. M. A. Richter, "Grotesques and the Mime," *AJA* XVII (1913) 149-156, pls. V-VI.
G. M. A. Richter 1915, 81-83, no. 127.
G. H. Chase 1924, 128, fig. 159.
W. Lamb 1929, 204, pl. 77b.
M. Bieber 1939, 419-420, figs. 554a-c; (1961) 247-248, figs. 817a-c.
H. Goldman, "Two Terracotta Figurines from Tarsus," *AJA* XLVII (1943) 24, n. 8.
G. M. A. Richter, *Handbook of the Greek Collection* (Cambridge, Mass., 1953) 126, n. 42, pl. 105a.
J. Cooney, "Siren and Ba, Birds of a Feather," *BClevMus* LV (1968) 270-271, n. 19.

NOTES: I thank Richard Stone for his analysis of the copper and silver alloy inlays present on this bronze. This material was taken by Richter to be niello.

For the grotesque as a charm against the evil eye, see A. J. B. Wace, "Grotesques and the Evil Eye," *Annual of the British School at Athens* X (1903-1904) 103-114; and also D. Levi, "The Evil Eye and the Lucky Hunchback," *Antioch-on-the-Orontes*, III (Princeton, N.J., 1941) 220-232.

For comparable terracotta grotesques, both masks and figures, see S. Mollard-Besques 1963, pls. 174-176; M. Bieber 1961, 248-249, figs. 819-822, 825-827.

On the Alexandrian realism and grotesques, see N. Himmelmann-Wildschütz 1983, 60-64, col. pls. I-III, pls. 8-10, 13-15, 18-22, 24-29, 33-35, 44-47, 50-55.

On the Hellenistic Mimes, see G. M. A. Richter, "Grotesques and the Mime," *AJA* XVII (1913); M. Bieber 1961, 106-107.

For a translation and discussion of Theophrastus' *Characters* and fragments of Herodas and other Hellenistic mimes, see J. M. Edmonds and A. D. Knox, *The Characters of Theophrastus, Herodes, Cercidas, Choliambic Poets*, Loeb Classical Library no. 225 (Cambridge, Mass., 1967).

For the Atellan farce, see *DarSag* I:513-515; M. Bieber 1939, 247-248.

For source of the image of the Devil, see M. Bieber 1939, 147-148.

29. Zeus

The mature man stands without attribute, serene and magnificent in his nudity. His weight is fixed comfortably on his right leg, while his relaxed left leg, turned out to the side and placed slightly behind his right, provides stability to his pose. He holds his left arm out to the side to be level with his shoulder, and his hand—raised to the level of his head—is loosely closed, originally to support an upright attribute. His right arm is extended out before his torso, and his now-missing hand most likely held another object. His head is turned toward the right, and his noble facial features, framed by long curling locks of hair and beard, express the same calm dignity as his pose.

Even without an identifying feature, there is no doubt that he is an immortal, and among the Olympians, there are only two possibilities for a bearded nude image: Zeus or his brother Poseidon. The left hand could have held either the regal scepter appropriate to the king of the gods or the trident of the lord of the seas. The advanced right hand is more appropriate to the iconography of Zeus, however, as he often holds out the thunderbolt of the lord of the skies, and it is thus that the gesture may be reconstructed.

The extended positions of the arms, justified by the presence of attributes, gave the artist the perfect device for focusing attention on the extraordinary modeling of the well-developed torso. The broad pectorals, the nipples inlaid in copper, stand out noticeably over the abdominal arch, within which the quadrants of the abdominal muscles are clearly defined over the hollow of the navel. The external oblique bulges noticeably over the right hip in response to the engagement of the leg, forming an obvious crease above the iliac crest that continues around to the back of the figure, ending only near the small of the back, where it converges with the descending contour of the latissimus dorsi. Though the individual details are exaggerated, the impression created by the overall appearance is convincingly life-like and far more effective visually than any precise representation of the human figure could be.

Nor is the surface of the back any less lively or interesting. The spine's sinuous curve emphasizes the sway of the torso to the proper right, and the massive breadth of the shoulders is balanced by the muscular buttocks, hollow on the sides and full at the back. The arms and legs are sculpted with the same sensitivity and obvious pleasure in the human anatomy, while the finest details of fingers and toes have not been overlooked.

In contrast to the dynamism of the body, the head is oddly disappointing. The face appears small in proportion to the total size of the figure, and much of the head's volume is taken up by the elaborate frame of locks. Radiating from a stylized pinwheel at the crown, the hair lies fairly flat until the ends turn into a thick mass of soft curls encircling the head. A hole drilled in the top of the head, just above the upswept locks over the forehead (anastole), must have originally anchored a diadem that held the hair in place, and a tiny trace of gilding among the locks at the back suggests that the hair was originally golden. The beard is composed of shorter, tighter curls, but the effect is equally luxuriant.

Beneath the upswept locks, the forehead thickens just over the bridge of the nose and the horizontal eyebrows, adding a sense of gravity to the otherwise placid expression. The eyes, though inlaid in silver, are almost lost between the heavy lids, and their shallowly drilled pupils add little to the rather unfocused expression. Surrounded by a thick mustache, the lips are inlaid as well, apparently in copper. Though no effort or expense has been spared in creating a regal bearded head, the lack of interest in rendering the features is more suggestive of academic repetition than inspiration.

ROMAN WORK OF
IST C. AD.
INSPIRED BY GREEK
ORIGINAL OF 4TH
C. BC.
H. 24.7 CM.
MR. AND MRS.
LAWRENCE A.
FLEISCHMAN
COLLECTION

The statuette, which made its first appearance in the San Francisco installation of *The Search for Alexander* exhibition, was published in a very thorough and provocative article by Volk, who argued that the statuette is a fourth-century work based on Lysippus's statue of Zeus at Sicyon, perhaps a product of that master's workshop. The multitude of bronze and marble figures of the same iconographic type has elsewhere been associated with the colossal Zeus by Lysippus at Tarentum (by Dörig) and the Zeus Thunderer of Leochares that was taken to Rome and placed in the temple of the Capitoline Jupiter (by Boucher and earlier, Charbonneaux). No certain reproduction of these originals exists, but on the basis of the characteristics common to all versions, a fourth-century original may generally be accepted as their source of inspiration. Boucher's arguments in favor of the Capitoline statue are the most persuasive, given the documented fate of the statue in Roman times, the widespread series of Roman bronzes, and representations in other media reproducing this image throughout the empire.

Although the manner in which the expansive pose of the Fleischman Zeus incorporates space is characteristic of sculpture associated with the fourth century, the details of the anatomy that Volk eloquently describes are actually closer to the style of the great fifth-century sculptor Polyclitus, by whom Lysippus was much influenced, as are the heavy overall proportions of the figure, its calm stance, and the radial star at the crown. Copies of the Doryphorus in particular share a number of features with the Zeus, from the balanced, frontal posture and turn of the head to the specific delineation of the musculature in the hips, abdomen, and lower back. Such significant details as the anastole of hair over the forehead and the scale of the head are surely un-Polyclitan, however.

This particular combination of features drawn from different periods is rather more suggestive of a masterful eclectic creation of a classicistic workshop than a fourth-century Lysippan original. The Fleischman Zeus may therefore be dated in the last half of the first century BC or the early first century AD, a date that would seem to be borne out by the very high lead content in the bronze (33 plus or minus 7 percent).

The popularity of this image of Zeus Thunderer obviously created a demand for reproductions, most likely to serve as votive offerings or as images in private shrines. With greater or lesser degrees of skill and interest, the craftsmen of the late Hellenistic and early Imperial periods met their customers' requests. The Fleischman Zeus is one of the most eloquent of these copies. The sophisticated execution of its mobile surfaces and its delight in the beauty of the mature male physique are no less satisfying here than they are in the classical image of Apollo. Only the slightly vacant, handsome facial features and the anomalous combination of stylistic details have betrayed the artist's lack of originality. His interest in the Classical past was not unique, however, for either his time or ours. As he drew his image from the models of great fifth- and fourth-century sculptors, he merely participated in a tradition of reflection and revival that continues to the present day.

CONDITION: The figure is missing the right arm from just above the elbow, the penis, the end of the big toe on the right foot, the entire scepter except for the small portion preserved within the left hand, and the diadem or crowning attribute originally inserted in the hole at the top of the head behind the anastole. The solid-cast figure has suffered extensive surface corrosion that has left a number of large craters, and there is a large gouge in the surface beneath the left breast.

The once superbly finished surface is now very irregular, with a basically brownish-black patina overlaid with a soft gray-green in the crevices of the face and a bluish-green malachite in the hair. The bare bronze shows through in places, especially on the torso at the shoulders, the abdomen, the left thigh and knee, and the backs of both thighs, the left buttock, and the right calf. The upper back is particularly mottled, with large areas of red cuprite exposed on the left scapula and in the center back.

EXHIBITED: San Francisco, Calif., M. H. de Young Memorial Museum, February 20-May 16, 1982, *The Search for Alexander*, Supplement to the Catalogue by J. Geary Volk (San Francisco, The Fine Arts Museums of San Francisco, 1982) no. S-10, n.p.; Supplement to the Catalogue (Toronto, The Royal Ontario Museum, 1983) 12-13, no. S-14.

PUBLISHED: J. Geary Volk, "A Lysippan Zeus," *California Studies in Classical Antiquity* III, 2 (1984) 272-283, pls. I-XI, XIX.

NOTES: The condition statement draws on a report by Pieter Meyers on the condition of this bronze.

For the Zeus Thunderer motif and references to the collected examples of this type, large and small, see S. Boucher 1976, 67-68.

For the discussion of the identification as Leochares' Zeus, see J. Charbonneaux, "Le Zeus Brontaios de Leochares," *MonPiot* LIII (1963) 9-17; also J. Charbonneaux et al., *Hellenistic Art, 330-50 B.C.*, tr. P. Green (New York, 1973) 210-211, fig. 221.

For the discussion of the type as Lysippus' Tarentine colossus, see J. Dörig, "Lysipps Zeuskoloss von Tarent," *JdI* LXXIX (1964) 257-278.

For other versions of the image, see also S. Reinach, *Rép.stat.* I:184, 681A, the Ince Blundell marble Jupiter; and idem, IV:1-5; and H. Menzel, "Les ateliers des artisans bronziers," *Dossiers de l'archéologie* XXVIII (May-June 1978) 58-63. (I thank John Herrmann for bringing this last article to my attention.) Also, a silver statuette in the J. Paul Getty Museum (77.AM.26) reproduces the image in another medium.

For Polyclitan features, see H. von Steuben, *Der Kanon des Polyklet; Doryphoros und Amazone* (Tübingen, 1973).

On the typically Roman combination of classical and Lysippan elements in statuettes of Zeus, see H. Menzel, "Observations on Selected Bronzes in the Master Bronzes Exhibition," in *Art and Technology* (1970) 231.

For the reference to Leochares' statue of Zeus Thunderer taken to Rome and set up on the Capitoline, see Pliny, *NH*, XXIV.19.79.

For a parallel to the high lead content of the statuette and the arguments for the Roman date of the British Museum's bronzes from Paramythia, which include Volk's closest comparison for the Fleischman Zeus Thunderer, see J. Swaddling, "The British Museum Bronze Hoard from Paramythia," *Bronzes hellénistiques* (1979) 103-105, pls. 49-57, esp. discussion of the composition of the Dione figure on p. 105.

For an expanded discussion of the high proportion of lead in Roman bronzes, see E. R. Caley, "Chemical Composition of Greek and Roman Statuary Bronzes," in *Art and Technology* (1970) 37-49.

For the presence of gilding and techniques for its application on ancient bronzes, see W. A. Oddy, T. G. Padley, and N. D. Meeks, "Some Unusual Techniques of Gilding in Antiquity," *Proceedings of the 18th International Symposium on Archaeometry and Archaeological Prospection* (London, 1978) 230-242, with extensive bibliography, and W. A. Oddy, "Gold in Antiquity: Aspects of Gilding and of Assaying," *Royal Society of Arts Journal* CXXX (1982) 730-743. I thank Jerry Podany and Susan Lansing for these references.

30. Antiochus IV Epiphanes as Heracles

The diademed King Antiochus IV Epiphanes (175-164 BC)—in a statue heretofore thought to represent Seleucus IV Philopator, King of Syria (187-175 BC)—stands holding in his outstretched left hand the lionskin, and probably once also the club, of Heracles. The iconographic traditions are thus those of the Macedonian conqueror, Alexander the Great, who claimed to be descended on his father's side from Heracles.

Seleucus IV, born in 218 BC, was the son of Antiochus III, the Great (223-187 BC). On becoming king, Seleucus IV had to maintain good relations with the Roman Republic and pay the Romans the great indemnity exacted after the defeat of Antiochus III at Magnesia in 190 BC and the treaty of Apamea in 188 BC. He also maintained friendly contacts with the kingdoms of Macedonia and Egypt. One of his advisors had him assassinated and his baby son declared ruler, but in a short time

GRECO-ROMAN, EARLY IMPERIAL, 50 BC-AD 50. H. 57.8 CM. THE NELSON-ATKINS MUSEUM OF ART, NELSON FUND, 46-37

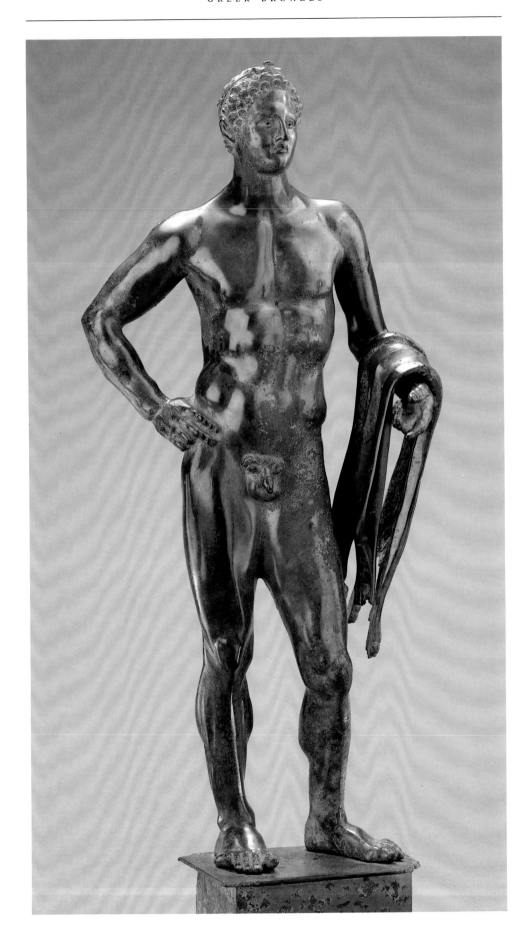

his younger brother, Antiochus IV Epiphanes, became his real successor. This Antiochus spent his student days in Athens and undertook the continuation of the Olympieum, a building left unfinished since the time of the sons of Pisistratus in the late sixth century BC, as a Hellenistic Corinthian temple. He died fighting in the East.

This figure of the young king has a majestic pose and stance suggesting that a life-sized or larger prototype existed in antiquity for this noble presentation. The statue is placed on the type of rectangular, altar-like base that also evokes a grander scale. Although slightly obscured by its present surface condition (mud and corrosion), the naturalistic details of hair, face (an idealization of a haughty prince), and veins on the right hand speak of early to middle Hellenistic observation in the scientific traditions of Lysippus. The stance, the zigzag from chest to legs, and the counterpoise of the arms, however, seem too unsubtle for Lysippus. The Greek sculptor of the original statue, working in Athens when Antiochus IV was in the city or at Antioch-on-the-Orontes at a slightly later date, took dramatic liberties with the fourth-century traditions. These modifications show that the originator of this royal Seleucid image was really part of the new tides of Hellenistic drama and sculptural pretensions radiating from the court art of Pergamum in northwest Asia Minor.

This statue was fashioned, probably in the Augustan or Julio-Claudian period of the Roman Empire, at a time when so many similar "historical" bronze figures and busts were treasured by wealthy households in Pompeii, Herculaneum, and the countryside that was devastated by the eruption of Vesuvius on August 21, AD 79. The Greco-Roman world, which followed the extinction of Ptolemaic Egypt in 31 BC and was annexed by Octavian to Rome after the Battle of Actium, had a

strong sense of visual history where the nostalgia of Greek freedom and power was concerned. Prominent Greeks recalled their ancestors' proud pasts, while romantic Romans cherished images of the rulers prominent in the histories or in the records of the Roman Senate.

The Kansas City statue has been known for decades as Seleucus IV Philopator, but comparison with the Seleucid tetradrachms (Figure 30a), the only true basis for identification, confirms that it represents his younger brother, Antiochus IV Epiphanes, who was occasionally restrained by the Romans and who had every reason to be loved by the Athenians. Antiochus IV was also the Seleucid king who appears to have tried to Hellenize the Jews and who initiated the events leading to the Hasmonean Revolt in 167 BC.

Perhaps a Roman administrator in the East, such as the Procurator Pontius Pilate, commissioned this statue and somehow left it in Benevento on his way back to Rome. The alleged findspot suggests that the statue might have been brought to a Roman villa near one of the roads like the Via Traiana that led from the ports for the East to the Bay of Naples and beyond to Rome. *C.C.V. III*

Figure 30a. *Antiochus IV Epiphanes* (175-164 BC), Obverse of a silver tetradrachm. Minted at Antioch, ca. 173/2-169 BC. After *Auction XX* (Los Angeles, Calif., 1988) no. 773. Photo: Andrew Daneman, Courtesy Numismatic Fine Arts International, Inc., Los Angeles, California.

CONDITION: The figure was hollow cast in five sections in leaded bronze. The proper left arm, both legs, and the head were cast separately from the body. The lionskin is a separate piece, made in two sections and welded together. Remains of chaplets(?) are visible in places, as are numerous casting flaws. The nipples appear to have been inlaid with copper. The core may have been removed through the back where there remain many patches.

Damage occurred and repairs to the damage were made in antiquity as corrosion was found in the cracks and on the patches. Additional damage (spade marks?) occurred in modern times probably at the time of unearthing. The club is missing from the open left hand, as is a small section of the lion's tail. The presence of a small corroded pin suggests that the end of the tail was originally separate and attached mechanically. The right hind foot of the lionskin is missing.

The surface is covered with black, green, and red corrosion products. The proper left arm is nearly black in color in contrast to the green-black of the rest of the figure. This does not mean, however, that the arm is a later addition. Similar x-ray fluorescence analyses and microscopic examination show that the arm is original to the figure, and the cause of the differentiation of color is not known.

PROVENANCE: Said to have been found at Benevento.

EXHIBITED: Cambridge, Mass., Fogg Art Museum, December 18, 1954-February 15, 1955,

Hellenistic Art in Asia, cat. by B. Rowland, Jr., no. 2.

PUBLISHED: *ArtQ* IX (1946) 178, 181.
Art News XLV (February 1947) 40, 60.
FA II (1947) no. 1841.
AJA LX (1956) 338.
Handbook of the Collections in the William Rockhill Nelson Gallery of Art and Mary Atkins Museum of Fine Arts, Kansas City, Missouri, 4th ed. (Kansas City, Mo. 1959) ed. Ross E. Taggart, 34, 2 illus.
C. C. Vermeule 1980, 74-75, 129, 239, pl. 92A.
H. G. Martin, *Römische Tempelkultbilder: Eine archäologische Untersuchung zur späten Republik* (Rome, 1987) 97-98, fig. 24.

NOTES: I would like to thank Bruce Christman for sharing his examination report on this bronze.

For iconography, see G. M. A. Richter 1965, III:269-273, figs. 1880-1891; R. R. R. Smith 1984, 241-242, citing H. Kyrieleis, *Ein Bildnis des Königs Antiochos IV von Syrien*, Winckelmannsprogramm der Archäologischen Gesellschaft zu Berlin CXXVII (Berlin, 1980); N. Davis et al., *The Hellenistic Kingdoms: Portrait Coins and History* (London, 1973), figs. 78, 79 (Seleucus IV), 80, 81 (Antiochus IV), pls. 84, 85.

For history, see O. Mørkholm, *Antiochus IV of Syria* (Copenhagen, 1966); "The Municipal Coinages with Portraits of Antiochus IV of Syria," *Congresso internazionale di numismatica, Roma 1961*, II (Rome, 1965) 63-67; M. Stern, in *A History of the Jewish People*, ed. H. H. Ben-Sasson (Cambridge, Mass., 1985) 202-210.

Figure 30b. *Seleucus IV* (187-175 BC). Obverse of a silver tetradrachm. Minted at Antioch, 187-175 BC. After *Auction XX* (Los Angeles, Calif., 1988) no. 773. Photo: Andrew Daneman, Courtesy Numismatic Fine Arts International, Inc., Los Angeles, California.

Etruscan Bronzes

Etruscan Bronzes

The elusive Etruscans have long fascinated and perplexed us, but gradually, as excavations and study continue, answers to some of the many questions about them have begun to emerge. The people whom we call the Etruscans (to the Greeks they were the Tyrsennoi, to themselves the Rasenna, and to the Romans—from whom we have derived their modern name—the Tusci or Etrusci) inhabited the portion of Italy bounded by the Arno and Po rivers to the north and south, the Apennines to the east, and the Tyrrhenian Sea to the west. This region appears to have been inhabited continuously since the Bronze Age. The Iron Age saw a highly developed culture, known as the Villanovan, prosper. Significant Villanovan remains have been discovered, among which are magnificent bronzes showing a high degree of technical competence. During the seventh century BC, the people of this region learned to write from their neighbors at the Greek colonies in Cumae and Pithecusae, and began to make records in their own unique language. It is at this time that we consider the Etruscan culture to have begun, and it continued until the region fell entirely under Roman domination, a lengthy process that was only completed in the first century BC. The bronzes in this exhibition, however, were made between the sixth and second centuries BC, during the fullest flowering of the Etruscan civilization. Most are from Etruria proper, but a few, such as the warrior from the Nelson-Atkins Museum of Art, Kansas City [40], and the satyr from the Walters Art Gallery [42], may have been made in contiguous parts of the Italian peninsula, under Etruscan influence.

Even ancient historians argued about the origins of the Etruscan people. The Greek historian Herodotus suggested that they were Lydians; Hellanicus, a fifth-century Greek chronicler, believed that they were the Pelasgians; and yet another Greek scholar, Dionysius of Halicarnassus in the first century BC, took the stance that they were simply the indigenous people of the Italian peninsula. Modern scholars would tend to support the latter view, as the archaeological record shows a continuous and gradually evolving culture, with no evidence of invasions or significant disruptions throughout the prehistoric and protohistoric periods. If in fact settlers arrived from elsewhere, they appear to have been assimilated without wreaking any radical changes on the existing local culture.

The wealth of Etruria derived not only from its abundant agricultural resources but also from its "metal-bearing" hills, which were mentioned frequently by ancient authors. The quest for ores brought many people to its shores. The Phoenicians had established active trade relations by the eighth century BC, when the Greeks established their first colony at Pithecusae. By the seventh century, Greek trading posts were established along the Tyrrhenian coast, and both Ionian and Corinthian pottery is found in Etruria. Etruscan bronzes from this period have been found as far afield as Gaul and the Celtic settlements to the north. Rich Phoenician luxury goods, including metal vessels decorated with motifs based on Egyptian and Assyrian styles, were discovered in the Barberini, Bernardini, and Regolini-Galassi tombs of this date. The "orientalizing" qualities of early Etruscan art draw on these traditions as well as those of the Ionian Greeks.

By the sixth century the Etruscans had become a major sea power; Etruscan bucchero—the local heavy-walled polished black pottery—bronze tripods from Vulci, and the distinctive spouted pitchers known as *Schnabelkannen* from this period have been found in such widely scattered sites as Sicily, Magna Graecia, the Greek mainland, the coastal Greek cities of Spain and France, the Hallstat settlements in Gaul, and Punic North Africa. Similarly numerous Greek imports, particularly Attic black-figure vases, have been found in Etruria. Toward the end of the century and into the early decades of the fifth, close contact with the colonial Greek

178

towns to the south in Campania provided yet another avenue for the transmission of Greek artistic ideas into Etruria and vice versa [32, 42]. Often it can be difficult to tell on which side of the border a given bronze was made.

During the fifth century, imports from Greece itself appear to have declined, perhaps reflecting a deterioration of Etruscan naval power after the Syracusan naval victory in 474 BC, although the Etruscans still imported Attic red-figure vases in quantity. Much of the Greek trade seems to have been by way of a newly opened port at Spina on the northern Adriatic coast of Italy. The trade in finished objects went in both directions, however, as Etruscan bronze utensils continued to find markets abroad.

Toward the end of the century, Greek pottery imports increased again and the Etruscans developed their own imitations of these wares. Torelli[1] has described a fourth-century renaissance, a vigorous burst of construction and artistic activity in Etruria, which was again colored by Greek influence, being largely transmitted by way of the Greek cities in South Italy. As early as the late fifth and fourth centuries BC, Gallic invasions and Roman incursions had begun to weaken the Etruscan civilization. In 396 BC Rome defeated the Etruscan city of Veii, and in mid-century Rome went to war against the city of Tarquinia. After an uneasy period of peace, warfare broke out anew in 311 between the Etruscan League and Rome. Raids and hostilities flared fitfully in the succeeding decades, culminating in the dramatic Etruscan defeat at the battle of Sentinum in 295 BC, after which the Etruscan cities fell under Rome's dominion in rapid succession.

Conventionally art historians have tended to consider Etruscan art as a kind of poor provincial attempt to replicate the glories of Greek art. Prone to evaluate Etruscan work in terms of its success in approaching Greek ideals, they usually concluded that it remained inferior. The "best" Etruscan art was that most closely approximating Greek artistry. Occasionally, Etruscan bronzes were mistaken for Greek [39], although when their true identity was established, they were less prized by collectors than they had been while considered to be Greek. The comparative slimness of this section of the exhibition is in part a reflection of the relative lack of interest in Etruscan art among American collectors in the early decades of this century, when the works that today form the backbone of American museum holdings were being acquired.

As the historical synopsis makes clear, however, Etruscan art was a product of many cultural influences, of which the Greek—though important and recurrent—was but one. It seems apparent that the Etruscans forged their own aesthetic from these many influences and that their art should be evaluated on its own terms, not against a Greek cultural yardstick.

Similarly, the Etruscans appear to have had a much less distinctly defined progression in the evolution of their style than did the Greeks. Whereas in Greek art there is a readily perceptible and quite consistent development from what art historians designate as the Archaic to the Classical to the Hellenistic style, with well-established transitional phases as well, the Etruscans seem to have comfortably retained older styles at the same time that they were instituting new ones. They tended to be conservative, retaining time-honored formulations for generations rather than setting them aside in favor of the new. Often such features coexist in the same object. The warriors on Cleveland's cosmetic box (cista) handle [45], for example, have faces in an Archaic style not unlike those of the Getty's Tinia [39] of half a century earlier, but their bodies reflect an understanding of anatomy and an interest in complex movement that is much more "advanced." The problem of dating can be further complicated by revivals of earlier styles, such as the second-

and first-century figures of Hercle, the Etruscan Heracles, that reiterate fourth-century types like Toledo's statuette [46]. For these reasons, placing Etruscan bronzes in a specific time frame is often difficult. It has been traditional to date Etruscan figures by referring to Greek works that exhibit similar characteristics. Besides considering the Etruscan tendency to retain older styles, however, it is important to remember that communication was not instantaneous in antiquity. The sources through which the Etruscans became familiar with developments in Greek art were probably not monumental sculptures but rather more portable items such as painted vases, bronzes, and luxury goods, or possibly drawings or models in materials that no longer survive. Innovations in large-scale sculpture would influence the style of these smaller objects, which would then have to find their way into the trade and make a lengthy voyage before even being seen by an Etruscan craftsman. There may, of course, have been itinerant artisans from Greece who could have transmitted the tradition personally—or Etruscan travelers who visited Greece—but still any adoption in Etruria would hardly have been immediate. Thus, although it may be useful to consider the date of an innovation in Greek art as an optimistic determinant of the earliest possible date for an Etruscan piece, such comparisons are rarely helpful in establishing the latest likely date of its creation.

What features can be identified as components of a distinctly Etruscan aesthetic? What qualities should be understood as having been deliberately sought rather than representing failed efforts at aping Greek models? If one looks at characteristic bronzes of the Etruscan Archaic such as the Morgan kore [33] and the Cleveland dancer [34], it is possible to identify several interrelated characteristics: an essentially two-dimensional quality; an emphasis on the elegant silhouette and the use of repeating curving forms; and a love of decorative surface patterning and descriptive detail.

Whereas at this period the Greek artist was struggling to represent the human figure—although an idealized version, to be sure—as naturalistically as possible, as a tangible, three-dimensional integral being, the Etruscan focused on the overall decorative effect. His subject was often conceived in terms of a front view joined to a back view, the sides largely neglected. It may be that the Etruscan sculptor was drawing on a two-dimensional representation as a source—perhaps a vase painting, wall painting, or relief plaque—but in turning his model into a sculpture in the round, he did not strive to rethink it in three dimensions as a Greek sculptor would doubtless have done.

In the interest of a lively silhouette, the figure was freely distorted by the Archaic Etruscan artist—hands and feet elongated and curled in unlikely ways, head turned 180 degrees, garment hems flaring. It is not that the Etruscan artist was incapable of making a lifelike figure, but he was fascinated instead with the patterns that could be imposed on the human form. In particular, he experimented with the replication of curves, almost to the extent of turning the human figure into an extension of the plant world. The love of pattern in the silhouette carried over to a fascination with surface ornament and, by extension, with superficial descriptive detail as well. Yet, although he might show exactly how a costume was made down to the individual stitches, the Etruscan sculptor was not concerned with representing the way in which the neck relates anatomically to the shoulders or how the drapery actually falls as it moves over the forms of the body beneath, as was his Greek counterpart. The result of this selective descriptivism, stylization, and emphasis on pattern—much as in the Art Nouveau or Art Deco styles closer to our time—is often highly pleasing to the eye, but its goals must be seen as very different from those of the contemporary Greek culture.

These fundamentally Etruscan traits can be found in work both earlier and later than the Archaic period. In the early "Apollo" in the Boston Museum of Fine Arts [31] the anatomical structure of the body is reduced to a dramatic pattern of chevrons and diamonds. In the fifth century and later, the Etruscans and their Italic neighbors produced series of stylized warriors (Figure XII) and elongated votive figures (Figure XIII), not represented in this exhibition, in which the emphasis on silhouette and exaggeration of proportions for aesthetic reasons are carried to extremes.

The preoccupation with descriptive detail is also pervasive. In the late fifth- or early fourth-century woman from the Walters [44], the patterning of the dress rather than the anatomy has preempted the artist's imagination. Elaborate hairdos and beards on many of the statuettes [36, 39] are described with loving care. One could probably actually duplicate an Etruscan shoe or sandal from the detailed depictions on several bronzes, which faithfully render the shoelaces, straps, and seams [43, 44, 48, 50]. Even on a highly Classical, essentially nude figure such as Toledo's Hercle [46], the artist has lavished great effort on depicting the fall of the hair on the lion's pelt, while in a moving narrative such as that found on the cista handle in Cleveland [45], the sculptor offers an elaborate digression on the construction of the foot-soldiers' body armor.

The emphasis on front and back views only, which we have noted in the Archaic bronzes, also continues to some degree. The Walters' woman [44], for example, is extremely thin front to back, so that the side views scarcely exist. There are awkward unfinished passages on the sides of the Smithsonian kouros [38]. Given the fine quality of the fronts and backs of these bronzes, it is unreasonable to conclude that the artist could not creditably treat the sides as well; he simply

Figure XII. *Umbrian Warrior.* Bronze, H. 24.5 cm. Etruscan, 4th century BC. From Ancarano, province of Perugia, Italy. Providence, Museum of Art, Rhode Island School of Design, Mary B. Jackson Fund, 34.011.

Figure XIII. *Elongated Woman with Crown.* Bronze H. 22.8 cm. Etruscan, 5th century BC. Cambridge, Harvard University Art Museums (Arthur M. Sackler Museum), Bequest—Marian H. Phinney, 1962.64.

181

did not feel that it was necessary. Such an approach to the human form would, however, be anathema to the Greek artist, who beginning with the earliest kouroi dealt with the figure in its entirety, as an organic volume in space. Even in Etruscan sculptures treated fully in the round—such as the Kansas City warrior [40], the Toledo Hercle [46], or the Fleischman votive youth [47]—the figure is more a compendium of parts than a truly integrated whole.

Figure XIV. *Candelabrum*. Bronze, H. 121.3 cm. Etruscan, late 5th or 4th century BC. The Saint Louis Art Museum, Museum purchase, 187:1954.

Although the Etruscans adopted the early Greek alphabet in the seventh century and numerous short inscriptions survive (see [46, 47]), none of their literature has persisted and their language is only imperfectly understood. As a result, our knowledge of their religion is sketchy. A bronze model of a sheep's liver from Piacenza,[2] dating from the Hellenistic period, is one of the more valuable remaining documents. Livers were used for divination by priests. This model, possibly designed for their instruction, is divided into 44 sections, each assigned to a divinity. It thus provides a sort of Etruscan cosmological diagram. Etruscan engraved mirrors of the fourth and later centuries are also helpful, since they show gods and goddesses in mythological scenes, often with the participants conveniently labeled. Besides enabling us to connect a deity with his or her typical iconography, they also help us to learn something about the roles they played. Nonetheless, these sources are not only late but also fragmentary, which means that it is simply not possible, on the basis of current knowledge, to do more than speculate about whether many of the known bronze statuettes represent deities, heroes, or mortals. In instances where the archaeological context is unknown, we cannot be certain whether the object was a votive dedication or simply an object created for enjoyment [43].

Besides statuettes that were probably votive—such as the Getty and Smithsonian kouroi, the Getty Tinia, and the Fleischman youth [37, 38, 39, 47]—other bronze figures served to enhance utilitarian objects—such as incense burners [36], skillet-like paterae [48-50], or cistae [45]. Although the general notion of using human figures to embellish utensils and vessels can be found in many earlier cultures—Egyptian, Near Eastern, and Greek (see [6, 7]) among them—the Etruscans adopted it wholeheartedly, and elaborately ornamented Etruscan bronze utilitarian wares became well known and coveted items of trade. The Etruscans enjoyed such luxury at home, as well, as is glimpsed in their tomb paintings. Banqueting scenes set with candelabra, incense burners, stands for a drinking game called "kottabos," and elaborate vessels show their fondness for their own bronze productions. Possessions treasured in life were also buried with the dead, and much of the Etruscan art in museums today has come from tomb excavations. We are not certain, however, whether some types of objects found in graves—such as paterae—were made exclusively for use in burial rites, or whether they also had a function in everyday life, perhaps for bathing after athletic activities (see [48, 49]).

Greek versions of some of these devices exist, but the Etruscan translations are usually more elaborate and more likely to have figurative ornament. To the simple shape of a Greek kottabos stand, the Etruscans added a figure at the top (see the Boston silenus [41]); the routine, architectonic man-with-ram patera handles of Greece became, in Etruscan hands, a variety of maidens and Lasas in inventive poses (see [48-50]). Some types of bronzes were purely Etruscan inventions, notably the candelabra (Figure XIV) and rod-tripods (Figure XV) of Vulci and the cistae that were a specialty of Praeneste (Figure XVI). The cast handles (see [45]) and feet of cistae provided rich opportunities for figurative sculpture, while the hammered bronze sides and lids of the vessels were incised with complex scenes taken from myth and legend. Other bronzes are certainly attachments, but what they once belonged to is not certain [31, 32].

Besides problems of stylistic development and dating, and unresolved questions about the identities and uses of many Etruscan bronzes, there is also considerable difficulty in determining where a given bronze was made. The hilly topography of central Italy, with few natural harbors, made communication even among places close to each other quite difficult. Also, the Etruscan cities were never even as loosely united politically as were the Greek city-states. Instead, they guarded their independence, engaging in shifting patterns of alliances and animosities over the centuries. Even when faced with the growth of Rome's power, they failed to unite. With the exception of Populonia, a metal-refining center on the mainland opposite the island of Elba, the Etruscan coastal cities were actually located somewhat inland, on high ground and adjoining waterways that led to the sea, and often in sight of it. The southern coastal cities—Caere, Tarquinia, and Vulci—and Veii, on a tributary of the Tiber, controlled trade to the interior and prospered at an early date. Being closest to the Greek colonies of South Italy and the first points of contact with traders arriving by sea, they tended to be more quick to absorb foreign influences.

Caere (known today as Cerveteri), one of the oldest cities, had strong ties with Greece, maintaining a treasury at Delphi and the practice of consulting the oracle there. It was known for its fine painted pottery, including the Caeretan hydriae of the middle Archaic period, which likewise show strong Greek influence, and a series of painted terracotta plaques used as wall decorations, as well as for handsome terracotta sarcophagi. Tarquinia, another city dating back to Villanovan times and, like Caere, strategically located on a bluff a few kilometers from the sea, is perhaps best known for its elaborate painted tombs of the sixth century BC. Hammered

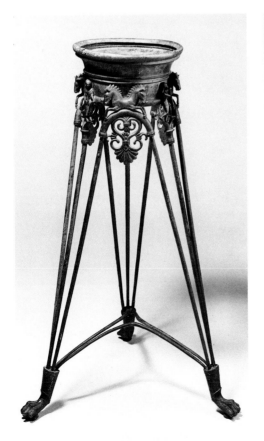

Figure XV. *Tripod*. Bronze, H. 61.28 cm. Etruscan, ca. 530-510 BC. From Vulci. The Saint Louis Art Museum, Museum purchase, 37:1926.

Figure XVI. *Cista*. Bronze, H. of body 29.85 cm.; H. of lid 16.19 cm. Etruscan, 4th century BC. From Praeneste. Baltimore, Walters Art Gallery, 54.132.

bronze decorative "shields" with repoussé masks in their centers were also made there in the late sixth century.

Pride of place among the Archaic bronzeworking centers must belong, however, to the neighboring city, Vulci, famed for its tripods (Figure xv), incense burners [36], and other decorative objects [32]. A major importer of Greek goods, Vulci also housed the first Etruscan workshops producing vases in the manner of Corinthian Greek wares and, later, both black-figure and red-figure pottery, including the handsome, if misnamed, "Pontic" vases. A lively artistic center for sculpture and jewelry as well in the sixth and early fifth centuries, Vulci declined around the middle of the fifth. In the fourth century the local stone sculpture tradition was revived. Production of bronzes continued throughout the fifth and fourth centuries and into the third, but it did not regain the level of quality or quantity attained in the Archaic and early Classical periods.

Veii, another important southern city, slightly north of Rome, was a major artistic center of the late Archaic period, particularly for the manufacture of large-scale terracotta sculpture. Few bronzes have been found there, but they may have been melted down or carried off after the sack of Rome in 396 BC.

Clusium (Chiusi), a newer city located inland in northeast Etruria, was likewise a major bronzeworking center, particularly after the late sixth century. Its products tend to be more retardataire in style, perhaps because of its distance from the coast and the influx of foreign influences.

Remains of a major Etruscan city have been found at what is today Orvieto; it may have been Volsinii Veteres, although the precise location of that settlement is open to debate (see [46, 47]). Bronzes from this region, ranging from the fifth century until the mid-third, show strong Classical Greek influence, perhaps by way of South Italy. Other sites in the region, including the area around Lake Bolsena, have yielded bronzes of contemporary date and related style.

Finally, mention should be made of Palestrina (Praeneste), a Latin city in the Sabine Hills east of Rome. Palestrina had close connections with southern Etruria as early as the eighth century BC and controlled important trade routes between the coast and the Appenines. During the fourth century, it became a center for the manufacture of elaborate engraved hand mirrors and cistae. The style of Praenestine bronzes of this date, related to that of Greek Tarentum, and the contents of rich tombs in the city attest to its good relations with Magna Graecia.

Although the broad outlines of styles associated with specific cities at certain periods are emerging, the picture is clouded by the knowledge that a bronze was not necessarily made in the region where it was found; and for many objects taken in clandestine or unsystematic excavations, even the information about findspot is lacking. Much work remains to be done before it is possible to make such regional attributions with any certainty.

A tremendous amount of research is going on in the field of Etruscan studies, however. Within the last five years a number of significant publications have appeared, adding measurably to our understanding of Etruscan bronzes. Certain important classes of objects are receiving systematic analysis in publications such as the *Corpus Speculorum Etruscorum* (mirrors) and the corpus of Praenestine cistae,[3] both of which will continue beyond the initial volumes now in print. To these volumes should be added Hostetter's careful study of the bronze candelabra from Spina[4] and Richardson's monumental *Etruscan Votive Bronzes*, which groups and analyzes votive statuettes through the Archaic period by type.[5] Dohrn has published a thoughtful examination of Etruscan sculpture during the Greek Severe Style period,[6] while Haynes presents an overview in *Etruscan Bronzes*, complete with much new data about metallic composition, and attempts to distinguish regional schools.[7] Cristofani's survey[8] offers information on manufacturing methods and many excellent new color reproductions. Among museum catalogues, Adam's work on the Etruscan and Italic bronzes in the Bibliothèque Nationale, Paris,[9] is exemplary. A series of exhibitions in Tuscany and Perugia, 1985-1986, under the auspices of the Progetto Etruschi, has brought wider exposure to the rich holdings of Italian museums, which are often inadequately published.[10] *Etruscan Life and Afterlife*, a compendium of articles by distinguished Etruscologists, is a highly successful summary of the current state of Etruscan studies, designed to point those interested toward the specialized literature.[11]

Through these publications and the continuing excavations, the "mysteries" of the Etruscans are gradually being explained. A clearer sense is developing about the Etruscans' unique creative contributions, not merely as pale imitations of Greek models but as a vigorous, integral tradition of their own. The impact of this tradition on other Mediterranean cultures and in particular on the civilization of Rome, which came to supplant that of the Etruscans, is another fascinating area for study.

Suzannah Fabing

1. M. Torelli, "History: Land and People," in *Etruscan Life and Afterlife: A Handbook of Etruscan Studies*, ed. L. Bonfante (Detroit, 1986) 57.

2. Now in the Museo Civico, Piacenza. See L. B. van der Meer, *The Bronze Liver of Piacenza: Analysis of a Polytheistic Structure* (Amsterdam, 1987).

3. The following volumes of the *Corpus speculorum etruscorum* have appeared to date: *Denmark* I: *Copenhagen, Ny Carlsberg Glyptotek* (Odense, 1981); *Italia* I, *1-2: Bologna, Museo Civico* (Rome, 1981); *Netherlands* (Leiden, 1983); *DDR* I: *Berlin, Staatliche Museen, Antikensammlung;* II: *Dresden, Staatliche Museen* (Berlin, 1986); *Belgique* I: *Bruxelles, Institut Royal du Patrimoine Artistique* (Rome, 1987); *USA* I: *Midwestern Collections* (Ames, Iowa, 1987). One volume on cistae has appeared thus far: G. Bordenache Battaglia, *Le ciste prenestine,* I: *Corpus* (Florence, 1979).

4. E. Hostetter 1986.

5. E. Richardson 1983.

6. T. Dohrn, *Die etruskische Kunst im Zeitalter der griechischen Klassik: Die Interimsperiode* (Mainz, 1982).

7. S. Haynes, *Etruscan Bronzes* (New York, 1985).

8. M. Cristofani 1985.

9. A. -M. Adam, *Bronzes étrusques et italiques.* Bibliothèque Nationale (Paris, 1984).

10. These catalogues include: *Fortuna degli Etruschi* (Florence, 1985); *Civiltà degli Etruschi* (Florence, 1985); *L'Accademia etrusca* (Milan, 1985); *La Romanizzazione dell'Etruria: Il Territorio di Vulci* (Milan, 1985); *Artigianato artistico in Etruria* (Milan, 1985); *L'Etruria mineraria* (Milan, 1985); *Santuari d'Etruria* (Milan, 1985); *Case e palazzi d'Etruria* (Milan, 1985); *Scrivere Etrusco* (Milan, 1985); *La Formazione della città in Emilia Romagna dalle origini all'età romana* (Bologna, 1986); and *Bibliotheca etrusca* (Rome, 1986).

11. L. Bonfante, ed., 1986.

31. Apollo

ETRUSCAN,
CA. 550-520 BC.
H. 21.3 CM.
MUSEUM OF FINE ARTS,
BOSTON, H. L. PIERCE
FUND, 98.653

This youthful male nude confronts the world directly, his gaze aimed steadily and levelly forward. His confident frontality and symmetry are emphasized by the position of his arms, with elbows out and hands on hips.

The triangles created by the arms akimbo are repeated in the chevron form given to his prominent collarbone, the trio of grooves articulating his rib cage, his triangular pubic hair, and the diamonds into which his kneecaps have been stylized. His eyes, edged with a double groove, are also nearly triangular in shape. His nose is a triangle, and his unusual beard, hatched on the chin only, forms yet another insistently projecting triangular form. His straight, broad mouth adds to the severity of his expression. Prominent straight grooves down the front of both thighs help emphasize the figure's angular geometry and its symmetry. Below the knees this line is continued by the distinct edge formed by the meeting of two planes in the lower legs. On the outside of each thigh another deep straight diagonal line helps to define the limbs and offers a schematic idea of the musculature. As is characteristic of Etruscan art, however, the love of pattern prevails over any attempt at naturalism.

Offsetting its geometric severity, on the other hand, the figure's hair is parted slightly off center and crosses its forehead in gentle waves. It emerges from behind the ears in two locks that fall over the shoulders in front. These are bound at intervals with fillets, tightly wrapped at their lower ends. The grooves outlining the muscles in the arms, while similar in function to the lines on the thighs, curve to reiterate in linear fashion the rounded forms of the youth's flexed biceps. His left foot is advanced slightly, bringing some sense of movement into his otherwise static pose. The eyelashes are delicately incised. The dots on the chest may be intended to represent chest hair, as they certainly represent hair in the pubic region.

Although conceived in the round, with prominent buttocks and heavy thighs, the figure has no decorative detail or incision on its back, and the fingers at the small of the back are shown only schematically. The upper body and head are unnaturally thin in comparison with the heavy legs, and the rear of the right arm is flat or even concave in places. Evidently the object was made to be seen only from three sides, and its upper part may have rested against some other surface. Its function is not clear from the rectangular plinth, the post that emerges horizontally from the back of the head, or the fragment of an attachment surviving on the top of the head. Jantzen has suggested that it may have been part of a tripod, while Comstock and Vermeule propose that it came from a bucket-shaped vessel called a "situla."

There seems to be no basis for the historical designation of the figure as Apollo, other than its seeming self-possession and mastery of its surroundings—traits that might not be so evident in a mere mortal. Apollo was a popular subject of statuettes in Greece at this period, but with many Etruscan statuettes it is in fact virtually impossible to tell whether they represent deities or votaries. Richardson has pointed out that, with a single exception, only Hercle (Heracles) and Menrva (Minerva) can be positively identified in statuettes before the late Archaic period. It is more likely, therefore, that the Boston statuette represents a mortal youth, related to the Greek kouroi (e.g., see [2]).

As Richardson has indicated, the Greek kouroi can be divided into an older, "active," group, which hold their arms away from their bodies and frequently grasp something in each hand, and the subsequent more stately, empty-handed, and aloof figures, whose hands rest at their sides. Richardson postulates that the livelier figures are worshippers, offering-bearers, or temple attendants, rather than "true kouroi." Both types were dedicated in sanctuaries, but only the true kouros was used for funerary monuments and cult images.

The Etruscans first borrowed the "true kouros" type from Greece, and it became the most common type among their sixth-century votive bronzes. As the Greek type evolved stylistically, the style of the Etruscan bronzes changed in imitation, allowing a rough gauge for dating. Nonetheless, the Etruscan bronzes never fully copy their Greek models. As Richardson states, "the Etruscan tradition of the body as a decorative support for the head is too strong to be replaced by the Greek tradition of the body as an equal partner with the head in a balanced composition based on observation of nature." The Boston bronze, with its emphasis on symmetry and pattern, betrays the Etruscan fondness for the decorative over the naturalistic. The thick, long neck, relatively small head in proportion to the body, nipped waist, and sharp shin-line reflect the Greek kouroi of the middle Archaic period. The aesthetic of the Mantiklos Apollo [2], nearly two centuries earlier, has also left its mark.

The pose, with both hands on hips and elbows out, is highly unusual. Jucker has discussed the far more common gesture among Archaic Etruscan statuettes—that with left hand on hip and right hand extended—but cites several Campanian bronzes and one Etruscan example that have arms akimbo.

The place of manufacture of the Boston youth has been open to debate. Jantzen assigned it to Locri, on the basis of somewhat unconvincing comparisons with later objects. Mansuelli suggests that it may not be Etruscan but proposes no specific place of manufacture. Riis has maintained that it is Campanian, probably Capuan, based on similarities to some terracotta antefixes. Indeed, the closest parallels do appear to be works in clay, either terracotta or bucchero (Italic black

ceramics). The facial features—notably the wide-open eyes, rimmed all around, the straight nose, horizontal mouth, and pointed chin beard—recall the relief heads on bucchero vessels of the mid-sixth century or terracottas such as one from San Biagio delle Venella, near Metapontum. The hairdo, with single locks falling in front of the shoulders, can be seen on another bucchero vessel, a pitcher (oinochoe) from Orvieto; the center part and gentle wave over the forehead is worn by the male figure on the famous sarcophagus in the Louvre, from Caere.

Ultimately, however, it is to Crete that we must look for the artistic impetus behind the Boston figure. Contact had been established between Crete and both Etruria and South Italy quite early, and the influence of the so-called "Dedalic style"—stylistic conventions for representing the human figure of the late seventh century BC—lasted a long time on the Italian peninsula. It was not uncommon for Etruscan and South Italian artists in the mid-sixth century to look to Cretan monuments of the seventh century for inspiration. Cut-out relief plaques such as one now in the Louvre and the elaborately decorated panoplies from Afrati offer a source for the linear delineation of muscles and for the leggy proportions of the Boston figure. A head on a Cretan relief pithos offers further parallels. Reinterpreting these Dedalic models as much as a century or so later, with the influence of the Greek kouros tradition also at hand, the artist of the Boston youth created a synthesis that is both forceful and unique.

CONDITION: X-ray fluorescence indicates that the alloy for this figure, which was solid cast in one piece, is leaded bronze. Patina varies from light green to black. Red cuprite is visible under the green corrosion; the thin black layer lies over the green in places, particularly on the lower chest and legs. Small casting flaws are present in many places, particularly on the right rear calf, another high on the left thigh at the rear. Some abrasion appears on the back. The nose has been flattened in modern times, and the tip of the beard is broken off. A long, cylindrical projection from the back of the head shows that the figure was attached to something. Some iron corrosion products may be present in the indentation at the end of the projecting element. There are traces of other attachments at the top of the head and the back of the base, now broken off. There are lightly punched dots on the chest, which form circles with a center dot, above the breast on each side. Other dots form a "necktie" down the center of the chest. A double or single row of dots runs under the breast. The figure bears scratch marks down each side, the remnants of the making of a gelatin mold at some point in its recent history.

PROVENANCE: Bought in Naples by Edward Perry Warren.

EXHIBITED: Worcester Art Museum, Mass., April 21-June 4, 1967, *Masterpieces of Etruscan Art*, 27-29, illus. 28, 120, no. 13, fig. 13, cat. by R. S. Teitz.

PUBLISHED: E. Robinson in Boston Museum of Fine Arts, *Annual Report* (Boston, 1898) 25, no. 11.
"Erwerbungen des Museum of Fine Arts in Boston im Jahre 1898," *AA* (1899) 136, no. 11.
E. Langlotz, "Ein Votivrelief aus Tarent," in *Antike Plastik; Walther Amelung zum sechzigsten Geburtstag* (Berlin, 1928) 115, n. 3 (as Campanian).
K. A. Neugebauer 1931-1951, I: 107, n. 3.
A. Rumpf, *Griechische und römische Kunst*, 4th ed. (Leipzig, 1931) 16.
U. Jantzen, *Bronzewerkstätten in Grossgriechenland und Sizilien* (Berlin, 1937) 3, 7, 69, no. 1; pl. I:1.
P. J. Riis, "Some Campanian Types of Heads," *From the Collections of the Ny Carlsberg Glyptotek*, 2 vols. (Copenhagen, 1938) II:152-153, fig. 18.
P. J. Riis, *An Introduction to Etruscan Art* (Copenhagen, 1953) 41f., pl. 16, fig. 24.
P. J. Riis, "The Danish Bronze Vessels of Greek, Early Campanian, and Etruscan Manufactures," *ActaA* XXX (1959) 44.
G. A. Mansuelli, *The Art of Etruria and Early Rome* (New York, 1965) 86.
G. A. Mansuelli, "La recezione dello stile severo e del classicismo nella scultura etrusca (Note problematiche)," *RA* (1968) fasc. 1, 80.
V. Poulsen, *Etruskische Kunst* (Königstein im Taunus, 1969) 11, illus. 10.
H. Jucker, "Etruscan Votive Bronzes of Populonia," in *Art and Technology* (1970) 200-203, figs. 10a-b.
S. Settis, "Su un kouros da Medma," *Archeologia classica* XXIII (1971) 67, pl. 21: 1-3.

M. Comstock and C. Vermeule 1971, 156-157, no. 178.

E. Schmidt, *Geschichte der Karyatide: Funktion und Bedeutung der menschlichen Träger und Stützfigur in der Baukunst* (Würzburg, 1982) 182, n. 285.

B. B. Shefton, ''Phoenizier im Westen,'' *Madrider Beiträge* VIII (1982) 362, n. 68.

NOTES: I am grateful to Arthur Beale for his assistance in examining the object and have also drawn on a report by Richard Newman.

E. Richardson 1983, 1:96-97, discusses the distinction among Greek kouroi between the older, ''active'' group and the later true kouroi, and the Etruscan adoption of the type.

The classic discussion of the Greek sculptures of this genre is G. M. A. Richter (*Kouroi*) 1970.

The arms akimbo pose is analyzed by H. Jucker (*Art and Technology*) 1970, 200-203. The unusual pose led G. A. Mansuelli 1965, 86, to doubt the authenticity of the MFA piece, although his article (*RA* 1968) implies that it is authentic but not Etruscan.

On the single hand on hip, see also J. -C. Balty, ''Un centre de production de bronzes figurés de l'Etrurie septentrionale, Volterra ou Arezzo?'' *Bulletin de l'Institut Historique Belge de Rome* XXII (1961) 5 ff., and E. Richardson 1983, 1:37.

The attribution to Locri is made in U. Jantzen 1937, 3, no. 1; that to Campania, probably Capua, in P. J. Riis 1938, 153.

For related heads on bucchero vessels, see, for example, a pitcher from Chiusi in the Museo Archeologico, Florence: M. Sprenger and G. Bartolini, *Die Etrusker: Kunst und Geschichte* (Munich, 1977) 87, no. 42 (English ed., *The*

Etruscans: Their History, Art and Architecture [New York, 1983]) 92, pl. 42); a drinking cup in the Ny Carlsberg Glyptotek: V. Poulsen 1969, 29; for another pitcher, from Chiusi, Musées Royaux d'Art et d'Histoire, Brussels (acc. N. 1434-A), see G. Q. Giglioli, *L'arte etrusca* (Milan, 1935) pl. LI:1.

For the terracotta head from Metapontum, see W. Hermann, *AA* (1966) 328, fig. 103, center of top row.

For the oinochoe in Orvieto, Museo dell' Opera, no. 438, see G. Q. Giglioli 1935, pl. LIV, who also illustrates the well-known Louvre sarcophagus, pl. CXVI:2.

On contact between Crete and Etruria in the sixth century, see L. B. Warren, ''Riflessi di arte cretese in Etruria,'' in *Studi in onore di Luisa Banti* (Rome, 1965) 81-87. For the Cretan parallels, see H. Hoffmann and A. E. Raubitschek, *Early Cretan Armorers* (Mainz, 1972) esp. pl. 49:2 (Louvre plaque), pls. 1, 2 (Schimmel helmet). See also A. Lembessi, *To Hiero tou Herme kai tis Afroditis sti simi Viannov: I, 1, Khalkina Kritika Torevmata* (Athens, 1985).

The kriophoros in Berlin (inv. 7477) shows similar treatment of the kneecaps and faceting of the lower leg. See K. A. Neugebauer 1931-1951, I: pl. 19, no. 158, and G. M. A. Richter (*Kouroi*) 1970, 68-69, figs. 166-168. See also P. Blome, *Die figürliche Bildwelt Kretas in der geometrischen und fr

üharchaischen Periode* (Mainz, 1982) pls. 22:1 (Berlin) and 22:2 (Louvre plaque).

For the relief pithos (Ny Carlsberg Glyptotek, I.N. 3380), see ibid., pl. 50; and M. Gjødesen, ''The Artistic Context and Environment of Some Greek Bronzes in the Master Bronzes Exhibition,'' in *Art and Technology* (1970) 146-151, figs. 1-4.

32. Kneeling Archer

The . . . Scythians had on their heads tall caps, erect and stiff and tapering to a point; they wore breeches, and carried their native bows, and daggers, and axes withal.

Herodotus, *Historiae* VII.64

The exotic Scythians clearly fascinated the Greeks and, in turn, the Etruscans, both of whom depicted them on their pottery. In Greece the bow was used only occasionally in hunting before the fifth century, but the Athenians began to recruit Scythian archers for their army about 530 BC. Greek vases of the second half of the sixth century represent Scythians, the majority of these coming from the period of 530-490, which coincides with their being hired for the Greek imperial army as it fought against Darius' army in the Persian wars. Etruscan vases occasionally depict Scythians as well, probably in imitation of their Greek prototypes. In bronze

ETRUSCAN,

530-500 BC.

H. 5 CM.

RHODE ISLAND

SCHOOL OF DESIGN

MUSEUM OF ART,

PURCHASE, MUSEUM

WORKS OF ART FUND,

47.792

the foreign archers appear more frequently, notably in a series of Campanian dinoi (large bowls for mixing wine and water), which feature groups of figures in Scythian dress, mounted or occasionally on foot, wielding their bows as they chase around the lids of these large cauldrons.

This tiny archer offers evidence of the extreme care in detailing and finishing that the Etruscan bronzeworker was willing to lavish on even the smallest object. The unusual Scythian costume is presented in elaborate detail. The figure wears a distinctive cap that comes to a tall, curved point, with flaps in front of the ears that cover the cheeks and flow out over the shoulders, and a pointed flap covering the neck and extending down the center of the back. Made of leather, these caps were part of the standard gear of a Scythian archer. The short tunic ends just below the waist in the back, its hem ornamented with a row of zigzags; in the front, folds of an underskirt cover the genitalia. The long trousers with close-fitting legs are indicated by patterns of large zigzags and dots, representing the appliqué decorations favored by the Scythians. In the crook of his left arm is nestled a gorytos, a kind of combination quiver and bow case, also decorated, here with incised crosshatching. His right hand probably originally held a bow. His feet are bare, the toes on his left foot being indicated, even on this minute scale.

The archer's face shows the influence of Ionian Greek art on the Etruscan canon of beauty at the end of the sixth century: slanting oval eyes, full cheeks, a small mouth drawn up slightly in an Archaic smile. Broad shoulders, heavy thighs, and muscular lower legs lend a sense of mass to so small a figure and link it to contemporary products of the Vulcian workshops.

The same sort of costume was used in Campania and Etruria to depict Amazons (probably because they were "barbaric" and reputedly skilled archers), and indeed it is not clear whether many of the bronze figures, including this one, are male or female. Mitten has cited closely related statuettes in Berlin, Dresden, and at Smith College (Northampton, Massachusetts), calling attention to a candelabrum figure of a Scythian in Kansas City as well; another is in Bologna.

The archer kneels on a volute which protrudes at right angles from a pair of flanking seven-petaled palmettes between volutes; beneath the center element is a shell motif with eleven ribs. The back of this slightly curved supporting bracket is unfinished, although the figure of the archer is carefully finished on all sides. Clearly, the bracket was intended for attachment to an object from which the archer would have stood out in the round. Mitten has suggested that this object might have been a small vessel analogous to later spouted situlae, or a pot-shaped helmet (pilos).

CONDITION: This solid-cast figure has a reddish patina. It is missing the tip of the point of the hat, and possibly a bow from the right hand. The piece has been mechanically cleaned.

PUBLISHED: D. G. Mitten 1975, 102-105, figs. a-g. A.-M. Adam, "Bronzes Campaniens du Vᵉ siècle avant J-C," *Mélanges de l'école française de Rome. Antiquité* XCII, 2 (1980) 649 and n. 34.

NOTES: On the Scythian costume and weapons, see M. F. Vos, *Scythian Archers in Archaic Attic Vase-Painting* (Groningen, 1963) 40-49, 65-66, and passim.

L. Bonfante, *Etruscan Dress* (Baltimore, 1975) 76-77, discusses the "Phrygian" hat. After 490 BC images of another group of oriental barbarians who dressed similarly, the Persians, begin to appear in Greek vase painting, a consequence, undoubtedly, of contact with these people during the Persian wars. The Etruscans also occasionally represented a deity in a Scythian cap, with bow and quiver, but clad in an animal skin. He has traditionally been called Heracles, but E. Richardson, *The Etruscans: Their Art and Civilization*, rev. ed. (Chicago, 1976) 234, has suggested that he may represent Silvanus, while L. Bonfante 1975, 76-77, proposes that he may be a specifically Etruscan hero or deity for whom a particular iconography was devised in the late sixth century BC. See T. Campanile, "Statua di Eracle in bronzo d'arte etrusca," *BdA*, 2nd ser., III (1923-24) 453-463; E. Galli, "Hereklu," *Studi etruschi* XV (1941) pl. 6:2 and 3.

A principal source for the Greek view of the Scythians is Herodotus, whose *Historiae* Book IV is largely devoted to them. In Book I.73 he attests to their proficiency with the bow and recounts that the Medes asked the Scythians to teach archery to their youth. The translation cited here is reprinted by permission of the publishers and the Loeb Classical Library from Herodotus, *Historiae,* translated by A. D. Godley (Cambridge, Mass.: Harvard University Press, 1946).

Among the well-preserved Campanian dinoi with mounted Scythians or Amazons are two in the British Museum, see H. Busch et al., *Etruskische Kunst* (Frankfurt, 1969) XLI, illus. 116 and 117; and O. Brendel, *Etruscan Art* (Harmondsworth, Eng., 1978) fig. 155; also Metropolitan Museum of Art: see O. Brendel 1978, fig. 154, and G. M. A. Richter, *Handbook of the Etrus-can Collection* (New York, 1940) fig. 81; and Berlin, Staatliche Museen, Antikenabteilung: see O. Brendel 1978, fig. 153.

A list of such mounted archers can be found in P. J. Riis 1938, 156-157, 158, nos. 15-20. See also A.-M. Adam (*MEFRA*) 1980, 642-649, who discusses both the mounted figures and those on foot.

On the relationship between Campania and South Etruscan art, particularly that of Vulci, see O. Brendel 1978, 226-228.

For the similar figures in Dresden, Berlin, and Northampton, and the candelabrum figure in Kansas City, see D. G. Mitten 1975, 105, nn. 8-11; K. A. Neugebauer, "Erwerbungen der Antiken-Sammlungen in Deutschland. Berlin Antiquarium. I: Bronzestatuetten," *AA* (1922) cols. 77-78, no. 27, illus.

For the candelabrum figure in Bologna see R. Pincelli, "L'arciere scita della Certosa," *Strenna storica Bolognese* VII (1957) 89-94.

Some tiny helmet ornaments showing scenes of combat, two above palmettes, are in the Villa Giulia, Rome: G. Q. Giglioli 1935, pl. CIV:2-5. A pot-shaped (Negau type) helmet with appliqués at the top, from the Tomba del Guerriero at Vulci (525-500 BC), is in the same museum, inv. 36579: M. Cristofani, ed., *Gli etruschi in Maremma: Popolamento e attività produttive* (Milan, 1981) 62, fig. 43; S. Haynes 1985, 267, no. 60, illus. 28.

See also the helmet in Berlin (G. Q. Giglioli 1935, pl. CCCV:2), which has an appliqué on the forehead. Other possible helmet ornaments are in the Bibliothèque Nationale, Paris: E. Babelon and J.-A. Blanchet 1895, nos. 580, 800, 895, 896, 897; note also the archers, nos. 892 and 903; see also M. Comstock and C. C. Vermeule 1971, 169, nos. 195, 196. They cite a helmet of a different type, with hinged cheekpieces and a nosepiece, which has figurative attachments on its sides that project out at an angle: Ny Carlsberg Glyptotek, *Bildertafeln des etruskischen Museums (Helbig Museum)* (Copenhagen, 1928) no. H229, pls. 97-99.

33. Kore

ETRUSCAN,
LATE 6TH C. BC
H. 29.4 CM.
METROPOLITAN
MUSEUM OF ART,
GIFT OF
J. PIERPONT MORGAN,
17.190.2066

One of the most engaging Etruscan statuettes in America, this standing maiden has been widely published and exhibited. The Etruscan sculptor has doubtless taken as his model the Archaic korai, which evolved during the later half of the sixth century in Greece and which were representations of votaries rather than goddesses. This bronze may have been a votive dedication at a sanctuary. Like her Greek cousins, she stands confidently before us, with her left foot very slightly advanced, daintily grasping a fold of her skirt and drawing it out to the side (see also [7, 44]). She probably clasped some sort of offering in her outstretched right hand, now lost. She greets the viewer with a straightforward gaze and a slight Archaic smile.

As Richter and others have pointed out, the sculptor wanted to dress his maiden in the height of Greek fashion. He must have been using a vase painting or relief as his model (see also [34]), however, for although the front of the statuette shows a fairly accurate rendering of the then-stylish Ionic chiton over which is wrapped a heavier diagonally draped himation, the side and back views reveal that the artist did not know how such a costume would look. The statuette was apparently designed to be seen from all sides, since the body is modeled in the round and the long hair is carefully and lovingly detailed as it spills down the maiden's back. The garment in back, however, is completely unbroken by folds of any kind, and there is no trace of the himation. As a result, the artist ran into real trouble on the sides, where the transitions are awkward and confused.

The heavier-weight himation would have been draped around the body—over one shoulder and under the opposite arm, falling in a diagonal across the chest and back. The artist has treated it, instead, as a sort of apron across the front only, its ends forming nearly symmetrical swallowtails on either side of an elaborate symmetrical set of zigzag folds. A tassel or weight hangs from each of the swallowtails, one modeled plastically, the other incised. Along the diagonal upper edge and the lower edge, the himation is decorated with a wide, crosshatched band, bordered by a single row of dots. From the evidence of statuettes such as this and vase and tomb paintings, Bonfante has concluded that the Ionian costume, which was universally worn by women in Greece and South Italy in the late Archaic period, was never adopted in Etruria.

Purely Etruscan, however, are the maiden's shoes, laced in front and featuring pointed, turned-up toes. This fashion was introduced in Etruria around 550 BC. It was worn consistently—by men and women—until about 475 BC. After that point it went out of use as everyday wear, being reserved for depictions of goddesses and what are probably female religious celebrants or priestesses, who are shown wearing what was by then an "old-fashioned" style. The Morgan maiden's preserved right shoe is very carefully and elaborately detailed; a row of dots surrounds the clearly drawn laces and curves into a floral decoration at the point of the shoe.

Also Etruscan is the maiden's penchant for jewelry. She wears rosette-shaped earrings, a necklace composed of a double row of punched circles, and a fillet in her hair adorned with three roses. Although the Greek korai also affected jewelry such as this (cf. [2, 6]), the taste for heavy jewelry remains a prominent feature in Etruscan costume throughout the centuries.

The bronzeworker has lavished much attention on the decorative details added in cold working after the bronze was cast. At the neck of the chiton is an incised border of zigzags, with a row of tiny punched dots at their lower extremities. The shoulder seam of the garment is represented by a double incised line, bordered on both sides by a row of dots; a single row of dots encircles the hem of the sleeve, possibly meant to represent decorative stitching. Thin, wavy lines, radiating in groups from the shoulder seam across the chest, are doubtless meant to indicate wrinkles in the thin chiton fabric, as it pulls away from buttons or pins that would have secured the shoulder. There are places where the lines along the shoulder seam curve, as though pulling away from a pin, but no pin is shown; again, the artist was probably attempting to imitate a model he did not understand. Beneath the right breast, three rows of tiny dots march diagonally across the drapery folds, creating a decorative but artificial surface pattern that ignores the play of the drapery beneath.

The skirt of the chiton—visible beneath the himation—has a pattern of triple spirals, composed of punched dots. The spirals recur across both front and back, but do not respond to the folds that the parallel raised ridges across the skirt are intended to represent. The chiton's lower edge is decorated with an elaborate crosshatched border, all around the figure. The ankle-length skirt was typical of Etruscan dresses [35], whereas the Ionic costume would have had a longer skirt. In Greece the gesture of lifting the skirt with one hand was a logical one; with the shorter Etruscan style, it is somewhat superfluous. The mannered gesture of the hand, its long fingers outstretched and bent backward to form a curve, is a familiar feature in Etruscan art.

The unfortunate corrosion of the face somewhat obscures its wide-eyed intensity. The eyes are almond-shaped, the mouth full, and the face quite rounded above a heavy neck. The hair is rendered with elaborate detail. Strands of hair on either side have been looped up under the fillet, much as on Greek statues like the Acropolis korai, but they are bluntly cut off rather than continuing back behind the ears in the Greek manner.

X-radiographs of the bronze (Figure 33a) show that it was a thick-walled hollow cast and had a sort of crude U-shaped armature inside it, which probably helped

support the core. Both the hollow casting and the use of an armature are highly unusual for Etruscan or Greek figurines at this date. As Brendel has pointed out, the bronze's relatively large scale reflects the affluence of Etruria in the last years of the sixth century. The partial core, however, would have served to reduce the mass of metal somewhat, allowing more even cooling and reducing the chance of damage in casting.

Riis has proposed that the Metropolitan kore might have been produced in Chiusi, relating it to Neugebauer's Chiusine group. Others have thought it probably Vulcian. The curious, ridged diagonal folds in the skirt, crosshatched borders, and a more successful attempt at rendering the fabric pulling away from pins on the sleeves are found on a female figure from an incense burner in the Ny Carlsberg Glyptotek, ascribed by Riis and Haynes to Vulci. The two also share the heavy neck, rounded face, and almond-shaped eyes, although the figure in Copenhagen appears somewhat more Archaic. The two bronzes were probably made in the same locality.

An elegant kore in the Bibliothèque Nationale, Paris, generally assigned to Chiusi, shares with the Metropolitan girl the carefully detailed hairdo, long and straight in back, with short pieces in front of the ears and scallops over the forehead. It also exhibits a predilection for symmetry and an elaboration of patterns on the drapery, although not the raised ridges representing folds. Both the Copenhagen and Paris figures wear typical Etruscan costume, however, so that the artist could detail the back as carefully as the front.

Both Vulci and Chiusi were active bronzeworking centers in the late sixth century, noted for their decorative bronzes. Vulci traded actively with Greece and would have kept abreast of artistic developments there. Its generally stocky, mus-

 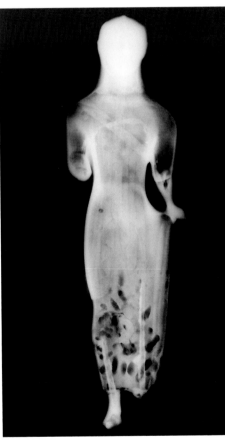

Figure 33a. X-radiograph showing ancient armature. A surviving ancient armature is rare and provides valuable information about how ancient bronzes were made. X-radiograph by Carlie Cleveland.

cular figures with small mouths drawn into Archaic smiles retained much of the middle Archaic aesthetic even into the fifth century (see Figure xv). Bronze figures assigned to Chiusi tend to be taller and thinner, slightly mannered, with a concern for revealing the anatomy beneath the garments.

Chiusi, whose earlier art had been heavily influenced by local traditions, toward the end of the sixth century achieved a sudden influx of wealth and power and, concurrently, in its art began to look more closely at Greek models. Being situated well inland, however, Chiusi received external artistic influences only through intermediaries—often from Vulci earlier in the sixth century but increasingly through Capua and Greek South Italy toward the end of the century. There was frequently a time lag before new styles took hold in Chiusi, and even then they may have been mixed with older styles or local traditions. Although the kore reflects aspects associated with both Chiusi and Vulci, her very modishness may tip the scales in favor of Vulci. Only when more is learned about the various schools of Etruscan bronzeworking in the Archaic period, however, will a definite assignment become possible.

CONDITION: For casting, see discussion above. The figure's right hand and left foot are missing. The left foot is restored in wax. The right foot is original but has been dowelled on with a brass rod in modern times. A very smooth brown-black patina covers much of the figure. It was adjudged by conservators at the Metropolitan to be a cassiterite patina, a "water patina" more commonly found in Chinese than in Mediterranean bronzes. Tin oxide also occurs on the face. There is considerable pitting of the surface on the face—especially the right side—on the right shoulder, along the decorated garment folds in front, and in portions of the hair and buttocks. X-radiographs taken in July 1986 (Figure 33a) reveal long rods in both legs, presumably added in modern times. They also show what appears to be an ancient armature running across the clavicles and down from neck to lower torso, with an inverted U-shape supporting the upper sections of the legs.

Small lenticular areas scattered over the body are places where core supports, or chaplets, were affixed during the casting and were later polished off. An ancient plug is visible on the right lower leg, over which there is a punched design element in an S-shape. Another, larger repair is visible on the back, between the lower legs. This is probably also ancient and was very carefully done. X-radiographs (Figure 33a) show that the bronze in the lower part of the skirt has considerable porosity, probably resulting from gasses trapped during the casting process.

PROVENANCE: J. Pierpont Morgan, New York (acquired ca. 1910).

EXHIBITED: Buffalo, N.Y., Albright Art Gallery, February 1937, *Master Bronzes: Selected from Museums and Collections in America*, no. 78. Zurich, Kunsthaus, January 15-March 31, 1955, *Kunst und Leben der Etrusker*, cat. by H. and I. Jucker, 81, no. 170. Cologne, Römisch-Germanisches Museum, April 29-July 15, 1956, *Kunst und Leben der Etrusker*, cat. by H. and I. Jucker, 117, no. 283. Worcester Art Museum, Mass., April 21-June 4, 1967, *Masterpieces of Etruscan Art*, cat. by R. S. Teitz, 44-45, no. 30, illus. 146, 147.

PUBLISHED: *BMMA* V (April 1910) 103.
G. M. A. Richter (*AJA*) 1912, 343-349, pls. 3-4.
G. M. A. Richter 1915, 34-38, no. 56.
A. A. Bernardy, "Collezioni etrusche nei musei di New York e Boston," *StEtr* I (1927) 472, fig. 69.
F. Poulsen, *Aus einer alten Etruskerstadt*, Det Kgl. Danske Videnskabernes Selskab. Historisk-filologiske Meddelelser XII, 3 (Copenhagen, 1927) 33, no. 2.
P. Ducati, *Pontische Vasen*, vol. V of *Bilder griechischer Vasen*, ed. J. D. Beazley and P. Jakobsthal (Berlin, 1932) 9, 11, n. 23.
G. M. A. Richter 1940, 28, fig. 71.
P. J. Riis, *Tyrrhenika, An Archaeological Study of the Etruscan Sculpture in the Archaic and Classical Periods* (Copenhagen, 1941) 123, n. 1.
E. Homann-Wedeking (*RM*) 1943, mentioned 90.

O. W. Von Vacano, *Die Etrusker: Werden und geistige Welt* (Stuttgart, 1955) pl. 70.
V. Poulsen 1969, 80, illus.
L. B. Warren, "Etruscan Dress as Historical Source: Some Problems and Examples," *AJA* LXXV (1971) 278-281, pl. 65, figs. 1 and 7.
L. Bonfante 1975, 53, 200, figs. 132-133.
M. Bieber 1977, 183, figs. 777-778.
O. Brendel 1978, 223, illus. 150; 224, 226.
E. Richardson 1983, I:297, II: pl. 208, fig. 706.
S. Haynes 1985, 281, mentioned under no. 96.

NOTES: I would like to thank Carlie Cleveland, who examined the bronze with me.

For the kind of Greek models on which the Etruscan artist patterned this work, see, for example, the Acropolis korai: G. M. A. Richter 1968, 68 ff., figs. 328-438, esp. figs. 393, 397. The most complete analysis of the problem of the costume is G. M. A. Richter (*AJA*) 1912, 345-347; see also her later publications cited in the bibliography; L. B. Warren 1971, 278-279, and L. Bonfante 1975, 53. The shoes are also discussed by L. B. Warren 1971, 279-282.

On the affluence of Etruria at this time, see O. Brendel 1978, 224. On the hollow casting of large statuettes, see M. Cristofani, ed., *Civiltà degli etruschi*, exh. cat. (Florence, Museo Ar-cheologico, 1985) 39 ff.; E. Richardson 1983, I:92. P. J. Riis 1941, 123, n. 1, relates the kore to the Chiusine group postulated by K. A. Neugebauer, "Kohlenbecken aus Clusium und Verwandtes," *RM* LI (1936) 194 and 196, which Riis expands. Vulci is proposed by E. Homann-Wedeking (*RM*) 1943, 90, while O. Brendel (1978) localizes it in South Italy, as "probably Vulcian."

The incense burner in Copenhagen (H223 [H.I.N. 477]) is connected by P. J. Riis 1941 (p. 79) with his Vulcian B 4 group, and in *Etruscan Types of Heads: A Revised Chronology of the Archaic and Classical Terracottas of Etruscan Campania and Central Italy* (Copenhagen, 1981) appendix 83 f., he suggests that it may actually have come from Vulci. See also S. Haynes 1985, 266, no. 57, illus. 159, fig. 57A, who enumerates other bronzes of Vulcian style in the British Museum on which the ridgelike folds are also found.

For the kore in Paris, see A.-M. Adam 1984, no. 225. Adam in turn relates this piece to the Chiusine group assembled by M. Cristofani, "La 'Testa Lorenzini' e la scultura tardoarcaica in Etruria settentrionale," *StEtr* XLVII (1979) 85-92, which includes the "Artemis" from Falterona, now in the British Museum (his pl. 28a).

34. Dancer or Maenad

This elegantly stylized dancer initially functioned as part of a thymiaterion, an elaborate incense burner. The Etruscans loved to decorate household utensils, and many of the figures in this section of the catalogue were not created as self-contained statuettes but rather as segments of more utilitarian objects.

Silhouette was of paramount importance to the Archaic Etruscan artist, and this elegant figure has been conceived as front and back silhouettes affixed to each other. It is so shallow in depth that it has virtually no "side views." The body has been twisted to keep the arms, the legs, and the head all in the same plane. Its silhouette is a rhythmic succession of curved projections ending in points: the pointed-toed shoes, the fillip of the hem, the swallow-tailed ends of the sash tied at the hips, the elongated points of the sleeves at the elbows, the impossibly boneless and backward curving fingers, and even the forms of the spool-like element on her head. Both positive and negative spaces within the figure bristle with sharp curves and pointed extremities.

This flatness and emphasis on silhouette, seen repeatedly in Archaic Etruscan art, may reflect the bronzeworker's dependence on two-dimensional sources such as wall paintings and vases for his compositions. The Etruscans eagerly imported Greek vases, which would have provided some of the most readily portable models for their art, and produced their own painted vases at Caere, Vulci, and elsewhere. Wall painting in Etruria, as evidenced by the tombs of Tarquinia and by painted terracotta slabs from Caere, had reached its heyday in the last half of the sixth century. Repoussé metal reliefs also treated the figure essentially in two dimensions, with an emphasis on profile. The Cleveland dancer seems to draw on these formulations, rather than on models among independent sculpture in the round.

ETRUSCAN,
LATE 6TH C. BC.
H. 18.7 CM.
THE CLEVELAND
MUSEUM OF ART,
PURCHASE FROM THE
J. H. WADE FUND,
53.124

A similar sort of costume, distinguished by the prominent knotted sash over the hips, is worn by two other bronze female figures, both from utensils. One, on an incense burner in the British Museum, shares the Cleveland dancer's planar orientation, although she looks forward rather than back. The second, a candelabrum figure in the Louvre, is frontal and conceived more fully in the round, but shares the back-curved fingers and pointed sleeve-tips that enliven its contours. The 180-degree turn of the head, to look back over the shoulder, is likewise found on a handsome incense burner with a female castanet-player, also in the Louvre. There are male dancers and acrobats, too, who embody the same vocabulary of forms, notably a trio of incense burner figures in Paris, Berlin, and Karlsruhe. All these figures are assigned to the school of Vulci, the principal center for the manufacture of candelabra and other elegantly decorated utensils in the last decades of the sixth and early fifth centuries BC. The Cleveland dancer's facial features, particularly the profile with receding forehead and chin, demonstrate the strong debt of this bronzeworking school to the Ionian Greek style.

The candelabra and incense burners that these figures once adorned are composed of a limited number of forms recombined in imaginative variations. The circular base on which the dancer stands, edged with beading and an egg-and-dart motif, is like the top of one in the Louvre (Br. 1477). It apparently rested, in turn, on a tripod base of three vigorously curved animal-like legs ending in lions' paws, as in the Bastis thymiaterion [36]. An old photograph in the curatorial files at The Cleveland Museum of Art shows it on such a base, supposedly excavated with the figure. Both the base and fragments of the dish that would have held the incense were reported to be in the Cigliano collection in Rome in 1953 and were at one time intended as gifts to the Cleveland Museum.

The spool on top of the dancer's head would have been the first stage of a many-tiered shaft, punctuated at intervals with discs or floral "umbrellas" of various diameters, and ending, probably, in a spray of spiky leaves and flower buds (cf. [36]). (The metal pin that would have supported the shaft can still be seen inside the spool-shaped element.) A shallow pan to hold the incense would have rested on the top of the floral crest; in the case of a candelabrum, which followed much the same form as an incense burner, candles would have been impaled on some of the floral elements, which would have ended in horizontal forked projections for this purpose. The castanet-player incense burner in the Louvre is well preserved and suggests in general what this piece might have looked like. The wall paintings of banquets in Etruscan tombs illustrate the use of incense burners and candelabra in daily life.

Like [35] and many of the dancers cited above, the Cleveland dancer wears pointed shoes with turned-up toes, big disc earrings, and a soft headdress that comes to a point—here it supports the shaft she balances on her head. Her hair emerges from the headdress in scallops, framing her neck and cheeks. Her ears are extremely large and sit high on her head. Her lips are very thick, her chin exaggerated and bulbous, and her cheeks full. Although both profiles are very elegant, the face is not symmetrical from the front and is, in fact, quite distorted—not unlike a head by Matisse or Duchamp-Villon.

The figure has been identified as a maenad—a female follower of Dionysus—by virtue of the fact that she stands with one foot on a tortoise, which has been interpreted as a symbol of music as well as of her woodland environment. (Hermes, according to the Homeric Hymn [IV, 23-59], first used a tortoise's shell as the sound-box for a lutelike instrument, a practice continued by his followers from early antiquity onward.) She may, however, simply represent a dancer, entertaining at a banquet. Tomb paintings show dancers with the same lively curving silhouettes as the bronzes; some even depict such performers actually balancing incense burners on their heads as they dance. Thus, the utensil's form may reflect actual practice. The dancer holds a flower bud or fruit, possibly a fig, which is pointed at both ends. The sinuous curves of her elongated fingers and the bulbous, almost gourdlike volumes of her forearms echo its contour.

CONDITION: The figure, base, and tortoise are solid cast in one piece. The plate which is the foundation for the spool is cast onto the hand and hat. The apparently hollow spool and its sheet metal top are attached to the plate with an iron rivet which probably also continued up to a larger assembly. The surface was apparently smoothed by filing and polishing, and cast details were sharpened with chasing tools. The figure is intact, except that a modern break at the thumb and index finger of the left hand was mended with liquid solder in 1957. The surface has green malachite and red cuprite corrosion products.

EXHIBITED: The Cleveland Museum of Art, September 11-October 10, 1965, *Juxtapositions*. Worcester Art Museum, Mass., April 21-June 4, 1967, *Masterpieces of Etruscan Art*, cat. by R. S. Teitz, 38-39, no. 23, illus. 134.

PUBLISHED: *ArtQ* (1953) 346 (brief mention). S. E. Lee, "An Etruscan Dancing Maenad," *BClevMus* XLII (1955) 186-188, illus. 182. W. M. Milliken, *The Cleveland Museum of Art* (New York, 1958) 12, illus. S. Glubok, *The Art of the Etruscans* (New York, 1967) illus. 34. O. Alvarez, *The Celestial Brides: The Visions of the Eastern Paradise Infiltrate the Mediterranean Afterlife. A Study in Mythology and Archaeology* (Stockbridge, Mass., 1978) 141, pl. 56. O. Brendel 1978, 461, n. 16.

NOTES: I am grateful to Bruce Christman for his assistance in examining this bronze.

For the incense burner in the British Museum (48.6-19.11), see H. B. Walters 1899, no. 598; and S. Haynes 1985, no. 56, illus. p. 158.

For the Louvre candelabrum figure in similar dress (Br. 1477) and the castanet-player from an incense burner (Br. 3145) as well as the British Museum piece, see L. Banti, *Etruscan Cities and Their Culture*, tr. E. Bizzari (London, 1973) 244-246, pl. 44a, c. She cites parallels for the costume and hands in Greek vase paintings and Tarquinian wall paintings.

The male figures are Bibliothèque Nationale: A.-M. Adam 1984, 42, no. 44; Berlin, Antiquarium: G. Q. Giglioli 1935, pl. CCX:2; Badisches Landesmuseum, Karlsruhe (662/93): S. Haynes

1985, no. 54, illus. p. 156. Here and in the subsequent entry, no. 55, she outlines others in this group.

On the symbolism of the tortoise and the identification as a maenad, see S. E. Lee (*BClevMus*) 1955, 186-187. Although maenads are frequently found in the company of satyrs in bronze and terracotta groups of this period, it is difficult to segregate a maenad from any other dancer without her bearded companion, in the absence of such attributes as an ivy wreath, fawn skin, or thyrsus.

Paintings showing dancers with incense burners on their heads are in the Tomb of the Jugglers and Tomb of the Monkey, cited and discussed by O. Brendel 1978, 461, n. 18. See also the discussion under [36] below.

In an inadequately supported hypothesis, O. Alvarez 1978, 141, interprets the pose of moving in one direction but looking back as a gesture of enticement and the fruit as a betel-nut, the Indian symbol of "loving intimacy." He postulates an infiltration of Indian symbolism into Italy, where the betel-nut was unknown.

35. Dancer

With sprightly step, this maiden—perhaps a nymph—executes part of an ancient dance. Her hem and sleeves swirl outward, emphasizing her movement. Their curving, pointed forms are echoed in the stylized curves of her oversized hands and her equally elongated pointed-toed boots. The maiden wears a form-fitting ankle-length dress, unbroken by any folds but decorated with elaborate patterns. This chiton was originally an orientalizing fashion and was adopted by many cultures, including the Greeks, in the later seventh century. The Etruscans modified it by making it shorter, so that it would not need a belt, and by lengthening its sleeves. The dress here appears to have a band of embroidery at the neckline, rendered as pairs of confronted teardrop shapes, the tiny depressions probably made with a punch. This motif continues along the shoulder seams and, as a single row, around the edges of the sleeves and hem. Trios of incised lines radiating downward from the neck edge must be intended to represent wrinkles in the thin fabric. On the sleeves they become wavier, perhaps indicating the pull of the fabric from the pins that would have closed the shoulder seam.

Beginning below the breast and continuing to the hemline in front, the dress is decorated with several lines of ornament, presumably intended to represent a textile pattern. A row of circles lies above a line bordered by a single row of dots on either side, a row of crosses comes next, and then the sequence repeats itself. The bands of design undulate across the body in a generally horizontal direction but are not always parallel, adding to a sense of flow and rhythm in the figure. The maiden also wears an elaborate necklace, rendered on the front of her neck as three rows of punched circles above a band of triangles.

On the back, the decorative bands on the skirt are fewer and tend to be simply single lines or bands of paired confronted teardrop shapes; the necklace disappears. On the sides of the figure only the neck, sleeve, and hem decoration continues. The curves of the woman's body show clearly beneath her garment, and although she is appropriately rounded in front and back, the figure is quite slender when viewed from the side. Rather than thinking of the figure entirely in the round, the Etruscan artist has conceived it in terms of front and back planes. Because of the figure's deliberate stride sideways and to the front, the principal view becomes a frontal three-quarter one, a feature that is shared by contemporary depictions of striding or dancing ladies.

The head is rather small in proportion to the body, with inordinately large eyes set high in the head. The eyes are almond-shaped and flat, with incised circles for pupils. Their prominent rims may be an attempt to represent kohl or cosmetic lines. The mouth is very small, scarcely wider than the nostrils. The prominent ears are also set high, above a stocky neck.

ETRUSCAN,
CA. 500 BC.
H. 13.3 CM.
MUSEUM OF FINE ARTS,
BOSTON, PURCHASE
BY CONTRIBUTION,
01.7482

An elongated cap, with its point slightly rounded off, covers most of the lady's hair, with the exception of a double row of curls in front, and makes her head seem in better proportion when viewed from the side. In the back, however, there is no line of demarcation between the hat and the neck; one flows directly into the other. This type of headdress originated in the Near East as a male fashion but was adopted by women, becoming very popular in the second half of the sixth century. It is often erroneously called a "tutulus," a term which actually describes a hairstyle of roughly the same profile—a high bun or chignon—worn until about 480-470 BC in Etruria and preserved in Roman times as the ritual hairstyle of the wives of the priests, who assisted at sacrifices (flaminica).

The lady's long pointed-toed shoes, the fashionable Etruscan calcei repandi, are left plain. Although her feet are firmly planted on the ground, as was characteristic of Archaic art, the curves and the breadth of her stride already begin to impart a feeling of motion to the figure, which is accentuated by the flip of the hem. The elongated fingers of the left hand, indicated by incised parallel lines, curve backward in the affected fashion so characteristic of Etruscan art. The arcing points of the long sleeve ends form complementary curves. The silhouette of the figure thus has a series of spiky waves that seems almost organic. Indeed, figures with this same kind of silhouette are found on Archaic Etruscan candelabra and incense burners, carrying on their heads tall plant stalk forms with spiky leaves and branches continuing this organic, "vegetative" silhouette. Schiering has likened the tonguelike shapes instead to flames and has spoken of an "electrical" energy surging through these figures. However it is described, this vocabulary of curving, echoing pointed forms lies at the heart of the Etruscan aesthetic during the Archaic period.

In their 1971 catalogue Comstock and Vermeule state that the Boston statuette comes from the same workshop and same tomb as a kouros in the Schimmel collection, a piece which Jucker attributes to Populonia. Richardson has pointed out, however, that the eyes of the Boston maiden are unusual and unlike those of the kouros. She notes the resemblance of the face to a kouros in Dresden and relates the Boston dancer to other similarly dressed late Archaic striding figures of Ionian inspiration, such as a maiden in London and a dancer in Vienna. Schiering has discussed it together with a statuette in Göttingen, whose eye form appears to be similar, and one in Berlin, which shows equally elaborate decorative detailing on the skirt. Neither, however, is close enough to be clearly attributable to the same workshop.

Roughly contemporary with the Cleveland dancer [34], the Boston bronze appears to be a country cousin. Her dress is more simple, although reflecting the same fashions. Her gestures and silhouette, while participating in the same aesthetic, are less elegant and refined, even a bit awkward. The bronzeworker has relied on the use of the graver after casting to create the patterning of her garment, rather than designing a pattern of folds in relief into the wax model from which the bronze was cast. These distinctions suggest a provincial workshop for the Boston bronze. Despite Jucker's efforts to establish its outlines, the school of Populonia is too ill-defined for a definite attribution there; no other clear assignment can be made for this energetic and charming, but idiosyncratic statuette. The use of the figure is likewise uncertain. It does not appear to have been part of a utensil, but our knowledge of the other purposes to which the Etruscans put their bronzes is limited. For want of evidence to the contrary, she has been considered a votive statuette by scholars.

CONDITION: The figure was solid cast in one piece. The toe of the right foot has been filed off. The surface is moderately corroded, especially on the back. There is abrasion on the tips of the breasts. The bronze has a fine, smooth surface which appears to be a tin oxide patina, rather brownish on the head and olive green on the body. There is a tang under each foot. The patterns in the dress, necklace, and other details were incised and punched in cold working; the grooves of the hair were probably cast and later cleaned up by chasing. A prominent scratch exists on the left leg above the knee, and fine scratches have been made down the sides in the process of making a gelatin mold from the figurine in modern times.

PROVENANCE: Bought in Rome by Edward Perry Warren.

EXHIBITED: Buffalo, N.Y., Albright Art Gallery, February 1937, *Master Bronzes: Selected from Museums and Collections in America*, no. 76, illus. Detroit Institute of Arts, March 23-April 20, 1947, *Small Bronzes of the Ancient World*, 8, no. 39, illus. 23.
Zurich, Kunsthaus, January 15-March 31, 1955, *Kunst und Leben der Etrusker*, cat. by H. and I. Jucker, no. 171.

PUBLISHED: "Archaeological News," *AJA* VI (1902) 377.
E. Hill, "Etruscan Dancing Figures," *Magazine of Art* XXXIII (1940) 470 f., figs. 1a, 1b.
O. W. Von Vacano, *Die Etrusker: Werden und geistige Welt* (Stuttgart, 1955) 445, pl. 67.
W. Schiering, "Etruskische Bronzestatuetten in Göttingen," *AA* (1966) 374 f., fig. 10.
Master Bronzes (1967) 66, under no. 57.
H. Busch et al. 1969, xli-xlii, pl. 118.
Art and Technology (1970) 235.
M. Comstock and C. Vermeule 1971, 170, no. 197, illus.
Small Sculptures in Bronze (1976) under no. 44.
C. C. Vermeule, *Roman Art: Early Republic to Late Empire* (Boston, 1978) 7-8, 185, 211, 225, fig. 8.
F. Jurgeit, "Aussetzung des Caeculus—Entrückung der Ariadne," in *Tainia. Roland Hampe zum 70. Geburtstag*, ed. H. A. Cahn and E. Simon, 2 vols. (Mainz, 1980) 1:279, n. 45.
E. Richardson 1983, I:293-294, no. 4; II: pl. 205, figs. 693-694.

NOTES: Arthur Beale kindly examined the bronze with me; I have also drawn on a report by Richard Newman.

On the Etruscan modification of the Greek chiton, see L. Bonfante 1975, 42; on 75-76, she discusses the tutulus and conical cap.

For elaborate utensils with vegetative forms, see, for example, the objects from Vulci discussed under [34]. W. Schiering (*AA*) 1966, 375-377, discusses these vegetative forms.

The suggestion of a relationship with the Schimmel bronze was first made by G. Ortiz and responded to by E. Richardson in a discussion session at a symposium; see *Art and Technology* (1970) 235. For the Schimmel kouros, formerly in the Simkhovitch collection, see *The*

Beauty of Ancient Art, exh. cat. (Mainz, 1964) no. 40, illus.; *Master Bronzes* (1967) 162, no. 159, illus. H. Jucker associates it with Populonia in the same symposium, pp. 210 and 211, figs. 29a-c. E. Richardson 1983, I:293-294 and II: pl. 205, figs. 693-694, compares it with Dresden ZV 491 (her pt. III, chap. 3, Series A Group 3A no. 4); British Museum: H. B. Walters 1899, 74, no. 538 (her p. 293); and Vienna, Kunsthistorisches Museum (inv. 110) (her p. 294, no. 5 and fig. 695). Schiering (*AA*) 1966 illustrates the Göttingen (figs. 1-4) and Berlin (figs. 6-7) comparisons.

36. Thymiaterion with a Dancer

ETRUSCAN, 500-475 BC. H. 33.3 CM. H. OF FIGURE 16.8 CM. CHRISTOS G. BASTIS

So many thymiateria have been preserved that they must have been common appointments in Etruscan households from the late sixth through the third centuries BC. In those of the Archaic period, such as this one, the composition usually features a three-legged base, on which is mounted a large single figure. On its head, the figure balances a shaft (sometimes broken by horizontal discs, leafy "umbrellas," or projecting leaf and stem forms). This is topped with a support for the semicircular phiale, or bowl, that held the incense, the support frequently being composed of vaguely vegetal forms suggesting leaves and buds on stems.

In this example, a dancer, accompanying herself with castanets (krotala), executes a dance step on a small round platform. Her serenity and inward focus give her an almost oriental cast. Despite the fact that she only lifts one heel in the dance, the figure conveys an extraordinary sense of vitality. The rounded forms of her body show through her tight costume, and the lively flare of the skirt at the hem expresses her motion. The elegantly curved line over the left leg, extending to the hem, serves both to define the thigh beneath the skirt and to enhance this sense of movement. There is, moreover, a very subtle asymmetry and torsion within the figure. The axis gently spirals from feet to torso to shoulders to head. Her forward stride is quite pronounced, an emphatic break with the rigidly parallel limbs of earlier Etruscan sculpture. The element she carries on her head is slightly off-center, contributing to the overall impression of asymmetry.

The head is beautiful. In an almost triangular face prominent brows and almond-shaped eyes with incised circular irises are separated by a long, straight nose which is continuous with the brow-line in profile. Her lower lip and chin recede in a manner typical of Etruscan figures at this time. The small mouth is drawn up in an Archaic smile.

The dancer's elaborate hairdo is described in painstaking detail. The hair comes from an unseen center part and is bound by a twisted fillet or braid of hair. Separate small curls are arranged over the forehead. A braided loop emerges beneath the fillet in front of each ear; locks from behind the ears are caught up in a double fold at the back of the head, creating a krobylos, which is held in place by the fillet. This type of complicated hairstyle is found on Greek and South Italian statues and bronzes of about 475 BC. The style was worn, with some modifications, by both men and women. Her large round disc earrings, on the other hand, are typically Etruscan. They have a punched circle in the center and are delicately hatched all around the edge.

The dancer's costume seems to have been typical for castanet-players, to judge from representations in tomb paintings and stone reliefs, as well as in bronze. It consists of a short jacket (ependytes) worn over a chiton that comes to mid-calf. Over the shoulders and crossing front and back are bandolierlike straps, here represented by an incised pattern of alternating plain and checked rectangles. A serpentine ridge over her hips may represent the lower hem of yet another shirtlike garment worn under the ependytes.

The neck of the ependytes is ornamented with a band of zigzags enclosed by a pair of parallel lines, and its hem is indicated by parallel hatching, as is the hem of the skirt. Along the shoulder seam of the sleeves, two rows of zigzags run together. The dancer appears to be wearing sandals or, as Oliver suggests, ribbons wrapped around her ankles. Crossed straps are incised at the ankles, and the sole of the raised foot is flat.

The elongated hands and feet appear to have been the Etruscan canon of beauty in Archaic times. She holds the castanets in her fingertips, and her hands are stylized into almost perfect U-shaped curves. The thumb was not meant to be seen and is as wide as the castanet itself.

The maiden has very broad shoulders. Her breasts are high and small, her waist is low, and her torso is generally quite flat in front. She has large, heavy thighs and projecting buttocks akin to those on many contemporary male figures, however, and is conceived fully in the round.

The base of the incense burner has three leonine legs, ending in claw feet resting on thick discs. At the junctures of the legs, there are palmettes with nine petals. On her head the figure balances the support for the bowl of the incense burner, which sprouts into vegetal forms at its top. The springy curvature of the legs and the taut curves of the plant form at the top both serve to intensify the feeling of vital energy in the figure. An aesthetic of controlled energy is sustained throughout the ensemble.

Many thymiateria were produced in late Archaic Etruria, along with closely related candelabra and tripods. No systematic study has yet been undertaken to group them into workshops, although Vulci is widely acknowledged to have been the center for the manufacture of all three types.

Among objects that seem to have much in common with this example is a handsome thymiaterion in the Louvre, also showing a dancer with castanets, on a similar base and with a similar foliate member at the top, although with a longer and more elaborate shaft. A thymiaterion in the Hunt collection, featuring a satyr who likewise lifts one heel off of his round platform, is virtually identical in height and shares the abbreviated shaft, similarities in the base, and the same general type of bowl-like form as a transition between head and shaft. The satyr and the castanet-player also have the same lithe proportions, long waist, long legs, and aura of vital energy. The similarities are so striking that the two may possibly be ascribed

to the same workshop. That both have only recently come to light raises the suspicion that they may have come from the same tomb or site.

A standing nude male figure with similarly posed arms, holding a blossom, on a thymiaterion ascribed to Vulci now in the Vatican, also seems particularly close in style and may be grouped with these two, even though it has a different kind of base and appears to be slightly earlier.

Although dancers, acrobats, and satyrs abound on incense burners, the conceit of using a castanet-player may have been particularly appropriate. A wall painting in the Tomb of the Jugglers shows a young woman in the chiton, ependytes, and bandoliers of the castanet-player, balancing on her head a candelabrum or thymiaterion whose shaft is ornamented with horizontal discs. A young man next to her is about to toss a smaller disc at the object on her head, possibly in an attempt to have it land in the dish at the top, while the musician behind her accompanies their performance on a double "flute" (aulos). To dance or play music while balancing such an instrument on the head may thus have been part of Etruscan entertainment, re-created in this thymiaterion as a sophisticated double entendre.

CONDITION: The object is in excellent condition. The bronze has been mechanically cleaned, leaving a very smooth mottled dark red and green patina. The thymiaterion is composed of four separate parts: starting from the bottom, the first is the tripod base which flares out slightly at the top. Next is a ring-shaped element between the base and the disc on which the dancer stands. The third piece is the central portion of the thymiaterion, beginning with the disc under the dancer's feet, including the figure and the element on her head, apparently up to and including the leaves at the top. The fourth is a separate piece composed of a thin pierced triangular plate, with a stem and bud extending from each point of the triangle. This element sits inside the crown of leaves at the top of the piece. Originally there would have been a small bowl for the incense, made as yet another separate piece, resting on top of the entire assemblage. The bowl survived into relatively modern times, as a photograph of the object with the bowl is in the owner's possession (reproduced in *Antiquities from the Collection of Christos G. Bastis* [New York, 1987] fig. 122a). A modern screw attaches the first element to the second, and another modern screw joins the second and third elements. A pin in the top of the third element, over which the fourth element is placed, may be modern as well.

PROVENANCE: Acquired in New York in the 1970s.

EXHIBITED: New York, Metropolitan Museum of Art, November 20, 1987-January 10, 1988, *Antiquities from the Collection of Christos G. Bastis*, entry by A. Oliver, Jr., 214-216, no. 122, figs. 122a-g.

NOTES: For a somewhat similar hairstyle, see a Greek bronze athlete pouring a libation, dated ca. 470-450 BC, in the collection of Mount Holyoke College, South Hadley, Mass.; *Master Bronzes* (1967) 86-87, no. 83. *Antiquities* 1987 cites other examples from major Greek sculpture. The locks falling over the cheeks in front of the ears are frequently worn by both male and female castanet-players. See, for example, a male figure in Berlin, from Chiusi: E. Hill (*MagA*) 1940, 475, fig. 12, and the Louvre thymiaterion discussed below, Hill's fig. 17.

On the castanet-player's costume, see E. Hill (*MagA*) 1940, 476-477, 492, figs. 17-19. Also L. Bonfante 1975, 38 and 120, n. 36.

For elaborate disc earrings in gold, from the same period as this bronze, see G. M. A. Richter 1940, 33-34, figs. 106-107; she also published them in *BMMA* XXXV (1940) 223-226 and idem IX (1914) 257, 259, fig. 3, respectively. On the way such discs were attached to the ear, see R. A. Higgins, *Greek and Roman Jewellery* (London, 1961) 138-139.

Examples of castanet-players in bronze include one in Orvieto from a candelabrum: M. Bizzari, *Orvieto etrusca: Arte e storia* (Orvieto, 1967) pl. 24. A looser example from a utensil stand found

at Spina but probably made at Vulci, now in the Museo Archeologico, Ferrara: T. Dohrn 1982, pl. I; E. Hostetter 1986, 32-33, no. 8, pl. II. Others are cited in E. Hill (*MagA*) 1940, 492, n. 19. Note also a castanet-player on a limestone cippus base from Chiusi, ca. 460, in Palermo, Museo Nazionale: O. Brendel 1978, 280, fig. 196; on an engraved mirror of ca. 475 BC: L. Bonfante, "Daily Life and Afterlife," in *Etruscan Life* (1986) 239, fig. VIII-8.

On sandals in Etruria, see L. Bonfante 1975, 59-60.

For the heavy thighs and prominent buttocks on male figures of the period, compare, for example, the figure on a four-wheeled cart in the Louvre: L. Banti 1973, 44a, right; illustrated in profile in *Het Geheim der Etrusken*, exh. cat. (The Hague, Gemeentemuseum, 1955) no. 181, fig. 31; *Il Museo Nazionale di Villa Giulia*, ed. G. Proietti (Rome, 1980) 164, figs. 205-206; Badisches Landesmuseum, Karlsruhe (inv. 62/93): S. Haynes 1985, no. 54; Bibliothèque Nationale: A.-M. Adam 1984, 45 f., no. 46, and the example in the Vatican cited below.

A. Hus, *Les bronzes étrusques* (Brussels, 1975) 88-89, has attempted a preliminary grouping of the Etruscan thymiateria into three categories, based on characteristics of the caryatid figures. The fundamental article on Vulcian bronze-working remains K. A. Neugebauer, "Archaische Vulcenter Bronzen," *JdI* LVIII (1943) 206-278. E. Hostetter 1986, I: ch. 3, attempts to establish typologies for the various parts of candelabra and utensil stands, most of which are later than this piece; no comparable study of thymiateria has been undertaken.

The castanet-player in the Louvre, also cited above, is Br. 3145, called Vulcian. The scalloped line at mid-thigh may represent the same sort of extra shirt as on the Bastis piece. It is also reproduced by G. Q. Giglioli 1935, pl. CCXI:2.

For the male figure, see F. Magi, *La raccolta Benedetto Guglielmi nel Museo Gregoriano Etrusco*, II (Vatican City, 1941) 165-171, pls. 47-49; O. Brendel 1978, 217, fig. 144, and 461, n. 13. Note especially the similarity of the stem-and-bud forms on the base to those at the top of the Bastis thymiaterion.

For the figure in the Tomb of the Jugglers, Tarquinia, see G. Q. Giglioli 1935, pl. CCIV:2, and M. Sprenger and G. Bartoloni, *The Etruscans: Their History, Art and Architecture* (New York, 1983) 105 and pl. 92. Another is in the Tomb of the Monkey, Sprenger's pl. 99.

37. Kouros

Striding forward boldly, this engaging young man holds one hand out, palm-downward, while originally grasping some object with a cylindrical shaft in his other hand. He wears a semicircular tebenna, the forerunner of the Roman toga, its lower border ornamented with a row of punched circles and its upper border indicated as a thick, ropelike roll of cloth.

The heart-shaped face is dominated by large lentoid eyes, their upper and lower lids carefully delineated but with no indication of iris or pupil. The eyebrows are high and arched, further emphasizing the eye sockets. The nose is small, the mouth rather deeply cut and gently upturned in an Archaic smile. The influence of Ionian Greek facial types is pervasive.

The hair is exquisitely worked. A comb tool has been used to produce the fine grooves that radiate in all directions from the crown. Although the ears are exposed, locks fall in front of them, joining with the heavy fringe of bangs to frame the face. The ends of the hair around the face are rendered with a series of tiny parallel hatched strokes, creating an effect almost like a row of architectural beading. The strong shadow cast by the protruding cap of hair becomes a major compositional element in the face. In the back, the hair falls in a neat, shoulder-length mass.

The body has that taut, bursting-with-life quality that we have observed in other Etruscan bronzes. In general, it is well proportioned and works effectively in the round. The broad expanse of chest is naturalistically rendered; the collarbones and musculature are indicated but not exaggerated. On the back, at the base of the neck, a slight ridge marks the beginning of the thoracic vertebrae, evidence of the sculptor's sophisticated observation of the body. The calves are heavy, but the hands and feet are only slightly elongated, lacking the extreme exaggeration of earlier Archaic pieces. The forms of the body can be seen clearly through the drapery, their gentle curves subtly reflected in the linear pattern of the incised lines that represent the drapery folds. These lines are an abstraction of the way the cloth would really fall. Fanning out from the draped left arm and spreading at regular intervals as they wrap around the figure, they reinforce the sense of movement set up by the stride and serve to enliven the surface as well.

The diagonal lines that create the twisted effect along the upper edge of the cloak were made in the wax model, not added by later incising, as were the fold lines. We find these heavy rolled edges on other statuettes as well, notably the handsome male figures from Monteguragazza and Uffington, as well as the Getty Tinia [39]. Perhaps they represent an embroidered or appliquéd band applied to the straight edge of the tebenna, or even an applied cord or work in a trapunto technique. On the front of the Getty bronze, the band almost seems to be an independent element; where the section coming over the shoulder intersects with that wrapping around the waist, the band from the shoulder section overlaps the one from the waist, whereas in the body of the cloak itself, the section covering the shoulder lies under the part that crosses in front of the body and over the forearm. This is probably the bronzeworker's error, however, rather than a record of a real garment.

Although this bronze is part of the same tradition represented by the Getty Tinia [39] and the Smithsonian kouros [38], it appears to be somewhat earlier. The strongly Archaic face, the stiff-kneed stride, the absence of the stylization of the thorax musculature that comes with the influence of the Greek Severe Style, all point to a date around 490-480 BC. As discussed in [38], however, one cannot reliably date Etruscan bronzes on the basis of a presumption of a straight-line progression from Archaic to Classical forms. Even within this bronze, the face and

ETRUSCAN, CA. 490-480 BC. H. WITH TANG, 25.4 CM. H. OF FIGURE 22.5 CM. J. PAUL GETTY MUSEUM, 85.AB.104

treatment of the garment folds are considerably more Archaic than the hairstyle, the naturalistic proportions, and the subtle handling of the bodily forms. Etruscan artists continued to employ Archaic formulas, particularly in rendering faces, well after the Archaic style had lost favor in Greece.

A comparison with the roughly contemporary Greek athlete in Cleveland [12] is instructive. The Greek artist's theme is the perfection of the male nude, beautifully proportioned. The athlete's stance is relaxed and fully understood by the sculptor; the transitions from one part of the body to another are organic and naturalistic. The pensive mood causes the viewer to speculate about the athlete's thoughts, so that the body is depicted as a housing for the equally admirable human mind. In contrast, the Etruscan figure, clothed, as was the preference in Etruria, is more stiff, with the emphasis on the pattern of drapery folds and hair rather than on the way the body works. His engaging smile is outwardly directed rather than introspective, an animating device that helps compensate for the fact that the body is not fully naturalistic.

Although Richardson does not include this bronze in her compendium, it would appear to belong to her group of late Archaic figures wearing the semicircular cloak without a tunic under it (togatae effigies sine tunica). Comparisons have been suggested to the bronze from Pizzirimonte in the British Museum and to a nude kouros in Frankfurt, but none is so close as to be compelling.

CONDITION: The solid-cast figure is covered with a smooth light blue-green copper carbonate patina, containing malachite with isolated areas of azurite. Traces of cuprite appear on the rear between the shoulder blades and on the center front at the collarbone. An area of abrasion on the back, beginning at the right shoulder, has been inpainted. The damaged area behind the left elbow and on the rolled edge of the drapery below the left shoulderblade may result from damage to the wax model from which the piece was cast, as the bronze does not show the kind of displacement that would result from later damage in these areas. The right thumb was broken and repaired in modern times. Most of the object originally held in the left hand is missing.

EX COLLECTION: Private collection, New York.

UNPUBLISHED.

NOTES: I am grateful to Jerry Podany, who examined this bronze with me.

For the male figure from Monteguragazza (Monte Acuto Ragazza), see E. Richardson 1983, I:240, no. I, II: pl. 165, figs. 546-548.

See also the related bronze, P. J. Riis, "The Bronze Statuette from Uffington, Berkshire," *Journal of Roman Studies* XXXVI (1946) 43-47 and pl. 7. Also M. Cristofani 1985, 285, no. 102, illus. p. 208.

The relationship to the Pizzirimonte bronze, "but about twenty years later," was suggested by C. C. Vermeule, that to the Frankfurt piece by D. G. Mitten, both in unpublished manuscripts in the Getty curatorial files. For these comparisons see E. Richardson 1983, I:233-234, no. 4, II: pl. 159, figs. 526-528 (Pizzirimonte) and I:153, II: fig. 346 (Frankfurt).

38. Kouros

Whereas in Greece the Archaic style virtually gave way to the Severe Style around 480 BC, and style is therefore a useful indicator of date of execution, in Etruria the situation was much less clear cut. The Archaic style persisted well into the late fifth century, coexisting with more classicizing features—sometimes even in the same object, as here. The Classical idiom took only shallow root in Etruria, although some scholars have discussed a "near-Classical" style there. While the development of certain features in Greece becomes a useful terminus post quem for their appearance in Etruscan art, style is a much less reliable predictor of date on the Italian peninsula than in Greece.

Draped in a rounded tebenna, this figure is in the same tradition as the Getty kouros and the Getty Tinia [37, 39], standing kouroi of the early fifth century. Their function is unknown, but they were probably votive dedications and may have represented votaries or priests. Unlike the Greek kouroi on whom they were undoubtedly patterned, the Etruscan figures in most instances wear a garment draped over at least the lower part of their torsos.

With an overly large head, trace of an Archaic smile, and extremely large almond-shaped eyes, this figure stands at the crossroads between the Archaic style—heavily influenced by Ionian Greek prototypes—and the early Classical or Severe Style that occurs in Etruria in a limited way. As Richardson puts it, "no other figure is quite like this: the head is more 'Ionian' than 'Severe,' the musculature of the body more 'Severe' than 'Ionian.'"

Because of its more Archaic facial features, it is tempting to date this bronze slightly earlier than the Getty Tinia [39], although, as observed above, it is perilous to presume an orderly progression from Archaic to Classical in Etruscan art. The figure's shoulders are broad above narrow hips; its clavicles form a prominent

ETRUSCAN,
CA. 480 BC.
H. 28 CM.
NATIONAL MUSEUM
OF NATURAL HISTORY,
SMITHSONIAN, 66-5172

ridge. The right nipple stands out so clearly that one suspects that it might be a rod set into the chest. The musculature of the thorax is stylized in the Severe mode but is less prominently articulated than on the Getty Tinia. Virtually identical in all these respects, however, is a nude youth in the Antikenmuseum, Basel, from the Käppeli collection. So similar are the two pieces that it seems reasonable to assign them to the same workshop, if not even the same hand.

Despite a certain amount of modern restoration of limited areas, the object's high quality is evident in the well-articulated volumes and beautiful tooling and chasing in the areas that have not been reconstructed. The figure's hairdo is quite elaborate. A double fillet runs around the head, behind the ears. The hair in the back is rolled up and over it. In front of the ears and across the forehead, parallel strands of hair with horizontal striations create a kind of heavy set of bangs that come in close around the face, establishing a square line across the brow that mirrors his square jawline. The eyebrows are well defined. The large almond-shaped eyes have incised iris and pupil.

The tebenna falls in fairly flat folds, depicted in relief, along its upper edge and in gentle raised ripples over the rest of its length. The genitalia show beneath the garment, as on the Getty Tinia [39]. At the left side and back, the artist has carefully rendered the fall of the cloth into elegantly disposed zigzag folds. Care has also been lavished on the fashionable pointed-toed boots with high flaps covering the ankles in back, their laces neatly picked out by incision. According to Richardson, such boots appear to be a sign of rank. Both hands and feet are exaggerated in length, another throwback to Archaic Etruscan conventions.

In type the kouros seems to be descended from the so-called ''Vertumnus'' from Isola da Fano, now in the Museo Archeologico, Florence, who also wears pointed shoes but is draped more completely. That figure represents the full flowering of the Archaic style and does not seem touched by the influence of the Greek Severe Style. Another handsome togatus, from Pizzirimonte, now in the British Museum, also bears comparison. It shares with the Smithsonian kouros the large head with Ionian-inspired features, the hairdo framing the face in a dense cap of parallel waves, and the lavish attention to the zigzag fall of drapery folds. The London bronze's collarbones are even more prominent, however, and its shoulders broader. The hand that made it seems more assured. Although they are part of the same tradition, the Smithsonian and Käppeli bronzes are somewhat more provincial.

Like the Getty Tinia [39] and the Fogg Turan [43], this piece reportedly was found near Piombino, which is twelve kilometers from ancient Populonia. According to Jucker, art market gossip was that a stone plinth with traces of the attachment of feet was shown with the three when they were put up for sale in a place northwest of Siena, which was otherwise not active in the art trade. The fact that the soles of this kouros's boots have been reworked lends credence to the report that it was at one time affixed to such a plinth.

Scholars have differed in their views as to where and when the piece was made, but the consensus would place it in that general vicinity in about 480-470 BC. Teitz dates it before 480 and attributes it to Populonia. Jucker also postulates the possibility that it was made in Populonia. Cristofani says it comes from the same workshop as the Pizzirimonte bronze and places it in the first phase of a cluster of related pieces, dating it about 480 BC. In support of the possibility of a location in Populonia, Volterra, or the surrounding area, he points to the many trade contacts between these towns and the Greco-Orient, offering an explanation for the strong

Ionian cast to the features of the sculptures in his group. Richardson notes the extremely close relationship with the Käppeli piece and classifies it with her late Archaic, Severe, fine group, dated 520-470 BC. Maule puts both these pieces and the Pizzirimonte one into his "Group 1" and implies a date later in the century. He sees a "presumption in favor of the Po Valley" as the place of manufacture, pointing out that Piombino and Pizzirimonte (which is near Prato) are not far away.

Populonia (ancient Fufluna) was the only major Etruscan city located on the coast. With a good harbor and access to the mineral resources of the nearby hills, it was active in trade—with Cypriots and Phoenicians, and later the Greeks—from Villanovan times or even before. Copper-mining was a principal industry there, as ancient writers tell us. Iron was refined on the nearby island of Elba, which Populonia controlled, and later—presumably when the wood supply ran out—at Populo-

nia itself, as the extensive slag heaps at the site attest. Lead and tin were also mined in the hills nearby.

Given its long tradition of involvement with metallurgy and its apparent wealth, one would expect a major bronzeworking operation in Populonia. Yet, although some utilitarian bronze objects have been found, the documented finds of figurative bronzes at Populonia are remarkably few and uneven in style and quality. In fact, the city seems to have no local tradition in any of the arts, although imports of high quality have been found there. There is not sufficient evidence, on the basis of our present knowledge, to assign the Smithsonian figure and the bronzes associated with it to Populonia, although it must have been made at some center in North Etruria that was heavily influenced by Ionian Greece.

CONDITION: The surface of this solid-cast figure is mottled, primarily medium green and brown. The patina is chipped off to expose the bronze in places, but elsewhere it shows relatively thin but normal corrosion products: malachite, cuprite, some azurite on the face, and a black substance, probably tenerite. It is missing the object formerly held in the right hand. The fingers of the left hand were broken off and re-attached. There is a deep gash in the right thigh. Substantial modern repairs have been made, especially on the left side of the face. The tip of the nose is rebuilt, the left forehead is inpainted, and the left eye heavily restored. There is superficial retouching on the torso. Substantial repairs exist along both upper arms and both shoulders. There are small spots of retouching on both ears and the chin.

PROVENANCE: Said to have been found near Piombino.

EX COLLECTIONS: Joseph H. Hirshhorn; bequeathed 1966 to the Hirshhorn Museum and Sculpture Garden, Smithsonian Institution, Washington, D.C., by which transferred 1986 to the National Museum of Natural History, Washington, D.C.

EXHIBITED: On extended loan to the Royal Ontario Museum, Toronto, 1956-1959. Baltimore, Md., Walters Art Gallery, 1958, *The Etruscans: Artists of Early Italy.* Worcester Art Museum, Mass., April 21-June 4, 1967, *Masterpieces of Etruscan Art,* cat. by R. S. Teitz, 58-59, illus. 8, 157, no. 47.

PUBLISHED: Royal Ontario Museum, *Bulletin of the Division of Art and Archaeology* no. XXV (June 1957) 13, pl. 14A.
G. A. Mansuelli (*RA*) 1968, 81.
H. Jucker, "Etruscan Votive Bronzes of Populonia," in *Art and Technology* (1970) 212-213; also Discussion Session 3, p. 235.
M. Cristofani (*StEtr*) 1979, 85-92.
E. Richardson 1983, I:235-236; II: pl. 162, fig. 537.
M. Cristofani 1985, 151, color illus.; 267, no. 41.
Q. Maule, "The Montaguragazza Style," *StEtr* LIV (1988) (forthcoming).

NOTES: I am grateful to Bruce Christman for assistance in examining the bronze, and to Quentin Maule, who shared the manuscript of his forthcoming article.

On the overlapping styles that occur in 5th-century Etruria and the way they have historically been analyzed by scholars, see Q. Maule, "A Near-Classical Sculptural Style in Italy," *AJA* LXXXI (1977) 487-505, esp. 487-488, nn. 2-4; also G. A. Mansuelli (*RA*) 1968, 73-84 passim.

For the Käppeli kouros (Basel, inv. 515), see E. Richardson 1983, I:153, no. 14, II: pl. 98, fig. 345. For the "Vertumnus" (Florence, inv. 72725), see ibid., I:237, no. 1, II: pl. 163, figs. 539-540, and for the Pizzirimonte bronze (London, inv. 509), see I:233-234, no. 4, II: pl. 159, figs. 526-528. She discusses the boots, I:220 and n. 20.

39. Tinia (Zeus)

Although very few Etruscan bronzes can be firmly identified as representing deities, this one has been known in modern times as "Zeus," largely because it is bearded, like Greek representations of Zeus, and resembles a Greek bronze statuette of this god found at Olympia. The Getty statuette was itself at one time considered to be Greek by Charbonneaux and others. Scholars more recently seem generally to agree that it is Etruscan, and hence the god it has been proposed as representing would be more properly called Tinia, the Etruscan counterpart of the Greek Zeus. The figure once held something in its outstretched left hand. If he is indeed Tinia, it was probably a thunderbolt or a staff.

It seems more likely, however, that this figure is another in an extensive series of toga-clad male figures, inspired by East Greek figures draped in himations, that constitutes a peculiarly Etruscan type that emerged in the late Archaic period, ca.

ETRUSCAN,
CA. 480-470 BC.
H. 17.5 CM.
J. PAUL GETTY
MUSEUM, 55.AB.12

520-470 BC. Although ultimately related to the standard Greek kouroi, these Etruscan figures differ in being clothed and holding something in their hands or making very specific hand gestures. They have been recently analyzed and classified by Richardson. Their identity remains a puzzle, although she concludes that they are mortals. They may be worshippers, temple attendants, or priests. A striding male figure excavated at Gabii who carries a lituus—a curved staff associated with augurs, priests, and persons of distinction—may offer a clue as to what the Getty figure originally held in his hand.

Richardson identifies the figure's garment as the semicircular Etruscan toga (tebenna) rather than a rectangular himation such as was worn by the Greeks. Indeed, the corner visible at the back may support that interpretation, although the

other corner and hem cannot be examined because of the break at the bottom. The garment has a heavy, rolled upper border ornamented on the front of the figure with zigzags, perhaps intended to represent folds in the cloth. Drapery folds on the remainder of the toga are indicated partly in relief, partly by a series of wavy incised lines. As on so many Etruscan bronzes, these lines fade out on the right side, which was considered an unimportant view by its maker.

The toga, worn extensively by the Romans, was apparently taken over from the Etruscan kings, for whom it was a symbol of royalty. Pliny (*N.H.* XXXIV.10.18 and XI.23) states that the statuary type of a standing male wrapped in a toga, such as the togatae effigies of the kings erected on the Capitoline Hill in Rome, also derived from the Romans' Etruscan ancestors. Richardson has assembled examples of Etruscan togatae effigies both with and, as here, without a tunic under the toga.

She classifies this bronze as part of the late Archaic Severe group sine tunica, which also encompasses the Smithsonian kouros [38]; a pipe-player in the Museo Archeologico, Florence; a youth formerly in Marzabotto; and another in a private collection in Santa Barbara. The first is bearded, and all share the feature of the hair forming a sort of cap with a distinct line across the brow, although in none of the others is the hair so elaborately articulated as here.

Indeed, one is immediately struck by the complex treatment of the hair and beard. The hair radiates from the crown and is tied with a fillet. Over the forehead, it forms finely striated bangs. At the rear, wavy paired locks are pulled up and out from the nape of the neck and wrapped over the fillet. Another swag, from behind each ear, is drawn up over the ear and under the fillet, ending in a curly fringe over the temples. The beard is equally meticulously and stiffly detailed, complete with its handlebar mustache and the small extra tonguelike tuft of beard just under the lower lip. It appears that some sort of a comb tool was used to render the hair, as groups of three or four strands seem to run parallel but then diverge slightly from the adjoining groups of strands. Elaborately detailed hairdos such as this are a feature of the Greek Severe Style.

The torso is squarish and solid. The clavicles are accentuated. The artist stylizes the abdominal muscles into a sort of round-cornered rectangle divided into quadrants by a vertical and a horizontal depression, much as do the Greek Severe Style sculptors. The modeling of the upper chest and the subtle articulation of the spinal column and shoulder blades, however, show a sophisticated understanding of human anatomy. The forms of the body can be discerned beneath the drapery. The navel is naturalistically handled; the nipples are schematically indicated by punched circles.

The Getty bronze has been related to a magnificent reclining banqueter in the British Museum and to a so-called Dionysus in Modena. They share the same prominent eyebrows, full cheeks with high cheekbones, caplike hairline over the forehead, and neatly trimmed beards with the characteristic mustache. The banqueter sports a Zungenbart ("tongue-beard") like the Getty piece. Neugebauer attributed the banqueter to Chiusi, while Homann-Wedeking adopted this designation for the Dionysus as well; both authors also added other pieces to the core group.

More recently, Cristofani has discussed these pieces in the context of a group of objects localized in the area around Volterra, Arezzo, and Populonia, descended from the so-called Lorenzini head. He construes the Getty Tinia as part of a second stylistic phase, later than the banqueter, the Dionysus, and the Smithsonian kouros [38]. His later group also includes the male and female standing figures from Monteguragazza and the well-known Ajax committing suicide, which was excavated at Populonia. Jucker proposes that the Tinia, the Smithsonian youth [38], the Turan [43], and a kouros in Basel—all said to come from Populonia and having appeared on the market at about the same time—may represent an active bronzemaking school in this ore-rich city during the fifth century about which little is yet known.

CONDITION: It is missing the lower right arm, both legs below the knees, and the object in the right hand. The solid-cast figure has a gray-green patina with areas of cuprite and malachite throughout.

PROVENANCE: Said to have been found at Piombino.

EX COLLECTION: J. Paul Getty.

EXHIBITED: Worcester Art Museum, Mass., April 21-June 4, 1967, *Masterpieces of Etruscan Art*, cat. by R. S. Teitz, 55-56, no. 44, repr. 152. University of California at Santa Barbara, The Art Gallery, February 7-March 15, 1967, *Etruscan Art from West Coast Collections*, cat. by M. del Chiaro, 39, no. 42, entry by R. Teitz. Cambridge, Mass., Fogg Art Museum, December 4, 1967-January 23, 1968; St. Louis, Mo., City Art Museum, March 1-April 13, 1968; Los Angeles County Museum of Art, May 8-June 30, 1968, *Master Bronzes from the Classical World*, cat. by S. F. Doeringer and D. G. Mitten, 166, illus., no. 164, entry by S. F. Doeringer. Chapel Hill, N.C., William Hayes Ackland Memorial Art Center, March 7-April 18, 1976, *Small Sculptures in Bronze from the Classical World*, ed. G. K. Sams, no. 50, illus., entry by J. B. Adler.

PUBLISHED: *ArtQ* XVIII (1955) 403. H. Stothart, *Handbook of the Sculpture in the*

J. Paul Getty Museum (Malibu, Calif., 1965) 11, pl. 2, as Greco-Etruscan.

J. P. Getty, *The Joys of Collecting* (New York, 1965) 49, col. illus. (text by J. Charbonneaux), as Greek.

G. A. Mansuelli (*RA*) 1968, 82.

H. Jucker, "Etruscan Votive Bronzes of Populonia," in *Art and Technology* (1970) 212-213; also Discussion Session 3, p. 235.

M. Sprenger, "Die etruskische Plastik des v. Jahrhunderts v. Chr. und ihr Verhältnis zur griechischen Kunst," *Studia archaeologica* XIV (1972) 52-53, pl. 24:1.

M. Sprenger and G. Bartoloni 1977, 129; also *The Etruscans: Their History, Art and Architecture* (New York, 1983) 115 and pl. 129.

O. Brendel 1978, 249, fig. 174; 464 n. 12; 469, n. 26.

M. Cristofani (*StEtr*) 1979, 88-89, pl. 25.

E. Richardson 1983, I:235, no. 3, II: figs. 533-535.

A.-M. Adam 1984, 157-158, mentioned under no. 232.

M. Cristofani 1985, 186, no. 81, illus.; 277.

S. Haynes 1985, 281, mentioned under no. 96. *Civiltà degli etruschi*, exh. cat. (Florence, Museo Archeologico, 1985) 287, mentioned under no. 10.33.

Q. Maule (*StEtr*) forthcoming.

NOTES: On Tinia, see M. Cristofani 1985, 277. For the Zeus from Olympia, now in the National Museum, Athens, see W. Lamb 1929, 88, pl. 28c. The most complete discussion of figures grouped with this bronze is in E. Richardson 1983, esp. I:220, 223-224, 231-236 and II: figs. 529-531 (her Severe group). See also I:239-240 on the togate orantes; I:338 on the question of whether human or divine figures are represented; I:96-97 on the Etruscan reinterpretation of the Greek kouros type.

The bronze from Gabii is in the custody of the Soprintendenza archeologica di Roma (inv. scavo G 601): *Civiltà* 1985, 287-288, no. 10.33, illus.

On the toga in Etruria, see L. Bonfante, 1975, 48-50. For the hairstyle, compare the large head in the British Museum, from the Tyszkiewicz collection (reg. 98.7-16.2): S. Haynes 1985, 274, no. 77; illus. 170.

For the banqueter in the British Museum, see H. B. Walters 1899, 79, no. 556; and M. Cristofani (*StEtr*) 1979, pl. 29a. See also K. A. Neugebauer (*RM*) 1936, 194 ff.

The Dionysus in Modena, Galleria Estense, is discussed by E. Homann-Wedeking (*RM*) 1943, 87-91, pl. 7; and M. Cristofani (*StEtr*) 1979, pl. 27, who discusses all three pieces together with the pipe-player in Florence, Museo Archeologico (inv. 12), and the Lorenzini head.

H. Jucker discusses the possibility of a Populonia school in *Art and Technology* (1970) 195-219, esp., for the later group, 212-213. M. Sprenger (*StArch*) 1972 suggests that a group of terracottas from Satiricum may be stylistically dependent on this piece.

40. Warrior

Scholars have long debated the identity of this striking figure. On analogy with Greek statues of Zeus hurling a thunderbolt, such as the famous large-scale Zeus (or Poseidon?) from Cape Artemisium, some have proposed that he represents Tinia, Zeus' Etruscan counterpart, although Zeus was not ordinarily depicted as holding a dagger. Photographs published in 1913 show a short segment of a rod, bent and apparently pointed at the end, in his upraised hand (Figure 40a). It was described as a lance by contemporary viewers, suggesting that the bronze may represent an Etruscan warrior god such as Maris (Ares/Mars), Laran, or Hercle (Heracles), or simply a mortal warrior, hero, or hunter.

The famous bronze sculptural group of the Tyrannicides—Harmodius and Aristogeiton, the heroes who slew the tyrant Hipparchus—made by the Greek sculptors Kritios and Nesiotes in 477-476 BC and erected prominently in the Agora in Athens, showed Aristogeiton in a broad stride, his outstretched left arm draped

ETRUSCAN,
CA. 460-450 BC.
H. 40.5 CM.
THE NELSON-ATKINS
MUSEUM OF ART,
NELSON FUND, 30-12

in a rounded cloak and holding a short scabbard, his lowered right holding a sword. Such a composition may have served as a basis for the Etruscan artist's conception. Any Etruscan visitor to Athens at that time would certainly have seen it, and it was no doubt widely discussed.

Whatever the direct source of inspiration, the Etruscan artist who modeled this bronze was greatly influenced by the early Classical sculpture of Greece. He has not, however, succeeded in capturing the real innovation represented by such masterworks as the Aristogeiton and the Zeus from Artemisium. For the early Classical Greek artists who made these two sculptures, the challenge was to represent a figure in action. In their radical new conceptions, the symmetry and timid step forward that characterized the Archaic kouroi have been set aside; lunging forward, their figures shift their weight to the bent forward leg. Their torsos twist as they raise their weapons, and the play of their muscles responding to that effort is carefully depicted. Their heads turn to follow the weapon's thrust, and their feet are at right angles to each other, adding stability to their stances.

By comparison, the stride of this Etruscan warrior is much less bold. The outward thrust of the right buttock suggests that his straight rear leg bears his weight, but the artist has shown that heel lifted, creating a confusing sense of weightlessness in the statuette. Although the right shoulder is drawn back slightly, creating some twist in the torso, the feet remain very nearly parallel and the head is only slightly turned. The Etruscan artist has gone beyond the frontality and symmetry of such statuettes as the Getty kouros and Tinia [37, 39] and has attempted to incorporate the innovations of his Greek counterparts, but he has not fully grasped the dynamics of motion and balance that underlie their dramatic new sculptural concepts.

Figure 40a. Nelson-Atkins warrior [40] holding short segment of rod. After *Gazette des Beaux-Arts* X (1913) 71.

The Etruscan artist's understanding of human anatomy also seems to be less fully developed than his Greek counterparts? The warrior's body is somewhat elongated, his head perhaps too small in relation to his long torso and legs, although in comparison with sculptures of the Archaic period such as Boston's dancer [35], the proportions are reasonably naturalistic and the figure is shown fully in the round. The modeling of the warrior's body—perhaps that of an older man—is much simpler than that of the Aristogeiton or the Zeus from Artemisium. The musculature of chest and torso are shown only summarily. There is a depression under the breasts, another at the waist, and one vertically along the ventral midline. The belly projects slightly; the navel was cast as a raised knob within a soft, fleshy depression. A few horizontal grooves below the navel may be intended to represent wrinkles. The pubic hair is a stylized fringe of wavy parallel lines. The genitalia are generalized.

In the head, the influence of the Greek Severe Style is evident. The cap of hair, combed forward over forehead and temples and turned under at the nape, is textured with wavy striations individually incised rather than made with a comb tool. A neat beard and long mustache frame the bow-shaped mouth. The incised lines on the beard are slightly coarser than those on the mustache; finer still are the tiny wavy incised lines that represent the sideburns. The eyebrows form a distinct bony ridge on the well-modeled skull. Both upper and lower eyelids are carefully rendered, but the eyes are open so wide that they reveal the entire round form of an inlaid iris, now missing. A few parallel lines on the forehead impart a sense of intense concentration, lending further seriousness to the expression that has already shed the Archaic smile.

The warrior wears a short semicircular cape, or chlamys, one end of which is wrapped around his left arm. The straight inner edge has a band raised in relief and

ornamented with a row of closely placed concentric circles and a narrow row of zig-zags. The outer, curved edge is crosshatched at the hem, with a double groove and then a band of more loosely spaced concentric circles inside that. As it widens across the back, the cloak has four and even five rows of circles, with grooves between the rows in some places. The grooves and the crosshatching at the hem are fairly crude and uneven, showing evidence of where the incising tool slipped in places. The circles, in contrast, are uniform in size and unbroken, even though their spacing and alignment is irregular. That they were made with a punch tool is betrayed by the one instance where the tool was double-struck but slipped slightly between strikes, registering two sets of circles that overlap. The intricacy of the incised decoration, although here concentrated largely on the cloak, betrays the persistent Etruscan love of ornament and decorative pattern even in the face of the strong Greek influence that informs the figure as a whole.

The cloak adheres closely to the body, revealing its forms beneath. The folds are only schematically suggested through ridges, not convincingly represented naturalistically as on Greek sculpture of the early Classical period. The Etruscan artist retains the Archaic form-fitting drapery even as he attempts to imitate the new early Classical style in his figure.

Why, where, and when was this statuette made? Its large size and careful finish indicate that it was an object of importance, probably intended as a votive dedication by a wealthy man. (It was found with a smaller but equally handsome statuette of Menrva, now in Berlin, which has been dated to the early fourth century.) Richardson notes that in the middle Archaic period in both Greece and Etruria fine figurative bronzes about 40-45 centimeters in height began to appear; they persisted into later decades, this being one of the finest examples of the group. The

findspot, Apiro, is in the Marches, in the hills above the Potenza River, not far from the coast. Nearby lie the Esino River and Ancona, the major Greek port on the middle Adriatic coast. The dagger is a form found in Picenum, the mountain region slightly to the south, which lay between southern Etruria and the Adriatic. We know that Greeks and Etruscans coexisted farther north on the Adriatic coast, at Spina. The evidence of the findspot, dagger type, and strong Greek influence on this figure may suggest that it was produced in some center on the northern segment of the Adriatic coast of Italy. Scholars have proposed dates for the sculpture ranging from 500 to mid-century. The Aristogeiton would seem to provide a useful terminus post quem of 476, and the degree to which the Archaic conventions have been set aside makes a date of ca. 460-450 seem plausible.

CONDITION: The sculpture is solid cast in two sections. The left forearm, hand, and sword were made as a separate piece and attached where the garment wraps over the arm by means of a tang inserted into a socket in the arm. A pin at the wrist holds the hand in place. There are tangs under the feet. The fairly even greenish-brown patina is estimated to contain malachite, cuprite, and tenerite; there are patches of brighter green, especially on the rear of his shoulders, arms, and legs. The sculpture is missing the implement originally held in the right hand, and inlay from the eyes. A large repair has been made to the left knee in modern times. The dagger in the left hand has been bent inward at the bottom since burial, as evidenced by stress lines and the loss of brittle corrosion products in this area. Tiny casting bubbles exist on the cape at the back lower left, and on the underside of the left arm, just above the elbow. The piece has been mechanically cleaned, but some encrustation remains on the inside of the right leg and on the elbows. Scratches and a deep gash appear on the left thigh. X-radiographs reveal a shrinkage crack in the right thigh and voids in the casting in both feet and below the knee in the right leg.

PROVENANCE: Excavated at Apiro (Macerata).

EX COLLECTIONS: Eugen Miller von Aichholz, by 1913, Vienna; Camillo Castiglioni, by 1923, Vienna.

EXHIBITED: Paris, Hôtel de Sagan, 23 rue de Constantine, May-June 1913, *Exposition d'objets d'art du moyen âge et de la Renaissance . . . organisée par la Marquise de Ganay . . .*, unpaginated, pl. 12.
Detroit Institute of Arts, March 23-April 20, 1947, *Small Bronzes of the Ancient World*, no. 40.
University of Chicago, Oriental Institute, December 1, 1955- January 6, 1956.
Seattle Art Museum, 1957, *2500 Years of Italian Art and Civilization*.
Detroit Institute of Arts, 1958, *Ancient Italic and Etruscan Art*.
Baltimore, Md., Walters Art Gallery, 1958, *The Etruscans: Artists of Early Italy*.
Kansas City, Mo., Nelson Gallery-Atkins Museum, 1960, *Anatomy and Art*, no. 45.
Worcester Art Museum, Mass., April 21-June 4, 1967, *Masterpieces of Etruscan Art*, cat. by R. S. Teitz, 63-64, 80, illus. 154, no. 51.

PUBLISHED: S. de Ricci, "L'art du moyen âge et de la Renaissance à l'hôtel de Sagan," *Gazette des Beaux-Arts*, 4th per., 2ᵉ semestre, X (1913) 71, illus. (See Figure 40a.)
I. Dall'Osso, *Guida illustrata del Museo Nazionale di Ancona* (Ancona, 1915) 105, illus.
L. Planiscig, *Sammlung Camillo Castiglioni: Bronzestatuetten und Geräte* (Vienna, 1923) 17, no. 1, pl. 1, as Italic, 5th century BC.
S. Reinach, *Rép.stat.* V, 264:3.
C. Albizzati, *Rendiconti della Ponteficia Accademia Romana di Archeologia*, 3rd ser., III (1924-25) 79-81, pl. 2.
Sale: *Collections Camillo Castiglioni, II: Bronzes antiques et de la Renaissance*, Amsterdam, Frederik Muller et Cie., November 18, 1925, I, no. 1, pl. 1
P. Ducati, *Storia dell'arte etrusca*, 2 vols. (Florence, 1927) I: 317, II: pl. 135, fig. 349.
Catalogue of the William Rockhill Nelson Gallery (Kansas City, Mo., 1933) 116.
Pantheon (December 1933) 367, CXXIII.
G. Q. Giglioli 1935, pl. CXXIII:1.
G. M. A. Hanfmann, *Etruskische Plastik* (Stuttgart, 1956) 14, pl. 22.
G. A. Mansuelli (*RA*) 1968, 73-84.
H. Busch et al. 1969, xli, illus. 115.
M. Sprenger and G. Bartoloni 1977, 136, pl. 184; also *The Etruscans: Their History, Art and Architecture* (New York, 1983) 130, pl. 184.
O. Brendel 1978, 311.
T. Dohrn 1982, 22, 23, pl. 7.
E. Richardson 1983, I:206-207, II: pl. 144, figs. 479-480.
L. Manino, *Il classicismo nella scultura etrusca: Appunti delle lezioni* (Turin, 1984) 90 ff.
M. Cristofani 1985, 164, fig. 55; 270-271, 277.
E. Hostetter 1986, mentioned 201, n. 70.

NOTES: I am grateful to Frederick Hollendonner and Bruce Christman, on whose examination report for this bronze I have drawn.
In the 1913 exhibition catalogue and *Gazette des Beaux-Arts* illustrations (Figure 40a), apparently unknown to later commentators, the figure holds a rod in the upraised hand, which de Ricci describes as a lance. It appears to be considerably thinner than what the opening in the hand would admit, but to have a thicker section where it passes through the hand. In this it seems analogous to the preserved fragments of the iron

lance once held by the Mars of Todi: F. Roncalli, ''Il 'Marte' di Todi,'' *Atti della Pontificia Accademia Romana di Archeologia, Memorie*, 3rd ser., XI:2 (1973) 28-29, fig. 39. The rod could have been bent and broken by the same damage that bent the dagger, which is already bent in the 1913 photographs; it may, however, not be original at all. According to the dealer, Jacob Hirsch, the bronze was formerly in the collection of Conte Ferretti, Cortona (identified elsewhere, in an anonymous document in the Museum's records, as having excavated it at Cortona).

E. Richardson 1983 (1:336-337) offers a convenient summary of documented Etruscan divinities. She points out that Maris is represented on four Etruscan mirrors in forms anything but warlike, and that according to Pfiffig, the Etruscan and Roman forms of the name are not linguistically related. Thus, Maris may not in fact have been a war god. On p. 198 she discusses the javelin thrower in Greek and Etruscan art.

For the Aristogeiton and the Zeus from Artemisium, see G. M. A. Richter, *A Handbook of Greek Art*, 3rd rev. ed. (London, 1963) 88-90, figs. 117-119.

On the ''forty centimeter group,'' see E. Richardson 1983, I:91-92.

For the Menrva found with this piece (Misc. 10819), see U. Gehrig et al., *Führer durch die Antikenabteilung, Staatliche Museen Preussischer Kulturbesitz, Berlin* (Berlin, 1968) 99, pl. 23.

E. Hostetter 1986 (p. 201 and n. 70) discusses the more southerly trade routes across the Apennines, as well as the possibility of communication along the Adriatic coast from Spina southward.

41. Silenus with Drinking Horn

The vitality of this ithyphallic satyr, or silenus, derives largely from his lively silhouette. He takes a sprightly step, his right arm upraised to cradle the end of a long drinking cup, while his left arm stretches out behind him, continuing the diagonal set up by the cup and the left leg. The extended right leg intersects on an opposing diagonal, to create an X-like composition. Both hands are disproportionately large with overly long fingers, a common Etruscan trait. The fingers are incised on the left hand, but are not delineated on the right. The right hand and drinking horn end squarely at the same level, creating a small flat surface that may give a clue as to the figure's use. As Hill first suggested, the satyr may have graced the top of a kottabos stand.

Kottabos was a game enjoyed by the Greeks and avidly borrowed by the Etruscans. Played at symposia—drinking parties at which the guests amused themselves in more or less ribald fashion—it involved trying to displace a metal disc balanced atop a high, thin metal stand, using the dregs of one's wine. The banqueter had to twirl his kylix—a shallow, footed drinking cup—by one of its handles and, at just the right moment, let the last few drops of wine from the cup fly across the room onto the plastinx, or disc. It would then fall and clatter against the manes, another disc farther down the shaft.

The Greek kottabos stands appear to have been composed of tripod bases topped by straight shafts, punctuated along their length by a disc or two. The Etruscans, however, delighting as always in adorning their utensils with figures, introduced a human figure at the top of the shaft to support the plastinx. Acrobats were popular for the purpose, since they evoked the delicate balancing act of the disc itself. Satyrs, often tipsy with drink, were another favorite; as the fun-loving

ETRUSCAN,
CA. 450 BC.
H. 13 CM.
MUSEUM OF FINE ARTS,
BOSTON, GIFT OF
E. P. WARREN, 13.112

companions of Fufluns (Dionysus), the god of wine, they were highly appropriate to a drinking game.

Games of kottabos are portrayed on over a hundred red-figure Greek vases; the Etruscans are depicted playing the game on fifth-century tomb paintings. As Hill has pointed out, the introduction of figures on kottabos stands seems to postdate the first Etruscan candelabra bearing figures at the top, and it seems likely that the similar general forms of the two types of utensils—tripod bases topped by long, slim shafts (see Figure XIV)—suggested the addition of figures to the kottabos stands. The type continues down to the late third or early second century BC with a well-defined series of acrobats from Perugia.

Like the satyr from the Walters Art Gallery [42], this one has a bald pate, animal ears, a hoof, and a tail. His bald spot is surrounded by a semicircular ring of hair which comes in front of the prominent ears and forms a ridge just above where his beard begins. His hair is rendered with short, discontinuous striations that are not carefully ordered, and some of which have been made in modern times. The hair is rolled under at the nape but has no incised detail there. The satyr has bushy eyebrows, a long, thin, asymmetrical mustache, and a pug nose. His eyes show no indication of pupils. His body is slim and lithe, its proportions reasonably naturalistic with the exception of the elongated fingers, typical of the Etruscan canon. The treatment of the musculature of his torso and the openness of his pose suggest a date nearer the middle of the fifth century than the first decades, as Vermeule and Comstock proposed.

The very long horn is unusual. Satyrs carrying rhyta—drinking horns—are known, as well as satyrs playing horns or flutes.

No particular workshop has been proposed for this satyr in the literature, and indeed satyrs were so widely present in Etruscan art that localizing them is difficult. The loss of surface detail on this bronze further complicates the issue. The satyr from a satyr-maenad group in the Museo Nazionale, Naples, bears similarities in body proportions and the form of his tail, but his head is larger in relation to his body and his hands are not elongated. A near duplicate of the Boston bronze is in Brindisi; Comstock and Vermeule have suggested, however, that it might be a forgery.

CONDITION: This solid-cast bronze has a fairly even green patina with traces of red (cuprite). It has been mechanically cleaned rather vigorously—causing the loss of much of the surface finish and detail—and chatter-marks from this process can be seen on the surface. Some of the striations in the hair were made during the modern cleaning. The left foot was broken off at the ankle and restored. The tip of the tail is missing. The tail was bent at some point in antiquity, as indicated by stress seen in the corrosion. Casting flaws are evident at the left wrist and inside the right ear. There are gashes on the top and back of the head. Both navel and nipples are punched.

EX COLLECTION: Edward Perry Warren.

EXHIBITED: Worcester Art Museum, Mass., April 21-June 4, 1967, *Masterpieces of Etruscan Art*, cat. by R. S. Teitz, 53, illus. 130, no. 40.

PUBLISHED: L. D. Caskey, Boston Museum of Fine Arts, *Annual Report* (Boston, 1913) 88.
E. Hill (*MagA*) 1940, 474 f., fig. 8.
M. Comstock and C. Vermeule 1971, 160, no. 182, illus.
M. I. Davies, "The Suicide of Ajax: a Bronze Etruscan Statuette from the Käppeli Collection," *AntK* XIV (1971) mentioned 149, n. 8.
C. A. Di Stefano, *Bronzetti figurati del Museo Nazionale di Palermo* (Rome, 1975) 46, under no. 77.

NOTES: The proposal that the figure might come from a kottabos stand is made in E. Hill (*MagA*) 1940, 75-76.

For other kottabos stands, see G. Q. Giglioli 1935, pl. CCCXII, especially figs. 4 and 5, a stand with a satyr from Vetulonia, in the Museo Archeologico, Florence.

For another satyr from a kottabos stand (CMA 74.16), see *BClevMus* LXI (1974) 240, figs. 1, 2.

For the Louvre's satyr playing kottabos, possibly from a candelabrum, see A. de Ridder, *Les bronzes antiques du Louvre*, 2 vols. (Paris, 1913-1915) I: 27, no. 136, pl. 15. De Ridder's no. 275, p. 46, pl. 24, is a satyr playing kottabos and probably also from a kottabos stand, though later than the figures cited above.

For the later series of kottaboi from Perugia, see R. Zandrino, "I kottaboi di Perugia," *RM* LVII (1942) 236-249; A. von Gerkan and F. Messerschmidt, "Das Grab der Volumnier bei Perugia," *RM* LVII (1942) 169-180, with list 173-175; A.-M. Adam 1984, 74-75, no. 77.

On the game of kottabos, see *DarSag* 1877-1919, III:1: 866-868, s.v. "kottabos"; G. M. A. Richter 1915, 460-462, under no. 1830.

On Etruscan musical horns and trumpets, see E. Richardson 1976, 225-226. Satyrs with short drinking horns: Louvre: A. de Ridder 1913-1915, I:26, no. 131, pl. 15; on the rim of a basin from Chiusi in the Museo Archeologico, Florence: A. Hus, *Les bronzes étrusques* (Brussels, 1975) pl. 32: 1, 2. Playing the flute: Louvre: A. de Ridder 1913-1915, I:46, no. 274, pl. 24; playing the double flute, in Florence: S. Reinach, *Rép. stat.* II, 140:6. Reinach, passim, illustrates dozens of such satyrs; see esp. II, 48:1-9; II, 49:4-5; III, 16:1-8.

The satyr and maenad group in Naples is illustrated in G. Q. Giglioli 1935, pl. CCIX:1. For the bronze in Brindisi, see B. Sciarra, *Brindisi, Museo archeologico provinciale* (Bologna, 1976) 9, no. 41, illus., where it is called Roman. Comstock and Vermeule also compare a running silen found in South Italy (now in Munich, *AA* XXV [1910] cols. 49-50, fig. 4), although its proportions are different: a chunky body and small head. The relationship suggested by C. A. Di Stefano 1975, 46, to a silenus from Himera, does not seem particularly compelling.

42. Satyr with Amphora

Satyrs (or sileni) were beloved by the Greeks and the Etruscans and were frequently represented on vases, in terracotta, and as small bronzes. The half-animal, half-human followers of Dionysus, they represented the more animal side of human nature, lustily enjoying their wine, women, and song. This muscular satyr skips along under his heavy load—an amphora filled with wine—balancing some of the weight on his squirrel-like tail. His torso is twisted in the effort, and he extends his right arm to help offset the weight of his burden. He is recognizable by his horse's ears and tail. One foot has been restored as a hoof, probably correctly. Hill has speculated that the other foot may have been human, seeing in the right ankle a slightly different shape from that of the left. Although this author does not find a significant difference between the ankles, satyrs are known with two hooves, two feet, or one of each.

This satyr's physiognomy—round face, bushy eyebrows, a pug nose, balding crown, and full beard and mustache—is also typical for the satyr type. His hair springs from a clearly demarcated horseshoe-shaped bald spot and is indicated by careful long parallel striations. It turns under at his neck. The same sort of striations characterize his beard and tail. The even, elliptical form of his beard mirrors his hairline in reverse.

The artist has gone to great pains to represent the anatomy of the torso and the bulging muscles of calves and upper arms. One shoulder blade thrusts out severely as the body twists, and even the tendons of the neck protrude with the strain. There is no single central axis to the figure, and no "front view." Rather, the artist achieves an almost baroque spiraling motion that forces the viewer to examine all sides of the piece in order to experience it fully.

This figure's purpose is not evident. Since its feet are missing, we cannot determine whether it was conceived as a decorative attachment to some sort of utensil, such as a candelabrum or vessel. Satyrs were frequently used to adorn the rims of large wine vessels (lebetes) and censers, for example, although an upright figure such as this would have been more likely used as a handle or atop a candelabrum. Some authors have suggested that if he were mounted differently, so that both feet were flat on the ground, this satyr might have stood at the top of a kottabos stand with a small disc teetering on the mouth of the amphora, into which banqueters would attempt to sling the dregs from their wine cups. The subject matter would certainly be appropriate for such a game! (For more on the game of kottabos, see Boston's silenus [41].)

Satyr plays were an important Greek theatrical medium, performed along with tragedies to furnish the same sort of comic relief that Shakespeare later employed in working comic interludes into his dramas. Brommer has demonstrated that many of the representations of satyrs on painted vases are in fact scenes from such satyr plays. Satyrs are also represented on vases imitating the everyday actions of people, creating humorous parodies of human experience apparently without the sort of religious, funerary, or mythological significance of other, weightier themes. It may be that these small bronze figurines existed, either singly or in groups, to illustrate satyr plays or simply for their owners' amusement.

The satyr is so ubiquitous in the art of Greece, Etruria, and South Italy in the fifth century that no scholar has been willing to assert a specific point of origin for this particular statuette. Greek parallels that have been cited include an acrobatic satyr found at Thebes and now in the Louvre, and the vase paintings of the Brygos Painter and Douris. Etruscan comparisons include somewhat earlier satyrs in the British Museum and Berlin, which have been assigned to Chiusi. Hill favors a Campanian attribution, citing the similarities between the satyr's head and Campanian

CAMPANIAN(?), MID-5TH C. BC. H. 9.5 CM. WALTERS ART GALLERY, 54.2291

head types identified by Riis and the later preoccupation with satyrs in the bronzes of Praeneste, in Latium, whose artistic tradition derives from that of Campania.

Although none of the parallels is so striking as to be definitive, the attribution to Campania seems plausible. The sculptor's interest in convincing anatomy and in a figure portrayed fully in the round shows a stronger influence of the Greek ideal than do most Etruscan figures at this time, more closely approximating the approach to the human form of contemporary Campanian bronzes. Rendering the musculature of the torso in action was a preoccupation of Greek artists during the transitional period between the Archaic and Classical styles, and the Campanian sculptors shared their interest. The face has lost its Archaic smile and Archaic stylization, despite the rather archaizing treatment of the hair and beard. A date in the middle of the fifth century would seem appropriate.

CONDITION: The solid-cast bronze is covered with an even green-black patina. The left foot is restored. Right foot, lower right arm, tip of tail, and phallus are broken off. A gash on the right side of the head aligns with others on the right upper arm and thigh, and was probably made by the same excavator's tool.

EX COLLECTIONS: De Nolivos; probably John E. Taylor; Henry Walters, Baltimore; Mrs. Henry Walters, New York.

EXHIBITED: Worcester Art Museum, Mass., April 21-June 4, 1967, *Masterpieces of Etruscan Art*, cat. by R. S. Teitz, 68-70, illus. 165, no. 57. Cambridge, Mass., Fogg Art Museum, December 4, 1967-January 23, 1968; St. Louis, Mo.,

City Art Museum, March 1-April 13, 1968; Los Angeles County Museum of Art, May 8-June 30, 1968, *Master Bronzes from the Classical World*, 85, cat. by S. F. Doeringer and D. G. Mitten, no. 80, entry by S. F. Doeringer. Chapel Hill, N. C., William Hayes Ackland Memorial Art Center, March 7-April 18, 1976, *Small Sculptures in Bronze from the Classical World*, ed. G. K. Sams, no. 24, illus., entry by C. J. Watson.

PUBLISHED: Sale: *De Nolivos Collection*, Paris, Mannheim, January 19-20, 1866, no. 14. Sale: *John E. Taylor*; London, Christie's, July 1-4 and 9-10, 1912, 4th day, 91, no. 358, as Ionic Attic, end of 6th century BC.

Sale: *Estate of Mrs. Henry Walters*, New York, Parke-Bernet, December 1-4, 1943, 3rd session (December 2) 88, no. 503.

D. K. Hill, "A Silene with an Amphora," *Art in America* XXXIV (1946) 8-13, illus.

D. K. Hill, review of H. C. Van Gulik, *Catalogue of the Bronzes in the Allard Pierson Museum at Amsterdam*, in *AJA* L (1946) 504.

D. K. Hill 1949, 42-43, no. 86, pl. 20.

M. Pallottino, review of D. K. Hill 1949, in *StEtr* XXIII (1954) 459.

NOTES: On satyrs and sileni, which are interchangeable through the fifth century, see C. Houser, *Dionysos and His Circle: Ancient through Modern*, exh. cat. (Cambridge, Mass., Fogg Art Museum, 1979) 14-15 and passim; F. W. Hamdorf, *Dionysos, Bacchus: Kult und Wandlungen des Weingottes* (Munich, 1986) passim.

On the different feet, see D. K. Hill (*AJA*) 1946, 504. She cites three examples of satyrs which, she believes, have one human foot and one hoof. D. K. Hill advanced—and withdrew—the kottabos proposal in (*ArtinAm*) 1946, 10, observing that such a mounting would unnaturally tip the figure; the suggestion was, however, repeated by R. S. Teitz in *Masterpieces of Etruscan Art* (1967) 69.

On Greek satyr plays, see F. Brommer, *Satyrspiele, Bilder griechischer Vasen*, 2nd enl. and rev. ed. (Berlin, 1959). His fig. 34, p. 39, shows a cup in the Vatican featuring a satyr similarly burdened by a heavy amphora; an Etruscan copy of the vase is in the Musée Rodin, Paris. A. D. Trendall, reviewing Brommer's book in *Gnomon* XXXI (1959) 647, speaks to the role of satyrs as comic mimics of human activity. Another superb depiction of a satyr with an amphora slung over his shoulder occurs on the red-figure calyx krater by the Kleophrades Painter at Harvard (1960.236), for which see *The Frederick M. Watkins Collection*, exh. cat. (Cambridge, Mass.,

Fogg Art Museum, 1973) 50-53, no. 20, illus. For a group of Boeotian terracotta satyrs believed to illustrate a satyr play, see *The Beauty of Ancient Art* (1964) no. 20 (unpaginated), also *Ancient Art: The Norbert Schimmel Collection*, exh. cat. (Mainz, 1974) no. 46 (unpaginated).

For the Louvre bronze, a satyr balancing on one hand and one foot, cited by Hill and others, see A. de Ridder 1913-1915, I: no. 132, II: pl. 14; J. Charbonneaux, *Les bronzes grecs* (Paris, 1958) pl. 16:2. A. de Ridder's pls. 14, 15, and 24 afford several examples of Greek and Etruscan bronze satyrs in a variety of attitudes.

A similar acrobatic satyr from the Walter C. Baker collection, now at the Metropolitan Museum of Art, was tentatively called Etruscan by D. von Bothmer, *Ancient Art from New York Private Collections*, exh. cat. (New York, Metropolitan Museum of Art, 1961) 39, no. 151, and pl. 54, where several other small satyrs can be found as well.

The Chiusine bronzes are treated by K. A. Neugebauer (*RM*) 1936, 181-211.

P. J. Riis 1938, II:140-168, deals with the Campanian facial type.

For the British Museum piece, see H. B. Walters 1899, 66, no. 473; the Berlin example is inv. no. Fr. 715b. Compare also another lively satyr in Berlin (misc. 8581): K. A. Neugebauer (*RM*) 1936, pl. 27:1-2; U. Gehrig et al., *Führer durch die Antikenabteilung, Staatliche Museen Preussischer Kulturbesitz, Berlin* (Berlin, 1968) 93, pl. 24, right, where it is designated as Italic, ca. 500 BC.

The above comparisons and the Praenestine fascination with satyrs are discussed at length by D. K. Hill (*ArtinAm*) 1946, 9-13, which remains the most thorough discussion of this satyr.

A set of three cista feet showing satyrs with amphorae, from the Scheurleer collection, The Hague, is published in *AA* (1922) cols. 226-227, fig. 21.

43. Turan (Aphrodite)

Whether this figure represents a goddess or a human votary has been debated. Hanfmann proposed that she represents Turan, the Etruscan equivalent of Aphrodite, goddess of love and beauty. He based that identification on the pomegranate that she holds and analogies in her costume to a figure labeled as Turan on an Etruscan mirror. Richardson, however, has pointed out that the same type of costume appears on many other divinities and on mortals as well. Besides being sacred to Hera, the pomegranate was also apparently used as a funerary offering to Persephone, so its presence only narrows the field of possiblities.

Whatever her identity, this bronze stands near the beginning of an extensive series of statuettes of draped female figures, produced in Etruria from about 475 BC through the fourth century. Like her sisters, she wears an ankle-length chiton,

ETRUSCAN, CA. 450-430 BC. H. 20.3 CM. HARVARD UNIVERSITY ART MUSEUMS, PURCHASE—ALPHEUS HYATT FUND, FRANCIS H. BURR FUND AND THROUGH THE GENEROSITY OF 24 FRIENDS OF THE FOGG, 1956.43

over which is draped a heavier woolen himation, which is wrapped over the left shoulder and has its end slung over the left arm. A heavy band of ornamentation at the neck of the chiton becomes a double band as it continues down the seamline of the right sleeve. The edges of the himation are decorated with a hatched band. The sculptor has gone to great pains to render the way the upper border of the himation falls in zigzag folds at the waist, over the left shoulder, below the left arm, and—especially—down the back.

Again, as is typical for her type, the lady wears soft pointed-toed shoes, on the front of which the laces are clearly shown. These "calcei repandi," as we believe they were called in Latin, can be useful in dating Etruscan works of art. The fashion first appeared soon after 550 BC and is found represented on both male and female figures almost universally until ca. 475 BC. After that time, the pointed-toed shoes are shown only on female figures—often on those identified as goddesses and mythological personages, but also on this series of draped standing female statuettes. As Warren has pointed out, quite frequently deities are represented in "old-fashioned" dress as a means of showing that they are not of our world. At some point after the third century BC, the pointed-toed shoes became associated exclusively with divinity; by the first century BC they are shown only on images of Juno Sospita. In the transitional period, between 475 and the third century BC, however, they may have been the costume of priestesses—those associated with the world of the dead—or individuals who had been heroized, and thus were seen as living both in the realm of the gods and among the living. The Harvard statuette, then, does not simply represent a fashionable matron, but rather someone whose other-worldly status causes·her to wear a special costume.

At her neck Turan wears a choker of heavy beads. Either this kind of necklace or a ropelike torque, often with a heavy bulla, is always part of the dress of these figures. Her elaborate garland, or stephane, however, is somewhat unusual. While these figures almost always wear a fillet or some sort of diadem, the scalloped form of this headdress is not repeated elsewhere. It may represent a wreath of gold leaves; actual examples of this type of adornment have been found in fourth-century tombs. Beneath the diadem, her hair is disposed in bangs that echo its scallops over her forehead. A lock in front of her ears on each side ends at her earlobe. In the back, the longer hair is wrapped up neatly and tucked under the hair ornament.

Brendel has commented on Turan's stance: her feet are nearly parallel, her left foot only slightly advanced, and her orientation is severely frontal. He points out that it is not like a Classical Greek stance, in which the weight would be shifted to one leg and the opposite leg would be relaxed, setting up a rhythm and balance in the body that is not dependent on symmetry. Nonetheless, he finds that the figure "is not devoid of a Classical quality."

The sculptor has clearly broken with the Archaic figurative conventions. Rather than an emphasis on a mannered, decorative silhouette, we find here a new sense of monumentality, of broad areas of form, of weighty solidity. Ornament, such as the patterns in the garment folds, has been brought under control and used to help define the volume of the figure. The heavy-lidded eyes and the absence of the Archaic smile make this Turan seem more pensive and inwardly oriented than the wide-eyed, gaily smiling Archaic figures. The relative quiet of her stance and simplicity of her gesture seem to partake of the spirit of the Greek Severe Style.

The influence of Greek Classicism on Etruscan art was pervasive. It did not, however, consist of direct borrowing, but rather of a reinterpretation in Etruscan terms. It lasted from about 460 BC into the early decades of the third century, complicating the dating of Etruscan objects.

The series of draped female figures to which this Turan belongs includes unusually fine pieces. Several of them are discussed below in conjunction with the splendid headless woman from the Walters Art Gallery [44]. Among those that are closer to Turan are two in the Bibliothèque Nationale, smaller in scale and dated ca. 440 BC. They share with Turan the draping of the himation so as to leave a large amount of chiton exposed over the chest; the zigzag band decoration on the heavy upper edge of the himation; and the fairly elaborate rendering of the fall of the himation in back, emphasizing elaborate but essentially flat zigzag folds. They also have neat short hairdos contained by a diadem, although the two in Paris lack the scalloped bangs of Turan. All share the same quiet stance and introspective mien. Although the curves of their bodies can be read beneath the drapery, there is an almost boyish flatness to their silhouettes. Related in feeling, although doubtless later in execution, is an unusual mirror handle in the Bibliothèque Nationale. Its female figure is winged and appears to be holding a dove. The treatment of hair, drapery, and overall silhouette recall the Fogg Turan and her sisters.

The Turan appeared on the art market in the mid-1950s, at the same time as two other important large-scale bronze statuettes, the Getty Tinia [39] and the Smithsonian kouros [38]. The dealer said they all came from Populonia, and scholars have speculated that they all may have come from the same tomb or find. Populonia, on the Tyrrhenian coast, was famous in antiquity as a copper- and iron-mining and refining area. Although many bronze utensils and vessels have been found in that vicinity, the evidence for the manufacture of figurative bronzes there, particularly for a workshop capable of producing statuettes of the size and sophistication of these three pieces, is slim. Chiusi—suggested by Adam for the two pieces in Paris, by Neugebauer and others for the Getty Tinia, and by Cristofani for Turan herself—may be the more likely place of production. The somewhat archaizing drapery folds, general conservatism of the figure, and a mood akin to the Greek Severe Style are consistent with contemporary bronzes and stone sculpture from that area. An important road led from Chiusi to Populonia by way of the valley of the rivers Orcia and Ombrone, so that bronzes from the thriving workshops of the inland center could have found their way to the coastal city.

CONDITION: The figure was solid cast. It has a bright red and green patina. Accretions show spots of malachite, azurite, and cuprite. Missing are the fingers of the right hand, tips of the fourth and fifth fingers and part of the third finger on the left hand, tang under right foot, and part of tang under left. The nose has been damaged. A deep gash appears on the rear of the right leg just above the knee. Breaks on the left heel and the right wrist have been glued. Modern tinted infill is located in bubbles on right shoulder and in drapery overfold on chest near left elbow.

PROVENANCE: Allegedly found at Populonia.

EXHIBITED: Baltimore, Md., Walters Art Gallery, 1958, *The Etruscans: Artists of Early Italy.* Worcester Art Museum, Mass., April 21-June 4, 1967, *Masterpieces of Etruscan Art*, cat. by R. S. Teitz, 71-72, 155, no. 59.
Cambridge, Mass., Fogg Art Museum, December 4, 1967-January 23, 1968; St. Louis, Mo., City Art Museum, March 1-April 13, 1968; Los Angeles County Museum of Art, May 8-June 30, 1968, *Master Bronzes from the Classical World*, cat. by S. F. Doeringer and D. G. Mitten, 169, no. 168, illus., entry by S. F. Doeringer.

PUBLISHED: G. M. A. Hanfmann, "An Etruscan Goddess," *Archaeology* IX (1956) 230-232, illus. 231 and cover.
G. M. A. Hanfmann 1956, 7, pl. 28.
E. Richardson, review of G. M. A. Hanfmann 1956, in *AJA* LXII (1958) 344.
M. Pallottino, *The Etruscans*, 6th ed. (Bloomington, Ind., 1965) 281 and pl. 33.
The Pomerance Collection (1966) mentioned 109, under no. 125.
H. Jucker, "Etruscan Votive Bronzes of Populonia," in *Art and Technology* (1970) 212-213; also Discussion Session 3, p. 235.
L. B. Warren 1971, 281, n. 27; pl. 67, fig. 16.
Small Sculptures in Bronze (1976) mentioned under no. 54.
Classical Art from a New York Collection, exh. cat. (New York, André Emmerich Gallery, 1977) mentioned under nos. 98, 101.
O. Brendel 1978, 309, fig. 227; 360.
A.-M. Adam 1984, 157-158, mentioned under no. 232.

M. Cristofani 1985, 162, no. 53; 270.
Q. Maule (*StEtr*) forthcoming, mentioned n. 17.

NOTES: On the figure's identity, see the debate between G. M. A. Hanfmann ([*Archaeology*] 1956, 230-232) and E. Richardson ([*AJA*] 1958, 344). On the association of the costume with divinity, see L. B. Warren 1971, 280-282.
The stephane as a headdress is discussed by E. Richardson 1976, 151-152. A similar diadem and scalloped hairline are found on a female figure of the first quarter of the century, possibly Chiusine, in the British Museum (reg. 73.10-20.1). Although her costume and stance are more Archaic, the lavish use of flattened zigzag folds and boyish body type presage this bronze: E. Richardson 1983, 1:298-299, II: pl. 210, figs. 709-710; S. Haynes 1985, 281-282, no. 99, illus. 180.
On the stance, see O. Brendel 1978, 309.
For an analysis of the impact of the Greek Severe Style on Etruscan art, see T. Dohrn 1982.
For the two pieces in the Bibliothèque Nationale, see A.-M. Adam 1984, 157-158, nos. 231, 232. Two figures of lesser quality, formerly in the de Kolb collection (Emmerich 1977, nos. 98, 101), appear to belong to a slightly different series of votive women, many holding a dove. See also A.-M. Adam 1984, 158, no. 233; *The Pomerance Collection* (1966) 109, no. 125.
For the mirror handle, see E. Gerhard et al. 1843-1897, IV: pl. 348:2,3; D. Rebuffat-Emmanuel, *Le miroir étrusque d'après la collection du Cabinet des Médailles*, 2 vols. (Rome, 1973) II: pls. 44 and 44 bis, dated ca. 400 BC.
H. Jucker in *Art and Technology* (1970) 195-219, has attempted to outline the production of a group of Archaic figurative bronzes in Populonia. He stops short, however, of firmly attributing the later Turan and pieces associated with her to the city. See also the discussion under [38, 39] above.

44. Woman

ETRUSCAN,
LATE 5TH-
EARLY 4TH C. BC.
H. 38.9 CM.
WALTERS ART
GALLERY, 54.99

This unusually large and carefully detailed statuette is surely one of the finest Etrus-can bronzes to have found its way into an American collection. It is unfortunate that the head has been lost, but even by analyzing the body we can determine that this piece was executed several decades after Turan [43] and represents a perpetua-tion of that type; from the specialized costume, we can deduce that she probably represents a priestess or votary.

The woman stands at ease, her left leg bent at the knee and her right hip thrust out slightly, in a sort of contrapposto, but with both feet firmly on the ground. Her right hand lightly touches her hip with two extended forefingers in what might be interpreted as a vestigial form of the gesture of lifting the garment that is so characteristic of the Archaic chiton-clad korai (see [7, 33]). Her left arm is bent at the elbow, her hand outstretched in a gesture of making an offering, although the object offered has been lost.

The proportions of the body are unusual—unlike any other known Etruscan statuette. The upper body is quite short in relationship to the lower torso and long legs. The distance from shoulder to waist equals that from waist to hip joint; the span from waist to knee is the same as that between knee and foot. Despite her broad hips and substantial thighs when viewed from the front, the figure is strangely thin when seen in profile. Again, as in many of the earlier statuettes dis-cussed here, the Etruscan artist seems to have conceived his representation as a front view affixed to a back view rather than as a sculpture to be seen fully in the round.

Like Turan and the kore, the lady wears a thin chiton, over which she has wrapped a heavier himation. The artist, unlike the earlier sculptor of Turan, has emphasized rendering the different textures of the garments and the ways in which the cloth would fall; the woman's small, prominent breasts with erect nipples show clearly through the gathered diaphanous chiton fabric. The weighty wool hi-mation, which wraps about her hips and drapes over the left arm, falls in heavier catenary curves over her groin and left leg. Small rounded weights can be seen at two of the corners. The borders of the himation are decorated with a narrow row of diagonal hatching (perhaps a decorative overstitch used to bind the hem), inside of which is a band of triangles. A pattern of groups of three dots recurs over the surface of the himation, probably representing a woven pattern. On the back, the artist has indulged in a profusion of drapery folds, trying to depict very accurately how the zigzag border would appear here and disappear there in the undulation of the cloth. Some of these clusters of folds are quite successful, such as the groups at the left below the elbow. Elsewhere, as behind the right ankle, they are less con-vincing. All remain quite flat, although in places, such as over the upper arm, they are more plastic than elsewhere.

From the woman's right shoulder hangs a long thin band composed of four parallel vertical strips with regularly spaced horizontal crosspieces. This is appar-ently some sort of woven sash or fillet, and it is found on representations of women in this particular costume appearing in various media in Etruscan art around 400 BC. The significance of these sashes is not fully understood, but Richardson and Bonfante have postulated that they may be a sign of rank or part of a special costume, such as that of a priestess.

On her feet, the figure wears elaborate pointed-toed boots, laced and bound about the ankles. Their construction is carefully portrayed, down to rows of tiny dots that indicate stitches. An extra seam in the leather at the instep is even shown.

The lady wears a heavy necklace, a ropelike choker (torque), from which hangs a central disc (bulla). A bracelet on her right wrist is indicated simply by two deeply

cut parallel lines. That on her left arm, however, is a raised cast ridge with parallel lines cut across it at intervals, probably to suggest beads.

This statuette's large size is remarkable among Etruscan bronzes of this date and would have required a high degree of technical competence on the part of the bronzecaster. Without the head, it is difficult to speculate on a regional attribution. Statuettes from the end of the fifth century or the early fourth, wearing the same sort of costume, are known. Many of them also tend to be of substantial size and/or very carefully and elaborately detailed, which indicates the importance attached to them by their owners.

The series of draped women to which the Baltimore bronze belongs differs from the group around the Turan [43] in their looser poses—often with bent knee or wide stride causing the drapery to fall in deep, three-dimensional folds that heighten the sense of movement. The principal members of this group are discussed here, in relation to the Walters statuette.

Perhaps closest is a woman with her hands outstretched in an attitude of prayer, formerly in the Castellani collection, now in the British Museum. Here, too, the breasts are prominent and the contrasts in drapery textures have been emphasized. The flexed left knee sets up a lively rhythmic play of drapery folds. A second figure in London, possibly from the same find, wears the same type of costume but appears slightly later in date. She holds what may be a bunch of flowers. Also quite close in feeling to the Baltimore piece is the so-called "Proserpina" in Florence, who holds a pomegranate. Another figure in Baltimore, also dated about 400 BC, holds her garment in one hand, as does this figure, but seems much more closely aligned to Greek prototypes.

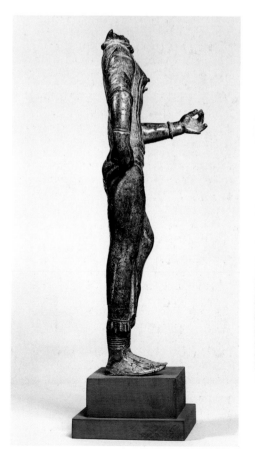

A second figure in Florence, known as "Ilithye," also holding a pomegranate and bearing a dedicatory inscription, takes a large sideways stride, setting up an even more dramatic feeling of motion within her drapery. She is almost as large as the Walters figure and appears to be slightly later because of her more baroque quality. A handsome figure in the Bibliothèque Nationale holds a fruit but lacks the pointed shoes and shoulder bands peculiar to the special costume of many of the figures. Her hipshot pose shows the strong influence of Classical Greek art. A piece in the Louvre, from Syria, and one in Lyon are chronologically near the end of the series. The costume—complete with diadem, necklace, shoulder bands, and pointed shoes—is also frequently found on engraved fourth-century Etruscan mirrors.

None of the statuettes mentioned, however, is close enough to the Walters woman to be identified with the same workshop or local school. In its high degree of finish, impressive scale, careful cold working, and in the insistent naturalism of such details as the drapery folds and nipples, the Walters figure has much in common with a bronze reclining male figure from a cinerary urn, found at Perugia and now in Leningrad. Scholars have argued about its attribution, but most have suggested a date about 400 and Chiusi as a place of manufacture. In the latter decades of the fifth century the economy of many of the Etruscan cities was in decline because of reverses at sea. By contrast Chiusi, whose economy was based on agriculture rather than trade, enjoyed great prosperity, and its bronze industry flourished. One of its wealthy citizens might well have commissioned this superlative, massive votive female from a leading local workshop.

CONDITION: The object is at least in part a thick-walled hollow cast, as is evident at the break in the neck and at the large hole in the left forearm. It has a smooth olive green and black patina. Missing are the head and possibly an object from the left hand. Several deep cracks on the back and left foot, and a deep small hole near the hem of the cloak over the right lower leg appear to have been made during the casting process. There is a dent in the back at the right side. Tangs under the feet are bent into hooks, one curving forward and the other backward. The piece has been mechanically cleaned, but encrustation remains in the deep fold along the left side.

EX COLLECTIONS: Stefano Bardini, Florence; Henry Walters, Baltimore.

EXHIBITED: Worcester Art Museum, Mass., April 21-June 4, 1967, *Masterpieces of Etruscan Art*, cat. by R. S. Teitz, 78-79, illus. 170, no. 69. Cambridge, Mass., Fogg Art Museum, December 4, 1967-January 23, 1968; St. Louis, Mo., City Art Museum, March 1-April 13, 1968; Los Angeles County Museum of Art, May 8-June 30, 1968, *Master Bronzes from the Classical World*, cat. by S. F. Doeringer and D. G. Mitten, 171, no. 171, illus, entry by S. F. Doeringer.

PUBLISHED: Sale: *Stefano Bardini*, London, Christie's, June 5, 1899, no. 191, pl. 3. S. Reinach, *Rép.stat*, III, 197:2. D. K. Hill 1949, 107, no. 240, pl. 46.

G. Fogolari, "Monumenti etruschi ed italici nei musei italiani e stranieri: Conclusioni," *StEtr* XXIII (1954) 389, n. 30.
Art of Ancient Italy: Etruscans, Greeks and Romans, exh. cat. (New York, André Emmerich Gallery, 1970) mentioned 12, under no. 18.
S. Boucher 1970, mentioned under no. 60, n. 2.
L. B. Warren 1971, 281, pl. 67, fig. 17.
L. Bonfante 1975, 39, 53, 63, 77, 182, fig. 82.
Small Sculptures in Bronze (1976) mentioned under no. 54.
O. Brendel 1978, 310, fig. 228.
A.-M. Adam 1984, mentioned 159, n. 3, under no. 234.

NOTES: On the Etruscan resistance to adopting the Greek Classical stance and the experiments with a more naturalistic stance in Etruscan art, see O. Brendel 1978, 305-310 and 315-317. On the woven shoulder bands, see E. Richardson 1976, 134, and L. Bonfante 1975, 39 and n. 37.

On the significance of the shoes and the costume, see [43] (Turan) and L. B. Warren 1971, 279-282; L. Bonfante 1975, 60-64. The torque was so-named after *torqueo*, "twist." It was a fashion borrowed from Gaul and appears frequently on Etruscan figures from about 400 BC onward. See L. Bonfante 1975, 77-78 and 144, n. 98. On bullae, see ibid., 143-144, n. 95.

For the piece from the Castellani collection, see H. B. Walters 1899, 91, no. 613, pl. 14; for the other London one, see his no. 612, pl. 14; both also illus. in T. Dohrn 1982, pl. 25. The "Proserpina" is Florence, Museo Archeologico (inv. 280): T. Dohrn 1982, 81, pl. 48:1.

For the Baltimore piece, see D. K. Hill, "Etruscan Woman," *BWalt* XVII (December 1964). Yet another figure in Baltimore (54.91), D. K. Hill 1949, no. 242, can also be related to this group. The "Ilithye" in Florence is Museo Archeologico (inv. 553): L. B. Warren 1971, pl. 67, figs. 18-19; T. Dohrn 1982, pl. 49:1-2. For that in the Bibliothèque Nationale, see A.-M. Adam 1984, 158-159, no. 234. For the piece in the Louvre, see A. de Ridder 1913-1915, I: no. 323, pl. 28. That in the Musée des Beaux-Arts, Lyon (inv. A 2008), is published with citation of further comparisons in S. Boucher 1970, no. 60; also in Lyon is a handsome bust, broken from a larger piece, in the same genre: S. Boucher 1970, no. 61. The reclining male figure is Hermitage B 485 (L. 69.5 cm.), made in several pieces: A. J. Vostchinina, "Statua cinerario in bronzo di arte etrusca nelle collezione dell'Ermitage," *StEtr* XXXIII (1965) 317-328; T. Dohrn 1982, 40-42, pl. 22:2. Dohrn declines to assign it with certainty either to Perugia or to Chiusi, the center of development of cinerary urns. He dates it about 400 BC. O. Brendel 1978, 322-323, fig. 245, and 470, n. 32, suggests that the artist had southern, perhaps Faliscan, tendencies.

45. Sleep and Death Carrying off the Slain Sarpedon (Cista Handle)

This dramatic figural group once formed the handle of a cylindrical bronze cista, a box for holding cosmetic articles and jewelry. Two winged figures in full armor hold the dead body of a nude youth. The group has been interpreted as representing Sleep and Death carrying off the slain Sarpedon or Memnon. Homer's *Iliad* tells the story of "godlike Sarpedon of the brazen helmet," lord of the Lycians and son of Zeus by Laodameia, daughter of the hero Bellerophon. After fighting fiercely on the Trojan side and killing Tlepolemos, Sarpedon meets his match in Patroclus.

Patroclus threw his brazen spear, which "struck where the beating heart is closed in the arch of the muscles. He [Sarpedon] fell, as when an oak goes down, or a white poplar, or like a towering pine tree which in the mountains the carpenters have hewn down with their whetted axes to make a ship-timber..." (XVI.481-485).

ETRUSCAN, EARLY
4TH C. BC.
L. 17.2 CM.
THE CLEVELAND
MUSEUM OF ART,
PURCHASE FROM THE
J. H. WADE FUND,
45.13

"But the Achaians took from Sarpedon's shoulders the armour glaring and brazen, and this the warlike son of Menoitios gave to his companions to carry back to the hollow ships. And now Zeus who gathers the clouds spoke a word to Apollo: 'Go if you will, beloved Phoibos, and rescue Sarpedon from under the weapons, wash the dark suffusion of blood from him, then carry him far away and wash him in a running river, anoint him in ambrosia, put ambrosial clothing upon him; then give him into the charge of swift messengers to carry him, of Sleep and Death, who are twin brothers, and these two shall lay him down presently within the rich countryside of broad Lykia where his brothers and countrymen shall give him due burial...'" (XVI.663-674).

The other protagonist who has been proposed as the central figure in this group, Memnon, was the son of Aurora (goddess of the dawn) and Tithonus, the

son of Laomedon, King of Troy. He was king of the Ethiopians and came to assist Priam in the Trojan War, but Memnon was killed by Achilles. His mother, who had witnessed his death, directed his brothers the Winds to carry his body to the banks of the river Esepus in Paphlagonia. At her urging, Zeus caused the flames of his funeral pyre to turn into flocks of birds which fought until they fell into the pyre as funeral offerings. Each year they return at the anniversary of his death and repeat the struggle. As for Aurora, "to this day She weeps, at times, and dews the world with tears" (Ovid, *Met.* XIII.620-621).

The three-figure group—two vertical figures and one horizontal—was popular with cista-makers, affording a convenient handle composition. Sometimes the figures are acrobats, but more often they are, as here, two persons carrying a dead body. The figures may be male or female, or a combination. They may be dressed or nude, in armor or in regular dress, winged or not. What places the Cleveland handle in a class by itself, however, is the extraordinary expressiveness of the figures. Usually they stand ramrod-straight, staring directly ahead, the body between them often stiffly horizontal and frontal, supported implausibly and impassively by the vertical figures with one hand each. In the Cleveland handle, however, the winged figures turn toward each other, bending their knees as they move the body gingerly, their backs bent under the weight of their load, and their gazes turned toward their task with concern and gravity. The body slumps convincingly, its arms hanging down limply, head rolled back and hair trailing in a languid drape forming a convenient thumb grip. Even the dead man's limp penis echoes the pendant diagonals of his hair and arms, bespeaking lifeless weight. His eyes are closed, but his face remains extremely expressive in death.

246

The piece represents a tour-de-force of bronzeworking, because it was made in a number of separate sections that have been so carefully joined that the seams are virtually invisible. Extensive cold working was done after casting. Details such as the fine hatching on the helmet crest and the elaboration of the patterns of feathers in the wings, as well as the patterns on the armor, attest to the craftsman's patience and skill.

The warriors are dressed in the style of armor that first came into vogue for Greek hoplites in the fifth century BC and was readily adopted by the Etruscans. They wear Attic helmets with long horsehair crests and hinged cheekpieces that are turned up. Incised spirals, terminating in palmettes on the figure at the head of the dead man, decorate the sides of the helmets behind the ears. Over short-sleeved, short-skirted chitons they wear heavy leather cuirasses, onto which rectangular bronze plates have been sewn.

Beneath the waist lies a crenelated band of leather, creating a row of rectangular flaps (pteryges), which also probably would have been covered in bronze. The individual plates on the cuirass of the figure holding the feet are simply outlined with a narrow line incised inside their edges, the bottoms of the pteryges ending in a delicate row of hatching; those on the figure supporting the head read as horizontal bands, decorated with, from the top, Greek key designs, running spirals or rectangles incised with X's, tongues, and, on the pteryges, double spirals. Broad straps over the shoulders fasten the cuirass over the breast, forming a V at the neck and revealing a serpentine design on the chiton beneath. These bands over the shoulders are further decorated with groups of parallel lines, triangles, and X's. The warriors wear no greaves and are barefoot.

The nude youth's torso is generally and subtly modeled; his muscles form a diamond-shaped pattern above the rib cage. His kneecaps are carefully rendered. On all the figures, parallel ridges are used on the front and side of the lower legs to represent muscles. The calf muscles of the supporting figures bulge convincingly as they lift their heavy load. Hands and feet are summarily treated.

Cistae were high-sided cylindrical, oval, or occasionally rectangular bronze boxes (see Figure XVI). They are often found in tombs of women, apparently having been prized personal possessions. Cistae came into existence early in the fourth century, achieved their canonical three-footed cylindrical form by mid-century, and continued in popularity through the third century and even into later years. Usually the surfaces of the box itself and of the cover were decorated with elaborate incised mythological scenes. The feet and handle were made separately and attached with rivets. It appears that the manufacture of the handles and feet was done by craftsmen other than those responsible for the incised decoration. In most instances the subjects of feet and handle seem to bear no relation to that of the incised scene, and the attachments are often placed so that they obscure the incised decoration—little thought having been given to how the various components would work together. In addition, the style of the handle and foot groups is often more retardataire than that of the drawing on the box. Stylistically, the handles can be analyzed in the context of contemporary statuettes, while the drawing bears analogies to the graphic arts, as represented in contemporary engraved mirrors or vase painting.

The principal place of manufacture for cistae was Praeneste (Palestrina), in the Sabine hills. A major center for the manufacture of engraved mirrors, the city appears to have also made various utensils with figurative handles (see discussion under Fleischman Lasa [48]). Although some of its products were carelessly produced and of mediocre quality, at their best they achieved the level of the finest masterpieces of Etruscan art. The Cleveland handle certainly ranks among the superb examples of this distinctly Etruscan genre.

The earliest cista handles seem mostly to be single figures, frequently acrobats doing a backbend. Three-figure compositions such as this one appear to have been introduced slightly later. The ultimate source for the composition of the Cleveland handle may well have been a Greek vase painting. The scene occurs on black-figure vases, while the splendid red-figure kalyx krater by Euphronios in the Metropolitan Museum of Art is astonishingly close in iconography, composition, and mood. Schefold has suggested that the dependence on Greek vase models may explain the difference between the relatively Archaic style of the faces and the style of the bodies, which reflect developments in Greek sculpture in the latter half of the fifth century.

CONDITION: The handle is a complex assembly of cast parts with a great deal of careful cold working. Each figure was solid cast in sections that were welded together. The figure supporting Sarpedon's feet was made in three sections. Each of his arms was cast separately and welded to the third part, the remainder of the figure. His left hand was cast as part of Sarpedon; the weld at the wrist has broken. The figure supporting Sarpedon's head is cast in two sections— his right arm, from the middle of the upper arm, being a separate piece. His left arm is cast with Sarpedon. A repair to his proper left leg appears to have been made at the foundry: a piece from just above the ankle to the middle of the calf was welded in place. His right wing is bent slightly to his left. Sarpedon was cast in three sections. His left arm has been welded at the shoulder; his right forearm has been welded at the elbow. His left thumb is missing. The rectangular base was another separate casting, and the clasp and ring in its center are two additional pieces.

An ancient pin between Sarpedon's head and the hip of the figure behind it attaches the two. It appears that Sarpedon's right leg was once welded to the arm of the figure at his feet. Pins would have attached both vertical figures to the flat base. The base, which would originally have been more curved, following the convex surface of the cista lid, has been bent away from the figures. The warrior at Sarpedon's feet has been reattached; the other warrior's right foot remains raised. There is a small crack in the base near the left foot of the figure supporting the head. Small casting flaws can be seen just above his right ear and at his right elbow.

After casting, the handle was finished by filing, polishing, and chasing. It is now covered with black, green, and red corrosion products. Photographs reveal that a great deal of corrosion has been removed since the piece left the Castellani collection at the end of the nineteenth century. The cleaning has been careful, however, and the elaborate incised decoration is well preserved.

EX COLLECTIONS: Alessandro Castellani, Rome; private collection, England.

EXHIBITED: Detroit Institute of Arts, March 23-April 20, 1947, *Small Bronzes of the Ancient World*, 9, 26, no. 48, illus.
Seattle Art Museum, November 8-December 8, 1957, *Survey of Italian Art*.
Montreal, Expo 67, April 28-October 27, 1967, *Man and His World*, International Fine Arts Exhibition, 304-305, no. 144, illus.

PUBLISHED: Sale: *A. Castellani: Catalogue des objets d'art antiques...*, Rome, 1884, 47, no. 282, pl. 8 (before cleaning).
S. Wunderlich, "A Bronze Cista Handle," *BClevMus* XXXII (1945) 39 ff.
"Art and Archaeology at the Cleveland Museum of Art," *Archaeology* VI (Winter 1953) 195-202, illus. 197.
S. E. Lee, "The Art Museum and Antiquity," *Apollo* LXXVIII (1963) 439-441, fig. 5.
H. Jucker in K. Schefold 1967, 325, pl. 417.
R. Ross Holloway, "Figure corazzate ed alate nell'Italia preromana," *Miscellanea di studi classici in onore di Eugenio Manni*, 6 vols. (Rome, 1980) VI:1939-1944, pl. IV, figs. 4-5.
D. von Bothmer, "The Death of Sarpedon," in *The Greek Vase: Papers Based on Lectures Presented to a Symposium Held at Hudson Valley Community College at Troy, N.Y., in April of 1979*, ed. S. L. Hyatt (Latham, N.Y., 1981) 78, n. 32, fig. 84.

NOTES: I am grateful to Bruce Christman for help in determining how the piece was made.
On Sarpedon, see Homer, *Iliad* II.876; V.627-667; VI.197-198, and esp. XVI.419-547 and XVI.659-683. The translation cited here is that of R. Lattimore (Chicago, Ill., 1951). Memnon's story originated in the lost *Aithiopis*, and a version is retold by Ovid, *Metamorphoses* XIII.576 ff., tr. Rolfe Humphries (Bloomington, Ind., 1960).
A corpus of the Praenestine cistae is in preparation. The first volume, *Ciste Prenestine* (1979) by G. Bordenache Battaglia, contains a number of cistae with three-figure groups in which two figures support a third who is wounded or dead. The groups exist in many permutations. A sampling of the types includes:

Two women supporting a nude youth: Bibliothèque Nationale: A.-M. Adam 1984, 25-26, no. 24. She cites another in the Armand-Valton collection.

Youth and woman supporting a nude youth: Ex collections Warneck and de Kolb: *Art of Ancient Italy* (1970) 12, no. 18.

Two winged men supporting a nude youth: Metropolitan Museum (22.84.1): G. M. A. Richter 1940, 51, fig. 155; *Corpus* I, B-42, pl. 174.

Two winged women supporting a nude warrior with helmet: Museo Archeologico, Florence (628): S. Haynes 1985, 289-290, no. 120, illus. p. 192, as central Etruscan, possibly Orvietan.

Two Amazons supporting a nude Amazon: Villa Giulia, from Palestrina: G. Q. Giglioli 1935, pl. CCCXCI; *Villa Giulia* (1980) 292-293, figs. 413, 414.

Two warriors supporting a warrior: Museo Archeologico, Florence: *Le città etrusche*, ed. F. Boitani et al. (Milan, 1973) unpaginated. Villa Giulia, Rome (25210): *Corpus* I, A-7, pls. 16, 17; *Villa Giulia* (1980) 289, fig. 408. Berlin, Charlottenburg, Staatliche Museen, Antikenabteilung (inv. misc. 6239): *Corpus* I, B-5, pl. 61.

Two warriors supporting a nude youth: Rome, Villa Giulia: G. Q. Giglioli 1935, pl. CCLXXXIII:1. London, British Museum (inv. 738.20-263): *Corpus* I, A-4, pl. 10.

Two nude youths supporting a nude youth: Walters Art Gallery (54.136): *Corpus* I, B-1, pl. 44; R. S. Teitz, *Masterpieces of Etruscan Art* (1967) fig. 77. Metropolitan Museum of Art (09.221.11 and 13.227.7): G. M. A. Richter 1915, 77-78, nos. 122, 123. Berlin, Charlottenburg, Staatliche Museen, Antikenabteilung (inv. misc. 6236): *Corpus* I, A-1, pl. 1. Copenhagen, Ny Carlsberg Glyptotek (inv. H 241): *Corpus* I, A-3, pl. 6.

Two nude, helmeted youths, supporting a nude youth: Palestrina, Museo Archeologico (inv. 1494): *Corpus* I, A-6, pl. 13.

Two nude youths, one with helmet, supporting a nude youth: Villa Giulia (inv. 51208-51209): *Corpus* I, A-9, pl. 26.

L. B. Warren, "A Latin Triumph on a Praenestine Cista," *AJA* LXVIII (1964) 35-42, has argued that cistae were being produced as late as 100 BC.
On the armor, see S. Doeringer and G. M. A. Hanfmann, "An Etruscan Bronze Warrior in the Fogg Museum," *StEtr* XXXV (1967) 645-653, citing further bibliography; also F. Roncalli, "Il 'Marte' di Todi," *MemPontAcc*, 3rd ser., XI:2 (1973) 58-65.
For the Euphronios vase, see *BMMA* XXXI (1972) 34-39, and D. von Bothmer, in *The Greek Vase* (1981) 63-80, who discusses distinctions between representations of Sarpedon and those of Memnon.
The relationship of the Euphronios krater and other vase paintings to the Cleveland handle is discussed by R. R. Holloway 1980.

46. Hercle

ETRUSCAN,
EARLY 4TH C. BC.
H. 24.2 CM.
TOLEDO MUSEUM OF
ART, GIFT OF
EDWARD DRUMMOND
LIBBEY, 78.22

If one judges solely from the number of votive statuettes preserved, Hercle would certainly seem to be the most popular divinity in pre-Roman Italy. Although Heracles was admired as a hero in Greece, in Etruria Hercle was primarily worshipped as a god. He was seen as a protector not only of men but also of mountains, streams, and gateways. As such, he was frequently depicted on gables and temple pediments, as well as on gems and coins.

Hercle is one of the few identifiable gods to be represented in Etruria before the middle Archaic period. His exploits form the subject of works of art in several media in the sixth and fifth centuries, most notably on the famous Vulcian tripods. Although votive statuettes are known from the late sixth century onward, during the fourth century they became more common. The Etruscans appear to have developed several distinctive types, melding the Greek tradition of the heroic nude figure with local folk traditions. Among them are the standing Hercle, such as this one, the fighting type, similar to this but with the weight shifted to the leg with the bent knee, and the club ready to strike; and the Hercle at rest, his arms lowered, often holding the apples of the Hesperides, which he obtained after many adventures as the eleventh of his twelve labors. Small Hercle statuettes of later periods, many of inferior quality, are found in profusion in antiquities collections, although most of them were apparently made in provincial centers outside Etruria proper. The fighting type seems to be the usual basis for these.

This Hercle is one of the finest examples extant, representing the full flowering of Etruscan classicism. The figure stands solemnly, his left knee bent, his right hand raised up and holding the club behind his back, the left hand extended and grasping a bow and arrow. He is nude except for a lionskin, which he wears as sort of a hooded cape. The lion's head covers his own like a helmet, his face actually projecting from its jaws. The lion's forepaws are knotted about his neck in what is known as a "Hercules knot." The skin continues down his back and is looped over his left forearm, ending with the hind paws and tail neatly arrayed at the level of his knees.

Hercle's face conveys his belligerence as effectively as do his weapons. His low, furrowed forehead radiates seriousness. Both eyelids are prominent; the iris and pupil are incised. His nose is straight, fleshy, and broad at the base. His full lips are set in a grave expression but show no trace of the "pout" that became fashionable in Greek Heracles figures of the age of Alexander the Great. Delicate incision is used to show the eyebrows and sideburns. A row of tight curls, much more stylized than the remainder of the figure, frame Hercle's face below the lion's teeth. The lion's jaw curves around the side of the face, its teeth covering Hercle's ears. Its mane is stylized into a short ridge articulated by radiating lines which form a sort of nimbus behind the hero's head. The lion's ears are small and round, and do not protrude beyond the mane. At the back of Hercle's head, the mane becomes a heavy raised median band incised in a herringbone pattern, which continues down Hercle's back and onto the flap draped over his arm. The body of the hero shows the influence of Polyclitan classicism. The musculature of his torso is very elaborately developed, particularly over the rib cage.

This type of standing Hercle, brandishing a club, continues in use down to the second century. A number of handsome examples, all dating from around 400 BC, are known, including those in Bologna, Kansas City, and Princeton. Seemingly related pieces have been found at various sites in France. The type continues with a late flowering in the Etrusco-Roman culture of the second half of the second century BC. Compare also the Hercle and Iolaos figures on the feet of the Ficoroni cista and the satyrs on the handle of this and the Napoleon cista in the Louvre, which show the same classicism of form and seriousness of expression that characterize

the Toledo Hercle statuette. In contrast to this bellicose image, an elegant fourth-century Hercle at rest, in Florence, holds a drinking horn in his lowered right hand and seems to follow the fluid, somewhat elongated Praxitelean canon of proportions rather than the Polyclitan. This type, too, seems to have spawned followers as late as the second and first centuries BC.

Although no Etruscan sanctuaries to Hercle have been found, the Toledo bronze must have been a votive dedication. The prominent inscription on his right side reads in retrograde: *hercales mi*, which Richardson has translated as "I belong to Hercale." She points out that the letter forms are those used in southern Etruria no later than the fourth century BC and that the spelling of the name, although unique among preserved inscriptions, would be an appropriate genitive form. The letter forms belong to the Etruscan Intermediate (fifth-fourth centuries BC) or Younger (fourth-first centuries) alphabet, and the last letter is a form used in southern Etruria only as far north as Vulci or Volsinii.

In his fundamental study, Bayet identified two basic types of votive Hercle figures, an Archaic type inspired by Cypriot models and a later Italic type. Transitional between these two was the type to which this statuette belongs. Richardson has suggested that both the Archaic and the transitional types were developed by the Etruscans. Because of the letter forms used in the inscription, she proposes a south Etruscan city, possibly Orvieto (near ancient Volsinii), as a conceivable site for the manufacture of this bronze.

Etruscan Volsinii was reputedly a city of great wealth, and judging from Pliny's report that the Romans carried away over 2,000 bronze statues after they took the city (*N.H.*, XXXIV, 16), it must have had a thriving bronzeworking industry. Scholars have differed on where the Etruscan city was, but modern Orvieto is presently

gaining in favor. Strategically located, with access to major Etruscan centers, and in a lush agricultural plain, it shows evidence of habitation from the eighth century BC until a radical destruction of the city took place in the early third, congruent with the recorded destruction of Volsinii Veteres ("old Volsenii") by the Romans in 265 BC.

Finds from Orvieto and the surrounding territory show the strong influence of Greek fifth-century sculpture, possibly transmitted by way of Greek South Italy. This classical style is found both in terracottas and in such large-scale bronzes as the famous "Mars" from nearby Todi, although comparatively few small-scale bronze statuettes have been found. Aristocratic burials of the fourth century, with extensive and lavish grave goods, attest to the existence of a wealthy class during the time the Hercle would have been made.

The inscription identifies the bronze as a votive dedication to Hercle. Although Orvieto encompasses the remains of several Etruscan temples, the only cult that can be definitely identified there was of Tinia, attested to by votive inscriptions on cippi—low stone pillars usually decorated in relief and inscribed and used as boundary or grave markers. Roman historians report that Noritia and Vertumnus were worshipped at Volsinii. Although there is no documentation of a sanctuary to Hercle there, Richardson's proposal of Volsinii/Orvieto as a place of manufacture for this strongly classicizing fourth-century Hercle seems quite plausible.

CONDITION: This solid-cast figure is missing both feet at the ankles and the ends of the arrow. An examination at the Museum of Fine Arts, Boston, in February 1978 provided the following information: even dark green cassiterite patina on figure; cuprite, cassiterite, malachite, and some paratacamite on bow. Many of the ancient corrosion products have been removed in modern cleaning; in places, particularly on the legs, the figure was overcleaned, necessitating repatination. The club has a thick artificial patina, and the bow appears to have an applied patina as well. Club, bow (two pieces), and arrow are each made separately and inserted into the statuette's hands. The bow-string appears to be a modern replacement. The carving in the "knots" on the club is very sharp and does not show wear, indicating possible modern recutting. The carving of the hair and inscription may also have been retouched. Calcium carbonate accretions were removed mechanically in August 1978; gouges on the right buttock and left leg, and cuprite patches on the right wrist and lion's nose were inpainted. Spectrochemical analysis at that time showed that the bronze contains 5 percent lead and low tin.

PUBLISHED: N. Thompson de Grummond, "Rediscovery," in *Etruscan Life* (1986) 21, fig. 1,1 and frontispiece.

NOTES: I am grateful to Emeline Richardson for sharing with me the manuscript for an article she is preparing on this bronze and the development of the Heracles type in general. She, in turn, has consulted with Helmut Rix and Carlo de Simone on the translation and interpretation of the inscription, which she has kindly allowed me to include here.

One of the earliest striding Hercle figures is in Baltimore: D. K. Hill 1949, 44-45, no. 90, pl. 23. Among the closest parallels to the Toledo piece is the Hercle in Bologna, Museo Civico, excavated at the Villa Cassarini outside the Porta Saragozza. See G. Gulandi in G. Colonna, ed., "Scavi e scoperte," *StEtr* XLIV (1976) 380, pl. LX:a; M. Cristofani 1985, 260, no. 7.4, illus. 120, 121.

For the Kansas City Hercle, Nelson-Atkins Museum (49-76), see *Master Bronzes* (1967) 179, no. 183. For the piece in the Art Museum, Princeton University (73-7), late 4th-3rd century BC, see *Small Sculptures in Bronze* (1976) no. 55, illus. In both of these the lionskin forms a sort of high collar standing away from the face. Among the French examples are: S. Boucher, *Vienne. Bronzes antiques* (Paris, 1971) 68-69, no. 24; and H. Oggiano-Bitar, *Bronzes figurés antiques des Bouches-du-Rhône* (Paris, 1984) nos. 19 and 20. See also her nos. 15 and 16, striding types.

From the 3rd century, note the examples in Minneapolis *(Minneapolis Institute of Arts Bulletin* LV [1966], 60) and Cassel (U. Hockmann, *Staatliche Kunstsammlungen Kassel. Antike Bronzen* [Cassel, 1972] 28, nos. 49, 50, pl. 15).

Two examples in the Bibliothèque Nationale—one standing, one fighting—have been attributed to a late Hellenistic Sabellan workshop: A.-M. Adam 1984, 188-189, nos. 289-290, illus., although M. Cristofani 1985 dates the former to 400-350 BC. See also A.-M. Adam 1984, nos. 288, 290, 291.

For the 4th-century Hercle at rest, in the Museo Archeologico, Florence (inv. 5), from Poggio Castiglione, see G. Q. Giglioli 1935, 47, pl. CCLX:3; M. Cristofani 1985, 283, no. 98, illus. 203. Among its descendants are a bronze in Karlsruhe, J. Thimme, "Badisches Landesmuseum Neuerwerbungen 1969," *Jahrbuch der Staatlichen Kunstsammlungen in Baden-Württemberg* VII (1970) 126-127, no. 10, illus., and a handsome Hercle formerly in the Coats collection, now owned by Lawrence Fleischman, New York: J. P. Uhlenbrock, *Herakles, Passage of the Hero Through 1000 Years of Classical Art*, exh. cat. (New Rochelle, Bard College, 1986) no. 32, illus. See also D. K. Hill 1949, no. 95.

J. P. Uhlenbrock 1986 offers a good overview of Heracles' role in classical art and literature. The basic study of representations of Hercle in Etruria is J. Bayet, *Herclé; Etude critique des principaux monuments relatifs à l'Hercule étrusque* (Paris, 1926) esp. 34-49, where he analyzes the cult statuettes of the god. The late Hercle figures are discussed by G. Colonna, "Problemi dell'arte figurativa in età ellenistica nell'Italia adriatica," *Atti 10 Convegno studi sulle antichità adriatiche* (Chieti-Francavilla al Mare, 1971) 172-177.

On the debate over the location of Etruscan Volsinii, see L. Banti 1973, 118-127; S. Haynes 1985, 91-92; also [47] below.

The Toledo Museum also possesses a lathe-turned cylindrical stone base (83.46; H. 15 cm.; Diam. at top 9.5 cm., at bottom, 11.8 cm.). It is one of two bases, the other one higher and square in section, said to have belonged to this statuette and to the bronze in Karlsruhe. It is inscribed in retrograde, "Laris dedicates [this] to Dionysus." There is no proof that the sculpture and the base go together.

47. Youth

This muscular youth, bearing a long dedicatory inscription, shows how the Etruscans modified the classicizing idiom represented by the Toledo Hercle [46] in the subsequent period, under the influence of the new canon of proportions introduced in Hellenistic Greece. One notices immediately that the head is quite small in relation to the body. The torso has been elongated, particularly the pelvic region, and the legs are longer, too. These new proportions reflect the work of the Greek sculptor Lysippus, as transmitted to the Etruscan artist no doubt through small-scale works influenced by the Greek's style.

The stance, too, is an exaggeration of that of the Hercle and shows the intervention of Lysippan influence. The hip above the weight-bearing left leg is thrust out dramatically, and the projection of the buttocks is pronounced. The right shoulder is brought forward and the elbow bent back, creating an exaggerated S-

ETRUSCAN,
LATE 4TH C. BC.
H. 19.7 CM.
MR. AND MRS.
LAWRENCE A.
FLEISCHMAN
COLLECTION

curve within the torso that is emphasized by the curve of the mid-ventral line and the furrow of the spinal column. This motion, reinforced by the three-quarter turn of the head to the left side, sets up a slight spiral within the figure, establishing a more complex sense of movement than was found in the more frontal Hercle; it represents another indirect inheritance from Lysippus.

Despite a fairly effective disposition of the masses of the figure in space, the artist was less concerned with rendering the details of anatomy. Although interested in featuring the athlete's muscular body, he depicted the muscles in a considerably more simplified and stylized way than was the case in the Hercle. The kneecap is reduced to a Y-shaped groove; an incised triangle serves to articulate the tendons of the neck. The hand shows similar cursory treatment; the fingers were crudely delineated in the wax with little cold working to articulate them.

Likewise the head betrays a degree of summary treatment and rough finish. The hair is swept back from the face and tucked behind the ears, turning under at the nape of the neck. It is rendered with relatively few strokes, quite different from the elaborate hairdos on the Archaic male statuettes (cf. the Getty kouros and Getty Tinia [37, 39]). The face has high, rounded cheekbones and a smooth jawline. The eyebrow ridge runs into the nose, which in profile continues the line of the forehead almost without a break. The mouth is small and full. Although the eyelids are modeled, the long pointed oval eyes are vacant. The ears are simple in form and mounted high and at an angle, giving the figure a slightly faunlike air. The face is a distinctly Etruscan type, related to many of the figures on Praenestine cistae and related utensils. It shows no awareness of the distinctive facial type introduced in portraits of Alexander the Great, which came to be widely dispersed throughout his empire.

The inscription runs in three lines from just under the right breast down along the right side of the torso and the inside of the right leg. It reads: *ecn: turce: avle: havrnas: tuthina: apana: selvansl[:] tularias.* This has been translated by de Simone and Bonfante as: "Avle Havrnas gave (turce) this (ecn) . . . to Selvans [Silvanus] of the boundaries." *Apana,* derived from *aps,* apparently means "paternal" or "of the father." The meaning of *tuthina* is debated. Van der Meer proposes that it may indicate a district; Colonna elsewhere has read it as "village," while de Simone interprets it as "votive gift." The word *tularias* seems to relate to *tular,* which means "boundary." In other inscriptions as well, Selvans (Silvanus) seems to be connected with the concept of protecting and establishing boundaries.

A figure such as this would probably have been a votive dedication at a sanctuary. It appears to represent neither a god nor a priest, but rather a fine specimen of masculinity, possibly an athlete. Numerous statuettes like this have been found in Etruria, dating from the fourth and later centuries. Many wear a short mantle draped about their hips, but others are nude. The gesture of the right hand on the hip is common; the left hand may either be empty or hold an offering of some kind. For the pose, compare two fourth-century statuettes in the British Museum—one draped and one nude—and a third-century figure in the collection of Emeline Richardson. Van der Meer dates the Fleischman youth to the fourth century and suggests, with de Simone, that it may come from Bolsena.

The remains of an Etruscan city have been found in the hills above modern Bolsena, surrounded by a wall of fourth- to third-century date. Some scholars believe that this was Volsinii Veteres, "old Volsinii," one of the most important Etruscan cities. Roman historians report that after this town was sacked by the Romans in 265 BC, its inhabitants were moved to "another place," called Volsinii Novi, new Volsinii. Inscriptions have shown Volsinii Novi, which continued into Roman times, to be located on the lake at Bolsena, very near the Etruscan remains. The proximity of the two argues against identifying Bolsena as Volsinii Veteres since, as Haynes points out, the Roman settlement "could hardly be described as 'another place' in relation to a site only a few hundred yards up the hillside."

Whatever its identity, the Etruscan town at Bolsena may have been a center for the worship of Selvans. On the western boundary of the Pozzarello sanctuary, within the walls, a cippus dating from the third or second century BC was found, bearing an inscription to Selvans as god of boundaries. A bronze statuette of a draped youth, also inscribed to Selvans, comes from Bolsena as well; it is now in the Villa Giulia, Rome. The cippus may indicate that the cult enclosure was devoted to the worship of Selvans, and it is conceivable that the Fleischman youth was intended as a votive dedication in this very sanctuary.

CONDITION: It is solid cast. The missing left arm appears to have been cast separately and welded on. A ring of gas bubbles at the shoulder and a band of metal of a different color indicate the location of the weld. Many trapped gas bubbles are seen over the entire surface of the sculpture. The cast details appear to have been sharpened with chasing tools and the inscription to have been chiseled. Ancient hammer marks can be seen on the right shoulder blade and the back of the upper right arm. Both legs are missing from the knee. Some damage has occurred to the right ear. A modern mounting rod is in the left leg. The surface is covered with malachite and a brown corrosion product.

PUBLISHED: C. de Simone, in *Atti II congresso internazionale di etruscologia, Firenze 1985* (forthcoming).
L. B. van der Meer 1987, 61, 63, 181 n. 6.
C. de Simone, *StEtr* LIV (1988) forthcoming.
L. Bonfante, *StEtr* forthcoming.

NOTES: The condition statement is based on an examination report by Bruce Christman.
For the statuettes in the British Museum, both also inscribed with dedications to Selvans, see S. Haynes 1985, 302, nos. 154 (draped) and 155, illus. 214; L. B. van der Meer 1987, 60, figs. 26 and 25, respectively. Mrs. Richardson's bronze is published in *Small Sculptures in Bronze* (1976) no. 57, illus.

An elongated figure in the same stance, called Italic-Etruscan, formerly in the Stafford collection, is published in *Master Bronzes* (1967) 177, no. 180. L. B. van der Meer 1987 illustrates several other examples (figs. 22, 23, 26, 29). For a draped figure with both hands extended, in which the facial type is influenced by portraits of Alexander the Great, see S. Haynes 1985, 316, no. 186, illus. In "The Bronze Priests and Priestesses from Nemi," *RM* LXVII (1960) 43 f., she relates this piece to other Hellenistic materials in Etruria. Compare also *Master Bronzes* (1967) 183, no. 187, with additional parallels.

On the location of Etruscan Volsinii, see S. Haynes 1985, 91-92 and [46] above.

For the bronze in the Villa Giulia (inv. 59459), see van der Meer 1987, 62, fig. 29.

I am deeply grateful to Larissa Bonfante for the references to the inscription's interpretation and to Carlo de Simone for permission to draw on his forthcoming article in *Studi Etruschi*. Bonfante is preparing a detailed publication of the bronze for the same journal to complement de Simone's publication of the inscription. The word *apana* had been read as *epana* in de Simone's 1985 paper, where he suggested that *tuthina epana* represents a noun and modifying adjective that describe the object given, for example, "bronze figure." G. Colonna's interpretation of *tuthina epana* as "village of Epana" in another inscription appears in *Atti e memorie della Accademia Petrarca di Lettere, Arti e Scienze*, n.s., XLVII (1985) 184-185, and is commented on by C. de Simone (*StEtr*) forthcoming.

48. Lasa (Patera Support)

Like the Boston girl and the Cleveland Lasa [49, 50], this statuette must have served as the handle for a patera. Winged female figures like this one have frequently been identified as Lasas, but the role and nature of Lasa within the Etruscan pantheon is only imperfectly understood.

Since there is virtually no literary evidence, the narrative scenes that appear on engraved mirrors from the fourth and third centuries BC are among the principal sources for information about Etruscan divinities—particularly in the later periods. Here, the participants are sometimes identified by inscriptions and can be associated with particular costumes, attributes, or other deities in what are often stock scenes. On these mirrors, figures labeled "Lasa" are often shown in the company of the goddess Turan (the Etruscan Aphrodite, see [43]), where they are involved in feminine preoccupations such as marriage rites or the toilette. Lasa figures may be shown nude or clothed, winged or not. Among their attributes are frequently a mirror or, as here, an alabastron (perfume or oil vessel), but also occasionally a scepter or lance. Some scholars have held that Lasa is a major goddess, while others consider her a type of minor divinity of which there might have been many—such as the Greek nymphs—who would have played a role subsidiary to Turan. Although the alabastron may have held perfume for Turan's toilette, some scholars have suggested that it might have contained ointments for annointing the dead. They have speculated that Lasa was associated with funeral rites, although this role is usually ascribed to Culśu and Vanth, other Etruscan deities, both of whom may also be winged.

The confusion over the role of Lasa is compounded by the difference of opinion about what paterae were used for: were they objects of daily use, or were they associated with religious activities? Many have been recovered from tombs, which

ETRUSCAN,
LATE 4TH OR
EARLY 3RD C. BC.
H. OF FIGURE 14.7 CM.
MR. AND MRS.
LAWRENCE A.
FLEISCHMAN
COLLECTION

has led to speculation that they were used to pour libations in funerary rites. Sometimes the bowls or the handle figures bear the inscription *Suthina*—usually translated "sacred to the burial cult." This does not necessarily preclude their having performed other functions as well; a person's treasured possessions might well have been buried with him. The possibility that paterae were used in daily life, perhaps in bathing related to athletic activity, is discussed further in the entry on the Boston girl [49]. A better understanding of the use of this patera might help us learn whether the handle figure is a handmaiden of beauty or a messenger from the afterlife.

Gjødesen has studied the relationship between Greek paterae with anthropomorphic handles and the standing mirrors whose handles are figures in the round, produced by Greek, South Italian, and Etruscan workshops. The idea of the human figure on handles can be traced to ancient Egypt, which produced standing mirrors of this type, as well as spoons and vessels. The motif was taken up by the Phoenicians. The Greeks extended the idea to include patera handles. Production of figurative patera handles was particularly prolific in the Greek colonies of South Italy, where a type of handle in the form of a nude youth supporting two rams over his head became commonplace in the early fifth century. The Etruscans borrowed the anthropomorphic motif from their South Italian neighbors, but in the late Classical period they broke with the rigid, symmetrical, frontal poses of the South Italian models, developing relaxed figures such as this, which shift their weight to one leg and turn their bodies with new freedom. In the third century, under the influence of the Hellenistic style, the figures become even more baroque, as in the Cleveland Lasa [50].

Nude female figures are rare in Etruscan art until the fourth century, when they began to appear on engraved mirrors and cistae, whose style was in the vanguard of the more conservative statuettes. Soon nudes began to be used for cista handles, and it is probably through this channel that they came to be employed for handles on other types of vessels and utensils. The focus on the female nude in Etruria to some extent parallels the intensified Greek interest in the theme during the Hellenistic period (see [15]), and once again trends in Greece may have provided the impetus for change in Etruria, although the conceptions are quite different.

The Fleischman Lasa stands at ease, her contrapposto pose well handled. Her left leg is relaxed, causing her right hip to project and setting up an S-curve within her body that is particularly well rendered in the back view. Her heels are closer together than her toes, her feet creating a triangle parallel to the triangle of the base on which she stands. She raises one hand to her head, perhaps evoking the weight-bearing caryatid function of figures such as the Boston girl [49] and the South Italian patera handles, but the gesture is languid and clearly not supportive. It serves, rather, to inject further enlivening asymmetry into the figure, despite its basic frontality. The Lasa's face has a rounded jaw and the vacant expression typical of many bronzes from Praeneste made at this time. Her eyelids are shown, but the pupils are delineated only by very shallow punched circles. Her mouth is small and unsmiling. Her hair, swept back and looped up in back over a barely visible band, is finely detailed except for the area just above this knot of hair in back, where her head is left plain with no indication of hair at all.

Her figure is well proportioned. With muscular upper arms, a torso more athletic than sensuous, and small, high breasts, she has an almost boyish appearance. She is nude except for her jewelry and shoes, which the artist has rendered in detail. We can see exactly how her necklace and armlet were made, the pendants having wide tubelike sleeves at the top, through which a band of metal—here given a different texture with tiny hatched strokes—was passed. She wears a plain armlet above the one with pendants, with some sort of rectangular element projecting upward from it. Her soft slippers (socci) are also carefully rendered, with their separate tongues, raised flaps at the ankles, and even the stitches that outline their upper edges all clearly shown. In contrast to this elaborate detailing of the sparse costume elements, the modeling of the body is quite generalized. The nipples are punched circles. A shallow groove defines the mid-ventral line, and a small punched dot represents the navel. One shallow curved line demarcates the top of the pubic triangle, which is otherwise left plain.

The wings are somewhat summarily executed. In some places, feathers are individually depicted as having a central rib from which lines radiate in herringbone fashion, but in others the wing becomes a mass of ribs and parallel hatched lines, no longer discernible as individual feathers. The backs of the wings are left completely plain, although the back of the figure itself is just as carefully finished as the front.

The support for the bowl of the patera ends in two simple rosettes in front. On the back, its curved form is decorated with a pair of facing ribbed elements (perhaps based on shells or sea-monster fins?) rather than the more customary palmette. The inner edges of the forms are shown as heavy raised ribs with diagonal hatching. The outer margins are scalloped and slightly raised above the background but otherwise left plain. Within the elements there are gently raised ribs, articulated further by double rows of dots. As Turan-Aphrodite was born from the sea, an aquatic motif would be appropriate for her attendant.

The Lasa stands on a triangular base, its edge beaded and its sides ornamented with a simple tongue pattern. The U-shaped lug under the base projects below its bottom edges and would have made it impossible for a heavy patera to stand up-

right on the base. A suspension ring probably originally passed through the lug, enabling its owner to hang the patera when it was not in use. Depressions in the lower rim of the base, either worn in or intentionally filed to allow the ring to turn freely, seem to corroborate this hypothesis. Most of these later paterae were furnished with suspension rings; the bases on which the figures stand are often simply flat round or triangular platforms, without appreciable height.

For the subject, comparison can be drawn with the handsome Lasa from Perugia in Florence, probably a support for an incense burner. A wingless figure of similar function in the Harvard University Art Museums, complete with sea monster, also holds an alabastron and has the same head type and boyish body as the Fleischman bronze. Numerous examples of nude or partially nude winged female figures as patera handles survive. They have close cousins among handles of Etruscan standing mirrors and a hand mirror handle in the British Museum. Among the patera handles, one of the closest is an example in the Metropolitan Museum that shares the same type of wings (including the blank backs), the rosettes on the mounting bracket, and the gesture of the right arm, although the head is somewhat different.

These handles have not been systematically studied, but there are significant differences among them in the proportions of the figures, treatment of drapery, elaborateness of pose, and degree of finish, indicating that they come from a variety of workshops and span a considerable period of time. Those with the more chunky, athletic proportions—such as this one and the Metropolitan example cited above—seem to form a group distinct from those with elongated proportions influenced by Lysippus. Both in their body types and in their faces and hairstyles they bear strong analogies to many of the handle figures on the elaborate decorated cistae manufactured in Praeneste beginning in the early fourth century BC. Compare, for example, the handle of the Ficoroni cista, perhaps the finest example extant, or the figure of a maenad in a handle group in the British Museum. A cista handle from Praeneste in the Villa Giulia consists of a male and a female figure—the male holding an alabastron and both bearing flamboyant wings analogous in character to this Lasa's— and dates from the second half of the fourth century. It seems likely that the well-established workshops that manufactured these fine cista handles would have produced patera handles as well.

CONDITION: The wings were cast separately and attached with a rivet in the center of the back. The figure is solid cast; the base is hollow and open at the bottom, with a U-shaped lug in the center, both cast in one with the figure. The surface has been cleaned, leaving only a thin layer of corrosion products and exposing much of the cuprite layer. It is a smooth surface of mottled green with areas of red, brown, and black. A few feather tips and the bowl of the patera are missing.

PUBLISHED: Sale: *Ancient Art*, New York, Sotheby Parke Bernet, December 11, 1980, lot 181, col. illus.
S. Haynes 1985, mentioned 320, under no. 195.

NOTES: I am grateful to Bruce Christman, who examined the object with me.
On Lasa, see R. Enking, "Lasa," *RM* LVIII (1943) 1-15. A. Rallo, *Lasa; Iconografia e esegesi* (Florence, 1974), analyzes pictorial images with inscriptions (usually on mirrors) and inscriptions without images, and concludes that Lasa has no association with funerary scenes and is a category of divine being but a minor, rather than a major figure.
For more about the winged female deities associated with the dead, see R. Enking, "Culśu und Vanth," *RM* LVIII (1943) 48-64; O. W. Von Vacano, "Vanth-Aphrodite," in *Hommages à Albert Grenier* (Brussels, 1962) III, 1531-1553; L. Bonfante in *Etruscan Life* (1986) 267.

On the relationship between paterae and standing mirrors, see M. Gjødesen, "Bronze Paterae with Anthropomorphous Handles," *ActaA* XV (1944) 101-187.

For an elaborate bulla of the type shown here, see G. M. A. Richter 1940, 54, fig. 170; G. Q. Giglioli 1935, pls. CCCLXXV:4, CCCLXXVI:3.

On sea monsters, see K. Shepard, *The Fish-Tailed Monster in Greek and Etruscan Art* (New York, 1940); M. Boosen, *Etruskische Meeresmischwesen: Untersuchungen zu Typologie und Bedeutung* (Rome, 1986).

For the bronze Lasa incense burner in the Museo Archeologico, Florence, see G. Q. Giglioli 1935, pl. CCCX:4. The Harvard piece (1966.109) is published in *The Frederick M. Watkins Collection*, exh. cat. (Cambridge, Mass., 1973) 80, no. 33, illus.

For the patera handle in the Metropolitan, see G. M. A. Richter 1940, 52, figs. 157, 158; *Masterpieces of Etruscan Art* (1967) 93-94, no. 84, illus. 202.

Other patera handles in the form of winged female figures include: Vatican: G. Q. Giglioli 1935, pl. CCCXIII:3 and 4; Volterra (inv. 90/1902): E. Fiumi, *Volterra: Il Museo Etrusco e i monumenti antichi* (Pisa, 1969) fig. 167 (note also the ceramic example, inv. 527, Fiumi's fig. 124); another in the Metropolitan Museum more Lysippan in inspiration: G. M. A. Richter 1940, 53, fig. 161, from a tomb at Bolsena; Walters Art Gallery: D. K. Hill, *Greek and Roman Metalwork in the Walters Art Gallery*, exh. cat. (Baltimore, 1976) no. 41; Royal Scottish Museum, Edinburgh:

M. A. Johnstone, "Etruscan Collections in the Royal Scottish Museum, Edinburgh, and the National Museum of Antiquities of Scotland, Edinburgh," *StEtr* XI (1937) 392, pl. 49:1; Museo Nazionale di Umbria: A. E. Feruglio, "Rivista di epigrafia etrusca," *StEtr* XL (1972) 458, no. 73, pl. 84, from Orvieto; Musée Borély (inv. 2333): H. Oggiano-Bitar 1984, 49, no. 44, illus. (the wings are a modern reconstruction); British Museum (reg. 68.6-6.6): S. Haynes 1985, 320, no. 185, illus., also from Bolsena; Florence, Museo Archeologico: L. A. Milani, *Il R. Museo Archeologico di Firenze: Sua storia e guida* (Florence, 1912) pl. 23, from Todi.

See also two examples in the Bibliothèque Nationale, less closely related in type: A.-M. Adam 1984, nos. 38-39, with further comparisons. A standing mirror handle is illustrated by M. A. Johnstone (*StEtr*) 1937, pl. 49:2; for an unusual hand mirror with a winged figure as handle, in the British Museum, see E. Gerhard et al. 1843-1897, IV: 330; A. Rallo 1974, pl. 36:1.

For the Ficoroni cista, see T. Dohrn, *Der Ficoronische Ciste in der Villa Giulia in Rom* (Berlin, 1972). For the British Museum piece (Br. 638), see S. Haynes, *Etruscan Bronze Utensils* (London, 1965) pls. 12, 13. Note also the head on a contemporary shovel from Praeneste, her pl. 14.

The cista handle in the Villa Giulia, formerly in the Barberini collection, is illustrated in M. Moretti and G. Maetzke, *The Art of the Etruscans* (New York, 1970) pl. 209, and in *Villa Giulia* (1980) 295, figs. 418, 420.

49. Nude Girl (Patera Support)

This rather athletic young woman holds both hands up to support some heavy object, undoubtedly the bowl of a patera. She seems to bear the weight easily, as indicated by her relaxed contrapposto pose, her right knee slightly bent. She wears soft Etruscan slippers (socci), which rise up the ankle in back, and a heavy necklace with a circular bulla in the center, flanked by two crescent-shaped pendants. Her stephane is rather elaborate in front, with an incised diamond pattern, centered with small punched dots; at the back of the head, it becomes a simple fillet. Her hair, centrally parted, falls in soft waves across the forehead and is drawn back over the ears; in back it ends at the nape of her neck. An extra flap over each ear, although not incised as hair, is probably so intended.

The girl's proportions are naturalistic, and her body is softly modeled, the flex of her biceps contributing to its athletic character. The anatomy is well understood. Contrast, for example, the realistic depiction of the curve of her breasts with

ETRUSCAN,
LATE 4TH OR
EARLY 3RD C. BC.
H. OF FIGURE 14.8 CM.
MUSEUM OF FINE ARTS,
BOSTON, H. L. PIERCE
FUND, 98.679

their generalized handling on earlier statuettes such as the Turan [43]. Yet, although the figure is fully formed in the round, it is presented frontally, with the position of the arms emphasizing its caryatid function.

The support on her head curves back at an angle that suggests that the patera had a deep bowl. On the back the attachment plate is decorated with a seven-petaled palmette in high relief. This is set into a scallop-edged element that has strong similarities to the motif on the back of the attachment plate for the Fleisch-man Lasa [48], which has been interpreted as perhaps representing a sea-monster's fins. Like that piece, this one has raised ribs within the scalloped motif, outlined by paired rows of dots. The "fins" become a pair of spiral whorls at their lower extremities, taking on a vaguely shell-like character. This scalloped shell-like motif is repeated on the front, the ridges of the whorls also being decorated with parallel rows of deeply punched dots.

Unlike the Fleischman bronze and the patera support from Cleveland [50], whose wings suggest that they belong to the supernatural realm, this young lady seems very much of this world. Her face shows the influence of Polyclitan forerunners, her heavy eyes tilting down slightly at the outer corners and her full lips forming a modified pout.

Johnstone and Gjødesen have both speculated that one use for paterae might have been for pouring water over the body when bathing, making representations of human athletic figures, rather than gods, quite appropriate as handle adornments. That figurative handles also are found on strigils in Hellenistic Etruria seems to bolster this connection. In Pompeii an athlete's grooming kit was found, consisting of an aryballos, four strigils, and a patera, all strung together on a ring. It

is possible, however, that like the other two patera handles here, the girl represents a Lasa, since Lasa could be shown with or without wings. The fin/shell decoration on the attachment, if indeed we are interpreting it correctly, does not help much with identifying the girl. It could allude to an association with the watery world of Aphrodite, or simply to the vessel's use in bathing.

The surviving paterae with nude female figures similar to this in stance, athletic body type, and treatment of the facial features include one in the Walters Art Gallery, with the pan preserved, and a handle in Vienne. An example from Vulci, now in the Vatican, has similar proportions but shows the woman looking at herself in a mirror.

Ever since its acquisition by the Museum of Fine Arts, this figurine has been called Faliscan. Ancient Falerii Veteres (modern Città Castellana) is not known, however, to have been a bronzeworking center. The handsome fifth-century bronze vessels found there have generally been thought to have been imported. During the fourth century, in spite of repeated skirmishes with Rome, Faliscan culture seems to have flourished, producing architectural terracottas and a wide range of red-figure vases that were influenced by the Hellenized culture of Tarentum in Magna Graecia. In 241 BC Falerii Veteres was destroyed by the Romans; the inhabitants founded Falerii Novi at a new site. Hoffmann has associated the Boston piece with a flat basin in the Menil collection, on which the handles are in the form of reclining youths, reportedly found in the region of Ancona. He also relates a group of spouted jugs said to have come from Todi. Indeed, findspots indicate that there was a considerable production of paterae with figured handles of this type in the area of Todi, Bolsena, and Orvieto. Given its stylistic similarities with these handles, a workshop in that region may prove more likely to have manufactured this patera support than one in the Faliscan territory.

CONDITION: The figure was solid cast in one piece with its base and attachment member. Its very thin, even dark patina has traces of red-brown on the upper torso. The object appears to have been recently cleaned to a nearly bare surface, and the black surface layer, which lies over a layer of red corrosion, is probably modern. There are small casting flaws on the left buttock, right thigh just above the back of the knee, and the right calf. There is a stress crack across the center of the back. A deep gouge above the proper left knee appears to have been filled in antiquity. The attachment member carried on her head has a groove on the inside, which would have supported the bowl of the patera, now missing.

EX COLLECTION: Edward Perry Warren.

EXHIBITED: Worcester Art Museum, Mass., April 21-June 4, 1967, *Masterpieces of Etruscan Art*, cat. by R. S. Teitz, 93, 96, illus. 195, no. 87.

PUBLISHED: E. Robinson, Boston Museum of Fine Arts, *Annual Report* (Boston, 1898) 33, no. 37.
AA (1899) 138.
M. Comstock and C. C. Vermeule 1971, 382, no. 529, illus. 383.
C. A. Di Stefano 1975, 95, under no. 170.
Sale: *Ancient Art*, New York, Sotheby Parke Bernet, December 11, 1980, mentioned under lot 181.
Masterpieces from the Boston Museum (Boston, 1981) no. 17, col. illus.
M. del Chiaro, *Re-Exhumed Etruscan Bronzes*, exh. cat. (Santa Barbara, Calif., 1981) mentioned 29, n. 6.

NOTES: I am grateful to Arthur Beale and Richard Newman for assistance in preparing the condition statement.
On the socci, see L. Bonfante 1975, 62-63. She discusses the jewelry, 143-144, n. 95.
On the uses of paterae, see M. A. Johnstone (*StEtr*) 1937, 392; M. Gjødesen (*ActaA*) 1944, 171: "The only hint of an implied concrete motive and thereby a hint at the use of the patera might lie in the athletic apparition of the figures; it is natural and obvious as far as the male figures are concerned, but remarkable for the females." For other theories on the use of paterae see the Fleischman Lasa [48].

Figurative handles on Hellenistic Etruscan strigils include British Museum: S. Haynes 1985, 228, no. 176, and Praenestine comparanda cited there; *Villa Giulia* (1980) 296, figs. 421-422; G. Q. Giglioli 1935, pl. CCCVIII:3,4. A nude female patera support figure in the British Museum (47.11.10; S. Haynes 1985, 314, no. 179, illus. 229) holds a strigil in her hand.

Closest parallels are the paterae in Baltimore (54.162; *Master Bronzes* [1967] 220, no. 223) and Vienne (S. Boucher 1971, 167, no. 360, illus.). For the one from Vulci now in the Vatican, see G. Q. Giglioli 1935, pl. CCCXIII:1. Note also his pl. CCCXIII:2, with a male figure, discussed with the Cleveland Lasa [50].

Among other paterae with wingless nude female figures as handles, less closely related stylistically to this piece, are Palermo: C. A. Di Stefano 1975, 95, no. 170, pl. 36; one formerly on the art market, Ars Antiqua, *Auktion* II (Lucerne, 1960) 38-39, no. 89, pl. 40, where it is assigned to Magna Graecia, possibly Locri, early 4th century BC.

On the 5th-century vessels from Città Castellana, see *The Frederick M. Watkins Collection*, exh. cat. (Cambridge, Mass., 1973) 77-78, under no. 32; G. M. A. Richter 1915, 180-181 and nos. 488-490, 570-573, 578-580; M. Comstock and C. Vermeule 1971, 381, no. 527; I. Krauskopf, "La 'Schnabelkanne' della collezione Watkins nel Fogg Art Museum e vasi affini," *Prospettiva* XX (January 1980) 7-16.

H. Hoffmann, *Ten Centuries That Shaped the West: Greek and Roman Art in Texas Collections*, exh. cat. (Houston, Tex., 1970) 193, under no. 90, discusses the connection with the Menil dish and Todi jugs.

50. Lasa (Patera Support)

Poised almost on tiptoe, this partially draped female figure admires herself in a hand mirror. Her elaborate, graceful wings sweep upward behind the fragmentary element that rests on her head, which at one time supported the bowl of a patera. The sculptor has maintained something of the concept of support by bringing the wings up to brace the basin in visual terms, if not in actuality. At the same time, this device ingeniously allows the Lasa to lower her arms and engage in another activity. It also liberates the sculptor from the frontality and symmetry that characterized the earlier patera handles [48, 49] and enables him to set up a radical torque within the figure, unlike anything produced previously. With her knees bent, her front leg crossing over the back one, and her right shoulder thrust forward, the Lasa twists around an imaginary central axis.

Brendel has christened this complex positioning of the legs, which recurs frequently in statuettes of this period, the "eccentric stance." He interprets it as the Etruscan response to the Polyclitan dilemma of incorporating both walking and standing in the same pose. The composition reflects in spirit the aesthetic innovations of Hellenistic Greece, in which a variety of complicated, often dramatic poses were introduced—although this particular conception does not rely on any known Greek prototype. No longer is there a "front view" at all; in order to understand the figure entirely, one has to move around it and see it from all angles. The baroque torsion enlivens the Lasa's contour and animates the composition on all sides.

The twist of the torso is accentuated by the animal-skin drapery in front, which is modeled with distinct folds in high relief that curve around the body, radiating out from a knot at the shoulder. The abdomen is softly modeled, the navel sunken, and the body forms generalized. The legs are stocky and simplified.

A silver-inlaid diadem in a guilloche pattern encircles the maiden's head; she wears an earring in the form of two concentric circles in her right ear and two necklaces, also in silver. Her garment is a leopard (or "panther") skin, its spots and the leopard's ruff also rendered in silver inlays. The leopard-skin garb is unusual. Wunderlich has suggested that the artist may have confused a Lasa's attributes with those of a maenad.

Although the silver spots on the leopard-skin are flush with the surface of the bronze and may be inlaid, they are quite thin, almost applied. An elaborate cista handle from Praeneste, now in the Louvre, shows Dionysus supported by two satyrs whose panther-skin garments show numerous small cavities, from which the inlays in another metal are now missing. These may give us some idea how the Lasa's silver spots were made, although the cavities there are probably deeper than those beneath this Lasa's spots. In the other areas, however, such as the headband, jewelry, and ruff, the silver is laid over a rounded, raised area of bronze, rather than being set into a recess. Probably the surface of the bronze was roughened and thin sheet silver was pressed over it and burnished, making a mechanical bond. The present very dark patina of the bronze is probably not original, since the object shows evidence of a rigorous cleaning in modern times. Nonetheless, it may not be unlike the ancient patina in color. Although we know very little about what the Greeks and Etruscans wanted their bronzes to look like, there is evidence that bronzes decorated in silver or copper may have had their surfaces artificially darkened to increase the coloristic effect and make the metallic decoration stand out more vividly.

The Lasa wears thick-soled sandals. Their construction is made plain: a thong runs between her first two toes, splitting into two straps that run diagonally, one to the instep, the other to the outside of her foot, just in front of the heel; another

ETRUSCAN,
3RD OR EARLY
2ND C. BC.
H. 21.6 CM.
THE CLEVELAND
MUSEUM OF ART,
PURCHASE FROM THE
J. H. WADE FUND,
47.68

strap goes around the heel and along the outside of her foot to the base of the little toe; a third one runs across the base of her toes.

The triangular base and the support she carries on her head indicate that this figure was the handle of a patera. Most of the bowl of the patera is now lost, as frequently happens because it would have been fashioned separately, of thinner, hammered bronze. Part of it can still be seen, however, gripped by the attachment bracket. It has a dentillated edge. On the front the support is decorated with two opposing leaf forms terminating in rosettes; from the rear the leaf forms are surmounted by a nine-petaled palmette in relief, which served to reinforce the attachment point.

The Cleveland patera handle continues the tradition of human supports for paterae [cf. 48, 49], although the complex pose, soft—almost sfumato—modeling, and dreamy expression are all new. It is not atypical in figures associated with objects of daily use for this mixture of continuity and change to occur at the transition from the Classical to the Hellenistic style in the third century. Many of the types of vessels and utensils popular in the fourth century continue in use: incense burners, cistae, paterae. Their figurative elements, however, take on a new mannerist or baroque aura. For example, the elegant exaggerated hipshot pose and crossover stance of this patera handle are paralleled among the figures on a class of baroque Etruscan incense burners with elaborate vegetal shafts such as those in the Villa Giulia and Berkeley. To see how this new aesthetic affected such figures in a widespread fashion during the third century, compare also the strigil handle in the Villa Giulia which has a leggy, mannered female figure; a cista handle such as that with Dionysus and a satyr in Palestrina, which is an elaborate triangular composition of two figures; or such Lasas on patera handles as an elegant one in the

Metropolitan Museum with one arm languidly draped over her head and the other cradling a rhyton.

Many of the comparisons cited here have more mannered, elongated proportions than the Cleveland Lasa, while none share the elaborate silver decorations. A patera found in the necropolis of Peschiera, at Todi, however, is supported by a nude youth. Like the Lasa, he stands on a triangular base, this one decorated with a meander band in silver. Like the Lasa's, the support for the bowl of his patera ends in a rosette at either end and the rim of the bowl has a beaded edge. In their dreamy expressions, soft fleshy forms, and body proportions the two figures resemble each other, although the Lasa's pose is more complex than the youth's contrapposto. The same necropolis yielded a bronze oinochoe with a handle in the form of a satyr in which the cross-legged stance and fluid, twisting pose are taken to new extremes. It also produced a quantity of elaborate gold jewelry, such as the Cleveland Lasa would have delighted to wear. Proietti has postulated the existence of an active local school of bronzeworkers and goldsmiths at work during the heyday of Etruscan Todi in the late fourth and third centuries BC. Indeed, the preponderance of examples of this kind of figure, usually decorating a utensil or vessel, seem to come from the area around Todi, Orvieto, and Bolsena, and despite its purported findspot at Kerch in South Russia, the Cleveland patera handle falls squarely within this tradition.

Kerch lies in the Crimea, on the western shore of the strait between the Black Sea and the Sea of Azov. This key location, a sort of second Bosporus, was the site of the Greek settlement of Panticapaeum. Archaeological evidence indicates a Greek presence in the area from the seventh century BC on. Although by the fourth century and later, direct commercial dealings between Etruria and Greece had declined considerably, a few Etruscan objects have been found at South Russian sites dating from the fourth and third centuries BC. Thus, the undocumented tradition that the Lasa was found at Kerch, is not wholly without plausibility.

CONDITION: The figure is solid cast; both wings were apparently cast separately and welded to the figure. The base was separately cast, with holes in the top through which tangs under the figure's feet were inserted and then flattened to attach the two. It is open at the bottom. The cast sections were finished by filing and polishing, and the cast details were sharpened by chasing. The object has a black-brown patina with some areas of cuprite corrosion. It has been mechanically cleaned and presumably repatinated thereafter; little of the original patina remains. The bowl of the patera and the figure's right index finger are missing. Both feet have been broken at the ankles and repaired. The left wing has been reattached with lead solder. The back of the attachment bracket has been bent downward.

PROVENANCE: Said to have been found at Kerch, South Russia.

PUBLISHED: *Fasti Archeologici*, II (1947) 183, fig. 41; 184, no. 1542.
S. A. Wunderlich, "A Bronze Patera Handle," *BClevMus* XXXIV (1947) 164-166, cover illus.
J. D. Cooney, "Siren and Ba, Birds of a Feather," *BClevMus* LV (1968) 262-271, fig. 13.
O. Brendel 1978, 411-412, fig. 312.
M. del Chiaro, *Re-Exhumed Etruscan Bronzes*, exh. cat. (Santa Barbara, Calif., 1981) mentioned 29, under no. 25, n. 7.
S. Haynes 1985, mentioned 320, under no. 195.

NOTES: I am grateful to Bruce Christman, who examined this object with me.

For inlays in "panther" skins on the Louvre cista handle (the so-called "Ciste Napoleon") from Praeneste, see S. Haynes 1985, 311, no. 173, illus.

O. Brendel 1978, 411-412, discusses the "eccentric stance."

For the elaborate thymiateria with twisting supporting figures, see Villa Giulia (inv. 24415): S. Haynes 1985, no. 183, illus. 231; R. H. Lowie Museum, University of California, Berkeley (8-3406): *Master Bronzes* (1967) 221, no. 221, also citing other examples. The strigil handle is published in *Villa Giulia* (1980) 296, figs. 421-422.

For the cista handle in the Museo Archeologico Prenestino, Palestrina (inv. 1499), see O. Brendel 1978, 411, fig. 311. For the Metropolitan Lasa patera handle, see G. M. A. Richter 1915, 217-218, no. 598, illus.; G. M. A. Richter 1940, 53, fig. 161.

The male figure from Todi is *Villa Giulia* (1980) 309, no. 438. For the satyr from the same site, see pp. 312-313, no. 449. On pp. 303-304, G. Proietti discusses the possibility of a major workshop at Todi.

Clearly related to this group, and also sporting an inlaid silver guilloche on a triangular base, is a utensil-holder from Orvieto in the British Museum (reg. 47.11-1.7): S. Haynes 1985, 306, no. 164; 220, fig. 164. For a 3rd-century tomb group from Todi, see L. Milani 1912, 1:134; II: pl. 23. It contained several utensils and vessels in this style, of 4th- and 3rd-century date.

On Greek settlements at Kerch and elsewhere on the Black Sea, see M. I. Rostovtseff, *Iranians and Greeks in South Russia* (Oxford, 1922) esp. 61-82; J. Boardman 1980, 225 ff., esp. 253; on later Etruscan finds in the area, see J. Macintosh Turfa, "International Contacts: Commerce, Trade, and Foreign Affairs," in *Etruscan Life* (1986) 81; J. G. Szilágyi, "Zur Frage des etruskischen Handels nach dem Norden," *Acta Antiqua Academiae Scientarium Hungaricae* I (1952) 432, n. 40. All offer useful further bibliographies.

Roman Bronzes

In the narrowest, geographical sense, a Roman work of art is an object produced in the city of Rome—or in its immediate environs, the region of Latium—from the eighth century BC to the fifth century AD. It is not necessarily, however, the product of a native Roman, since ancient Rome was host to multitudes of foreign artists coming from Etruria or the Greek-speaking world. Imported works of art found at Rome can also be included in the concept of a Roman statuette. As Rome's political influence expanded and cultural contacts intensified, moreover, the definition grows ever looser and more problematic. Rome's conquest of the Aegean world in the second century BC led to a love affair with Greek art that has caused the late Hellenistic period to be alternatively termed the "Greco-Roman period."[1] The borderline between so-called "Greek" and "Roman" becomes so vague in this time span that several relatively early pieces in *The Gods Delight* could as easily be classified in one category as the other.

Most works in the Roman section of the exhibition, however, are placed here for unambiguous chronological reasons. These works have been ascribed to the Roman Imperial period: that is, the time of the uncontested rule of the first emperor, Augustus, and thereafter. In the first centuries of the Imperial era, artistic developments in Rome or central Italy had strong repercussions throughout the entire Empire. Even though regional traditions survived, production throughout this vast territory tended to go through a common series of phases.[2] After 31 BC, then, almost any more-or-less realistic bronze statuette coming from a region extending from Mesopotamia to England can be considered Roman.

Although the known provenances of the exhibited works are clustered in the eastern half of the Mediterranean—from sites ranging from Italy through Asia Minor and Lebanon to Egypt—the objects themselves offer an international rather than a regional picture. High quality statuettes fully in the Classical tradition appear throughout the Roman world, including the northern and western regions of the Empire—modern England, France, Belgium, Switzerland, and western and southern Germany. Low quality production is equally widespread. The percentage of poor work may be higher in the western provinces than in traditionally Classical lands, but the difference is one of degree rather than principle. Economic integration contributed to the spread of common standards; statuettes, which are, after all, highly portable, were often shipped from one end of the Empire to the other. Nearly identical statuettes of Jupiter, which must stem from the same workshop if not the same molds, have come to light in Padua and Lyon, and other pairs of duplicates have been found in England and Switzerland, and in Morocco and Switzerland.[3] A Jupiter recently retrieved from Spanish coastal waters is practically identical with two figures in Austria, and all three must come from the same source.[4] The case of the Cleveland Hercules and Lar [61, 62] is in its way equally illuminating about the cultural unity of the Roman world; the Cleveland figures are presumably from the Mediterranean basin, but a very similar Hercules and Lar have been excavated at Weissenburg north of the Danube in Germany (Figures XVII, XVIII).[5] A comparable situation holds true for the Walters Palaemon [72]. The Walters figure is said to come from Sidon in Lebanon, but a somewhat earlier replica has been found in Velleia in northern Italy.

This cosmopolitan situation makes it difficult to establish the locations of workshops that produced statuettes in Imperial times, although some regional schools have been delineated.[6] Only one piece in the exhibition—the running Hercules from the Brooklyn Museum [73]—seems to represent a distinctly local phenomenon: a rough but vigorous Egyptian folk art in the service of official Imperial ideology.

Compared to the rich finds of Etruria, lying on the north and east side of the Tiber, relatively few early statuettes have been discovered in Latium, either because of a different attitude toward votive gifts[7] or else because of accidents of preservation. The few votive bronzes that have been found are of Etruscan workmanship, like the late second-century pieces from the Latin sanctuary of Diana at Nemi.[8] Production of what could be called "post-Etruscan" character might maintain a marginal presence down to the end of the Republic,[9] but powerful new stimuli were coming from the Greek world. By the later second century BC, Rome had become a major patron for Greek artists, and the process of Hellenization had reached and was to remain at an intense level, at least in patrician circles.[10] Statuettes were surely among the cultural trappings of the time in Rome, as they were in contemporary towns in nearby Campania. As has been reaffirmed recently by Zanker, the mansions of second-century Pompeii were from the beginning embellished with masterful small-scale bronzes like the famous dancing satyr or the satyr with wineskin.[11]

A few works discussed here throw light on artistic cross-currents at Rome in the late Republic and at the beginning of the Imperial period. To judge from these statuettes, Greek artists migrated to Rome where they established new workshops. The evidence is both stylistic and technical. The Metropolitan Museum's brilliant figure of a mime [28], apparently discovered in Rome, for instance, seems to have been made by an artist fully conscious both of Hellenistic Greek artistic fashion and native Italic customs. He may have been a migrant, but a fully assimilated one, perhaps from no farther away than the Greek regions of southern Italy. The Metropolitan's statuette of the philosopher found at Ostia, Rome's port [26], is a Hellenic work that betrays a trace of coloring from an Italic environment in its handling

Figure XVII. *Hercules.* Bronze, H. 14.9 cm. (with base 20.8 cm.) Roman, later 2nd century AD. From Weissenburg, Bavaria. Prähistorische Staatssammlung, Munich.

Figure XVIII. *Lar.* Bronze, H. 20.4 cm. (with base 25.9 cm.). Roman, later 2nd century AD. From Weissenburg, Bavaria. Prähistorische Staatssammlung, Munich.

of ornament. The statuette of the warrior wearing a Corinthian helmet now in the collection of the Wadsworth Atheneum in Hartford [58], which was retrieved from the Tiber River near Rome, is almost purely Greek in outlook. The many unfilled casting flaws, however, make it unlikely that the figure was an import.

The difficulties of dating bronze statuettes of the Roman Imperial period or, for that matter, in even distinguishing them from Hellenistic works have been stressed in recent literature. Boucher has gone so far as to argue that all examples considered Hellenistic are simply misdated Roman pieces and that the production of statuettes essentially stopped in the Greek world for roughly four centuries until it was revived by the Romans. Following her theory, the Etruscans would have kept the tradition alive and then passed it on to the Romans. Manfrini-Aragno has, on the other hand, taken the position that statuettes were cast in the Hellenistic period but they are indistinguishable from Roman works.[12]

Although an attempt to separate works of these two closely related phases does, indeed, involve subtle distinctions and the possibility (or likelihood) of occasional error, the operation does not seem impossible or arbitrary. A firm point of reference is offered by several high quality Greek statuettes from shipwrecks of late Hellenistic times: the Mahdia wreck of about 100 BC recovered off the Tunisian coast (Figure XIX) and the wreck datable between 75 and 50 BC off the Greek island of Anticythera. More evidence comes from statuettes or busts in Hellenistic sites that were either impoverished or semi-abandoned in Roman Imperial times, like Pella in Macedonia and the island of Delos.[13] Their Roman Imperial counterparts are the bronzes found in Gaul, in the north Italian town of Industria, and in shipwrecks like those of Lake Nemi (Figure XX) and one recently recovered off the Spanish coast at Cavallo.[14]

Figure XIX. *Dancing Dwarf with Castanets.* Bronze, H. 32 cm. Hellenistic Greek, late 2nd century BC. From the Mahdia shipwreck. Tunis, Bardo Museum. Photo: Deutches Archäologisches Institut, Rome, 61.456.

Neither group of bronzes, of course, presents a stylistically unified picture, but certain tendencies seem to emerge. In general, the Hellenistic works appear to be modeled with a softer, gentler, and more fluent touch. They tend to be vivacious and immediate. Roman works more often display a sharpness and elaboration of detail. Their effect is harder and more emphatic, based in part on a widely diffused admiration of High Classical art, a phenomenon well known from marble sculpture. Attributes take on a greater role, increasing the narrative, declarative side of the work of art. Eventually, this kind of emphatic definition leads to outright anti-naturalistic stylization. Etruscan statuettes, with their bold spontaneity and periodic lapses into primitivism, are easily distinguished from bronzes produced in this environment of elaborate classicism.

The style and treatment of hair can be of great help in dating works within the Imperial period. The portraits of living (or more-or-less recently deceased) persons can be related to the likenesses of magistrates, the Imperial family, and Imperial favorites, whose chronology is certain. Portrait heads on coins and in monumental marble reliefs have helped to date the magistrates of the Getty relief [63], the Getty singer [55], the Bloomington child actor [71], and the Brooklyn running Hercules [73]. These works in turn have served as reference points for dating others in the exhibition.

Small-scale bronze portrait busts are important sources of information for the techniques used by Roman bronzeworkers in various phases of the Imperial period. Portraits are, as pointed out, datable with relative ease, and the way that hair is modeled in these works returns in statuettes of ideal or grotesque types that otherwise might be difficult to fix in time.[15] A miniature bronze portrait of a woman found in the Villa of the Papyri at Herculaneum (Figure XXI),[16] for exam-

Figure XX. *Double Herm of a Silenus and Satyr.* Bronze. Roman, ca. AD 25-50. From the shipwreck of Lake Nemi. After G. Ucelli, *Le navi di Nemi* (Rome, 1940) fig. 236. Photo: Courtesy, Museum of Fine Arts, Boston.

ple, makes use of a special coloristic treatment also employed in many of the finest Roman statuettes; curls of hair are given emphasis by small circular perforations, probably made by twirling the point of a stick in the wax model. The resulting spots of shadow parallel the effects created by drillwork in marble. Since the lady's hair is styled like that of Agrippina, Caligula's mother, who appears on coinage in the span AD 37-54, the technique was evidently established in bronzeworking shops by middle Julio-Claudian times. In all likelihood, it was used even earlier. The Herculaneum bust is an undistinguished work, and the indentations are large and heavy-handed. The delicate application of the technique in fine statuettes, like the Hartford warrior [58] or the Cleveland Hercules [61], is probably earlier. If an analogy with the use of drilled shadow-holes in marble sculpture is permitted, such indentations could be earlier still. Drill-holes can be seen in the Zoilos relief in Aphrodisias of the 30s BC,[17] in the Stephanos athlete of the mid-first century BC,[18] and in a marble head of Heracles from Capua,[19] attributed to the early first century BC. The absence of indentations for coloristic effect in the bronze statuettes found in shipwrecks of the first half of the first century BC, however, cautions against over-stressing the importance of analogies with marblework.

The treatment of hair undergoes another series of changes in the course of the first century AD. Sharp linear description is gradually replaced by more fluent, sketchy modeling. In the early Empire, locks of hair are frequently defined as tapering forms that turn into a curl, giving them the curvature of a C, a J, or an S (sickle-like, hooked, or reversing curves). In late Augustan works like the Cleveland Lar [62], the locks on the crown of the head stand out in relief and are carefully striated with incisions. Parallels can be found in such large-scale bronzes as the herm of the Doryphorus by Apollonius of Athens in the Villa of the Papyri at Herculaneum.[20] In the more emphatic treatment given the hair of the Polyclitan athlete in the Levy collection [59], probably at a slightly later date, the curls have been reinforced with the circular indentations discussed above. But by mid-century, sickle-like locks of hair flow more restlessly and fluently, as on the older magistrate of the Getty relief [63]. Definition, although still entirely linear, has become sketchier and more suggestive. The hair of a miniature bronze portrait of Caligula (AD 37-41) in a private collection in Zurich (Figure XXII)[21] is quite similar.

The development in the second half of the first century has been traced by Leibundgut. Linear finishing tends to be given up; hair is modeled either as a soft, smooth surface or else in more rounded, cordlike forms.[22] There is an obvious parallel with the incipient baroque of late Julio-Claudian times that becomes fully baroque under the Flavians (AD 69-96) and into the reign of Trajan (AD 98-117). This

Figure XXI. *Bust of a Woman*. Bronze, H. 14 cm. Roman, ca. AD 50. From the Villa of the Papyri at Herculaneum. Naples, Museo Nazionale. Photo: Deutsches Archäologisches Institut, Rome, 37.969.

Figure XXII. *Caligula*. Gilded bronze, H. 20 cm. Roman, ca. AD 40. Zurich, Schinz collection. After *Ancient Portraits in the J. Paul Getty Museum* (Malibu, 1987) 31, fig. 18b.

looser, more amorphous treatment of hair, characteristic of the High Empire, appears in small bronze portrait busts like that of the Emperor Domitian (AD 81-96) in Copenhagen (Figure XXIII) or that of an unknown general from Velleia (Figure XXIV).[23] It can also be seen in the Getty Penthesilea [68], the Bloomington child actor [71], and the Levy dancer [69].

An excellent measuring rod for the transformation of technique between around 100 BC and AD 100 is offered by a series of grotesque heads and theater masks in the exhibition. They illustrate the transition from a sketchy, suggestive Hellenistic style through the clear linear definition of Julio-Claudian times to the softness and amorphousness of the Flavio-Trajanic baroque. The sequence starts with the comic actor from the J. Paul Getty Museum [54], probably of the mid-first century BC, who wears a mask with subtly modeled knotted brows, recalling the grotesques of the late second century BC from the Mahdia shipwreck (Figure XIX). The phallic dwarf [56], probably of the early first century AD, has a harder and more emphatic face, although the linear-featured face of the boxing dwarf [57], also from Boston, goes much farther in this direction and dates from about AD 25-50. This same emphatic definition can be found in the contemporary herm from Lake Nemi (Figure XX). The comic mask worn by the boy actor [71], cast about AD 90-120, on the other hand, is defined almost completely in terms of contrasted masses of doughy material without a linear component. Once the outlines have been established, this same progression can be traced in other aspects of the modeling of statuettes from these centuries.

Bronze statuettes in the Roman Imperial period continue Greek traditions in the kinds of figures used as well as in their stylistic approach. Ideal figures—whether of gods, athletes, generalized children, or actors in their masks—constitute the basic repertory of the bronzeworker; grotesques are simply the reverse side of the Hellenic coin. All have their roots in the Greek past. The exploitation of the Greek artistic repertory in Roman Imperial times was comprehensive to the point of being encyclopedic. All periods of Greek art were drawn on from the late Archaic to the Hellenistic. All kinds of subjects were presented, ranging quite literally from the sublime to the ridiculous. The process involved not only copying, revivals, and survivals, but it also led to complex recombinations of different stylistic traditions. The rich, eclectic visual culture of the late Republican and the Imperial periods offered an extremely complex extension of Greek artistry. It should be noted that both literal copying and thorough modification are not unique to Roman Imperial times; both practices seem to have come into existence in the second century BC, probably in the environment of the Hellenistic kingdom of Pergamum.[24] Eclecti-

Figure XXIII. *Emperor Domitian*, AD 81-96. Bronze, H. 15 cm. Roman, AD 90-100. Copenhagen, Ny Carlsberg Glyptotek.

Figure XXIV. *Bust of a General*. Bronze, H. 17.5 cm. Roman, ca. AD 100. From Velleia. Parma, Museo di Antichità. After H. Jucker, *Das Bildnis im Blätterkelch* (Olten, 1961) pl. 16, B6.

cism was not uniquely Roman; it simply became more important and took on a more specifically Roman character as time progressed.

Relatively few Roman bronze statuettes can be considered faithful replicas of earlier Greek masterpieces, and in cases where several Roman replicas of the same model are known, each reflection tends to diverge significantly in detail or treatment.[25] In the exhibition, perhaps only the Levy athlete [59], the Hartford warrior [58], and the Getty Venus [65] can be said to present compositions of the fifth century BC with relative consistency. Early or middle Hellenistic prototypes seem to be reflected with some accuracy in the Getty comic actor [54], the Penthesilea from the Levy collection [68], and perhaps also the begging girl in the Getty [70]. To varying degrees, however, the execution of all these figures is colored with a Roman period tint, and several are fitted out with costumes or ornaments that probably stem from later Hellenistic or early Imperial revisions of the designs; this kind of alteration is particularly evident in the case of the Getty beggar [70], who can be compared with a Hellenistic original presenting a similar composition (Figure XXV).

In part, the scarcity of faithful replicas of famous works of the past is due to the physical and technical characteristics of the bronze statuette. Most of the opera nobilia were presumably life-sized or larger. A reproduction in the same scale could be much more accurate since there was no need to telescope detail and since mechanical aids like the pointing machine or casts could be used. A sculptor producing a miniature version of another work, in contrast, had to take a more independent viewpoint, as he summarized freehand.

Recent studies of Roman bronze statuettes have de-emphasized the role played by copies of early prototypes. Instead, bronzeworkers usually seem to have engaged in a process that was more continuous, ongoing, and flexible than that of copying.[26] Similar compositions were apparently produced in relatively close chronological succession; craftsmanship and artistry evolved within a cohesive framework. In such cases, it is preferable to speak of examples of a figural type rather than of models and copies. Technical procedures may have much to do with this state of affairs. At times, all-but-identical replicas were created in the same studio, as is the case with the genii [51, 52] and the Hellenistic Pans [23]. In these replicas created within the same workshop for the same project, a single wax model may have been used to produce several clay or plaster molds for the casting process. Normally, however, when figures of the same type were cast at a certain distance—whether in time or space—from one another, some detail is changed, if only the position of a limb or an attribute. The relative ease with which a small bronze could be produced made continuity and flexibility characteristic of the medium. Cases

Figure XXV. *Statue of a Girl.* Bronze, H. 40 cm. Hellenistic Greek, ca. 2nd century BC. Found in the harbor of Bône (Hippo), Algeria. Present location unknown. After *Bulletin archéologique du Comité des Travaux Historiques et Scientifiques* (1912) pl. 85. Photo: Courtesy, Museum of Fine Arts, Boston.

of steady production of typologically identical pieces over the centuries from Hellenistic into Roman Imperial times have been described by Barr-Sharrar in her study of the bronze busts attached to various sorts of furniture and by Manfrini-Aragno in the realm of bronze images of Bacchus.[27] The Hercules and the Lar in Cleveland [61, 62], which were replicated with only small variations over a century later at Weissenburg in modern Bavaria (Figures XVII, XVIII), are good examples of how durable a type could be when established in the Roman bronzeworker's repertory.

Many Roman statuettes with Hellenic antecedents are, therefore, likely to be late manifestations of a continuous, evolving tradition rather than copies of a specific prototype. This is especially true of statuettes whose roots lie in the Hellenistic period. Continuity is evident in the case of the early Imperial boxing dwarf in Boston [57]; his composition stands in the same tradition as the Hellenistic dancing dwarf from the Mahdia shipwreck (Figure XIX). To change dancers to boxers, little more was required than a turn of the head and the addition of a pair of boxing gloves. The other dwarf from Boston [56], the Getty begging girl [70], and the Baltimore dolphin rider [72] are also Roman variations on light, popular Hellenistic themes. The Getty actor and the singer, both seated on altars [54, 55], present two different approaches to basically the same Hellenistic type; the former is quite close to a famous Greek masterpiece, while the latter is an original Roman reinterpretation of the composition. In all these cases, elasticity is a primary characteristic of tradition.

Statuettes in which Greek models of various periods were combined are as numerous as the more consistent productions, and these composite works can be considered eclectic classicistic originals in their own right. The Walters Mercury [60] is based on a Severe Style Hermes, but he has a hairstyle and sideburns of the later fifth century. The modeling of his face seems Praxitelean and his cloak is, in all likelihood, cut to a Hellenistic length. Classical and Hellenistic prototypes are intermingled in the Levy dancer [69], the Cleveland Victory [66], and the Getty Artemis [53].

Some of these stylistic mixtures, like the Cleveland Victory [66], change a tender, feminine image of Hellenistic descent into something more austere and majestic, but just the reverse process can be at work—an idealized image can be made much more naturalistic. The standing Hercules from Cleveland [61] seems, for example, to be based on a fourth-century prototype, but he has been given a beard and an unclassically massive belly. This transformation in a late Hellenistic or early Imperial manner is also in a sense a more naturalistic reinterpretation of the Classical hero; the hardworking demigod is given the anatomy of a laborer or heavyweight fighter. The "realistic" intent becomes even more evident when ideal figures are equipped with portrait heads, as in the case of the Getty singer [55] and the Bloomington child actor [71]. The running Hercules in Brooklyn [73], on the other hand, uses a portrait head to give a mythological figure a contemporary political message. The Imperial likeness grafted onto the hero must have been conditioned by the divine pretensions of emperors like Commodus and Caracalla, whom the image distinctly resembles.

Some works in the exhibition place Greek types in new contexts to create truly Roman themes. Bristly-haired aliens dressed, like the Cleveland barbarian [67], in trousers and floppy caps had been a major subject of early Hellenistic art. From the age of Alexander in the late fourth century through the golden age of the Pergamene kingdom in the late third and early second centuries BC, Persians from the East and Gauls from the North had been shown in essentially these terms as they

Figure XXVI. *Kalathiskos Dancer.* Silver stater minted Abdera, 411-385 BC. After G. Apparati and F. Sternberg, *Antike Münzen Auktion XIX* (Zurich, 1987) no. 86.

battled Greeks in major state monuments.[28] The Cleveland barbarian, however, is not engaged in heroic combat; instead he seems to be portrayed in the act of negotiation or surrender. The context has been broadened into a descriptive narrative, undoubtedly within a triumphal framework much more characteristic of Roman than of Greek official art. In keeping with this new, less noble role as subject rather than threatening adversary, the Cleveland barbarian has been portrayed in almost caricatural, ethnographic terms.

New themes for ideal sculpture were created under Roman influence from late Hellenistic times on into the Imperial period. The areas in which this innovative spirit manifested itself, it should be noted, lay as often in the East as in Italy. In the Getty Roma [64], the Imperial city is personified as a vigorous Amazon wearing a short skirt. Such Amazonian geographic personifications are a Greek tradition going back to the early Hellenistic image of Aetolia (Figure 68a). The Getty statuette, however, is treated with a simplified Classical austerity characteristic of one side of the art of the early Roman Empire. The Lar, a Latin god of ancient origin, is an unequivocally Italic creation. Statuettes like the Cleveland Lar [62] or the Weissenburg Lar (Figure XVIII) began to be produced only after the cult of the Lares was reorganized by Augustus in the late first century BC.

A special approach to allegorical figures seems to have emerged in the East at the very end of the Hellenistic period or at the beginning of the Roman Empire. Smiling children were loaded with the most ornate and portentous trappings of maturity and become genii or embodied spirits. The pair of boys found together in Egypt and now in the Metropolitan Museum and the Walters Art Gallery [51, 52] are fitted out with the costume of eastern Anatolian royalty; they are probably geographic spirits intended more for decorative than for serious religious or politi-

Figure XXVII. *Genius of Jupiter Dolichenus.* Bronze, H. 19.1 cm. From Marash in Southeast Anatolia, early 3rd century AD. Staatliche Museen, Stiftung Preussischer Kulturbesitz, Antikenabteilung, Berlin, 11865.

Figure XXVIII. Detail of the so-called *Ara Pietatis.* Marble. Roman, mid-1st century AD. Rome, Villa Medici. Photo: Deutsches Archäologisches Institut, Rome, 2375.

cal purposes. A child, who runs forward eagerly and incongruously wears full armor (Figure XXVII), seems to personify the spirit of Jupiter Dolichenus, a cult stemming from southeastern Asia Minor.

These new types of the later first century BC, probably created in or shortly before the age of Augustus, have a number of features in common. Both the Anatolian genii [51, 52] and the Lar [62] are youthful, ingratiating minor deities who combine the unpretentious with the ornate. Part of the ornamental effect comes from fluttering drapery, which billows out in symmetrical waves. Since the figures are basically static, the drapery patterns are in a sense illogical (unless the presence of a strong wind is reconstructed), but the demigods thereby gain not only decorative interest but also an almost magical aura. In the case of the Genius of Jupiter Dolichenus (Figure XXVII), the date of whose formulation is unclear, the blowing drapery is better motivated by the figure's action. This motif, so characteristic of these new types, is borrowed from the art of the late fifth century BC, a phase after the High Classical moment usually referred to as the "Rich Style." The most significant early sources for these Roman statuettes are the famous Laconian dancers of the Athenian sculptor Callimachus.[29] The pose of one of Callimachus's dancers appears in a nearly contemporary coin of the northern Greek city of Abdera (Figure XXVI); her body is erect and seemingly stationary as drapery fans out on either side of her. Her tiptoeing posture and ornate headdress are further points of comparison with the Anatolian genii [51, 52]. This process of borrowing somewhat arbitrarily from the most ornamental aspect of the art of fifth-century Greece is characteristic of the Neo-Attic movement, which flourished from late Hellenistic through earlier Imperial times and which may have reached its apex under Augustus.

The vocabulary of the Roman public monument, celebrating public benefactions and official piety, has a significant presence in the realm of the Roman bronze statuette. Compared with the symbolic language of Greek commemorative reliefs, terms are consistently realistic. The Getty magistrates [63] wear dignified contemporary costume and hairstyles, and their facial types are individualized. Although the Roman taste for the factual provides the framework for such a composition, the artistic formulas of the time also strongly conditioned its conception. In presenting the two magistrates, who were undoubtedly intended to represent specific persons, the sculptor fell back on compositional types juxtaposing an aged intellectual with his son or youthful follower, a scheme familiar from large-scale official monuments (Figure XXVIII).

The sites covered by Mt. Vesuvius in AD 79 have provided the best information on the use of statuettes in antiquity,[30] but groups of bronzes buried in times of trouble can also help to reconstruct the original settings for bronze figures. Notable hoards have been found, as at Weissenburg in south Germany, Arezzo, or in Athens itself.[31] Inscriptions on statuettes or on their bases can also clarify their original purpose.

As they had been for almost a millennium in the Greek world, statuettes continued to be dedicated in public sanctuaries by private individuals, as the Levy Discophorus [59] must have been. Votive figures seem rare in Imperial Italy, but in the northern and western provinces, they were more common. The hoard at Weissenburg in Bavaria (including Figures XVII and XVIII), for example, has been interpreted as the treasury of a temple buried during the invasions of the third century.

Art for art's sake was not an unknown concept in Roman times. Masterpieces of the past were reproduced, perhaps with particular frequency in the first century BC, probably as pure cultural evocation. The statuettes from the Anticythera wreck, the Hartford warrior [58], and perhaps the Levy Discophorus [59] could have been made for such purely artistic purposes, although they might eventually have been put to other uses.

The most common role for a statuette in the Roman Imperial West was to stand as an object of veneration and as a good luck charm in the family household shrine, the lararium. Such a shrine takes its name from the household deities, but the Lares (e.g., [62]) could be flanked by many other images according to the family's beliefs and interests. These various figures—which might include Olympians, barbarian gods, and portrait busts (e.g., [53, 60-62])—would collectively be considered the Penates. The flowering of the lararium with its attendant paintings and statuettes seems to date from the century following Augustus's reorganization of the cult in 12-7 BC. A bronze that might have been made for its art historical associations, like the Hartford warrior [58], could also have served as a Mars in a household shrine. The popularity of lararia in the earlier Empire may well be responsible for the abundance of bronze statuettes from that time.

The cult of the Lares spread into barbarian areas beyond Rome's northern frontier and was taken up in areas of the East that had undergone a strong degree of Italic penetration, like Epirus on the east coast of the Adriatic and the island of Delos in the Aegean.[32] There were independent traditions of accumulating religious images in Greek households as well.[33] The lararium need not contain only objects of devotion. Statuettes of dancers wearing a cylindrical headdress (kalathiskos dancers) were found in a hoard of bronzes from a household shrine in Arezzo.[34] These evocations of the religious dances of the Spartans probably contributed to the sense of ceremonial tradition. The Levy dancer [69] might have served a similar role.

Official religion was flanked by superstition in popular practice. Comic and phallic good luck charms were common in the East, where they were called "baskania," as well as in the West. Mysteriously endowed with beneficent protective powers, such statuettes—like the Mahdia dancer (Figure XIX), whose phallic character has been concealed in its present display, the crouching dwarf [56], or the boxing dwarf [57], the latter both in the Boston Museum of Fine Arts—would be suspended in places particularly vulnerable to the effects of the evil eye. Metalworkers, for example, would place them over their furnaces.[35] In the Latin West, bells were often hung from such phallic images, presumably as part of the charm.

Many Roman statuettes were produced as adjuncts to pieces of functional equipment, which may range in their connotations from religious through ceremonial to purely decorative. Incense burners were made in the form of altars surmounted by singers or by slaves taking refuge [55, 54]. Perhaps the comic effect and the incense were intended as a more cultivated type of defense against the evil eye. They might also have been votive offerings; a bronze statuette of a comic slave on an altar (in this case, not an incense burner) is said to have been found below the ruins of the Temple of Neptune at Salerno, where it originally may have been dedicated.[36] Others served as a coin bank [70] or perhaps part of a lamp stand [72]. Small statuettes often decorated lamps or embellished pieces of household furniture.

Statuettes for lararia tended to be relatively small. Larger statuettes would be used for decorative purposes in domestic fountains or in garden niches; in the latter case, they might have had a religious value as well. Small bronze figures also played a role in public monuments or equipment for public display. Harnesses for horses were turned into fields for narrative sculpture; bronze panels were attached to the breastplates (baltei) and became relief grounds on which small statuettes of battling Romans and barbarians [67] were mounted.[37] Chariots, like the remains of one discovered in the forum of Herculaneum, were encrusted with figures that could be almost fully in the round and only loosely linked to the background.[38] Bronze relief figures might also stem from domestic shrines, as probably did the Minerva or Roma found in a Roman villa near Lausanne.[39] At Augst in Switzerland, appliqués with griffins and a cantharus were excavated in the precinct of a temple, which the figures may originally have embellished.

To judge by the statuettes in this exhibition, the production of fine bronze figures may have declined in both quality and quantity after the Julio-Claudian period. The impression may not be entirely illusory. Mass production during the great age of the lararium figure could well have given the craft a certain disrepute. The increasing availability of marble may also have led to a shift of interest around the shores of the Mediterranean. Certainly, the military and social crises of the mid-third century caused a drastic retrenchment in the role and availability of the bronze statuette. As barbarian armies burst through the frontiers, many statuettes went underground in the form of hoards. In the embattled and eventually Christian world of the late Roman Empire, conditions never again favored the large-scale production of refined bronze figures of the kind assembled for *The Gods Delight*.

John J. Herrmann, Jr.

1. On this cultural intermingling, see J. J. Pollitt 1986, 150-163.

2. As in the case of architectural decoration: W.-D. Heilmeyer, *Korinthische Normalkapitelle, RM,* Suppl. XVI (1970) 16-17.

3. S. Boucher 1976, 68, 69, figs. 102-103; H. Menzel, "Römische Bronzestatuetten und verwandte Geräte: Ein Beitrag zum Stand der Forschung," *Aufstieg und Niedergang,* II, 12, 3 (Berlin, 1985) 160, pls. 13-14.

4. M. Corsi-Sciallano and B. Lion, "Les épaves de Tarraconaise à chargement d'amphores Dressel 2-4," *Archaeonautica* V (1985) 127, 129, fig. 102; S. Boucher 1976, figs. 128, 129.

5. H.-J. Kellner and G. Zahlhaas, *Der römische Schatzfund von Weissenburg,* 2nd rev. ed. (Munich and Zurich, 1984) nos. 23, 25.

6. S. Boucher has circumscribed both a primitive vein and a vein of diluted classicism in Gaul, both of which stand apart from fine classicistic work and sorry mass-production (1976, 50-54, 205-223).

7. As pointed out by E. Richardson (pers. com.).

8. M. Comstock and C. Vermeule 1971, nos. 155-164; S. Haynes 1985, nos. 196-197; for other finds from Latium, see ibid., nos. 147, 188. For an Etruscan statuette of the 3rd or 2nd century BC with a Latin votive inscription found at Orvieto, see M. Torelli in *Roma medio repubblicana* (Rome, 1977) 340, no. 493, pl. 106.

9. For an Etruscan-looking genius from Torre Annunziata, see H. Kunckel, *Der römische Genius, RM,* Suppl. XX (Heidelberg, 1974) 29, 93, F III 3, pl. 43, 2.

10. F. Coarelli, "Architettura e arti figurative in Roma: 150-50 a.C." in P. Zanker, *Hellenismus in Mittelitalien: Kolloquium in Göttingen vom 5. bis 9. Juni 1974* (Göttingen, 1976) 24-29.

11. M. Bieber 1961, 39, figs. 95-96; T. Kraus et al., *Pompeii and Herculaneum, The Living Cities of the Dead,* tr. R. Wolf (New York, 1975) figs. 91, 99-100; P. Zanker, "La scultura" in F. Zevi, ed., *Pompei 79* (Naples, 1984) 202.

12. S. Boucher 1976, 7; I. Manfrini-Aragno, *Bacchus dans les bronzes hellénistiques et romains: Les artisans et leur répertoire* (Lausanne, 1987) 21.

13. W. Fuchs 1963. For an assessment of the varying opinions on the Mahdia find, see B. Barr-Sharrar, *The Hellenistic and Early Imperial Decorative Bust* (Mainz, 1987) 23-26; P. C. Bol, *Die Skulpturen des Schiffsfundes von Antikythera* (Berlin, 1972); M. Siganidou, in N. Yalouris et al., *The Search for Alexander,* exh. cat. (Boston, 1980) no. 154 (Pella); G. Siebert, "Grèce: Délos, l'île d'Apollon," *DossArch* CV (May 1986) 60-66; B. Barr-Sharrar 1987, 20-23.

14. Late 1st and 2nd century, H. Menzel in *DossArch* XXVIII (May-June 1978) 66-67; G. Moretti in G. Ucelli, *Le navi di Nemi* (Rome, 1940) 199-217. For these and other chronological reference points, see S. Boucher 1976, 241-260; in general, see H. Menzel, "Problèmes de la datation des bronzes romains," *Actes du IVᵉ colloque international sur les bronzes antiques* (Lyon, 1977) 121-126; idem, "Römische Bronzestatuetten und verwandte Geräte: Ein Beitrag zum Stand der Forschung," in *Aufstieg und Niedergang* 1985, II, 12, 3:160-161, pls. 15-18, 25; B. Barr-Sharrar 1987, 19-32; M. Corsi-Sciallano and B. Lion (*Archaeonautica* V) 1985, 127, 129, fig. 102, statuette of Jupiter.

15. For good collections of miniature bronze portraits, see H. Jucker, *Das Bildnis im Blätterkelch: Geschichte und Bedeutung einer römischen Porträtform* (Olten, 1961) 48-60, B1-B10, pls. 12-18; *Master Bronzes* (1967) nos. 229-232, 236.

16. D. Comparetti et al., *La villa ercolanese dei Pisoni: I suoi monumenti e la sua biblioteca* (Turin, 1883) 267, no. 31, pl. 12, 3; M. R. Wojcik, *La Villa dei Papiri ad Ercolano* (Rome, 1986) 135-136, no. E5, pl. 70.

17. K. T. Erim in A. Alföldi, *Aion in Mérida und Aphrodisias* (Mainz, 1979) 35-37, pls. 22, 28. On another technique paralleling drillwork, see the introduction by D. G. Mitten, above.

18. As pointed out to me by M. True (pers. com.); see P. Zanker 1974, 49-51, pls. 42, 1; 43, 1.

19. W. Johannowsky, "La situazione in Campania" in P. Zanker 1976, 285, figs. 8-9.

20. D. Comparetti et al. 1883, 261, no. 6, pl. 8, 3; P. Zanker 1974, 8-9, pls. 7, 1; 31, 2; M. R. Wojcik 1986, 171-173, no. G1, pl. 90.

21. H. Jucker 1961, 48-49, no. B1, pl. 12; A. Leibundgut, "Der 'Traian' von Ottenhusen," *JdI* XCIX (1984) 269, fig. 12; F. Johansen in J. Frel et al. 1987, 96, fig. 18b.

22. A. Leibundgut (*JdI*) 1984, 263-269, figs. 6-15.

23. H. Jucker 1961, 54-56, B5, pl. 15, and 56-57, no. B6, pl. 16; F. D'Andria, "I bronzi romani di Veleia, Parma e del territorio parmense," *Contributi dell'Istituto di Archeologia* III (1970) 46-47, no. 22, pls. 14-15.

24. J.-P. Niemeier, *Kopien und Nachahmungen im Hellenismus: Ein Beitrag zum Klassizismus des 2. und frühen 1. Jhs. v. Chr.* (Bonn, 1985) esp. 157-163.

25. S. Boucher, "A propos de l'Hermès de Polycèlte," *BCH* C (1976) 95-102; A. Leibundgut (*JdI*) 1984, 258-259; H. Menzel 1985, 157-160.

26. S. Boucher 1976, 61-63; A. Leibundgut (*JdI*) 1984, 258-260; I. Manfrini-Aragno 1987, 23-27.

27. I. Manfrini-Aragno 1987, passim; B. Barr-Sharrar 1987, passim.

28. For example, the Alexander Sarcophagus and the dedication of Attalus I on the Acropolis, Athens: J. Charbonneaux et al. 1973, figs. 248-250; M. Bieber 1961, 108-110, figs. 432, 433, 435, 437.

29. W. Fuchs, ''Die Vorbilder der neuattischen Reliefs,'' *JdI*, Suppl. XX, (1959) 91-96, fig. 2; L. Kahil, *ArchDelt* XX, B' 2 (1965) 283-284, pl. 335; J. Boardman 1985, fig. 242.

30. See E. Dwyer, *Pompeian Domestic Sculpture: A Study of Five Pompeian Houses and Their Contents* (Rome, 1982) 121-126; idem in *Pompeii and the Vesuvian Landscape: Papers of a Symposium Sponsored by the Archaeological Institute of America, Washington Society and the Smithsonian Institution* (Washington, 1979) 60-64; P. Zanker in *Pompei 79* (1984) 202-208.

31. H.-J. Kellner and G. Zahlhaas 1984, passim; H. Kunckel 1974, 85, pls. 54-55; with a listing of other group finds, pp. 86-89; Ph. Stavropoullos, *ArchDelt* XX, B' 1 (1965) 103-107, pls. 58-70; G. Daux, *BCH* XCII (1968) 741, figs. 15-22.

32. H. Menzel in *Master Bronzes* (1967) 228; idem (*Aufstieg und Niedergang*) 1985, II:12, 3, 155, pl. 6, 1; J. Swaddling 1979, 103-105, pl. 53, 10; M. Bulard, "Peintures murales et mosaïques de Délos," *MonPiot* XIV (1908) 33-56.

33. In houses of the 4th century BC at Olynthus, figural vases were found with small altars; M. Trumpf-Lyritzaki, *Griechische Figurenvasen* (Bonn, 1969) 124-125. On arrangements for dedications of statuettes in Delos, see M. Kreeb, "Figürliche Ausstattung delischer Privathäuser," *BCH* CVIII (1984) 328-329.

34. A. Minto, *Notizie degli Scavi di Antichità* (1934) 53-54, figs. 7-8; H. Kunckel 1974, 85, pl. 55.

35. A. Wace (*BSA*) 1903-1904, 109; D. Levi 1941, 225.

36. J. A. Scott, in *Master Bronzes* (1967) no. 275.

37. B. Andreae, *The Art of Rome*, tr. R. E. Wolf (New York, 1977) fig. 83.

38. E. Gabrici, ''La quadriga di Ercolano,'' *BdA* I (1907) 179-190.

39. A. Leibundgut, *Die römischen Bronzen der Schweiz*, III: *Westschweiz, Bern und Wallis* (Mainz, 1980) no. 105. The sword favors an identification as Roma.

51. Genius in Eastern Anatolian Costume

The ornately clad figure sways forward on tiptoe, poised between movement and immobility. In his raised right hand he grasps a rodlike handle, while in his lowered left he held a now-missing, separately cast object. His trousers (anaxyrides or bracae) and tall cap characterize him as an oriental, but his elaborately layered costume is unusual, even by the standards of Eastern exotica. His shoes are tied with long bows, and a tongue with a three-pointed end is pulled down over the knot. He wears two short tunics; the inner one has long sleeves, but the outer is sleeveless. The outer tunic is very elaborately arranged, folded under his belt and pulled back up at the center and sides. In front of the tunic's skirt, a sash is threaded through a pair of loops suspended from a second, concealed belt. Over the tunic a third garment, a cloak, is fastened by pulling one corner through a slit in another.

GRECO-ROMAN (LATE HELLENISTIC) OR EARLY ROMAN IMPERIAL, CA. 50-20 BC. H. 64 CM. METROPOLITAN MUSEUM OF ART, EDITH PERRY CHAPMAN FUND, 1949, 49.11.3

The front and sides of the remarkable wedge-shaped hat are divided horizon-

Figure 51a. Incised ornament on wedge-shaped hat. Drawing by John Herrmann.

Figure 51b. *Artavasdes II of Armenia*, 56-34 BC. Obverse of a silver tetradrachm. Photo: Courtesy of Numismatic Department, Bank Leu, A.G., Zurich.

tally into three panels by ridges, and each of the two larger sections is decorated with an incised palmette and tendrils (see Figure 51a). On the front, the palmettes are mounted on a vertical shaft; on the sides, they are enclosed in the involutions of an undulating tendril. The palmettes themselves spring from a horizontal bar. In the narrow middle fields of the hat, tendrils bearing leaves undulate out from the main stem. Corrosion has effaced or obscured much of the incision. The vegetation may have been inlaid with silver, but no clear trace of it survives. The hat has a weighted triangular back flap that hangs down between the figure's shoulder blades. A flange on the left side of the hat and a smaller protuberance at the right suggest that lappets or side flaps also existed originally. A hole, roughly square in shape, is just below the hat at the right. Three blunt projections surmount the hat.

Prototypes for this unusual and unclassical costume can be found on the eastern borders of the Greco-Roman world in monumental stone sculpture of around 50 BC at Nimrud Dagh and at Arsameia on the Nymphaios, the heart of the Commagenian kingdom. In these works, the Commagenian king has a wedge-shaped, ornamented tiara with lappets, topped with a row of five points. He is also dressed in a tunic, a long-sleeved undertunic, a cloak, and leggings tied at the ankles. A heavily ornamented sash is suspended from his belt. At least some features of this costume, however, are not unique to Commagene; a nearly identical tiara is worn by Armenian kings of the first century BC on their coins (Figure 51b). In the process of Hellenization, the costume, as represented by the Commagenian reliefs, has been somewhat modified; the tiara has been elongated and angularized from its original rounded plan, and its crowning points have been reduced from five to three; the tunic has been given a Classical belting with overfold. The stiff sash hanging from the belt of the Commagenian king has become loose drapery.

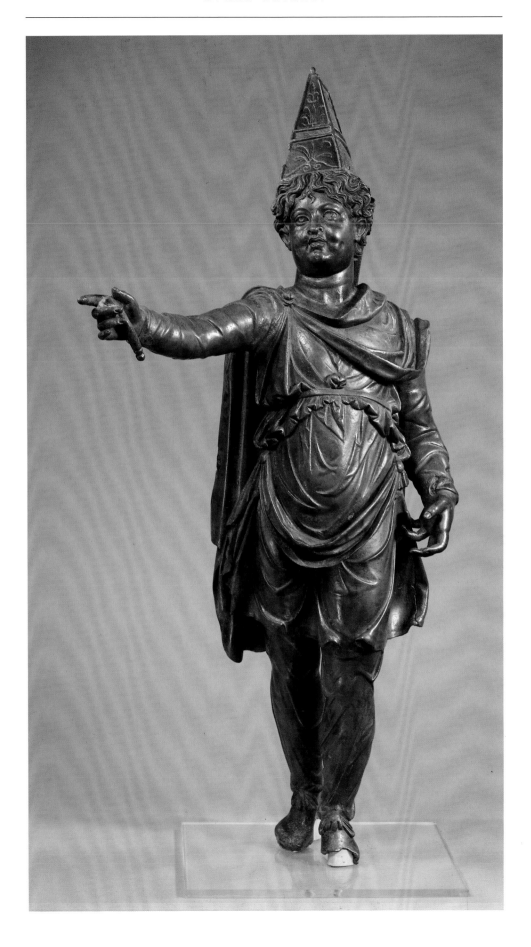

Without the sash, the costume was taken up in a Greco-Roman idiom by female personifications on Arretine pottery and by defeated barbarians on coinage. Generally these works celebrate the Armenian victories of Antony and of Augustus. In an unpublished fragmentary Arretine bowl attributable to L. Avillius Sura, however, the female in the exotic costume laments the dragging of Hector's body at Troy (Figure 51c). In this context, she probably symbolizes Asia in general. After the incorporation of Armenia into the Roman Empire at the beginning of the second century AD, personifications of Armenia wearing the same costume enjoyed a new phase of popularity in coinage and state monuments at Rome and in a few small bronze statuettes of unknown provenance.

Although the costume has geographical associations generally focused on the area to the north of Mesopotamia, its meaning for this statuette of a child and the companion piece in the Walters Art Gallery [52] is much less evident. The figures are not mature females, as is customary for personifications of conquered provinces, nor is their duplication easily understandable. The figures have been interpreted as unusual images of the Asiatic divinity Attis, who is also shown as a child in elaborate Eastern costume. The upraised hand, in fact, parallels a typical gesture of Attis. The nicely finished handle with its knobbed end in the Metropolitan figure's hand could not, however, have belonged to a shepherd's staff like that carried by Attis. In all other representations, moreover, Attis wears a Phrygian cap. Most of all, this interpretation does not explain why two identical figures should be found together. In attempting to interpret them, Hill has suggested that the two bronzes represent the Dioscuri, Castor and Pollux. These demigods, however, are customarily shown as athletic youths, and their caps are the bulletlike pileus (the Greek pilos).

Figure 51c. *Asia or Hecuba*. Fragment of terra sigillata bowl. L. Avillius Sura, Arezzo, late first century BC. Private collection.

The double image might reflect a double geographic reference. The kings of Armenia and Commagene could wear similar costumes, and personifications of their kingdoms might well look alike. Armenia Minor, moreover, adjoined Armenia Maior, a situation that could also have led to a double presentation. The figures would thereby represent somewhat ephemeral geographic genii rather than full-fledged personifications, if such a distinction can be made.

The two figures being essentially exact duplicates, however, suggests that the artist's intention was more decorative than seriously iconographic; an effort to personify two adjoining regions or two semi-divine brothers would have led to more variation and contrast. Instead, the extreme similarity of the two brings to mind sets of bronzes for domestic use of a kind known from Pompeii. Two identical pairs of bronze statuettes of placentarii—naked vendors hawking their wares and carrying silver trays for sweets—for example, were found in a box in the House of the Ephebe. They were evidently to be used as serving dishes. A pair of identical bronze Pans of Hellenistic date in the Levy collection [23] probably served as co-attachments to a piece of furniture. It is not impossible that the statuettes in the Metropolitan and the Walters also served a functional purpose; they might have originally held lamps or incense burners. In their combination of ingratiating youth and pretentious costume, the two "Armenians" recall the bronze statuettes of children dressed in full armor and holding incense burners or lamps in the form of poppies found at Straubing in Austria, Augst in Switzerland, and Marash in southern Anatolia, not far from Commagene (see Figure XXVII). Another such figure is preserved in the Bibliothèque Nationale in Paris. These running armored children, identified as genii, fit into the tradition of running, lamp-carrying Erotes. Full-size bronze statues of nude youths based on Classical Greek prototypes were

also provided with bronze appliances, usually vines, to support lamps in early Imperial times. The handle in the right hand of the Metropolitan figure might have belonged to some such piece of equipment. The cupped left hand of the figure may only have supported the now-missing left end of his sash.

Stylistically, the figures stand in the late Hellenistic tradition of large, elaborately modeled Erotes and grotesques like those from the Mahdia shipwreck of about 100 BC (see Figure XIX). The knobby articulation of their cheeks is a strikingly similar characteristic. The Armenian children are, however, fuller and more emphatic, and they lack the fluid, spiraling movement of the Mahdia figures. The more ornate and more static terracotta figures produced at Myrina in Asia Minor in the first century BC, themselves related to the Mahdia bronzes, are even closer in feeling. The taut, tiptoeing poses of the Armenians, however, have a new component of Neo-Atticism; they recall the Laconian dancers created at the end of the fifth century BC by the Athenian sculptor Callimachus, compositions known through contemporary coins and Roman replicas (Figure XXVI); the comparison even extends to the fluttering draperies and the elaborate headgear. The Laconian dancers had their greatest influence in Roman art of the Augustan period, when they appeared frequently in Arretine pottery and when they also seem to have inspired the restyled Lares.

The hat's vegetal ornament suggests a date close to the beginning of the Imperial period, when inlaid ornament became popular. Bronze bed fittings of Hellenistic date, for instance, were apparently not inlaid, while their Imperial descendants often were. The ornament itself, to be sure, is highly unusual in terms of the Imperial vocabulary. None of the naturalistic ornament (enriched with leaves or figures) so characteristic of Hellenistic times or later is present. Abstract palmettes and scrolls belong to a Classical vocabulary best known from Greek vases. A comparably abstract lotus and palmette band is inlaid into the base of a statuette of Aphrodite fastening her sandal from Herculaneum, dated by Menzel to the end of the first century BC. The drawing of the petals is even quite similar to what is seen here. The vertical compositions of ornament on the hat, however, evoke much earlier forms quite specifically; round five-petaled palmettes enclosed in a stem, as on the sides of the hat, are actually best paralleled in Archaic vase painting of the late sixth or early fifth century. The stack of palmettes on the front also recalls the filigree work of early Hellenistic jewelry, as on a gold pyramidal pendant from Varna, on the Black Sea coast of Bulgaria.

It should be noted, however, that this retrospective vocabulary is applied very roughly and arbitrarily; it is fragmented and interrupted by the middle sections of the hat. The loose overall effect has more in common with Imperial inlaid beds than with earlier precedents. The stack of palmettes on the front of the hat has a central shaft like Roman floral candelabra. The ornament seems, therefore, to be an archaistic throw-back, and should be dated in the first century BC, before the Imperial vocabulary became firmly established.

A date as early as 55 BC, after the Armenian victories of Pompey, is possible for these outstanding figures. In all likelihood Armenia was among the statues of conquered nations sculpted at that time by Coponius for the Theater of Pompey at Rome, and these genii may have been influenced by that project. Armenian campaigns under Antony and again under Augustus could also have been the occasion for this kind of figure. They are not likely to have been made after Armenia was lost to the Parthians under Tiberius. The region became topical once more under Nero. These figures' thick necks and the deep backs of their heads, as well as their fleshy chins, even recall numismatic portraits of Nero (see Figure 63a). Second-century victories again led to an interest in personifications of the region, but these dates seem too late for the post-Hellenistic style and archaistic ornament of this statuette. A pre-Augustan or early Augustan date would best reflect their relationship to the Mahdia bronzes. In spite of the Roman influences on the iconography of the Metropolitan and Walters genii, they were certainly executed in the East. They were found there and reflect an Eastern stylistic world as well.

CONDITION: The pupils of the eyes are pierced. The arms and the back-flap of the hat were cast separately. The top of the object in the right hand is broken away, as is the left end of the sash suspended from the belt. A rectangular hollow in the left wrist might reflect either a casting flaw or a clamp to fasten the object supported by the left hand, which may have only been the end of the sash. The patina alternates red-brown and green areas. A hole on the right side of the head just below the hat and a projecting flange on the lower left side of the hat suggest that ear flaps were originally present.

PROVENANCE: Said to have been found in Egypt (either just east of the Suez Canal or else in Alexandria) in 1912 together with [52].

EXHIBITED: Cambridge, Eng., Fitzwilliam Museum, May 9-June 20, 1944, *Exhibition of Greek Art, 3000 B.C.-A.D. 1938*, 25, no. 256 (cited in D. K. Hill, "Bracatae nationes," *JWalt* VII-VIII [1944-1945] 80, n. 14).
Tokyo National Museum, August 10-October 1, 1972; Kyoto Municipal Museum, October 8-November 26, 1972; *Treasured Masterpieces of the Metropolitan Museum of Art*, no. 39.

PUBLISHED: A. H. Smith, "A Bronze Figure of a Youth in Oriental Costume," *JHS* XXVII (1917) 135-139, pl. 2.
S. Reinach, *Rép. stat.* V:222, 4.
P. Bienkowski, *Les celtes dans les arts mineurs gréco-romains* (Cracow, 1928) 62.
D. Hill, "Bracatae nationes," *JWalt* VII-VIII (1944-1945) 75-81, figs. 4-5.
Sale: *Joseph Brummer Collection*, New York, Parke-Bernet Galleries, June 8-9, 1949, pt. III, 6-7, no. 37, illus.
J. R. Mertens (*BMMA*) 1985, no. 33, col. illus.
M. Vermaseren and M. de Boer, in *LIMC* III, "Attis," 35, no. 261.

NOTES: On the costume of Armenia and Commagene and its adaptation in Roman art, see A. H. Smith (*JHS*) 1917, 136-139, figs. 1-2; H. Ingholt, *Archaeology* XXII (1969) 315-317; E. Akurgal, *Ancient Civilizations and Ruins of Turkey* (Istanbul, 1970) pls. 109-110; J. Balty, in *LIMC* II: "Armenia" 610-613, pl. 439; M. Colledge, *Parthian Art* (Ithaca, N.Y., 1977) pls. 32, 39e; J. M. C. Toynbee, *Roman Historical Portraits* (Ithaca, N.Y., 1978) 131-137, illus. 251-262; E. Akurgal, *Griechische und römische Kunst in der Türkei* (Munich, 1987) pl. 192; R. R. R. Smith in *Journal of Roman Studies* (1987) 117-120, pl. 16.
For the bronze statuettes, here identified as Armenia, see M. Vermaseren and M. de Boer,

in *LIMC* III: "Attis," 27, pl. 16, no. 51; J. Eisenberg, *Art of the Ancient World*, IV (New York, 1985) no. 300.
For the placentarii, see A. Maiuri, *BdA* V (1925) 268-269; S. Boucher 1976, 189, 280, fig. 339; *Pompeii A.D. 79* (Boston, 1978) no. 93; W. F. Jashemski, *The Gardens of Pompeii, Herculaneum and the Villas Destroyed by Vesuvius* (New Rochelle, N.Y., 1979) 93, fig. 149.
For the armored genii from Straubing, Augst, Marash, and Paris, see J. Keim, *Der römische Schatzfund von Straubing* (Munich, 1951) no. 24, pl. 38; A. Kaufmann-Heinimann 1976-, I: no. 49; K. Vierneisel, *Römisches im Antikenmuseum. Berlin, Staatliche Museen* (Berlin, 1978) 63, fig. 49; E. Babelon and J.-A. Blanchet 1895, no. 197.
On classicistic lampadophori or lychnouchoi, see A. Rumpf, "Der Idolino," *Critica d'arte* XIX-XX (1939) 17-27; Jashemski 1979, 92 f., 113, figs. 148, 184.
For comparably ornate figures in bronze and terracotta, see W. Fuchs 1963, 16-18, nos. 5-7, pls. 14-16; D. Burr, *Terra-cottas from Myrina in the Museum of Fine Arts, Boston* (Vienna, 1934) 13, 38-40, nos. 17, 18; J. Herrmann in J. Fontein, *Masterpieces from the Boston Museum* (Boston, 1981) no. 16.
For the contrast between plain Greek bronze furniture and silver-inlaid Roman furniture, see G. M. A. Richter, *The Furniture of the Greeks, Etruscans, and Romans* (London, 1966) figs. 306-308, 534, 537-538, 543, 548, 565-566; B. Barr-Sharrar 1987, pls. 5, 6, 9, 16, 19, 20, 31, 33, 34, 77-79, 81.
For the inlaid base from Herculaneum, see H. Menzel in *Actes du IVe Colloque international sur les bronzes antiques* (Lyon, 1977) 123, fig. 9; idem in *DossArch* XXVIII (May-June 1978) 63.
For the vertical band of palmettes enclosed in an undulating tendril, see J. Boardman, *Athenian Red Figure Vases: The Archaic Period, A Handbook* (London, 1975) figs. 40-41, 129; P. Jacobsthal, *Ornamente griechischer Vasen* (Berlin, 1927) pl. 61a.
For a stack of palmettes, see P. Jacobsthal 1927, pls. 124b, 125; I. Venedikov and T. Gerassimov, *Thracian Art Treasures* (London, 1975) fig. 191.
For the statues by Coponius in the Theater of Pompey, see F. Coarelli, "Architettura e arti figurative in Roma: 150-50 a.C.," in P. Zanker 1976, 28, fig. 25.
For the Armenian successes of Tiberius and Nero, see Suetonius, *Lives of the Caesars*, tr. J. C. Rolfe (Loeb ed., Cambridge, Mass., 1970) Tiberius, 41; Nero, 13: 40, 2, pp. 106-107, 160-161.

294

Since the figure is almost identical with the example in the Metropolitan, see [51] for the description and discussion. The objects that the figure originally held are here entirely missing. The bottom of the cap bends out on the right side with an almost tonguelike projection. The left side of the hat is straight. A small irregular surface at the center suggests that a small flap might have been broken off. The presence of side flaps is again uncertain but possible.

GRECO-ROMAN
(LATE HELLENISTIC)
OR EARLY ROMAN
IMPERIAL,
CA. 50-20 BC.
H. 62 CM.
WALTERS ART
GALLERY, 54.1330

CONDITION: The back of this figure is open from the shoulder blades to the buttocks. This void is covered by the separately cast cloak. The surface patina is part dark red and part dull green with small patches of bright green. The pupils of the eyes are pierced. No trace of inlaying remains.

PROVENANCE: Said to have been found in Egypt (either just east of the Suez Canal or else in Alexandria) in 1912 together with [51].

EXHIBITED: The Detroit Institute of Arts, March 23-April 20, 1947, *Small Bronzes of the Ancient World*, no. 92.

PUBLISHED: D. K. Hill, *JWalt* VII-VIII (1944-1945) 80 ff., fig. 6.
D. K. Hill 1949, no. 49, pl. 13.
M. Vermaseren and M. de Boer, in *LIMC* III: ''Attis,''no. 261 35, pl. 30.

53. Diana (Artemis)

The tall, slender goddess stands languidly with her relaxed left leg placed well back and to the side. Even without her almost obligatory quiver, Diana is identifiable from the short chiton and boots appropriate for a classical huntress. Her firmly confined hair, tied up into a knot on top and pulled into a bun behind, is also suitable for an active life. The rather tight and severe arrangement is, however, softened by the locks of hair that escape in front of and behind each ear. The elaborate gestures recall Diana's traditional pose of drawing an arrow from a quiver. Stothart has suggested that her quiver and bow have disappeared because they were made separately. Simon, on the other hand, interprets the pose as Diana looking at herself in a mirror. In this case, only the mirror would have been executed separately. Diana's association with beautification led, as Simon has pointed out, to Lake Nemi being known as the "mirror of Diana" (speculum Dianae). A comparably far-sighted Aphrodite also holds a mirror in a low position as she adjusts her hair in a bronze statuette found in the sea near the Greek island of Astypalea. The parallel lends support to Simon's reconstruction.

The costume is shown in unusual detail. The chiton has a long overfold fastened with an ovoid pin at the shoulder. The neckline is reinforced with a double braid, and rectangular weights in front and back pull the neckline down in a sharp V. Her mantle, which is a broad band quite unlike Diana's usual rolled mantle, is wrapped tightly around her middle and over her left shoulder. Its elaborately fringed end hangs down at her right. Her open-toed boots are particularly ornate. They are laced up the front; the laces are turned around spiky studs and then hang down at the sides. An acanthus leaf embellishes the heel of each boot, and tendrils spread out at each side, bearing round flowers in their involutions. The boots are lined with animal skins whose head and paws emerge at the top.

The style is sharp, disciplined, and decisive. Drapery folds are pulled tight as in Hellenistic sculpture, an influence already noted by Simon, and the combination of taut ridges and loose fringes even echoes figures like the Baker dancing woman [14]. The drapery patterns here, however, form a severely rectilinear grid, crossed by a few sharp diagonals, that has moved beyond Hellenistic softness and complexity. The patterns have their best parallels in late Classical, fourth-century funerary statues and reliefs from Athens. The work is, thereby, subtly classicistic. The bronze relief with Artemis at an altar from Delos, however, already shows some of this severity in a Hellenistic context. There are other fourth-century allusions as well. The hairstyle is a variation on that of Praxiteles' Lycian Apollo; only in that work a roll of hair at the sides is drawn back to a bun at the same time that hair is pulled directly up over the forehead. The crowning braid of the Apollo Lykeios has, however, been replaced with a more feminine bowknot. Crowning knots of hair are, in fact, highly characteristic of Artemis from early Hellenistic times onward. The languid gestures also recall the Lycian Apollo.

The splendid boots are an important index of how far this figure has gone beyond its Classical and high Hellenistic sources. Vine-decorated boots appeared on the Great Altar of Pergamum, but open-toed boots are an Italic type that was not taken up in Hellenistic sculpture and combined with vine decoration until the late second or early first century BC. The acanthus leaf, from which the vines spring, stands out prominently on the heel, as in works of the Imperial period. Such acanthus-decorated footgear appears on a fragmentary bronze statuette of Dionysus in Boston from the tomb of Prince Arikankharēr at Meroë (buried ca. AD 15), a relief in the Palazzo dei Conservatori of ca. AD 160, and a bronze statue of Septimius Severus in Brussels.

GRECO-ROMAN
(LATE HELLENISTIC)
OR EARLY ROMAN
IMPERIAL,
IST C. BC.
H. 29.8 CM.
J. PAUL GETTY
MUSEUM, 57.AB.15

296

An important framework for dating the Getty statuette is provided by the bronze busts of Diana (Artemis) that are used to embellish chests and headboards of couches (fulcra) in Hellenistic and Imperial times. Both the V-shaped neckline, with hem and central weight, and the folds radiating out from the breast appear on a bust from Priene of around 100 BC. The fine detail on the hem of the neckline is found on another late Hellenistic piece from Cyparissia in Greece. The eclectic hairstyle is worn by an Artemis on a chest from Pompeii dated by Barr-Sharrar to the Augustan period. This latter piece must be derived from works like the Getty Diana, which could be substantially pre-Augustan.

CONDITION: The main torso and head are hollow cast as one piece. X-radiographs indicate the remains of a sprue at the central upper interior surface of the head. It is uncertain whether the right leg was poured with the torso and head or cast on later.

The left leg is an addition which appears to have been soldered on, joining at the underside surface of the garment. Both arms are solid additions, possibly soldered on in ancient times; the contact points are too abrupt and smooth for a mechanical joint and no bronze residue from casting-on was seen in the x-radiographs.

The fringed tail of drapery hanging from the figure's right side was soldered on. An equivalent piece is missing from the left side, where the garment has been smoothed to accept it. The left arm shows signs of reshaping to correct considerable damage. The arms are now reattached with an adhesive. Their similar patina confirms that they originally belonged to the figure. The entire statuette is extraordinarily light in weight.

The little finger of the left hand is missing. There are minor abrasions from cleaning. The eyes were left hollow to receive inlays. Chiseling in the hair is sharp. The locks on the neck are outlined with incisions. There is an ancient mounting pin below the right sandal toe. Traces of another appear below the left sandal toe.

The patina is dark green to black, dense, and smooth. The patina over the entire surface is extremely thin. A golden brown tone emerges below the black on the rear and on the right leg where the patina has been abraded.

PROVENANCE: Said to come from Ephesus or from Konya, along with bronze statuettes of a dog and a stag.

PUBLISHED: *Art Quarterly* XX, 4 (1957) 469, 471 (1st century BC).
P. Wescher, "New Acquisitions 1956-1957," *BGettyMus* I (1957) 12-13, fig. 5 (Augustan).
J. Charbonneaux in J. P. Getty, *The Joys of Collecting* (New York, 1965) 72-73 (1st century BC).
H. Stothart, *Handbook of the Sculpture in the J. Paul Getty Museum* ([Malibu, Calif.,] 1965) 15-16, pl. 7 (Augustan).
E. Simon in *LIMC* II: "Artemis/Diana," 814, 844-845, no. 82 (1st century AD).

NOTES: The condition statement for this bronze is adapted from a conservation report by Jerry Podany.
For the Aphrodite arranging her hair from Astypalea, see J.-P. Michaud, *BCH* LXXXV (1971) 1043, fig. 530.
For 4th-century BC Athenian statues with similar drapery, see M. Bieber 1961, figs. 206, 208-209.

For the bronze relief from Delos, see M. Bieber 1961, 153, fig. 651.

For the hairstyle of the Apollo Lykeios and Roman variations, see *LIMC* II: "Ápollon," no. 39 (O. Palagia); *LIMC* II: "Apollon/Apollo," no. 75 (E. Simon).

On open-toed boots and vine decoration, see K. D. Morrow 1985, 123-139, figs. 112-121, 124.

On the Dionysus in Boston, see M. Comstock and C. Vermeule 1971, no. 68.

On the Septimius Severus in Brussels, see A. Furtwängler, *Sammlung Somzée* (Munich, 1897) 46 ff., pl. 30.

For the bronze busts of Artemis, see B. Barr-Sharrar 1987, C54, C56, C67.

54. Incense Burner in the Form of a Comic Actor Seated on an Altar

The actor wears a type of mask associated by Bieber with the role of a leading slave of New Comedy. Typical are the megaphone-like mouth and the rolled arrangement of hair known as "speira." His knotted brows and broad nose are also characteristic of the role, but they are rendered in unusually restrained, elegantly naturalistic terms. His silver-inlaid eyes roll expressively upward. The clothing is typical of ancient comedy: long-sleeved, long-legged tights; a short, sleeveless tunic; and a short, skimpy mantle (palla). The modeling is subtle and naturalistic. His lingula-type sandals have a thong extending up to the cross straps. It then folds back as a tongue (lingula), which has a wide three-pointed end fastened by a button. The soles are indented between the first and the second toes.

The actor leans back on his right hand and places his left in his lap. His left hand is pierced so that he can hold a separately cast wig by an attachment wire. The round altar on which he sits is circled by three babies carrying garlands of fruit, ears of grain, pine cones, and sheaths of pine needles tied together by fillets with gaily fluttering loops and tails. Above, the altar is topped by an S-curve molding (Lesbian cymatium) and a fillet, and below, it is finished with a fillet, a Lesbian cymatium, and a concave molding (cavetto). The entire composition is mounted on a platformlike base that is modeled by a cavetto and fillet above and a Lesbian cymatium and fillet below. The base is mounted on four lion paws, each of which terminates in a leaf flanked by scrolls.

The top of the altar is a removable lid. Within the altar, the base is perforated with ten irregularly shaped holes arranged in roughly circular fashion around a central hole. This provision for ventilation has suggested that the object was an incense burner; draft would enter below, and fumes would issue from the mouth of the mask.

GRECO-ROMAN
(LATE HELLENISTIC)
OR EARLY AUGUSTAN,
CA. 75-25 BC.
H. 23.2 CM.
J. PAUL GETTY
MUSEUM, 87.AB.143

The comic actor seated on an altar is not an uncommon theme in Hellenistic and especially Roman art in both bronze and marble. Bieber has interpreted such figures as slaves taking refuge from their persecutors, a situation alluded to in verse 975 of the Roman dramatist Terence's *Self Tormentor (Heauton Timoroumenos)*. A less obscure interpretation has been proposed for two South Italian Greek terracotta comedians on altars in the British Museum. The actors would be playing Priam taking refuge on an altar at the sack of Troy. The two British Museum pieces, whose composition is quite similar to that of the Getty bronze, date from the mid-fourth and the mid-second century BC. In the case of a Hellenistic figure like the Getty bronze, however, it is unclear why a comedian would play King Priam in the mask of a slave.

The detachable wig or wiglike object that the Getty actor holds suggests a situation involving disguise. A parallel is offered by a figure in Berlin of a seated comedian with a mask beside him. Bieber has connected the Berlin statuette with the lost comedy *Verpus* (a circumcised man) by Livius Andronicus and conjectured that the verpus is contemplating transvestitism.

Two marble statuettes of comic slaves in the Vatican are almost identical to the Getty bronze in pose and costume; only the extra wig is missing. The marbles in the Vatican are thought by Lippold to copy an original stemming from the most creative moment of New Comedy during the early Hellenistic period (ca. 300 BC). The sandals of the Getty piece, however, suggest a date for the model no earlier than the second century BC, when the lingula type seems to have passed from the Italic world to the Aegean. The execution of the Getty incense burner is not likely to be before the first century BC. Erotes wrestle with garlands in the same twisting strides on black-glazed Pergamene pottery of the late second and earlier first cen-

tury BC. Similar garlands carried by Erotes also appear on silver cups of the mid-first century BC, as in an example in the Getty Museum. There are only slight differences from these compositions; on the bronze the Erotes have lost their wings to become normal babies, and they have a somewhat more awkwardly upright position. They still move freely in space, however, as in Hellenistic times, rather than being compressed into a denser, firmer composition characteristic of an Imperial date. A date like that of the silver cup in the third quarter of the first century BC seems plausible.

A bronze statuette in the Wadsworth Atheneum in Hartford is very similar to this in its composition. A comic slave again sits on a cylindrical altar mounted on a lion-footed platform; the object might likewise be an incense burner. The moldings have, however, become bulky and inflated, the handling is much rougher and cruder. It reflects a lively stylization of the Getty type during Imperial times, perhaps the second century. A clear contrast also emerges in a comparison with high quality works of the later first or early second century AD like the child actor [71]. The child's comic mask lacks the subtle linear detail of the Getty incense burner; forms are rendered in terms of fluidly rounded masses.

The treatment of the Getty incense burner has an elegant naturalism that stands strongly in the Hellenistic tradition. Although it is more detailed and solidly constructed than the modest bronze statuette of a comic slave seated on an altar from the Mahdia shipwreck, its workmanship has much in common with that of the finer Mahdia pieces, like the dancing dwarf (see Figure XIX); the handling of cheeks, brow, and nose is quite similar. Still, the Getty piece has a refinement and classicism that set it off from Hellenistic robustness. A characteristic detail is the texturing of wigs with regular parallel striations. The adaptation of the composition as a practical device (an incense burner) is a decidedly Roman approach.

CONDITION: The figure including the lid was hollow cast with the left hand and right leg cast on. The altar was cast from a wax sheet pressed into a mold. It may then have been attached to the stand, but corrosion now makes it impossible to be certain. The stand was manufactured from sheet wax. The four corner feet have been added in modern times and may have been part of the ancient piece. The eyes are inlaid with silver. The irises are incised and the pupils are indented. The patina is predominantly dark green to dense black.

PROVENANCE: Probably found with [55] and a statuette of Hypnos.

UNPUBLISHED.

NOTES: The condition statement for this bronze draws on a conservation report by Jerry Podany.

On sandals of the lingula type, see K. D. Morrow 1985, 118-120, figs. 106-107.

For statuettes and a relief of slaves seeking refuge on altars, see M. Bieber (*Theater*) 1961, 104-105, 150, 162, figs. 406, 410-413, 556-558, 587.

For the Hartford statuette, see M. Bieber (*Theater*) 1961, fig. 412; L. H. Roth, *J. Pierpont Morgan, Collector: European Decorative Arts from the Wadsworth Atheneum* (Hartford, 1987) 198.

On the Vatican statuettes, see G. Lippold, *Die Skulpturen des Vaticanischen Museums* III, 2 (Berlin, 1903-1956) 322, 329-330.

The British Museum actors are GR1865.1-3.45 (terracotta 1359) and GR1873.10-20.2 (D322). R. A. Higgins, *Catalogue of the Terracottas in the Department of Greek and Roman Antiquities, British Museum* (London, 1954) 369, no. 1359, pl. 189. M. Bieber (*Theater*) 1961, 104-105, fig. 411 (D322); T. B. L. Webster, *Monuments Illustrating New Comedy*, 2nd rev. and enl. ed. (London, 1969) 139, no. IV 4 (D322). The interpretation was noticed on a visit to the museum's new South Italian display. For a phlyax actor as Priam on an Apulian bell-krater in Berlin, see M. Bieber (*Theater*) 1961, fig. 493.

For the Berlin statuette and the interpretation as Verpus, see M. Bieber (*Theater*) 1961, 148-149, fig. 547.

For similar garlands on architectural decoration of 126-120 BC and on vases, see J. Schäfer, *Hellenistische Keramik aus Pergamon* (Berlin, 1968) 83-84, 91-92, fig. 15, 2; pls. 37, 38, 1; A. Oliver, "A Set of Ancient Silverware in the Getty Museum," *GettyMusJ* VIII (1980) 158-159, figs. 1-9.

For the dwarf and the actor from the Mahdia wreck, see W. Fuchs 1963, pls. 16, 21, 1.

A man with long locks of straight hair combed down onto his forehead wears clothing associated with comic actors. Like the preceding figure [54], he is clad in long-sleeved, long-legged tights and a sleeveless tunic, which this time reaches to a more dignified length below his knees. Under the outer tunic he wears a second sleeveless tunic, whose woolly hem is visible. His costume is belted with a firmly knotted double cord. His tongued sandals are also much like those of the comic slave. Here, however, the sole is not indented between the first two toes; the lingula has a much more prominent button; a strap crosses the toes; and the knotted laces are much more conspicuous. The singer's pose is a reversed and varied version of the comedian's. He crosses his ankles rather than his legs. He leans back with his mouth open, supporting himself with his left hand. He carries a knobbed loop in his right hand—probably a stylized rattle (sistrum). Its puzzling downward inclination may, however, be due to a misunderstanding or to damage; the handle is bent at a sharp angle.

The circular altar is decorated with garlands of fruit, grain, and pine cones. The garlands are tied with bows over the skulls of three bulls (bucrania). The altar is topped by an overhanging cornice formed by a convex molding (quarter-round) supported by a cavetto. The moldings are bordered above and below by very slender convex moldings (astragals). The lower part of the altar is finished with a fillet, a Lesbian cymatium, and another slender astragal. The entire composition is mounted on a platformlike base that is modeled by a fillet, a Lesbian cymatium, and a slender astragal above and below. The base is supported on legs that are continuous with the lowest fillet of the base and are finished with a Lesbian cymatium and a fillet.

ROMAN,
EARLIER IMPERIAL,
IST C. AD.
H. 19 CM.
J. PAUL GETTY
MUSEUM, 87.AB.144

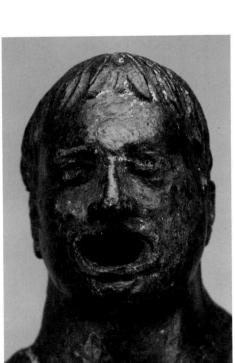

The upper surface of the altar is a detachable lid. The bottom of the altar is a separately made plate pierced with a round central hole and four teardrop-shaped surrounding holes. Like the preceding comic actor, the object was probably an incense burner, with ventilation below the altar and egress for fumes through the mouth of the figure.

The singer wears clothing associated with the world of the theater, but the absence of a mask—an obligatory piece of equipment for Greek tragic or comic performance—is unusual. He may be a mime, who performed without mask or theatrical clothing. The sistrum is connected with the cult of Isis and has no evident links with the theater. It may be, therefore, that the mime portrays a priest of Isis chanting or singing.

Marion True has pointed out another bronze performer without mask who was similarly seated on top of an incense burner. The figure, included in an exhibition in Paris in 1931, was slightly varied in costume and pose, much simpler in style, and probably later in date. He was interpreted by Sambon as an actor reciting a prologue, an activity that would not explain the sistrum of the Getty piece.

The Getty incense burner can be dated in the Imperial period on the basis of the altar decoration. Garlands strung from bucrania descend from those of the Altar of the Augustan Peace (Ara Pacis Augustae) of 13-9 BC. The singer's long, straight hair with its central fork resembles hairstyles of Roman portraits from both Julio-Claudian and Trajanic times. Coins of the young Nero and of Trajan seem especially similar, while sculpted portraits from these periods show the relationship even more closely. Particularly characteristic of the later period is the way the long locks spread without interruption from the crown of the head. The striations of the individual locks, however, are sharply incised in a way that is unusual in small

portrait busts of Flavian or Trajanic times (Figures XXIII, XXIV). The Levy dancer [69] shows the softer technique that emerges late in the first century. Incised locks, on the other hand, are characteristic of earlier works, like the portrait of Caligula (Figure XXII).

The style of the piece is bluffer and less suave than that of the late Republican incense burner with comic actor purchased with it [54]. The garlands do not have the graceful sag, the figure's pose is more frontal, and the singer's neck is thick and less natural than in the earlier work. In both, however, garments are modeled with skillful understatement. The moldings on the altars and bases also have much in common. The two incense burners were probably found together and clearly belong to the same tradition and possibly to the same workshop. Although they may stem from different periods, an interval of a century or more seems troublingly large. The singer should, therefore, be dated as early as possible; the hairstyle might even be a retardataire late Republican fashion carried into the very early Empire.

CONDITION: The figure including the lid was hollow cast in one piece, but the left leg and right arm were made separately. The right arm has been reattached in modern times. The leg has a squared tenon end which assures a proper fit into the squared hole in the figure's knee area. A small excess of bronze pour on the interior suggests that it was fitted and then cast on. The altar was cast from a wax sheet that was pressed into a mold. The cylinder was then soldered onto the stand. The altar and the stand have two register "nubs" which assure proper alignment of the altar on the stand. The stand was assembled from wax sheets and then cast. The patina is dark yellowish-green to black, very thin. Red-brown spots appear on the altar and base.

PROVENANCE: Probably found with [54] and a statuette of Hypnos.

UNPUBLISHED.

NOTES: I have drawn on reports by Karen Manchester and Jerry Podany in describing the physical condition of this bronze.

On mime, see M. Bieber (*Theater*) 1961, 164-165.

For the performer without mask in Paris in 1931, see A. Sambon, *Aperçu général de l'évolution de la sculpture depuis l'antiquité jusqu' à la fin du XVIᵉ siècle* (Paris, 1931) pl. XV.

For portrait coins with long straight hair, see J. Kent et al., *Roman Coins* (London, 1978) nos. 96 (M. Antony), 119 (Octavian), 156 (sons of Drusus), 180, 188-189 (the young Nero), 208 (Galba), and 259, 265 (Trajan).

For sculptural portraits with a central fork in long straight hair, see V. Poulsen, *Les portraits romains*, I: *République et dynastie Julienne* (Copenhagen, 1962) nos. 23, 65, 82, 87; idem, II: *De Vespasien à la Basse-antiquité* (Copenhagen, 1974) nos. 36, 51-56; A. Leibundgut (*JdI*) 1984, 264-267, figs. 7-11.

For small bronze portrait busts of about AD 100, see H. Jucker 1961, 56-58, nos. B6-B8, pls. 16-17.

56. Phallic Dwarf

The man stands in a stooped position clutching his ridiculously short mantle around him; muffled in drapery, both his hands are pressed to his chest. A sash is twisted around his waist; it is unusual in lacking projecting ends. Folds radiate out below the sash in an axially symmetrical pattern. An enormous phallus projects out between his knees, the remains of another project backward from his testicles. Another set of genitalia, complete with curly pubic hair, emerges from the back of his head and curves forward to form a loop. His bald head is greatly enlarged. He has a large hooked nose and big ears. His thick lips fill his thin, unsymmetrical face from side to side. Disfiguring warts appear on his forehead, right jaw, and chin, and he wears pendant globe earrings. His arching brows are contracted as he gazes apprehensively upward. His mouth gapes open foolishly, revealing a prominent row of upper teeth.

ROMAN,
EARLY IMPERIAL,
LATE AUGUSTAN
OR TIBERIAN,
1ST 3RD OF
1ST C. AD.
H. 15.1 CM.
MUSEUM OF FINE
ARTS, BOSTON, GIFT
OF E. P. WARREN, RES.
08.32D

The figure was clearly intended to be funny as well as shocking. The various features of this unfortunate creature make up an inventory of inappropriate, unattractive, ignoble, and undesirable characteristics; everything is wrong with him. Besides his obvious lecherousness and his generally grotesque and disfiguring proportions, his facial features are as far from the Classical norm as possible. Baldness was, if anything, more unpopular then than now. His gaping mouth is indecorous. He may have a component of effeminacy as well as lecherous exhibitionism. His skimpy mantle is pulled about him in a way that is far more common for representations of women than of men, and the gesture of the muffled arms recalls the famous pudicitia stance, used throughout the Hellenistic and Roman Imperial periods for female portrait statues. The earrings as well as his beaklike nose mark him as an Easterner; Armenian kings are shown wearing earrings on their coins

(Figure 51b). His apprehensive upward glance and his crouching stance may have been intended to suggest the "crafty cringing look of a household slave," a characterization praised by Pliny the Elder in a work by Leochares.

An x-ray examination revealed that two bronze loops hidden in the yellow marble (giallo di Siena) base project downward from the bottoms of his feet. This arrangement helps to explain the loop formed by the phallus on his head. The loops under the feet would originally have supported bells hanging from chains, while the loop on the head could have served for suspending the entire figure. Parallels are provided by the many variously phallic bronze objects with bells buried by the eruption of Mt. Vesuvius in AD 79. The Hellenistic dancing dwarf from the Mahdia wreck (Figure XIX) was also to be suspended and was likewise phallic—his exaggerated member is concealed by the modern support. He does, however, lack the bells under his feet found in the Roman grotesques. The purpose of such outrageous dangling objects was to ward off the effects of witchcraft or the evil eye. In Greek such apotropaic images were called *baskania*, while the Latin term was probably *fascina*. In archaeological literature, they are often termed *tintinnab-ula* from the bells associated with them.

In spite of the harshly laughable characterization, this piece is an outstanding example of its brutal genre. The drapery is full of torsions and reveals the forms of the body beneath it. The head is richly and emphatically modeled as well as being vividly and expressively detailed. The figure belongs to a tradition going back to terracotta statuettes of actors of the fourth century BC. In Attic figures of Old and Middle Comedy, actors frequently muffle their upper bodies in a cloak, below which hangs an artificial phallus. The frontal, crouching stance with nervously clenched arms can be paralleled in an actor in the Syracuse Museum. The masks

with huge megaphone-like mouths of the fourth-century figures, however, have been replaced by a lean caricatural head with hooked nose. Such heads frequently appear on Hellenistic and Imperial figures identified at times as actors of mime and at other times as caricatures of Asiatic slaves. In this case, multiple phalluses have been overlaid on this caricatural-theatrical basis, which had itself already been conspicuously phallic.

The forceful tensions of the drapery and the splendid characterization of the head strongly recall late Hellenistic bronzes like the Metropolitan "mime" [28] or dancing dwarfs from the Mahdia shipwreck. On the other hand, the figure is strongly echoed in works like a bronze mime or slave found at Nyons in France and a terracotta jug from Herculaneum made in the form of an old man wearing the costume of a schoolboy that are probably Imperial in date. The sash is like that of a Lar (see [62]), whose basic design was created between 12 and 7 BC. The proliferation of bells and phalluses seems more "Pompeian" than Hellenistic. The frontal, symmetrical composition suggests a relatively early chronology. The eyebrows, which have been stylized to independent, earlobe-like forms, recall busts of Silenus dated by Barr-Sharrar to late Augustan and Tiberian times.

CONDITION: The object was hollow cast in one piece. X-radiographs show that two rings (each with an outer diameter of approximately 12 millimeters) were cast in place on the bottoms of the feet. The metal is relatively thick and x-ray fluorescence analysis of some abraded areas shows a high lead content (30-35 percent) and moderate tin (10-15 percent). The casting is fairly porous, with many small holes from gases evolved during cooling visible on the surface. The legs and arms are probably solid.

Visual examination shows an apparent join just below the right knee, now partially separated with a few spots of metal overlapping from the lower part of the leg onto the upper part. The overlap suggests that the leg may have been cast onto the upper part; rather than being an intended procedure, the second step may have been required because of a casting problem.

The pupils of the eyes are lightly drilled. There is a small squarish hole (about 4 x 5 millimeters) on the left buttock; this is now filled with a soft reddish material (perhaps iron oxide). It was probably the site of a patch to repair a casting flaw. There is a larger square opening on the back, near the right shoulder. The purpose of this feature, which may have been cast in, is not clear. It may have been related to an attachment (R.N.) or to a repaired casting flaw (J.H.).

Some red and green corrosion is present on the surface. Overall the surface is covered by a thin black patina, which appears to have been applied and is flaking away in a few areas. The age of the patina is uncertain.

PUBLISHED: H. Licht, *Sittengeschichte Griechenlands*, Suppl. III (Zurich, 1928) 72 (as "Berlin, Antiquarium").
M. Comstock and C. Vermeule 1971, no. 143.
M. I. Davies, *AJA* LXXXVI (1982) 117, n. 16.

NOTES: The condition statement for this bronze is adapted from a report by Richard Newman.

For Pliny's mention of the cringing youth of Leochares, see *Natural History*, XXXV, 79, tr. H. Rackham (Loeb ed., Cambridge, Mass., 1968).

For tintinnabula from Vesuvian sites and their relationship to the evil eye, see *Pompeii A.D. 79* (1978) 64, 188, nos. 205-206; C. Johns, *Sex or Symbol, Erotic Images of Greece and Rome* (Austin, Tex., 1982) figs. 52-54.

For phallic and comic images for apotropaic purposes in the East, see A. Wace (*BSA*) 1903-1904, 109-110; D. Levi 1941, 224-225.

For figures of comic actors, see M. Bieber (*Theater*) 1961, figs. 135-138, 530.

For mimes with hook-nosed heads, see M. Bieber (*Theater*) 1961, figs. 415, 817-822, 825-827.

For the slave from Nyons, see S. Boucher 1976, 200, figs. 454, 456.

For the comic jug from Herculaneum, see *Pompeii A.D. 79* (1978) no. 33.

On the sash of the Lares, see M. Bieber 1977, 78-79, figs. 305-310.

For busts of Silenus with similar eyebrows, see B. Barr-Sharrar 1987, nos. C19, C20, C22, pp. 37, 38, pls. 5, 6.

57. Boxing Dwarf

The muscular but short-legged figure strides forward, raising his left fist as if to block a blow and cocking his right for a counterpunch. He wears boxing gloves (caesti) tied with straps at the wrist and having a knoblike attachment. His leather cap is a type worn especially by wrestlers to keep opponents from pulling their hair. In ancient athletic festivals, since there were no weight classifications, all boxers were heavyweights. To emphasize the comic effect of this small combatant, he is given a grossly exaggerated phallus. For an Alexandrian version of a boxer, see [24].

In spite of the deformities, the dwarf is beautifully modeled; his muscular anatomy is richly detailed, and his vaguely African head has a balanced, if rather diabolical intensity. Several other figures of boxing dwarfs in just this stance are known. Examples in the former Gréau collection and in the former Fouquet collection have normal-sized genitals, while one in the British Museum has the comic

ROMAN,
EARLY IMPERIAL,
AD 25-50.
H. 11.1 CM.
MUSEUM OF FINE
ARTS, BOSTON,
GIFT OF E. P.
WARREN, RES. 08.32K

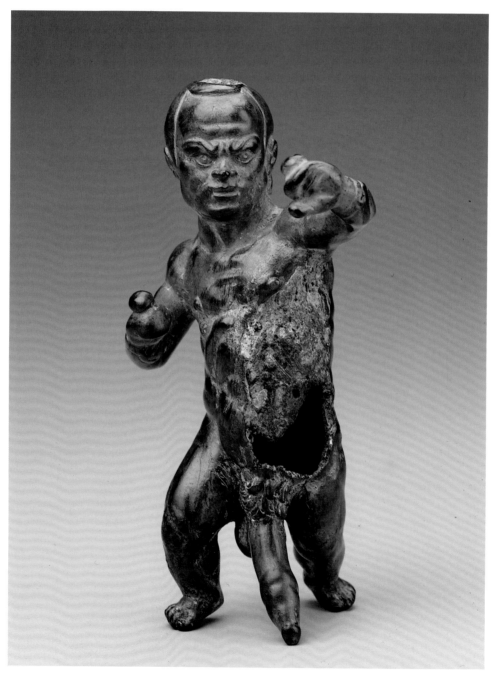

310

exaggeration of this piece. None, however, can rival the elegant line, anatomical detail, and handsome head found here. The pieces from the Gréau and Fouquet collections are both bottles; a small neck with a pair of handles emerges from the top of the head. Some such arrangement may have existed in this figure too, but if so, the bottleneck was removed, leaving the present hole in the top of the head. The object was later filled with lead, and a rod was inserted. These arrangements may have been intended to convert the bottle into a suspended charm against the evil eye (a baskanion or fascinum).

The general conception of this type of figure has Hellenistic roots. The striding-defending pose strongly recalls the Borghese Warrior signed by Agasias of Ephesus and usually dated around 100 BC. The pose returns with a different twist of the head in the dancing dwarf from the Mahdia shipwreck of about the same

 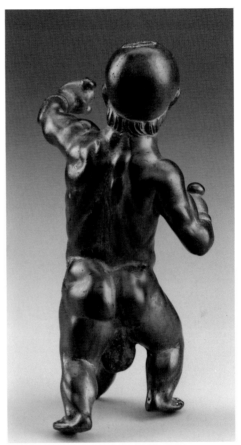

date (see Figure XIX). The Mahdia dwarf, however, outdoes all the boxing dwarfs in force, freshness, and sheer size, but the Boston figure retains a rather similar demonic expression conveyed through almost S-curve eyebrows. The elaborate anatomy of the Boston figure, for that matter, also recalls the Borghese Warrior.

The precise linearity of the Boston boxer, on the other hand, partakes of the classicism of the early Imperial period. This combination of linearity and baroque dynamism is probably early Julio-Claudian. Barr-Sharrar has dated a rather comparable bust of a triton from Pompeii to the time of Tiberius or Caligula. This chronology is supported by a head of a satyr on a bronze double-herm from the Nemi ships, sunk in the time of Nero (AD 54-68) and probably built in the second quarter of the century (Figure XX). Both the dwarf and the Nemi herm-head have S-curve eyebrows and a network of paired horizontal and vertical wrinkles in their foreheads. Deep wrinkles lead down from the nose; all features are rendered in sharply linear terms. The profiles also have much in common; the noses have a low bridge and an offset tip. The sickle-like locks split by sharp incisions curving low onto his neck, moreover, are similar to those of the older magistrate from the Getty Museum [63] datable around the middle of the first century AD. This same treatment of locks appears in the bust of Caligula in Zurich (Figure XXII).

CONDITION: The statuette was hollow cast in one piece. Radiography suggests that most of the arms, the feet, and part of the lower legs are solid metal. The metal is 1-1.5 millimeters thick around the loss in the chest. An elliptical hole in the head (about 15 millimeters across in the longest direction) appears to have been intentionally cast. The left side of the chest and abdomen is missing, probably the result of an ancient damage. Also in ancient times the head and part of the chest cavity were filled with lead, and a pin was fastened in the top of the head, perhaps for suspension. The pupils of the eyes are marked lightly. There is an abrasion on the left hand, and numerous scratches occur on the body, particularly around the large loss (probably from the filling of the lead plug). X-ray fluorescence analysis shows that the alloy is a leaded high-tin bronze (lead varies 8-18 percent).

Local patches of red and green corrosion are present. Over much of the surface a thin black patina appears to sit directly on the bare metal.

EX COLLECTION: Stefano Bardini, London, sold 1899; E. P. Warren.

PUBLISHED: S. Boucher 1970, 54, n. 1.
M. Comstock and C. Vermeule 1971, no. 145.

W. Hornbostel, *Aus Gräbern und Heiligtümern: Die Antikensammlung Walter Kropatscheck* (Mainz, 1980) 143, under no. 83.
J. Petit, *Bronzes antiques de la collection Dutuit* (Paris, 1980) 105, n. 1, under no. 40.

NOTES: I have drawn on a report by Richard Newman in describing the physical condition of this bronze.

For the wrestler's leather cap, see a bronze head in the British Museum: J. Swaddling, *The Ancient Olympic Games* (London, 1980) 58.

For other bronze boxing dwarfs, see: P. Perdrizet, *Bronzes grecs d'Égypte de la collection Fouquet* (Paris, 1911) 62, pl. 24, no. 99; Sale: *Collection Julien Gréau. Les bronzes antiques,* Paris, Hôtel Drouot, April 20, 1881, 81, 83, no. 383; cited in Petit (*Bronzes antiques*) 1980, 105, n. 1; British Museum 1824.4-31.2.

For the Borghese Warrior, see M. Bieber 1961, 162, figs. 686, 688, 689.

For the dwarf from the Mahdia wreck, see W. Fuchs 1963, 17-18, no. 7, pl. 16; J. J. Pollitt 1986, 138-140, fig. 149.

For the Pompeian triton, see B. Barr-Sharrar 1987, no. C106.

For the Nemi satyr-herm, see G. Ucelli, *Le navi di Nemi* (Rome, 1940) fig. 236.

58. Warrior in a Corinthian Helmet

The bearded, nude figure wears his helmet pushed back on his mane of hair, either in anticipation of or in a sequel to combat. The pose establishes fluid shifts of axis, but his limbs are arranged in a contrast of mobility and stasis that is in the Polyclitan tradition; the figure is supported on his right leg, his left is set back slightly and the heel is raised in movement. His right arm points downward with a slight flex, while the left is bent sharply. His head is turned from the static to the mobile side, which creates a sense of smooth, continuous flow. Transitions in the simply but intelligently rendered anatomy are soft and gentle, and contours have a curvilinear elasticity. The expression is altered by the loss of inlays in the right eye and the lips. A faint circular line on the right pectoral, nearly concealed by the modern patination, suggests that the nipples were originally inlaid with copper. Curls of the beard are rendered with circular indentations.

ROMAN, LATE
REPUBLICAN OR
EARLY IMPERIAL,
40 BC-AD 30,
AFTER STATUE OF
END OF 5TH C. BC.
H. 26.8 CM.
WADSWORTH
ATHENEUM,
J. PIERPONT
MORGAN, 1917.820

Bielefeld has hypothesized that the figure copies the lost statue of Pericles by the Athenian High Classical sculptor Kresilas. Boardman has observed that the head is not a portrait but that a military commander of 430-420 BC could have been presented in these generic terms. He noted that the stance is Polyclitan, a suggestion that might lead to a slightly later date and different identification. The pose is associated particularly with statues ascribed by Arnold to the first generation of pupils of Polyclitus: the Pan (best represented by the copy in Leiden) and the Dresden Youth. The modeling of the musculature also has a reticent quality that differs from earlier robustness. Only the angle of the head, turned up rather than down, differs from these post-Polyclitan figures, whose prototypes were apparently created in the span 420-405 BC. Arnold has connected other Roman bronze statuettes of Greek generals similar to this one with the monument to Lysander and a multitude of other Spartan and allied commanders set up at Delphi in 405-401 BC after the end of the Peloponnesian War. This piece has at least as good a claim as any of them to reflect that project—carried out largely by pupils of Polyclitus. The suave elegance of the composition does, indeed, have an Attic flavor, but such influences have often been noted in the work of the Argive school in their own version of the Rich Style of around 400 BC.

The figure probably supported a shield on its left arm and held a spear with its right hand, but no clear-cut evidence of such attachments is visible on the pitted and encrusted surface. The arms of most bronzes of helmeted warriors, from the monumental fifth-century warriors of Riace to Roman statuettes, are held in just this position, presumably in order to bear weapons.

The Hartford statuette has a refreshing originality in its soft but anatomically sure modeling and could be pre-Imperial; it lacks the elaborate academic definition

of high quality Imperial work, like the Paramythia statuettes in the British Museum or the Levy athlete [59]. A few details, however, make it clear that the execution is post-Classical; the upturned head gives the figure an anachronistic Lysippan or Hellenistic expression, and the indented centers of the curls of the beard reflect an illusionistic approach more at home in Roman Imperial times. The technique appears, for example, in a bust from the Villa of the Papyri at Herculaneum (Figure XXI). The broad surfaces and gentle simplicity of the anatomy, however, strongly recall the three classicistic statuettes from the Anticythera shipwreck of 75-50 BC; the treatment is even gentler and less sharply defined here. They, too, make use of inlays in eyes, lips, and nipples. The relationship is close enough to suggest a workshop connection.

Although the workshop that produced the figure must have come from the Aegean, in all likelihood it must have transferred itself to Rome. The piece is a failed cast filled with bubbles, and surely would not have been deemed fit for export, even though it was evidently passable in a local market.

CONDITION: The surface is severely pitted due to a porosity caused by gases (not corrosion) according to Clifford Crane (1980). The greenish-black patina, which allows much yellow metal color to show through, is soluble in organic solvents and therefore modern. The two base plates are separate from the figure and modern. The right foot is smaller than the left, again due, presumably, to the failed casting. The hands are filled with concretions. The left cheek plate of the helmet is broken, the right bent. Heavy concretions fill the area below each projection. The iris of the left eye is inlaid in a black material. A slight circular line seemingly inscribed on the right pectoral could reflect a copper inlay in the nipple; a corresponding circular concavity is found in the left pectoral, presumably where a copper inlay was intended. The lips may also have been inlaid. The casting appears to be one piece and solid.

PROVENANCE: Found in the Tiber near Rome.

PUBLISHED: E. Bielefeld, "Bronzestatuette des Wadsworth Atheneums in Hartford, Connecticut," *AntP* I (1962) 39-41, pls. 30-37.
M. Robertson 1975, 336, pl. 112b.
J. Boardman 1985, fig. 236.

NOTES: On the Leiden Pan and the Dresden Youth, see D. Arnold, *Die Polykletnachfolge* (Berlin, 1969) 49-68, pls. 1b-2b, 6a, 7a, 8a.
On the Monument to Lysander, see D. Arnold 1969, 97-109.

On Roman bronze statuettes of commanders in Munich, Vienna and Paris, see D. Arnold 1969, p. 108; J. Sieveking, *Die Bronzen der Sammlung Loeb* (Munich, 1913) pl. 15; E. Berger, *RM* LXV (1958) 19, 20; R. V. Schneider, *Album ausserlesener Gegenstände in der Antikensammlung des Allerhöchsten Kaiserhauses* (Vienna, 1895) pl. 25, lower middle; A. de Ridder 1913-1915, I: no. 1045, pl. 61. For the warriors of Riace, see *Due bronzi da Riace: Rinvenimento, restauro, analisi ed ipotesi di interpretazione*, 2 vols. (Rome, 1984); J. Boardman 1985, 53-54, figs. 38-39.
On the Paramythia hoard, see J. Swaddling 1979, 103 ff., pls. 49-55.
For the Anticythera statuettes, see P. C. Bol 1972, 11-17, pls. 1-4.

59. Athlete with Headband: Variation on the So-Called Discophorus of Polyclitus

ROMAN,
EARLY IMPERIAL,
AD I-40.
H. 22 CM.
SHELBY AND
LEON LEVY

The youth stands quietly with his weight on his right leg and his relaxed left flexed. His weight-bearing hip is skewed far to the side. His right arm is bent at the elbow; the forearm is extended diagonally forward and outward. His right hand—fingers bent and thumb partly missing—is extended with open palm. The palm itself has an uneven surface from the attachment of some object. His left arm hangs at his side; a circular hole for a now-missing object passes horizontally between its thumb and index finger. The youth's head is bent toward his active right hand, but oddly his eyes are cast upward. A ribbon or fillet rings his head and is knotted in front. A projection above and below the line of the ribbon might be either its ends or else a separate rectangular object of wood or metal. The ribbon is probably a piece of athletic apparatus since the figure is both youthful and nude; athletes frequently have their stephane knotted in front in fifth-century BC Attic vase painting.

A votive inscription is incised on his right leg: ΠΟΥΒΛΙΣ ΑΧΑΕΙΚΟΣ ΕΙΞ-ΜΕΝΟΙ ΑΝΕΘΗΚΑΝ; "Publi[o]s Achaiikos, having vowed, dedicated [this]." A six-rayed star is incised on his left leg. Several abbreviations or misspellings make the brief text somewhat puzzling: *achaeikos* for *achaiikos* is a recognized alternative. *Poublis* for *Poublios* can be paralleled in a bronze plaque in the Museum of Fine Arts, Boston (1983.222), in which *Antonis* is substituted for *Antonios*. *Eixamenoi* replaces *euxamenoi*; the participle *euxamenos* is so common in dedicatory formulas and changes in diphthongs are so frequent in inscriptions of the Imperial period that the emendation seems reasonable. The plural verbs and the singular subject are more troubling. A second name may have been placed on another statuette in a joint dedication. The star is frequently used as an emblem of the Dioscuri, and the two statuettes (if two there were) could have been dedicated to this pair of divinities. The inscription was cut after the statuette had been cast. Small lumps of material pushed up by the chisel can be seen at the end of the strokes of many letters. The letter *ksi* has a form found in Roman Imperial times.

The workmanship is highly Classical and refined. The anatomy is elaborately articulated, and the hair is built up of a multitude of carefully striated J- and S-shaped locks. In wavelike succession they march back along his forehead, hooking outward along the left side and alternating inward and outward curls on the right. The curling ends of the locks are given decorative emphasis by circular cavities, probably made by twirling the end of a pointed stick in the wax of the model. With the exception of the enormous eyes, the facial features are small and delicate. Curiously, the soles of the feet do not follow a plane perpendicular to the axis of the body; the figure seems designed for a sloping base or mounting.

The composition is clearly derived from a famous lost statue known through many replicas and variants, universally attributed to Polyclitus. It has been conjectured, on insufficient grounds, that the fifth-century statue was an athlete carrying a discus. Since many bronze statuettes of this type are equipped with the attributes of Hermes, Boucher has argued that this was also the identity of the Polyclitan original. Rejecting the idea that any of the trappings of the Roman Mercury (Hermes) could go back to the fifth century, Berger has recently attempted to show that the prototype was a figure of Theseus.

The stance and the positions of the limbs of the Levy bronze generally agree with those of the putative Classical model. The squarish, sharply defined musculature of the torso and the curly locks of the hair are quintessentially Polyclitan. The variations are themselves interesting; as in a bronze statuette in Basel, the back is relatively broad and tall, and the hips are boyishly narrow. The left shoulder is level with the right, rather than tilted upward as is usual. Most radically changed is the head; the headband (without a knot) and the essentials of the hair arrangement are

ΠΟΥΒλ
ΙϹΑΧΑϹ
ΙΚΟϹΕΙ
ΣΑΜΕΝ
ΟΙΑΝΕ
ΘΗΚΑ
Ν

found in the marble variant of the Discophorus in Aphrodisias. A headband with a central roundel appears in a Discophorus from Gaul, now in Boston. The headband probably does not belong to the original, since it is present in only one of the full-sized marble versions of the figure. The distant, upward cast of the eyes is seen in the famous bronze statuette in the Louvre, probably of Augustan date. The sheer size of the Levy statuette's eyes can be paralleled in the youthful Asclepius found in Volubilis, Morocco.

The meaning of the statuette is somewhat unclear. Unlike most of the other Discophori, it does not seem to have been a Hermes; no wings sprout from the head, and it is very unlikely that the right hand held a moneybag. It seems much more probable that the figure was simply a decorative creation evoking athletes and artists of the fifth century BC. It has much in common with one of the classicistic statuettes recovered from the Anticythera wreck of 75-50 BC. The figure in question stands in a very similar pose, wears a headband and probably poured a libation from a phiale in its outstretched right hand. Its left seems to have once held an object that has not been reconstructed.

The refined workmanship in general and the sharply articulated overlay of well-defined locks in particular suggest a date in Julio-Claudian times. The circular perforations marking the ends of curls are a decorative approach best paralleled from Tiberian times on, as in the bust of a lady from Herculaneum (Figure XXI). Although the figure seems to lie in the tradition of the Anticythera statuettes, the elaborately emphatic detailing of its hair and anatomy is far from their sketchy simplicity. The inscription's large, roughly formed letters suggest re-use at a somewhat later date.

CONDITION: The eyes are inlaid with silver, and the pupils are deeply drilled. Rather rough straight incisions separate the toes. The big toes are large and cut free from the others. The arms are separately cast. The tip of the right thumb is missing. The palm of the right hand is rough, probably from the attachment of an object (a phiale?). The patina is dark green.

PROVENANCE: Said to come from Lebanon.

PUBLISHED: *House and Garden,* October 1987, 151, col. illus.

NOTES: For athletes with headband knotted in front, see N. Yalouris et al., *The Olympic Games* (Athens, 1976) figs. 91, 96.

For a stephane with vertical peak, see N. Yalouris et al. 1976, fig. 16; D. Finn and C. Houser, *Greek Monumental Bronze Sculpture* (New York, 1983) 102-107 (boy from Marathon).

For headbands with a knot or ornament in front in a royal context, see J. Boardman 1985, fig. 141 (Arkesilaos IV of Cyrene?); R. R. R. Smith 1984, 64, fig. 28; A. Herrmann, in N. Yalouris et al., *The Search for Alexander,* exh. cat. (Boston, 1980) no. 14 (Lysimachos?).

For the form of the *ksi* and the use of *euxamenos,* see M. Guarducci, *L'epigrafia greca* (Rome, 1967-1978) I: 382; II: 125.

For other examples of the composition, see E. Berger, "Der sogenannte Diskophoros: Eine Theseusstatue(?) des Polyklet," *Quaderni ticinesi di numismatica e antichità classiche* IX (1982) 59-105.

For the Discophorus as Hermes, see S. Boucher (*BCH*) 1976, 95-102.

For the Boston Discophorus as Hermes, see S. Boucher (*BCH*) 1976, 102, fig. 7; M. Comstock and C. Vermeule 1971, no. 109.

For the Asclepius from Volubilis, see C. Boube-Piccot, *Les bronzes antiques du Maroc,* I (1969) no. 205; H. Menzel, "Römische Bronzestatuetten und verwandte Geräte: ein Beitrag zum Stand der Forschung," in *Aufstieg und Niedergang,* 1985: II, 12, 3:160, pl. 14, 2.

For the Anticythera statuette, see P. C. Bol 1972, 11-13, pl. 1, 4, 1-3.

60. Mercury in a Cloak

Mercury, identifiable from the remaining wing in his hair, stands at rest and looks downward with a benevolent expression. He wears elaborate sandals and a long cloak that almost entirely covers his body: the Greek chlamys, the costume of travelers and warriors. The cloak is fastened with a round pin (fibula) on his right shoulder and is pulled tight by a weight at the lower corner. Mercury's bent left arm lifts the hem and frees itself, undoubtedly to hold a herald's staff, the caduceus. The god's weight is carried on his left leg. His relaxed right leg is placed to the left with his foot flat on the ground, while his empty right hand hangs calmly at his side. His head is inclined to the weight-bearing left side.

Modeling and detail are handled with great subtlety and seriousness. The cloak adheres to the body, revealing the forms below almost as if it were transparent. The collar falls loosely, and a cascade of long catenary and short straight secondary wrinkles articulate the cloak's surface. Nowhere does the cloak's modeling develop a plasticity that distracts from the anatomical understructure. Hair and wing are finely worked; the hair flows back from a central part, and many curls have individually drilled centers. Delicate sideburns creep down the cheeks and onto the jaw.

The figure is derived from a Severe Style image of Hermes created around the middle of the fifth century BC. The type is known from several Boeotian terracotta statuettes roughly contemporary with the large-scale archetype. One headless large-scale marble copy of the figure is preserved in the Sala della Biga of the Vatican. As in this figure, a weight-bearing left side is contrasted with a relaxed right. An intaglio by Dioscourides shows that it originally wore a sun-hat (petasus).

There are, however, major changes in this image; the old compositional scheme has been reworked in a remarkably eclectic way. The petasus has been omitted, and the short cloak, which ended above the knee in the Severe Style figure, has been

ROMAN, LATE JULIO-CLAUDIAN OR EARLY FLAVIAN, AD 40-80. H. 29.5 CM. WALTERS ART GALLERY, 54.605

replaced by one reaching almost to the ankle. The long cloak is rare in the Classical period, although it can be found in an East Greek statuette of the Severe Style in the Museum of Fine Arts, Boston. It apparently became much more popular in Hellenistic times. Worn with the left hand covered, the long chlamys appears in many terracotta figures of the early Hellenistic period and in the Zoilos relief at Aphrodisias of the 30s BC. The long cloak is worn with the left hand free, as in the Walters statuette, by a votary in a late Hellenistic relief in Athens. Perhaps, then, the longer cloak represents an updating of the costume of the Severe Style Hermes in Hellenistic terms. A variety of other influences are also at play in the treatment of the figure. There is a touch of late Classical style; the pose has a delicacy and relaxation that seems influenced by early fourth-century images like the Hermes attributed to Naukydes. The face has a softness that also has fourth-century, in this case Praxitelean, associations. A clear allusion to the High Classical sculpture of Polyclitus, on the other hand, occurs in the central part in the hair. The sideburns allude to the Diomedes of the late fifth century BC.

This kind of eclectic play with fifth- and fourth-century styles would be perfectly at home in the mid- to late first century BC, whether in the pre-Augustan Pasitelean environment or in the Augustan climate that produced the San Ildefonso group. The introduction of a kind of cloak popular especially in Hellenistic times suggests a date for the classicistic archetype before the late first century BC. The execution of this statuette has hitherto been dated roughly in the last third of the first century BC, and such a chronology seems doubly reasonable since Polyclitan styling appears to have suppressed alternate approaches under the early Empire. On the other hand, some details of the treatment suggest that the figure was made in post-Augustan times; the illusionistic effects of transparency in the cloak

recall figures like the marble Isis at Pompeii, which may, like so much of the marble sculpture of the town, date from the early Imperial period. As pointed out by Comstock, the arrangement of the hair with masses of curls on either side of a central part has a resemblance to female hairstyles of the mid-first century AD, a resemblance that seems more than coincidental. The earliest datable example of curls of hair accented, as here, by circular indentations is in a small bust from the Villa of the Papyri at Herculaneum whose hairstyle resembles that of both Caligula's mother, Agrippina I, and Claudius' wife, Agrippina II (cf. Figure XXI). The individual locks, moreover, lack plasticity; the grooves between them are as important as the locks themselves. The resulting intensification of shadow pattern is a step in the direction of the illusionism of the Flavian period (AD 69-96).

Quite aside from its high quality, the figure has a unique position among Roman statuettes of Mercury (Hermes) with a cloak. It is the only figure so far known that preserves the stance of the Severe Style prototype, and it presents a uniquely rich set of stylistic allusions. The other Mercuries, whether with long cloak or short, are totally dominated by Polyclitan models; their stance is almost invariably derived from that of the Doryphorus, with its more robust movement and reversed direction. Splendid examples of the Polyclitan remodeling have been found at Delphi and Pompeii, and another is in Lyon. Numerous less distinguished pieces were diffused throughout western Europe. The Walters figure is also rare in omitting both the traveler's hat (petasus) and the moneybag (marsupium) that are almost obligatory attributes of the Roman Mercury. The omissions give him a grander and more ideal air.

CONDITION: Missing are the caduceus and one wing. The sandal straps are inlaid with silver. The patina is black with much corrosion on the right side. Spots of blue-green corrosion appear on the inside of the elbow, the forearm, and a fold beside the right knee. The figure is said to have been electrolytically treated, but the brassy color associated with this process is nowhere in evidence. Observers have thought that the figure might have been entirely silvered.

PUBLISHED: D. K. Hill 1949, 19, no. 33, pl. 8. A. Linfert, *Von Polyklet zu Lysipp* (Giessen, 1966) 67. P. Zanker 1974, 104.

NOTES: On the Severe Style prototype (''Hermes/ Phokion''), see A. Furtwängler, *Masterpieces of Greek Sculpture* (London, 1895) 233, fig. 94; idem, *Sammlung Somzée* (Munich, 1897) 74, no. 102; L. R. Farnell, *Cults of the Greek States*, V (Oxford, 1909) 46-47, pls. 12-16; G. Lippold 1903-1956, 83, no. 616; W. Fuchs in W. Helbig, *Führer durch die öffentlichen Sammlungen klassischer Altertümer in Rom*, I (Tübingen, 1963) 398, no. 502; W.-H. Schuchhardt, *Göttingische gelehrte Anzeigen* (Göttingen, 1960) 177; M.-L. Vollenweider, *Die Steinschneidekunst und ihre Künstler in spätrepublikanischer und augusteischer Zeit* (Baden-Baden, 1966) 114, pl. 66, 1, 2; G. Horster, *Statuen auf Gemmen* (Bonn, 1970) 57 ff.; B. S. Ridgway 1970, 68-69, fig. 113.

For the East Greek cloaked youth in Boston, see M. Comstock and C. Vermeule 1971, no. 30. For early Hellenistic terracotta youths in long cloaks, see R. Higgins, *Tanagra and the Figurines* (Princeton, 1986) 150, figs. 179, 181, 186-189. On the early archaistic relief, Athens, National Museum 1966, see D. Willers, ''Zu den Anfängen der archaistischen Plastik in Griechenland,'' *AM*, suppl. IV (1975) 27, 29-30, pl. 6. For the Zoilos relief, see K. T. Erim in A. Alföldi, *Aion in Mérida und Aphrodisias* (Mainz, 1979) 35-37, pl. 21a. For the Hermes of Naukydes, see D. Arnold 1969, 123-126, 263-265, pl. 10a. For the Classical head of Diomedes, see M. B. Comstock and C. C. Vermeule 1976, no. 149; B. Vierneisel-Schlörb, *München, Glyptothek: Katalog der Skulpturen*, II: *Klassische Skulpturen* (Munich, 1979) no. 9. On Roman bronze statuettes of Mercury covered by his cloak, see S. Boucher, *Bronzes romains figurés du Musée des Beaux-Arts de Lyon* (Lyon, 1973) nos. 133-135; idem 1976, 102, 112-113, 235-236, 270-271, figs. 185-189, 210, 351-352, 446-452. For the marble Isis from Pompeii, see *Pompeii A.D. 79* (1978) no. 191.

61. Hercules

The hero stands in a quiet yet fluid pose. The stance is frontal, Hercules looks directly forward, and his relaxed left leg is scarcely advanced beyond his weight-bearing right. Yet his right hip projects strongly to the side, and his upper body sways back toward his bent, outstretched arm, over which the skin of the Nemean lion is draped. The knotty, swollen musculature ripples powerfully to intensify the fluid effect, as do his elegantly asymmetrical genitals. Hercules' outstretched left hand originally held the apples of the Hesperides, and his lowered right once carried his club, projecting forward at a 45-degree angle as if to balance the tilt of his torso. He is crowned with a diadem formed by a twisted ribbon, made of a twisted silver wire.

ROMAN, EARLY IMPERIAL, CA. 30 BC-AD 20. H. 14.5 CM. THE CLEVELAND MUSEUM OF ART, PURCHASE FROM THE J. H. WADE FUND, 87.2

The hero's expertly rendered anatomy has been turned into that of a weight-lifter or a workman accustomed to the heaviest manual labor. His belly is massive in a way usually confined to representations of the drunken Hercules or the closely related theme of Hercules urinating. Even the hero's head—with its swelling forehead, puffy, curly beard, and tiny eyes—looks muscle-bound. At the same time, there is a refinement and even elegance in the characterization. The closely cropped hair, slim nose, small ears, and piercing glance turn the muscle-man into a formidable champion on more than one level. This is not one of the hero's well-publicized weaker moments; he is alertly in control of himself.

The workmanship is unusually refined and subtle. The back is as beautifully finished as the front. The lion's pelt is filled with turbulent asymmetries and rich modeling. Details are finely shaped from the lion's teeth to the hero's toes, genitals, and facial features. The massive locks at the front of his beard gradually shrink to tiny curls at the back of his jaw. The hair of his head and pubes is suggested impressionistically in contrast with the careful chiseling of the beard.

A club-carrying Hercules standing quietly extending the apples of the Hesperides with an arm draped in a lionskin is a sculptural theme popular ever since Myron's lost masterpiece of the mid-fifth century BC. Hercules appears with these attributes and in just the stance of this bronze in large-scale statues, whose original has been attributed to the fourth century. These statues, however, generally depict the hero as youthfully beardless and with a relatively trim, athletic waistline, as in a colossal bronze in the Vatican or a basalt colossus of Flavian date from the Palatine. The bearded version is more difficult to document in large-scale sculpture, and it may be a late Hellenistic variation on the composition. The heavy belly of our statuette probably reflects the influence of drunken Herculeses popular in Hellenistic and early Imperial times. Examples in marble and bronze come from Herculaneum, and a fine fragmentary bronze statuette from Smyrna (Izmir) is in the Metropolitan Museum. The fat, bearded version of Hercules with the apples may then have been created around the end of the Hellenistic period.

Although the Cleveland bronze is hard to parallel exactly in large-scale sculpture, it does represent a well-established type in the repertory of craftsmen producing small-scale bronze statuettes. Recently, an almost identical Hercules, complete with base, was found at Weissenburg on the Danubian frontier in Bavaria (Figure XVII). The two are even the same size; the Weissenburg Hercules is a mere three millimeters taller. A clumsier version from Rimini is in the British Museum. The Weissenburg statuette is thought to have been made in the second half of the second century AD and was buried in a hoard of bronzes around the middle of the third century. In spite of the close physical and typological similarities, there are significant stylistic differences. The Weissenburg figure is more emphatic and overt; not only does he wear a flamboyant laurel wreath, but he also glances out in the direction of his more pronounced step, giving him a stormy, aggressive

quality that has much in common with portraits of the later Antonine emperors. His musculature is sharply outlined, and he has a more conventionally acceptable waist.

Although the two are probably the products of a single workshop, the shop may well have been a long-lived one. Cleveland's bloated-but-refined Hercules may be substantially earlier and stem from a time close to the formulation of the type. A similar mixture of bulky body and refined head is found in a terracotta relief of Hercules in the Museum of Fine Arts, Boston. The relief, said to come from Capua, continues the Italic middle Republican tradition of fine terracottas, probably not later than the early first century BC. The modeling of the Hellenistic drunken Hercules in New York also has much in common with that of the Cleveland statuette. The almost archaistic frontality and delicacy of detail in the Cleveland piece may reflect a date that is later, but not necessarily after the second half of the first century BC. Its association with the following Lar [62], however, makes it likely that the Hercules was produced after 12 BC.

CONDITION: The figure is light for its size which indicates that the statuette is hollow cast or filled with a core. The lionskin is a separate cast section attached to the arm, possibly with solder. The wreath is a twisted silver wire. The lips and nipples are inlaid with copper. The eyes are also inlaid with some gray to black metal and may be silver. The pupils of the eyes are very lightly drilled.

Bronze corrosion products, malachite and cuprite, cover the surface of the sculpture. The right arm has been damaged with "warts" of corrosion. The arm has expanded and cracked due to the expansion of the corrosion products. The club in Hercules' right arm is broken and missing as is the end of the lionskin.

PROVENANCE: Purchased together and conceivably found with [62].

EXHIBITED: New Rochelle, N.Y., Bard College, March-May 1986, *Herakles: Passage of the Hero Through 1000 Years of Classical Art*, cat. by J. P. Uhlenbrock, xii, illus. (reversed).
The Cleveland Museum of Art, February 24-April 17, 1988, *The Year in Review*, 65, illus. 30, no. 3.

PUBLISHED: *Architectural Digest*, October 1986, 208, illus.

Artemis S. A., *Annual Report* (Luxembourg, 1986-1987) 8, illus. cover, 9.

NOTES: I have drawn on a report by Bruce Christman in describing the physical condition of this bronze.

For Hercules from Capua in Boston, see G. Chase, rev. by C. Vermeule and M. Comstock, *Greek, Etruscan and Roman Art* (Boston, 1972) 170, fig. 166; C. C. Vermeule 1980, pl. III.

For Hercules in Herculaneum (marble in the House of the Stags, bronze statuette in Naples) see A. Maiuri, *Ercolano, i nuovi scavi (1927-1958)*, I (Rome, 1958) 302-323; M. Grant and W. Forman, *Cities of Vesuvius: Pompeii and Herculaneum* (New York, 1976) 89; *Pompeii A.D. 79* (1978) no. 204; C. C. Vermeule 1980, pl. 112.

For the drunken Hercules in New York, see G. M. A. Richter, *BMMA* x (1915) 236 f.; M. Bieber 1961, 140, figs. 577-578.

For the Weissenburg Hercules, see H.-J. Kellner and G. Zahlhaas 1984, no. 23.

For the statuette in the British Museum, see H. B. Walters 1899, no. 1303, pl. 27.

For another bronze statuette of this type in the J. Paul Getty Museum, see J. P. Uhlenbrock 1986, no. 49

For the Vatican bronze colossus, see G. Lippold 1903-1956, III, 1, no. 544, pls. 37, 44; W. Fuchs in W. Helbig 1963, I, no. 38.

For the basalt colossus from the Palatine, see B. Andreae 1977, 180, 472, fig. 397.

For headless large-scale bodies of this type, see D. Candilio in A. Giuliano, ed., *Museo Nazionale Romano, le sculture*, I, 2 (Rome, 1981) 339 f., 351 f.

For further examples, either beardless or headless, see S. Howard, *The Lansdowne Herakles* (Malibu, 1978) 23, 25-29, figs. 79-80, 83-89.

A few marble Herculeses with this stance seem to have had bearded heads; see S. Reinach, *Rép. stat.* v: pls. 81, 1, 83, 2.

For an example of the Myronian Heracles, see M. B. Comstock and C. C. Vermeule 1976, no. 139.

62. Lar

The youth stands quietly erect with his weight-bearing right leg contrasted only slightly with his relaxed left. He wears a short tunic which has copper-inlaid stripes descending vertically from his shoulders front and back. In spite of the motionless pose, the skirt of the tunic mysteriously blows back in three deep, wavelike folds beside each leg. His scarflike mantle passes over his left shoulder and hangs down to his boot-tops in front, where it falls in a pattern of exactly repeated undulations. His waist is circled by a sash, which might be a part of the mantle, but its mechanics are difficult to follow. The high boots have open toes and animal-skin liners. The youth has an almost feminine hairdo; locks flow back around his face and are fastened by a diadem or ribbon.

The Lares were popular, domestic divinities without a special mythology. They were spirits connected with particular localities, especially households, crossroads, and fields. Bronze statuettes and painted images of the Lares were placed in domestic shrines called *lararia*. Their cult seems to have had roots in the propitiation of the dead, but as they are presented in numerous images like this one, they are cheerful bringers of prosperity: gods of a full larder. The best-known Lares are the pairs of lively figures advancing on tip-toe and normally carrying a phiale and a rhyton; they were used in both household and public shrines, and have been identified as the Lares Compitales or Lares Augusti (Lares of the crossroads or of Augustus). Their cult was linked to that of the genius of the emperor by Augustus between 12 and 7 BC, and the dancing pose was remodeled at that time.

The Lar in this quiet pose has been identified as the Lar Familiaris (the household Lar). He generally offers a libation from a patera and carries a cornucopia; the missing arms of this statuette undoubtedly held the same attributes. Bieber has argued that the dangling, patterned sash of the Lar Familiaris is an irrational form

ROMAN,
EARLY IMPERIAL,
CA. IST QUARTER
IST C. AD.
H. 16.2 CM.
THE CLEVELAND
MUSEUM OF ART,
PURCHASE FROM THE
J. H. WADE FUND, 87.3

that originated in the Imperial period. It is likely that the entire figure type was created in Augustan times in connection with a general revision of the cult. This standing Lar, as has been noted by Alcock, is a composite of the dancing Lar and the Imperial Genius; he wears the short tunic and the sash of the dancing Lar, and like the Genius of the Emperor, he carries the cornucopia and pours a libation. Perhaps this hybrid standing figure has the best claim to being the Lar Augusti.

This statuette is an outstanding representative of its standardized type, of which very few examples come from closely datable contexts. A poor quality, stylized standing Lar was found in Herculaneum, while a beautifully crafted one was recovered in the hoard at Weissenburg (Figure XVIII). In spite of the great similarities between the Cleveland and Weissenburg figures, the differences of interpretation are significant. The general effect of the Weissenburg Lar is more robustly

Classical and more emphatic in tone. He takes a more vigorous, Polyclitan stride (with a reversal of the supporting leg) and has broader shoulders and a wider skull. The Cleveland piece, on the other hand, excels in delicacy and refinement. Its anatomy and drapery are unmatched in elaboration. Subtle secondary folds animate the fabric where it is blown against the legs and in the dangling end of the mantle. The liners of the boots, the toes, and the tendons in the legs are beautifully rendered. In comparison, the modeling of the boots in the Weissenburg Lar is stiff and harsh.

One detail seems particularly relevant for the chronology of this figure. On top of the head, each curl stands out in relief and is carefully striated. In a few cases, their curling tips seem formed with a drill-like twist of a stick in the wax model. The treatment of the hair is a miniature version of what is seen on large-scale heads—both portraits and ideal sculptures—in Augustan or Tiberian times. A head of Augustus in the Vatican Library and a late Augustan or Tiberian portrait statue of a boy in the Metropolitan Museum offer good parallels. The bronze head of the Diadumenus in Oxford, which has been given a similar date, is even closer. The modeling of the legs and feet of the Lar is very similar to that of the Hercules that has traveled with it through the art market [61]; in all probability, the two were found together and stem from the same workshop.

CONDITION: A small hole (a casting flaw) in the back reveals that the body is hollow. The sculpture was cast in four sections: the torso, the two arms, and a section of drapery hanging from the waist in the front. The arms were inserted into holes in the drapery. How these sections may have been attached is not obvious, but they may have been soldered on. Inlays of copper probably form the stripes of the tunic. Recessed areas are seen on both boots which may also have been for inlays. The eyes are inlaid with gray to black metal which may be silver. The irises are drilled.

The patina is a light, matte green. The sculpture is covered with malachite and cuprite corrosion products. Several small areas of bronze disease are also seen. Both arms below the elbows are now missing. The drapery hanging from the waist on the front and the bottom end of the drapery in front have been broken off and reglued recently. A small fill of a green plastic material has been made to the back of the drapery on the left side.

PROVENANCE: Purchased together and conceivably found with [61].

EXHIBITED: The Cleveland Museum of Art, February 24-April 17, 1988, *The Year in Review*, 65, illus., 46, no. 7.

PUBLISHED: Artemis S.A., *Annual Report*, II (Luxembourg, 1985-1986) (as late 1st or early 2nd century AD).

NOTES: I have drawn on a report by Bruce Christman in describing the physical condition of this bronze.

For other comparable Lares, see H. Menzel, *Die römischen Bronzen aus Deutschland*, I: *Speyer* (Mainz, 1960) no. 16; A. Leibundgut, *Die römischen Bronzen der Schweiz*, II (Mainz, 1976) no. 15.

For the association of the dancing Lares with the cult of the Genius of Augustus, see I. Ryberg, "Rites of the State Religion in Roman Art," *Memoirs of the American Academy in Rome* XXII (1955) 55-63, figs. 28b, 37c.

On the dangling sash of the standing Lar, see M. Bieber 1977, 79-80, fig. 312.

For the Pompeian standing Lar, see *Pompeii A.D. 79* (1978) no. 213.

For the composite origins of the standing Lar, see J. Alcock, "The Concept of Genius in Roman Britain," in M. Henig and A. King, eds., *Pagan Gods and Shrines of the Roman Empire*, Oxford University Committee for Archaeology, monograph VIII (Oxford, 1986) 127.

For the Weissenburg Lar, see H.-J. Kellner and G. Zahlhaas 1984, no. 25.

For the head of Augustus in the Vatican, see K. Kluge and K. Lehmann-Hartleben, *Die antiken Grossbronzen*, III: *Grossbronzen der römischen Kaiserzeit* (Berlin, 1927) pl. 3.

For the statue in the Metropolitan, see G. M. A. Richter 1915, no. 333; L. Curtius, "Ikonographische Beiträge VIII," *RM* L (1935) 298, fig. 22.

For the Oxford Diadumenus, see P. Zanker 1974, 15, no. 13, pls. 12, 2; 13, 2,4.

63. Relief with Two Togate Magistrates

A wrinkled older man with flowing locks of hair partly covering a balding forehead stands holding a scroll in his left hand. He is seconded by a younger man placed deferentially behind his right shoulder. The younger man's hair is short, and his hairline is deeply indented at the temples. They glance back at some action, almost certainly an official ceremony, going on to their right. Both wear the proper costume for a patrician at a public function: a toga draped generously over a short-sleeved tunic. The older man holds the overfold (sinus) of his toga in his right hand. More material is tucked in at the waist to form a loop (the umbo). The younger man's right arm and part of the sinus of his toga are missing. Their shoes (calcei) are fastened by broad straps of material that are wrapped around the ankles.

The magistrates probably belonged to a frieze of considerable extent. Not only do they seem to be gazing to their right, but a break along the older man's left side

ROMAN, LATER JULIO-CLAUDIAN, PROBABLY REIGN OF CLAUDIUS OR NERO (AD 40-68). 26 X 13.8 CM. J. PAUL GETTY MUSEUM, 85.AB.109

also suggests that figures continued on that side as well. Analogies with marble Julio-Claudian reliefs like the so-called "Ara Pietatis" make it probable that the older man is a priest, and his scroll could contain ritual formulas to pronounce at the ceremony. The main scene of the relief probably was the sacrifice of a bull or a libation at an altar, or both. Some comparable bronze reliefs certainly showed such sacrifices. The most informative are two reliefs found near Lausanne, one depicting a togatus who holds a pitcher and leads a bull and the other a sacrificial attendant (camillus). Reliefs in Paris represent a flute-playing togatus and a victimarius. Lictors, like those known from several other bronze reliefs, could have completed the scene with the Getty magistrates.

Few bronze ceremonial reliefs have been found in a context that helps to reconstruct their original setting. A Minerva in Lausanne from the ruins of a Roman villa suggests that such friezes could have been attached to a piece of furniture for religious or decorative purposes. Figural appliqués with griffins and a cantharus were found in a temple precinct at Augst, indicating that this kind of decoration might have been employed in the furnishings of public buildings. Menzel attributed a relief togatus in Bonn to the frieze of a temple. Bol thinks that a togatus from Rome, now in Frankfurt, could have been attached to a bronze chest, perhaps for incense. Vermeule has suggested that the Getty magistrates could have embellished a funerary wagon. A chariot is another possibility. A monumental sculptural group of a four-horse, relief-decorated chariot together with driver from Herculaneum offers a good parallel; the embellishments of the Herculaneum chariot included high relief figures of both divinities and Roman officials, as does the group of magistrates and goddesses [64, 65] in the Getty.

The magistrates' heads are highly individualized. The older man, as Vermeule has pointed out, has much in common with portraits of Cicero. There are enough differences in detail, however, to make a definite identification impossible. Rather than the portraits of specific persons, the heads in the bronze relief are probably generic characterizations. The older man with his broad brow, furrowed cheeks, and lanky, flowing hair stands in a tradition of aging intellectuals that goes back to the early Hellenistic image of the Athenian playwright Menander. The tradition was continued in marble state reliefs of the Julio-Claudian period, like the Ara Pietatis, where the long-haired, wrinkled older figure is frequently juxtaposed with a youthful companion (Figure XXVIII). A date for the bronze in the later Julio-Claudian period is indicated by the costumes; the older man's toga has a sinus that is much fuller than in earlier times, falling below his knee. One of the early datable occurrences of this fashion is the monumental bronze statue of Lucius Mammius Maximus from the theater at Herculaneum, probably from just after the middle of the first century. The toga of the younger man in the relief is still draped in the older fashion; the sinus is well above the knee.

A detail of the older man's hairstyle suggests the same chronological range for the work; his hair is brushed so far forward on his neck that it can be paralleled only in the portraits of Caligula, Claudius, Nero (Figure 63a), and their contemporaries. The treatment of his flowing, sickle-shaped locks that are split by incised striations is extremely similar to what is seen in a small bronze bust of Caligula in Zurich (Figure XXII). There too, hair is brushed far forward onto the neck. The staccato pattern of chips and scratches used to render the hair of the younger man, as well as the hairline indented at the temples, strongly recalls the miniature bronze bust of an imperator in Madrid, dated by Jucker to the second quarter of the first century. The modeling of the figures is broad and fluid, while the drapery is drawn in sharp, summary diagonals. The style is confident, mature, and almost informal.

It stands far from official classicism and has the fluent surface play of early Flavian works in marble like the altar of Vespasian at Pompeii.

Figure 63a. *Emperor Nero.* Obverse of a gold aureus, minted AD 64-68. Boston, Museum of Fine Arts, 1973.640.

CONDITION: The two figures were probably cast in one piece, heads pointing downward since the cast becomes more porous toward the feet and there is evidence of a riser (or vent) on the right hand of the left figure. The right arm and toga sleeve of the left figure have clearly been cast on; this area has corroded somewhat differently and in places is separated from the main body of the figures by as much as three to four millimeters.

The pupils of the eyes are drilled. Hair is defined with fine chiseling. Backs are open, but the head of the older man is fully in the round. Thickness of the wall varies from 17 millimeters in the body of the older man to 5 millimeters in the head of the younger. There is a casting flaw in the chest of the younger. The left side of the older man's drapery is incomplete or damaged, possibly from another adjoining figure at this point. There are four diamond-shaped marks on the back surface, almost in the center. These marks were made in the wax, perhaps to serve as a sort of register or numbering system.

The smooth areas of surface range in color between green, yellow-green, and brown. The patina is predominately iron-stained carbonates with some isolated dense patches of azurite and tin oxide in the intergranular corrosion areas.

This suggests a burial condition which was mixed and continuously or repeatedly wet.

PROVENANCE: Traveled through the art market and conceivably found with [64-66]. The similar patinas support the association.

PUBLISHED: C. C. Vermeule, *Catalogue of a Collection of Greek, Etruscan and Roman Antiquities* (Cambridge, Mass., privately printed, 1984) no. 21.
GettyMusJ XIV (1986) 185, no. 15.

NOTES: The condition statement for this bronze is adapted from a conservation report by Jerry Podany.

For the bronze reliefs from Lausanne, see A. Leibundgut 1976-, III: nos. 103-105.

For the attendants in Paris, see E. Babelon and J.-A. Blanchet 1895, nos. 880, 886.

For lictors, see S. Boucher, *Bronzes romains figurés du Musée des Beaux-arts de Lyon* (Lyon, 1973) nos. 207-208; E. Babelon and J.-A. Blanchet 1895, no. 889; K. Vierneisel, 1978, 56-57, fig. 45; Sale: *Catalogue of Antiquities*, London, Sotheby's, December 12-13, 1983, no. 297a (now British Museum).

For the reliefs with griffins from a temple in Augst, see A. Kaufmann-Heinimann 1976-, I: no. 177.

For the bronze chariot group from Herculaneum, see E. Gabrici (*BdA*) 1907, 179-190.

For a survey of Roman historical reliefs, see I. S. Ryberg, "The Rites of the State Religion in Roman Art," *MAAR* XXII (1955) 65-75, figs. 34-36.

For the Ara Pietatis, see A. Bonanno, *Portraits and Other Heads on Roman Historical Relief up to the Age of Septimius Severus*, BAR Supplementary Series VI (1976) 31-41, pls. 81-88; G. M. Koeppel, "Die historischen Reliefs der römischen Kaiserzeit I: Stadtrömische Denkmäler unbekannter Bauzugehörigkeit aus augusteischer und julisch-claudischer Zeit," *Bonner Jahrbücher* CLXXXIII (1983) 98-116, nos. 12-23, figs. 13-28; F. Albertson, "An Augustan Temple Represented on an Historical Relief Dating to the Time of Claudius," *AJA* XCI (1987) 440-458.

On Mammius Maximus, see *Pompeii A.D. 79* (1978) no. 38.

For Menander, see R. R. R. Smith 1984, 160-163, figs. 121-126.

For Cicero, see J. M. C. Toynbee, *Roman Historical Portraits* (Ithaca, N. Y., 1978) 28-30, illus. 22, 23.

For the bronze busts of Caligula in Copenhagen and an imperator in Madrid, see H. Jucker 1961, 48-49, 53-54, nos. B1, B4, pls. 12, 14.

For numismatic portraits from Caligula through Nero, see J. Kent et al., *Roman Coins* (London, 1978) pls. 48-57.

For the togati in Bonn and Frankfurt, see P. C. Bol and T. Weber, *Liebighaus Museum Alter Plastik, Antike Bildwerke*, II (Messingen, 1985) 136, no. 64; H. Menzel, *Rheinisches Landesmuseum Bonn. Römischen Bronzen* (1969) 62, no. 42.

For other bronze relief togati, see O. Picard and C. Rolley, *Collection Hélène Stathatos*, IV (Athens, 1971) 34-37, St. 701, pl. 8; H. Menzel, *Die römischen Bronzen aus Deutschland*, III: *Bonn* (Mainz, 1986) no. 118; E. Babelon and J.-A. Blanchet 1895, no. 876; G. Hafner, *Die Bronzen der Sammlung Dr. Heinrich Scheufelen in Oberlenningen* (Mainz, 1958) no. 343. Another is in the Indiana University Art Museum (63.103.61). A pair of togati like the Getty piece is in Munich.

64. Roma (Chariot Attachment?)

Roma wears the Amazonian short tunic unfastened on the right shoulder to permit her arm to move freely. She is distinguished from the Amazons by her helmet, which is of the Attic type with a visor topped by a knob and a short, simple crest. Short curls of hair blow back at Roma's temples and behind her ears, while a flat, tapering mass of hair descends down her neck and is fastened with a clasp on her shoulders. The soles of her sandals are indicated, but the straps are not.

Roma was shown standing in this costume on coinage from the time of Galba (AD 69) onward (Figure 64a), and the numismatic parallels suggest that she supported a spear with point downward in her left hand and carried a small figure of Victory in her right. The bronze statuette and the coins were probably inspired by a major statue of Roma. Such a statue could well have been pre-Imperial. Geographic personifications like the seated Aetolia had been shown as Amazons wearing short skirts ever since the third century BC (Figure 68a). A marble statuette of a seated Amazonian Roma in the Vatican might well be based on a Republican archetype. On coinage, Roma is more ornately presented than in the Getty statuette; she wears a cloak and high boots, and the crest of her helmet is much more elevated. Plain as she is, the figure is highly Classical in inspiration. Although she takes a robust Polyclitan stride, her head seems to go back to Phidian models. The unadorned Attic helmet with minimal crest and the hair blowing back at the temples and clasped on the shoulders are based on the Athena Medici, best represented by the head from the Pnyx (the open-air assembly ground on the hill west of the Acropolis) in Athens. A helmet and an arrangement of curls around the ear almost identical to the Getty statuette appear in a head of Ares in the Louvre, whose original has also been ascribed to Phidias or his circle. Elements of

ROMAN, LATER
JULIO-CLAUDIAN,
AD 40-68.
H. 33.1 CM.
J. PAUL GETTY
MUSEUM, 84.AB.671

the composition are echoed in a classicistic work like the Athena Parthenos from Pergamum and in several marble heads that have been identified as Roma.

Close to this figure both iconographically and stylistically is the bronze statuette of an Amazon fighting on horseback from Herculaneum. Both are severely classicistic in conception, and anatomy and drapery are shown in firmly defined yet economical terms. The Herculaneum Amazon also has an unornamented helmet with minimal crest. For all her Classical spareness, however, she is still somewhat more ornate than the Getty Roma. Her sandals still have straps and her tunic is more richly folded. The slightly broader, barer, and somewhat heavier treatment of the Roma appears, as pointed out privately by Martin Robertson, in a similarly classicistic figure of a wounded warrior in the Musée Saint Germain-en-Laye. All three figures might well have been produced by the same atelier or by associated ateliers over a span of a few decades in the early Empire. A small bust of a lady from Herculaneum (see Figure XXI) is a chronologically relevant comparison for some details of Roma's technique, like her crisply incised locks and her indented curls.

The Getty statuette could well have come from a chariot. Similar high relief figures of divinities were also used to ornament the chariot of the monumental sculptural group from Herculaneum. The style of the "relief statuettes" from the Herculaneum chariot is also somewhat similar to that of the Roma, but their drapery is more elaborate, and their volumes are less firmly controlled.

Figure 64a. *Roma.* Reverse of bronze sestertius, minted under Vespasian, AD 69-79. Boston, Museum of Fine Arts, 60.1434.

CONDITION: The torso and head were hollow cast in one piece with the left arm and a small part of the left leg just above the knee. The right arm was attached by casting on or solder. The legs and feet were then cast on. This procedure might have been carried out as follows. A wax sheet applied to the underside of the garment sealed the opening into the figure. Wax "pillars" were attached, one directly to the wax sheet and the other to the bronze nub making up part of the left leg above the knee. Precast bronze legs and feet were affixed to the wax pillars and all was cast on in place. The texture of the outer surface, the various tool marks, and variations in surface corrosion and porosity observed in the x-radiographs of these areas support this general method of manufacture. In addition, there is a large flow of bronze on the interior right side of the figure (which flowed toward the head before it solidified) which must have been caused by casting on the feet and sheet section mentioned above.

A metallurgical cross section indicates the bronze has been well annealed, consistent with a cast-on technique. The large rectangular hole in the back may have been used to remove core material after casting and/or for mounting the bronze with a pin or shaft in ancient times. What seems to be lead is smeared around the opening. The thickness of the wall varies from four to eight millimeters in back. Filling material, probably lead, visible on the right interior, gives the object substantial weight.

335

The irises of the eyes are lightly indented. The hair is beautifully incised, and centers of the curls are marked with circular indentations. There are two rectangular patches on the back of the right upper arm. Work is rough and irregular at the backs of the knees. The right hand is missing two fingers, and there may be an ancient repair in one. The left hand seems to be missing the tips of two fingers, but in fact these were never completely finished or modeled. What may be solder appears on the underside of the right foot.

The surface is a smooth olive green, becoming brown or red-brown in many areas. There is a striking similarity to that of the other figures said to come from the find. The patina is predominantly malachite with iron staining. The form of the malachite ranges from smooth and compact to mammillary and botryoidal. There are isolated patches of tin oxide corrosion in an intergranular form. Thin compact areas of azurite are present in isolated areas. Pseudomorphs are present on some areas such as the left elbow, revealing contact of the bronze with plant material. The patina suggests the burial conditions were fairly consistent and the immediate material in contact with the bronze surface was fairly homogeneous and protective of the bronze.

PROVENANCE: Traveled through the art market and conceivably found with [63, 65, 66].

PUBLISHED: *GettyMusJ* XIII (1985) 166, no. 11.

NOTES: The condition statement for this bronze is adapted from a report by Jerry Podany.

For Roma in this pose on the coins of Galba, see H. Mattingly, *Coins of the Roman Empire in the British Museum,* 6 vols. in 8 (London, 1923-) I: pl. 56, 3; C. C. Vermeule, *The Goddess Roma in the Art of the Roman Empire* (Cambridge, Mass., 1959, 1974) pl. 5, nos. 20-22.

For the seated marble Roma in the Vatican, see below under the Levy Penthesilea [68].

For the Athena from the Pnyx, see B. Theophanidos, "I Athina tis Pnikos," *ArchDelt* XIII (1930-1931) 171-176, figs. 1-3; G. Becatti 1951, 175-184; F. Canciani, in *LIMC* II: "Athena/Minerva," 1085, no. 144c, pl. 796.

For a very similar head from Salonika, see S. Pelekidi, *ArchDelt* IX (1924-25) 121-124, figs. 1-2.

For the Phidian Ares in the Louvre, see S. Reinach, *Recueil de têtes antiques* (Paris, 1903) 67, pls. 81-82.

For the Athena Parthenos from Pergamum, see J.-P. Niemeier, *Kopien und Nachahmungen im Hellenismus: ein Beitrag zum Klassizismus des 2. und frühen 1. Jhs. v. Chr.* (Bonn, 1985) 20, 24, 26-27, figs. 1-2.

For Roma in marble, see the list in C. C. Vermeule 1959, 104-105. See especially a head restored as Roma in Toronto and heads in the Vatican and Spain; C. C. Vermeule, *Greek and Roman Sculpture in America* (Malibu, Calif., 1981) no. 186 (Toronto); G. Kaschnitz-Weinberg, *Sculture del magazzino del Museo Vaticano* (Vatican City, 1937) 148, no. 313, pl. 30; P. Arndt, *Photographische Einzelaufnahmen antiker Skulpturen* (Munich, 1893-1940) no. 1848 f. (San Lúcar de Barrameda).

For the bronze Amazon from Herculaneum, see V. Spinazzola, *Le arti decorative in Pompei e nel Museo Nazionale di Napoli* (Milan, 1928) 245.

For the bronze chariot group from Herculaneum, see E. Gabrici (*BdA*) 1907, 179-190.

For the warrior in the Musée Saint Germain-en-Laye, see G. M. A. Richter, *The Sculpture and Sculptors of the Greeks,* 4th ed. (New Haven, 1970) 43, 180, fig. 135; J. Boardman 1985, fig. 238.

65. A Goddess, Perhaps Venus

The figure is clad in a long tunic fastened with six buttons down the right upper arm but unbuttoned down the left. Over this is wrapped a palla with a heavy roll at the waist and a hanging, apronlike flap. One end of the palla is draped loosely over the left arm, and its lower left corner is pulled taut by two weights. The soles but not the straps of the sandals are shown. The divinity wears a crescent-shaped diadem and her partially unbuttoned garment and discreetly bared shoulder allude to her irresistible female charms. In her left hand she held a staff, which projected obliquely forward. In her open right, whose fingers are missing, she offered a libation from a patera. Her hair is parted centrally, pulled back into a roll at the sides, and folded into a loose bun at the back. Locks may have escaped beside the fold.

The pose and drapery are inspired quite directly from High Classical Attic statuary of the span 430-410 BC. The Kore Albani, one of the Grimani statuettes,

ROMAN, LATER JULIO-CLAUDIAN, AD 40-68.
H. 32 CM.
J. PAUL GETTY MUSEUM, 84.AB.670

and the so-called Hera Borghese, all provide ingredients of the final version. Most of the compositional elements of our figure were brought together in a statue on the Roman art market in the mid-nineteenth century, which may have copied a Classical original. A heavily restored marble statuette in Villa Doria Pamphili is another near replica of this figure, and in addition it presents a chiton unfastened on the shoulder, a detail that was missing in the work on the market. A fourth-century Greek relief found in Italy and preserved in the Museo Baracco, Rome, depicts a similarly clad female, again with a bare shoulder, but the Baracco figure has a more generously draped mantle.

The Getty bronze statuette has a blunt simplicity and a frontality not encountered in major Greek masterpieces. Yet these qualities are to a degree found in some minor Classical statues and statuettes, like the youth from Rhamnus of 420-410 BC, who has much the same draping of the mantle, and even has a similar broad face, narrow mouth, and puffy roll of hair.

Although the strongly Greek background leading to such a figure is clear, it is also equally evident how the Roman artist has simplified and rationalized his statuette beyond even the most understated of minor Classical works. Fluttering borders of drapery have been eliminated, and each basic unit has been turned into a well-characterized volume. Drapery folds and hair patterns are continuous and symmetrical. The diadem is large and conspicuous. The intention must have been to render the figure more forceful, compact, and easily intelligible.

The meaning that this modest divinity had in her Roman setting is not entirely clear. Numismatic evidence raises the possibility that she was a personification rather than one of the Olympian goddesses. The closest parallels for the pose and the costume (tunic and palla, diadem, outstretched patera and scepter held with elbow close to the body) are provided by the figures of Clementia Augusta (Figure 65a), popular on the coinage of Hadrian, or Salus (Figure 65b), who was common throughout the middle of the second century. Many other numismatic personifications carried a different attribute in their right hands but are otherwise identical (Aeternitas, Pax, Felicitas, Libertas, Aequitas, Laetitia Publica). Clemency, an attribute of victors and emperors, would have been particularly appropriate in company with Roma [64] and mounted on a chariot or some other conveyance for display, as this figure probably was. Salus (Hygeia) has a mythological association with Roma; in Pergamene tradition, the two were sisters and were worshipped together.

The possibility that the figure is an Olympian goddess cannot, however, be discarded. Juno appears in the same scheme on coins of Faustina the Elder, where the goddess, as usual, has a modestly veiled head. On coins of Faustina the Younger, Venus also appears in the costume and pose of this statuette, but she holds a globe or apple. Strong support for an identification as Venus comes from the unbuttoned sleeve; although the detail is not found in any numismatic parallel, it had been characteristic of the goddess of love ever since the Parthenon. Venus' attribute, however, is rarely the banal patera, which must have been held here.

Although this pose and costume are popular in coinage of around AD 120-150, it seems likely that the statuette is substantially earlier. It was probably found with the bronze relief of magistrates [63], which can be confidently dated in the middle of the first century AD. Larger in scale and in higher relief than the magistrates, the goddess could have come from a separate composition, yet the modeling of the drapery is so similar that it seems likely that both were produced in the same workshop. The calm balance of drapery patterns here, however, contrasts with the

Figure 65a. *Salus.* Reverse of bronze sestertius, minted under Antoninus Pius, AD 140-143. Boston, Museum of Fine Arts, 60.145.

Figure 65b. *Clementia.* Reverse of bronze as, minted under Hadrian, AD 119-138. Private collection.

sweep and angularity in the magistrates' togas, and two different, albeit closely associated artisans were probably involved.

Like the magistrates with which it was presumably found, the figure may well have been attached to a chariot. Similar high relief figures of divinities were also used to ornament the chariot of the monumental sculptural group from Herculaneum.

CONDITION: The body was hollow, direct cast; x-radiographs indicate the head was cast with the torso. Corrosion currently makes it impossible to determine whether the solid-cast arms and the draped area of the garment that hangs free from the left side of the figure and over the left arm were added by casting-on or by soldering. What remains of an attached object in the left hand appears to be iron oxide. A pin still in the right hand supported the now-missing object it once held. A large rectangular hole in the back may have been used to remove the core and/or to secure the bronze with a wood or metal pin (shaft) in ancient times. The back of the figure is incomplete and flattened; it was evidently meant to be placed against a back-

ground. There are numerous chaplet repairs over the surface of the figure. An ancient residue in the right eye is either an amber inlay, a resin inlay, or the residue of a resin adhesive used to adhere the now lost inlay in place. The irises of the eyes are lightly indented, and the waves of hair are finely chiseled.

The smooth areas of the surface range from green through greenish-brown to red-brown patina. Large areas of thick green, blue-green, and red-brown corrosion products overlie the surface. The patina is predominantly carbonates (malachite, with isolated dense patches of azurite) which vary in form from smooth and dense to highly voluminous and botryoidal or mammillary. Iron staining of the carbonates is common and is especially predominant in the lower half of the front and upper half of the back. Isolated patches of tin oxide are present in areas where intergranular corrosion can be seen without magnification. Isolated areas of mammillary-form grains over much of the surface are especially obvious on the back. These large grain forms may be representative of the high degree of reheating of the bronze in the process of casting-on the added parts, allowing massive growth of the alloy grains. The patina suggests a continually or repeatedly wet burial condition. The surrounding matrix of the burial material was highly heterogeneous since some of the bronze surface has been well protected and preserved while other areas have been aggressively corroded.

PROVENANCE: Traveled through the art market and conceivably found with [63, 64, 66].

PUBLISHED: *GettyMusJ* XIII (1985) 166, no. 10.

NOTES: The condition statement for this bronze draws on a report by Jerry Podany.

On Classical statues with a triangular himation overfold, see S. Karusu, *AM* LXXXII (1967) 158-169, Beilagen 85-89; B. S. Ridgway 1981, 176-177, 194-198, figs. 115, 125; R. Kabus-Jahn, "Die Grimanische Figurengruppe in Venedig," *AntP* XI (1972) 1-20, figs. 1-9; 81-85, figs. 1-4, pls. 1-9, 49-51; J. Boardman 1985, 214, figs. 143, 196, 202, 210, 214.

For Roman copies and variants of the type, see M. Bieber 1977, 121-122, figs. 543-553. On the so-called "Hera Borghese" now the "Aphrodite Borghese," see P. Zancani Montuoro, *Bollettino della Commissione Archeologica Comunale di Roma* LXI (1933) 25-58; C. von Hees-Landwehr, *Griechische Meisterwerke in römischen Abgüssen: Der Fund von Baia*, exh. cat. (Frankfurt, 1982) 36-37.

On the Baracco relief, see H. Süsserott, *Griechische Plastik des 4. Jahrhunderts vor Christus* (Frankfurt, 1938; reprint, Rome, 1968) pl. 21, 5.

On the statue on the Roman market, see C. Clarac, *Musée de sculpture antique et moderne*, 12 vols. (Paris, 1826-1853) III:5, 86-87, pl. 419, no. 736; S. Reinach, *Rép.stat.* I: pl. 201, 4.

For the statuette in the Villa Doria, see B. Palma in R. Calza et al., *Antichità di Villa Doria Pamphilj* (Rome, 1977) no. 8, pl. 8.

For the youth from Rhamnus, see S. Karusu 1967, 160, Beilage 89; B. S. Ridgway 1981, 119, 127, fig. 93; J. Boardman 1985, 177, fig. 143.

For the bronze chariot group from Herculaneum, see E. Gabrici (*BdA*) 1907, 179-190.

For Clementia, see T. Hölscher in *LIMC* III: 295-299, pl. 230, 4,5.

For Junos of this type, see H. Mattingly 1923-, IV: pls. 10, 15; 36, 12.

For Venus, see H. Mattingly 1923-, IV: pl. 23, 13, 15.

For Aphrodite with a bare shoulder, see *LIMC* II: pls. 18-30, 32, 137, 138 (A. Delivorrias, G. Berger-Doer, and A. Kossatz-Deissmann).

On Salus and Roma, see C. Fayer, *Il culto della Dea Roma* (Pescara, 1977) 60-61.

66. Victory with a Cornucopia (Chariot Attachment?)

Victory flies with her peplos fluttering about her in undulating S-curves and deep concavities. The motion blows the garment back from her forward leg. She carries an elongated horn of plenty that sprouts an acanthus leaf at its middle and from which brim a cluster of grapes, apples, ears of grain, a pine cone, and an elongated pyramidal cake. In spite of her flight and her awkward burden, which she supports with her left hand and steadies with her right, the goddess carries herself with erect dignity. On the outer faces of the wings, feathers are drawn with great turbulence and variety.

Victory alighting from flight had been one of the most popular themes of terracotta sculpture in Hellenistic Asia Minor; the charming Nikes found in graves around the coastal site of Myrina have draperies blowing about them in a multitude of variations that include most of the basic patterns seen here. The theme was rarer, but not unknown in Hellenistic Italy; a terracotta Victory very similar to this figure in pose and costume has been excavated in a tomb at Tarentum; the essential differences are that one breast is bared and the gown is fastened by a belt just below the breasts. The broken right arm is extended, as if to offer a wreath, while the left hand is empty. The spirit of the Hellenistic images is, however, quite different; all are sweeter and—to a degree at least—more sensuously physical. This early Imperial transformation of the theme is firmer, more dignified, and more majestic. A conscious revival of fifth-century sculpture plays a strong role in this change. The broad face and strong features with their sharply delineated contours, which seem based on Polyclitan models, contrast with the softer, smaller features, and the oblique glances of the Hellenistic figures. The drapery has taken on a new decorative intelligence. In place of the patterns that tend to fan outward in the Hellenistic terracottas, undulating lines of curvature pass smoothly down the Cleveland figure,

ROMAN, IMPERIAL, LATER JULIO-CLAUDIAN, AD 40-68. H. 42 CM. H. TO TOP OF CORNUCOPIA 36.7 CM. THE CLEVELAND MUSEUM OF ART, LEONARD C. HANNA, JR., FUND, 84.25

as the overfold of the peplos swings out to the right and is counterbalanced by the skirt at the left. Again, there is a Classical association; the swinging, unbelted overfold recalls figure G from the east pediment of the Parthenon.

The similar layout of the Tarentine terracotta may not be an unrelated coincidence; on his return to Rome in 28 BC after the battle of Actium, Augustus took a celebrated image of Victory from Tarentum and placed it in the Senate House in Rome. Both the terracotta and the Cleveland bronze are probably to some degree derived from that transported figure.

The cornucopia gives the Cleveland Victory a more mature Roman Imperial message; Nike is not just a goddess of military success or—as in the case of the Myrina funerary terracottas—bearer of the Dionysiac delights of paradise, she also brings peace and prosperity. This image first appeared on the coinage of Augustus and was linked to the end of the prolonged civil wars concluded at Actium.

Bronze statuettes of Victory with a cornucopia had a certain popularity in workshops of the mid- to late first century. In the examples from Pompeii and Avenches, however, right and left are reversed, and Nike has one bared breast, as in the terracotta from Tarentum and perhaps in the Victory in the Senate House. The Cleveland version did, however, gain a certain currency; it reappears again in triumphal reliefs from Carthage of about AD 160. These Western parallels, moreover, tend to confirm a report that the Cleveland figure has an Italian origin. The Cleveland piece is still relatively early in date; it is said to have been found with a group of bronzes that includes portrait statuettes datable to around the middle of the first century. The message of peace and prosperity embodied in a Victory with a horn of plenty would well suit the mood of Nero's reign, when the doors of the Temple of Janus were closed with great fanfare to symbolize the establishment of peace throughout the Empire.

The figure might originally have surmounted a globe. Like the pieces possibly

found with it, it may have formed part of the decoration of a wagon or chariot. If so, it would have stood at some point on the railing.

CONDITION: Originally, the missing left ankle and foot must have provided support for the figure, since there is no other trace of a mounting. The left arm, the right leg, and the wings were cast separately from the body, which is hollow. X-radiographs show the core is still present. The cornucopia was cast in one piece. The casting was refined by smoothing and polishing the metal. Details were sharpened with chasing tools.

In an ancient restoration, the wings were repositioned, being moved farther apart and lower; it has been suggested that they were entirely remade at this time. The roll of hair at the back of the head was chopped away to accommodate the wings in their new locations. The wings have now been reattached at their first position. A pit below the left wing is a casting flaw. Gray stains, similar to lead corrosion products, can be found on the back, possibly a residue from the lead-tin solder used to fasten the wings in antiquity. It is not evident how the arm, leg and cornucopia were originally attached to the figure. In recent times, the wings and cornucopia have been attached with modern glue and the left arm and right leg with pins.

Rust has been deposited on the surface, particularly on the fruits. Iron buried near the statuette plus a substantial component of tin in the metal itself may have been responsible for the coloring of the patina. The smooth surface patina ranges from light olive green to light brown with a few spots of bright green.

PROVENANCE: Traveled through the art market and conceivably found with [63-65].

EXHIBITED: The Cleveland Museum of Art, April 3-May 5, 1985, *The Year in Review*, 200, illus. 168, no. 7.

PUBLISHED: See exhibition above.

NOTES: The condition statement for this bronze incorporates a report by Bruce Christman.

For the terracottas of Myrina, see S. Mollard-Besques 1963, pls. 80-91.

For the Taranto terracotta, see T. Hölscher, *Victoria romana* (Mainz, 1967) 14, n. 65; E. De Juliis and D. Loiacono, *Taranto, il Museo Archeologico* (Taranto, 1985) fig. 467.

For Classical prototypes, see B. S. Ridgway 1981, figs. 23, 147; J. Boardman 1985, 102, fig. 80.2; 207.

On the Victory in the Senate and Victory with a cornucopia, see T. Hölscher 1967, 6-22, 109, 163, pls. 1, 6; 13, 4.

For bronze Victories, see A. Leibundgut 1976-, I: no. 30.

For the Carthage relief, see S. Reinach, *Rép. stat.* II:379, 4; G. Ch. Picard, *Karthago* I (Paris, 1950) 67 ff.; I. Tillessen, *Die Triumphalreliefs von Karthago* (Hamm, 1987) passim.

67. Barbarian (from a Relief)

A bearded man wears non-classical clothing: a stocking cap, whose top falls forward; a short, belted tunic; a shirt or under-tunic with long sleeves; trousers (anaxyrides or bracae); rather ill-defined shoes; and a cloak fastened on the right shoulder with a circular pin. His costume is generally that of a barbarian of either the North or the East. His bushy hair, which radiates up from his forehead and flows onto his neck, tends to suggest that he is a northerner—whether a Dacian or a German—and the absence of ear-flaps on his cap, which would characterize it as "Phrygian" or eastern, points in the same northern direction. His right hand, missing two fingers, is raised in salutation. His lowered left held the staff of a separately made object, perhaps a standard or a spear, which was inserted into a drilled opening.

The modeling is rich and delicate on this miniature scale. Drapery folds are loose and free, down to the rippled hems and cuffs of tunic and trousers. The tunic

ROMAN,
IST C. AD.
H. 8.5 CM.
THE CLEVELAND
MUSEUM OF ART,
PURCHASE FROM THE
J. H. WADE FUND,
87.64

344

even has a side vent. Best of all are his elongated face and beard: slight wrinkles furrow his brow, and his eyebrows seem knotted with anxiety. His nose is flattened and indented in a way that may be intended as an ethnic characterization; the effect is somewhat Slavic. His narrow mouth has arched lips framed by a long drooping mustache. A lump of material between his lips gives him a caricatural snaggletoothed expression.

The figure was evidently intended to be set against a background. Flattened zones appear on the back of the left shoulder and the left rear side of the cap. Another flattened area goes down the center of the back. The model for the figure seems to have been worked fully in the round and then cut down to fit into its setting. A circular hole for a mounting pin five millimeters in diameter enters the back in a diagonal direction. As both the cuttings and the hole indicate, the figure would

have been placed obliquely against the background. The barbarian would have looked toward another figure rather than out toward the viewer. The background might have curved out above his head.

The barbarian's gesture probably signifies submission to a Roman general or emperor. On the Column of Trajan, many figures advance with one hand forward and the other down to indicate surrender, allegiance, or a willingness to negotiate. In one scene, the right is fully raised, much as here. The problem arises from the object once held in the Cleveland figure's left hand. Normally, submissive barbarians come empty-handed. On the Column of Trajan, however, one surrendering Dacian carries a tray with objects on it, and in Augustan art, Parthians present the recovered standards of Crassus. These standards are, however, extended toward the victorious Roman rather than held in the proprietory way seen here.

A few bronze statuettes from reliefs show submissive barbarians, usually engaged in more theatrically desperate acts of surrender. Bushy-haired barbarians in combat with Romans are a well-known decoration for equine breastplates (baltei) of bronze equestrian monuments; the best-preserved piece is in Aosta in northernmost Italy. Fighting and dying barbarians disconnected from their backgrounds have been found in the forum of Herculaneum. The rarer figures of submissive barbarians may well also come from the baltei of bronze horses.

The fluid elongation of the Cleveland barbarian recalls late Antonine art, but an Augustan marble relief also has an elongated head of a barbarian. The elegance of detail in the Cleveland piece, which outdoes that of both the Pompeian and the Aostan barbarians, suggests a date in the first century.

CONDITION: The pupils of the eyes are drilled. The patina is a smooth dark green with areas of rough bright green. Small areas of red-brown appear on the front. There is coarse rusty brown encrustation in back. See also above.

PROVENANCE: Said to have been found near Taranto.

EXHIBITED: The Cleveland Museum of Art, February 24-April 17, 1988, *The Year in Review*, 65, no. 1.

PUBLISHED. See exhibition above.

NOTES: For the Column of Trajan, see S. Reinach, *Rép.stat.* I:338, 343, 346, 350, 356, 366, sects. 24, 40, 49, 60, 79, and esp. 109.

For Parthians returning standards, see A. C. Levi, *Barbarians on Roman Imperial Coins and Sculpture* (New York, 1952) pls. 1, 3; 2, 2.

For the balteus from Aosta, see B. Andreae 1977, pl. 83.

For the bronze barbarians from Herculaneum, see A. de Franciscis in *Pompeji: Leben und Kunst in den Vesuvstädten* (Essen, 1973) nos. 167-175; idem (Zurich, 1974) nos. 249-257.

For barbarians surrendering detached from bronze reliefs, see E. Babelon and J.-A. Blanchet 1895, nos. 911, 915.

For the Augustan relief with a barbarian, see G. M. Koeppel (*BonnJbb*) 1983, 88-89, no. 3.

68. The Amazon Queen Penthesilea Seated on a Rock

The woman is characterized as an Amazon by her chiton being fastened only on her left shoulder, leaving her right breast bare and her right arm free for fighting. In other respects she is also dressed for an active life; her high-belted chiton is itself rather short, and she wears firmly laced, high-topped, open-toed boots, which have cloth liners draped over the top. Her crescent-shaped diadem, which was set with five silver studs and is bent forward at the top, identifies her as Penthesilea, the Amazon Queen and Trojan ally. Her hair is swept back in a roll at the sides and looped into a bun behind. Her cloak is draped over her left shoulder and covers her back. Her upraised left hand probably held a spear and her right a sword.

The modeling of the figure is of great naturalism and elegance. The drapery folds flow like water across the forms of the body, breaking into a multitude of fine secondary wrinkles. The garments themselves seem to have weight and substance.

ROMAN, EARLIER IMPERIAL, PROBABLY CA. AD 50-80. H. 17 CM. SHELBY AND LEON LEVY

The hair is richly interwoven. Hands and feet are carefully detailed. The effect of the face, however, is marred by damage to the nose and lips.

The figure's composition goes back to an early Hellenistic prototype. Geographic personifications, like the Fortune (Tyche) of the newly founded city of Antioch, were shown as draped ladies seated in complicated positions on rocks as early as 300 BC. Aetolia in western Greece was personified in terms almost identical to this figure well before the middle of the third century BC. On third-century coins of the Aetolian League, Aetolia wears a short, slipped tunic, boots, and holds a spear and sword (Figure 68a). She is, however, seated on a pile of weapons and usually wears a Macedonian cap (kausia). The image goes back to a statue at Delphi erected shortly after 278 BC following the defeat of the Gallic invaders. The coinage of Nicomedes I of Bithynia (ca. 279-255 BC) has an almost identical figure, who has

Figure 68a. *Aetolia.* Reverse of silver tetradrachm, minted under the Aetolian League, ca. 279-168 BC. Boston, Museum of Fine Arts, 58.1180.

been identified as the Thracian goddess Bendis and who is seated on a rock and wears a Phrygian bonnet. The composition was later taken up for an image of Roma; in a marble statuette of Imperial date in the Vatican, the personification of the Imperial city is shown with a helmet, the position of the arms reversed, and a slightly varied mantle treatment.

Although the general composition of the Levy Amazon repeats that of its early Hellenistic (third century) prototypes quite exactly, details have been revised in late Hellenistic (second to first century) terms. The hairstyle is one seen on innumerable coins of the second century BC. The interwoven strands of hair pulled back from a central part can be found in the Apollo by Timarchides of 179 BC. The open-toed boots seem to be an Italic fashion taken up in the Aegean area only in

the later second century. The flowing wrinkles of the drapery recall nothing so much as the garments of Rhodian nymphs and Muses in Hellenistic rococo taste.

Although this figure fits well into late Hellenistic art typologically, its closest relatives from a technical point of view are from the Imperial period. The splendidly academic bronze statuettes found at Paramythia in Epirus and preserved in the British Museum offer highly similar treatment of detail. The chiton flowing in a myriad of fine wrinkles across breasts and belly is paralleled in the Dione from Paramythia. Penthesilea's interwoven hair reappears in Dione, in the sandalbinding Aphrodite, and in the Apollo from Paramythia. Since the Paramythia find includes a Lar of a well-known Imperial type, the group is certainly no earlier than the late first century BC. Comparisons for the Paramythia figures have ranged from the mid-first century AD (Avenches lararium) on into Hadrianic times.

A late Julio-Claudian date for the Levy Amazon might be argued on the basis of a general similarity to the bronze statuette of Mercury seated on a rock from Ottenhusen; the Mercury has a portrait head datable in Neronian times. Although the Mercury was cast by a less accomplished craftsman working in the western provinces, he has comparably complex drapery and slender proportions. The treatment of hair in the Amazon leads to much the same conclusion. The twisting undulations of the hair in front recall the modeling of hair in a small bronze bust of Domitian in Copenhagen (see Figure XXIII). The incised striations of the individual locks, however, still stand in the Julio-Claudian tradition and suggest a somewhat pre-Domitianic date.

CONDITION: The eyes are inlaid with silver. The crown has five circular hollows for inlays. One inlay, apparently silver, remains at the right. There is an inscribed circle at the right side of the crown that seems to continue the sequence of inlays. The lips are inlaid with copper, and the belt is copper wire, which was set into grooves in the belly. The arm and the drapery over the left shoulder are cast as a separate unit. The legs might be cast on. The detachable base is hollow below and is pierced by a (mounting?) hole 5-millimeters square placed diagonally in the upper surface. The flattened seat of the figure has a rectangular opening 1.7 by 1.3 centimeters oriented normally. A rectangular hollow in the back of the neck may be a once- plugged casting flaw.

The patina is greenish-black. The figure was placed on a square foil of bronze with bent-up corners. A bronze figure of Hercules in the Levy collection of comparable dimensions but different workmanship also stands on such a foil.

PROVENANCE: Perhaps from Syria or Lebanon.

UNPUBLISHED.

NOTES: For Aetolia, see J. M. C. Toynbee, *The Hadrianic School: A Chapter in the History of Greek Art* (Cambridge, 1934) 7, 52, pl. 9, 1; C. Arnold-Biucchi, in *LIMC* I: "Aitolia," 432-433, nos. 2-4, pl. 335.

For Bendis-Artemis on coins of Nicomedes, see J. M. C. Toynbee 1934, 52, pl. 11, 22; Z. Gočeva and D. Popov, in *LIMC* III: "Bendis," 96-97, no. 6, pl. 73.

For the Vatican Roma, see G. Lippold 1903-1956, III, 2, 179, pl. 85.

For the Apollo of Timarchides, see J. J. Pollitt 1986, 174, fig. 182; H. G. Martin, *Römische Tempelkultbilder: Eine archäologische Untersuchung zur späten Republik* (Rome, 1987) 60-86, figs. 11-13, pl. 2.

For boots of this type, see the discussion under the Getty Artemis [53].

For similar drapery on Hellenistic statues of Rhodian derivation, see A. Linfert, *Kunstzentren hellenistischer Zeit* (Wiesbaden, 1976) 89-91, figs. 192-199.

For the Paramythia bronzes, see J. Swaddling 1979, 103-105, pls. 49-57; A. Delivorrias, G. Berger-Doer, and A. Kossatz-Deissmann, in *LIMC* II: "Aphrodite," no. 184, 28-29, pl. 21 (ca. 100 BC).

For Mercury from Ottenhusen, see A. Leibundgut (*JdI*) 1984, 257-289.

On the treatment of hair in small-scale bronzes of late Julio-Claudian times, see A. Leibundgut (*JdI*) 1984, 269, figs. 12-15.

For the bust of Domitian, see H. Jucker 1961, no. B5, pl. 15.

69. Female Dancer

The dancer advances on tiptoe lightly in an upright, weightless pose, as if alighting from flight. Her peplos with belted overfold blows in the breeze. Her broad but shapely lower body is set off by the wavelike patterns of drapery beside her legs. Below the belt, the overfold fans out in an arbitrarily regular calyx of folds. With upraised arms she carries a pair of semi-cylindrical objects, as if both to display them and to clap them together as noisemakers. Her glance is given a smoldering intensity by the forward tilt of her head and the upward gaze of her deep-set eyes. A headband fastens her hair, which is pulled back in loose waves to a bun. A heavy lock swings forward onto her cheek, and strands of hair are pulled above the headband over her forehead. The dancer looks directly forward in the line of her advance, while her body axis is skewed at an angle; her right side is forward. The front is clearly the principal view, as the figure's back is only summarily finished.

ROMAN, LATE
FLAVIAN OR
EARLY TRAJANIC,
LATE 1ST C. AD.
H. 32.4 CM. H. OF
FIGURE 24.9 CM.
SHELBY AND
LEON LEVY

The noisemakers (if that is indeed what they are) are highly unusual and puzzling. They do not resemble the customary castanets at all. Ariel Herrmann has evoked a passage from the Roman historian and biographer Suetonius' *Lives of the Caesars* in which Nero was said to have organized groups to applaud in the Alexandrian style; one of the groups was called the "rooftiles" (imbrices): ('Nero,' XX,3). The translator suggests that clapping with cupped hands was intended. In this statuette, the idea seems applied literally; the dancer may be beating out a heavy rhythm with actual imbrices.

The sources for the figure lie in High Classical Greek art of the second half of the fifth century. The broad headband recalls Phidias' Athena Lemnia or a Polyclitan Hera. The figure type is clearly derived from Nikai descending to earth, like the Nike of Paionios at Olympia. The theme of an ecstatic dancer evokes the often-copied maenads or the Laconian dancers whose originals are usually ascribed to Callimachus (Figure XXVI). The symmetry of the figure along with the tiptoeing stance seems, in fact, to derive from and exaggerate the characteristics of the Laconian dancers in a decorative way typical of the Neo-Attic trend in Roman art.

Although many essentials of the composition can be found in a span of forty or fifty years in the fifth century, the piece is nonetheless eclectic. There is, apparently, no single prototype, nor is it likely that one existed; the relatively early and severe head type meshes strangely with the looser and freer body. The gesture seems more suited for a figure that supports another object (like a mirror) than for a dancer. The head has many eccentric and unclassical details; to some degree they may be the result of crossbreeding with works of later origin, but they also reflect the expressive and decorative intentions of the object's Roman maker. The parted lips are an evident Hellenistic borrowing. The strands of hair tucked up above the headband, on the other hand, recall the classicistic dancers from the Villa of the Papyri at Herculaneum (where waves of hair appear above the headbands at the sides). Here the tucked-up locks of hair suggest the bows of hair tied on the crown of the head in many Praxitelean and Hellenistic figures. The head has an especially close kinship with a marble head of Dionysus in Leiden. Again, hair is pulled up above a broad headband, this time in a mass of vertical strands. At the sides and rear, the treatment of the hair is almost identical in the two pieces. The lips of the Leiden Dionysus are again parted, and the face is full and fleshy, with a short chin and upper lip. The highly baroque marble sculpture in Leiden, which was purchased in Izmir, was formerly considered to be a Hellenistic original, but more recently it has been dated around AD 100. The Hellenistic component in the bronze dancer may be derived from such a work, and it may stem from the same Western Asiatic school.

The dancer stands out for its mixture of baroque softness and Neo-Attic axiality. It also has a solid physicality rarely found in Roman draped figures in motion. Fluttering drapery tends to overwhelm anatomy in dancing Lares, like those from Mainz or Pompeii, in the Hora from Avenches (ca. AD 50), and the Victory from Augst (ca. AD 200). The late Julio-Claudian Victory in Cleveland [66] likewise falls short of the substantial corporeality of this figure. The drapery patterns and the relationship of body to drapery of the Levy figure, on the other hand, find a good though not closely datable parallel in a Victory in Constantine (Algeria).

The treatment of surface in the Levy statuette strongly suggests a late Flavian or early Trajanic date. The hair is without the linearity so typical of Julio-Claudian figures. The fluid undulations where it swells out below the headband are comparable to what is seen in the miniature bronze bust of Domitian in Copenhagen

(Figure XXIII). The softly striated lobes of hair on the crown of the head strongly recall a miniature bronze portrait bust of a man in armor in Parma datable around AD 100 (Figure XXIV). The short, overhanging upper lip of the Levy figure also appears in these portrait busts.

CONDITION: The eyes are inlaid with silver, and the pupils are pierced. The lips, headband, and belt (in front only) are inlaid with copper. The figure is supported on a peg that projects 3.1 centimeters below the left foot. The patina is red-brown with large areas of bright green.

PROVENANCE: Perhaps from Syria or Lebanon.

UNPUBLISHED.

NOTES: Suetonius, *Lives of the Caesars*, tr. J. Rolfe (Loeb ed., Cambridge, Mass., 1970) XX, 3, pp. 116-117.

For the High Classical sources, see J. Boardman 1985, figs. 139, 183, 207, 242, 243.

For the Herculaneum dancers, see B. S. Ridgway 1970, 134, figs. 170-171; D. Pandermalis, *AM* LXXXVI (1971) 181-182, 192-193, pls. 85-89; W. Trillmich, "Zur Erforschung der römischen Idealplastik," *JdI* LXXXVIII (1973) 256-264.

For the Dionysus from Leiden, see S. Reinach, *Recueil de têtes antiques* (Paris, 1903) pls. 244-245; F. L. Bastet and H. Brunsting, *Corpus signorum classicorum, Musei Antiquarii Lugduno-Batavi* (Zutphen, 1982) 260, no. 380 (with bibliography).

For the dancing Lares, see M. Bieber 1977, 78-79, pl. 51.

For the Hora from Avenches, see A. Leibundgut 1976-, no. 32.

For the Victory from Augst, see A. Kaufmann-Heinimann 1976-, I: no. 75.

For the Victory from Constantine, see L. Leschi, *Algérie antique* (Paris, 1952) 77.

For the portrait busts of Domitian in Copenhagen and the armored man in Parma, see H. Jucker 1961, nos. B5, B6, pls. 15, 16; F. D'Andria 1970, 46-47, no. 22, pls. 14-15.

70. A Girl Begging (Coin Bank)

A chubby girl, perhaps four or five years old, is seated cross-legged on the ground. She stretches out her right hand, palm up, and pulls at the top of her belted tunic with her left. A slot, presumably for the insertion of coins, opens along the neckline. A braid of hair runs along the crown of her head to an unkempt knot at the upper rear. Curls twist out along her face and around her neck. Three more curls are incised on her forehead and another curves onto each cheek. Her tunic is embellished with colored stripes and incised ornament. The stripes run down from the shoulders to the belt in front and down to the ground behind. The neckline has an incised, striated hem and zigzag ornament, presumably imitating embroidery. She apparently wears an under-tunic, since a second strap can be seen on her left shoulder.

ROMAN,
JULIO-CLAUDIAN,
CA. AD 25-50.
H. 12.2 CM.
J. PAUL GETTY
MUSEUM, 72.AB.99

Figures of children seated on the ground and reaching out with lively gestures are a tradition stemming from early Hellenistic times. A marble baby from Ephesus, now in Vienna, with one hand on a fox goose and the other reaching forward presents an assemblage of frontal thrusts quite comparable to the Getty bronze. The Ephesus statue is a Roman work thought to copy a lost sculpture of the last quarter of the third century BC. Compositions in this vein may have continued to be invented into Roman times; an example might be a bronze girl holding a puppy in New York, which has an even closer relationship to the Getty piece. The Getty bronze, however, is in some sense a replica; a magnificent headless statue of Hellenistic date found in Bône (Hippo) in Algeria (see Figure XXV) presents the same action—a girl seated on the ground again reaches out with her right hand and this time also tugs at her neckline with her left. The position of the feet is slightly varied, but the two probably stem somehow from a common source.

The complicated, tangled hairdo of the Getty statuette is also common in early Hellenistic representations of children and Erotes. This rather disorderly version of the hairstyle has a particularly close parallel in a marble statue in the Capitoline Museum at Rome showing a girl protecting a dove from another pet. The Capitoline statue is usually thought to derive from an archetype of around 230 BC, but its hair and face seem somewhat remodeled in Julio-Claudian taste. The Getty statuette has locks that project out in a spiky composition that is extremely open and baroque. A statue of the late third century BC probably lies behind it.

Any Greek sources, however, have been strongly Romanized. The high-belted tunic of thin, crinkly material of the Algerian bronze has been changed to a low-belted embroidered tunic that falls in broad, simple folds in the Getty statuette. The stripes and pattern-work seem to have no Hellenistic parallels. Borders of tri-

angles inlaid with copper, on the other hand, appear on the garment of one of the "dancers" from Herculaneum. The features of this little rich girl have been coarsened, perhaps to characterize her as greedy; her nose is short and broad, and her lips heavy. The hair is stylized into a very neatly incised plain surface and wild, knoblike curls. A similar treatment appears in a statuette of a baby in Autun, dated because of its excellent quality to the "first century of the Empire." The modeling of the Getty statuette is simplified but bold and broad. At first glance, this departure from classical naturalism suggests a middle Imperial date. Yet, the disciplined linear finishing of the hair has the dryness of earlier Julio-Claudian times. A small bronze bust, in New York, of a matron from the time of Claudius has a very similar harsh, linear stylization. The aggressively projecting corkscrew curls of the Getty girl may have been inspired by Neo-Attic stylizations, as seen in the curls of a Medusa mask on a door handle from Pompeii.

The significance of the gesture is unclear. Cornelius Vermeule has suggested that she is exposing boils on her chest (a plea for pity and alms?). Ariel Herrmann has pointed out that children can keep playthings, like knucklebones, in the fronts of their tunics, and whatever this girl extorts may be similarly stowed there. The embroidered tunic, well-fed physique, and elaborate hairstyle suggest prosperity; the action apparently lies in a playful realm. If she is begging, it is probably out of greed rather than need. She may simply be reaching for an apple, as in a votive statue in the sanctuary of Asclepius at Cos described by Herondas, a third-century BC writer; the vivid rendering of the child's eagerness for the trivial prize excited the admiration of the onlookers.

CONDITION: The bronze was an indirect cast (cast from a wax positive which was itself cast in a mold). It was done in two steps using both a pour of molten wax for the upper torso and a thin sheet for the lower torso. The drip marks found on the interior surface point to an indirect method. No major parts have been added, but a vertical rounded bronze plate approximately 40 millimeters at the widest point and approximately 0.7 millimeters in thickness is attached below the head on the interior using molten lead. X-radiographs show that the lead has filled the figure's head cavity. The plate is most probably modern since the highly uniform thickness is unknown in ancient bronze sheet or plate.

Six copper inlay strips approximately two to two and a half millimeters in width create two strips front and back on the right and left side of the garment. These appear to have been hammered into the pre-cast grooves in the body, which seem to have been cut in the wax. The copper strip inlays may have been acid cleaned.

The hair and the hem of the tunic are finished with regular parallel incisions. The toes and fingers are separated with simple strokes of the chisel. The slot in her chest is 32 by 7 millimeters—barely large enough to admit a second-century sestertius—but sufficient for smaller pieces. The statuette is open underneath. At the back of the base is a protrusion of 4 by 13 millimeters. A one-millimeter hole is drilled into its underside, apparently to no great depth. The arrangement suggests a socket for a pin to anchor or position the figure on top of another object. The eye sockets are hollow enough to permit shallow inlays.

The patina consists of a rough bubbly surface and black crust which is relatively soft and flaky, cleaving away cleanly from the bronze surface with little effort in crumbled sheets. The bronze surface that remains is relatively fresh and reveals an undistorted, deeply etched dendritic structure except along the front edge of the garment and the underside of the left arm. In some areas, particularly the back of the neck and the end of the hair at the back, the patina consists of the black layer with highly reflective black granules similar to pyrite in sheen. There are also isolated spots of unexplained light blue powder and numerous areas of encrusted sand and larger quartz grains. The patina is not unlike some water burials or early nineteenth-century flame patinas. The right hand and right leg have lost patina due to abrasion. The golden brown surface of the metal is revealed where the thin black patina has worn or flaked away.

PROVENANCE: From Rome, said to have been found in the Tiber.

UNPUBLISHED.

NOTES: The condition statement for this bronze draws on a conservation report by Jerry Podany.

For the treatment of children in Hellenistic art, see H. Rühfel, *Das Kind in der griechischen Kunst* (Mainz, 1984) 185-309, esp. figs. 93, 110.

For the Capitoline girl and the child with the fox goose, see Rühfel 1984, 252-254, 258-262, figs. 106, 110; J. Pollitt 1986, 128, fig. 133. Zanker (1974, 73, n. 9) has identified the head of the Capitoline girl as a Julio-Claudian portrait. This view has been rejected by Rühfel and H. Lauter: *Gnomon* LII (1980) 158.

For the statuette in New York, see G. M. A. Richter 1915, no. 375.

For the statue in Bône, see M. Babelon in *Bulletin archéologique du Comité des Travaux historiques et scientifiques* (1912) CCLXXXII-CCLXXXIV, pl. 85; S. Reinach, *Rép. stat.* V: pl. 191, 5.

For the bronze baby in Autun, see P. Lebel and S. Boucher, *Musée Rolin: Bronzes figurés antiques* (Autun, 1975) no. 13.

For the embellished peplos of a Herculaneum Dancer, see D. Comparetti et al. 1883, 269, pl. 14, 3; B. S. Ridgway 1970, fig. 170; R. Tölle-Kastenbein, *AntP* XX (1986) pls. 70-71.

For the representation of the child reaching for the apple in the Aesculapium of Cos, see Herondas, *Mime: Offerings and Sacrifices*: IV. 20-34, as cited by J. J. Pollitt, *The Art of Greece 1400-31 B.C.: Sources and Documents* (Englewood Cliffs, N.J., 1965) 203-204.

For a Hellenistic bronze moneybox from Egypt, see M. Comstock and C. Vermeule 1971, no. 456.

For the bust in New York, see H. Jucker 1961, 49-51, B2, pl. 13.

For the door handle from Pompeii, see V. Spinazzola 1928, pl. 255, top right.

71. Child with Comic Mask

The boy is nude except for a mantle carried over his left shoulder. His mask is that of a slave of New Comedy, with contorted eyebrows, rolled hair (speira) and megaphone-like mouth. The mask is pushed back on the child's head as if he were relaxing after a performance, but his open mouth suggests that he is reciting. The child's hair is combed forward onto his temples and forehead in curving, concentric arcs. The hairstyle can be paralleled in portraits from Neronian through Trajanic times. The softness of modeling and the lack of sharp incision in the hair favor a date at the end of this span. Late Flavian portrait busts, like those in Copenhagen and Parma (Figures XXIII, XXIV) offer the best points of chronological reference.

Children with theater masks are a favorite theme of early Hellenistic terracotta sculpture, where conventionally dressed boys hold them like favorite pets or toys. Eros too, for reasons unknown, often plays with a mask. At times, nude children

ROMAN, LATE
FLAVIAN OR TRAJANIC,
CA. AD 90-120.
H. 7.6 CM.
INDIANA UNIVERSITY
ART MUSEUM, 76.132.2

hold or put on masks of Silenus or Pan. Occasionally at least—as in marble statues in Sperlonga and the Capitoline Museums—the child is the infant Bacchus, his play mysteriously prefiguring the dramatic art that he will create.

The Indiana figure stands out from all these playful babies and children, most of whom are sprawled on the ground, for his mature, dignified posture as well as his Roman hairstyle. His balanced, Classical composition contrasts flexed limbs on the left with extended limbs on the right (he is almost a plump, babyish version of the Hero with a Chlamys in the British Museum). The combination of Classical dignity with a contemporary hairstyle might be explained if the figure were a commemorative portrait of a deceased precocious child. On the other hand, the figure belongs to a relief and presumably formed part of a larger composition. In this case, the theme is almost certainly Bacchic. The childhood of Bacchus with attendant nymphs and silens is a possibility. The mask of a slave, however, ill-becomes the god himself; it is possible that this unusual figure represents a historic individual inserted into the divine retinue.

CONDITION: The figure was originally mounted on a relief. Its back is flat; only the left (relaxed) leg, the right hand and wrist, and the back of the mask are worked fully in the round. The back of the neck and lower back are roughly modeled. The right hand gripped a now-missing, separately cast object.

PUBLISHED: A. Calinescu in J. Leslie, *Indiana University Art Museum, Guide to the Collections* (Bloomington, 1980) 57.

NOTES: On slaves and their masks in New Comedy, see M. Bieber (*Theater*) 1961, 102, figs. 388-393.

For early Hellenistic terracotta statuettes of boys with theater masks, see R. Higgins 1986, 150, 155, fig. 190.

For a similar composition of Eros with a mask, see K. Gschwantler et al. 1986, no. 172.

For nude children with masks, see S. Reinach, *Rép. stat.* II: pl. 434, 1; 4, pl. 283, 3.

For the infant Bacchus with a Silenus mask, see H. Stuart Jones, ed., *A Catalogue of the Ancient Sculptures Preserved in the Municipal Collections of Rome: The Sculptures of the Museo Capitolino* (Oxford, 1912) pl. 79; G. Jacopi, *L'Antro di Tiberio e il Museo Archeologico Nazionale di Sperlonga* (Rome, 1965) 13, fig. 26; H. von Steuben in W. Helbig 1966, II: no. 1404.

A child of about three or four years of age sits in an unstable position, with one leg kicking forward and the other back. He leans his torso backward and flails his arms as if to maintain his balance. In spite of his animated pose, he stares rather fixedly forward. Flattened areas on the inside of his calves and his open seat make it clear that he was meant to be mounted astride some creature. His upraised right hand is perforated to hold an object. His hair is arranged in a typical child's fashion; it is caught up into a braid and a topknot (see [21]) above his forehead and hangs down in long ringlets around his neck. His solemn expression is almost paradoxically dignified. The modeling of the plump juvenile anatomy is firm and emphatic, and the hair has crisply chiseled detail.

The backward tilt of his body and the sloping shape of the opening make it very likely that the child was riding a dolphin plunging downward (for contrast, see

ROMAN,
JULIO-CLAUDIAN,
CA. AD 20-60.
H. 17 CM.
WALTERS ART
GALLERY, 54.724

[13]). The composition is known from a bronze lamp stand found in Pompeii and from many marble statuettes used as fountain ornaments. In most cases the rider is a winged Cupid, but in Parma a bronze replica of the Walters figure is also wingless. The Parma rider, who was excavated at the nearby site of Velleia, is somewhat smaller and has his limbs in slightly different positions.

The interpretation of the two wingless riders is somewhat unclear. Stories of humans saved by dolphins abounded in antiquity, but normally they did not involve children. The principal childish dolphin-rider of mythology was Palaemon; the child was thrown into the sea by his mother Ino-Leucothea, who had been driven mad by Hera. The dead Palaemon was carried back to Isthmia (near Corinth) on the back of a dolphin, but his spirit survived as a god who protected sailors. Virgil has Palaemon following in the retinue of Neptune accompanied by "cete," which may be either whales or dolphins. It is probably this benevolent spirit that is intended here.

The rider in Parma has been attributed to the late Hellenistic period. The sharply emphatic definition of the Walters figure has something in common with the Nemi bronzes (see Figure xx) and could well be from around the second quarter of the first century AD.

CONDITION: The eyes are inlaid in silver; the pupils incised, the irises pierced. A crack appears at the top of the left leg, probably from an ancient joint. The smooth surface has a blackish-green patina with a few bright green spots.

PROVENANCE: Said to have been found in Sidon.

EXHIBITED: Baltimore, Md., Walters Art Gallery, May 15-June 25, 1939, *The Greek Tradition in Painting and the Minor Arts*, 70, no. 71.

PUBLISHED: S. Reinach, *Rép.stat.* V:183, no. 4. D. K. Hill 1949, 35, no. 67, pl. 16. F. D'Andria 1970, 50, under no. 25.

NOTES: For the Pompeian lampstand with Cupid on a dolphin, see V. Spinazzola 1928, pl. 291.

For a smaller putto in a very similar pose, riding a pantheress on a lampstand, see V. Spinazzola 1928, pl. 293.

For cupids riding dolphins as fountain figures, see B. Kapossy, *Brunnenfiguren der hellenistischen und römischen Zeit* (Zurich, 1969) 38-39; A. Herrmann in *Pompeii A.D. 79* (1978) no. 73.

On Palaemon, see Virgil, *Aeneid*, tr. H. R. Fairclough (Loeb ed., Cambridge, Mass., 1974) V, lines 822-823, pp. 500-501; P. Weizsäcker in W. H. Roscher, *Ausführliches Lexikon der griechischen und römischen Mythologie* III, 1 (1902) 1260-1262; K. Shepard, *The Fish-Tailed Monster in Greek and Etruscan Art* (New York, 1940) v, 85-86; B. S. Ridgway, *Classical Sculpture, Museum of Art, Rhode Island School of Design* (Providence, R. I., 1972) 58-59, no. 21.

73. Hercules Running

Hercules runs carrying a lionskin draped over his extended forearms. The pelt wraps around the hero's body so that mask, tail, and paws all hang over his left arm. He is crowned with a wreath which seems to alternate laurel leaves and flowers, and is tied with broad ribbons fluttering down onto his shoulders. His broad, lumpy face is given a fiercely leonine expression by a pattern of crossing diagonals; the massive frown lines in his brow are continued by furrows in his cheeks extending down from the corners of eyes and nostrils. Much use is made of incision to render the anatomy, particularly in the tendons and muscles of the lower legs. The pectorals, shoulder muscles, and shoulder blades are sharply outlined in emphatic, conceptualized fashion. On the back, anatomical detail is scarcer, and the surface is rougher. The hero's hair and beard are rendered with rough, chunky locks, while the hair of the lion's pelt is indicated with rough dots and slashes. The texturing does not continue behind Hercules' arms or back, thereby making it clear that the figure was meant to be viewed either directly from the front or from slightly to his left. In back, a pair of vertical grooves segregate the area of the pelt over the hero's buttocks.

The action is quite uncharacteristic for Hercules; he runs forward as if to present the trophy of one of his assigned labors: killing the Nemean lion. The running pose with frontal chest and symmetrically flexed arms recalls marble statues of runners in the Palazzo dei Conservatori at Rome, whose original is ascribed to a fourth-century BC follower of Polyclitus. There, however, the front leg is flexed, while the back is straight. The tensile strength of bronze makes it possible to lift the back foot from the ground here, as in the life-sized Hellenistic bronze runner in the Izmir Museum from the Aegean Sea near Kyme. Oddly, the position of the lionskin seems dictated as much by modesty as by the demands of narration; the

ROMAN, LATER IMPERIAL, LATE SEVERAN OR EARLY IN TIME OF SOLDIER-EMPERORS, AD 215-250. H. 31.2 CM. BROOKLYN MUSEUM, FRANK L. BABBOTT FUND AND HENRY L. BATTERMAN FUND, 36.161

hero is shrouded front and back as if by a pair of shorts or a bath towel. Although there are precedents for some aspects of the pose, as a whole the composition is highly original.

His battered and ferocious face is the focus of the composition. The X-shaped pattern of lines slashing across a secondary grid of horizontals is extremely dynamic and expressive. This X-pattern emerged in the portraits of Caracalla, and its influence, as traced by Wood, continued into the time of Gallienus. It is within this time span that the Brooklyn statuette should be placed. The turbulent plasticity of hair, beard, and face suggests a date under Caracalla himself. Lower relief and less stormy effects characterize the following reigns. Several considerations, however, indicate that the piece was cast somewhat later. The impressionistic, linear texturing of the lionskin recalls techniques seen in marblework of the time of Severus Alexander (AD 222-235) and thereafter. The deep indentations of the hairline at the temples evoke hairlines in portraits of the Soldier-Emperors (AD 235-285). Perhaps an ideal date of about AD 235 might be imagined.

The rough technique and primitive rendering of anatomy can seem surprising in an age of such suave marblework in the city of Rome. The arts of Egypt, however, offer excellent parallels. A colossal granite head of Caracalla from Coptos, now in the University Museum, Philadelphia, presents very similar harsh simplifications while focusing on the X-pattern of wrinkles. Hair is shown in similar lumpy balls. The Brooklyn statuette manifests this provincial style in particularly vivid, spontaneous terms. The running Hercules is one of the few pieces in the exhibition that seems to represent a distinctly local phenomenon: a vigorous Egyptian folk art at the service of Imperial ideology.

CONDITION: The figure was solid cast in three sections. The bottom of the left foot is perforated with a small, round hole in the heel. The patina is red-brown flecked with green.

PROVENANCE: Probably from Alexandria in Egypt.

EXHIBITED: Brooklyn Museum, January 23-March 9, 1941, *Pagan and Christian Egypt*, no. 80.
The Detroit Institute of Arts, March 23-April 20, 1947, *An Exhibition of Small Bronzes of the Ancient World*, no. 33.
Baltimore, Walters Art Gallery, April 25-June 22, 1947, *Early Christian and Byzantine Art*, no. 200, pl. 34.
Waltham, Mass., Brandeis University, Rose Art Museum, December 18, 1968-February 16, 1969, *Art of the Late Antique from American Collections*, 50, no. 23.

PUBLISHED: *Annual Report of the Brooklyn Museum* (1935) 49.
J. D. Cooney, *Late Egyptian and Coptic Art* (Brooklyn, 1943) 18, pls. 25-26.

A. Badawy, *Coptic Art and Archaeology* (Cambridge, Mass., 1978) 119, 121, no. 3.6.

NOTES: For the Conservatori Runners, see D. Arnold 1969, 141-146, 267-268, pls. 18-19c, no. G 1-2.
For the Izmir Runner, see Rijksmuseum van Oudheden, Leiden, *Schatten uit Turkije/Treasures from Turkey* (Leiden, 1986) no. 213.
On the portraits of Caracalla and their influence, see S. Wood, *Roman Portrait Sculpture 217-260 A.D.: The Transformation of an Artistic Tradition* (Leiden, 1986) 27-48, pls. 1-9, 25.
For the granite head of Caracalla from Coptos, see H. B. Wiggers, *Das römische Herrscherbild*, III, pt. 1: *Caracalla, Geta, Plautilla* (Berlin, 1971) 76; P. Graindor, *Bustes et statues-portraits d'Égypte romaine* (Cairo, 1939) 145-146, pl. 61; *Art of the Late Antique* (1968) 46, no. 2; S. Morgan in *Romans and Barbarians* (Boston, 1976) no. 31.

Adam, A.-M., 1984: *Bronzes étrusques et italiques. Bibliothèque Nationale.* Paris.

Andreae, B., 1977: *The Art of Rome.* Translated by R. E. Wolf. New York.

Arnold, D., 1969: *Die Polykletnachfolge: Untersuchungen zur Kunst von Argos und Sikyon zwischen Polyklet und Lysipp.* Berlin.

Art and Technology (1970): *Art and Technology: A Symposium on Classical Bronzes.* Edited by S. Doeringer, D. G. Mitten, and A. Steinberg. Cambridge, Mass.

Babelon, E., and J.-A. Blanchet, 1895: *Catalogue des bronzes antiques de la Bibliothèque Nationale.* Paris.

Banti, L., 1973: *Etruscan Cities and Their Culture.* Translated by E. Bizzari. London.

Barr-Sharrar, B., 1987: *The Hellenistic and Early Imperial Decorative Bust.* Mainz.

Becatti, G., 1951: *Problemi Fidiaci.* Milan.

Bieber, M., 1939: *The History of the Greek and Roman Theater.* London.

Bieber, M., 1955: *The Sculpture of the Hellenistic Age.* New York.

Bieber, M., 1961: *The Sculpture of the Hellenistic Age.* Revised edition. New York, 1961.

Bieber, M. (*Theater*), 1961: *The History of the Greek and Roman Theater.* Second revised and enlarged edition. Princeton.

Bieber, M., 1977: *Ancient Copies: Contributions to the History of Greek and Roman Art.* New York.

Blome, P., 1982: *Die figürliche Bildwelt Kretas in der geometrischen und früharchaischen Periode.* Mainz.

Boardman, J., 1964: *Greek Art.* London.

Boardman, J., 1973: *Greek Art.* Revised edition. New York.

Boardman, J., 1980: *The Greeks Overseas: Their Early Colonies and Trade.* New and enlarged edition. New York, 1980.

Boardman, J., 1985: *Greek Art.* New, revised edition. London.

Bol, P.C., 1972: *Die Skulpturen des Schiffsfundes von Antikythera.* Berlin.

Bonfante, L., 1975: *Etruscan Dress.* Baltimore.

Bothmer, D. von, 1961: *Ancient Art from New York Private Collections.* Exh. cat. New York, Metropolitan Museum of Art.

Boucher, S., 1970: *Bronzes grecs, hellénistiques, et étrusques (sardes ibériques et celtiques) des musées de Lyon.* Lyon.

Boucher, S., 1973: *Bronzes romains figurés du Musée des Beaux-Arts de Lyon.* Lyon.

Boucher, S., 1976: *Recherches sur les bronzes figurés de Gaule pré-romaine et romaine.* Rome.

Boucher, S., (*BCH*) 1976: "A propos de l'Hermès de Polyclète." *BCH* c.

Brendel, O., 1978: *Etruscan Art.* Harmondsworth, Eng.

Brilliant, R., 1973: *The Arts of the Ancient Greeks.* New York.

Bronzes hellénistiques (1979): *Bronzes hellénistiques et romains: Tradition et renouveau.* Lausanne.

Busch, H., et al., 1969: *Etruskische Kunst.* Frankfurt.

Chase, G. H., 1924: *Greek and Roman Sculpture in American Collections.* Cambridge, Mass.

Civiltà degli Etruschi (1985). Edited by M. Cristofani. Exh. cat. Florence.

Comparetti, D. P. A., et al. 1883: *La villa ercolanese dei Pisoni: I suoi monumenti e la sua biblioteca.* Turin.

Comstock, M., and C. Vermeule 1971: *Greek, Etruscan and Roman Bronzes in the Museum of Fine Arts, Boston.* Greenwich, Conn.

Comstock, M. B., and C. C. Vermeule 1976: *Sculpture in Stone: The Greek, Roman and Etruscan Collections of the Museum of Fine Arts, Boston.* Boston.

Congdon, L. O. K., 1981: *Caryatid Mirrors of Ancient Greece: Technical, Stylistic and Historical Considerations of an Archaic and Early Classical Bronze Series.* Mainz.

Cristofani, M., (*StEtr*) 1979: "La 'Testa Lorenzini' e la scultura tardoarcaica in Etruria settentrionale." *StEtr* XLVII.

Cristofani, M., 1981: editor. *Gli etruschi in Maremma: Popolamento e attività produttire.* Milan.

Cristofani, M., 1985: editor. *Civiltà degli etruschi.* Exh. cat. Florence, Museo Archeologico.

D'Andria, F., 1970: "I bronzi romani di Veleia, Parma e del territorio parmense." *Contributi dell'Istituto di Archeologia* III.

de Ridder, A., 1913-1915: *Les bronzes antiques du Louvre.* 2 vols. Paris.

Di Stefano, C. A., 1975: *Bronzetti figurati del Museo Nazionale di Palermo.* Rome.

Dohrn, T., 1982: *Die etruskische Kunst im Zeitalter der Griechischen Klassik: Die Interimsperiode.* Mainz.

Frel, J., et al. 1987: *Ancient Portraits in the J. Paul Getty Museum.* Malibu, Calif.

Fuchs, W., 1963: *Der Schiffsfund von Mahdia.* Tübingen.

Fuchs, W., 1969: *Die Skulptur der Griechen.* Munich.

Fuchs, W., 1979: *Die Skulptur der Griechen.* Munich.

Gabrici, E., (*BdA*) 1907: "La quadriga di Ercolano." *BdA* I.

Gerhard, E., et al. 1843-1897: *Etruskische Spiegel*, 5 vols. Berlin.

Giglioli, G. Q., 1935: *L'arte etrusca*. Milan.

Giulia, Villa, (1980): see Proietti, G., editor.

Grace, F. R., 1939: *Archaic Sculpture in Boeotia*. Cambridge, Mass.

Gschwantler, K., et al. 1986: *Guss und Form: Bronzen aus der Antikensammlung*. Vienna.

Hanfmann, G. M. A., 1956: *Etruskische Plastik*. Stuttgart.

Hanfmann, G. M. A., 1967: *Classical Sculpture*. Greenwich, Conn.

Haynes, S., 1985: *Etruscan Bronzes*. New York.

Helbig, W., 1963: *Führer durch die öffentlichen Sammlungen klassischer Altertümer in Rom*, I. Tübingen.

Herfort-Koch, M., 1986: "Archaische Bronzeplastik Lakoniens." *Boreas*, Suppl. IV.

Higgins, R., 1986: *Tanagra and the Figurines*. Princeton.

Hill, D. K., (*ArtinAm*) 1946: "A Silene with an Amphora." *ArtinAm* XXXIV.

Hill, D. K., 1949: *Catalogue of the Classical Bronze Sculpture in the Walters Art Gallery*. Portland, Me.

Hill, E., (*MagA*) 1940: "Etruscan Dancing Figures." *MagA* XXXIII.

Himmelmann-Wildschütz, N., 1983: *Alexandria und der Realismus in der griechischen Kunst*. Tübingen.

Hoffmann, Herbert. *Ten Centuries That Shaped the West: Greek and Roman Art in Texas Collections*. Exh. cat. Houston, 1970.

Homann-Wedeking, E., (*RM*) 1943: "Bronzestatuetten etruskischen Stils." *RM* LVIII.

Hommes et dieux de la Grèce antique (1982): Edited by K. van Gelder. Exh. cat. Brussels, Palais des Beaux-Arts.

Hostetter, E., 1986: *Bronzes from Spina*, I: *The Figural Classes*. Mainz.

Jucker, H., 1961: *Das Bildnis im Blätterkelch; Geschichte und Bedeutung einer römischen Porträtform*. Olten.

Kellner, H.-J., and G. Zahlhaas, 1984, *Der römische Schatzfund von Weissenburg*. Second revised edition. Munich and Zurich.

Koeppel, G. M., (*BonnJbb*) 1983: "Die historischen Reliefs der römischen Kaiserzeit I: Stadtrömische Denkmäler unbekannter Bauzugehörigkeit aus augusteischer und julisch-claudischer Zeit." *BonnJbb* CLXXIII.

Lamb, W., 1929: *Greek and Roman Bronzes*. London.

Langlotz, E., 1927: *Fruehgriechische Bildhauerschulen*. Nuremberg.

Leibundgut, A., (*JdI*) 1984: "Der 'Traian' von Ottenhusen." *JdI* XCIX.

Leibundgut, A., 1976-: *Die römischen Bronzen der Schweiz*. Mainz.

Leon, C., 1968: "Statuette eines Kuros aus Messenien." *AM* LXXXIII.

Levi, D., 1941: "The Evil Eye and the Lucky Hunchback." In *Antioch-on-the-Orontes*, III: *The Excavations of 1937-1939*. Princeton.

Lippold, G., 1903-1956: *Die Skulpturen des Vaticanischen Museums*. Berlin.

Mansuelli, G., (*RA*) 1968: "La recezione dello stile severo e del classicismo nella scultura etrusca (Note problematiche)." *RA n.s.* XI.

Master Bronzes (1967): See Mitten, D. G., and S. F. Doeringer, editors.

Masterpieces of Etruscan Art (1967): See Teitz, R. S.

Mattingly, H., 1923-: *Coins of the Roman Empire in the British Museum*, 6 volumes in 8. London.

Maule, Q., (*StEtr*) forthcoming: "The Montaguragazza Style." *StEtr.*

Mertens, J. R., (*BMMA*) 1985: "Greek Bronzes in the Metropolitan Museum of Art." *BMMA* XLIII.

Mitten, D. G., 1975: *Classical Bronzes*. Providence, R.I.

Mitten, D. G., and S. F. Doeringer, editors. *Master Bronzes from the Classical World*. Exh. cat. Cambridge, Mass., 1967.

Mollard-Besques, S., 1963: *Catalogue raisonné des figurines et reliefs en terre-cuite grecs, étrusques et romains* II, *Myrina*. Paris.

Morrow, K. D., 1985: *Greek Footwear and the Dating of Sculpture*. Madison, Wisc.

Muthmann, F., 1982: *Der Granatapfel, Symbol des Lebens im Alten Welt*. Bern.

Neugebauer, K. A., 1921-1951: *Katalog der statuarischen Bronzen im Antiquarium. Staatliche Museen, Berlin*. Berlin.

Neugebauer, K. A., (*RM*) 1936: "Kohlenbecken aus Clusium und Verwandtes." *RM* LI.

Pollitt, J. J., 1986: *Art in the Hellenistic Age*. Cambridge.

Pompei A.D. 79 (1978): See Ward-Perkins, et al., editors.

Pompeii 79 (1984): See Zevi, F.

Pomerance Collection (1966): *The Pomerance Collection of Ancient Art*. Exh. cat. Brooklyn, The Brooklyn Museum.

Praschniker, C., (*OJh*) 1912: "Bronzene Spiegel-stütze im Wiener Hofmuseum." *OJh* XV.

Proietti, G., editor. *Villa Giulia: Il Museo Nazionale di Villa Giulia*. Rome, 1980.

Reinach, S., *Récueil de têtes antiques*. Paris, 1903.

Reinach, S., *Rép.stat: Répertoire de la statuaire grecque et romaine*, 6 volumes. Paris, 1904-1930.

Richardson, E., 1976: *The Etruscans: Their Art and Civilization*. Revised edition. Chicago.

Richardson, E., 1983: *Etruscan Votive Bronzes*, 2 vols. Mainz.

Richter, G. M. A., (*AJA*) 1912: "An Archaic Etruscan Statuette." *AJA* XVI.

Richter, G. M. A., 1915: *Greek, Etruscan, and Roman Bronzes*. New York.

Richter, G. M. A., 1940: *Handbook of the Etruscan Collection*. New York.

Richter, G. M. A., 1949: *Archaic Greek Art Against Its Historical Background*. New York.

Richter, G. M. A., 1950: *Sculpture and Sculptors of the Greeks*. Revised edition. New Haven, Conn.

Richter, G. M. A., 1951: *Three Critical Periods in Greek Sculpture*. London.

Richter, G. M. A., 1953: *Handbook of the Greek Collection*. Cambridge, Mass.

Richter, G. M. A., 1955-: *Greek Portraits*, 4 vols. Berchem-Brussels.

Richter, G. M. A., 1956: *Catalogue of the Greek and Roman Antiquities in the Dumbarton Oaks Collection*. Cambridge, Mass.

Richter, G. M. A., 1959: *A Handbook of Greek Art*. New York.

Richter, G. M. A., 1963: *A Handbook of Greek Art*. Third revised edition. London.

Richter, G. M. A., 1965: *The Portraits of the Greeks*, 3 volumes. London.

Richter, G. M. A., 1966: *The Furniture of the Greeks, Etruscans, and Romans*. London.

Richter, G. M. A., 1968: *Korai: Archaic Greek Maidens*. London.

Richter, G. M. A., 1929: *Sculpture and Sculptors of the Greeks*. London; Fourth edition. New Haven, 1970.

Richter, G. M. A., (*Kouroi*), 1970: *Kouroi*. Third edition. New York.

Ridgway, B. S., 1970: *The Severe Style in Greek Sculpture*. Princeton.

Ridgway, B. S., 1972: *Classical Sculpture, Museum of Art, Rhode Island School of Design*. Providence.

Ridgway, B. S., 1981: *Fifth Century Styles in Greek Sculpture*. Princeton.

Riis, P. J., 1938: "Some Campanian Types of Heads." *From the Collections of the Ny Carlsberg Glyptotek*, 2 vols. Copenhagen.

Riis, P. J., 1941: *Tyrrhenika, An Archaeological Study of the Etruscan Sculpture in the Archaic and Classical Periods*. Copenhagen.

Robertson, M., 1975: *A History of Greek Art*. 2 volumes. London.

Rolley, C., 1967: *Greek Minor Arts*, I: *The Bronzes* (or *Les arts mineurs grecs* I: *Les bronzes*). Leiden.

Rolley, C., 1986: *Greek Bronzes*. Translated by R. Howell. London.

Sams, G. K., 1976: editor. *Small Sculptures in Bronze from the Classical World*. Exh. cat. Chapel Hill, N.C., William Hayes Ackland Memorial Art Center.

Schefold, K., 1967: *Die Griechen und ihre Nachbarn*. Berlin.

Search for Alexander: See Yalouris, N., et al.

Small Sculptures in Bronze (1976): See Sams, G. K., editor.

Smith, R. R. R., 1984: editor. *The Portraits of the Greeks*. Abbreviated and revised edition. Ithaca, N.Y.

Snowden, F. M., 1970: *Blacks in Antiquity; Ethiopians in the Graeco-Roman Experience*. Cambridge, Mass.

Spinazzola, V., 1928: *Le arti decorative in Pompei e nel Museo Nazionale di Napoli*. Milan.

Sprenger, M., and G. Bartoloni, 1977: *Die Etrusker: Kunst und Geschichte*. Munich (also English edition: *The Etruscans: Their History, Art and Architecture*. New York, 1983).

Swaddling, J., 1979: "The British Museum Bronze Hoard from Paramythia, North Western Greece: Classical Trends Revived in the 2nd and 18th Centuries A.D." *Bronzes hellénistiques et romains, tradition et renouveau*. Lausanne.

Teitz, R. S. *Masterpieces of Etruscan Art*. Exh. cat. Worcester Art Museum, Mass., 1967.

Ten Centuries That Shaped the West. See Hoffmann, Herbert.

Uhlenbrock, J. P., 1986: *Herakles, Passage of the Hero Through 1000 Years of Classical Art*. Exh. cat. New Rochelle, N.Y., Bard College.

Vermeule, C. C., 1959: *The Goddess Roma in the Art of the Roman Empire*. London, 1959; reprinted Cambridge, Mass., 1974.

Vermeule, C. C., 1978: *Roman Art: Early Republic to Late Empire*. Boston.

Vermeule, C. C., 1980: *Greek Art, Socrates to Sulla*. Cambridge, Mass.

Vermeule, C. C., 1981: *Greek and Roman Sculpture in America*. Malibu, Calif.

Vermeule, C. C., 1982: *The Art of the Greek World: Prehistoric through Perikles, From the Late Stone Age and the Early Age of Bronze to the Peloponnesian Wars*. Boston.

Vermeule, C. C., 1984: *Catalogue of a Collection of Greek, Etruscan and Roman Antiquities*. Privately published. Cambridge, Mass.

Vierneisel, K., 1978: *Römisches im Antikenmuseum. Berlin, Staatliche Museen*. Berlin.

Villa Giulia (1980). See Proietta, G., editor.

Wace, A. J. B., (*BSA*) 1903-1904: "Grotesques and the Evil Eye." *BSA* x.

Walters, H. B., 1899: *Catalogue of the Bronzes, Greek, Roman, and Etruscan, in the Department of Greek and Roman Antiquities, British Museum*. London.

Ward-Perkins, J. B., et al., editors. *Pompeii A.D. 79: Treasures from the National Archaeological Museum, Naples, and the Pompeii Antiquarium*. 2 vols. Exh. cat. Boston, 1978.

Warren, L. B., 1971: "Etruscan Dress as Historical Source: Some Problems and Examples." *AJA* LXXV.

Frederick M. Watkins Collection (1973): *The Frederick M. Watkins Collection*. Edited by D. G. Mitten and S. F. Doeringer. Exh. cat. Cambridge, Mass., Fogg Art Museum.

Yalouris, N., et al. *The Search for Alexander*. Exh. cat. Boston, 1980.

Zanker, P., 1974: *Klassizistische Statuen*. Mainz.

Zanker, P., 1976: *Hellenismus in Mittelitalien: Kolloquium in Göttingen vom 5. bis 9. Juni 1974*. Göttingen.

Zevi, F., editor. *Pompei 79*. Naples, 1984.

Glossary

ACROPOLIS. The citadel of a Greek city-state, the site of the main sanctuary and associated buildings; Acropolis, the citadel of Athens, site of the Parthenon.

AESCULAPIUS. See **Asclepius.**

AGORA. Marketplace and civic center; Agora, the marketplace and civic center in Athens.

ALABASTRON. Small, round-bottomed slender vessel often with two small opposing handles at neck, used to hold perfumes.

AMPHORA. Tall, footed, usually high-necked, vessel with two opposing handles, used to hold liquids (such as wine or oil).

APHRODITE. Greek goddess of love and fruitful reproduction. The Etruscans called her Turan; the Romans, Venus.

APOLLO. One of the most important of the Greek and Roman gods; god of prophecy, divination, healing, music, and light.

ARRETINE WARE. Mold-made red-glazed ware with finely molded decoration produced in the city of Arretium (around Arezzo) from ca. 30 BC to AD 30.

ARTEMIS. Greek goddess of archery and hunting, protectress of wild animals and children, sister of **Apollo**; the Romans called her Diana.

ARYBALLOS. Spherical narrow-necked oil flask with a small handle.

ASCLEPIUS. God of healing and medicine, son of **Apollo**; Roman name is Aesculapius.

ATHENA. Greek goddess of war, also of crafts, city goddess of Athens; the Etruscans called her Menrva; the Romans, Minerva.

AULOS. A reed instrument usually played as a pair but referred to in the singular, generally translated as ''flute.''

BACCHUS. See **Dionysus.**

BOUSTROPHEDON. An early way of writing in a line that alternately runs from right to left, then left to right. The word comes from the Greek meaning ''turns like an ox,'' as in plowing fields.

BUCCHERO. Etruscan ceramic ware of black body, fired with a glossy, polished black surface.

BUCRANIA. Bulls' skulls from sacrifices, a common decorative motif in later Greek and Roman art.

CADUCEUS. See **kerykeion.**

CANALIS. Wide, shallow channel forming the major space in the spirals of an Ionic capital.

''CANON.'' The sculptor Polyclitus' codification and explanation of his system of proportions; name also often given to his statue, the **Doryphorus** (''spearbearer'').

CANTHARUS. See **kantharos.**

CARYATID. Female figure used in art and architecture as a support; male figure is telamon or atlantid.

CERES. See **Demeter.**

CHAPLETS. Iron pins used to hold core in place during bronzecasting.

CHARON. Greek god of the underworld who ferries dead souls across the River Styx; the Etruscans called him Charun.

CHITON. Short-sleeved Greek undergarment worn by both men and women which is often partially visible beneath the overgarment.

CIPPUS (pl. cippi). Low stone pillar usually decorated in relief and inscribed; used as a boundary or grave marker.

CIRE-PERDU (French). Lost-wax technique of bronzecasting.

CLASSICAL. Refers to the period of time from the beginning of Greek history to the end of the Roman Empire and to the cultures and lands dominated by Greek and Roman influences; Classical, the fifth and early fourth centuries BC in Greece.

CLEMENTIA AUGUSTA (Latin). Imperial pardon or mercy.

CONTRAPPOSTO (Italian). In statuary, a stance with weight on one leg which sets up answering rhythms through the body. Pose in which the movement of the torso opposes that of the lower body.

CYBELE. Phrygian mother goddess.

DACTYLIC HEXAMETER. Verse of six metrical feet, each having three syllables, the first accented, the second and third unaccented; the meter in which were written the Homeric epics and the dedicatory inscription on the Mantiklos Apollo [2].

DEMETER. The Greek earth goddess; the Romans called her Ceres.

DIANA. See **Artemis.**

DINOS (pl. dinoi). Ovoid, nearly spherical, footless, wide-mouthed vessel used for mixing wine and water; see also **lebes.**

DIONE. Goddess, consort of **Zeus** at Dodona; mother of **Niobe.**

DIONYSUS. Greek god of wine, ecstasy and rebirth; the Etruscans called him Fufluns; the Romans, Bacchus.

DIOSCURI. Twin sons of **Zeus**: Castor, the horseman, and Pollux, the boxer.

DORYPHORUS. Statue of a spearbearer by the Greek sculptor Polyclitus, ca. 450 BC, known from numerous copies of Roman date, perhaps the embodiment of his ''**canon.**''

EPHEBE. An Athenian youth of military age, around eighteen years old.

EPIMETHEUS (Greek: afterthought). Brother of Prometheus (Greek: forethought), husband of Pandora.

ETHOS (GREEK). Inner psychological state.

FUFLUNS. See **Dionysus**.

GENIUS (pl. genii). Protective spirit, especially of the Roman family or emperor.

GREAVES. Pieces of armor that protect the shins.

HADES. Lord of the Greek world of the dead, the lower world; husband of **Persephone**.

HALTERES. Jumping weights, used in the Greek broad-jumping contest.

HELIOS. The Greek sun god; the Romans called him Sol.

HEPHAESTUS. Greek god, divine smith and metalworker; patron of metalworkers and artisans; the Romans called him Vulcan.

HERA. Greek goddess, wife of **Zeus** and queen of heaven; the Etruscans called her Uni; the Romans, Juno.

HERAION. See **Samian Heraion**.

HERACLES. Most popular Greek hero who overcame all odds to accomplish seemingly impossible deeds and labors assigned to him; the Etruscan god Hercle is somewhat his equivalent; the Romans called him Hercules.

HERM. Pillar statue, originally with bearded head and phallus, later with portrait heads.

HERMES. The Greek messenger god; the Romans called him Mercury.

HESPERIDES, APPLES OF. Golden apples given as a wedding present by Earth to the goddess **Hera**. The tree from which they came was kept in a garden inhabited by the Hesperides (in some accounts daughters of Atlas). As one of his Labors, **Heracles** had to slay the serpent guarding the apples and steal them.

HETAIRA (PL. HETAIRAI). Greek prostitute or hired high-class entertainer, courtesan.

HIMATION. Large, wrapped overgarment, usually draped diagonally over the chiton, worn by both men and women.

HIPPOLYTUS. Hunter, follower of **Artemis**, and son of Theseus, subject of one of the Greek dramatist Euripides' works.

HOPLITE. Heavily armed Greek foot-soldier.

HORA. One of the Horae, female divinities who guarded the order of nature and succession of seasons.

HYDRIA (PL. HYDRIAI). Footed vessel with three handles (one vertical) for carrying and pouring water.

HYGEIA. See **Salus**.

HYPNOS. Winged god of sleep.

ISMENION (AT THEBES). Ancient oracular sanctuary of **Apollo**.

JUNO. See **Hera**; Juno Sospita, a goddess of state shown armed and wearing a goatskin cloak.

JUPITER. See **Zeus**; Dolichenus, a local Commagenian god shown in Roman costume with a thunderbolt and double-axe, standing on a bull, descended from a Hittite god of thunder and fertility.

KANTHAROS. A footed drinking cup with two high vertical opposing handles, one of **Dionysus**' attributes.

KERYKEION. Herald's staff, the rod entwined with snakes and winged near the top, an attribute of **Hermes** (Mercury); called caduceus in Latin.

KORE (PL. KORAI). Young Greek woman; Archaic Greek sculpture of the standing draped female figure; Kore, another name for **Persephone**.

KOUROS (PL. KOUROI). Greek male youth; statues of the ideal nude male youth sculpted in the Archaic period.

KRATER. Large footed vessel with wide mouth and two opposing handles, used for mixing wine and water; kalyx krater has flaring lip and outwardly curving handles resembling the silhouette of a flower.

KRIOPHOROS (pl. kriophoroi). Rambearer.

LAR (PL. LARES). Popular Roman domestic divinities without specific mythology: Lar compitales, of the crossroads; Lar Augusti, of Augustus; Lar familiaris, household Lar, dressed as youths wearing short tunics and holding drinking horns and libation saucers.

LARAN. Etruscan warrior god, son of Earth, connected with Turan.

LARARIUM (PL. LARARIA). Roman domestic shrine where statuettes of the household Lares, among others, were kept for private devotion.

LEBES (PL. LEBETES). A deep, rounded bowl, used for mixing wine and water, sometimes it has handles; see also **dinos**.

LICTOR. Carrier of the Roman fasces (standards) who accompanied high Roman magistrates.

LYCURGUS. Mythical Thracian king who tried to prevent young **Dionysus** and his nurses from seeking refuge in his kingdom and whom Dionysus then drove insane.

MAENAD. Ecstatic female attendant of **Dionysus**.

MAGNA GRAECIA. The Greek provinces in South Italy.

MARIS. Etruscan version of Ares, god of war; Latin name is Mars.

MEMNON. Son of the dawn, Aurora; leader of the Ethiopian forces to aid Priam at Troy; slain by Achilles in Homer's *Iliad*.

MEN. Phrygian moon god.

MENRVA. See **Athena**.

MERCURY. See **Hermes**.

MINERVA. See **Athena**.

NEMEAN LION. Fierce beast sent by **Hera** to ravage Nemea, was killed by **Heracles**, who is often depicted wearing a lionskin in reference to this feat.

NEW COMEDY. Produced in Athens after 325 BC, plots involved love stories and domestic comedies, restrained in humor compared to raucous 5th-century Old Comedy by Athenian dramatist Aristophanes.

NIELLO. A black silver-sulfur alloy, used for inlay in metals.

NIKE (PL. NIKAI). Greek name for the female personification of victory, shown as a winged woman; the Romans called her Victoria.

NIOBE. Daughter of Tantalus, the legendary king of Lydia, and **Dione**; had six sons and six daughters (Niobids) whom she compared to **Apollo** and **Artemis**, the children of the Titaness Leto, and all of whom were killed by **Apollo** and **Artemis** in revenge.

NORTIA. Local Etruscan god at Volsinii.

NYMPH. Lesser female divinity who inhabited forests, meadows, and springs.

OINOCHOE. Greek name for a wine pitcher, usually having a trefoil mouth.

ORANTES. Figures standing in praying position with hands raised.

ORPHEUS. Mythical Thracian poet, singer, and lyre player able to charm wild creatures with his music.

OVOLO. Molding usually carved with egg-and-tongue pattern in Greek architecture and egg-and-dart in Roman; a rounded, convex molding of ninety degrees.

PALLA. Mantle worn by Roman women.

PALUDAMENTUM. Short red mantle of Roman generals fastened at the left shoulder and worn over armor.

PARTHENON. Temple to Athena Parthenos on Athenian Acropolis.

PARTHENOS. Most often referring to Phidias' colossal gold and ivory statue in the **Parthenon**; see also **Athena**; Athena Parthenos, Athena the virgin goddess.

PATERA (PL. PATERAE). Pan or saucer with handle used for pouring liquid offerings.

PEPLOS. Short-sleeved or sleeveless overdress, symmetrically draped and worn by women, often wool, sometimes belted.

PERSEPHONE. Daughter of **Zeus** and **Demeter**; wife of **Hades**; allowed to return to earth once each year, bringing spring with her.

PHIALE. Shallow, handleless saucer for pouring liquid offerings to the gods.

PHOEBUS. Epithet of the sun god, **Apollo**; in Greek, Phoibos.

PHRYGIAN CAP. Floppy peaked cap, usually worn by easterners or foreigners in Roman works of art.

PILOS (PL. PILOI). Brimless conical hat or helmet worn by warriors; in Latin, pileus, pilei.

PITHOS (PL. PITHOI). Large handleless storage vessel.

POLIS (PL. POLEIS). Greek city-state.

POSEIDON. Greek god of the sea, flowing waters, and underground places, lived in the sea.

"PONTIC." Name given to a type of Etruscan vase painting which imitates Eastern Greek black-figure vase painting; was once thought to have come from Pontus in northeastern Asia Minor.

PROSERPINA. See **Persephone**.

PTOON. Mountain in western Boeotia, with a sanctuary of Apollo where many Archaic **kouroi** were found; G. M. A. Richter classified these kouroi into numbered Ptoon types.

RHYTON (PL. RHYTA). Curved drinking horn often shaped like the head and shoulders of an animal.

SALUS. Goddess of health; the Greeks called her Hygeia.

SAMIAN HERAION. Sanctuary and temple of the goddess **Hera** on Samos.

SATYR. Male companion of **Dionysus,** sometimes endowed with animal features: pointed ears, tail, sometimes hooves.

SELEUCID. Dynasty of rulers founded in 312 by Seleucus, follower of Alexander the Great, in Syria and Babylonia.

SERAPIS. During Hellenistic and Roman times, a widespread composite god originating in Alexandria, associated especially with healing and combining attributes of Osiris as king of the underworld, **Asclepius**, and **Zeus**-Jupiter.

SESTERTIUS. Large bronze or brass Roman coin.

SILEN, SILENUS (PL. SILENS, SILENI). Elderly pointy-eared, snub-nosed companion of **Dionysus**; an older **satyr**, often gifted musically.

SITULA (PL. SITULAE). Bucket-shaped wine vessel sometimes with swinging handle.

SOL. See **Helios**.

SOPHISTS. Philosophers who encouraged cynical disbelief in moral restraints and taught rhetoric as the road to success.

STEPHANE. Greek women's diadem.

STRATEGOS (PL. STRATEGOI). Greek general.

STRIGIL. Scraper used by athletes for removing excess water, oil, and perspiration after exercise.

TETRADRACHM. Greek silver coin.

THIASOS. Group of individuals, sometimes a society, that chose a particular god as patron; usually applied to the retinue (**satyrs, maenads, silens,** etc.) of **Dionysus.**

THYRSOS (PL. THYRSOI). Ritual staffs wrapped in grape or ivy vines and topped with pine cones carried by **Dionysus** and members of his **thiasos.**

TINIA. See **Zeus**.

TOGA. A large draped garment worn by Roman male citizens on formal and official occasions, also serving as their shrouds. It was roughly a semicircle of fine white woolen cloth.

TOGATUS (PL. TOGATI). Male figure wearing a **toga**.

TRAPUNTO. Technique of decorating clothing used by the Etruscans featuring a quilted design worked through at least two layers of cloth. The design is outlined with a running stitch, then padding is inserted.

TURAN. See **Aphrodite**.

TYCHE. Goddess of Fortune, seated on a rock with legs crossed, leaning back on one hand; personification of a city in the guise of its fortune or prosperity.

UMBO. Bunched folds of a **toga** gathered on the chest of a wearer.

UNI. See **Hera**.

VENUS. See **Aphrodite**.

VERTUMNUS. Complex deity, according to Roman author Varro, the chief god of Etruria, probably of Etruscan origin; perhaps god of Volsinii; Roman god of vegetation and growth of plants, associated with gardens and fruit.

VICTIMARIUS. An assistant at Roman sacrifices.

ZEUS. Father and supreme ruler of the Greek gods, the sky god; Etruscan version is Tinia; Roman version is Jupiter.

ZEUS AMMON. The deity, with strong Egyptian components, of Greek cities of North Africa; worshipped especially at Cyrene and at Zeus' oracle in Siwa Oasis, which is west of the Nile Delta in the desert; depicted as a bearded man with ram horns.

Photography credits

Justin Kerr, pp. 111, 112, 169; Otto E. Nelson, pp. 143, 145, 146, 316, 318, 348, 350, 352; David A. Loogie, p. 209; Sarah Wells, p. 347; Ken Strothman, Harvey Osterhoudt, p. 357; E. Irving Blomstrann, p. 364.